American History

Second Edition

Irving L. Gordon

Author of:

American Studies: A Conceptual Approach
Review Text in American History
Review Text in World History
World History, Second Edition

When ordering this book, please specify
either **R** 473 **P**
or AMERICAN HISTORY, SECOND EDITION

Dedicated to serving

AMSCO
our nation's youth

AMSCO SCHOOL PUBLICATIONS, INC.
315 Hudson Street / New York, NY 10013

To my dear ones
Who make everything worthwhile
Lois, my wife and companion
Our children, Meryl, Scott, Jesse, Reena
And our grandson, Joshua

ISBN 0-87720-852-2

Printed in the United States of America

PREFACE

In every generation, Americans have encountered and solved problems besetting the nation. Today, Americans must contend with both domestic and foreign problems of great urgency. They must determine our national goals and the appropriate means for moving toward these goals. Americans can gain perspective and guidance for this task through an understanding of our past and our national heritage.

High school students delve into these topics in their course in American history. There, they now face new interpretations, shifts in emphasis, and growing amounts of historical information. Consequently, they need a text that surveys our history in a concise and accessible manner.

To meet this need, *American History, Second Edition*, offers the following features:

1. Relevant History and Current Issues. In addition to the traditional historical topics, the text deals with contemporary political, economic, and social history. Irrelevant data have been omitted so as to focus attention upon significant developments and concepts in American history since the Civil War. The text places considerable emphasis upon current U.S. problems, including those faced by urban dwellers, farmers, senior citizens, minorities, and women. International affairs, and American leadership in the search for world peace, are also given their full due.

2. Historical Scholarship. The text draws upon the latest historical scholarship and seeks to present differing points of view fairly. This approach is meant to enrich the subject matter and to stimulate students' interest.

3. Clear and Unbiased Language. Every effort has been made to facilitate understanding by providing crisp and clear language. Nevertheless, the text conveys the complexity of our historical development. It is mature, not simplistic, and it is geared to the high school level.

4. Constitutional Issues. Historic and present-day case studies dealing with Constitutional issues and interpretation are included in the narrative. The full texts of the Declaration of Independence and the Constitution follow the final unit.

5. Extensive Illustrative Materials. The text contains much illustrative material. Historical maps show the development of the United States and highlight important events. Cartoons illuminate and comment upon recent events and problems. Graphs and tables provide information for analyzing economic and social trends.

6. *Individual Achievements.* Significant contributions by Americans to literature, the sciences, the arts, historical scholarship, and public affairs since the nation's earliest days are clearly presented.

7. *Abundant Test Materials.* The book contains ample test materials. A variety of short-answer and essay questions appear at the end of appropriate unit sections. The questions probe significant information, measure students' mastery of the content, and reinforce social studies skills. Many questions require logical reasoning and mature comprehension—major objectives of the teaching of social studies.

— I. L. G.

CONTENTS

West Europeans Spread Their Culture in the New World

PART 1. Old World Developments Lead to the West European Discovery of America

THE VIKINGS THRUST WESTWARD (9th TO 12th CENTURIES A.D.)

1. Leif Ericson Reaches Vinland. A Norse people, the Vikings were warriors, traders, and seafarers from western Europe's northernmost region, Scandinavia. From there some Vikings sailed westward across the Atlantic Ocean, arriving at Iceland and Greenland. Around the year 1000, Leif Ericson led a Viking crew that headed west from Greenland and reached a region of abundant grapes, grain, fur-bearing animals, and forests. The Vikings named this region *Vinland*. Later, the Vikings made other voyages from Greenland to Vinland for trade. They were chiefly seeking timber for home- and shipbuilding. Historians believe that Vinland was probably part of the North American mainland somewhere between Newfoundland in Canada and Massachusetts. Leif Ericson and his crew thusly had reached the New World almost 500 years before the voyage of Christopher Columbus.

2. Effects of the Vikings' Voyages. Why did the Vikings' discovery and expeditions have so little influence on the New World and on western Europe? *(a)* The Vikings probably did not realize that they had reached a previously unknown continent. *(b)* The Vikings were not interested in establishing permanent settlements far from their homelands. *(c)* The peoples of western Europe, living far from Greenland, heard little or nothing about the Vikings' voyages to Vinland. Under the feudal system, most people were preoccupied with the struggle to survive. They were concerned with religious matters and had little curiosity about distant lands. Books were scarce, and few people could read. The invention of movable type and the circulation of printed news reports lay far in the future. *(d)* Western Europe at the time of the Viking voyages lacked the knowledge of navigation and geography needed for successful long-distance voyages. Also, western Europe lacked a strong middle class interested in investment and trade, and lacked powerful national states to finance overseas voyages.

Before western Europeans could carry their culture to distant lands, these conditions had to be overcome. They were overcome as a result of three major Old World developments: the Crusades, the Renaissance, and the rise of absolute monarchs ruling national states.

CRUSADES (1095–1291)

1. Brief History. Pope Urban II in 1095 called upon western Christendom to wrest the Holy Land, Palestine, from Muslim Turks by undertaking a military expedition, the first Crusade. Over a period of almost 200 years, western Europe launched seven major Crusades, during which thousands of Crusaders reached the Middle East and came in contact with the advanced Muslim and Byzantine civilizations. Despite some temporary successes, the Crusades failed to establish permanent Christian rule in Palestine.

2. Results of the Crusades. The Crusades weakened feudalism and revived trade in western Europe. They aroused European demand for the products of the East: spices, sugar, silk, rugs, paper, glassware, metals, and precious stones. This profitable trade became the monopoly of (a) Middle Eastern traders, who brought goods by overland caravan from China to eastern Mediterranean ports, especially Alexandria and Constantinople, and (b) Italian merchants from city-states such as Genoa and Venice, who shipped the products from the eastern Mediterranean ports to the cities of western Europe. Eastern goods remained high-priced luxuries. One reason was the service costs added to the price of the products by the many intermediaries. The Italian city-states developed a merchant class and grew prosperous.

By reviving trade in western Europe, the Crusades contributed to the formation of a strong middle class, to the rise of national states, and in a limited way, to the Renaissance and to the strengthening of royal power.

RENAISSANCE (14th THROUGH 17th CENTURIES)

1. Meaning and Distinctive Features. The term "renaissance" means "rebirth or revival." The Renaissance was a period of growing intellectual interest by West Europeans in worldly, or nonreligious, aspects of civilization. Renaissance scholars emphasized reason, questioned authority, and pursued free inquiry. They showed interest in the advanced Muslim and Byzantine civilizations of their time, and in the Greco-Roman civilization of ancient times. The Renaissance arose in the Italian city-states because (a) Italy had been a center of Greco-Roman culture, (b) Italians were in close contact with the Byzantine and Muslim worlds, and (c) Italy had wealthy merchants and rulers who supported literature, art, and science.

2. The Renaissance Stimulates Interest in Geography and Navigation. During the Middle Ages, west Europeans traveled little, and travel was mainly by foot, horse, or riverboats, or along the Atlantic and Mediterranean coasts in small ships. Geographic knowledge was limited to Europe, northern Africa, and western Asia. When the Renaissance directed attention to scientific matters, west Europeans wanted to know more about the world's size, shape, and diverse peoples. In order to reach distant lands by water, west Europeans drew more precise maps, built faster and safer ships, and achieved greater accuracy in using the compass to determine direction and the astrolabe to determine latitude. By the 15th century, educated Europeans accepted the belief, held by the ancient Greeks, that the world is not flat but round.

RISE OF ABSOLUTE MONARCHS RULING NATIONAL STATES

1. Brief History. Under the feudal system of the Middle Ages, most monarchs exercised little power. They ruled only their royal domains and had little control over their feudal lords, who held most of the land. Near the end of the Middle Ages, monarchs began to extend their authority over the lords and eventually became absolute rulers. Royal power was strengthened by *(a)* the Crusades and other wars, which killed many feudal lords, *(b)* the rising merchant or middle class, which supported monarchs to assure protection of property and trade, and *(c)* the awakening spirit of nationalism, which considered the monarch the symbol of national unity. By the end of the 15th century, monarchs in western Europe had united peoples of a common nationality and molded unified national states such as England, France, Portugal, and Spain.

2. Encouragement of Overseas Voyages. The rise of national states in western Europe led to the undertaking of voyages of discovery because *(a)* national states possessed sufficient wealth to finance such voyages, *(b)* their absolute monarchs sought colonial empires, and *(c)* their middle classes wanted increased investment and trade. Portugal and Spain, desiring to smash the monopoly of Italian city-states, sought an all-water route to the Far East and took the lead in sponsoring voyages of discovery.

COMMERCIAL REVOLUTION

By the late 15th century, western Europe stood at the threshold of a new era to be marked by (1) overseas exploration and colonization, (2) expansion of world trade, and (3) the shift of major trade routes from the Mediterranean Sea to the Atlantic Ocean. These developments have been termed the *Commercial Revolution.*

PORTUGAL REACHES THE FAR EAST

Prince Henry the Navigator inspired Portugal to search for an all-water route around Africa and on to the Far East. Portuguese sea captains gradually pushed southward along the Atlantic coast of Africa. *Bartholomew Diaz* in 1488 reached the southern tip of Africa, named the Cape of Good Hope. *Vasco da Gama* in 1497–1498 rounded the Cape and sailed on to India. Because he returned with a cargo of spices worth 60 times the cost of the voyage, his trip excited western Europe.

SPAIN FINANCES AN EXPEDITION BY COLUMBUS

Christopher Columbus, an Italian navigator, in 1492 led an expedition for Spain's King Ferdinand and Queen Isabella. Convinced that the earth was round, Columbus planned to reach the Far East by sailing westward across the Atlantic Ocean. After a two-month voyage he came upon several islands in the Caribbean Sea. Columbus thought he was in the Indies off the coast of Asia, and conse-

Spanish and Portuguese World Explorations in the 15th and 16th Centuries

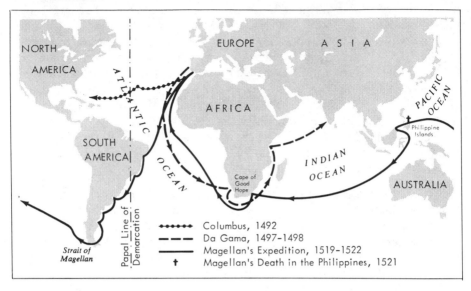

quently he named the natives of the Caribbean islands "Indians." Columbus actually had stumbled upon the New World. *Amerigo Vespucci,* an Italian explorer, who soon after reached the mainland, was the first person to declare it a new continent. In his honor, the New World was named America.

THE EARLIEST AMERICANS—THE PRE-COLUMBIAN INDIANS

When Columbus reached the New World, it was inhabited by some 15 million to 20 million people.

1. Indian Origins. Many thousands of years ago, the first people to enter the Western Hemisphere came from Siberia in Asia into Alaska in North America. Scientists believe that the two continents were once connected by a land bridge. (Today, the waters of the *Bering Strait* separate Asia from North America.) Over long periods of time people crossed the land bridge and spread out over the two American continents and adjacent islands.

2. Named "Indians." Columbus gave the name "Indians" to the reddish-skinned people with whom he first came in contact. Later explorers used this name for most other people of the New World.

3. Complex Pre-Columbian Indian Civilizations. The Indians of Central and South America created three highly developed civilizations. *(a)* The *Mayas* in present-day Mexico (A.D. 4th to 10th centuries) devised a system of hieroglyphic writing, constructed buildings of stone, observed the stars, and devised an accurate calendar. *(b)* The *Incas* of Peru (A.D. 13th to 16th centuries)

Pre-Columbian Indian Civilizations in the New World

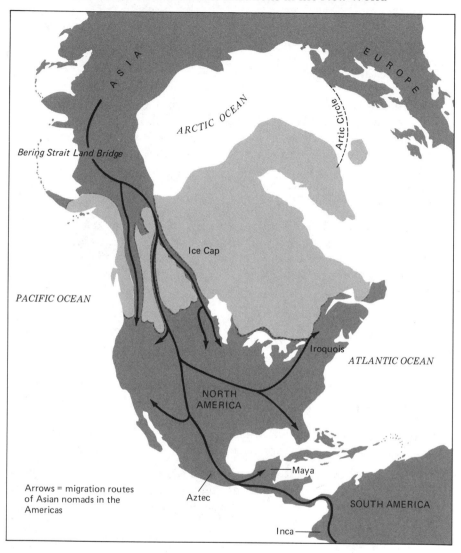

conquered a 2500-mile strip of land along the west coast of South America and created an empire. The Incas built roads, bridges, public buildings, and irrigation systems. They wove fine textiles and shaped elaborate gold and silver ornaments. The Inca empire was overthrown in 1532 by the Spanish *conquistadors* (conquerors) under *Francisco Pizarro*. (c) The *Aztecs* of Mexico (A.D. 14th to 16th centuries) conquered many peoples in Central America and established a sizable empire. The Aztecs built irrigation systems, pyramids, temples, and palaces of stone. Aztec rule ended in 1510 with the Spanish conquest led by *Hernando Cortes*.

4. Other Pre-Columbian Indian Civilizations. The Indians of North America consisted of many separate tribes. Each tribe was headed by a chieftain who was usually advised by the warriors, the elders, and the religious leader— the "shaman," or "medicine man." Some tribes glorified warfare.

THE IROQUOIS OF NEW YORK STATE

1. Background. The Iroquois were a group of tribes living in the Northeast and speaking related languages. They lived in villages and used tree poles and bark to construct *longhouses*. The Iroquois lived by hunting, fishing, and farming. Their major crops were corn, beans, and squash. They viewed the land as belonging to the entire tribe—an inalienable community property—available for use by all tribal members. They held that people must live in harmony with their natural environment.

2. Iroquois Tribal Organization. The best-known Iroquois tribes lived in central New York. They were the Mohawks, Oneidas, Onondagas, Cayugas, Senecas, and Tuscaroras. Known as the *Six Nations,* they dealt with common problems through a confederacy called the *League of the Iroquois.* The Iroquois were feared by other tribes as fierce warriors.

3. Status of Women. Iroquois society, to some extent, was *matriarchal.* Family descent was traced through the mother. Women headed the family groups that made up the clans. In addition, women helped choose the men who served on the tribal councils and in the League of the Iroquois.

4. Religious Beliefs. The Iroquois held that the universe was created and ruled by the Great Spirit, who represented peace and justice. The Great Spirit constantly struggled against the Evil Spirit—sometimes considered its twin—who represented war and wrongdoing. The Iroquois took part in elaborate rituals and ceremonials in their religious expressions and in other aspects of tribal life.

5. In the American Revolution and Afterward. The League of the Iroquois split apart during the American Revolution. Two tribes sided with the colonists and four tribes sided with the British. After the war, tribes who had sided with the colonists remained in New York State. The tribes who aided the British moved to Canada.

PART 2. West Europeans Explore and Settle in the New World

PERIOD OF EXPLORATION (LATE 15th TO EARLY 17th CENTURY)

REASONS FOR VOYAGES OF EXPLORATION

Spurred by Columbus' trip, the leading west European nations sent explorers to the New World to (1) seek a passage through or around the Americas to the Far East, (2) secure gold, silver, precious gems, and other valuable products, (3) establish claims to new lands, (4) convert the Indians to Christianity, (5) satisfy the spirit of adventure and intellectual curiosity, and (6) pave the way for trading posts and settlements.

IMPORTANT EXPLORERS AND THEIR ACHIEVEMENTS

EXPLORERS	DATES	ACHIEVEMENTS
For Portugal		
Cabral	1500	While en route around Africa to the Indies, Cabral was blown westward off course and accidentally reached Brazil.
For Spain		
Balboa	1513	Hearing rumors of gold and "another sea," Balboa crossed the Isthmus of Panama and was the first European in America to see the Pacific Ocean.
Ponce de Leon	1513	In search of the legendary "Fountain of Youth," Ponce de Leon explored Florida.
Cortes	1519–1521	An adventurer and fortune hunter, Cortes conquered the Aztecs in Mexico.
Magellan	1519–1522	The expedition that Magellan headed was the first to circumnavigate the world, although he was killed en route, in the Philippines.
Cabeza de Vaca	1528–1536	Attempting to colonize Florida, Cabeza de Vaca was shipwrecked off Texas and traveled to Mexico.
De Soto	1541	While searching for gold from Florida westward, de Soto reached the Mississippi River.
Coronado	1541–1542	Searching for legendary cities of gold, Coronado explored New Mexico, Texas, and Kansas and made contact with the Zuñi and Quivira Indians.
Cabrillo	1542	Leading an expedition that sailed north from New Spain (Mexico), Cabrillo was the first European to sight the coast of California and land at San Diego Bay.
For France		
Verrazano	1524	Looking for a "northwest passage" through the Americas to Asia, Verrazano explored the Atlantic coast of North America and sailed into New York Harbor.
Cartier	1535	In search of riches and a "northwest passage" to Asia, Cartier sailed up the St. Lawrence River.
Champlain	1603–1608	Interested in empire-building, Champlain explored northern New England, northern New York, and eastern Canada. He founded a settlement at Quebec.

For Holland

Hudson	1609	Instructed to locate a "northwest passage" to Asia, Hudson entered New York Harbor and sailed up the river later named after him—the Hudson River.

For England

Cabot	1497–1498	Authorized to claim new lands, Cabot explored Labrador and other parts of the northeastern coast of North America.
Drake	1577–1580	An explorer and adventurer, Drake led the second expedition to circumnavigate the world.

PERIOD OF COLONIZATION
(EARLY 16th TO MID-18th CENTURY)

ADVANTAGES OF EUROPEAN SETTLERS OVER THE INDIANS

(1) *Weapons.* The European settlers had firearms and gunpowder, which were far more powerful than the Indians' spears and bows and arrows. (2) *Agricultural Output.* Using improved agricultural methods, settlers were able to increase food output and support many people. (3) *Manufactured Goods.* Settlers had available a variety of manufactured goods, which they bartered with the Indians for valuable furs and lands. (4) *Immunity to Certain Diseases.* Europeans had developed immunity to diseases such as measles, smallpox, and influenza that they brought to the New World. The Indians, having had no previous contact with these diseases, had no such immunity. Whole Indian tribes died when exposed to them. (5) *Political Organizations.* Colonial governments were organized to deal with the Indians. By contrast, the Indians were separated into numerous tribes. Many of the tribes had long histories of rivalries and conflicts.

PORTUGUESE COLONIZATION

In 1493–1494, by a *Line of Demarcation,* drawn by the pope, and by a subsequent Portuguese-Spanish treaty, Portugal received title to eastern South America, or Brazil. To control the territory and to cultivate the sugar crop, the Portuguese soon established Brazilian settlements.

SPANISH COLONIZATION

1. Motives. Spain encouraged settlements in the New World to strengthen its claims to territory; to secure gold, silver, and valuable agricultural produce, such as sugar and indigo (a blue dye); and to convert the Indians to Catholicism. Spanish settlers were chiefly government officials, soldiers, nobles, merchants, and missionaries.

2. Extent. The papal decision and the subsequent treaty assigned the entire New World, except for Brazil, to Spain. The Spanish first settled in the islands of the West Indies: Cuba, Puerto Rico, and Hispaniola (Haiti and Santo Dom-

Spanish Explorations in the Americas in the 16th Century

ingo). From these bases, Spain proceeded to colonize Mexico, Central America, and most of South America.

Spain also established colonies in territory that today is part of the United States. In 1565, in Florida, the Spanish founded St. Augustine, the oldest city in the United States. In 1605, in New Mexico, they founded Santa Fe, the second oldest city in the United States. Other settlements were made throughout Florida, New Mexico, Arizona, Texas, and California.

In 1600, before the English had made their first settlement, Spanish colonists in the New World numbered about 200,000.

3. Life in the Spanish Colonies

a. Culture. Spain gave the New World its culture, notably its language, religion, and architecture. Spain permitted only Catholics to settle in its colonies. In the major cities, Spain built impressive cathedrals and church-run universities. Missionaries labored, with much success, to convert the Indians to Christianity. Spanish settlers and Indians intermarried and raised their children within the Spanish culture. Such persons of mixed Spanish and Indian ancestry are known as *mestizos*.

b. Economy. The Spanish introduced wheat, barley, and fruit and nut trees to their colonies in the New World. They also brought with them horses and cattle, domesticated animals that would form the basis of the ranch system. The Spanish introduced the feudal European landholding practice by which the ruler granted large estates to Spanish nobles. These estates were first worked by the Indians, who were often enslaved and treated cruelly. Later, plantation owners used black slaves brought from Africa, as well as mestizos, who were little more than slaves.

Colonial merchants were permitted to trade only with Spain. This restriction accorded with the prevailing idea that colonies exist to enrich the mother country, an idea basic to the economic doctrine of *mercantilism*. From its colonies, Spain obtained a treasure of gold and silver that helped maintain it, during the 16th and most of the 17th century, as a leading world power.

c. Government. The rulers of Spain permitted no self-government at home or in the colonies. They exercised strict control over the colonies by giving absolute powers to the officials they sent from Spain to serve as royal governors, or *viceroys*.

4. Decline of the Spanish Empire. After the defeat of the Spanish Armada in 1588 by the English, Spain slowly declined as a world power. In the 19th century, Spain lost all its American colonies, most by revolution during the Napoleonic era and the rest as a result of the Spanish-American War. Although its political control ended, Spain left the New World an extensive heritage: literature, music, architecture, the Spanish language, and the Roman Catholic religion; and also concentrated landownership and wide class distinctions.

FRENCH COLONIZATION

1. Motives. When the king of France heard that the pope had apportioned the New World between Spain and Portugal, he demanded to see "the clause in Adam's will" that excluded his country. The French wanted to acquire an empire in the New World, to fish for cod on the Newfoundland banks, to trade with the Indians for furs, and to convert the Indians to Catholicism.

2. Extent. The French used the vast inland waterways to explore and settle in North America. In 1608 *Samuel de Champlain* established the first permanent French settlement, at Quebec on the St. Lawrence River. In 1673 the missionary *Jacques Marquette* and the fur trader *Louis Joliet* canoed across Lake Michigan and down most of the Mississippi River. In 1681–1682 the explorer *Sieur de La Salle* descended the entire length of the Mississippi. Along the St. Lawrence, the Great Lakes, and the Mississippi, the French established many fur-trading posts and settlements, notably Montreal, Detroit, St. Louis, and New Orleans.

3. Few Settlers. In 1750 *New France*—the name of the extensive French colonial territories in North America—held only 80,000 settlers. The reasons for

French Explorations in North America in the 16th and 17th Centuries

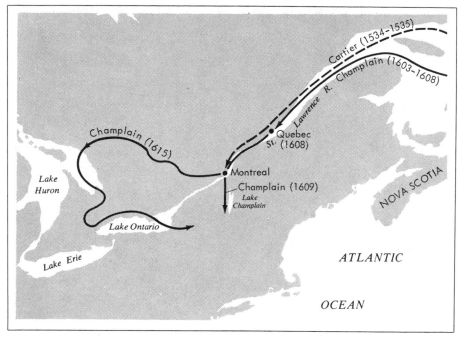

this small number were: *(a)* New France contained no gold and silver to lure fortune seekers. *(b)* France restricted immigration to Catholics, thereby excluding French Protestants. *(c)* French settlers engaged primarily in the fur trade and were little interested in farming. *(d)* Like France, the colonies were under the strict rule of the monarch, who opposed the growth of self-government.

4. Decline. France lost its possessions in North America as a result of the French and Indian War (1754–1763). (Check the index.) However, French influence in the New World has remained strong in the province of Quebec, with its predominantly French-Canadian population, and in the state of Louisiana.

DUTCH COLONIZATION

1. Motive and Extent. Interested in the fur trade, the Dutch West India Company in 1621 founded the colony of *New Netherland*. It included trading posts and settlements along the Hudson River, notably at Albany and New Amsterdam, now New York City. In 1626 *Peter Minuit*, the Dutch governor, gave the Indians goods reputedly worth $24 for Manhattan Island. The Dutch also settled on Long Island and in New Jersey. In 1655 they annexed New Sweden, a Swedish settlement in Delaware.

Dutch and Swedish Settlements in the 17th Century

2. Limited Population. Since Holland was prosperous and few Hollanders were willing to migrate, the Dutch West India Company tried to attract settlers by offering a *patroonship*, a huge tract of land, to any of its members who would transport 50 tenants to the colony. Also, the company raised little objection to non-Dutch immigrants. By the 1660s the colony contained settlers speaking some 18 different languages. Nevertheless, the total population did not exceed 10,000.

3. Decline. Holland and England were commercial and colonial rivals, and England considered the Dutch colony an obstacle to its ambition to control the Atlantic seaboard of North America. In 1664 an English naval force appeared before New Amsterdam and compelled the surrender of the colony by the Dutch governor, *Peter Stuyvesant.*

Dutch influence in New York State is evidenced by family- and place-names and by a number of old houses and churches.

ENGLISH COLONIZATION

1. Extent. England founded ten colonies along the northern Atlantic seaboard and fashioned three colonies out of New Netherland, seized from the Dutch. These 13 English colonies formed the basis of our country, the United States of America.

2. Motives of the English Settlers

a. Religious. King Henry VIII broke with the papacy and in 1534 established the independent Anglican Church, or Church of England. During the reign of Henry's daughter, Queen Elizabeth I (ruled 1558–1603), Anglicanism became firmly established as the English religion. Catholics as well as dissenting Protestants, such as Puritans and Quakers, suffered discrimination and sometimes persecution. To gain religious freedom, many English migrated to the New World.

b. Political and Military. In the 17th century, England was torn by strife between Parliament and the Stuart kings, who sought absolute rule. In succession, England experienced civil war (1642–1645), the beheading of King Charles I (1649), a Puritan military dictatorship under Oliver Cromwell (1649–1658), the restoration of the Stuarts (1660), and the final overthrow of Stuart rule by the Glorious Revolution (1688–1689). To escape governmental tyranny, political unrest, and civil strife, many English migrated to the colonies.

c. Economic. Starting in the 16th century, many English lords, seeking sheep pastures, illegally fenced in lands formerly held in common by all farmers and also fenced in their own lands. Thus, tenant farmers were driven off the land. Many landless peasants moved to the cities, where they were unable to find work and fell into debt. Under England's severe criminal code, debtors faced imprisonment. To start life anew, and perhaps acquire their own farms, many impoverished English people looked to the New World.

3. Motives of the English Government

a. World Power. In striving for world leadership, England came into conflict with Spain. English sea captains, notably John Hawkins and Francis Drake, raided Spanish treasure ships and Spain's colonies in the New World. In 1588 an English navy under Drake and other sea captains completely defeated, off the English coast, a huge Spanish invasion fleet, the "invincible" Spanish Armada. This victory marked the emergence of England as a world power and as the "mistress of the seas." Equating a colonial empire with world power, the English government generally encouraged colonial settlement.

b. Economic Benefits. England, like other European governments, accepted the doctrine of mercantilism, especially the idea that colonies should serve to enrich the mother country. According to mercantilist theory, colonies should assure raw materials and markets for English manufacturers, trade for English merchants, and revenues for the English treasury.

THE THIRTEEN ENGLISH COLONIES

THE FIRST COLONIES—VIRGINIA AND MASSACHUSETTS— FOUNDED BY JOINT-STOCK COMPANIES

The joint-stock company was a form of business organization that preceded the present-day corporation. The joint-stock company received a charter from the English Crown granting it, for a period of years and a specific area, a monopoly over trade and colonization. In return the company was to give the Crown a portion of the profits earned and the precious metals acquired. The joint-stock company sold stock to numerous investors who provided the needed capital and shared in the company's profits or losses.

1. Virginia

a. Founding of Jamestown (1607). The first permanent English settlement in the New World was undertaken as a business venture by a group of merchants organized into a joint-stock company, the *Virginia Company of London,* also called the *London Company.* In 1607, after the company secured a charter from King James I, a group of more than 100 settlers founded Jamestown.

b. Early Mistakes. The first settlers included too few farmers and artisans and too many "gentlemen" unaccustomed to work. They located the colony on low, marshy ground infested with malaria-carrying mosquitoes. They began to search for gold instead of undertaking the tasks necessary for survival. Thereupon, *John Smith,* a practical-minded soldier, forced his way into control. He secured food from the Indians and compelled the settlers to build fortifications, plant food crops, and stock firewood. Nevertheless, fewer than half the settlers survived the early years. In 1610 the colony was saved from abandonment only by the arrival of new settlers and supplies.

c. Tobacco Cultivation. In 1612 *John Rolfe* began cultivating a West Indian species of tobacco in Virginia. Tobacco grew well in the soil of Virginia and commanded a good price in Europe. The raising of tobacco was further encouraged when, in 1619, the Virginia Company permitted each settler to claim a farm of 50 or more acres.

d. Survival Assured. As the Virginia Company went bankrupt and lost its charter, Virginia in 1624 became a *royal colony.* Despite its history of inexperienced leadership, disease, and Indian attacks, Virginia had survived. By 1624 the colony contained over 1200 settlers, most of them engaged in the flourishing tobacco culture. Virginia thus faced the future with confidence.

2. Massachusetts

a. Plymouth (1620). The Pilgrims, a small group of Protestant dissenters, determined to escape religious persecution by establishing a New World colony. They organized a joint-stock company, selling stock to a group of London merchants who hoped to make a profit and also giving stock to each person who

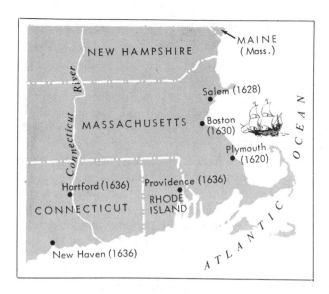

New England Settlements in the 17th Century

became a colonist. The Pilgrims received permission from the Virginia Company to settle in its territory, but their ship, the *Mayflower,* was blown northward off course and landed at Plymouth. They were beset by cold, hunger, and disease, and only half of the group lived through the first winter. However, under the leadership of *William Bradford* and with the help of friendly Indians, the Plymouth colonists farmed, fished, traded for furs, and survived. In the fall of 1621 the Pilgrims held a celebration to give thanks to God for their well-being—the origin of our Thanksgiving Day. In 1627 the Pilgrims arranged to buy up, at a nominal price, the interests of the London merchant stockholders. Plymouth did not attract many settlers and finally was absorbed by the Massachusetts Bay Colony.

b. Massachusetts Bay (1630). The Puritans, so named because they wished to purify the Anglican Church of practices remindful of Roman Catholicism, suffered discrimination at the hands of Anglican Church leaders and King Charles I. A Puritan group organized a joint-stock company, the Massachusetts Bay Company, and managed to secure a royal charter. Many of the leading Puritans were wealthy merchants and bought up the stock of the company. They emigrated to the New World and established company headquarters in the colony. The company thus was converted from a business enterprise into a religious haven with significant powers of self-government.

In 1630, led by *John Winthrop,* 1000 Puritans settled in the Massachusetts Bay area, mostly at Salem, Cambridge, and Boston. The settlers had enough food and were equipped with tools and valuable skills. With these advantages the colony prospered almost immediately. During the 1630s, as Puritans in England suffered greater persecution and as England moved toward civil war, more Puritans emigrated. By 1640 the Massachusetts Bay Colony had grown to 20,000 inhabitants. The colonial government supported the Puritan church and did not tolerate disagreement with Puritan beliefs and practices.

THE PURITAN ETHIC

As Puritan believers migrated throughout colonial New England and into the Middle Colonies, they brought along a moral and ethical code which historians later called the *Puritan Ethic*. It stressed the following beliefs: that those elected beforehand by God would achieve eternal salvation; that those so elected for salvation could be recognized by how they lived on earth; that they would shun idleness, extravagance, and vanity; that they would avoid frivolous pastimes such as dancing, cardplaying, and theatergoing; that they would read the Bible regularly for religious and moral guidance; and that they would devote their lives to working hard, being thrifty, achieving business success, and accumulating material wealth. In recent years Americans have referred to the Puritan ethic as the "work ethic."

THREE COLONIAL OFFSHOOTS OF MASSACHUSETTS

3. Rhode Island (1636). *Roger Williams,* minister of the church in Salem, challenged Puritan rule. He condemned the seizure of land from the Indians without payment and denied the right of the Massachusetts government to interfere in religious matters. Expelled from Massachusetts in 1635, Roger Williams and his followers went to Rhode Island, where a year later they founded *Providence.* Another Massachusetts religious rebel who went to Rhode Island was *Anne Hutchinson.*

In 1644 Williams secured from the English Parliament a charter for Rhode Island Colony and set up a government which permitted religious freedom for all people and provided for the separation of church and state. Rhode Island's enlightened religious policy attracted many settlers.

4. Connecticut (1636). *Thomas Hooker,* pastor of the church at Cambridge, led his congregation to Connecticut and settled at *Hartford.* These settlers were not religious reformers but desired better farmlands and a government less restrictive than that of Massachusetts. In 1662 Connecticut received a royal charter confirming the settlers' right to self-government.

5. New Hampshire (1638). This area was settled chiefly by colonists who left Massachusetts for political, religious, and economic reasons. For a while New Hampshire was under the control of Massachusetts, but in 1679 it received its own charter as a royal colony.

SEVEN PROPRIETARY COLONIES

From the experiences of the Virginia and Massachusetts colonies, English investors concluded that no quick profits—if any—could be realized from buying stock in joint-stock companies planning New World settlements. Subsequent English colonization efforts were undertaken mainly by individuals called proprietors.

Proprietors were wealthy persons, usually friends or relatives of the king, who received royal grants of New World lands to colonize and rule. The major restriction upon the proprietors was the requirement that the laws for the colony must be made "by and with the consent of the freemen," that is, a colonial legislature. The proprietors faced financial risks to bring settlers to the colony, but they expected to make large profits from the rental and sale of land and from the crops raised on their New World estates. The best-known proprietors, who also had religious motives for founding colonies, were Lord Baltimore (Maryland) and William Penn (Pennsylvania).

6. Maryland (1634). *George Calvert,* the first *Lord Baltimore,* a convert to Catholicism, secured a royal grant of land around Chesapeake Bay for the colony of Maryland. Lord Baltimore hoped that the colony would improve his family finances and would also afford a place of refuge for English Catholics. His son, the second Lord Baltimore, in 1634 sent the first group of settlers to the colony. They were capably led and well equipped, and they treated the Indians fairly. Turning quickly to growing tobacco, the settlers prospered from the start. Maryland attracted Protestants as well as Catholics and soon granted freedom of religion to all Christians.

7 and 8. North and South Carolina (1663). A group of proprietors received a royal grant to the Carolinas. The northern portion was settled chiefly by pioneers from Virginia; the southern portion, including Charles Town (later Charleston), was settled by colonists from the British Isles and other European nations. The settlers earned a living by raising rice and tobacco, producing *naval stores* (pitch and tar) from the pine forests, and trading for furs with the Indians.

The proprietors attempted to rule according to a document entitled the *Fundamental Constitutions of Carolina* (1669–1670). It was a curious mixture of some democratic with many feudal and aristocratic principles. Presumably it was the product of an English writer later to be hailed for other works as a great philosopher, *John Locke.*

The Carolina settlers long opposed proprietary rule, chiefly because the proprietors rebuffed demands for greater self-government. The proprietors finally surrendered their charter to the crown, and North Carolina and South Carolina each became a royal colony.

9. New York (1664). Shortly before the English navy seized New Netherland from the Dutch in 1664, King Charles II assigned the region to his brother James, then Duke of York. Renaming the colony *New York,* James confirmed the right of the Dutch settlers to retain their lands, observe their religion, and speak the Dutch tongue. He also continued the Dutch practice of governing the colony without a legislative assembly, and he ruled autocratically. When James became king in 1685, New York became a royal colony. After James was deposed by the Glorious Revolution of 1688–1689, New York gained a representative assembly.

10. New Jersey (1664). Immediately after acquiring New Netherland, James granted the area between the Hudson and Delaware Rivers to two of his friends, *Lord John Berkeley* and *Sir George Carteret*. This area, named New Jersey, already had some Dutch and Swedish settlements. The new proprietors, eager for land rents, encouraged the coming of additional settlers but had difficulty governing them and collecting rents. Eventually, Berkeley and Carteret sold their interests to Quaker groups who hoped to use the colony as a religious haven. In 1702 New Jersey became a royal colony.

11. Pennsylvania (1681). *William Penn* received a charter to Pennsylvania as payment for money owed to his late father by King Charles II. Penn envisioned the colony not only as a business venture, but as a place of refuge for his persecuted coreligionists, the *Quakers,* or *Society of Friends.* The Quakers, a group of Protestant dissenters, had no formal church organization. They believed in humility, hard work, help for unfortunates, and brotherly love. They opposed war, violence, rank, and pride. In 1682 Penn came to the New World and for two years personally supervised the colony, which he called a "holy experiment." Penn himself planned the "city of brotherly love," *Philadelphia.*

Pennsylvania became renowned for religious freedom, a popularly elected legislature, fertile land, and fair treatment of the Indians. It attracted many settlers from the British Isles and also from the Continent, especially German and Swiss Quakers, Mennonites, and Amish—the ancestors of today's Pennsylvania Dutch. Pennsylvania soon became a most prosperous colony.

12. Delaware (1682). William Penn also received a grant to Delaware, already containing Swedish and Dutch settlers. These people did not want to be ruled by the Pennsylvania legislature, and so in 1701 Penn granted them their own representative assembly.

ONE MILITARY OUTPOST

13. Georgia (1732). *James Oglethorpe* headed a group of "trustees" consisting of military leaders and philanthropists and secured a charter from King George II for this last and southernmost English colony. Not seeking profits, the trustees planned Georgia as a military outpost against Spanish Florida and also as a haven for honest but penniless debtors. The trustees assigned each settler a small farm and forbade the importing of slaves. Soon, however, Georgia developed into a colony of large plantations employing slave labor. In 1752 Georgia became a royal colony.

—————————— MATCHING QUESTIONS ——————————

Select the letter of the item in Column B that matches each item in Column A.

Column A—Achievements

1. Was first to reach India by sailing around Africa
2. Was first European to sail into New York Harbor
3. Was first to identify the New World as a continent
4. Crossed Panama and saw the Pacific Ocean
5. Conquered the Aztec Indians in Mexico
6. Headed the expedition that first circumnavigated the world
7. Founded the city of Quebec
8. Led Viking expedition that reached Vinland
9. Was first European to reach Brazil
10. Explored eastern North America, where a major river was named after him

Column B—Explorers

a. Balboa
b. Cabral
c. Cartier
d. Champlain
e. Cortes
f. Da Gama
g. Ericson
h. Hudson
i. Magellan
j. Ponce de Leon
k. Verrazano
l. Vespucci

———— IDENTIFICATION QUESTIONS: WHO AM I? ————

For each description below, write the name of the person to whom the description best applies, making your selection from the following list:

William Bradford   James Oglethorpe   Peter Stuyvesant
George Calvert   William Penn   Roger Williams
Thomas Hooker   John Smith   John Winthrop

1. A practical-minded soldier, I compelled the first Jamestown settlers to undertake tasks necessary for their survival.
2. One of the Pilgrim leaders and governor of the colony, I made provision for a day of thanksgiving.
3. Expelled from Massachusetts, I founded a colony famed for separation of church and state.
4. As first Lord Baltimore, I planned a colony partly as a refuge for Catholics.
5. I founded a colony mainly to provide a place of refuge for Quakers.
6. As governor of New Netherland, I was compelled to surrender the colony to an English naval force.
7. I founded a colony in the South mainly to enable debtors to start life anew.

——————————— MULTIPLE-CHOICE QUESTIONS ———————————

Select the letter preceding the choice that best completes the statement or answers the question.

1. The Vikings' expeditions to Vinland (a) were deliberately kept secret from western Europe (b) took place before western Europe had a strong middle class interested in trade (c) excluded the west Europeans from the fur trade with the Indians (d) reported a barren land uninteresting to west Europeans.
2. By the Crusades, west Europeans sought to (a) control an all-water route to the East (b) drive the Turks from Constantinople (c) establish Christian rule over the Holy Land (d) further trade between East and West.
3. A result of the Crusades was the (a) increase in importance of the middle class (b) decline of the Italian city-states (c) establishment of European colonies in India (d) spread of the Muslim religion into Spain.
4. The Crusades helped to bring about the discovery of America by (a) stimulating European demand for goods of the East (b) encouraging the movement for a united Europe (c) reviving the power of the Catholic Church (d) encouraging Europeans to settle in the Middle East.
5. Which is most typical of the Renaissance spirit? (a) rejection of religion (b) lack of interest in humankind's past (c) questioning of authority (d) revolt against absolutism.
6. The Renaissance began in Italy because the (a) Italian city-states had conquered the nations of the East (b) Italian merchants and rulers became wealthy from trade with the East (c) Roman Empire was at its height (d) Italians are the most scientific of all peoples.
7. Which was a direct result of the Renaissance? (a) defeat of the Spanish Armada (b) spirit of inquiry as seen in the period of exploration (c) exclusion of non-Catholics from French colonies in North America (d) idea of separation of church and state.
8. Which would be characteristic of a culture encouraging a spirit of inquiry? (a) Leadership would be accepted without question. (b) Customs and traditions would change very little. (c) There would be few opportunities for individuality. (d) Changes would occur regularly in many areas of life.
9. An important cause for the rise of national states in Europe was the (a) development of the middle class (b) collapse of the Roman Empire (c) growth of democracy (d) aid given by the Roman Catholic Church.
10. In the 14th and 15th centuries, west Europeans sought an all-water route to Asia to (a) break the Italian trade monopoly (b) stimulate progress in agriculture (c) add new territory to their empires (d) transport surplus population to colonies in Asia.
11. An immediate result of the Commercial Revolution was the rise in importance of (a) Venice and Genoa (b) Constantinople and Baghdad (c) Lisbon and London (d) Hamburg and Bremen.
12. Which was a result of the Commercial Revolution in Europe? (a) domination of European trade by Italian city-states (b) emergence of the peasant class into positions of political and social power (c) rise in the political and economic importance of the middle class (d) support of free public education.
13. Spanish colonies in the New World were typified by (a) the prohibition of trade with any country but Spain (b) self-government (c) fair treatment of Indians (d) admission of peoples of all religions.

14. According to mercantilism, a world power should (a) not seek colonies (b) seek only colonies rich in gold (c) permit colonial self-government (d) regulate colonies so as to enrich the mother country.

15. The French did *not* establish a settlement in North America at (a) Detroit (b) New Orleans (c) St. Louis (d) St. Augustine.

16. The Puritan settlement in the Massachusetts Bay Colony resulted most directly from the (a) political and religious policies of King Charles I (b) ambitions of Dutch merchants (c) flight of the Huguenots from France (d) European demand for furs.

17. Which three colonies were offshoots of the Massachusetts Bay Colony? (a) New Jersey, Vermont, Maine (b) New York, New Jersey, Delaware (c) Virginia, Connecticut, Pennsylvania (d) Connecticut, Rhode Island, New Hampshire.

18. Early English settlements in the New World were largely financed by (a) the royal family (b) military leaders (c) private companies and individuals (d) the Anglican Church.

19. Proprietors did *not* found which one of the following colonies? (a) Virginia (b) Pennsylvania (c) Maryland (d) North Carolina.

20. The joint-stock companies that founded the earliest English colonies in America (a) made tremendous profits (b) sold out their interests to proprietors (c) made settlements without permission of the English king (d) showed that risky investments sometimes lead to losses.

21. Prince Henry the Navigator directed his sailors to (a) round Africa (b) go westward across the Atlantic (c) gain control of the Mediterranean (d) seize Constantinople.

22. What was the attitude of merchants and rulers toward overseas voyages? (a) Both groups supported them. (b) Both groups opposed them. (c) Merchants supported them; rulers opposed them. (d) Rulers supported them; merchants opposed them.

23. The American Indian was so named because (a) Indians had migrated to the Americas from India (b) American Indians followed Hindu religious practices (c) Columbus believed he had reached the East Indies (d) Columbus believed he had discovered a new world.

24. The horse and cattle were introduced into the New World by settlers from (a) Spain (b) Holland (c) England (d) France.

25. The Europeans who explored the world during the 15th and 16th centuries were motivated chiefly by (a) an interest in science, art, and literature (b) wealth, religion, and glory (c) curiosity, concern for peace, and love for the sea (d) a need for markets for manufactured products and outlets for surplus population.

———————————— **ESSAY QUESTIONS** ————————————

In developing your essay answers, be sure to (1) include specific factual information and evidence whenever possible, (2) keep to the questions asked, and (3) avoid overgeneralizations or sweeping statements without sufficient proof.

1. The Viking expeditions to Vinland (9th to 12th centuries) aroused little interest in western Europe. *(a)* Present *one* piece of evidence showing that the Vikings were excellent sailors. *(b)* Discuss *two* reasons why the Viking expeditions to Vinland aroused little interest in western Europe.

2. The European discovery of America resulted from developments in Europe, notably the *(a)* Crusades *(b)* Renaissance and *(c)* rise of absolute monarchs ruling na-

tional states. Select *two* of these developments and for each show how it (1) affected Europe and (2) related directly to the discovery of America.

3. In the late 1400s, western Europe entered upon the Age of Discovery and Exploration. Today, the world has entered upon the Space Age. Explain how these two periods are similar *or* different in regard to *(a)* leading nations *(b)* motives for exploration *(c)* financing of trips *(d)* vehicles and other necessary equipment *(e)* recruiting of explorers *(f)* actual and potential results.

4. *(a)* Name *four* west European countries that explored the New World and name *one* explorer who sailed for each country. *(b)* Of the four explorers named, state the one you would most have liked to accompany. Discuss *two* reasons for your choice.

5. By the 18th century, the white population in the New World colonies of England far exceeded the white population of the colonies of any other European power. Comparing the English colonies with either the Spanish *or* the French colonies, discuss *two* reasons why the English colonies attracted the greater number of settlers.

6. In discussing the English colonies, we must distinguish between the motives of the settlers and the motives of the government. *(a)* Discuss *two* motives that led English people to settle in the New World. *(b)* Discuss *two* motives that led the English government to encourage such settlement.

7. For *each* of the following pairs of colonies, show that their early histories were *(a)* in *one* way similar, and *(b)* in *one* way different: (1) Virginia and New York (2) Rhode Island and New Hampshire (3) Maryland and Georgia (4) Pennsylvania and Massachusetts Bay.

UNIT II

The English Colonies Evolve Into a New Nation

PART 1. The Colonists Develop Distinctive American Practices

Life in the colonies differed considerably from life in England and in continental western Europe. Settlers in the New World had to adjust to new conditions. They had to discard many old customs and gradually develop new ways of thinking and acting. In time, their way of life was no longer European, but American.

COLONIAL POLITICAL PRACTICES

COLONISTS' RIGHTS

In a number of royal charters authorizing the establishment of colonies, the colonists were assured their rights and privileges. These rights and privileges rested upon four major landmarks in English history:

1. Magna Carta (1215). King John was compelled by the feudal nobles to sign the *Great Charter,* or *Magna Carta.* In time Magna Carta came to mean that *(a)* the monarch is not an absolute ruler but is subject to the laws, *(b)* all persons are guaranteed trial by jury, and *(c)* Parliament alone may levy taxes.

2. Evolution of Parliament. By the 14th century, Parliament had divided into two houses: representatives of the higher clergy and nobility constituted the hereditary *House of Lords;* representatives of the wealthy middle class constituted the elected *House of Commons.* Also, by threatening to withhold tax laws, Parliament compelled English monarchs to accept its legislation, not only on taxes, but on all other matters.

3. English Common Law. By the 14th century, English courts had established the practice of referring to similar past cases and following the previous decisions of judges. These legal precedents collectively formed a body of judge-made law called the *common law.* Its principles, some of which in time became English *statute law* (enacted by a legislature), helped protect the individual against governmental tyranny. By the end of the 17th century, common law, as supplemented by statute law, had given all English people certain basic rights: *(a)* Life, liberty, and property could not be taken away arbitrarily. *(b)* If arrested, a person was entitled to a writ of habeas corpus (providing for a statement of charges and a speedy trial) and to a trial by jury. *(c)* Government officials could not search a private home without first securing from a court a search warrant specifically stating the articles being sought.

4. English Bill of Rights (1689). As part of the Glorious Revolution that ended Stuart rule in England, Parliament passed the Bill of Rights. It provided that *(a)* the monarch may not, without the consent of Parliament, make or suspend laws, levy taxes, or maintain an army, *(b)* the monarch may not interfere with Parliamentary elections and debates, and *(c)* the people are guaranteed the right to petition the government; the right to an impartial and speedy jury trial; and the right to protection against excessive fines and bails and against cruel and unusual punishments.

THE COLONISTS ESTABLISH DEMOCRATIC INSTITUTIONS

The colonies were far from democratic as we understand the term today, but they were significantly more democratic than continental western Europe and even England. The American colonists developed the following institutions:

1. Virginia House of Burgesses (1619). The landowning male colonists of Virginia received from the Virginia Company the right to elect representatives to a colonial legislature, the *House of Burgesses.* This was the New World's first elected legislature and its first institution of representative government. Other colonies followed Virginia's pattern in establishing lawmaking bodies.

2. Mayflower Compact (1620). Before disembarking from the *Mayflower* for their new home at Plymouth, the Pilgrims made plans for self-government. In a compact to further the general good of the colony, they pledged to enact and obey just and equal laws. The *Mayflower Compact* set an example of certain democratic principles: *(a)* direct democracy, wherein the citizens themselves, not their representatives, were the lawmakers, *(b)* rule by the majority, and *(c)* fair treatment of all persons under the law.

3. New England Town Meetings. The Pilgrims began the practice, which became typical of colonial New England, of building towns with farms at the outskirts and a church meetinghouse at the center. Town life concentrated around the church. The freemen, originally only men who owned property and belonged to the town church, conducted town affairs and enacted local ordinances in *town meetings.* They also elected town representatives to serve in the colonial assembly. The town meeting, an example of direct democracy and possible only in a small community, provided the colonists with training in self-government.

4. Fundamental Orders of Connecticut (1639). Led by Thomas Hooker, the settlers of Connecticut drew up the first successful written constitution of modern times. It permitted all loyal male citizens who owned property to elect a legislative assembly, which in turn would choose a governor. The Fundamental Orders implied that government rests upon the consent of the governed and that it should express the will of the majority.

COLONIAL GOVERNMENT IN THE 1750s

(1) *Eight Royal Colonies.* The monarch selected the governor and, except for Massachusetts, appointed the members of the governor's council, which was the upper house of the colonial legislature. The qualified voters elected the lower house, the colonial assembly. (2) *Three Proprietary Colonies.* In Delaware, Maryland, and Pennsylvania, the proprietor selected the governor; the eligible voters elected the colonial assembly. (3) *Two Self-Governing Colonies.* In Connecticut and Rhode Island, the colonists directly or indirectly elected the governor and members of both houses of the legislature.

The Thirteen English Colonies, About 1750

Historical Analysis. *How democratic were the colonies?* Historians have long debated this question.

Some historians insist that the colonies were controlled by the upper classes—the landed aristocracy, wealthy merchants, and representatives of the English crown. In this analysis, the lower and middle classes were engaged in a constant political struggle to have their voices heard and their interests furthered.

Other historians claim that since land was so easily obtained and so widely held, practically all men who wished to could take part in the political process. In this analysis, the colonists had achieved, and were determined to preserve, a middle-class democratic society.

In support of each of these contrary viewpoints historians cite the following data:

Undemocratic Aspects. In the royal and proprietary colonies (11 of the 13) the colonists had little voice in the selection of a governor. The royal or proprietary governor retained the power to veto laws passed by the colonial legislature and to appoint lesser colonial officials. Furthermore, the English crown claimed the power to review and reject any law passed in the colonies.

In many colonies, voters had to meet religious qualifications. In all colonies, landless urban dwellers could not satisfy property qualifications for voting. Frontier settlers, living in isolation, found it difficult to vote and were underrepresented in the colonial assemblies. Finally, in all the colonies membership in the assembly was restricted to the well-to-do by the high property qualifications for officeholding.

Democratic Features. The legal rights of the colonists were protected by colonial judges, who followed English common law. The colonists were also protected against tyranny by the separation of governmental powers. With power divided between a governor representing the crown or a proprietor and a colonial assembly representing the settlers, neither branch of government could become all-powerful.

The colonial assembly was elected by men who could meet the property qualifications—according to some historians, a majority. The assembly's consent was necessary to enact laws, such as to levy taxes and dispense funds. Often the assembly was able to bend the governor to its will by withholding funds for his salary or for running the government. Such use of a legislature's financial power was named the *power of the purse.*

COLONIAL RELIGIOUS PRACTICES

EARLY INTOLERANCE IN COLONIAL AMERICA

Following Old World practices, most colonies set up an official or *established church*—one supported by government funds and, especially in the 17th century, one in which church membership was required for voting. In the southern colonies and in New York, the official church was the Anglican Church. In the New England colonies, except for Rhode Island, the official church was the Puritan or Congregational Church.

The early Puritan leaders of Massachusetts were intolerant of dissent. They punished and exiled any religious nonconformists. In time, however, Massachusetts became more tolerant of other religious sects. (For the Salem witch trials as an example of religious intolerance, check the Index.)

FACTORS PROMOTING RELIGIOUS TOLERANCE

1. Number of Religious Groups. Because England had permitted members of all religions to come to the New World, the colonial settlers represented a great many religions. They were chiefly Protestants (Puritan, Anglican, Quaker, Presbyterian, Dutch Reformed, Baptist, and Lutheran), but there were also some Catholics and a small number of Jews. The settlers realized that if their own religion was to survive, other religions had to be tolerated.

2. Splits Within Existing Churches. Starting in the 1720s, America was shaken by a religious movement called the *Great Awakening*. This movement, under the intellectual leadership of *Jonathan Edwards,* stimulated religious conversions and strong religious emotion among large numbers of people. Itinerant (traveling) ministers conducted mass revival meetings, preaching that humans are sinful by nature and can be saved from Hell only by faith in God's love. By causing *schisms* (splits) in the existing churches, the Great Awakening promoted religious diversity and therefore tolerance.

3. Frontier Conditions. Faced with the difficulties of securing a living and withstanding Indian attack, frontier settlers had little time for theological disputes. Nor were they disposed to question the religion of their neighbors, who helped them in taming the wilderness and safeguarding the settlement.

STEPS TOWARD RELIGIOUS TOLERANCE

The advanced views of certain colonial founders also helped to promote religious tolerance.

1. Roger Williams—Rhode Island. In 1636 Roger Williams and his followers, fleeing from religious intolerance in Massachusetts, founded Rhode Island. Williams provided complete religious freedom for all people and did not set up an established church. The government of Rhode Island did *not* use public funds for religious purposes, did *not* require any person to join a church, and did *not* establish any religious qualifications for voting. This idea of *separation of church and state* was later incorporated in the First Amendment to the United States Constitution.

2. Lord Baltimore—Maryland. Although Lord Baltimore founded Maryland as a haven for Catholics, the colony soon attracted a majority of Protestants. To protect the Catholic minority and to prevent religious strife, Lord Baltimore in 1649 secured from the colonial assembly the *Maryland Toleration Act.* It granted religious freedom to all Christians.

   3. William Penn—Pennsylvania. William Penn founded Pennsylvania as a haven for Quakers but he opposed any established church. In 1682 he granted religious freedom to all colonists, no matter what their religion, as long as they believed in God.

COLONIAL ECONOMIC PRACTICES

GEOGRAPHIC CONDITIONS INFLUENCE COLONIAL OCCUPATIONS

   1. New England Colonies. New Englanders were discouraged from agriculture by the rocky, inhospitable soil and the cold climate. Farms were small, subsistence units and produced little beyond the needs of the farm family. On the other hand, the abundant forests, swift-flowing streams, and fine natural harbors such as Portsmouth, Boston, and Providence turned New Englanders to lumbering, shipbuilding, whaling, fishing for cod and mackerel, and the trans-Atlantic trade.

   New England merchants developed various trade routes, several involving a *triangular trade.* One profitable route took fish, grain, and lumber from the colonies to the West Indies for sugar and molasses, which, in turn, were exchanged in England for manufactured goods needed in the colonies. On another profitable trade route, New Englanders took rum to Africa and exchanged it for black slaves. The slaves were sold in the West Indies for sugar and molasses, and these products were shipped to New England to be distilled into rum.

   New England's merchants made substantial profits, but they also faced great obstacles: the hazards of the sea, the dangers of pirate attack, and the English

New England's Triangular Trade Routes

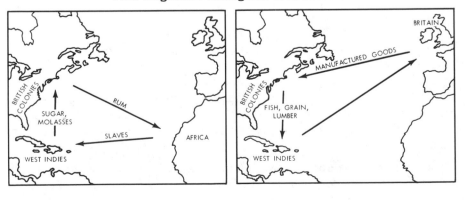

mercantilist laws—the *Navigation Acts*. These laws were designed to keep colonial ships trading with England and the British West Indies rather than with the European continent or the French and Spanish West Indies. For example, the *Sugar and Molasses Act* of 1733 required the colonists to pay a high import duty on these products if they were secured from any place but the British West Indies.

2. Middle Colonies. These colonists were encouraged by fertile, level land and a favorable climate to maintain family-size farms that produced surplus grain (wheat, corn, and oats) for export to the other colonies and to England. The Middle Colonies soon became known as the *bread colonies*. Long, navigable rivers such as the Hudson, Susquehanna, and Delaware promoted trade with the Indians for furs. First-class harbors, such as at New York and Philadelphia, stimulated trade with other colonies, England, and the continent.

3. Southern Colonies. From the abundant forests, Southerners obtained pitch and tar—naval stores vital to English and colonial shipbuilding and repair.

Southern colonists, spurred by fertile soil and a warm climate, developed a plantation economy producing *indigo* (a blue coloring substance), rice, and tobacco. These products were shipped mainly to England in return for manufactured goods.

As the planters became wealthy, they secured additional plantation land, in part because tobacco-raising quickly exhausted the soil. They imitated the ways of the English aristocracy and dominated southern colonial society. The planters' lives contrasted sharply with those of the small southern farmers and of the frontier dwellers struggling in the back country.

(For colonies included in each geographic division, see map, page 25.)

COLONIAL SHORTAGE OF LABOR

Planters and farmers had difficulty securing enough workers. Settlers were unwilling to work for others when they could easily acquire land and themselves become independent farmers. To overcome the labor shortage, colonists turned to indentured servants and slaves.

1. Indentured Servants. These impoverished persons from Britain and continental western Europe were landless farmers, unemployed workers, debtors, orphans, and paupers. They signed contracts called *indentures,* agreeing to work for four to seven years in exchange for passage to the New World. They were employed as household help, artisans, and farmhands. After their period of indenture, they became free and sometimes received a parting wage of land or tools.

2. Black Slaves. In 1619 a Dutch sailing ship brought 20 blacks to Jamestown, Virginia—the first in colonial America. The blacks were originally regarded as indentured servants, but by the 1660s most were legally held as slaves. Slavery became strongest in the South, where tobacco and rice planters came to depend upon black workers. By 1750 the colonies contained 400,000 black slaves, of whom three-fourths were in the South.

COLONIAL INDUSTRIES

1. Beginnings of Colonial Manufacturing. The colonists were overwhelmingly engaged in extractive occupations—extracting from the natural resources furs, fish, lumber, and farm produce.

The colonists also engaged in certain basic manufactures: weaving cloth and sewing clothes, tanning leather and making shoes, trimming lumber and making furniture, forging iron and shaping implements. These activities were at first performed on the farm or plantation as household industries.

As the colonial population grew and as manufactured goods came into greater demand, craftworkers founded small local shops. In time textiles, iron implements, and beaver hats became somewhat larger industries, and manufacturers sought to expand beyond local markets. The most important manufacturing activity, centered in New England, was shipbuilding.

2. Obstacles to Colonial Manufacturing

a. Scarcities. Colonial manufacturing remained limited because of (1) lack of capital, (2) lack of skilled workers, (3) lack of adequate inland transportation facilities for the distribution of goods, and (4) opposition from England.

b. English Mercantilist Laws. England passed laws in accordance with the mercantile theory—that colonies should produce raw materials and exchange them for manufactured goods from the founding country. The *Woolen Act* (1699) and the *Hat Act* (1732) prohibited any colony from exporting these manufactured goods to any other colony or overseas. The *Iron Act* (1750) encouraged the shipment of crude iron to England but prohibited the colonists from making finished iron products.

COLONIAL SOCIETY

COLONIAL POPULATION

1. Rapid Growth. In 1700 the English colonies contained 250,000 people. By 1750, only 50 years later, the population had increased sixfold to 1.5 million. This rapid growth was due both to a considerable immigration and to a high native birthrate.

2. Variety of Peoples. The English colonies admitted persons of diverse nationalities and cultures. Thus began the American tradition of the *melting pot.* (Check the Index.) From the British Isles came the English, Welsh, Scotch, Scotch-Irish (of Ulster in northern Ireland), and the Irish. Since the colonies accepted non-British immigrants too, many settlers came from western Europe, especially from France, the German states, and Switzerland. In Delaware and New York, both formerly part of New Netherland, the original settlers were Swedish, Finnish, and Dutch.

3. Family Patterns. Mirroring British and western European practice, most colonists maintained families consisting of the husband, wife, and children—the nuclear family. Some households, especially in the southern colonies, also included grandparents and other close relatives, thereby constituting the *nuclear extended form*.

Colonial families were *patrilineal*. A woman took her husband's family name, and their children traced their family line through the father. Colonial families were also *patriarchal:* the father ruled the family, made its important decisions, and exercised full authority over its members. The mother ran the household and took care of the children. In rural families, the mother also assisted with the farm work, and the many children were an economic asset, performing necessary chores. Within the patriarchal family, colonial women had a higher status than their European sisters. Colonial women were highly valued, being relatively scarce among the early settlers and, especially in rural families, being considered an economic asset.

4. Social Classes and Mobility. The colonists consisted of three broad classes: *(a)* the aristocracy of wealth (planters and merchants) and education (clergy, printers, and lawyers), *(b)* the middle class of small farmers and skilled workers, and *(c)* the lower class of indentured servants and slaves. Except for the slaves, however, colonial classes were not hereditary, and colonists moved easily up or down the social ladder.

COLONIAL CULTURE

ARCHITECTURE

Once secure in their settlements, the early colonists acted to construct permanent buildings. For materials, they used wood from nearby forests; in time they also used brick, stone, plaster, and glass. They constructed the following major architectural types: (1) *New England Colonial.* Following the pattern of their homes in England, the New England colonists built one- and two-story rectangular-shaped abodes. Their chief medium was wood, but they later added stone and brick fireplaces. An example, erected in 1676 in Boston, is the *Paul Revere House.* (2) *Georgian-Style Buildings.* Named for the first three Georges, who reigned in England during most of the 18th century, this style was employed to construct impressive private and public buildings. It featured massive size, symmetry of exterior design, and an elaborate center entrance. The Georgian style was used in homes for the wealthy—southern plantation owners and northern merchants. It also was used in many public buildings, such as Philadelphia's *Independence Hall.* (3) *Log Cabins.* Swedish settlers in Delaware were excellent carpenters who fitted together rough-cut logs to construct rectangular log cabins. In wooded frontier regions, the log cabin became the standard dwelling.

PAINTING

Well-to-do colonists sought cultural refinement by commissioning portraits of individuals and family groups. They employed the services of itinerant (traveling) portrait painters whose names generally are unknown to us. Called *limners,* these painters produced works of varying quality. In their best efforts they achieved good detail and character expression. An important limner work is entitled *Mrs. Elizabeth Freake and Baby Mary.*

John Singleton Copley of Boston was the best-known colonial painter. He produced some 300 portraits of the leading colonists of the day, most notably of Samuel Adams and Paul Revere. Loyal to Britain, Copley in 1774 fled to London and never returned home.

EDUCATION

1. Elementary Education. The colonists were better educated than the common people of England and western Europe. The quality and content of colonial schooling varied, however, depending on the colony and the family's social status. In general, upper-class children were educated by costly private tutors or in private schools. They learned basic academic skills as well as practical and classical subjects. Children of frontier dwellers had the least formal education but were often taught the three R's—reading, 'riting, and 'rithmetic—by their parents at home.

Especially in New England, the Protestant emphasis on personal Bible reading motivated parents to educate their children. Massachusetts in 1647 and later other New England colonies passed laws requiring towns to provide schools for the teaching of reading. These first public education laws were poorly enforced.

2. Higher Education. To prepare young people for the ministry, various Protestant groups established colleges and universities, including Harvard (1636), William and Mary (1693), Yale (1701), Princeton (1746), and Columbia (1754). Benjamin Franklin, a colonial printer and a self-educated person, founded the University of Pennsylvania (1751). Offering a broad, practical, and liberal arts education, it was the first nondenominational (not founded by a church) college in America. By the late 18th century most institutions of higher learning were training students for medicine, law, and other secular professions.

PRINTED MATERIALS

1. Books and Newspapers. Although books were expensive, a number of planters and merchants had large personal libraries. In Philadelphia, Benjamin Franklin in 1731 founded the first subscription library society. Each member contributed funds for the purchase of books and could borrow from the collection. Other colonial cities also established library societies.

Most colonists, however, relied heavily upon only two books: the Bible and an almanac containing a calendar and articles on agriculture, health, cooking, science, and politics. A popular almanac was Benjamin Franklin's *Poor Richard's Almanac.*

The first colonial newspaper, started in 1704, was the *Boston Weekly News-Letter.* Within 50 years, 27 newspapers were being published in 11 colonies. Printer-editors also turned out numerous pamphlets, especially on political matters.

2. Zenger Trial (1735). John Peter Zenger, publisher of the *New-York Weekly Journal,* was arrested for libel because he had printed articles criticizing New York's royal governor. Tried before a hostile judge, Zenger was acquitted by a courageous jury on the ground that he had published the truth. Henceforth publishers were free to criticize the government. Freedom of the press, the principle thus proclaimed by the Zenger case, was later reaffirmed in the First Amendment to the United States Constitution.

SUPERSTITION AND SCIENCE

1. Salem Witch Trials. At Salem, Massachusetts, the townspeople in 1692 panicked in their fear of witchcraft. The Puritan authorities arrested several hundred persons, and 20 were formally tried and hanged as witches. As the hysteria subsided and colonial leaders came to their senses, the trials were stopped. The Salem witch trials were a tragedy, but they involved fewer people and lasted a shorter time than similar trials in England and Europe.

2. Science. Benjamin Franklin, a man of many talents, was an 18th-century colonial model of scientific thinking and accomplishment. He devised the lightning rod, bifocal lenses, and a fuel-conserving iron stove; he studied the ocean currents and identified lightning as electricity. Franklin was unequaled as a scientist among the colonists. Several other 18th-century colonists were recognized by European scientific circles, especially in the field of biology.

THE NEW PERSON: THE AMERICAN

The colonists, British and non-British alike, brought from Europe certain customs, habits, and traditions. Their European way of living was modified by the American environment, especially by the frontier with its great tracts of available land, its danger from Indians, and its challenges from nature. In adjusting to the new environment, the colonists were forced to change. They developed a spirit of individualism, self-reliance, independence, and faith in the future. With the passing of time, a new person emerged—no longer a European, but an American in character and outlook.

———————— MULTIPLE-CHOICE QUESTIONS ————————

1. The traditional rights of English people do *not* derive from England's (a) Magna Carta (b) common law (c) Glorious Revolution (d) policy of mercantilism.
2. Which was a result of Magna Carta? (a) The monarch lost the power to impose taxes alone. (b) All classes were represented in Parliament. (c) No free man could serve on a jury. (d) Parliament could pass laws for the colonies.
3. "No free man shall be . . . imprisoned . . . except by the lawful judgment of his peers. . . . "—Magna Carta 1215. This quotation is the basis for the democratic principle of (a) freedom of speech (b) trial by jury (c) freedom of assembly (d) freedom from cruel and unusual punishment.
4. The Virginia House of Burgesses and the New England town meetings were similar in that both (a) originated in New England (b) were free from vetoes by colonial governors (c) were initially established by the English Parliament (d) represented colonial participation in the government.
5. The Mayflower Compact was an important step in the growth of democracy because it (a) guaranteed trial by jury to the Pilgrims (b) indicated that the people were the proper source of political authority (c) freed the indentured servants on the *Mayflower* (d) guaranteed religious freedom to all settlers.
6. "Direct democracy" is best illustrated by the (a) United States Congress (b) New England town meeting (c) House of Burgesses (d) English Parliament.
7. Which of these represents the first written constitution in North America? (a) royal charter granted to the Virginia Company (b) Fundamental Orders of Connecticut (c) Mayflower Compact (d) United States Constitution.
8. Which was the most common feature of government in the 13 colonies? (a) a legislature with an elected lower house (b) a legislature appointed by the monarch (c) a governor elected by the people (d) a governor appointed by the established church.
9. In the 18th century, the colonial assemblies frequently used the "power of the purse" to (a) obtain the royal governor's assent to laws (b) encourage political union among the colonies (c) promote economic dependence on Britain (d) extend suffrage on the frontier regions.
10. Some colonies maintained an established church, best described as a church that (a) is tax-supported (b) all people must join (c) owns much property (d) recognizes the leadership of the pope.
11. "My sermons demanded freedom of worship for all and just payment to the Indians for land. The authorities forced me to flee." This statement could have been made by (a) Roger Williams (b) William Penn (c) Thomas Hooker (d) Jonathan Edwards.
12. Which two colonies led the movement for separation of church and state? (a) Massachusetts and New York (b) Rhode Island and Pennsylvania (c) Virginia and New Jersey (d) Maryland and South Carolina.
13. By the early 18th century, religious developments in the 13 colonies indicated that the (a) Anglican Church was the established church in almost all the colonies (b) religious leaders were generally the civil administrators (c) principle of religious toleration had made significant headway (d) separation of church and state was the policy in most colonies.
14. The geography of a region will have the most direct influence on its people's (a) means of support (b) form of worship (c) system of education (d) system of government.

15. In colonial America, the "triangular trade" routes involved commerce in (a) sugar and molasses with the West Indies (b) silks and spices with China (c) gold and silver with Central America (d) furs and lumber with Canada.

16. The differences in the economic development of the New England, middle, and southern colonies resulted chiefly from (a) geographic conditions (b) customs of the immigrants (c) differences in colonial government (d) extent of education in the colonies.

17. During the 18th century, the basic purpose of the British mercantile system was to (a) increase the wealth and power of Great Britain (b) stimulate colonial initiative and self-sufficiency (c) guarantee the colonies a favorable balance of trade (d) encourage international economic cooperation.

18. Which colonial enterprise was *least* affected by the English mercantile system? (a) a shipyard in Connecticut (b) a distillery in Massachusetts (c) a subsistence farm in Pennsylvania (d) a tobacco plantation in Virginia.

19. Under Great Britain's policy of mercantilism, the American colonists were encouraged to (a) manufacture beaver hats (b) import sugar and molasses from the French West Indies only (c) ship tobacco and naval stores to Britain exclusively (d) export woolen goods to European countries.

20. The early colonists who worked for a specified number of years in exchange for their passage to America were called (a) slaves (b) patroons (c) indentured servants (d) sharecroppers.

21. The chief occupation of most American colonists was (a) farming (b) manufacturing (c) shipping and shipbuilding (d) fishing.

22. Before 1763 most colonial farmers wore clothing that was (a) imported from Europe (b) made in American factories (c) made by tailors in their shops (d) made by women in their homes.

23. In 1700 the most important export of Virginia was (a) cotton (b) tobacco (c) wheat (d) fish.

24. Large families were an asset to the early American colonists mainly because large families provided (a) social mobility (b) a closely knit social unit (c) a source of labor (d) military protection.

25. A characteristic of the 13 English colonies was (a) complete religious freedom (b) free compulsory public education (c) class distinctions (d) universal male suffrage.

26. The early leaders of Massachusetts Bay Colony emphasized education because they desired to encourage (a) democracy in government (b) an enlightened public opinion (c) the reading of the Bible (d) religious toleration.

27. In the New England colonies, elementary schools were generally maintained by the (a) towns (b) English government (c) Anglican Church (d) colonial legislatures.

28. The first colleges in New England were organized primarily to (a) teach medicine and law (b) teach the practical arts and sciences (c) prepare persons for the ministry (d) train farmers.

29. An important cultural achievement during the colonial period was the (a) development of a distinctive American music (b) printing of newspapers to influence public opinion (c) advance in medical science that eliminated colonial superstitions (d) establishment of schools for the children of factory workers.

30. Which principle was promoted as a result of the Zenger trial? (a) A newspaper must publish the replies of its critics. (b) A provable statement may be published without fear of punishment. (c) A newspaper may print the testimony given in criminal trials. (d) Newspapers may be operated under private ownership.

31. Which reinforced the principle established in the Zenger case? (a) Mayflower Compact (b) Fundamental Orders of Connecticut (c) Salem witch trials (d) First Amendment to the United States Constitution.

32. Benjamin Franklin, an outstanding colonist, did *not* win fame as (a) a frontier explorer (b) an educator (c) a writer (d) a scientist.

33. A pledge to "frame such just and equal laws . . . as shall be thought most meet and convenient for the general good" is contained in (a) the Mayflower Compact (b) the Maryland Toleration Act (c) the royal charter for Pennsylvania (d) Benjamin Franklin's *Poor Richard's Almanac.*

34. Which was the most important reason for the social mobility that existed in the 13 English colonies during the 18th century? (a) absence of racial prejudice (b) existence of a strong cultural heritage (c) emphasis on rapid industrialization (d) availability of land.

35. Which was a major difference between American colonial society and European society of the same period? (a) greater social mobility in Europe than in America (b) absence of a social class structure in America (c) greater emphasis in America on wealth rather than family background (d) lack of a merchant class in Europe.

36. In its *broadest* sense, the term "culture" is best defined as (a) a high level of technological achievement (b) the ideals and hopes of a nation (c) a people's total way of living (d) all of the fine arts, such as painting, sculpture, and music.

37. Which characteristic of an area is *not* considered part of its culture? (a) economy (b) religion (c) topography (d) language.

38. Which is the most accurate statement concerning American culture during the colonial period? (a) It was hindered by climate and geography. (b) It was a model of British society. (c) It was influenced by many different sources. (d) It was dominated by Puritan ideas.

39. Which statement best illustrates that colonial culture reflected multiple causation? (a) To each according to his or her needs. (b) Environment and heredity are constantly interacting. (c) Geographic differences account for variations in civilizations. (d) Wealth and power go together.

———————————————— **ESSAY QUESTIONS** ————————————————

1. Show in *one* way how the 13 colonies were influenced by their British heritage with respect to *each* of the following: *(a)* law and court procedures *(b)* individual rights *(c)* structure of government *(d)* religious beliefs.

2. Democratic government in the United States had its beginnings during our colonial period. Show how *each* of the following was an important step in the development of our democracy: *(a)* Mayflower Compact *(b)* House of Burgesses *(c)* New England town meetings *(d)* Fundamental Orders of Connecticut *(e)* General School Act of 1647 in Massachusetts *(f)* Maryland Toleration Act of 1649 *(g)* Zenger trial.

3. Choose *one* of the colonies. Compare life about 1750 in that colony with life today in the same area with reference to *three* of the following topics: *(a)* education *(b)* religion *(c)* means of earning a living *(d)* amusements and recreation *(e)* methods of communication. *(f)* social mobility.

4. The colonial period in United States history (1607–1776) provided new opportunities for developing (1) political democracy, and (2) social democracy. *(a)* Explain

why the colonial period offered new opportunities to the colonists. *(b)* Describe *two* developments in political democracy and *two* developments in social democracy that resulted from the colonists' taking advantage of these new opportunities.

5. Although the colonies developed certain democratic institutions, they also displayed undemocratic practices. *(a)* Discuss *one* political, *one* economic, and *one* social development that illustrate colonial democracy. *(b)* Discuss *one* political, *one* economic, and *one* social practice that illustrate colonial lack of democracy.

6. The 13 colonies usually are considered as three groups—*(a)* New England, *(b)* middle, *(c)* southern—chiefly because each group had its own distinctive geographic features. For *each* group of colonies (1) describe *two* of its distinctive geographic features, and (2) show how these features influenced the way its colonists earned a living.

PART 2. The Colonists Fight the American Revolution and Gain Independence

WORLDWIDE STRUGGLE BETWEEN FRANCE AND ENGLAND

Starting in 1689 England and France engaged in a series of wars for mastery in Europe, and for commercial and colonial supremacy throughout the world. The first three of these wars were indecisive, but the fourth—the Seven Years' War in Europe and its American counterpart, the French and Indian War—brought victory to England.

FRENCH AND INDIAN WAR (1754–1763)

In 1754 Virginia colonial militia clashed with French forces for control of the Ohio Valley. At first the French won many victories, the most important being their ambush of a British and colonial army under General Edward Braddock as it marched toward the French Fort Duquesne (at the present site of Pittsburgh). Braddock's forces might have been completely destroyed had it not been for the skill of a Virginia colonial officer, George Washington.

In 1757 William Pitt became Britain's prime minister and redoubled the war effort in North America. Additional British troops, together with additional colonial militia, turned the tide of battle. In 1759 General James Wolfe captured Quebec, the French fortress on the St. Lawrence River. In 1760 General Jeffrey Amherst captured Montreal, ending the war in Canada. These British victories in North America were paralleled by British triumphs in India and by the success of Britain's ally, Prussia, in Europe. France was completely defeated.

The Treaty of Paris (1763) eliminated France as a colonial power in North America. France ceded (1) to Spain: all French territory west of the Mississippi, as well as the city of New Orleans, and (2) to Britain: Canada and all French territory east of the Mississippi, except New Orleans.

EFFECTS OF THE FRENCH AND INDIAN WAR

1. On the Colonies. The American colonists were affected favorably. They *(a)* gained self-confidence and military experience, *(b)* saw the need for colonial unity to meet common problems, and *(c)* had the danger of attack by the French and certain Indian tribes removed from their frontiers and thus became less dependent on England.

2. On Britain. Concentrating on wars against France, Britain had followed a colonial policy of *salutary neglect*. Britain had permitted its American colonies to exercise virtual self-government and to evade British mercantilist restrictions. This neglect the colonists considered salutary, or beneficial. Britain now determined to change its policy, believing that the colonies *(a)* had not helped sufficiently with soldiers and supplies in the war against France, *(b)* had gained much from the victory over the French and the Indians, and *(c)* should pay at least part of the cost of the war.

BRITAIN'S NEW POLICY FOR COLONIAL AMERICA

Starting in 1763 the British government adopted a new colonial policy with three basic objectives: (1) place the colonies under strict British political and economic control, (2) compel the colonies to respect and obey English laws, and (3) make the colonies bear their part of the cost of maintaining the British Empire.

1. Strict Enforcement of Existing Laws

a. Navigation Acts. Reflecting mercantilist doctrine, these laws required the colonists to (1) transport their goods only in British (and colonial) ships (although Dutch freighters offered lower rates), (2) export certain *enumerated ar-*

Growth of the British Empire in North America

North America in 1689	North America in 1763

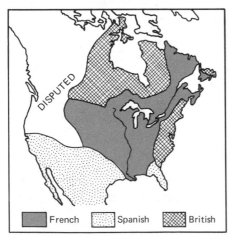 

French   Spanish   British   Spanish   British

ticles, such as tobacco, sugar, indigo, and furs, only to Britain (although western European markets offered higher prices), and (3) purchase their imports from Britain or, when colonial ships secured goods from Europe to stop at a British port and pay import duties. These laws sought to benefit British (and also colonial) shipbuilders, British merchants, and British manufacturers. Beginning in 1763, British Prime Minister *George Grenville* sent to the colonies an increasing number of customs collectors, royal inspectors, and naval patrols to enforce the laws.

b. Writs of Assistance. These general search warrants were court orders authorizing British officials to search colonial homes, buildings, and ships for smuggled goods. Unlike a search warrant in the United States today, which authorizes an officer to search only a particular place for specified goods, a writ of assistance permitted a British official to search any place and seize any smuggled goods.

2. New Taxes

a. Sugar Act (1764). This act reduced the existing duties on colonial imports of sugar and molasses from the Spanish and French West Indies, but called for strict enforcement.

b. Stamp Act (1765). This was the first *internal tax* (as contrasted with import and export duties) levied on the colonies. It required the purchase of stamps that were to be put on printed materials such as wills, mortgages, almanacs, pamphlets, and newspapers. It mostly affected influential groups such as lawyers, clergy, and printers.

c. Townshend Acts (1767). At the suggestion of Chancellor of the Exchequer *Charles Townshend,* Parliament levied new duties on colonial imports of paper, glass, paint, and tea. Part of the fines levied against colonists who violated these tax laws was to go directly to the royal governors so as to make them financially independent of colonial assemblies.

Colonists accused of violating the British tax laws were tried in admiralty (military) courts, where they were denied a jury trial. The colonists very likely would have found more sympathy from a jury in a colonial court.

3. Western Land Policy: Proclamation of 1763. This royal decree of George III prohibited colonists from settling west of the Appalachian Mountains. By prohibiting settlement in this region, the British government sought to *(a)* protect the fur trade, *(b)* remove a cause of Indian uprisings such as the 1763 rebellion led by the Indian chief Pontiac, and *(c)* prevent colonial settlements beyond the reach of British authorities.

4. Stationing of Soldiers: Quartering Act of 1765. This law, regarded by the colonists as a form of taxation, required them to provide food and living quarters for British soldiers. Supposedly, the soldiers were to protect the colonists from the Indians. Most of the soldiers, however, were stationed not in frontier settlements but in populous coastal cities such as New York and Boston.

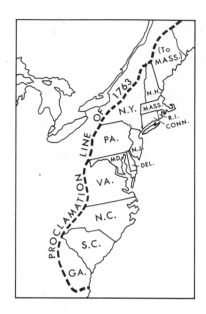

Proclamation Line of 1763

COLONIAL OPPOSITION

1. Violations of British Laws. Merchants and shipowners continued to smuggle goods into the colonies to avoid import duties. When the *Gaspee,* an English naval patrol vessel, ran aground off Rhode Island, colonists boarded the ship and set it afire. Frontier settlers and southern planters continued to occupy the fertile lands beyond the Appalachians.

2. Protests Against Writs of Assistance. Lawyers and writers protested the writs of assistance as illegal invasions of colonial property. *James Otis,* in a Boston court, eloquently but unsuccessfully denounced the writs as violating the English common law principle that "a man's home is his castle."

3. Cooperation Among the Colonies

a. Stamp Act Congress of 1765. At the urging of the Massachusetts assembly, delegates from nine colonies met in New York City to plan united resistance against the Stamp Act. The delegates asserted that the colonists could be taxed only by colonial legislatures, not by Parliament. They also began a colonial boycott of British goods.

b. Committees of Correspondence. Samuel Adams in Massachusetts in 1772 launched these committees to provide an intercolonial information network. The committees communicated with one another on mutual problems and helped organize the opposition to British policies.

4. Mass Action: Boycotts and Demonstrations. The Stamp Act Congress delegates urged and many colonial merchants supported nonimportation agreements. These were pledges not to import British goods until the repeal of the Stamp Act. In addition, resistance throughout the colonies prevented distribution of the tax stamps. Parliament finally repealed the Stamp Act in 1766 but reaffirmed its right to tax the colonies by passing the Declaratory Act.

When Parliament passed the Townshend taxes (1767), colonial merchants and consumers again boycotted British goods. The *Sons of Liberty,* an organization of colonial patriots, helped enforce the boycott. The colonists hoped that English business leaders would pressure Parliament to repeal the hated tax laws. In 1770 the British Parliament yielded and repealed all the Townshend import duties except the tax on tea.

In Boston, colonial demonstrators often clashed with British soldiers, or redcoats. In 1770 soldiers fired upon a hostile but unarmed crowd and killed five persons. The colonists named this event the *Boston Massacre.*

BOSTON TEA PARTY (1773)

Parliament passed the Tea Act (1773), exempting the East India Company from taxes on tea shipped from Britain to the colonies. By this act, Parliament offered the colonists the cheapest tea ever. Nevertheless, the colonists were resentful: (1) Colonial merchants, who were smuggling tea from Holland to avoid the import duty, would be undersold by the inexpensive tea of the East India Company. (2) The colonists would still be paying the hated Townshend import duty. In New York and Philadelphia, colonists turned back the tea ships with their full cargoes. In Boston, colonists disguised as Indians boarded the British ships and dumped the tea into the harbor. This action, defying British authority and destroying British property, was named the *Boston Tea Party.*

"INTOLERABLE" ACTS (1774)

To punish Massachusetts and assert British authority, Parliament passed a series of acts that the colonists termed "intolerable." These acts (1) closed Boston harbor until the colonists paid for the destroyed tea, (2) authorized the quartering of troops in any colonial town, (3) permitted British officials accused of crimes in Massachusetts to stand trial in Britain, and (4) drastically curtailed self-government in Massachusetts. By their severity, these acts solidified colonial support for Massachusetts.

FIRST CONTINENTAL CONGRESS (1774)

To unify colonial resistance to the Intolerable Acts, delegates from 12 colonies met at Philadelphia as the *First Continental Congress.* They addressed a "Declaration of Rights and Grievances" to King George III, asking for a redress (correction) of wrongs, especially for repeal of the Intolerable Acts. Meanwhile, they voted to impose a boycott on British goods.

Patrick Henry in Virginia acclaimed the work of the Continental Congress in a famous speech, concluding with: "Give me liberty, or give me death!" Realizing

Lexington and Concord: First Battles of the Revolutionary War   1775

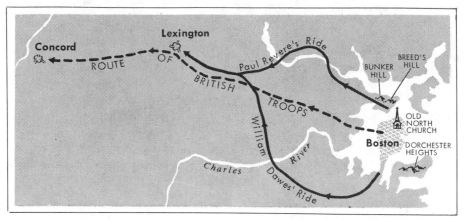

that liberty might require defense, colonial patriots began training militia and storing military supplies.

OUTBREAK OF THE AMERICAN REVOLUTION (APRIL 1775)

In Massachusetts British General Thomas Gage ordered a detachment of troops to seize colonial military supplies at Concord and to arrest the colonial leaders John Hancock and Samuel Adams, believed to be at Lexington. Forewarned by Paul Revere and William Dawes, *Minutemen,* who were Massachusetts militia pledged to be ready at a minute's notice, were waiting to resist the British troops. Fighting broke out. The poet and essayist Ralph Waldo Emerson later wrote, "Here once the embattled farmers stood and fired the shot heard round the world." Thus started the American Revolution.

BASIC CAUSES OF THE AMERICAN REVOLUTION

1. Economic Causes. Colonial manufacturers and merchants were indignant over British mercantilist laws, which hampered their industry and trade. They rejected the doctrine that colonies exist only to enrich the country that founded them. Plantation owners and frontier settlers, eager for new land, disliked the prohibition against westward expansion. Professional people opposed the stamp tax on printed matter, such as newspapers, pamphlets, and legal documents. Consumers resented import taxes, which raised living costs. The colonists were determined to free themselves from restrictions and exploitation by Britain.

The British argued that Britain's mercantilist laws assigned the colonies their proper role in the economy of the British Empire as producers of raw materials. They further pointed out that mercantilist laws encouraged colonial shipbuilding, provided bounties for colonial production of essential products such as naval stores, permitted colonial merchants to trade freely with Britain and the British West Indies, and helped colonial planters by requiring British merchants to buy tobacco only from the British colonies. Finally, Britain claimed that its armed might protected colonial shipping and frontier settlements.

2. Political Causes. The colonists maintained that they were entitled to self-government and could be taxed only by their own elected colonial legislatures. Their sentiments were expressed in the slogan, ascribed to James Otis: "Taxation without representation is tyranny." Further the colonists were incensed by the writs of assistance and the denial of trial by jury. These measures, they argued, deprived them of their rights.

In answer to the colonists' claim that they were being taxed without representation, the British pointed out that even in Britain itself, high property requirements allowed less than 5 percent of the adult male population to vote for Parliamentary representatives. The British asserted that the Parliament at London had the right to legislate for all parts of the Empire. They argued that members of Parliament represented not only the voters who had elected them, but all persons in the Empire. The British also maintained that the taxes levied in the colonies were used for colonial defense and government. To colonial charges that British laws were unduly harsh, the British replied that colonial defiance of authority made such laws necessary.

3. Misunderstandings. Separated by 3000 miles of ocean with contacts maintained only by slow-moving ships, the American colonies and Britain did not understand each other. Although most colonists were of British origin, their environment had transformed them into Americans. They proved unwilling or unable to understand the British viewpoint. Furthermore, many non-British colonists had come from countries traditionally hostile to Britain. Finally, a small but active minority resented the British monarchy and desired independence.

Likewise, the British authorities failed to comprehend the colonial position. King George III, seeking to revive royal executive power in Britain, considered the colonists ungrateful and disloyal, rejected efforts at compromise, and pursued a policy of suppressing the colonies by force.

REASONS FOR THE DECLARATION OF INDEPENDENCE

During the first year of active warfare, most of the colonists were not certain whether they were fighting for their rights as English citizens within the Empire or for complete freedom. By the summer of 1776, the colonists had decided that this was a war for independence.

1. The colonists were outraged by British military conduct and by the British use of German mercenaries, or hired soldiers—the *Hessians.*

2. The colonists believed that a declaration of independence would entitle captured American soldiers to the status of prisoners of war rather than traitors to the British crown.

3. *Thomas Paine,* a recent immigrant from England, published a persuasive

and widely read pamphlet, *Common Sense.* He declared that common sense forbade a continent to remain subservient to an island and forbade a people to remain loyal to a king who was spilling their blood. Paine convinced many colonists that independence was the only sensible goal.

4. American forces had fared well against British troops. The Americans had retreated from their positions around Boston—at Breed's Hill and Bunker Hill—only after inflicting heavy casualties on the British, and they had subsequently forced the British to evacuate Boston. These achievements gave the colonists confidence in declaring their independence.

5. Colonial leaders believed that independence would help the colonies to secure assistance from foreign nations, especially from France, which wanted revenge for its defeat by Britain in the French and Indian War.

AUTHORSHIP OF THE DECLARATION OF INDEPENDENCE

On July 4, 1776, the Second Continental Congress, speaking for the American colonies, formally adopted the Declaration of Independence. Although Benjamin Franklin and John Adams made some contributions, the Declaration was written chiefly by *Thomas Jefferson.* Claiming no originality, Jefferson asserted that he merely placed on paper the political beliefs widespread among the American people. In so doing Jefferson drew heavily upon the ideas of John Locke.

Locke had justified England's Glorious Revolution of 1689 in his work *Two Treatises of Government.* He had affirmed the democratic political theory that *(a)* the people possess *natural rights* to life, liberty, and property, *(b)* the people, by means of a *social contract* among themselves or with their rulers, create and grant authority to government for the purpose of protecting their rights, and *(c)* the people may replace a government that fails in this purpose, if necessary by revolution.

BASIC IDEAS OF THE DECLARATION OF INDEPENDENCE

1. Introduction. The Declaration states that as it has become necessary for the colonists to "dissolve the political bands which have connected them" with Britain and to declare their independence, "a decent respect to the opinions of mankind" requires them to "declare the causes which impel them to the separation."

2. Democratic Philosophy of Government. In simple yet eloquent language, the Declaration proclaims: *(a)* "All men are created equal" and "are endowed by their Creator with certain unalienable rights," including "life, liberty, and the pursuit of happiness." *(b)* "To secure these rights, governments are instituted [started] among men, deriving their just powers from the consent of the governed." *(c)* "Whenever any form of government becomes destructive of these ends, it is the right of the people to alter or to abolish it, and to institute new government." *(d)* However, "governments long established should not be changed for light and transient [temporary] causes."

3. List of Grievances. To prove that the colonists have sufficient causes, the Declaration enumerates the many "injuries and usurpations" committed against them by Britain's King George III.

4. Conclusion. The Declaration concludes that "these united colonies are, and of right ought to be, free and independent states."

SIGNIFICANCE OF THE DECLARATION OF INDEPENDENCE

1. Proclamation of New Ideas. The Declaration affirmed political concepts that, for its time, were revolutionary. To a world long accustomed to sharp and hereditary class distinctions, it stated that "all men are created equal" and are endowed with "unalienable rights." To a world long accustomed to absolute monarchs ruling by "divine right," it proclaimed that governments rule by "the consent of the governed." To a world long accustomed to countries ruling their colonies strictly, it announced that colonists have the right to overthrow such despotism and to "institute new government."

2. Effects Upon the American Revolution. The Declaration elevated the colonial struggle against the British armies into a war for independence. It encouraged France and Spain to assist the colonists.

3. Long-Term Effects Throughout the World. To peoples throughout the world, the Declaration became a source of inspiration. It inspired the French revolutionaries, who in 1789 rebelled against the old order or regime and adopted the *Declaration of the Rights of Man*. It encouraged Latin American leaders, in the early 19th century, to fight for independence from Spain. It inspired Asian and African nationalists, in the 20th century, to oppose imperialist control and to achieve national independence.

4. Long-Term Effects Within the United States. Although not part of the formal government of the United States, the Declaration influenced certain Constitutional provisions such as due process of law and the addition of amendments. Further, by providing Americans with a basic democratic philosophy, the Declaration inspired movements for democratic reforms, such as the abolition of slavery, equal rights for women, and full civil rights for blacks.

BRIEF SURVEY OF THE REVOLUTIONARY WAR

1. British Successes in the Middle States (1776–1777). Britain, a major military power, expected to subdue its rebellious subjects easily. Sir William Howe led a sizable British army that defeated George Washington's poorly trained forces and occupied New York City. Washington retreated into New Jersey, where he gained morale-boosting triumphs at Trenton and Princeton. Thereafter, the British redcoats defeated the colonial forces in several engagements near Philadelphia and occupied that city.

The Revolutionary War in the Middle States
1776–1777

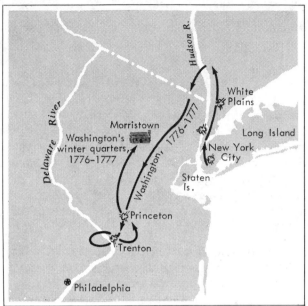

2. American Victory at Saratoga (1777). At Saratoga in upstate New York, the Americans captured a British army under General John Burgoyne that had come south from Canada. The Battle of Saratoga was the turning point of the war. It convinced the French government that the Americans had a chance to win. Until then, France had been providing the colonists with loans and munitions, but secretly. Now the French government, heeding our minister to France, Benjamin Franklin, recognized American independence and in 1778 signed a treaty of alliance with the new nation.

3. American Suffering at Valley Forge (1777–1778). Meanwhile, having lost Philadelphia to the British, Washington and his troops retreated some 20 miles away to Valley Forge. Inadequately fed and clothed, they suffered through an especially harsh winter. Washington held his army together only with great difficulty.

4. American Victory in the Northwest Territory (1778–1779). *George Rogers Clark* led a force of fewer than 200 frontier fighters down the Ohio River and into the Northwest Territory. Clark won a series of victories against British forces, climaxed by the recapture of Vincennes. Clark's victories ended British control of the Northwest Territory and established American claims to the area.

American Victory at Saratoga 1777

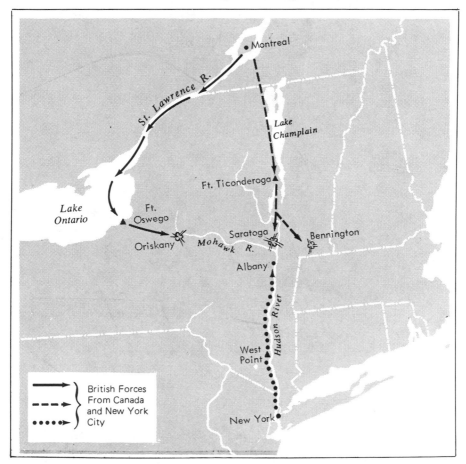

5. War in the South (1778–1781). The British left Philadelphia in 1778 and returned to New York City. British forces next moved southward, won several battles, and occupied the major seaports of Savannah and Charleston. However, they could not crush the American forces. By early 1781 in the interior of the Carolinas, the British had suffered a series of reverses. British General Charles Cornwallis eventually withdrew his forces northward to Yorktown, Virginia.

6. Yorktown: The Final American Victory (1781). Washington's forces in the New York area were augmented by a French army under the Count de Rochambeau. A French navy under Admiral de Grasse moved northward from the West Indies. With Cornwallis encamped at Yorktown, Washington quickly moved the American and French forces southward to overwhelm the

War in the Middle States   1777–1778

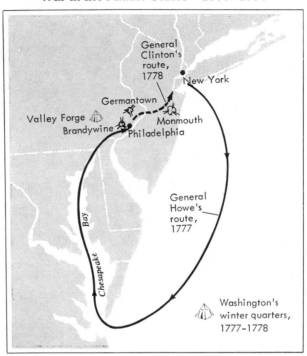

American Victory in the Northwest Territory
1778–1779

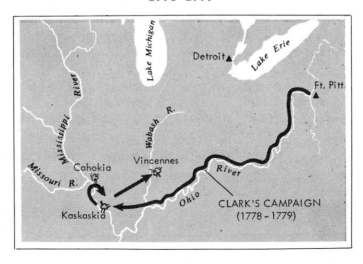

War in the South and American Victory at Yorktown 1778–1781

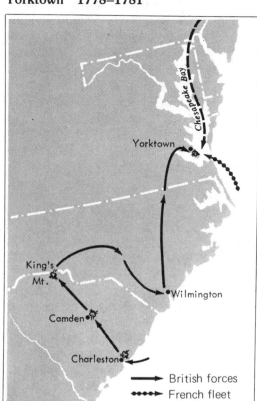

British on land while the French navy cut off any escape by sea. Cornwallis surrendered as the British military band played "The World Turned Upside Down." This American victory practically ended the war. Several months later peace negotiations began, and a treaty was signed in 1783 (see map, page 52).

REASONS FOR THE AMERICAN VICTORY

1. The Americans were fighting on their own soil, for their own homes, and for freedom. The British forces, consisting of British soldiers and Hessian mercenaries, were far from home and in enemy territory. They did not match the Americans in their determination for victory.

2. The Americans were superior wilderness fighters. Their frontier experience helped them defeat the British at Saratoga in upstate New York and at Vincennes in the Northwest Territory.

3. The American forces were led by men of courage and ability. Outstanding, of course, was *George Washington.* A leader with military experience and good judgment, Washington set an example of devotion, integrity, and steadfastness. By strength of personality, he instilled confidence and held his army together during its darkest days.

Other outstanding American military leaders were: *(a)* Colonel *George Rogers Clark,* who drove the British out of much of the Northwest Territory, *(b)* General *Nathanael Greene,* whose hit-and-run tactics exhausted the British army in the Carolinas, and *(c)* Captain *John Paul Jones,* who commanded the naval vessel *Bonhomme Richard* and upheld the American cause on the sea.

The British forces, although superior in numbers and equipment, were led by generals who were often incompetent and overconfident. For example, the British General William Howe moved south from New York City to occupy Philadelphia in 1777 instead of moving north to join Burgoyne. (See map, page 48, top.) This blunder made possible the American victory at Saratoga.

4. The Americans were aided by notable foreign volunteers who saw the colonial cause as a struggle for freedom. *(a)* The Marquis *de Lafayette* of France joined Washington's staff; *(b)* Baron *de Kalb,* who had served in the French army, led colonial troops in the south; *(c)* Baron *von Steuben* of Prussia served as drillmaster of the colonial army; *(d)* Count *Pulaski* was a cavalry leader who had headed an unsuccessful Polish uprising against Russia; and *(e)* Thaddeus *Kosciusko,* appointed a colonel of military engineers, later returned to his native Poland to become a great hero in that nation's unsuccessful struggle for freedom from Russia.

5. As the American Revolution progressed, other nations—first France, then Spain and Holland—entered the struggle against Britain. Now facing several enemies, Britain could not concentrate its full efforts on suppressing the colonists.

6. Public opinion in Britain was divided over the war against the American colonists. William Pitt and Edmund Burke, influential British statesmen, publicly defended the colonists as seeking only their rights. Such an attitude in Britain did not encourage wholehearted prosecution of the war.

WARTIME PROBLEMS FACING THE COLONISTS

1. Providing a Government. The Second Continental Congress acted as the central government for the 13 colonies, or states. From 1775 to 1781 it concerned itself primarily with one objective: winning the war. The Congress was handicapped because it *(a)* lacked essential governmental powers and could only request men, money, and cooperation of the states, but could not enforce its requests; *(b)* was inexperienced, inefficient, and wasteful; and *(c)* had some members who engaged in petty political bickering.

Nevertheless, the Second Continental Congress achieved an impressive record. It *(a)* held the 13 states together, *(b)* authorized an army and appointed

George Washington as commander in chief, *(c)* established a small navy, *(d)* issued the Declaration of Independence, *(e)* arranged the military alliance with France, *(f)* raised funds to finance the war, and *(g)* proposed the Articles of Confederation, which in 1781 became the framework for the government of the new nation.

2. Raising Funds. Congress needed large sums of money to feed, clothe, equip, and pay the Continental Army. Congress proceeded in many ways. *(a)* It issued paper money, called *continentals,* totaling nearly $250 million. This money was backed not by specie (metal), such as gold, but rather by public confidence in the American cause. As the British won victories in the early days of the war, this currency depreciated (fell in value) until it was practically worthless. (From this experience is derived the expression "not worth a continental.") *(b)* Congress requested funds of the states, but these requests were scarcely heeded. *(c)* Congress floated loans, both domestic and foreign—notably from the Netherlands, Spain, and France. However, these amounts were far short of the money needed. *(d)* Congress obtained some funds through the efforts of patriotic Americans. *Haym Salomon,* a Jewish refugee from Russian rule in Poland who had become a New York banker, gave his entire fortune to the American cause. *Robert Morris,* a Pennsylvania merchant and banker who served as superintendent of finance of the young nation, guaranteed government loans with his personal credit.

3. Maintaining an Army. During most of the war, the Continental Army numbered no more than several thousand troops. They were volunteers who usually signed up for short-term enlistments. Because of the constant turnover, most recruits were never properly trained or disciplined. Their food, shelter, and military equipment were inadequate, and their families received no government assistance while they were in service.

When the Continental Army faced battle, it was often reinforced by local militia. These were civilians who dropped their daily pursuits and served as temporary soldiers.

4. Dealing With the Tories. Not all the colonists supported the war. Historians are generally agreed that at the start of the war, the colonial population was divided as follows: *(a)* one-third, the organized Patriots, actively supported independence; *(b)* one-third were undecided, waiting to see what would develop; and *(c)* one-third, the unorganized Tories, or Loyalists, remained loyal to Britain and the king. The Tories consisted chiefly of the more prosperous and conservative groups, especially wealthy landowners and officeholders. During the war, most Tories fled to Canada and Britain but some remained to fight in the British armies. With most of the Tories gone, Patriots took control of the state governments and revised the state constitutions to provide for greater democracy. The Patriots also confiscated royal, proprietary, and Tory estates, subdividing and selling the lands.

The United States After the Treaty of Paris 1783

Areas in dispute with foreign nations

TREATY OF PARIS (1783)

The American negotiators—*Benjamin Franklin, John Jay,* and *John Adams*—secured a highly favorable treaty of peace from Britain.

1. Britain recognized the 13 United States as independent. The new nation was bounded *(a)* on the north by Canada and the Great Lakes, *(b)* on the south by Spanish-owned Florida, which extended then to the Mississippi River, *(c)* on the east by the Atlantic Ocean, and *(d)* on the west by the Mississippi.

2. The Americans regained their right to fish on the banks off Newfoundland.

3. All debts owed by citizens of either nation to creditors of the other were declared valid.

4. The United States agreed to recommend to the states the restoration of confiscated Loyalist properties and the payment of debts owed to British merchants. (This provision was little heeded by the states.)

EFFECTS OF THE AMERICAN REVOLUTION

1. In the United States

a. Political. The 13 American colonies became 13 independent states, loosely bound together by a central government under the Articles of Confederation. Although this government was not very powerful, it was an important step on the road to an effective national union.

Most states drafted new written constitutions containing many democratic features. "Bills of rights" guaranteed the people freedom of speech, press, and religion; assured trial by jury; and prohibited illegal search and seizure. As a result of colonial experiences with royal governors, the state constitutions granted most power to the legislatures and restricted the authority of the governors. The constitutions kept officeholders subject to the popular will by providing for short terms of office and frequent elections.

Most state constitutions retained, but at lower rates, property qualifications for voting. Property qualifications for officeholding remained high, and a few states retained religious qualifications.

b. Economic. The American Revolution resulted in (1) the end of British mercantilist restrictions on American trade and industry, and consequently the growth of an American merchant marine and American manufacturing, (2) the end of British restrictions on migration across the Appalachians and consequently the movement of land-hungry settlers westward, (3) the breakup of large estates—previously royal, proprietary, and Tory-owned—and consequently an increase in the number of independent small farmers, and (4) the end of *primogeniture*—the legal right of the oldest son to inherit the entire estate of his deceased father—and consequently the end of the legal superiority of the oldest son over his younger brothers.

The end of the Revolution also brought economic problems. American merchants were excluded from the British West Indies and lost their favored position in British markets. With the wartime demand for goods ended, American farmers and planters saw agricultural prices decline, and city workers faced unemployment. The new nation was plagued by two other economic problems: inflation, and the large public debt incurred to finance the war.

c. Social. (1) The Anglican Church was disestablished in all former colonies where it had previously been tax-supported. (2) All state constitutions but three guaranteed separation of church and state. In Virginia this separation became law in 1786 by passage of Thomas Jefferson's *Statute of Religious Free-*

dom. (3) Criminal codes were made more humane by the abolishment of severe punishments for minor infractions. (4) Slaves in the northern states were gradually freed. (Slavery, however, remained fastened on the southern economy.)

2. In France. The American Revolution encouraged many French citizens to hope that they might overthrow their absolute monarchy and establish a democratic government. Thus the French Revolution of 1789 was partly inspired by the American Revolution of 1775.

3. In Latin America. Throughout the Spanish colonies in the Western Hemisphere, people were thrilled by the success of the American Revolution. While Spain was involved in the Napoleonic Wars in Europe (1799–1815), the Spanish colonists followed the example of the United States and revolted for independence and democracy.

4. In the British Empire. The American Revolution *(a)* discredited King George III and his efforts to revive royal power, and *(b)* led to gradual changes in Britain's colonial policy. The British abandoned the mercantilist idea that colonies exist solely to enrich the founding country. To prevent colonial rebellion and encourage colonial loyalty, Britain gradually extended self-government throughout its empire, starting in 1867 with dominion status for Canada.

Historical Analysis. *How revolutionary was the American Revolution?* Historians have long disputed this question.

Meaning of Revolution. Historians are generally agreed that revolutions professing democratic goals exhibit the following similarities: (1) *political*—a shift of governmental power from one socioeconomic class to another, (2) *economic*—greater freedom for economic enterprise and wider ownership of land, (3) *social*—democratic reforms, and (4) *intellectual*—a proclamation of idealistic goals.

The classic example was the French Revolution of 1789, which achieved a shift of governmental power from the aristocracy to the middle class; removed guild and local restrictions on business enterprise; stripped the aristocracy and the church of their lands, which were eventually sold to many small, independent farmers; eliminated special privileges and class distinctions, and proclaimed the goals of "liberty, equality, and fraternity."

The American Revolution—Truly a Revolutionary Movement. Historians who support this point of view cite the following evidence:

(1) *Political.* The governments of the former colonies became more responsive to the popular will. There were no more royal and proprietary governors; aristocratic control ended; and with property qualifications for voting reduced, the poor and underprivileged lower classes gained a greater political voice. This analysis views the American Revolution in part as a class conflict for political control.

(2) *Economic.* American merchants and manufacturers were freed from British mercantilist restrictions on their trade and industry. With the seizure and sale of the landed estates of the aristocracy, more small farmers became landowners. Primogeniture was ended.

(3) *Social.* Religious freedom was expanded. In the northern states, slavery was ended.

(4) *Intellectual.* The colonists upheld English democratic ideals and saw themselves as defending liberty and human freedom.

The American Revolution—Mainly a War for Independence, Not a Revolutionary Movement. Historians who support this point of view cite the following evidence:

(1) *Political.* (a) Britain's colonies were democratic for their times. With land easily available and widely held, a large proportion of the adult males could satisfy the property qualifications for voting and vote for the members of their assemblies. (b) The assemblies, by use of the power of the purse, were able to check the royal and proprietary governors. (c) The leaders of the struggle against Britain were drawn from the middle and upper classes. They neither experienced a change in socioeconomic status themselves nor suffered a loss of power to members of another class. People such as planters George Washington and Thomas Jefferson, professionals John Adams and Benjamin Franklin, and merchant John Hancock were leaders in colonial government before the war, during the war itself, and in the state and national governments established after the war. Hence, according to this analysis, there was no class conflict inherent in the war for independence.

(2) *Economic.* Colonial merchants and manufacturers were relatively free and prospered before 1763 under Britain's policy of salutary neglect. In pursuing independence they were seeking not so much to remove long-standing restrictions on their economic enterprise as to prevent new and unacceptable restrictions.

(3) *Social.* The American patriots did not view the struggle against Britain as a social revolution. The movements for religious freedom and the abolition of slavery had preceded the war and existed apart from it. The Declaration of Independence did not condemn slavery, and slavery remained powerful in the southern states.

(4) *Intellectual.* These historians argue that ours was hardly a revolution at all and cannot be cast in the mold of the French Revolution. The colonists had already evolved into a new people before independence. Having outgrown colonial rule, they were in fact a new nation. They fought against Britain to assure independence for this new nation and for their right to live in freedom.

MATCHING QUESTIONS

Column A

1. Spoke for "liberty or death"
2. Secured new taxes on the colonists
3. Denounced the "writs of assistance" in a Boston court
4. Negotiated the American alliance with France
5. Won the Northwest Territory
6. Surrendered army at Yorktown
7. Gave fortune to the colonial cause
8. Wrote the Declaration of Independence
9. Surrendered army at Saratoga
10. Spoke for the colonial cause in Britain

Column B

a. John Burgoyne
b. Edmund Burke
c. George Rogers Clark
d. Charles Cornwallis
e. Benjamin Franklin
f. John Hancock
g. Patrick Henry
h. Thomas Jefferson
i. James Otis
j. Haym Salomon
k. Charles Townshend
l. George Washington

MULTIPLE-CHOICE QUESTIONS

1. A result of the French and Indian War was that it (a) ended the Indian menace in North America (b) caused France to cede its claims west of the Mississippi to Great Britain (c) encouraged a spirit of independence in the colonies (d) lessened British restrictions on the colonists.
2. The French and Indian War increased tension between Britain and the American colonies because the (a) colonists had not been allowed to participate in that war (b) colonists had hoped to win independence (c) British pressed the colonists to form Committees of Correspondence (d) British insisted that the colonists share the expenses of the war.
3. Which statement best describes the reaction of American patriots toward British colonial policy following the French and Indian War? (a) They rejected Parliament's right to manage their internal affairs. (b) They petitioned Parliament for independence. (c) They urged the colonial legislatures to enforce the tax program of Parliament. (d) They demanded colonial representation in Parliament.
4. The British contended that the American colonists were represented in Parliament because (a) members of Parliament spoke for all British people (b) colonial governors could communicate colonial demands to Parliament (c) colonial legislatures had the same power as Parliament (d) colonists had been given the rights of English citizens in their charters.
5. Immediately following the French and Indian War, the colonists opposed the British policy of (a) stricter enforcement of mercantilism (b) stricter adherence to "salutary neglect" (c) prohibition of emigration to the colonies (d) greater attention to new possessions in India and Canada.
6. Which legislation of the British Parliament concerning the 13 colonies most clearly illustrates the principles of mercantilism? (a) Intolerable Acts (b) Navigation Acts (c) Stamp Act (d) Proclamation of 1763.
7. The purpose of the Navigation Acts was to protect (a) New England merchants (b) the economic interests of the British Empire (c) colonial trade with the West Indies (d) the slave trade between Britain and the colonies.

8. The *primary* reason why the British Parliament repealed some of the laws to which the American colonists objected was that (a) the colonists used economic sanctions which hurt the merchants of Great Britain (b) the colonists were strongly represented in Parliament (c) Great Britain feared the military power of the colonies (d) colonial petitions were generally well written and therefore effective.

9. The British government felt that a policy of mercantilism also helped the American colonies because it (a) assured the American colonists a secure British market for their products (b) stimulated colonial manufacturing and self-sufficiency (c) encouraged colonial trade with the rest of the world (d) guaranteed the American colonists a favorable balance of trade.

10. Which action of the British government directly affected the people on the frontier? (a) Intolerable Acts (b) Stamp Act (c) Proclamation of 1763 (d) Townshend Acts.

11. The Intolerable Acts were passed as a result of the (a) Boston Massacre (b) Boston Tea Party (c) writs of assistance (d) Stamp Act Congress.

12. Which could best be a subtopic under the heading "Economic Causes of the American Revolution"? (a) British competition outselling American goods in the world market (b) devaluation of the American dollar in relation to the British pound (c) concern of colonists over British interference with their right to decide basic commercial matters (d) inability of colonial apprentices to get work in England.

13. In 1775–1776 one factor that tended to delay the separation of the colonies from Great Britain was the (a) publication of *Common Sense* (b) willingness of King George III to compromise (c) feeling of loyalty to Britain by many colonists (d) military aid supplied to the colonies by France.

14. The significance of Thomas Paine's *Common Sense* was that it (a) suggested a plan of reconciliation with Britain (b) pointed out the absurdity of continued loyalty by the American colonists to the king (c) argued that protests of the colonies should be made only to Parliament (d) outlined a "common sense" approach to commonwealth status.

15. In the Declaration of Independence, the statement "deriving their just powers from the consent of the governed" refers to the (a) source of governmental authority (b) right of trial by jury (c) need for limits on taxation (d) movement to abolish slavery.

16. According to the Declaration of Independence, the purpose of government is to (a) secure the people in their natural rights (b) equalize opportunities for all citizens (c) provide for the common defense (d) establish a system of free public schools.

17. Which is *not* a part of the Declaration of Independence? (a) a statement of the rights of the individual (b) a listing of grievances against King George III (c) a framework for a new government (d) an assertion of the freedom of the colonies.

18. The principles of the Declaration of Independence can be described as (a) part of America's debt to European thought (b) Roger Williams' contribution to political philosophy (c) concepts of government inconsistent with accepted American ideals (d) a defense of the Articles of Confederation.

19. The chief significance of the Declaration of Independence is that it (a) expressed for the first time the right of a people to petition the government (b) attracted thousands of Loyalists to the colonial cause (c) reflected the democratic ideals of the French government of 1776 (d) furnished a body of ideals which future generations could emulate.

20. In what sense was the American Revolutionary War a civil war? (a) Colonial troops fought the Hessians. (b) State militias fought to defend only their own states. (c) French troops helped the Americans fight the British. (d) Some Americans fought on the side of the British.

21. Which statement best explains the outbreak of the American Revolution? (a) The colonists wanted free land. (b) Colonial taxes were too low to pay governmental officials. (c) Radical colonial leaders aroused colonial opinion against British policies. (d) The Articles of Confederation assured a united opposition against Britain.

22. In which pair is the second event or development a direct result of the first? (a) British surrender at Saratoga—signing of the treaty of alliance with France (b) Intolerable Acts—Boston Massacre (c) publication of Declaration of the Rights of Man—signing of the Declaration of Independence (d) George Washington appointed commander in chief of the Continental Army—battles of Lexington and Concord.

23. The primary motive behind French aid to the United States during the Revolutionary War was the French government's desire to (a) regain Canada and Florida (b) promote the principles of the French Revolution (c) force British evacuation of French islands in the West Indies (d) obtain revenge against Great Britain for previous French colonial losses.

24. As a result of the Treaty of Paris (1783), the United States was bounded by all of the following *except* the (a) Atlantic Ocean (b) Great Lakes (c) Mississippi River (d) Gulf of Mexico.

25. The American Revolution resulted in all of the following *except* the (a) breakup of large estates (b) abolition of property qualifications for voting (c) inclusion of a bill of rights in the new state constitutions (d) emancipation of northern blacks.

26. Which is the most valid generalization that can be drawn from the study of our colonial period? (a) Domination by the Church of England was unacceptable to the 13 colonies. (b) Widespread desire on the part of ordinary people is the secret of a successful revolution. (c) Economic boycott is an effective means of expressing protest. (d) Crushing taxation breeds revolutionary discontent.

27. About how many years did our colonial period last? (a) 75 (b) 125 (c) 175 (d) 225.

28. A study of the American Revolution of 1776 best supports the generalization that revolution is most likely to occur when (a) those in power are resistant to change (b) a society has a lower standard of living than those around it (c) a society has become industrialized (d) stable governments are in power.

29. Americans have regarded the American Revolution as being of worldwide importance because it (a) was led by people of recognized intellectual ability (b) was won without outside assistance (c) ended European imperialism in the Western Hemisphere (d) marked the successful emergence of a new concept in government.

30. Which statement best reflects the "revolutionary" nature of the American Revolution? (a) It was led by George Washington, a Virginia planter. (b) It resulted in elected governors in place of royal and proprietory governors. (c) It enabled Americans to continue fishing off the Newfoundland banks. (d) It discredited the effort of Britain's king to revive royal power.

—————————— **DISCUSSION ANALYSIS QUESTIONS** ——————————

Base your answers to the questions below on the statements of the various historians and on your knowledge of the American Revolution.

Historian A: The War for Independence was a bourgeois revolution. Popular masses, in fact, won the war, yet the bourgeoisie and the planters turned the victory to their interests.

Historian B: The successful rebellion of the patriots profoundly affected the course of the future, not only for the Americans, but for all other peoples. The American Revolution brought the first break in the European colonial system. It inspired and continues to inspire colonials of all colors to seek freedom from European domination. It also brought into existence for the first time in modern history a republican system of government in a large nation.

Historian C: Primarily, the American Revolution was a political and constitutional movement and only secondarily one that was either financial, commercial, or social. At bottom the fundamental issue was the political independence of the colonies . . .

Historian D: The struggle was not over high-sounding political and constitutional concepts but over colonial manufacturing, western lands and furs, sugar, wine, tea, and currency.

Historian E: The American Revolution was not a popular revolution. . . . During the conflict itself the mass of people . . . were not seriously disturbed by the actual fighting, and many of the more isolated communities scarcely knew that a war was on.

1. The historian who interpreted the American Revolution in terms of a colonial class struggle was (a) *A* (b) *B* (c) *C* (d) *E*.

2. Historian *C's* views are most similar to those of historian (a) *A* (b) *B* (c) *E* (d) *D*.

3. Which historian is primarily concerned with the economic causes of the American Revolution? (a) *A* (b) *B* (c) *C* (d) *D*.

4. Which historian presents the most patriotic interpretation of the American Revolution? (a) *A* (b) *B* (c) *E* (d) *D*.

5. Which historian considers mercantilism the most important reason for the American Revolution? (a) *A* (b) *B* (c) *C* (d) *D*.

6. Which historian considers the American Revolution as primarily a movement for self-government? (a) *A* (b) *B* (c) *C* (d) *D*.

7. The suspension of the Massachusetts Charter could be cited in support of historian (a) *A* (b) *B* (c) *C* (d) *D*.

8. The Navigation Acts could be cited in support of historian (a) *A* (b) *B* (c) *C* (d) *D*.

9. The historian who interpreted the American Revolution as lacking widespread colonial support was (a) *A* (b) *B* (c) *C* (d) *E*.

10. Which is the most valid conclusion that may be drawn from the statements of the five historians? (a) The study of history is of limited value since there is little or no agreement among historians. (b) One should read only one historian in order to avoid becoming confused. (c) History is really an interpretation of available evidence. (d) Together, the five interpretations provide an accurate picture of the American Revolution.

——————————————— **ESSAY QUESTIONS** ———————————————

1. Show *one* way in which each of the following contributed to the revolt of the American colonies against Britain: *(a)* geography *(b)* mercantilism *(c)* rights of English people *(d)* Proclamation of 1763 *(e)* conflicts between royal governors and colonial legislatures *(f)* French and Indian War.

2. "The history of the present King of Great Britain is a history of repeated injuries and usurpations. . . . To prove this, let facts be submitted to a candid world."
   —The Declaration of Independence
   (a) State *three* examples of these "injuries and usurpations" that, in the opinion of the colonists, justified their decision to declare themselves independent. (b) Discuss *three* basic principles that the colonists advanced in the Declaration of Independence to justify their action.

3. (a) State *two* principles of the Declaration of Independence. (b) Describe *two* ways in which the United States has tried since the adoption of the federal Constitution to carry out *each* of these principles. (c) Giving specific illustrations, show how *one* foreign government pursues policies contrary to the principles of the Declaration of Independence.

4. The American Revolution, with its surprising victory by the colonists, had significant domestic and worldwide effects. (a) Discuss *one* reason why Britain expected to subdue its rebellious colonists easily. (b) Discuss *three* factors that enabled the colonists to achieve victory. (c) Describe *two* effects of the American Revolution within the United States. (d) Describe *two* effects of the American Revolution upon the rest of the world.

PART 3. Americans Surmount a Critical Period and Form a More Perfect Union

ONE NATION OR THIRTEEN?

With the Revolutionary War won, Americans had to decide whether they constituted a unified nation or 13 separate states. Several factors encouraged unity: (1) Most Americans shared a common English language and culture and had a growing sense of being one people. (2) Located along the North Atlantic coast, the states formed a single geographic unit. (3) The states had no tradition of hostility or war against each other. (4) The states had cooperated in a common effort to win independence from Britain.

Other forces, however, worked against unity: (1) The people were divided by strong loyalties to their individual states. (2) The states occupied a large area and lacked close contact because of poor roads and inadequate transportation. (3) The states were not interdependent economically, having traded more with the West Indies and Europe than with one another. (4) The states no longer faced a common enemy. Beset by economic distress and political weakness, the United States underwent a period (1781–1789) that many historians have called "critical."

THE ARTICLES OF CONFEDERATION—A "LEAGUE OF FRIENDSHIP"

The *Articles of Confederation,* proposed as a central government by the Continental Congress, came into existence in 1781 following ratification by all the states. Proclaiming that each state retained "its sovereignty, freedom, and independence," the Articles constituted for these states a "perpetual Union" but only as "a firm league of friendship"—in other words, a confederation with a weak central government. The fundamental weakness of any confederation is that power resides in the individual members, not in the central government.

WEAKNESSES OF THE ARTICLES OF CONFEDERATION

1. Defects in Governmental Structure

a. The Articles established a central government consisting only of a Congress—a one-house legislature of delegates from the 13 states, each state casting one vote. The Articles contained no provision for a chief executive to enforce the laws and no provision for courts to handle disputes between citizens of different states.

b. For Congress to enact laws, the Articles required not a simple majority, but a "yes" vote of nine out of the 13 states. With delegates from more than ten states rarely present at any one time, Congress practically was unable to legislate.

c. To add an amendment, the Articles required the approval of all 13 states— that is, a *unanimous vote.*

2. Lack of Essential Legislative Powers

a. Congress could not tax the people directly; it could only request the states to supply funds—which requests were mainly ignored.

b. Congress could issue money, but it could not prevent each state from issuing its own currency. Some states printed huge quantities of paper money unbacked by metal, thereby causing the value of money to fall and prices to rise. This *cheap money* pleased the debtor class of small farmers and city workers because it enabled them to repay their mortgages and other loans easily. Other states refused to cheapen the value of their money, thus pleasing the creditor class of bankers and merchants. Without a nationwide uniform currency, merchants were reluctant to do business outside their own states.

c. Congress could not directly recruit an army; it could only request the states to supply troops. The states were reluctant to do so, and the central government remained militarily helpless. In Massachusetts, *Daniel Shays* led debtors in an armed rebellion (1786–1787) seeking to end imprisonment for debt, halt the foreclosure of farm mortgages, and compel the state to issue cheap paper money. The debtors seized a number of courthouses and tried to seize the United States arsenal at Springfield. The central government stood by helpless. *Shays' Rebellion* was finally suppressed by the Massachusetts state militia.

d. Congress could not control commerce between the states, that is, interstate commerce. Each state established its own commercial regulations. New York taxed farm products from Connecticut and New Jersey, and these states retaliated by taxing goods from New York. Maryland and Virginia each claimed control of navigation on the Potomac, an interstate river. Such disputes disrupted trade between the states.

e. Congress could not control foreign commerce, and each state maintained its own tariffs on imports. Britain refused to enter into a commercial treaty with the United States, realizing that Congress could not enforce such a treaty.

f. Congress commanded little respect abroad and was ineffective in dealing with foreign nations. Britain, in violation of the Treaty of Paris, retained its military and trading posts in the Northwest Territory. The British justified their action on the grounds that the United States was violating the treaty in failing to restore Loyalist estates and repay British merchants. Also Britain closed its West Indies ports to American merchant ships, and Spain closed the lower Mississippi and New Orleans to American shipping of western farm produce. Both nations realized that the American government lacked the power to resist their actions.

3. Groups Most Dissatisfied. The failings of the Confederation most hurt the propertied and business groups: merchants, shippers, bankers and other creditors, lawyers, manufacturers, and large landowners. Also dissatisfied were western farmers and national patriots.

ACHIEVEMENTS UNDER THE ARTICLES OF CONFEDERATION

1. Groups Most Satisfied. The weak Articles of Confederation pleased many small farmers, frontier settlers, and city workers. They held this government least likely to threaten their rights and liberties. Also pleased were debtors, who enjoyed the prevalence of cheap money, and the advocates of state sovereignty.

2. Successful Efforts. Under the Articles, Congress *(a)* triumphantly concluded the Revolutionary War, *(b)* achieved the advantageous Treaty of Paris of 1783, *(c)* kept the states united in name, if not always in fact, through a period of great difficulty, and *(d)* passed the Land Ordinance of 1785 and the Northwest Ordinance of 1787.

ORDINANCES FOR WESTERN TERRITORIES

1. Background. Maryland had delayed its ratification of the Articles of Confederation until states with claims to western lands ceded those lands to the central government. When Virginia agreed to do so, the other states followed this example. The central government thus gained title to the Northwest Territory— an area bounded by the Mississippi River, the Ohio River, and the Great Lakes. To provide for the settling and governing of the Northwest Territory, Congress passed two laws: the Land Ordinance of 1785 and the Northwest Ordinance of 1787.

2. Land Ordinance of 1785. This ordinance provided that *(a)* the western lands be divided into square townships of 36 sections each, a section being a square mile (640 acres), *(b)* the income from one section of each township be used to support public education, and *(c)* the land be sold in 640-acre sections at no less than $1 per acre.

**Northwest Territory and Dates the States Formed From It
Gained Admission to the Union**

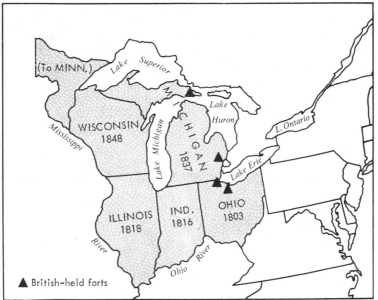

▲ British-held forts

3. Northwest Ordinance of 1787

a. The Northwest Territory would be divided into no fewer than three nor more than five territories, each eventually to become a state. (Five states were eventually formed from the Northwest Territory: Ohio, Indiana, Michigan, Illinois, and Wisconsin.)

b. As soon as a territory contained 5000 male adults, it could elect a territorial legislature. This legislature, together with a governor and judges appointed by Congress, would rule the territory.

c. As soon as a territory contained 60,000 inhabitants, it could adopt a constitution and apply for statehood "on an equal footing with the original states in all respects whatever."

d. For the Northwest Territory, the ordinance prohibited slavery, encouraged education, and provided a "bill of rights" guaranteeing basic civil liberties such as habeas corpus, trial by jury, and freedom of religion, speech, and press.

4. Significance. The Land Ordinance established national policy for the sale of western lands and encouraged public education. The Northwest Ordinance served as a model for the democratic treatment of territories and their admission to the Union as equal states. It contrasted sharply with Britain's handling of its 13 colonies.

Historical Analysis. *A Contrary View.* Historian Merrill Jensen in two books, *The Articles of Confederation* and *The New Nation,* concluded that the "critical period" was not really so critical. He emphasized the achievements of the Confederation and the favorable climate it provided for local and state democratic rule. Jensen further pointed out that American merchant ships had access to many foreign ports, state tariff wars were the exception, by 1786 the postwar economic depression was ending, and the states were considering a national tariff, with its funds to be reserved for the central government. Jensen concluded that the collapse of the Confederation resulted not from weakness but rather from the efforts of a determined group of nationalists to establish a strong central government.

CONSTITUTIONAL CONVENTION AT PHILADELPHIA (1787)

1. Background. With dissatisfaction mounting against the Articles, Congress, although reluctant to initiate any change, in 1787 issued a call for a convention at Philadelphia for the "sole and express purpose of revising the Articles of Confederation."

2. Absentees. The delegates to the Philadelphia Convention were appointed by state legislatures or governors. The convention thus included scarcely any representatives of over 90 percent of the country's population: small farmers, city workers, and frontier dwellers. Also, several leaders of the Revolutionary period were absent: Patrick Henry, who opposed a strong central government, refused to attend, and John Adams and Thomas Jefferson were abroad as our ministers in London and Paris.

3. Delegates. The Philadelphia Convention consisted of 55 delegates from all the states except Rhode Island. They were mainly lawyers, large landowners, bankers, and merchants; they reflected property and business interests. They were well-educated persons, widely read in history, government, and law, and many had considerable political experience.

Several outstanding leaders exercised great influence over the convention. *(a) George Washington* presided with dignity and fairness. *(b) James Madison,* a scholar of government, took detailed notes of the proceedings. Since the delegates conferred in secret to facilitate agreement, Madison's notes are our chief source of information about the convention. Madison played a major role in the proceedings and has been called the father of the Constitution. *(c) Alexander Hamilton,* a lawyer and son-in-law of a large New York landowner, spoke eloquently for a strong central government controlled by the educated and wealthy. *(d) Benjamin Franklin* employed his wisdom and prestige to bring about agreement on crucial issues.

4. Points of Agreement: Lessons Learned From Experience Under the Articles. *(a)* Agreeing that the Articles of Confederation were entirely inadequate, the delegates at Philadelphia proceeded to draw up a new constitution, thus turning the meeting into a Constitutional Convention. The members of the convention became known as the *Founding Fathers,* or the *Framers.* *(b)* The delegates wanted a government strong enough to govern effectively at home and to command respect abroad, yet not so strong as to become a tyranny, threatening the liberty and property of the people. *(c)* The delegates believed that such a government must have a visible executive head and an independent judiciary as well as a legislature. *(d)* The delegates believed that the central government had to have the power to levy taxes, control interstate and foreign commerce, raise an army, and protect property, and the sole power to coin money. Furthermore, it had to be able to exercise its powers directly on the people, not indirectly through the states.

THE CONSTITUTION AS A "BUNDLE OF COMPROMISES"

1. Representation. The more populous states supported the *Virginia Plan,* that representation in the national legislature be based on population. The less populous states supported the *New Jersey Plan,* that each state have equal representation. This issue, the most serious one dividing the delegates, was settled by the *Great Compromise,* or *Connecticut Compromise.* The legislature was to consist of two houses: *(a)* a House of Representatives, where representation was to be based on population, and *(b)* a Senate, where each state was to have equal representation.

2. Slavery. The southern states, in which slavery was extensive, proposed that *(a)* slaves be counted as part of the population for representation, which would increase the number of Southerners in the House of Representatives, and *(b)* slaves not be counted as part of the population for direct taxation, which would decrease the southern tax burden. The northern states, in which slavery was fast dying out, supported the opposite positions. The issue was settled by the *Three-Fifths Compromise:* five slaves were to be counted as three free persons for both representation and direct taxation.

By another compromise on slavery, Congress was forbidden for 20 years (until 1808) to interfere with the importation of slaves into the country.

3. Tariffs. The southern states opposed giving the central government the power to levy tariffs. Being chiefly agricultural, they feared that Congress would pass a tariff on their exports of indigo, rice, and tobacco. The northern states, being engaged in trade, wanted the central government to have the power to establish uniform regulations on navigation and protection of shipping. The issue was settled by granting Congress the power to control foreign commerce and to levy tariffs on imports but not on exports.

4. Presidency. The delegates disagreed over the term of office of the President and the method of choosing the President. Suggestions for a term of office ranged from three years to life. Some delegates wanted the President elected directly by the people; others suggested election by Congress. The issues were settled by *(a)* authorizing a four-year term and *(b)* establishing a complex procedure for electing the President through an electoral college. (Check the Index.) By this procedure, the delegates meant to allow the people only an indirect voice in choosing the President.

ADOPTION OF THE CONSTITUTION

1. Method of Ratification. The Framers provided that the new Constitution go into effect when ratified by conventions in nine of the 13 states. Thus they disregarded the Articles of Confederation, which had specified that all changes must be approved unanimously.

2. Debate Over Ratification. The *Federalists,* supporters of the Constitution, consisted of people with business and property interests, and of others who considered the nation more important than their state. They argued that the Constitution would provide a stable government capable of maintaining law and order, furthering economic prosperity, and commanding respect abroad. The *Anti-Federalists,* opponents of the Constitution, consisted of farmers, city workers, and others who gave their chief loyalty to their state or locality. They argued that the Constitution served the propertied classes, threatened the powers of the states, and left the people unprotected against federal encroachment upon their civil liberties. Acknowledging the last argument, the Federalists pledged to add a bill of rights to the Constitution.

3. Process of Ratification. Each state held its own Constitutional convention to consider ratification. The less populous states of Delaware, New Jersey, and Georgia quickly and overwhelmingly gave their approval. The more populous states approved ratification more slowly and by narrow margins. In Massachusetts, the sixth state to ratify, the convention voted 187 to 168. In Virginia, the tenth state, the convention vote was 89 to 79. In New York, the eleventh state, the convention voted 30 to 27.

After George Washington was inaugurated as first President of the new government, the Constitution was ratified by the last two states, North Carolina and then Rhode Island. The 13 states were now bound together in a strong federal union.

4. Reasons for the Success of the Federalists

a. Effective Organization. A well-organized group, the Federalists expended much energy and money toward achieving ratification. At various state ratifying conventions, the Federalists won the support of doubtful delegates and delayed the voting until they were assured a majority. The Anti-Federalists could not compare with them in funds, organization, and effectiveness.

b. Voting Qualifications. Most supporters of ratification could satisfy state property qualifications for voting and could therefore vote for state convention delegates. Some Anti-Federalist urban workers and poorer people lacked property qualifications and were unable to vote.

c. The Federalist Papers. Alexander Hamilton, James Madison, and John Jay argued persuasively for the new Constitution by writing a series of articles for New York newspapers. These learned essays helped swing New York public opinion in favor of ratification. The articles were later collected and published under the title *The Federalist.* They provide insights into the political thinking of the Framers, and the principles of the Constitution.

d. Influential Supporters. The Federalists enjoyed the support of two highly respected leaders: Benjamin Franklin and George Washington. Their approval of the Constitution won over many doubters.

Historical Analysis. *Was the Constitution essentially an economic document?* Historians have long debated this question.

Yes. Historian Charles A. Beard, in his influential study *An Economic Interpretation of the Constitution,* argues that the Constitution was designed to protect the economic interests of the propertied classes against any "popular majority" of poorer people. Beard claims that the Framers of the Constitution themselves were or represented persons whose major concern was to protect their economic interests by creating a strong central government. These persons included holders of public securities, who wanted their depreciated bonds paid off at face value; creditors, who wanted a stable currency; merchants, who wanted unhampered internal trade and uniform commercial regulations; manufacturers, who wanted tariff duties against foreign competition; and all property owners, who wanted protection against riots and insurrection. Beard, however, qualifies his argument by pointing out that he called his study "an economic interprepation," not "the economic interpretation"—implying that factors other than economic ones may be considered in evaluating the formation of the Constitution.

No. Historian Robert E. Brown attacks Beard for faulty historical research, such as accepting secondary sources without checking them, presenting unfounded rumors, and discarding data that contradicted his "economic interpretation." While not denying that economic factors were involved, Brown also condemns Beard for implying that the delegates at Philadelphia who owned public securities acted solely on that basis. Other historians point out that among the Anti-Federalists who opposed the Constitution, there were persons who also held large amounts of public securities and that the farmers—an overwhelming majority of the population—were not all chronic debtors; some even were creditors.

Historian Henry S. Commager strongly disputes Beard. Commager claims that the Constitution was essentially not an economic document but rather a political document. The Framers were concerned with the division of powers between the central government and the states, and with the separation of powers among the three branches of the central government. They wanted to establish a stable, efficient governmental system that could protect both property rights and civil liberties. Commager asks, if Beard is correct in claiming that the Philadelphia delegates wanted to place property rights "beyond the reach of popular majorities," then why did they not include in the Constitution provisions prohibiting the central government—not only the states—from impairing the obligations of contract, requiring property qualifications for voting and officeholding, and restricting the admission of new states? Since such provisions were not included, Commager argues, it is clear that the Constitution was designed not to protect the interests of property, but to extend to all citizens the blessings of liberty and happiness.

─────────── **MULTIPLE-CHOICE QUESTIONS** ───────────

1. In the government provided by the Articles of Confederation (a) the states exercised most of the power (b) Congress enforced its will by its power of taxation (c) the central government exercised most of the power (d) the consent of a simple majority of the states was necessary to amend the Articles.
2. Under the Articles of Confederation, the lack of adequate central authority to deal with national problems can *best* be explained by the (a) fear of the kind of rule experienced under the British (b) lack of concern for these national problems (c) absence of any feeling of American nationalism (d) failure to develop competent leaders.
3. Which was a weakness of the government under the Articles of Confederation? (a) ease with which laws could be passed in Congress (b) dictatorial power of the executive (c) the amount of power held by the federal courts (d) Congressional power to request, not demand, an army from the states.
4. Which best explains the dissatisfaction of the merchant class with the Articles of Confederation? (a) The power of Congress to tax was unlimited. (b) Individual states lacked the power to regulate commerce. (c) The President's treaty-making power was unchecked. (d) There was no provision for a uniform currency.
5. Under the Articles of Confederation, economic difficulties existed because of (a) continuous cheapening of the currency (b) high taxes levied by the central government (c) a revolt by indentured servants (d) the refusal of Americans to trade with Britain.
6. Shays' Rebellion was a protest against (a) debts and lack of currency (b) the tax on whisky (c) the closing of the lower Mississippi by Spain (d) the calling of the Constitutional Convention.
7. In 1786 which person would most likely favor Shays' Rebellion? (a) a Boston merchant (b) a New England sea captain (c) a Philadelphia banker (d) a Massachusetts farmer.
8. An important accomplishment of the government under the Articles of Confederation was (a) support of the principle of public education (b) free navigation of the entire Mississippi River (c) establishment of the domestic credit of the United States (d) recognition of the prestige of the United States by European governments.
9. The Northwest Ordinance has been regarded as nonimperialistic because it provided for the (a) establishment of public education in the territories (b) defense of the inhabitants from Indian attacks (c) permanent abolition of slavery in the territories (d) preparation of a territory for statehood.

10. Which provision of the Northwest Ordinance was based upon an established practice in Great Britain? (a) prohibition of slavery (b) admission of new states on an equal footing with the original states (c) guarantee of habeas corpus and trial by jury (d) encouragement of public schools.

11. Historians who claim that the years 1781 to 1789 were not really "critical" would cite the (a) tariff wars between states (b) lack of a powerful executive (c) beginnings of a recovery from the post-Revolutionary war depression (d) suppression of Shays' Rebellion.

12. The Philadelphia Convention (1787) was called for the purpose of (a) choosing a President for the new republic (b) revising the Articles of Confederation (c) making plans to suppress Shays' Rebellion (d) drafting a new Constitution.

13. At the Philadelphia Convention of 1787, on which issue was there the most agreement? (a) representation in a new Congress (b) importation of slaves (c) increased power for the central government (d) method of electing the President.

14. Which group was largely unrepresented at the Constitutional Convention (1787)? (a) lawyers (b) small farmers (c) large landowners (d) wealthy merchants.

15. The Great Compromise and the Three-Fifths Compromise at the Constitutional Convention were both concerned with (a) regulation of interstate commerce (b) representation in the Congress of the United States (c) admission of new states into the Union (d) the future of slavery in the United States.

16. Which decision reached at the Constitutional Convention represented a concession to the South? (a) Tariffs on exports were prohibited. (b) The President was to be chosen by an electoral college. (c) Revenue bills must originate in the House of Representatives. (d) Congress was given control of interstate commerce.

17. At the Constitutional Convention, the Great Compromise was agreed upon to settle the controversy between the (a) slave states and free states (b) southern states and northern states (c) farm states and industrial states (d) large states and small states.

18. One basic reason for the inclusion of democratic features in the original Constitution was the (a) influence of the small landowners (b) fact that some states already had democratic constitutions (c) ideas of Alexander Hamilton (d) work of Thomas Jefferson at the Constitutional Convention.

19. The Three-Fifths Compromise, which became a part of our Constitution, related to (a) the metric system (b) slavery (c) the tariff (d) the election of the President.

20. The Constitution was an improvement over the Articles of Confederation in that the Constitution (a) provided for a federal legislature (b) delegated to Congress the power to declare war (c) gave the national government control over United States territories (d) enabled the national government to act directly on the people.

21. Which power did the federal government *lack* under the Articles of Confederation? (a) issuing money (b) regulating territories (c) regulating interstate commerce (d) selling public lands.

22. The delegates to the Constitutional Convention were strongly influenced in their decisions by their (a) faith in direct democracy (b) distrust of the states (c) fear of unchecked majorities (d) belief in compulsory education.

23. *The Federalist*, a series of political essays, was written to urge (a) ratification of the Constitution (b) rejection of the Constitution (c) the election of Washington as President (d) adoption of the Northwest Ordinance.

24. Which was the basic reason that the Bill of Rights was added to the original Constitution? (a) Local governments demanded a listing of their powers. (b) There was a

need for a strong central authority. (c) Individuals needed protection from possible abuses of government powers. (d) The powers of Congress were not sufficiently defined.

25. Which argument against the ratification of the federal Constitution was used *least?* (a) The President would become too powerful. (b) The states would lose their power. (c) Senators would be elected by state legislatures. (d) A Bill of Rights was not included.

26. Which statement best represents the political ideology of Alexander Hamilton and the Federalists? (a) Only the wealthy will survive in the economic system. (b) A strong central government is essential for the economic growth of the nation. (c) No one should have to pay taxes to the national government. (d) Elected officials should give public jobs to those who helped them into office.

27. Historians who claim that the authors of the Constitution were motivated by economic interests point to the fact that (a) capitalism was introduced immediately before the writing of the Constitution (b) bankers controlled government offices in the early days of the United States (c) commercial businesses flourished under the policies of the new government established by the Constitution (d) consumer protection was denied in the original Constitution.

——————— MODIFIED TRUE-FALSE QUESTIONS ———————

If the statement is correct, write the word *true*. If the statement is incorrect, substitute a word or phrase for the italicized term to make the statement correct.

1. Under the Articles of Confederation, the states were *sovereign*.
2. Amendments to the Articles of Confederation required the approval of *three-quarters* of the states.
3. The issuance of huge quantities of paper money caused the value of money to *rise*.
4. The state of *Wisconsin* was formed from part of the Northwest Territory.
5. *Alexander Hamilton* was president of the Constitutional Convention.
6. In New York State, the Constitution was ratified by *an overwhelming* majority.
7. *Rhode Island* did not ratify the Constitution until after the new government was organized.
8. The Great Compromise at the Constitutional Convention was sponsored by the state of *New Jersey*.
9. The Constitutional Convention provided that the Constitution go into effect when ratified by *seven* of the 13 states.
10. The "father of the Constitution," who kept detailed notes of the proceedings of the Constitutional Convention, was *Benjamin Franklin*.

——————————— ESSAY QUESTIONS ———————————

1. Although the government under the Articles of Confederation had many weaknesses and was soon discarded, it also compiled a record of achievement. In regard to the government under the Articles of Confederation, *(a)* explain *three* of its weaknesses, and *(b)* discuss *two* of its achievements.

2. The Northwest Ordinance has been called a model for democratic treatment of colonies. Discuss *three* provisions of the Northwest Ordinance and show how each justifies this statement.

3. *(a)* Show how the Constitutional Convention of 1787 settled a dispute that arose over *each* of the following: (1) control of commerce (2) election of the President (3) representation of the states in Congress. *(b)* State *two* ways in which the organization of the government under the federal Constitution differed from its organization under the Articles of Confederation.

4. The Federalists and Anti-Federalists battled vigorously over the ratification of the Constitution. *(a)* Explain *two* arguments advanced by the Federalists in favor of ratification. *(b)* Explain *two* arguments presented by the Anti-Federalists against ratification. *(c)* Discuss *two* factors that enabled the Federalists to secure ratification.

5. The United Nations has often been compared to the American government under the Articles of Confederation. *(a)* Show *three* ways in which this comparison is justified. *(b)* Show *two* ways in which the situations are *different*.

UNIT III The Constitution Is the Basis of Our Democratic Government

PART 1. Introduction

MEANING OF DEMOCRACY

The word "democracy," derived from the Greek language, means the "rule of the people." Democracy rests upon the political principle that government is created by, derives its powers from, and exists to serve the people. In practice today, political democracy means a system of government characterized as follows: (1) Governmental powers are limited by a written constitution or by basic laws and historic traditions. (2) Governmental officials, chosen by secret ballot in free and frequently held elections, are responsible to the people. (3) The legislators debate issues, arrive at compromises, and, by majority vote, pass laws. (4) More than one political party exists, and each is free to present its views in seeking to become the majority party. (5) Minority groups, regardless of race, color, religion, or national origin, have the right to full and free existence. (6) The people are protected against possible governmental tyranny by basic civil liberties, especially (a) freedom of speech, press, religion, and assembly, and (b) the right to bail, impartial trial, and equal treatment under the law.

PREAMBLE—PURPOSES OF THE CONSTITUTION

The Preamble, or introduction, explains briefly why "we, the people of the United States" established the Constitution: (1) to form a more perfect union—by creating national institutions to bring the people and the states closely together, (2) to insure domestic tranquility—by assuring "law and order" so that people might go about their everyday routines in safety and without fear of violence, (3) to establish justice—by creating fair legal procedures and courts to protect the innocent, punish lawbreakers, and enforce valid contracts, (4) to provide for the common defense—by raising military forces to protect the people and promote the "national interest" against foreign threats, (5) to promote the general welfare—by enhancing the economic and social well-being of the people, and (6) to secure the blessings of liberty—by restraining the powers of government and guaranteeing civil liberties so that people may live in freedom.

PART 2. The Constitution Divides, Separates, and Limits the Powers of Government

CONSTITUTIONAL PHILOSOPHY UNDERLYING THE GRANTING AND LIMITING OF POWER

The Framers were concerned with establishing a government that would maintain a balance between power and liberty. James Madison, "father of the

Constitution," claimed "the truth was that all men having power ought to be distrusted to a certain degree." Madison further observed, "In framing a government which is to be administered by men over men, the great difficulty lies in this: you must first enable the government to control the governed; and in the next place oblige it to control itself."

To preserve liberty for the people and to prevent tyranny by government, the Framers provided for the distribution of power among many hands with each expected to resist encroachment of the others. They also denied powers to various governments. These two factors—the distribution of power and the denial of power—underlie the structure of government provided by the Constitution.

FEDERAL SYSTEM: DIVISION OF POWERS BETWEEN THE CENTRAL GOVERNMENT AND THE STATES

The Constitution set up a system of *federalism,* a dual system of government whereby powers are divided between the state governments and the central (also known as the national or federal) government. The Constitution limits the federal government to *delegated,* or *enumerated,* powers. These are powers specifically listed in the Constitution as being granted to the federal government. Powers not given to the federal government and not denied to the states are reserved to the states or to the people. These are called *reserved,* or residual, powers. Certain powers that may be exercised by both the federal government and state governments are called *concurrent* powers.

Under the federal system each government is supreme within its own sphere. Every American is a citizen both of the United States and of the state in which the citizen resides.

DELEGATED, OR ENUMERATED, POWERS

(Article I, Section 8)

1. Financial. To levy and collect taxes; borrow money; coin money and regulate its value; punish counterfeiters.

2. Commercial. To regulate interstate and foreign commerce; establish rules for bankruptcy; establish post offices and post roads; grant patents and copyrights.

3. Military. To declare war; raise, support, and make rules for an army and navy; call up the state militia to enforce federal laws; suppress insurrections and repel invasions; punish piracy.

4. Miscellaneous. To establish rules for the naturalization of aliens; provide for courts below the Supreme Court; control the seat of government (Washington, D.C.) and all federal property.

ELASTIC CLAUSE

(Article I, Section 8, Clause 18)

1. Statement. Concluding the list of delegated powers, the Constitution grants Congress the power "to make all laws which shall be necessary and proper for carrying into execution the foregoing powers." Because this statement enables Congress to expand its delegated powers (the "foregoing powers"), it is known as the *elastic clause.*

2. Applications: The Elastic Clause and Implied Powers. *(a)* Congress in 1791 authorized a national bank although the Constitution nowhere specifically grants this power. Nevertheless, Congress considered the law "necessary and proper" for carrying out its delegated powers to collect taxes, coin and borrow money, and regulate its value. *(b)* Congress, beginning in 1877, passed legislation to regulate railroad fares, although, when the Constitution was written, the railroad had not been invented. Since railroads go from state to state, such federal control is based upon the elastic clause together with the delegated power "to regulate commerce among the states."

Such powers, each derived from the elastic clause plus one or more of the delegated powers, are not specifically stated in the Constitution but are hinted at or can be inferred. Consequently, they are called *implied* powers.

3. Controversy Regarding the Use of the Elastic Clause. Throughout our history, Americans have debated the extent to which the federal government should use the elastic clause.

a. *Strict Construction or Interpretation.* Some Americans have held that the Constitution should be interpreted strictly and that Congress should be limited to its specific delegated powers. These people advocate restraints on the federal government and greater exercise of power by the states. That attitude is called "states' rights." Although states' righters have been found in all sections of the nation, they have been most numerous and influential in the South.

b. *Loose Construction or Interpretation.* Other Americans have held that the Constitution should be interpreted broadly and that Congress should exercise many powers not specifically given to it, but merely implied. These people, champions of a powerful federal government, have usually been in the majority.

4. Historic Trend Toward Loose Construction. Over the years, the central government has greatly increased its functions by using its implied powers. Today, the federal government utilizes the elastic clause: *(a)* together with the clause giving Congress control of interstate commerce, to regulate such matters as interstate transportation, communication, business practices, the sale of securities, labor unions, and minimum wages, *(b)* together with the power to tax for the general welfare, to maintain Social Security and Medicare, and *(c)* together with the power to raise and support armies, to further research for peaceful as well as military purposes.

GROWTH OF FEDERAL POWER: SINCE 1865

Federal power expanded as the Civil War marked the triumph of nationalism in America and ushered in an era of economic growth and social change. In time, federal power expanded to deal with the following matters:

1. Geography. American rivers such as the Mississippi and mountainous areas such as Appalachia extend over many states. To keep the Mississippi from overflowing its banks, and to improve conditions for the impoverished inhabitants of Appalachia—such programs called for interstate or federal action.

2. Industrialization. The growth of American industry brought problems such as prevention of monopoly, regard for unemployed persons, discrimination in hiring, and disposal of industrial wastes. Since industry was now nationwide, its problems could not be regulated effectively by state action but required federal attention.

3. Improvements in Technology. Modern means of transportation and communication tended to wipe out state lines. The products that people buy, the news they hear, the sports teams they follow—almost all involve interstate commerce and therefore are subject to federal supervision.

4. Urbanization: Growth of Metropolitan Areas. With Americans moving from rural areas to cities and suburbs, the nation has experienced the growth of huge metropolitan areas. As defined by the Census Bureau, a *metropolitan statistical area* consists of a central city of at least 50,000 population or an urbanized area of 50,000 population plus the surrounding areas of at least the same population. Of more than 280 metropolitan statistical areas, many overlap state boundaries. For example, the New York City metropolitan area includes parts of three states: New York, New Jersey, and Connecticut. Metropolitan areas face problems such as mass transportation and pollution control, but since many metropolitan areas encompass more than one state, their problems call for federal initiative.

5. National Crises: World Wars and Economic Depressions. With two world wars requiring total national involvement, the federal government increased its powers: conscripting men for military service, directing the economy toward war production, settling labor-management disputes, combating inflation, and developing new weapons. Also economic depressions have been national in scope. Since 1933 the federal government has assumed the responsibility of combating economic downturns.

6. Federal Income Tax. By the Sixteenth Amendment, the federal government was empowered to levy a tax on incomes. In the World War II years, the federal government raised income tax rates to such high levels as to effectively preempt this form of taxation. States and cities could levy an income tax but only at low rates, and their real estate, sales, and other taxes brought in relatively limited revenue. With states and cities facing mounting costs, they have been forced to look to Washington for federal aid.

RESERVED, OR RESIDUAL, POWERS

Adopted in 1791, the Tenth Amendment to the Constitution states: "The powers not delegated to the United States by the Constitution, nor prohibited by it to the states, are reserved to the states respectively, or to the people." The states consequently have retained control over such matters as education, voting requirements, intrastate (within the state) commerce, most intrastate crimes, traffic laws, marriage, and divorce. State powers directly concerned with protecting the health, welfare, safety, and morals of the people are called *police powers*.

CONCURRENT POWERS

Concurrent powers are exercised by both the federal government and the states. Concurrent powers include levying taxes, borrowing money, building roads, and maintaining courts.

POWERS DENIED THE FEDERAL GOVERNMENT

1. Article I, Section 9. The original Constitution specifically prohibits the federal government from *(a)* passing any commerce or revenue law favoring one state at the expense of another, *(b)* granting any title of nobility, *(c)* levying any tax on exports, *(d)* levying any direct tax not based on population, *(e)* spending money without an appropriation authorized by law, and *(f)* encroaching upon the civil liberties of the people by suspending the right of habeas corpus (except in time of rebellion or invasion) or passing a bill of attainder or an *ex post facto* law. (Check the Index for Civil liberties.)

2. Amendments to the Constitution. The first ten amendments, together known as the *Bill of Rights,* deny the federal government the power to interfere with various civil liberties of the people and assign the reserved powers to the states or people. (Check the Index for Bill of Rights.)

Four later amendments—the Fifteenth, Nineteenth, Twenty-Fourth, and Twenty-Sixth—prohibit the federal government (and the states) from denying voting rights of citizens on account of "race, color, or previous condition of servitude," "sex," "failure to pay any poll tax" in the election of federal officials, and "age" if at least 18 years old. (Check the Index for these amendments.)

POWERS DENIED THE STATES

1. Article I, Section 10. The original Constitution also denies certain powers to the states. *(a)* States may not coin money, enter into foreign treaties, or impair (lessen) obligations of contract. *(b)* Without the consent of Congress, states may not levy import or export duties, enter into agreements with each other, maintain troops in peacetime, or engage in war. *(c)* Like the federal government, the states may not grant titles of nobility or pass bills of attainder or *ex post facto* laws.

2. The 14th, 15th, 19th, 24th, and 26th Amendments. The Fourteenth Amendment prohibited states from abridging the privileges of citizens or depriving "any person of life, liberty or property without due process of law" or denying any person "equal protection of the laws." The other four amendments prohibit the states (and the federal government) from denying voting rights of citizens.

FEDERAL SYSTEM: FEDERAL-STATE RELATIONSHIPS

FEDERAL OBLIGATIONS TO THE STATES

(Article IV, Sections 3 and 4)

The Constitution empowers Congress to admit new states into the Union. It also requires the federal government to assure each state (1) a republican form of government, (2) protection against invasion, and (3) upon request of the state, protection against domestic violence.

FEDERAL-STATE DISPUTES TO 1865

1. Basic Issue: States' Rights and Nullification vs. Federal Supremacy. From the adoption of the Constitution, Americans disputed regarding the nature of the federal union. States' righters argued that (1) the states had entered into a compact creating the federal government to serve as their agent, (2) the states remained independent and sovereign entities with power to declare federal laws null and void, and (3) as a last resort the states could withdraw from the federal union, that is, the right of *secession*. National patriots insisted that (1) the people had created the federal government with full right to exercise its delegated and implied powers, (2) the Supreme Court was the only agency empowered to determine the constitutionality of federal laws, and (3) no state has the right to secede lest the union be an absurdity.

2. Historic Confrontations. This dispute of states' rights versus federal supremacy was at the heart of several historic confrontations, notably *(a)* the Alien and Sedition Acts (1798), *(b)* the tariff as a sectional issue (1828–1833), and *(c)* secession by southern states (1860–1861). (For these confrontations, check the Index.)

FEDERAL-STATE DISPUTES IN THE 20TH CENTURY

1. Basic Issue: States' Reserved Powers vs. the 14th and 15th Amendments. Conflicts have arisen regarding the manner in which states have employed certain reserved powers. States' righters have argued that the authority of the state is practically without limit. National patriots have insisted that the state may exercise its authority only within the limits set by the *Fourteenth Amend-*

ment: not to abridge the privileges of citizens; *not* to deprive "any person of life, liberty, or property without due process of law"; *not* to deny any person "equal protection of the laws"; and by the *Fifteenth Amendment: not* to deny voting rights on account of "race, color, or previous condition of servitude."

2. Historic Conflicts. The constitutionality of certain state and local laws was challenged before the Supreme Court. Some state and local laws were declared unconstitutional; others were superseded by federal laws. Notable conflicts dealt with *(a)* racial discrimination in education, outlawed by the Supreme Court in *Brown vs. Board of Education of Topeka* (1954); *(b)* discriminatory voting qualifications, outlawed by successive voting rights acts; and *(c)* unequal election districts, outlawed by the Supreme Court in *Reynolds vs. Sims* (1964). (For these conflicts, check the Index.)

FEDERAL-STATE COOPERATION IN THE 20TH CENTURY

The central government and the 50 state governments consistently work together, thereby (1) making possible the smooth operation of our system of federalism and (2) furthering their shared goal of providing for the needs of the people.

EXAMPLES OF COOPERATION

1. By Government Agencies. *(a)* The *Federal Bureau of Investigation* (FBI) assists state and local law-enforcement officers by providing data from its crime laboratory and fingerprint files and by offering criminal-investigation training courses. *(b)* The federal *Public Health Service* advises state and local officials on methods of preventing and controlling disease. Federal and state public health agencies exchange findings and sometimes coordinate efforts in medical research.

2. By Regionalism. To deal with regional problems that extend beyond state lines, the national government has devised federal regional agencies that cooperate with and coordinate the efforts of the states involved. *(a)* The *Tennessee Valley Authority* (TVA) pioneered in this regional approach. (Check the Index for Tennessee Valley Authority.) *(b)* The *Appalachian Regional Commission* consists of a representative of each state in the region and a federal official. The commission plans, coordinates, and supervises federal and state efforts to improve conditions for the people of Appalachia.

3. By Grants-in-Aid. *(a) Meaning.* Federal grants-in-aid are cash payments made by the central government to the states to finance specific state-run programs. Grants have supported some 1400 detailed programs, mostly classified under such broad categories as education; low-cost public housing; public health; aid to the aged, the physically handicapped, and dependent children; unemployment insurance; and highway and airport construction. *(b) Conditions.* To qualify for any specific grant-in-aid, the states must agree to (1) set up and administer the program, (2) accept federal supervision of the program, and (3) supplement federal funds, which may range from 50 percent to 90 percent of the cost, with state funds to provide the balance. The states are free to accept or reject any specific grant. *(c) Amounts.* After rising above 15 percent of federal expenditures in the 1970s, grants-in-aid have declined to about 10 percent of such expenditures in recent years. States depend on federal grants for about 20 percent of their revenues.

REVENUE SHARING

1. The Proposal. In 1971 President Nixon urged Congress to provide the states and localities with revenue-sharing funds not restricted as to use or limited only to broad categories. These funds would replace many grants-in-aid previously earmarked for specific programs.

2. Arguments For. President Nixon claimed that revenue-sharing would strengthen the state and local governments by *(a)* entrusting them with greater responsibility for the people's welfare, *(b)* freeing them from federal interference, *(c)* allowing them more initiative and greater flexibility in spending moneys, and *(d)* rescuing them from financial crises.

3. Arguments Against. Opponents of revenue sharing stated that the federal government *(a)* collects the tax revenues and therefore should determine the uses of the funds, *(b)* must exercise controls to insure that the moneys are spent honestly, efficiently, and for worthwhile purposes, *(c)* would be compelled to maintain high income tax rates and perhaps deficits to provide revenue-sharing funds, and *(d)* could better aid the states financially by lowering federal income tax rates so that the states could raise their rates or by assuming the total financial burden of welfare.

4. Revenue-Sharing Legislation. Congress approved revenue sharing in 1972. Over the following 14 years, the federal government distributed some $85 billion under the program, one-third to the states and two-thirds to cities and other local governments. The money was used as each recipient saw fit.

5. End of Revenue Sharing. Revenue sharing came to an end in 1986 as part of a general effort to hold down federal spending for domestic programs. By then, however, President Reagan and Congress had given the states greater freedom in their use of other grants from the federal government. The Reagan administration combined numerous grant-in-aid programs into so-called *block grants* for broad purposes, such as transportation. Each state wrote its own rules for how the money should be used.

The end of revenue sharing caused a severe crisis for many local governments, especially in rural areas, which had grown used to the annual receipt of revenue-sharing funds.

RELATIONS AMONG THE STATES

STATES' OBLIGATIONS TO EACH OTHER

(Article IV, Sections 1 and 2)

The Constitution specifies that each state shall (1) give "full faith and credit" to the legal actions of the other states (a couple married in New York is still considered married even though they move to California), (2) extend to citizens of other states the privileges of local citizenship, such as the right to own property and engage in business, and (3) honor requests from other states for *extradition,* that is, the return of a fugitive charged with committing a crime.

EXAMPLES OF STATE COOPERATION

1. Interstate Compacts. "No state shall," says the Constitution (Article I, Section 10), "enter into any agreement or compact with another state" without the consent of Congress. States have secured Congressional approval for interstate compacts dealing with port facilities, water resources, fishing rights, oil conservation, and economic development of metropolitan areas. *(a)* The Port of New York Authority, established by New York and New Jersey, has planned the unified development of the metropolitan harbor area. The authority has constructed piers, bridges, tunnels, airports, and the World Trade Center buildings. *(b)* The Ohio River Valley Sanitation Compact, composed of eight states, has sought to halt water pollution and prevent floods of the Ohio River.

2. Interstate Organizations and Meetings. The Governors' Conference, National Association of Attorneys General, National Association of State Budget Directors, and other similar organizations all enable officials of the 50 states to meet regularly, discuss common problems, and seek uniform solutions.

EXAMPLES OF STATE DISPUTES AND COMPETITION

1. State Disputes. States have quarreled with each other over such issues as boundaries, fishing rights, and ownership of water. For example, Arizona and California long disputed the division of Colorado River waters. In 1963 this dispute was settled, in favor of Arizona, by the United States Supreme Court.

2. State Competition. States have competed with each other to attract tourists, secure business enterprises, and assist local industries: *(a)* Nevada offers an "easy" divorce law so that persons seeking divorce come to the state and spend money there while meeting the minimal residence requirements. Other states, however, have rejected the validity of Nevada "quickie" divorces on the ground that the out-of-state persons were only temporary, not genuine residents of Nevada. *(b)* Delaware has long been known for its "easy" corporation charters which place few restrictions upon the business managers. Delaware benefits by collecting incorporation fees and by requiring the corporation to maintain head-quarters, even if only token, within the state. The Delaware-chartered corporation benefits from the Constitution's "full faith and credit" clause and may do business in all the 50 states. *(c)* The states compete with each other to attract business concerns that will provide jobs for local residents. The states have offered to provide land sites and low-cost loans for constructing factories, to train local workers, and to grant exemptions from state taxes.

EVALUATION OF FEDERALISM: STRENGTHS AND WEAKNESSES

1. Strengths. *(a)* The federal government can best handle matters of national interest. State governments, being closer to the people, are best qualified to handle local problems. *(b)* By dividing powers between the federal government and a group of independent states, federalism prevents complete centralization, which might lead to tyranny. Democracy survives best, it is argued, when powers are divided, not concentrated. *(c)* By preserving independent states, federalism prevents sole reliance upon national authority, provides a training ground for government officials, and encourages the people to exercise local initiative. *(d)* A state may serve as a laboratory for reform without involving the entire nation. For example, Wyoming experimented with woman suffrage and Wisconsin with unemployment insurance before these measures were adopted by the national government.

2. Weaknesses. *(a)* Conflicts arise between the federal government and the states because the Constitutional provisions dividing their powers have proved vague and subject to differing interpretations. For example, advocates of states' rights consider education an area reserved for the states. Nevertheless, the federal government has legislated on education, claiming that scientific knowledge is essential for national defense. *(b)* On matters reserved to the states, laws have varied considerably from state to state. For example, Nevada permits gam-

FEDERAL GOVERNMENT COMPARED WITH UNITARY GOVERNMENT

THE UNITED STATES (Federal)	GREAT BRITAIN (Unitary)
1. Powers are divided between the federal government and the states.	1. Powers are concentrated within the national government.
2. The states are supreme in matters of local government, and each state derives its authority from and is responsible to the people of the state.	2. Local governmental bodies are subordinate agencies, deriving their authority from and owing responsibility to the national government.
3. Federalism meets the diverse needs throughout the vast territorial extent of the United States.	3. Unitary government provides competent rule over the limited area constituting Great Britain.

bling casinos; most other states do not. New Jersey requires a minimum age of 17 for a driver's license; most states accept age 16, and some, age 15. *(c)* Federalism results in inefficiency, waste, and overlapping administration. For example, duplicate federal and state agencies exist in such areas as housing, agriculture, and law enforcement.

WITHIN THE FEDERAL GOVERNMENT: SEPARATION OF POWERS

THREE BRANCHES OF GOVERNMENT

The Framers provided that the powers of the federal government be separated among three distinct branches: (1) The executive branch, headed by the President, administers, or carries out, the laws. (2) The legislative branch, Congress, enacts, or makes, the laws. (3) The judicial branch, the court system, interprets the laws in specific cases.

The Constitution further provides that a member of Congress may not serve at the same time in another branch of the federal government. Thus, before John F. Kennedy took office as President, he was compelled to resign as Senator from Massachusetts. By tradition, a person may not simultaneously serve in the executive and judicial branches.

The three branches of government, however, are not separated rigidly as to powers, and to some extent their powers overlap. For the federal government to function smoothly, the three branches must work together with a considerable degree of harmony.

CHECKS AND BALANCES

The Constitution enables each branch of the federal government to brake and counteract the powers of the other two branches through a system of checks and balances.

1. Executive. *(a)* The President may check Congress by vetoing legislation. The President may influence Congress by calling it into special session, by recommending legislation, and by appealing to the people to pressure their Congressional representatives to support Presidential recommendations. *(b)* The President may check the federal courts by nominating judges, by granting pardons and reprieves (except in cases of impeachment), and by refusing to enforce court orders.

2. Legislative. *(a)* Congress may check the President by refusing to pass legislation and to appropriate funds, and by overriding the President's veto (a two-thirds vote of each house). In addition, the Senate may check the President by refusing to approve Presidential appointments (a majority vote) and refusing to ratify treaties (a two-thirds vote). The House of Representatives may bring impeachment charges of "high crimes and misdemeanors" against the President.

The Senate, acting as the jury, may find that the President is guilty (a two-thirds vote) and should be removed from office. *(b)* Congress may check the Supreme Court by passing a somewhat altered law to replace a law held unconstitutional, by initiating an amendment to the Constitution, by impeaching and convicting judges of "high crimes and misdemeanors," and by increasing the number of judges on the Supreme Court. The Senate may refuse to approve persons nominated by the President for judgeships. *(c)* The House of Representatives and the Senate may check each other, since approval of both houses is necessary to pass laws.

3. Judicial. *(a)* The Supreme Court may check the President by declaring actions of the executive branch unconstitutional. *(b)* The Supreme Court may check Congress by declaring laws unconstitutional.

EVALUATION OF CHECKS AND BALANCES

1. Strengths

a. Checks and balances prevent any branch of government from becoming too powerful and establishing a dictatorship. The Framers greatly feared the danger of tyranny. They derived the idea of checks and balances from (1) the

SEPARATION OF POWERS COMPARED WITH PARLIAMENTARY SUPREMACY

THE UNITED STATES (Separation of Powers)	GREAT BRITAIN (Parliamentary Supremacy)
1. The President is chosen by the voters in each state (as expressed through the electoral college). Regardless of how Congress responds to the President's requests for legislation, the President serves a fixed four-year term.	1. The Prime Minister secures office as leader of the majority party in Parliament and remains in office while retaining the support of a Parliamentary majority. If defeated by Parliament on a significant issue, the Prime Minister either resigns or calls for new elections in an attempt to regain a Parliamentary majority.
2. No Cabinet member may be, at the same time, a member of Congress. Cabinet members may be called to testify before Congressional committees. The Cabinet, however, exercises executive functions chiefly.	2. Cabinet members are also members of Parliament. The Cabinet exercises both executive and legislative functions. Its legislative duties include introducing bills into Parliament, defending them in debate, and guiding them to passage.
3. The President and the Cabinet may belong to one political party, while Congress (or either house) is controlled by another party. Thus, the executive and legislative branches may be in conflict.	3. The Prime Minister and the Cabinet must come from the majority party in Parliament and are responsible to Parliament. Thus, the executive and legislative branches work in harmony.
4. The Supreme Court may declare laws unconstitutional, that is, in violation of the written Constitution.	4. No formal written constitution exists, and so no court may declare laws of Parliament invalid.

political theory of the *Baron de Montesquieu,* the French philosopher, who in his book *The Spirit of the Laws* urged a three-part division of governmental powers to protect liberty, and (2) the experiences of the colonial legislatures that had fought the royal governors.

b. Hasty, ill-considered action is discouraged, since each branch is aware that its action is subject to checks by the other two.

c. In national emergencies, the branches temporarily and voluntarily suspend their powers of check and balance in order to work quickly and efficiently. In 1933, to combat the depression, President Franklin D. Roosevelt requested a considerable number of major New Deal laws, which Congress passed within a 100-day period. On December 7, 1941, Japan attacked Pearl Harbor; on December 8, President Roosevelt requested a declaration of war, which Congress passed the same day. In these instances, Congress abbreviated its usual slow procedures of debating, criticizing, and deliberating so as to accede quickly to executive requests.

2. Weaknesses

a. Checks and balances may paralyze the workings of government, especially if one party controls Congress and another the executive. For example, in 1947–1948, when President Harry S Truman, a Democrat, and Congress, controlled by Republicans, disagreed on most domestic matters, they accomplished little toward meeting the nation's domestic needs.

b. In case of an executive-legislative deadlock, no provision exists for calling a special election so that the voters may end the deadlock. Instead, the nation must await the next regular election.

c. Checks and balances may cause delay and uncertainty. For example, a law passed by Congress and signed by the President may be declared unconstitutional by the Supreme Court after an interval of several years.

————————— **MULTIPLE-CHOICE QUESTIONS** —————————

1. A necessary characteristic of a democracy is (a) a system of free public education (b) popular election of the chief judicial officer (c) a written constitution that guarantees people the right to earn a living (d) a system of majority rule and legal protection of individual rights.
2. The most useful indicator of the degree of democracy reached by a particular society would be whether it has a (a) formal method whereby people can effect changes in government policy (b) system of governmental checks and balances (c) two-house legislature (d) system of liberal and humane courts.
3. The ultimate source of all political power in the United States is the (a) people of the United States (b) laws made by Congress (c) state constitutions (d) United States Constitution.
4. Which basic principle of the Constitution has been involved in the controversy between those who advocate states' rights and those who favor an increase in federal

power? (a) separation of powers (b) division of powers (c) due process of law (d) concurrent powers.

5. In a federal system of government (a) all power is concentrated in the national government (b) powers are divided between the national and the state governments (c) the states are supreme (d) there is a system of Cabinet responsibility.

6. The Constitution of the United States guarantees to each state (a) an equal share of federal funds (b) federal aid for flood control (c) a republican form of government (d) the power to grant patents to inventors.

7. Which best illustrates a federal system of government? (a) Congress passes laws, but the President enforces them. (b) The President appoints Cabinet members, but the Senate must approve them. (c) The Supreme Court has the power to declare laws of Congress unconstitutional. (d) The national government regulates interstate commerce, but state governments regulate commerce within the states.

8. The expansion of federal power since the end of the Civil War has (a) threatened the existence of our republican system of government (b) weakened the system of checks and balances (c) altered the division of powers in our nation (d) strengthened the powers of the House of Representatives at the expense of the Senate.

9. The responsibilities of the federal government have increased during the 20th century primarily because of the (a) absence of interstate regional planning (b) complexity of problems cutting across state boundaries (c) government's commitment to social ideals (d) introduction of the idea of revenue sharing.

10. The Constitution contains "delegated powers," which are (a) found in the elastic clause (b) reserved to the states (c) the enumerated powers of Congress (d) the purposes listed in the Preamble.

11. The powers of Congress derived from the provision "to make all laws which shall be necessary and proper for carrying into execution the foregoing powers" are said to be (a) concurrent (b) implied (c) residual (d) enumerated.

12. According to the Tenth Amendment, the powers "not delegated to the United States by the Constitution, nor prohibited by it to the states," are reserved to the (a) Congress (b) Supreme Court (c) President (d) states or the people.

13. Which headline refers to an action that may be justified under the elastic (necessary and proper) clause? (a) President Vetoes Act of Congress (b) Congress Passes Minimum-Wage Law (c) President Appoints Ambassador to United Nations (d) Senate Ratifies Treaty.

14. A "strict constructionist" of the Constitution would favor (a) the institution of programs for social reform (b) annexation of territory by the United States (c) bypassing Constitutional restraints (d) limiting the power of the federal government.

15. The *most* frequent basis for legislation expanding the role of the federal government in our economy has been the elastic clause together with the delegated power of Congress to (a) coin money (b) issue patents and copyrights (c) promote the progress of science (d) regulate interstate commerce.

16. Which action by a state legislature would be permissible under the Constitution? (a) imposing a tariff on imported products that compete with local industry (b) establishing a quota for immigrants to reside in that state (c) licensing a merchant ship engaged in transporting goods from New York to Boston (d) lowering the voting age requirement in that state.

17. The rapid expansion of metropolitan areas in the United States has resulted in (a) the need for greater intergovernmental cooperation (b) a reduction in the

amount of federal aid needed by the cities (c) the disappearance of local government boundary lines (d) an increase in the power of city governments.

18. In contrast to federal grants-in-aid, the federal revenue-sharing program (a) cost the federal government nothing (b) set few restrictions on the states regarding use of the moneys (c) maintained strict federal supervision of state programs (d) required states and localities to lower real estate tax rates.

19. Which of the following could be considered a weakness of federalism? (a) State laws vary greatly on such matters as divorce and minimum age for auto drivers' licenses. (b) A state-chartered corporation can do business only in that state. (c) State law-enforcement agencies are denied assistance by the FBI. (d) No facilities exist for settling disputes between states.

20. A criminal suspect wanted in Georgia is found in New York. To have the suspect arrested in New York and returned to Georgia, the Georgia governor can (a) authorize the Georgia police to do so (b) require the FBI to do so (c) request New York authorities to do so (d) appeal to the Supreme Court for a certificate of arrest and return.

21. Which two functions are carried on by both the federal and state governments? (a) maintaining highways and operating a postal system (b) conserving natural resources and coining money (c) appointing ambassadors and financing schools (d) levying taxes and apprehending criminals.

22. Which is an example of a power denied both to the federal government and to the states? (a) enactment of *ex post facto* legislation (b) impeachment of judges (c) levying of tariffs (d) coining of money.

23. Appointments to the United States Supreme Court must be approved by the (a) House of Representatives (b) Senate (c) Supreme Court (d) state legislatures.

24. The system of checks and balances was made part of our federal government to prevent (a) the federal government from obtaining too much power over the states (b) the states from seceding (c) any one branch of the federal government from becoming too powerful (d) the Supreme Court from declaring laws void.

25. A member of Congress may *not* be in the President's Cabinet because such a practice would violate the principle of (a) separation of powers (b) division of powers (c) the federal system (d) Cabinet responsibility.

26. A bill may become a law over the veto of the President by a (a) two-thirds vote of Congress (b) three-fourths vote of Congress (c) judicial interpretation of the Supreme Court (d) three-fourths vote of the Senate.

27. Which illustrates the system of checks and balances? (a) An individual pays an income tax to both the United States and New York State. (b) New York State requires at least 180 school days per year. (c) The Senate approves a President's nominee to the Supreme Court. (d) The Senate censures one of its members.

28. Both the President of the United States and the Prime Minister of Great Britain are (a) presiding officers of the legislatures (b) persons responsible for declaring war (c) members of the legislatures of their countries (d) leaders of political parties.

29. One similarity between the United States and British political systems is that in both (a) the government is ultimately responsible to the electorate (b) one political party has sole responsibility for making and enforcing laws (c) the chief executive serves a four-year term of office (d) the chief executive is directly elected by the people.

30. The main *difference* between the Cabinet in the United States government and the Cabinet in the British government is that, under the British system, Cabinet members (a) are members of the legislative branch (b) are appointed by the chief executive (c) advise the chief executive (d) direct activities of government departments.

31. Parliamentary forms of government have often been considered more democratic than presidential forms of government because parliamentary forms may be (a) more stable (b) more responsive to public opinion (c) based on a written constitution (d) more rigid in separating the three branches of government.

——————————— APPLICATION QUESTIONS ———————————

Constitutional Powers: *(A)* Delegated *(B)* Reserved *(C)* Implied *(D)* Denied

For each of the following statements, select the *letter* of the power, chosen from the group above, that best applies to that situation.

1. New York State requires a course in American history in its high schools.
2. California issues a "Bear State Dollar" for use along the Pacific Coast area.
3. The Federal Communications Commission assigns television channels.
4. Congress decides to change the gold content of the dollar.
5. Wisconsin passes a law conferring the rank of baron on all former governors of the state.
6. The Interstate Commerce Commission regulates rates of an interstate busline.
7. Congress raises the salaries of members of the armed forces.
8. Congress places a tax on exports from the West Coast states.
9. In Georgia a driver seeking an auto license must be at least 16 years old.
10. Congress lowers tariff rates on goods imported through Charleston and Savannah.

——————————— ESSAY QUESTIONS ———————————

1. *(a)* By giving *two* examples, prove that the Constitution divided powers between the states and the national government. *(b)* Give *two* examples of the increase in power of the national government in the 20th century. *(c)* Give *one* argument for *or one* argument against the increase in power of the national government now.
2. *(a)* By giving *two* examples, illustrate the operation of the system of checks and balances in our federal government. *(b)* State *one* reason for including this system in our Constitution. *(c)* Explain *one* advantage and *one* disadvantage of this system. *(d)* By giving *one recent* example, illustrate the workings of this system.
3. Compare the English with the American system of government, illustrating *(a) two* ways in which they are similar, and *(b) two* ways in which they are different.
4. Agree or disagree with each of the following statements and present *two* arguments to support your opinion. *(a)* For federalism to succeed, the central government and the states must seek cooperation and avoid conflict. *(b)* In giving funds to states and localities, the federal government should allot the monies for specific programs and should exercise strict supervision over the programs. *(c)* In the 20th century the federal government has shown increasing concern for democratic reforms. *(d)* Social and economic developments in the United States since the Civil War have brought about the expansion of federal power.

PART 3. The President Is the Chief Executive

At the Constitutional Convention, the Framers had two opposing fears regarding the office of the Presidency: making it too powerful might lead to a tyranny; making it too weak might repeat the mistakes of the Articles of Confederation. They therefore created an independent executive with important powers and also with limitations upon those powers. They left unsaid, whether deliberately or accidentally, many details regarding the Presidential office. Evolving out of practical experience, such details now constitute our Presidential traditions and customs.

SELECTION OF PRESIDENTIAL CANDIDATES

CONSTITUTIONAL REQUIREMENTS

The Constitution requires that a candidate for the Presidency be a native-born citizen of the United States, at least 35 years of age, and for 14 years a resident within the United States.

BRIEF HISTORY OF NOMINATING PROCEDURES

The Constitution is silent regarding the nominating of Presidential candidates. This task was assumed, early in our history, by political parties.

1. Caucus System (to 1828). A *caucus,* or meeting of a small group of influential party leaders, mostly members of Congress, selected the party candidate for the Presidency. Because the rank-and-file party members had no voice in this process, it was condemned as undemocratic and called *King Caucus.*

2. Nominating Convention (Since 1832). Spurred by the democratic spirit of the *Jacksonian Era,* political parties began selecting their Presidential candidates by the *nominating convention.* Since a large group of party members attended the convention, it was considered a democratic advance over the caucus.

NATIONAL NOMINATING CONVENTION SYSTEM TODAY

1. Selection of National Convention Delegates

a. By District and State Conventions. In about one-quarter of the states, delegates are chosen by the political parties through district and state conventions. These procedures, operating within the party machinery, usually are controlled by local and state party leaders.

Evaluation. These procedures have been criticized as being undemocratic and enabling the party "bosses" to dominate the national convention; they have been defended as being practical and enabling informed political leaders to exercise their best judgment.

b. By Presidential Primaries. In about three-quarters of the states, delegates are chosen by the party members in preliminary elections, called *primaries.* Usually, delegates pledge to vote for a specific candidate on at least the first ballot of the convention. In recent years, the number of Presidential primaries has increased sharply.

Evaluation. Presidential primaries have been hailed as a democratic advance over district and state conventions, since primaries reflect the wishes not of a few party leaders, but of the many party members. However, the primaries have been criticized because they (1) generally attract a low voter turnout, so that an active minority of party members may gain delegates for their candidate while the majority of party members may remain apathetic, (2) involve considerable expense, thereby favoring the candidate with the greater campaign funds, and (3) tend to discourage qualified candidates who lack the money and time from actively seeking the Presidency.

In recent years, political parties have insisted that national convention delegates—regardless of how chosen—include more women, youths, and ethnic minorities. In this way the parties hope that the convention delegates will more accurately reflect the interests of all their members.

2. National Convention. Held in the summer preceding Election Day, the convention—full of noise, motion, and color, and broadcast over radio and television—has been called a "political circus." It serves to center public attention upon the party, to enthuse rank-and-file party workers, to reconcile differing party views and unite delegates on a statement of party policy or *party platform,* and to nominate the party candidates for President and Vice President.

3. Qualifications Considered in Selecting a Candidate

a. Party Criteria. Each party seeks to nominate a candidate who can win. Such a person, party leaders generally believe, should (1) possess great personal popularity and have few enemies, (2) reflect moderate views on controversial issues, and (3) come from a heavily populated and *doubtful state,* that is, a state that has not consistently voted for one major party. Since the Civil War, many candidates have come from such populous and "doubtful" states as New York, Ohio, Illinois, and California.

b. Types of Candidates. For the Presidency, no major political party has ever nominated a black, a Jew, or a woman. Twice only, the Democrats have nominated Catholics—in 1928 Alfred Smith, who lost the election, and in 1960 the victorious John Kennedy. With these two exceptions, the candidates of the major parties have been white, Protestant, and male.

4. The Convention Selects the Party Ticket

a. Presidential Candidate. The names presented to the convention include those of (1) *active candidates,* who have declared their intention to seek the nomination and possibly have won the support of delegates through Presidential primaries and political arrangements, and (2) *favorite sons,* who are state leaders honored by their delegations even though they may not be actively seeking the Presidency. To gain the nomination, a candidate requires a majority of the votes. If repeated balloting fails to give any candidate a majority, the convention is deadlocked and may unite behind a compromise choice, usually a person not previously considered and therefore called a *dark horse.*

If the President is seeking a second term, the convention usually loses the sense of battle and becomes "cut-and-dried" as it renominates the incumbent.

b. Vice Presidential Candidate. After the Presidential candidate is nominated, the convention selects the Vice Presidential candidate. Usually, the convention respects the wishes of the Presidential nominee as to his or her running mate. The Vice Presidential candidate is expected to bring strength to the ticket by attracting voters indifferent to the Presidential nominee. For example, the two candidates may come from different sections of the country and may be identified with different economic interests. The Vice Presidential candidate is said, therefore, to *balance the ticket.*

Since nine Vice Presidents—five in the present century—have moved into the Presidency, political scientists criticize national conventions for their "balance-the-ticket" motives in selecting the Vice Presidential candidate.

ELECTION OF THE PRESIDENT

ELECTION CAMPAIGN

1. Appeal to the Voters. For eight to ten weeks, the Presidential and Vice Presidential candidates "go to the people." They present their philosophies of government and their views on current issues. They travel extensively, deliver major addresses and brief talks, and appear on radio and television.

Evaluation. Some political scientists question the need of such long campaigns today. They argue that *(a)* the candidates actually engage in two campaigns—for the nomination and for the election; *(b)* by means of radio, television, and airplane, candidates today reach more voters in less time than ever before; *(c)* in Great Britain, national election campaigns last about three weeks; and *(d)* shorter campaigns would make possible reduced expenditures.

2. Campaign Finances—Federal Regulations. Running for federal office is expensive. Candidates for seats in the House of Representatives often spend more than $500,000 on a single election campaign. Senate candidates spend an average of more than $2 million. Candidates for President spend in the tens of millions.

To prevent politicians from being unduly indebted to large contributors, Congress has passed several "corrupt practices" laws in the past 80 years. But such laws contain many loopholes. For example, while federal law bars corporations and labor unions from contributing directly to candidates for federal office, indirect contributions from both sources are common.

a. The 1972 Federal Election Campaign Act. In 1972 Congress passed a law requiring federal candidates to make public the names of all individuals who contributed more than $10 to their campaigns, and to reveal all expenditures of more than $100. Those provisions are still in effect. However, another provision, placing limits on spending in House, Senate, and Presidential elections, was ruled unconstitutional by the Supreme Court in 1976. (See paragraph **c**, page 92.)

b. The 1974 Federal Election Campaign Act. An aura of scandal surrounded the 1972 Presidential election. An investigation by the Senate Committee on Presidential Campaign Activities found that corporations and milk cooperatives had made large and illegal campaign contributions, mainly to President Nixon's reelection committee. Intent on reform, Congress passed the 1974 *Federal Election Campaign Act.*

The law began a new program of federal funding of Presidential elections. Federal funds come from individual taxpayers who agree to let $1 of their taxes go to the Presidential campaign fund. During primary campaigns, candidates can draw funds from private donors and from federal funds. In the general election campaign, however, a candidate who is eligible for and accepts federal funding must stop taking contributions from other sources. The federal funds available to each major-party candidate in 1984 totaled $40.4 million. The amount varies from one campaign to another.

In the Presidential primaries, federal funds are provided on a matching basis. To become eligible for such funds, a candidate must first raise $100,000 in private contributions of $250 or less in at least 20 states ($5000 per state). The federal government matches each private donation of $250 or less up to a preset limit. In 1984, the limit was $10.1 million in federal funds to match $10.1 million in private funds for each candidate. Thus, each candidate could spend $20.2 million before the national nominating conventions. For their conventions that year, the Republican and Democratic parties each received $8 million in federal funds. After the conventions, private donations must stop.

A minor party may also be eligible for federal election funds, provided it gets at least 5 percent of the total vote. The more votes a minor party gets, the more federal money it can receive.

The 1974 Federal Election Campaign Act also limited spending by Presidential candidates on their own behalf to no more than $50,000. The law provided no federal funds for Senate and House candidates.

The law set caps on individual contributions to federal candidates and committees in any one year. For a single federal candidate, an individual is limited to a contribution of $2000—$1000 for the primaries and $1000 for the general election. Individuals may give a national party committee up to $20,000 and a political action committee up to $5000.

Political action committees, or *PACs,* are organizations that seek to influence political life, often by working to help elect or defeat a candidate. Since 1974,

PACs have become an increasingly important source of funds for Congressional races, increasing their donations from an estimated $12.5 million in 1974 to $100 million in 1984. PACs are organized mainly by corporations, trade and industry associations, labor unions, and political-issue groups.

The law established a *Federal Elections Commission* of six members—two named by the President and four by Congress. The commission receives reports from candidates of receipts and expenditures, investigates suspicious contributions, and institutes civil suits against suspected campaign law violators. Candidates who violate the law may be barred for a number of years from running again for federal office. All violators may be fined up to $50,000.

c. The 1976 Supreme Court Decision on the Campaign Reform Act. The Court's decision voided some aspects of the act and upheld others:

(1) The Court held unconstitutional the spending limits on Presidential candidates for themselves and on Senate and House candidates. Such limits, the Court reasoned, violated the First Amendment guarantee of free speech.

(2) The Court ordered the restructuring of the Federal Elections Commission to have all six members named by the President. The commission, the Court held, is an executive agency and must conform to the principle of separation of powers. (By law, the commission was so restructured.)

(3) The Court upheld *(a)* limits on individual and group contributions to political candidates as only a "marginal" restraint on free speech, outweighed by the need to insure the "integrity" of the election process; *(b)* requirements that political candidates provide detailed reports of contributions and expenditures; and *(c)* public financing of Presidential candidates. In upholding these provisions, the Court cited the need to avoid the "actuality and appearance of corruption" in federal elections.

d. The 1985 Supreme Court Ruling on Spending by PACs. In *Federal Elections Commission vs. NCPAC,* the Supreme Court in 1985 struck down a section of the 1974 law barring any PAC from spending more than $1000 on behalf of a Presidential candidate in a general election. Such a limit, the Court held, went against the First Amendment by restricting rights of free speech and association.

e. "Loopholes." Despite the reforms of the 1970s, many people feel that federal election campaigns remain subject to undue influence by "special interests." Two "loopholes" have come under special attack:

(1) A supposedly minor change in federal election law in 1979 gave corporations and labor unions a legal way to aid Presidential campaigns. They can do this by contributing to state and national parties for "party-building" activities such as voter registration drives and get-out-the-vote activities, thus freeing other party funds for direct aid to candidates. Contributions for party-building activities are known as "soft" money, and may include donations from individuals who have already reached the federal limit of $25,000 in "hard" donations.

(2) Presidential candidates may (and often do) avoid restrictions on early campaign spending by establishing "charitable foundations" to advance their political goals. Such foundations cannot directly support the candidate's campaign,

but they can pay for travel expenses and promote events such as seminars that help to publicize the candidate's name and ideas. Individuals, corporations, and unions can make unlimited donations to such foundations.

Efforts to bar such practices have run into stiff opposition. Many people defend the present law, saying it gives greater flexibility to the political process.

3. Election Day. On the first Tuesday after the first Monday in November each leap year, the voters go to the polls. They vote their choice of candidate not directly, but through a group of relatively unknown persons called *electors*.

ELECTORAL SYSTEM

1. Number of Electors. The *electoral college*—the term for all electors as a group—chooses the President and Vice President. For each state, the number of electors equals the total of the state's Representatives and Senators in Congress. Although the District of Columbia is not a state, by the Twenty-Third Amendment, it is currently entitled to three electors. Since the number of Representatives equals 435, the number of Senators equals 100, and the District of Columbia has three electors, the electoral college today totals 538.

2. Election Procedures. On the ballot, the voters see the phrase "electors for" followed by the names of the Presidential and Vice Presidential candidates. Thus, the voters actually choose from among several slates of electors, each slate being pledged in advance to support its party's candidates. The winning slate receives either *(a)* a *majority*—more than half the popular votes cast in the state, or *(b)* a *plurality*—the largest number of popular votes, though less than half, as may happen if more than two slates are contesting the election.

The Presidential and Vice Presidential candidates of the winning slate in each state receive that state's total electoral votes—the *winner-takes-all* principle. For election, a candidate needs an electoral college majority, now 270 votes.

3. Appeals From an Electoral College Deadlock

a. Constitutional Provisions. If the electoral college does not give any candidate the necessary majority, the House of Representatives chooses the President from among the top three candidates in electoral votes. In such a situation the House votes by states, with each state having one vote. To be elected President, a candidate must receive the votes of a majority of the states. For the Vice Presidency, if no candidate receives a majority in the electoral college, the Senate selects a Vice President from the top two candidates.

b. Case Studies. Twice the electoral college failed to elect a President and threw the election into the House: in 1800 between Thomas Jefferson and Aaron Burr, and in 1824 between Andrew Jackson and John Quincy Adams. (For these elections, check the Index for Jefferson and Adams.)

4. From Undemocratic Intent to "Rubber Stamp." The Framers devised the electoral system so as to reduce the voice of the people in electing the President. They intended that the electors express their own judgment. Since 1796, however, political parties have overcome this undemocratic intent by naming electors who were pledged in advance to vote for the party's Presidential candidate. Thus, the electoral college reflects the people's wishes. It has become a "rubber stamp."

5. Effects of the Electoral College System

a. The electoral vote distorts the popular vote. In 1980 Ronald Reagan defeated Jimmy Carter in the popular vote by 43 million to 35 million (55 percent to 45 percent), but the electoral vote of 489 to 49 indicated a landslide Reagan victory.

b. A candidate may lose the small states overwhelmingly in the popular vote while carrying the large states by narrow margins. The electoral votes of the large states may then give one candidate a victory in the electoral college though the opponent had more popular votes. In 1888, although Grover Cleveland outdrew Benjamin Harrison by 100,000 popular votes, Harrison received a majority of the electoral votes and was elected President.

c. Most minor parties are discouraged by the electoral system, since they rarely poll enough popular votes to capture any electoral votes. People often feel that a vote for a minor-party candidate is a "wasted" vote. In 1980 John Anderson, a third-party candidate, polled some 6 million popular votes but gathered no electoral votes.

d. In most states, electors are not legally pledged to vote for their party's candidates. In a few recent instances electors have broken their pledges, but these broken pledges have not affected the outcome of the election.

e. Candidates tend to campaign little in small states and rural areas. They concentrate upon the industrial states, and upon heavily populated cities and suburbs, aiming to win the states with the most electoral votes.

f. To carry closely contested or *doubtful* states, especially in the North, candidates seek to satisfy minority groups whose numbers could determine, that is, *swing* the electoral vote of an entire state.

g. When more than two strong candidates are running, the electoral college may convert a popular plurality into an electoral majority and so prevent a deadlock. In 1968 Richard Nixon led in a field of three strong candidates and, although he lacked a popular majority, was elected President.

6. Proposed Changes.
The 1968 Presidential election, with three forceful candidates, aroused the nation to the possibility of an electoral college deadlock. The House of Representatives therefore proposed a Constitutional amendment to (a) abolish the electoral college, (b) base the election upon the popular vote, (c) require the top pair of candidates for President and Vice President to secure at least 40 percent of the popular vote, and (d) if no pair secured this minimum, provide for a runoff election between the top two pairs. After two decades, this proposal has not received the required two-thirds vote in the Senate and has not been submitted for ratification to the states.

PRESIDENTIAL INAUGURATION

On the 20th of January following the election, the President takes office. In a solemn ceremony, the Chief Executive takes an oath or affirmation to "preserve, protect, and defend the Constitution of the United States."

PRESIDENTIAL TENURE AND SUCCESSION

TERM OF PRESIDENTIAL OFFICE

1. Two-Term Tradition. The Constitution sets the term of office at four years. George Washington, our first President, originated the tradition of serving no more than two terms.

2. Breaking the Two-Term Tradition. In 1940 Franklin D. Roosevelt broke the two-term tradition when he was elected to a third term. His supporters argued that the people *(a)* needed an experienced leader to deal with the critical problems of World War II and *(b)* had made and therefore could unmake traditions. His opponents insisted that the people *(a)* should not consider any one person indispensable and *(b)* needed the two-term tradition as a safeguard against dictatorship.

3. Twenty-Second Amendment (1951). Passed after Roosevelt's death, this amendment prohibits any one person from being elected President for more than two terms. A person who has served more than two years of another person's term may be elected for only one additional term.

SUCCESSION TO THE PRESIDENCY

1. Original Constitution (Article II, Section 1). In case of the death, resignation, or removal of the President, the Constitution provides that the President be succeeded by the Vice President.

2. Presidential Succession Act of 1947. In the event of a vacancy in both the Presidency and the Vice Presidency, the *Presidential Succession Act of 1947* provides the following order of succession: first the Speaker of the House of Representatives, then the President *pro tempore* of the Senate, and finally the Cabinet members, starting with the Secretary of State.

3. Problems of Presidential Disability and Succession. From 1955 to 1957, President Eisenhower suffered three serious illnesses. Eisenhower's Vice President, Richard Nixon, took an active part in maintaining the administration, but did not become Acting President—a position not foreseen by the Founders. Also, in 1963, following President Kennedy's assassination, Lyndon Johnson became President, and the Vice Presidency remained vacant for over a year. These events turned the nation's attention to the problem of Presidential disability and succession.

4. Twenty-Fifth Amendment (1967): Presidential Disability and Succession

a. In case the office of Vice President is vacant, the President shall nominate a new Vice President, subject to approval by a majority vote of both houses of Congress.

b. In case of Presidential disability, the President or—if the President does not or cannot—the Vice President, with a majority of the Cabinet members, may so inform Congress. Thereupon, the Vice President shall serve as Acting President.

c. When the President informs Congress that a Presidential disability no longer exists, the President shall resume the duties of office. In case the Vice President and a majority of the Cabinet officers dispute the President's ability to resume office, the President may be declared still disabled and kept from office by a two-thirds vote of Congress. The Vice President then continues as Acting President.

5. First Applications of the Twenty-Fifth Amendment. *(a)* In 1973 Spiro Agnew, pleading "no contest" to a charge of income tax evasion, resigned as Vice President. President Nixon then nominated and Congress approved a new Vice President, Gerald Ford. *(b)* In 1974, because of the Watergate investigation, Nixon resigned as President and Ford assumed that office. Ford nominated and Congress approved a new Vice President, Nelson Rockefeller. (For details, check the Index.)

6. The Vice Presidency

a. Constitutional Requirements. The Constitution requires that the Vice President (1) meet the same qualifications as the President—35 years of age, a native-born citizen, and 14 years United States residence, (2) be elected by a majority vote of the electoral college, and (3) if no candidate secures an electoral majority, be selected by the Senate from the two top candidates.

b. Powers. The Vice President is empowered by the Constitution (1) to serve as presiding officer of the Senate and (2) to vote in the Senate only if the Senators "be equally divided"—two unimportant duties. The Vice President is usually absent from Senate sessions, and the place of presiding officer is occupied by a Senate-elected temporary head, the president *pro tempore* (for the time being).

The Vice President is also empowered by the Constitution to assume the Presidency upon the resignation, removal, or death of the President. Thus, the Vice President is the "heir apparent" who may succeed to the Presidency but in the meantime is powerless—dependent on Congress and the President for assignments and responsibilities.

c. Early Disdain for the Vice Presidency. John Adams, our first Vice President, described the position as the "most insignificant office ever contrived." Other early leaders reinforced this critical appraisal by referring to the Vice President as the "superfluous excellency." (For the reasons behind Theodore Roosevelt's nomination in 1900 as Vice President, check the Index.)

d. Growing Respect for the Vice Presidency—In the 20th Century

(1) Succession to the Presidency. In this century, five Vice Presidents have succeeded to the Presidency: Theodore Roosevelt in 1901 upon the assassination of McKinley; Calvin Coolidge in 1923 upon the death from illness of Harding; Harry Truman in 1945 when a stroke ended the life of Franklin D. Roosevelt; Lyndon Johnson upon the assassination of Kennedy; and Gerald Ford upon the resignation of Nixon. These latter three successions awakened the American people to the importance of the Vice Presidency.

(2) Vice Presidential Assignments by Congress. By law Congress has assigned the Vice President to serve as a member of the National Security Council.

(3) Vice Presidential Assignments by the President. With the burdens of the Presidency becoming more onerous, recent Presidents have delegated certain duties to their Vice Presidents. President Truman used his "Veep," *Alben Barkley,* for liaison with Congress. President Eisenhower kept his Vice President, Richard Nixon, busy attending Cabinet meetings, undertaking foreign trips, campaigning in the midterm elections, and strengthening relations with Congress. Subsequent Presidents have continued this practice of training and utilizing their respective Vice Presidents. However, the President retains full power to decide if and to what extent the Vice President will be employed.

PRESIDENTIAL POWERS AND LIMITATIONS

POWERS OF THE PRESIDENT

The President of the United States is the most powerful democratically elected official in the world. The President's powers are derived from the Constitution and also from custom and tradition.

1. Executive Powers. *(a)* The President enforces the Constitution and the laws passed by Congress. *(b)* The President appoints all important government officials, including Cabinet officers. *(c)* The President is the ceremonial head of the government and symbol of national unity.

2. Legislative Powers. *(a)* In the "State of the Union" message, required by the Constitution, and in other messages, the President may request that Congress pass specific legislation. *(b)* If the President deems it necessary, Congress may be recalled into special session. *(c)* The President may veto legislation. *(d)* As head of a political party, the President may often influence the votes of these party members in Congress. The President may also use the power of *patronage;* that is, offer political jobs for distribution by those members of Congress who vote as the President wishes. *(e)* In radio and television talks and through press conferences, the President may appeal to the public for its support.

3. Judicial Powers. *(a)* The President may grant pardons and reprieves in cases involving federal crimes, except in cases of impeachment. *(b)* The President appoints all federal judges. *(c)* The President enforces or may refuse to enforce federal court decisions.

4. Powers Over Foreign Affairs. *(a)* The President determines foreign policy and is responsible for the conduct of foreign affairs. Today, the President is also considered the leader of the free nations of the world. *(b)* The President appoints officials to assist in foreign affairs: the Secretary of State, ambassadors, and ministers. *(c)* The President directs diplomatic matters and negotiates treaties with foreign countries. *(d)* The President receives foreign ambassadors, and may therefore recognize or refuse to recognize foreign governments.

5. Military Powers. *(a)* The President is commander in chief of the armed forces, thereby maintaining civilian control over the military. *(b)* The President appoints the top military commanders, may offer them military advice, and also may remove them from their commands. *(c)* The President may order the armed forces into action in case of disturbances within the United States and in foreign countries.

LIMITATIONS ON PRESIDENTIAL POWERS

1. Limits on Executive Powers. *(a)* The President's appointments of important officials require approval by a majority of the Senate. *(b)* Executive orders of the President may be challenged in the courts as to their constitutionality. *(c)* Chief Presidential assistants may be called before Congressional committees to testify regarding executive policies and actions.

2. Limits on Legislative Powers. *(a)* The President's requests for legislation need not be heeded by Congress. *(b)* A Presidential veto may be overridden by a two-thirds vote of each House of Congress. *(c)* Party members may refuse to back Presidential programs, especially, analysts believe, if the President is in the second and last term. *(d)* Public appeals for support may be futile if many citizens disapprove of the President's views.

3. Limits on Judicial Powers. *(a)* The President's appointments of federal judges require the approval of a majority of the Senate. *(b)* Federal judges have life tenure and decide cases independent of Presidential wishes. *(c)* The President may not grant pardons in cases of impeachment.

4. Limits on Powers Over Foreign Affairs. *(a)* The President's appointments of major foreign affairs officials require the consent of a majority of the Senate. *(b)* Treaties negotiated with foreign countries go into effect only if ratified by two-thirds of the Senate. *(c)* The President's foreign policies may be examined and criticized by House and Senate committees.

5. Limits on Military Powers. *(a)* The President's authority does not extend to declaring war, for that power resides exclusively in Congress. *(b)* The

President depends upon Congressional legislation authorizing such military programs as recruitment of personnel and development of weapons. *(c)* Funds to pay for military expenditures require Congressional appropriations of money.

In 1973 Congress limited the Presidential military power by enacting, over President Nixon's veto, the War-Powers Resolution. (For details, check the Index.)

6. Impeachment Power of Congress. The Congressional power of impeachment provides an extreme check upon the President. The House of Representatives by majority vote may bring impeachment charges against the President for "treason, bribery, or other high crimes and misdemeanors." The Senate, with the Chief Justice of the Supreme Court presiding, acts as the jury and hears the charges. The Senate requires a two-thirds vote to declare the President guilty and remove him from office.

(For the 1868 impeachment of President Andrew Johnson and the 1974 resignation of President Richard Nixon, check the Index.)

HISTORIC GROWTH OF PRESIDENTIAL POWERS

1. Overview. Over the years, the Presidency has grown tremendously in its functions and has become much more involved in solving the nation's problems. This growth of Presidential powers has been marked by an "ebb-and-flow" pattern. Strong Presidents who have expanded their powers have been followed frequently by weak ones who through lack of ability or indifference have constricted Presidential powers. Each strong President, however, has built upon the traditions of the earlier strong ones, and the historic trend has been toward greater Presidential powers.

2. Reasons

a. Rise of the Democratic Presidency. By the administration of Andrew Jackson (1829–1837), our seventh President, the Presidency had become a democratic office with its occupant the people's chief advocate. This transformation resulted largely from the rise of political parties, the recasting of the electoral system into a "rubber stamp," and the achieving of universal male suffrage, all of which enabled a greater expression of the popular will in Presidential elections. Andrew Jackson proclaimed that the President has the "duty to protect the liberties and rights of the people and the integrity of the Constitution against the Senate, or the House of Representatives, or both together."

b. Changes in Public Attitude Toward Government. As Americans demanded that the federal government accept greater responsibility for economic and social problems, they looked to the President for leadership. As a single decision-maker, the President is better able to act swiftly than either Congress or the Supreme Court.

c. Economic and Social Change. As the United States evolved into a large industrial and urbanized nation, it faced complex new problems. Many of these could not be solved by individuals or states acting separately. Federal efforts to deal with such problems focused on the President. For example, in 1902 Theodore Roosevelt dealt with a serious coal strike, and in 1957 Dwight Eisenhower dealt with a school integration crisis at Little Rock, Arkansas. (For details, check the Index.)

    d. Foreign Affairs. As the United States became increasingly concerned with foreign affairs, the President exercised greater leadership. (For the President's role in foreign policy, check the Index.)

    e. Emergencies. During crises, such as war and economic depression, the people have looked to the President for leadership. Strong Presidents have acted with speed and decision, stretched their authority, and exercised almost dictatorial power. Usually, they have received cooperation from the Congress which, during crises, voluntarily has suspended its powers to check the President. (1) For Presidential leadership in response to the crisis of southern secession in 1861, check the Index for Abraham Lincoln. (2) In 1917, before the United States entered World War I, unarmed American merchant ships were threatened by unrestricted German submarine warfare. President Wilson requested Congress to authorize the arming of American merchant ships, but a "little group of willful men"—so named by Wilson—filibustered the bill to death in the Senate. Thereupon, Wilson discovered an 1819 statute on piracy and, citing its provisions, ordered the arming of American merchant ships. (3) For Presidential leadership in response to the crisis of the 1929 economic depression, check the Index for "Franklin D. Roosevelt."

VARIATIONS AND CONTRASTS AMONG PRESIDENTS

THE PRESIDENTIAL "RATING GAME"

    Historians have long enjoyed "rating the Presidents." Although differences of opinion exist, historians generally are agreed—on the basis of Presidential record *only*—on the following ratings:

    Great Presidents: Washington, Jackson, Lincoln, Theodore Roosevelt, Wilson, Franklin D. Roosevelt.

    Near-greats: John Adams, Jefferson, Polk, Hayes, Cleveland, Truman.

    At the bottom: Pierce, Buchanan, Grant, Harding.

    (This listing omits Presidents since 1953 since their administrations are too recent for valid objective judgment; it also omits other Presidents who rate somewhere in the wide area between "near-greats" and "at the bottom.")

    The major factors that determine the performance record of the "person in the White House" are (1) the individual's personality and outlook, (2) the times during which the individual serves as President, and (3) the President's advisers and assistants.

PRESIDENTIAL PHILOSOPHY REGARDING THE USE OF POWERS

Each President has had substantially the same powers, but the extent to which each has used these powers has varied greatly.

1. Limited Use. This person sees the President as a purely administrative officer. This President follows Congressional initiative and uses the powers of office sparingly.

a. James Buchanan (1857–1861). In office for four months after the 1860 election of Lincoln as President, Buchanan denied the southern states the right to secede but declared that he was powerless to resist their secession.

b. Calvin Coolidge (1923–1929). In office during a prosperous era, Coolidge did nothing to prevent the oncoming 1929 depression. He held that "if the federal government should go out of existence, the common run of people would not detect the difference . . . for a considerable length of time."

2. Moderate Use. This person sees the President as an administrative officer and as a defender of executive power and public welfare against Congressional encroachment. This President uses the powers of office moderately. One exponent of this philosophy was Grover Cleveland.

3. Dynamic Use. This person sees the President as a forceful national leader. This President advocates a legislative program, rallies public opinion, and battles to secure Congressional enactment. Trying to anticipate the needs of the nation, this President uses the powers of office to the utmost. The earliest exponent of this philosophy was Andrew Jackson (check the Index). Other Presidents exemplifying this philosophy include the following:

a. Abraham Lincoln (1861–1865). Unlike Buchanan, Lincoln acted vigorously to prevent southern secession. Lincoln called for army volunteers, ordered a naval blockade of southern ports, suspended the writ of *habeas corpus* in certain states to keep southern sympathizers in jail, and issued the Emancipation Proclamation to weaken the South's war effort. Lincoln said that he availed himself of "the broader powers conferred by the Constitution" to suppress insurrection.

b. Theodore Roosevelt (1901–1909). In office during relatively crisis-free times, Roosevelt helped Panama gain its independence from Colombia, thereby speeding a treaty allowing America to construct the Panama Canal, curbed "bad trusts," promoted conservation, and protected the consumer. Roosevelt called the White House a "bully pulpit" and asserted that the President was the "steward of the people"—the stewardship theory.

c. Franklin D. Roosevelt (1933–1945). Taking office during the worst year of the Great Depression, Roosevelt acted vigorously to lift the nation out of the depression. He prevented a run on the banks and secured from Congress an amazing number of New Deal laws on economic matters. Roosevelt viewed the Presidency as a position of "moral leadership."

4. The Person in the White House: The Role of the Times. The record of each President depends in part upon the nature of the times. Presidents who have overcome crises have been rated as strong Presidents; those who have left little imprint upon crises have been rated as less successful. All Presidents have had ample opportunity for leadership. Even in crisis-free times the nation has faced problems that required solutions.

PRESIDENTIAL LEADERSHIP IN DOMESTIC MATTERS

1. George Washington (1789–1797). Our first President, Washington set important precedents: creator of our first Cabinet; signer of the National Bank bill, thereby supporting loose construction of the Constitution; and upholder of the authority of the government by using troops against western Pennsylvania farmers who refused to pay the excise tax on whisky—the so-called Whisky Rebellion.

2. Andrew Jackson (1829–1837). Jackson rejected South Carolina's nullification of the 1832 tariff laws. He planned to use the military, if necessary, to enforce the nation's tariff laws within South Carolina. An armed clash was averted as Congress enacted the compromise 1833 Tariff Act.

3. Lyndon Johnson (1963–1969). Johnson gave leadership to the movement for equal rights for black Americans. He secured from Congress three major civil rights laws protecting voting rights and prohibiting discrimination in employment, places of public accommodation, and the rental and sale of most housing.

PRESIDENTIAL LEADERSHIP IN FOREIGN AFFAIRS

1. Thomas Jefferson and the Louisiana Purchase (1803). 2. James Polk and the Mexican War (1846–1848). 3. Harry Truman and the Cold War Policy of Containment (Beginning 1946). 4. John Kennedy and the Cuban Missile Crisis (1962)

(For each President's handling of the specified foreign problem, check the Index.)

PRESIDENTIAL ADVISERS AND ASSISTANTS

As the nation's chief decision-maker, carrying heavy and diverse responsibilities, the President must rely upon many people for advice and assistance. They serve the President by: (1) gathering and organizing information, (2) undertaking special missions and conducting negotiations, (3) expressing opinions and providing new ideas, (4) administering government laws and policies, and (5) presenting the administration's viewpoint to the American people.

THE EXECUTIVE DEPARTMENTS

1. Number and Work. As our nation has grown in size and complexity, the number of executive departments has increased. There were three executive departments in the administration of George Washington. Today, there are 13, as follows:

(a) The Department of State furthers our foreign policies. *(b)* The Department of the Treasury manages the nation's finances. *(c)* The Department of Defense provides military protection. *(d)* The Justice Department handles the legal work of the federal government. *(e)* The Department of the Interior conserves the nation's natural resources. *(f)* The Department of Agriculture aids farmers. *(g)* The Commerce Department aids businesses. *(h)* The Department of Labor aids workers. *(i)* The Department of Health and Human Resources (formerly Health, Education, and Welfare) directs social welfare programs. *(j)* The Department of Housing and Urban Development (HUD) encourages housing construction and slum clearance. *(k)* The Department of Transportation supervises our transportation systems. *(l)* The Department of Energy deals with the regulation and conservation of energy. *(m)* The Department of Education coordinates and directs education programs throughout the nation.

2. Department Heads. The President, with the consent of the Senate, appoints the heads of the executive departments. In selecting these assistants, the President may consider the importance of *(a)* repaying political debts, *(b)* representing different factions in the President's political party, *(c)* satisfying interested economic and geographic groups, *(d)* gaining bipartisan support for administration plans, *(e)* avoiding weak, indecisive individuals who may discredit the administration, and *(f)* avoiding strong, determined individuals who may cause dissension.

Together, these department heads make up the group of top-level Presidential advisers called the Cabinet.

THE PRESIDENT'S CABINET

1. Origins. The original Constitution mentions executive departments but it says nothing about the Cabinet. George Washington began the practice of having executive department heads and other top advisers meet with the President as the Cabinet. These meetings became an American governmental tradition.

2. The President and the Cabinet. The President may call Cabinet meetings frequently or infrequently. The President may use the Cabinet to *(a)* dramatize policy or public issues, *(b)* enable departmental heads to coordinate their work, and *(c)* propose and evaluate new policies. As the final authority, the President may accept, modify, or reject any Cabinet recommendations.

3. Presidential Relationships to Cabinet Members. *(a)* George Washington supported his treasury secretary, Alexander Hamilton. Washington approved of Hamilton's financial plans, endorsed loose construction of the Constitution, and maintained peace with Britain—all policies reflecting Hamilton's advice. (Check the Index for Alexander Hamilton.) *(b)* Andrew Johnson dismissed his war secretary, Edwin Stanton, and faced impeachment. (Check the Index for Andrew Johnson.) *(c)* Woodrow Wilson overruled his secretary of state, William Jennings Bryan. In response to the German sinking of the *Lusitania* (1915), Wilson drew up a very strong protest note. Bryan refused to sign the note and resigned. Wilson appointed another secretary of state, who dispatched the strong *Lusitania* note.

PRESIDENTIAL ADVISERS OTHER THAN CABINET MEMBERS

Most Presidents look to their close personal associates for advice and companionship. These individuals rarely occupy Cabinet positions. The friends of the President have often held non-Cabinet government positions or no public office at all. But they have exercised considerable influence in past administrations. (1) Andrew Jackson, in his early Presidential years, rarely held Cabinet meetings. Instead, he sought the advice of a group of close friends, whom his opponents dubbed the "Kitchen Cabinet." (2) Woodrow Wilson depended greatly upon Colonel Edward House, a successful Texas business leader and Democratic politician. Wilson employed House in secret negotiations relating to World War I and in formulating the Fourteen Points, Wilson's statement of American postwar aims. (3) Franklin Roosevelt relied heavily upon the advice of a group of college professors soon dubbed by the newspapers as the "brain trust."

THE EXECUTIVE OFFICE OF THE PRESIDENT

In 1939, with the consent of Congress, President Franklin Roosevelt reorganized much of the executive branch into the Executive Office of the President. This reorganization set the broad outlines for the executive branch as it exists today.

1. White House Office. Members of the White House Office are in intimate contact with the President. They include the following: *(a)* Assistants to the President specialize in various problem areas such as domestic affairs, national security affairs, and Congressional relations. *(b)* The press secretary supervises public relations, prepares press conferences, distributes news releases, and plans radio and television broadcasts. *(c)* The appointments secretary budgets the President's time. *(d)* Speech writers translate the President's views into written form for messages to Congress and the public. *(e)* Other members of the White House Office include a correspondence secretary, science, and diplomatic and military aides, and advisers on specific areas such as urban affairs and consumer problems.

2. Major Agencies. Major agencies within the Executive Office that report directly to the President include the following: *(a)* The Council of Economic

Advisers studies our economy and proposes government economic policies. *(b)* The Office of Management and Budget prepares the annual estimate of federal income and expenditures and seeks efficient government operations. *(c)* The Council on Environmental Quality develops policies to deal with environmental problems. *(d)* The Central Intelligence Agency (CIA) evaluates intelligence data and directs undercover missions relating to national security. *(e)* The National Security Council advises in regard to "domestic, foreign, and military policies" that affect the nation's security.

SOME PROBLEMS REGARDING THE AMERICAN PRESIDENCY

(1) Is the job too much for one person? If so, what may be done to improve the situation? (2) Should any one President be limited to a single six-year term? (3) Should the Presidential inauguration date, now January 20, be moved closer to the early November election date? (4) Is a strong President necessarily a good President? (5) Does the growth of Presidential power threaten our democracy?

———————— MULTIPLE-CHOICE QUESTIONS ————————

1. Which statement concerning the national nominating conventions for the Presidency is true? (a) They are provided for in the federal Constitution. (b) They preceded the Congressional caucus as a nominating procedure. (c) They have been the basic Presidential nominating procedure since the early 1830s. (d) They are not held when a President seeks reelection.
2. The practice that Presidential electors vote for the candidate nominated by their political party is based upon (a) the Constitution (b) custom and tradition (c) a law of Congress (d) a decision of the Supreme Court.
3. A governor of New York State is likely to be a candidate for the Presidential nomination because (a) he or she is a "dark horse" (b) New Yorkers are well known nationally (c) his or her state has a large number of electoral votes (d) New York State is the most rapidly growing state in the nation.
4. Voters in a Presidential election cast their ballots for (a) their candidates directly (b) a slate of electors (c) candidates selected by a Congressional caucus (d) the state party committee.
5. The authors of the Constitution included the electoral college method of selecting a President because of their belief that (a) populous states should determine the outcome of Presidential elections (b) this system would eliminate the influence of private interests in choosing a President (c) voting procedures should be as democratic as possible (d) popular majorities could not be trusted to select the best leader.
6. Because of the electoral college system, the two major-party Presidential candidates (a) find it necessary to campaign in all 50 states (b) spend much of their time campaigning in states with large populations (c) use much of their time appealing to the electors, rather than to the people (d) make an effort to campaign chiefly in those states containing disadvantaged minorities.

7. Under the Presidential election system, which might a third-party candidate *most* likely be able to accomplish? (a) win a majority of the popular vote by capturing the rural states (b) gain an electoral majority by winning in ten urban states (c) force a major party candidate to name him or her Vice President (d) prevent either major party candidate from gaining a majority in the electoral college.

8. Which is true of a Presidential election under the electoral college system? (a) The winner of a plurality of the popular votes in a state wins all the electoral votes of that state. (b) The winner of the majority of the popular vote in the country is elected President. (c) The ratio of the electoral vote usually follows closely the ratio of the popular vote. (d) The winning candidate usually does not have a majority of the popular vote.

9. A major criticism of the electoral college system has been that it (a) encourages the emergence of numerous third-party candidates (b) convenes after the general election results have been tallied (c) may select a candidate different from the candidate with a majority of the popular vote (d) represents the political views of the minority instead of the majority of the electorate.

10. In a Presidential election, Candidate A secured 40 percent and Candidate B secured 38 percent of the electoral college vote. Therefore, (a) Candidate A was declared the winner. (b) Candidate A became President and Candidate B became Vice President. (c) Another Presidential election was held to determine a winner. (d) The President was chosen by the House of Representatives.

11. Which action would be needed in order to abolish the electoral college as a method of electing the President? (a) a national referendum (b) a decision by the Supreme Court (c) an amendment to the federal Constitution (d) passage of a law by Congress.

12. The influence that major campaign contributors have on elected officials might be reduced by (a) shortening the terms of office of elected officials (b) permitting one interest group to serve as the sole sponsor for a candidate (c) providing government funds to pay all campaign costs (d) lengthening the average time of political campaigns.

13. The 1974 Federal Campaign Reform Act (a) for the first time prohibited corporations from contributing campaign funds (b) failed to provide for a commission to enforce the law (c) for the first time provided for federal funds for Presidential candidates (d) prohibited labor union members from contributing campaign funds.

14. Political Action Committees (PACs) were established to (a) oversee the workings of the Federal Elections Commission (b) evade the financial limitations on campaign contributions set by the Federal Campaign Reform Act (c) coordinate business and labor support for political candidates (d) further reform of the electoral college system.

15. In the oath of inauguration, the President swears (affirms) to preserve, protect, and defend (a) the Constitution (b) democracy (c) the nation (d) the states.

16. According to a law of Congress, the person next to the President and the Vice President in line of succession is the (a) secretary of state (b) speaker of the house (c) secretary of the treasury (d) president *pro tempore* of the Senate.

17. The limitation on the number of terms a President may serve is based upon (a) a law of Congress (b) a Constitutional amendment (c) an agreement between the two major political parties (d) a decision of the Supreme Court.

18. Which best explains why most politicians do *not* favor popular selection of Vice Presidential candidates? (a) The politicians believe that a Vice Presidential candidate has an unimportant role in the campaign. (b) Most voters show little interest in

the candidates for the Vice Presidency. (c) Supreme Court approval would be required for the change to the popular selection method. (d) Politicians think that Presidential candidates should have some choice and an opportunity to balance the ticket.

19. The growing importance of recent Vice Presidents is *most* clearly shown by their (a) expanded roles defending administration policies (b) increased influence in the Senate (c) positions as national chairpersons of the political party in power (d) decisive voices in determining foreign policy.

20. In case the office of Vice President is vacant, the Twenty-Fifth Amendment provides that a new Vice President be nominated by (a) the President (b) a special meeting of the electoral college (c) the Senate (d) the President's Cabinet.

21. As commander in chief of the armed forces, the President can (a) declare war (b) lower the age for drafting men and women into the armed forces (c) establish a treaty of peace (d) order the Marines into foreign countries to protect American interests.

22. President Carter's recognition of Communist China in 1979 was based primarily on his Constitutional power to (a) sign or veto bills (b) receive ambassadors (c) command the armed forces (d) inform Congress on the "State of the Union."

23. The Constitutional power that was the basis for United States military involvement in Vietnam was the power of (a) the President as commander in chief of the armed forces (b) the President to extend diplomatic recognition (c) Congress to make alliances (d) Congress to declare war.

24. Which is a valid statement about the term of office of members of the President's Cabinet? (a) Their term of office is fixed by Congress. (b) They serve at the discretion of the President. (c) They have tenure for life. (d) Their term of office is limited by the federal Constitution.

25. The President's "State of the Union" message to Congress is an example of (a) a Constitutional requirement (b) a Presidential practice of recent years (c) the carrying out of a federal law (d) custom and tradition.

26. To secure Congressional support for a legislative program, the President may make use of (a) the merit system (b) police power (c) patronage (d) gerrymandering.

27. Which has been the most important factor in the increase of Presidential power during the 20th century? (a) the frequent occurrence of crises demanding immediate attention (b) a lack of Congressional leadership willing to exercise its authority (c) an expansion of the executive bureaucracy, especially the White House staff (d) the inability of the Supreme Court to place limits on Presidential power.

28. A President exercises political leadership without using a specific or implied Constitutional power when he (a) appoints a new chairperson of the Joint Chiefs of Staff (b) suggests a new national chairperson for his party (c) appoints an ambassador to another nation (d) nominates a Justice for the Supreme Court.

29. A major check on Presidential control of foreign policy is (a) Congress's power regarding appropriations (b) the power of the House of Representatives to reject treaties (c) the existence of immigration laws (d) Congress's power to appoint ambassadors.

30. In general, Presidents considered by historians to have been outstanding leaders are those who (a) had complete control of the judicial and legislative branches of government (b) distributed government jobs to members of their political party only (c) initiated new programs and new directions in government policy (d) were elected by an overwhelming majority of the people.

——————————————— **ESSAY QUESTIONS** ———————————————

1. Agree or disagree with *each* of the following statements regarding the process of Presidential elections. In *each* case support your opinion with two facts. *(a)* The system of primary elections serves a useful purpose. *(b)* The personal qualities and/or public image of the candidate have a greater impact on election outcomes than do issues. *(c)* An incumbent running for office has great advantages over an opponent. *(d)* Candidates must appeal to ethnic groups and their interests in order to win elections. *(e)* The national nominating convention system should be reformed. *(f)* Federal financing of Presidential candidates, as provided in the 1974 Federal Campaign Reform Act, is a well-thought-out and worthwhile reform.

2. *(a)* Explain fully the part played in selecting the President of the United States by (1) party conventions, (2) the electoral college. *(b)* Discuss *one* criticism that has been made of *each* of these procedures.

3. Discuss *two* facts to prove *each* of the following statements concerning the Presidency of the United States: *(a)* Amendments to the federal Constitution have affected the Presidency. *(b)* The process of electing the President encourages candidates to concentrate much campaign activity in certain states. *(c)* To fulfill the many responsibilities of office, the President is assisted by a number of individuals and agencies. *(d)* In recent years, the mass media have played a significant role in the election of the President. *(e)* A President may be considered as strong or weak not according to the powers of the office of President, but according to the way these powers are used by the President.

4. The problem of Presidential succession has received considerable attention. *(a)* Discuss *two* criticisms that have been voiced concerning the factors that at present help to determine the selection of a party's Vice Presidential nominee. *(b)* Discuss *one* argument for *and one* argument against the Presidential Succession Act of 1947. *(c)* State *one* provision of the Twenty-Fifth Amendment and explain whether or not you approve of this provision.

5. Discuss *two* powers by which the President may accomplish *each* of the following: *(a)* influencing Congress, *(b)* enforcing laws, *(c)* controlling his own political party, *(d)* determining foreign policy. For *each* power discussed, indicate whether it is stated in the Constitution or derived from custom and tradition.

6. It has been said that the President of the United States has one of the most difficult executive jobs in the world. *(a)* Discuss briefly *two* major responsibilities of the President. *(b)* Explain *two* ways in which the system of checks and balances limits the power of the President. *(c)* Discuss briefly *two* different reasons for the increase in the power of the President during the 20th century.

PART 4. The Congress Is the Legislature

The Framers believed, that the leading branch of government would be the legislature. They based this belief upon the history of England, whose Parliament (1) twice had overthrown Stuart kings, ending absolute rule, and (2) had served as the arena for great orators, brilliant thinkers, and decisive doers. The Framers further knew of resistance by colonial legislatures against royal governors.

The Framers consequently expected that the Congress would most clearly express the public will and most effectively further the public welfare. Their expectations did not prove wholly correct. Over the years the Congress has taken much criticism, fallen in esteem, and been surpassed as public champion by the executive. Congress nevertheless constitutes an essential and significant branch of our American government.

ORGANIZATION OF CONGRESS

The Congress consists of a *bicameral,* or two-house, legislature. The House of Representatives represents the people by population, and the Senate represents them by state.

HOUSE OF REPRESENTATIVES

1. Requirements for Office. The Constitution requires that a Representative be at least 25 years of age, a citizen of the United States for seven years, and an inhabitant of the state from which the person is elected to the House.

2. Apportionment of House Seats. As the American population grew, the number of Representatives increased from 65 in 1789–1790 to 435 in this century. To keep the House from becoming too large to conduct its business efficiently, Congress fixed House membership at 435. These seats are apportioned as follows:

a. Among the States. The number of Representatives for each state is calculated by the ratio of the state population to the national population. To provide population data, the Constitution directed the taking of an "enumeration," or census, every ten years. The first such census was taken in 1790.

The 1980 census disclosed a national population of 227 million, which when divided by 435 House seats meant one Representative for about 520,000 persons. The 1980 census also required a shift of 17 House seats among the states. The largest gainers were Florida, four more; Texas, three more; and California, two more. The largest losers were New York, five fewer; and Illinois, Ohio, and Pennsylvania, each two fewer.

b. Within Each State

(1) Political Considerations in Drawing Boundaries. The state legislatures, practically unchecked by Congress, assumed the task of drawing state boundaries for Congressional districts. In many states, the legislatures created unfair districts as follows: *(a) Gerrymandering.* The political party in control of the state often drew district boundaries so as to concentrate its opponent's strength in a few districts while spreading its own strength in order to give itself a majority in many districts. This practice, used in 1812 by Governor *Elbridge Gerry* of Massachusetts, became known as *gerrymandering. (b) Rural Overrepresentation.* Until the 1960s, state legislatures dominated by rural members failed to redraw election district boundaries so as to redistribute Congressional (and state legislative) seats as population shifted from rural to urban and suburban areas.

(2) More Equitable Election Districts. In 1964, in *Wesberry vs. Sanders,* the Supreme Court held that the Constitution requires equal representation in the

House for equal numbers of people. In 1965 Congress legislated (a) against gerrymandering by requiring Congressional election districts to be contiguous and compact and (b) against rural overrepresentation by requiring Congressional election districts to have a population that was not above or below the average by more than 15 percent.

3. Term of Office. Each Representative serves a two-year term, and the entire House membership is elected every two years. Theoretically, therefore, the entire House membership may be drastically altered in a single election. In reality, however, this is not so. Most Representatives who run for reelection are returned to office, partly because their names become well known to voters and partly because political funds tend to go mainly to incumbents.

4. Presiding Officer. The *Speaker of the House* serves as its presiding officer. Elected by the Representatives voting along strict party lines, the Speaker is always a member of the majority party.

THE SENATE

1. Requirements for Office. The Constitution requires that a Senator be at least 30 years of age, a citizen of the United States for nine years, and an inhabitant of the state electing the person to the Senate.

2. Membership. The Senate has 100 members, with each of the 50 states, regardless of population, entitled to two Senators.

3. Term of Office. Senators are elected to a six-year term, but elections are staggered so that only one-third of the Senators are chosen every two years. Senate membership thusly cannot be drastically altered by any one election.

4. Presiding Officer. Since the Vice President frequently does not attend Senate sessions, the Senators, voting along strict party lines, elect a *president pro tempore*.

SPECIAL PRIVILEGES OF MEMBERS OF CONGRESS

1. Remuneration. Members of Congress receive substantial salaries; membership in a pension system; travel allowances from home to Washington and back; special tax exemption for expenses while living away from home; free office space in Washington and in their home districts or states; funds for office expenses including supplies, telephones, clerical help, and administrative assistants; and the right to send official mail free of postage, called the *franking privilege*.

2. Senatorial Courtesy. A Senator of the same political party as the President expects to be heeded on important federal appointments (district attorneys, judges, revenue collectors) within the Senator's state. If the Senator objects to the President's nominee as "personally obnoxious," then the Senate will show "courtesy" to its member by not approving the appointment.

3. Immunities. *(a) Freedom From Arrest.* While attending sessions, members of Congress are free from arrest on civil charges and misdemeanors (but not on charges of treason or major crimes). Thus, members of Congress are protected against undue interference with their legislative duties. *(b) Freedom From Suits for Libel and Slander.* For any speech on the floor of Congress, members "shall not be questioned in any other place," that is, they shall be exempted from lawsuits for libel and slander. This means that members of Congress are free to speak and debate in Congress. (Members of Congress occasionally abuse this immunity and malign individuals by making personal attacks and unsupported charges.)

SESSIONS OF CONGRESS

Each Congress sits for a two-year term. By custom, beginning with the first Congress of 1789–1790, Congresses have been numbered consecutively.

Each Congress meets in two regular sessions, each session convening, in accordance with the Twentieth Amendment, on or soon after January 3. Congress remains in session as long as it has important work to do. In recent years, most sessions have run into late autumn.

GENERAL POWERS OF CONGRESS

Congress has the general powers to (1) regulate itself, especially judging its members and determining its procedures, (2) enact laws, legislating upon those matters enumerated in the Constitution and implied by the elastic clause, and (3) hold hearings and conduct investigations.

SPECIAL POWERS OF THE HOUSE OF REPRESENTATIVES

The House has the sole power to (1) start all revenue (tax) bills, which the Senate later may amend, (2) bring charges of impeachment against federal officials, including the President, and (3) elect the President if the electoral college fails to give any one candidate a majority.

SPECIAL POWERS OF THE SENATE

The Senate has the sole power (1) to ratify treaties negotiated by the President (needs a two-thirds vote), (2) when the House brings charges of impeachment, to sit as a jury and decide the guilt of the impeached person (two-thirds vote), (3) to approve Presidential appointments (majority vote), and (4) to elect the Vice President if the electoral college is deadlocked (majority vote).

CONGRESS REGULATES ITSELF

1. Ethical Conduct of Members. According to the Constitution, each house of Congress shall judge "the elections, returns, and qualifications of its own members," may punish its members for disorderly behavior, and by a two-thirds vote may "expel a member."

In past years, Congress has occasionally acted against individual members on the grounds of unethical conduct. Such cases, few in number and quite flagrant, have involved (a) excessive campaign spending to "buy" the election (William Vare in 1926 as Senator from Pennsylvania), (b) taking of public funds for personal use (Adam Clayton Powell in 1967 as Representative from New York; Charles Diggs, Jr., in 1979 as Representative from Michigan; Herman Talmadge in 1979 as Senator from Georgia), and (c) accepting bribes in the FBI's Operation Abscam—a probe of political corruption (a dozen members of Congress in 1980).

In general, Congress has been reluctant to investigate and punish its own members. In recent years, however, as the news media have unearthed and publicized cases of unethical conduct, Congress has been prodded into greater action.

2. Ethical Codes. In 1977 the House and the Senate both adopted more stringent "ethical codes": members of Congress were (a) limited as to the value of gifts they could accept, (b) limited as to earned outside income—no more than 15 percent of the annual Congressional salary, and (c) required to submit detailed financial disclosure statements. The codes were hailed as evidencing Congressional concern with maintaining ethical standards. The codes were criticized for containing loopholes and lacking adequate enforcement.

In 1979 the Senate and the House voted to ease the required annual financial disclosure statements.

3. Lawmaking Procedures. The Constitution states that in order to conduct its business, each house shall require the presence of a majority of its members—a minimum number called a *quorum.* In most other procedural matters, the Constitution permits each house to determine "the rules of its proceedings."

HOW CONGRESS MAKES LAWS: THE COMMITTEE SYSTEM

1. Introduction of the Bill. Except for money bills, which must originate in the House, any bill may be introduced by any member of Congress. The bill may reflect the thinking of the members of a special-interest group or of the executive branch, but all bills must be sponsored, or formally presented, by members of Congress. In the Senate, the bill is announced orally; in the House the bill is placed in a basket called the hopper.

2. Referral to Committee. Thousands of bills on many subjects are introduced during each session of Congress. Each bill is given a number preceded

HOW A BILL BECOMES A LAW
(When the bill originates in the House)

Representative introduces bill by placing it in hopper. Speaker refers bill to proper committee.

Committee studies bill, holds hearings, and may change provisions. If approved, bill goes to Rules Committee.

Rules Committee places bill on calendar for discussion by entire House.

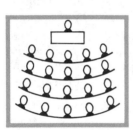

The bill is introduced in Senate, considered by committee, and debated by entire Senate. If Senate passes bill different from House version, bill goes to conference committee.

House debates bill and may pass it as is or with further change. If passed, bill goes to Senate.

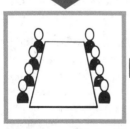

If conference committee, of House and Senate members, resolves differences, compromise bill is submitted to both House and Senate.

If both House and Senate pass compromise bill, it goes to President for signature.

If President signs, bill becomes law; if he vetoes, Congress may override veto by two-thirds vote of both House and Senate.

by the letters "HR" or "S" (identifying the originating house), its sponsors are listed, and it is printed.

Since neither house acting as a whole can adequately consider all these bills, each house is divided into small legislative bodies, called committees. In each house, the presiding officer refers each bill to the appropriate committee.

3. Number and Organization of Committees. The House of Representatives has 22 and the Senate has 16 standing or regular committees. House committees include Agriculture; Armed Services; Banking, Finance, and Urban Affairs; Education and Labor; Foreign Affairs; Judiciary; Rules; Science and Technology; and Ways and Means (taxation). Senate committees include Agriculture, Nutrition, and Forestry; Armed Services; Commerce, Science, and Transportation; Energy and Natural Resources; Environment and Public Works; Foreign Relations; Labor and Human Resources; and Judiciary.

Committee members are chosen from both political parties. House committees average about 30 members, Senate committees about 15. On each committee, the majority of the members belong to the majority party, which thereby should be able to control the committee. Committee members are expected to become experts in their respective fields. Committee chairpersons, always of the majority party, are usually chosen on the basis of length of service, or *seniority*.

4. Committee Proceedings. The committee disposes of most bills by deferring consideration indefinitely, that is, pigeonholing them. Some 90 percent of all bills introduced in Congress are killed in committee.

On a major bill the committee usually conducts research, holds hearings, and considers arguments for and against the measure. Then the committee, by majority vote, may approve the bill as introduced, or as amended, or it may reject the bill.

If a House committee delays action on a vital bill, a majority of the House membership can move the bill from the committee onto the House floor by signing a *discharge petition*. This rarely occurs.

5. Action in the Originating House. If approved by the committee, the bill is scheduled for consideration by the entire house by being placed on the calendar. (In the House of Representatives, this function is performed by the powerful *Rules Committee*. It also sets the rules for House consideration of the bill, regulating debate and restricting or permitting amendments from the floor.) The originating house debates the bill, possibly amends it, and finally takes a vote. If a majority votes against the bill, it is dead. If a majority approves, the bill goes to the other house.

6. Action in the Second House. Here the bill follows a similar path: introduction, referral to committee, consideration in committee, referral to the entire body, and decision.

7. Conference Committee. A bill is often approved by the two houses in versions that differ as to details. To adjust these differences, members designated by the presiding officer of each house meet as a temporary *conference committee.* Usually, they arrive at a *compromise bill,* and this bill is then submitted to each house for approval.

8. Presidential Action. After passage by Congress, the bill goes to the President. *(a)* If the President signs the bill within ten days, it becomes a law. *(b)* If the President holds the bill for ten days without signing it and Congress is still in session, the bill unsigned becomes a law. *(c)* If the President holds the bill for ten days without signing it and Congress is *not* in session, the bill is automatically killed. This is called a *pocket veto.* *(d)* If the President *vetoes* the bill, it is returned to the originating house with a statement of reasons for the Presidential veto. Congress may override the veto by a two-thirds vote in each house.

EVALUATION OF CONGRESSIONAL LAWMAKING PROCEDURES

1. Committee System. *(a) Merits.* The committee system provides a sensible way of handling the many bills proposed in Congress. It enables bills to receive careful consideration. Committee hearings permit interested parties to express their views. *(b) Criticisms.* The committee system is time-consuming. It involves needless duplication, as House and Senate committees cover essentially the same ground. The committee system prevents most bills from ever being considered by Congress. In killing some 90 percent of the bills, the committees do not necessarily reflect the views of Congress or the people.

2. Seniority and Committee Chairpersons. *(a) Merits.* Chosen by seniority, committee heads have much legislative experience. They are capable of exercising strong control so that their committees function smoothly. *(b) Criticisms.* Seniority does not necessarily mean ability. Committee heads usually represent "safe" districts and states, where voters consistently support the same party. They rarely come from "doubtful" districts and states, where voters often switch support, thus making it difficult for their Congress members to acquire sufficient seniority. Chairpersons exercise too much power over their respective committees. They hire secretarial and research staffs, call or postpone committee meetings, and determine the *agenda*—the list of matters to be discussed.

In 1975 three veteran committee heads, whose thinking was out of step with the House Democratic majority, were denied reassignment. The vacated positions went to persons with less seniority but whose views were more in harmony with the Democratic majority. This onetime violation of seniority was considered a warning to all committee chairpersons to be responsive to the will of their party's majority.

3. Rules Committee in the House of Representatives. *(a) Merits.* The Rules Committee arranges the orderly flow of bills for consideration by the entire House. It serves as a "traffic director." *(b) Criticisms.* Composed of senior Representatives, the Rules Committee does not necessarily reflect the views of the House majority but tends to resist new ideas. If it opposes a bill approved by a standing committee, the Rules Committee may prevent consideration by the entire House. It may serve as a "roadblock."

RULES ON DEBATE

The House maintains strict rules limiting debate. These House rules enable the Representatives to discuss bills and reach decisions without deliberate delay through debate. The Senate, however, usually permits its members the privilege of unlimited debate. This makes possible the *filibuster*.

FILIBUSTER IN THE SENATE

1. Purpose. A filibuster is a deliberate attempt sometimes used by a minority group of Senators (or a single Senator) to talk continuously so as to consume time and prevent a favorable vote on a bill. The filibustering members hope to compel the Senate leaders, concerned about the regular work schedule of the Senate, to return the disputed bill to committee, probably to be pigeonholed.

2. Cloture. A filibuster may be halted by *cloture,* a special vote to close debate. *Senate Rule 22,* adopted in 1917, permitted cloture by a two-thirds vote of the Senators present. Cloture was infrequently used because *(a)* southern Senators are opposed to cloture and often have mustered enough votes to block it, and *(b)* many Senators are unwilling to employ cloture against others for fear that, at some future time, it may be used against themselves.

In 1975 the Senate moved to ease its cloture rule. While still requiring a two-thirds vote of all Senators present for any further change in its cloture rule, the Senate adopted a new regulation permitting cloture on all other issues by a vote of three-fifths of its total membership. This regulation reduced from as many as 67 to 60 the number of votes needed to invoke cloture.

Scholars pointed out that from 1917 to 1975, only 24 cloture attempts were successful. If the new Senate rule had been in effect since 1917, the number of successful cloture attempts would have increased only by four.

3. Evaluation of the Filibuster. *(a) Merits.* A filibuster (1) permits thorough discussion of a bill, (2) allows time for the public to make known its views, and (3) protects the rights of the minority. *(b) Criticisms.* A filibuster (1) prevents meaningful discussion on a bill when filibustering Senators "talk a bill to death," by reading such extraneous materials as telephone directories and novels, (2) frustrates the will of the majority, and (3) wastes time and prevents the Senate from functioning. Critics of the filibuster point out that the rights of minorities are safeguarded by the Constitution and that minorities may appeal to the voters to elect Senators favorable to their viewpoint.

LOBBYING

1. Special-Interest Groups. To secure the passage of laws they desire or to defeat laws unfavorable to their interests, many economic and social organizations try to "pressure" members of Congress. Typical large, nationwide pressure groups include the National Association of Manufacturers (NAM), American Federation of Labor and Congress of Industrial Organizations (AFL-CIO), American Farm Bureau Federation, American Medical Association (AMA), and American Legion. Typical smaller, more specialized pressure groups represent interests such as postal clerks, chiropodists, teachers, cotton growers, dairy farmers, home builders, petroleum producers, and tobacco manufacturers.

2. Meaning and Methods of Lobbyists. Lobbyists are politically experienced persons employed by special-interest groups. The name "lobbyists" was derived from the practice originally of such persons buttonholing Congress members in the lobbies just outside the legislative chambers.

Lobbyists seek to influence Congress members by *(a)* drafting bills, testifying at hearings, and supplying data selected to support their views, *(b)* cultivating personal contacts with Congress members—arranging parties, granting favors, and providing campaign funds, *(c)* preparing for special-interest delegations to chat with Congress members, and *(d)* urging the public to deluge Congress with postcards, letters, and telegrams. Sometimes the work of one lobby, such as a business organization, is offset by the work of another lobby, such as a labor organization. Lobbyists also seek to influence executive agencies and regulatory commissions.

3. Arguments for Lobbies. *(a)* Lobbying is in accord with the Constitutional right of people to petition the government. *(b)* Lobbying enables special groups to make their views known. *(c)* Lobbyists may call attention to the need for laws. *(d)* Lobbyists may provide Congress with valuable information.

4. Arguments Against Lobbies. *(a)* Lobbyists sometimes utilize questionable methods, including the giving of lavish gifts and campaign contributions. *(b)* Lobbying gives well-organized groups, such as industry and labor, an advantage over poorly organized groups, such as consumers. *(c)* Lobbying may foster laws that benefit special-interest groups. *(d)* Lobbyists may provide information that is incomplete and one-sided.

5. Federal Regulation. By the *Regulation of Lobbying Act* (1946), Congress defined lobbyists as persons directly seeking to influence legislation and required that they *(a)* register with Congress and provide the names and addresses of their employers, *(b)* identify current legislation they support or oppose, and *(c)* file quarterly statements regarding the sources of their funds and the nature of their expenditures. Under this law, more than 5000 lobbyists have so registered. (This law has served as a model for many states to regulate lobbying in state capitals.)

6. Weaknesses of Federal Regulation. *(a)* The law defines lobbying in a limited way. Some lobbyists have claimed that their chief work is not to influence legislation but to educate the public and that they therefore need not register. *(b)* It sets no bounds on the activities and expenditures of lobbyists. *(c)* It lacks adequate enforcement powers, especially to compel the filing of reports and to check upon their accuracy.

CONGRESSIONAL COMMITTEES CONDUCT INVESTIGATIONS

1. Purposes. To assist Congress in its major functions, House and Senate committees hold hearings and conduct investigations. The committees may be the regular standing committees or their subcommittees or special investigating committees. These committees seek to *(a)* determine the effectiveness of existing laws, *(b)* measure the performance of the executive branch in enforcing laws, and *(c)* assess the need for new laws. The committee members may be aware in advance of what their investigation will reveal, but they use the hearings to gain publicity and arouse support for Congressional action.

2. The Hearings. Committees may hold hearings anywhere in the country, but usually they are held in Washington, D.C. The hearings usually are open to the public and press and sometimes may be broadcast on radio and television.

In some investigations, the committee may want to question persons who are not willing to testify. The committee may use the *subpoena*—a legal document ordering a person to appear for questioning. If a witness refuses to appear or refuses to answer legitimate questions pertaining to the investigation and not infringing upon the witness' civil rights, then the committee may have the witness cited for *contempt of Congress* and face the possibility of a jail sentence.

3. Criticisms of Investigating Committees. In the post-World War II years, Congressional committees investigating "sensitive areas," such as organized crime, labor racketeering, and Communist activities, were subjected to considerable criticism. These committees, critics charged, were *(a)* merely looking for publicity, *(b)* engaging in "fishing expeditions," that is, not seeking any specific information and not having any legislative purpose, and *(c)* "trying" witnesses in the newspapers without permitting courtroom legal safeguards such as the right to counsel, and the right to cross examine hostile witnesses and to produce friendly witnesses. Supporters argued that these committees had served to alert the nation to serious problems and that questionable committee procedures could be remedied.

4. Limitations Upon Investigating Committees

a. The Fifth Amendment. A number of witnesses called before Congressional committees investigating "sensitive areas" refused to answer questions. They pleaded the Fifth Amendment provision that no person "shall be compelled in any criminal case to be a witness against himself." Witnesses who "take the Fifth," some observers claimed, must have something to hide and therefore must be guilty of illegal activity. On the other hand, the federal courts held that witnesses employing the privilege against self-incrimination have the legal right to do so and without any inference of guilt.

b. House Rules for Investigations. To guide its investigating committees, the House in 1955 adopted the following rules: witnesses must be informed of the purpose of the investigation; also they may have counsel and may make brief sworn statements; the committee must hear defamatory evidence in closed session and then decide if such testimony is to be made public. (The Senate has permitted its investigating committees to set their own rules.)

OTHER CONGRESSIONAL PRACTICES

1. Pork-Barrel Legislation. Members of Congress are eager to provide their home districts and states with public works such as post offices, highways, and river and harbor improvements. Public works prove to the "folks back home" that their members in Congress are looking out for their best interests. If such bills provide public works—regardless of need—they are called *pork-barrel* legislation.

2. Logrolling. A member of Congress may sometimes say to another, "If you vote for my bill, I'll vote for yours." This trading of votes, despite shortcomings of the respective bills as in pork-barrel legislation, is called *logrolling*.

CONSIDERATIONS REGARDING CONGRESSIONAL REFORMS

1. Criticisms of Congress. The American people, according to public opinion polls, view Congress with considerable dissatisfaction. They criticize Congress for *(a)* working too slowly, *(b)* following inefficient and duplicatory procedures, *(c)* failing to cooperate with the President, and *(d)* passing unsatisfactory laws and neglecting vital legislation. To what extent are such criticisms justified?

2. Defense of Congress. Supporters point out that Congress is easy to criticize because *(a)* more than the other two governmental branches, Congress works in the public spotlight, *(b)* by its investigative and legislative functions, Congress is a center of controversy, and *(c)* Congress has little control over its members but is blamed for any individual misdeeds.

Supporters claim that the value of Congress is measured neither by the speed with which it works nor by the extent to which it cooperates with the President. Congress has value, supporters say, because it *(a)* serves to check and counterbalance the powers of the other two governmental branches, *(b)* arouses public concern over vital issues, *(c)* reflects diverse interests in the nation, *(d)* arrives at satisfactory compromises between such diverse interests, and so *(e)* enacts legislation that is workable and rooted in public acceptance. However, even supporters of Congress admit that its procedures can be improved.

3. Congressional Reforms Already Achieved

a. The Legislative Reorganization Act of 1946. This act (1) reduced the number of standing committees in each house, (2) authorized committees to employ additional research and professional help, and (3) required lobbyists to register and disclose their activities.

b. The Legislative Reform Act of 1970. This act (1) provided for radio and television broadcasting of House committee proceedings (as already allowed for Senate committee proceedings), and (2) empowered a majority of the members of any House or Senate committee to call a meeting if the committee head refuses to do so.

c. Other Reforms. Already achieved are reforms in legislative reapportionment, codes of ethical conduct, the discharge petition in the House, cloture in the Senate, and House rules for investigating committees.

4. Possible Further Reforms

a. Stronger Party Discipline. In the two major political parties, reformers urge that each national organization exercise effective control over the party members in Congress and assure votes for party programs.

b. Four-Year Term for Representatives. President Lyndon Johnson urged a Constitutional amendment extending the term of office for Representatives to four years. The longer term would enable Representatives to devote more time to their legislative duties and less to "politicking." On the other hand, Representatives might be less responsive to their constituencies.

c. Joint House-Senate Committees. By holding hearings and conducting research jointly, reformers claim, similar House and Senate committees could avoid needless duplication and speed up their work. On the other hand, by having committees function separately, each serves as a check upon the other.

d. Improved Relations With the Executive Branch. Reformers have proposed that the Congress and executive coordinate efforts in regard to legislation by (1) establishing a joint legislative council to meet regularly and (2) setting aside a definite time when legislators might question executive officials.

e. Item Veto. Congress has, at times, added to a vital bill an unrelated provision called a *rider*. Although this provision may be objectionable to the President, he has no power to veto a single item but must approve or veto the entire bill, including the rider. Reformers have proposed that the President be granted the power to veto single items, thereby checking riders. Congress, however, is reluctant to increase the powers of the President.

f. Other Proposed Reforms. (1) For cloture to halt filibuster in the Senate, reduce the vote needed from 60 to a simple majority of the Senators present, (2) for a discharge petition to move a bill out of a House committee, reduce the number of signatures needed from 218 to 150 Representatives, (3) limit the power of the House Rules Committee to delay bills, (4) strengthen disclosure requirements for lobbyists, and (5) in selecting committee heads, consider in addition to seniority such factors as ability and adherence to party programs.

———————— MULTIPLE-CHOICE QUESTIONS ————————

1. According to the Constitution, Congress is required to meet (a) twice a year -
(b) annually (c) once every two years (d) only when called into session by the President.

2. The Framers of the Constitution best expressed their faith in the people by the provision for choosing the (a) Justices of the Supreme Court (b) President and Vice President (c) Speaker of the House of Representatives (d) members of the House of Representatives.

3. According to the Constitution, a nationwide census is conducted every ten years in order to (a) establish trends of enrollment in the major political parties (b) determine the allocation of federal moneys for revenue sharing (c) determine the number of Representatives each state will have in Congress (d) study changes in social customs.

4. According to the Constitution, the House of Representatives has the sole power to (a) approve appointments (b) impeach federal officials (c) override Presidential vetoes (d) filibuster.

5. In the House of Representatives, the period of debate is likely to be shorter than in the Senate because the House (a) remains in session longer (b) has rules that limit discussion (c) considers bills only after the Senate has passed them (d) is generally composed of less experienced members.

6. The Senate *differs* from the House of Representatives in that (a) the Senate is continuously in session (b) a two-thirds vote is required to pass bills in the Senate (c) one-third of the Senate is elected every two years (d) Senators must be native-born Americans.

7. Which action of the Senate requires a simple majority vote? (a) ratification of a treaty (b) approval of an appointment (c) passage of a bill vetoed by the President (d) conviction of an impeached official.

8. The increasing influence of California in national politics is *best* explained by that state's (a) outstanding political leaders (b) increase in population (c) increased number of primary contests (d) peaceful campus life.

9. The term "gerrymandering" refers to the (a) unequal distribution of campaign contributions (b) unfair system of apportionment of districts for election purposes (c) unusual power of the southern states in Congress (d) unjust practice of dismissing officeholders for political reasons.

10. One argument for the election of Representatives biennially rather than every four years is to (a) secure more state electors for Presidential elections (b) make legislators more accountable to the people they represent (c) insure that legislators have adequate time to study bills (d) have all legislative elections coincide with the Presidential elections.

11. What is the *smallest* number of members of Congress that a state, regardless of its population, may have? (a) five (b) two (c) three (d) four.

12. By its *most* recent rule on debate, the Senate (a) outlawed filibusters (b) required a two-thirds vote of the Senators present and voting to end a filibuster (c) extended the right of unlimited debate to the House of Representatives (d) required the vote of 60 Senators to limit debate on any measure except a proposed Senate rules change.

13. According to the Constitution, which of the following must originate in the House of Representatives? (a) a bill to levy an excise tax on television sets (b) a proposed amendment to require a referendum for a declaration of war (c) a contempt of

court order against a witness refusing to answer questions of a Congressional investigating committee (d) approval of appointment of a new attorney general.

14. Filibustering is most likely to be used by a (a) lobbyist favoring a new federal law (b) majority attempting to override a Presidential veto (c) minority seeking to delay a vote (d) Congressional committee attempting to kill a bill.

15. According to the Constitution, the Senate has the exclusive power to (a) declare war (b) appoint committees (c) try impeachment cases (d) select a President when no candidate receives a majority of the electoral votes.

16. Suppose the President filled an important federal position in State X without consulting either of the two Senators from that state. Such a procedure would be (a) illegal because of the Constitutional provision governing appointments (b) appropriate if the Senators did not belong to the President's party (c) proof that the President would not engage in logrolling (d) proper because of the Corrupt Practices Act.

17. Congressional immunity protects members of Congress against (a) federal taxes on their salaries (b) prosecution for remarks made in Congress (c) expulsion from Congress (d) arrest while in a foreign country.

18. The statement "Lawmaking in a democratic society is often said to be the art of the possible" most nearly means that (a) government agencies may take any action that is necessary to achieve their objectives (b) most laws are the result of compromises of differing views (c) legislators generally vote the wishes of their constituents (d) the Constitution has provided for the smooth operation of government.

19. No bill may become a law without the approval of (a) the United States Supreme Court (b) the President (c) a two-thirds vote of the Senate (d) both houses of Congress.

20. The Constitutional justification for Congressional hearings on crime is that they (a) give Congress information on needed legislation (b) expose criminals to public disapproval (c) furnish information to the FBI (d) assist the Internal Revenue Service to collect income taxes from criminals.

21. Congressional investigating committees have been a source of public controversy mainly because these committees have (a) been used to determine the need for legislation (b) eliminated the influence of interest groups in the lawmaking process (c) been accused of abusing their power by using undemocratic procedures (d) publicized conflicts of interest of the members of Congress.

22. Usually, after a bill has been introduced into either house of Congress, it is first (a) signed by the presiding officer of that house (b) debated by members of that house (c) referred to a committee of that house (d) considered by a joint committee representing both houses.

23. In the legislative process, a conference committee is usually appointed when (a) Congress desires to investigate corrupt practices in government (b) the President calls Congress into special session (c) the President vetoes a bill of Congress (d) the Senate and the House pass different versions of the same bill.

24. The heads of Congressional committees get their positions by (a) a vote of committee members (b) appointment by the presiding officer (c) seniority on the committee (d) recommendation of the President.

25. Although many Democratic Representatives and Senators from the South have in recent years voted against their party's program, most have remained within the Democratic party *chiefly* because (a) the Republican party is hostile to Southerners (b) gerrymandering forces them to do so (c) they would lose their seniority on Congressional committees (d) they would lose their representation on the Supreme Court.

26. If an agricultural group from Kansas sends a member to Washington, D.C., to urge the passage of a flood-control bill, he or she is said to be engaged in (a) filibustering (b) logrolling (c) lobbying (d) gerrymandering.

27. According to federal law, all lobbyists must (a) confine their activities to the lobbies of Congress (b) refrain from influencing Senators (c) reside in Washington, D.C. (d) register with Congress.

28. Which statement *best* supports the contention that lobbyists perform a needed function in the legislative process? (a) They have a national, not a sectional, background. (b) They are recognized in the federal Constitution. (c) They provide information that might not ordinarily be available. (d) They usually reflect majority opinion.

29. Which statement about lobbies in the United States is most accurate? (a) Lobbies are discouraged by the Constitution. (b) Lobbies are usually concerned with local issues. (c) Lobbies are an important influence on the lawmaking process. (d) Lobbies are effective mainly in times of prosperity.

30. The Rules Committee of the House of Representatives is important because it (a) acts as a liaison between the House and the President (b) functions as an independent legislative body (c) censures members who are out of order (d) determines the order in which bills are to be put before the House.

31. A Senator from the Midwest votes in favor of higher government-supported prices for cotton in return for a Southern Senator's vote in favor of higher government-supported prices for corn. The two Senators are said to be engaged in (a) Senatorial courtesy (b) patronage (c) lobbying (d) logrolling.

32. "Because party lines are so lax in Congress, it is rare for all Democrats or all Republicans to vote the same way on any significant issue." Which conclusion can be drawn from this statement? (a) Senior members of Congress tend to control the votes of the junior members of their party. (b) There is a clear-cut party position on most issues before Congress. (c) Democrats and Republicans frequently form coalitions to pass laws. (d) Seniority leads to an equal sharing of power by committee chairpersons of both parties.

DISCUSSION ANALYSIS QUESTIONS:
———————— SENATORIAL ACTIVITY ————————

Base your answers to the following questions on the activities of the United States Senators described below and on your knowledge of American government.

Senator A is talking with a representative of the AFL-CIO concerning a labor bill about to be introduced.

Senator B has been speaking on the floor of the Senate for several hours in an effort to prevent a vote on a bill the Senator opposes.

Senator C is attending committee hearings on a treaty about to be submitted to the Senate for ratification.

Senator D is drafting a bill that will provide for a federal flood-control project in the Senator's home state.

1. Which Senator would be most opposed to cloture? (a) *A* (b) *B* (c) *C* (d) *D*.

2. Which Senator is most likely to be involved with pork-barrel legislation? (a) *A* (b) *B* (c) *C* (d) *D*.

3. Which Senator appears to be most directly involved with a lobbyist? (a) A (b) B (c) C (d) D.

4. Which Senator is most directly involved in evaluating an executive action? (a) A (b) B (c) C (d) D.

5. Which pair of Senators is engaged in activities that might also be typical of those carried on by members of the House of Representatives? (a) A and B (b) A and C (c) A and D (d) B and D.

6. In the early post-World War II years, Senator B would *most* likely have represented which section of the country? (a) Northeast (b) South (c) Midwest (d) Pacific Coast.

7. If Senator C opposed the treaty under consideration, what minimum number of votes in the Senate would he need to defeat its ratification? (a) one-third (b) one-third plus one (c) one-half (d) one-half plus one.

8. In regard to the measures under consideration above, how many of these four Senators might consider the use of logrolling? (a) one (b) two (c) three (d) four.

9. The AFL-CIO representative talking with Senator A might be expected to talk with all of the following *except* (a) the Speaker of the House of Representatives (b) the Secretary of Labor (c) a Justice of the Supreme Court (d) the chairperson of the Senate Education and Labor Committee.

——————————— ESSAY QUESTIONS ———————————

1. President Kennedy is said to have remarked, "It is very easy to defeat a bill in Congress. It is much more difficult to pass one." *(a)* Discuss *two* specific features of Congressional organization and procedures to support President Kennedy's point of view. *(b)* Explain *one* way in which the legislative process is affected by each of the following: (1) the President (2) public opinion (3) special-interest groups.

2. The practices of Congress have been both vigorously defended and vigorously attacked. *(a)* Discuss *two* Congressional practices to show why *each* has been defended. *(b)* Discuss *two* other Congressional practices to show why *each* has come under attack. *(c)* Explain *one* remedy proposed for *each* of these attacked Congressional practices. *(d)* Has criticism of Congress been overdone? Defend your answer.

3. Assume that you have heard these statements on radio or television: "Our taxes are twice as high as they should be. The reason is clear. Congress is wastefully squandering public funds. *Logrolling*, the *pork barrel*, and selfish *lobbies* must be swept out. I call on *every* citizen to help in doing this long-needed job."
   (a) Define *each* of the *italicized* terms. *(b)* Discuss *two* ways in which a citizen can determine to what extent these statements are true. *(c)* Explain *two* ways by which he could help remedy such conditions if they existed.

4. Present *one* argument to support *or one* argument to oppose *each* of the following statements: *(a)* Congress remains in session too long. *(b)* The requirements for members of Congress should include a college education. *(c)* The filibuster is undemocratic. *(d)* A majority vote of both houses of Congress should be required to ratify treaties. *(e)* The committee system of Congress is a sensible way of handling legislation. *(f)* Congress should outlaw all lobbying in Washington, D.C. *(g)* Our present two-house Congress should be replaced by a one-house Congress with each member representing an equal number of people. *(h)* The national party organization should exercise strict discipline over party members in Congress.

5. Assume that you are considering a career as a member of Congress. *(a)* Discuss *one* advantage and *one* disadvantage of such a career. *(b)* How would you prepare

yourself for such a career? *(c)* Explain how any *three* of the following items might further your Congressional career: (1) oratorical ability (2) tact (3) determination (4) devotion to a cause (5) luck (6) ability to reconcile conflicting interests.

PART 5. The Federal Courts Are the Judiciary

Of the Framers, half were lawyers and many others possessed strong legal backgrounds. During the Articles of Confederation, they had been dismayed by the confusion resulting from the existence of 13 independent state legal systems and the lack of any unifying national judiciary. They were aware that each state would maintain its own court system, but they were determined to create some measure of national legal uniformity. They declared that the Constitution "shall be the supreme law of the land," and they provided for a national judiciary.

JURISDICTION (AUTHORITY) OF THE FEDERAL COURTS

The federal courts have *jurisdiction,* or authority, over cases as follows:

1. By Matters Involved. *(a)* Determining Constitutional issues, which means the constitutionality of federal and state laws and executive actions, *(b)* interpreting federal laws and treaties, and *(c)* ascertaining treason, the only crime specifically defined in the Constitution—"levying war" against the United States, or giving "aid and comfort" to its enemies.

2. By Parties Involved. *(a)* Ambassadors and other representatives of foreign nations, *(b)* the United States government itself, *(c)* two or more states, *(d)* citizens of different states, and *(e)* American citizens or states in dispute with foreign citizens or nations.

(All other cases not under federal court jurisdiction are reserved for the state and local court systems.)

FEDERAL COURT SYSTEM

The Constitution specifically provides for one Supreme Court and empowers Congress to establish *inferior* (lower) courts. Accordingly, Congress passed the *Judiciary Act of 1789* setting the broad outlines of our federal court system. Today it consists as follows:

1. About Ninety District Courts

a. Jurisdiction. These lowest federal courts have *original jurisdiction;* that is, they hear and decide most cases first. They hear (1) *civil cases* in which individuals or corporations dispute each other (or the federal government) over property and personal rights, and (2) *criminal cases* in which the government accuses persons of violating federal law. Annually, the district courts handle over

100,000 cases—two-thirds civil and one-third criminal. In most civil and all criminal cases, the district courts provide trial by jury.

   b. Procedures. The federal district court judge presides over the selection of the jury and over the trial. Attorneys for each side (1) question members of a large jury panel so as to select 12 "impartial" trial jurors, (2) question and cross-examine witnesses, (3) raise objections to testimony and pose legal issues, and (4) conclude with oratorical addresses to the jury.

   c. Possible Jury Findings. After receiving instructions from the judge, the jury retires to consider the evidence and reach a decision—which must be *unanimous.* (1) If the jury decides "not guilty," the defendant is set free. (2) If the jury is unable to arrive at a unanimous decision despite lengthy deliberation, then the judge may declare a *mistrial* and dismiss the deadlocked or *hung jury.* Usually the case is retried with a new jury. (3) If the jury decides "guilty," the defendant is sentenced by the judge. In a civil case the sentence may be to pay a fine, while in a criminal case the defendant may have to pay a fine and serve a prison term.

   If a party to the case claims legal grounds for dissatisfaction with the district court trial or verdict, then that party's attorney may file an appeal to a higher court—as happens on average in one out of every 20 cases.

   2. Eleven Circuit Courts of Appeals. These intermediate courts have *appellate jurisdiction;* that is, they hear cases on appeal from the district courts. The appeals court has no jury and hears no witnesses; it does not retry the case. The appeals court reviews the record to determine if *(a)* the district court trial revealed any irregularities such as prejudice by the court, use of illegal evidence, or other violations of Constitutional rights, and *(b)* the law that the defendant violated is Constitutional. The circuit court may confirm or void the lower court judgment. Its decisions are made by a panel of three or more judges. In most cases, circuit court decisions are accepted as final. Some cases, however, may be further appealed to the Supreme Court.

   3. One Supreme Court

   a. Appellate Jurisdiction. The Supreme Court, the highest federal judicial authority, has appellate jurisdiction over cases coming from lower federal courts and from the highest state courts. The Supreme Court is not required to hear all cases appealed to it; of some 2500 cases annually appealed to it, the Supreme Court hears on average about 200—less than one case in ten. Usually, it considers only cases involving new or important legal principles. If an appeal is rejected by the Supreme Court, the decision of the preceding court remains in effect.

   b. Original Jurisdiction. The Supreme Court also has original jurisdiction in cases involving a state, ambassadors, foreign ministers, and consuls.

   c. Procedures. The Supreme Court "sits," or is in session, usually from October into June. It divides its work into alternating periods: two weeks to hear cases—in public—and two weeks to study the evidence, arrive at decisions, and write opinions—in private. In the public hearings, the Supreme Court Justices sit on the bench, the attorneys make their oral presentations limited to one hour for each side, and the Justices may interrupt to ask questions. The Justices also have available previously submitted written briefs, presenting the attorneys' detailed arguments. In private contemplation, the Justices review the case record and search for related past legal cases as *precedents*.

   d. Decisions. The Supreme Court today consists of one Chief Justice and eight Associate Justices, totaling nine judges. Decisions are made by a majority vote. One Justice of the majority writes an explanation of the decision, the *majority opinion* or the *opinion of the Court*. A Justice who agrees with the Court's decision but disagrees with its reasoning may write a *concurring opinion*. A Justice who disagrees with the Court's decision may write a *dissenting opinion*.

   4. Special Courts. The Court of Claims handles claims against the government of the United States. The Customs Court handles questions of tariffs on imports. The Court of Customs and Patent Appeals handles appeals from the Customs Court and the Patent Office.

FEDERAL JUDGES

   1. Appointment and Tenure. Federal judges are *not* required to meet any Constitutional qualifications. They are nominated by the President, who usually consults advisers—the attorney general, friends, judges, political leaders, and bar associations. After being named by the President, the federal court nominees must secure the consent of a majority of the Senate. They serve "during good behavior," meaning usually for life. Protected by life tenure, federal judges can render impartial decisions free from unwarranted pressures.

   2. Removal From Office: Impeachment. Federal judges may be removed for "treason, bribery, or other high crimes and misdemeanors" through the process of impeachment. Of thousands of federal judges, only four ever have been impeached by the House of Representatives and found guilty by the Senate.

   3. Philosophies Regarding the Use of Judicial Power

   a. Judicial Self-Restraint. Justices who advocate *judicial self-restraint* insist that the chief responsibility for setting public policy rests with elected officials—the national and state legislatures and executives. In deciding Constitutional issues, these Justices hold that they should set aside their own preferences and achieve objectivity, respect the Constitutional views of the other branches of government, and avoid broad, sweeping opinions in favor of narrow, limited decisions only on the specific issue. To keep the Supreme Court from expanding its power, these Justices urge judicial self-restraint.

   b. Judicial Activism. Justices who advocate *judicial activism* assert that the Supreme Court has the right to initiate public policy and to bring about constitutionally sanctioned changes. They deny that Supreme Court Justices can, or even should, achieve total objectivity. They insist that, with the ultimate responsibility of interpreting the Constitution, the Supreme Court must make political decisions that will help us move toward our national goals. In our earliest history, judicial activism was illustrated by Chief Justice *John Marshall,* notably in assuming for the Supreme Court the power of judicial review.

THE SUPREME COURT AND JUDICIAL REVIEW

1. Meaning. *Judicial review* refers to the power of courts, especially the Supreme Court *(a)* to determine whether or not laws are in harmony with the provisions of the Constitution and *(b)* for such laws as are in conflict with the Constitution, to declare them invalid, void, and unconstitutional.

2. Implied in the Constitution. The Constitution implies but nowhere specifically grants the power of judicial review. The Founders, many scholars believe, expected the Supreme Court to exercise judicial review.

3. Assumed by the Supreme Court Under John Marshall: Case of *Marbury vs. Madison* (1803)

a. **Issue.** *William Marbury,* a Federalist, was appointed justice of the peace for Washington, D.C., by outgoing President John Adams in 1801, but was denied his official papers, or commission, by James Madison, the incoming Democratic-Republican secretary of state. In accordance with the Judiciary Act of 1789, Marbury went *directly* to the Supreme Court for an order, called a *writ of mandamus,* to compel Madison to deliver the commission.

b. **Decision.** Speaking for a unanimous Court, Marshall declared that, although Madison was wrong in withholding the commission, the Court could not grant Marbury the requested writ. Marshall explained that the section of the 1789 Judiciary Act expanding the Supreme Court's original jurisdiction to include the issuing of writs of mandamus violated the Constitution. Marshall reasoned that (1) the Constitution is the supreme law of the land, (2) the Supreme Court is the final interpreter of the Constitution, and therefore (3) the Supreme Court may declare unconstitutional any law or provision of a law contrary to the Constitution. Acting boldly, Marshall thus established the precedent of *judicial review.*

4. In Subsequent Years. During Marshall's tenure (1801–1835), the Supreme Court did not invalidate another federal law but did declare several state laws unconstitutional. To the present, the Supreme Court has held fewer than 100 federal laws (out of 40,000) and some 1000 state and local laws unconstitutional. Among democratic nations this power of the Supreme Court remains unique.

THE SUPREME COURT: CENTER OF CONTROVERSY

At times the Supreme Court, by virtue of the leadership of its Chief Justice and its decisions upon vital public issues, has been at the center of controversy.

1. Marshall Court (1801–1835)

a. The Chief Justice. John Marshall, born in Virginia, fought for American independence in the Revolutionary War and thereafter became a lawyer. A leading Federalist, he deplored the Articles of Confederation, supported the new Constitution, and helped secure its ratification in Virginia. In 1801 Marshall was appointed by President John Adams as Chief Justice of the Supreme Court—the fourth Chief Justice. In 12 years his three predecessors had done little to enhance the status of the Court. Not so Marshall.

b. Direction and Decisions. For 34 years, Marshall dominated the Supreme Court and made it into a coequal branch of the federal government. Possessing a logical mind and an activist legal philosophy, Marshall (1) strengthened the Supreme Court at the expense of the other federal branches by assuming the power of judicial review (*Marbury vs. Madison*), (2) expanded federal power at the expense of states by declaring state laws unconstitutional (*Dartmouth College*), by denying a state the right to tax a federal agency (*McCulloch vs. Maryland*), and by upholding a broad interpretation of interstate commerce (*Gibbons vs. Ogden*), (3) protected the terms of business contracts against impairment by state law (*Dartmouth College*), and (4) upheld the loose interpretation of the Constitution's elastic clause (*McCulloch vs. Maryland*). (For details of these Supreme Court cases, check the Index.)

c. Center of Controversy. The Marshall Court, with its nationalist outlook, faced opposition as the Democratic-Republicans, who favored states' rights, gained control of the executive and legislative branches. Commenting on Marshall's decisions weakening states' powers, Jefferson wrote bitterly, "The Constitution is a mere thing of wax in the hands of the judiciary, which they may twist and shape into any form they please." States' rights supporters spoke of limiting the powers of the Court, but they did not do so.

2. Warren Court (1953–1969)

a. The Chief Justice. Earl Warren, born in California, graduated from the University of California with a law degree, and for three terms (1942–1953) served as governor of California. In 1953 he was appointed by President Eisenhower as Chief Justice of the Supreme Court.

b. Direction and Decisions. The Warren Court served during an era of democratic progress, especially in the area of rights for minority groups and for individuals. Reflecting those times, the Warren Court pursued a liberal and activist course. *(1)* In *Brown vs. Board of Education of Topeka,* the Warren Court unanimously held racial segregation in schools unconstitutional, thereby contributing to the movement for black civil rights. *(2)* In *Baker vs. Carr,* the Warren Court held legislative reapportionment to be a judicial matter, thereby furthering more equitable election districts. *(3)* In cases affecting persons accused of crimes, the Warren Court insisted upon protection of their rights to a lawyer (*Gideon vs. Wainwright*) and against self-incrimination (*Miranda vs. Arizona*). (For details of these Supreme Court cases, check the Index.)

c. Center of Controversy. The Warren Court was condemned by its opponents for violating precedents, delivering politically minded rather than legally justified decisions, and usurping powers of other bodies of government. President Eisenhower is reputed to have called his appointment of Warren the "biggest damfool mistake I ever made."

The Warren Court was hailed by its supporters for upholding the Constitution, protecting the rights of accused persons, and furthering democracy. President Lyndon Johnson labeled Warren "the greatest Chief Justice of them all."

3. Burger Court (1969–1986)

a. The Chief Justice. *Warren Burger,* born in Minnesota, worked his way through law school and thereafter combined a private legal practice with teaching law. In 1956 he became a judge of the United States Court of Appeals. In 1969 Burger was nominated by President Nixon to be the fifteenth Chief Justice of the United States. He retired in 1986.

b. Direction and Decisions. Conservatives felt that the Warren Court (1953–1969) had been overly activist, too eager to impose its own liberal social theories on the laws and the Constitution. During the 1968 election campaign, Richard Nixon promised to appoint judges who would "interpret the Constitution strictly and fairly and objectively." Conservatives hailed President Nixon's appointment of Burger as a return to "strict construction" and judicial self-restraint. But the Burger Court had a record of both activism and restraint, of conservatism and liberalism.

(1) The Burger Court did move away from the Warren Court's emphasis on the rights of people accused of crimes. It tended to rule on the side of the justice system rather than defend the rights of criminal suspects. Despite the urgings of conservatives, however, the Burger Court did not overturn the Miranda Rule, which gives suspects the right to have an attorney present during police questioning.

(2) On civil rights, the Burger Court was the first to approve of busing as a tool for school desegregation, in *Swann vs. Charlotte-Mecklenburg Board of Education* (1971). However, in *Milliken vs. Bradley* (1974), the Court held that a federal court could not order busing when segregation resulted from living patterns rather than from discrimination by school boards. The Burger Court took a cautious stand on affirmative-action programs to aid minority individuals. In *Regents of the University of California vs. Bakke* (1978), the Court sided with a white student who claimed he had been denied admittance to medical school because of his race. In the same case, the Court held that school admissions officers could constitutionally consider race as one factor in a carefully designed affirmative-action program. In *United Steelworkers of America vs. Weber* (1979), the Court allowed a voluntary affirmative-action program in employment.

(3) The Burger Court reinforced First Amendment press freedoms in *New York Times vs. United States* (1971), known as the Pentagon Papers Case, when it ruled against a government effort to block publication of secret documents

about the Vietnam War. In other cases, the Court weighed the First Amendment guarantee of press freedom against the Sixth Amendment guarantee of a speedy and public trial. In *Gannett Company vs. De Pasquale* (1979), the Court granted broad discretion to trial judges to close criminal pretrial hearings to the press and public. In *Richmond Newspapers, Inc. vs. Virginia* (1980), the Court reaffirmed the press's right to attend and report on criminal trials.

(4) One controversial decision of the Burger Court was *Roe vs. Wade* (1973), in which Chief Justice Burger joined a 7-to-2 majority in supporting a woman's right to have an abortion. The Court held that this right is part of the constitutional right to privacy.

(5) On church-state issues, the Burger Court gave mixed signals. In *Stone vs. Graham* (1980), it struck down a Kentucky law requiring that the Ten Commandments be posted in public schools. In *Wallace vs. Jaffree* (1985), it struck down an Alabama law providing for a moment of silent prayer in public schools. However, in *Lynch vs. Donnelly* (1984), it permitted the city of Pawtucket, Rhode Island, to put up a Christmas crèche, or Nativity display.

4. Rehnquist Court (1986–   )

a. The Chief Justice. Named to the Court as an Associate Justice in 1971, *William H. Rehnquist* was elevated to Chief Justice by President Reagan in 1986. Rehnquist was seen as a strong leader who could have a significant effect in shaping Court decisions along conservative lines. Before joining the Court, Rehnquist had served as a Supreme Court clerk, a lawyer in private practice, and a high official in the Justice Department.

b. New Directions? Conservatives had high hopes for the Rehnquist Court. On the day that he elevated Rehnquist, President Reagan appointed another conservative, *Antonin Scalia,* as an Associate Justice. That gave the Court two firm conservatives, two staunch liberals, and a shifting center of five Justices. Among the five was *Sandra Day O'Connor,* the Court's first woman Justice, appointed by President Reagan in 1981.

The unexpected resignation in June 1987 of Justice *Lewis F. Powell, Jr.,* a moderate, gave President Reagan the opportunity to add another conservative Justice to the Court.

PROPOSALS TO LIMIT THE SUPREME COURT: NONE ADOPTED

Opponents of the Supreme Court claim that the traditional checks upon judicial powers are insufficient, and propose other checks:

1. Increase the Number of Supreme Court Justices. The number of Supreme Court judges is not fixed by the Constitution, and Court membership has varied from as few as five judges (1801–1807) to as many as ten (1863–1867). In 1937 President Roosevelt requested Congress to permit him to appoint additional Supreme Court members, but Congress refused to "pack the Court" by passing such legislation.

2. Limit the Supreme Court's Appellate Jurisdiction and Voting Regulations. Congress is empowered by the Constitution to control the appellate jurisdiction of the Supreme Court by making "exceptions" and "regulations." Court opponents have urged Congress to limit the Supreme Court's appellate jurisdiction, especially denying it the right to consider matters involving national security. Opponents also have urged Congress to prohibit the Supreme Court from declaring a law unconstitutional by a bare majority, and to require a vote of at least 6 to 3 or of 7 to 2.

3. Permit Congress to Override an Adverse Supreme Court Decision. Court opponents also have urged a Constitutional amendment to permit Congress, by a two-thirds vote, to override a Supreme Court decision holding a federal law unconstitutional.

PART 6. The Courts Protect Rights and Liberties—Within Limits

ORIGINAL CONSTITUTION

The Framers, recalling colonial experience as well as English history, sought to protect the individual against possible governmental tyranny. They provided the following restrictions on the powers of government:

1. Protection of Writ of Habeas Corpus. Except during rebellion or invasion, the federal government may not suspend the privilege of the *writ of habeas corpus.* This writ is a document issued by a judge upon the request of a defense attorney that protects an arrested individual. It requires the police to bring the prisoner before the judge and to provide a statement of charges. If the judge determines that the prisoner is being held illegally, the prisoner is freed. If held legally, the prisoner may be released on bail or returned to jail pending a speedy trial.

2. Prohibition of Bill of Attainder. Neither Congress nor the state legislatures may pass a *bill of attainder.* Such a law would punish individuals without granting them a trial in court.

3. Prohibition of Ex Post Facto Law. Neither Congress nor the state legislatures may pass an *ex post facto* law. Such a law would punish persons for acts that were not criminal at the time the acts were committed.

4. Protection of Contracts. No state may pass a law impairing the obligation of contracts—that is, altering the terms of a valid business contract.

AMENDMENTS ONE THROUGH TEN—THE BILL OF RIGHTS

1. Historic Background. In the original Constitution, the Framers did not include a bill of rights. During the struggle over ratification, the Anti-Federalists, who opposed the Constitution, argued effectively that the lack of a bill of rights left the people inadequately protected against the federal government. To win popular support, the Federalists pledged to add a bill of rights to the Constitution. Our first Congress proposed a series of amendments and by 1791 the states had ratified ten of them, which constitute our *Bill of Rights*.

2. Applicability to the States. Originally, the Bill of Rights was intended to protect individual liberties against encroachment by the federal government. With the adoption of the Fourteenth Amendment after the Civil War, however, much of the federal Bill of Rights was made applicable to laws and actions of the states. The Fourteenth Amendment prohibits states from depriving "any person of life, liberty, or property without due process of law." According to subsequent Supreme Court decisions, many safeguards of individual liberties listed in the federal Bill of Rights apply to the states under the "due process of law" clause.

3. The First Ten Amendments—The Bill of Rights

The *First Amendment* prohibits Congress from abridging freedom of speech, press, and religion, and from abridging the right to assemble peaceably and to petition the government. By prohibiting any established religion, it signifies the separation of church and state.

The *Second Amendment* declares that, a state militia being necessary, the right of the people to bear arms shall not be infringed.

The *Third Amendment* forbids the quartering of soldiers in private homes in peacetime except with the owner's consent.

The *Fourth Amendment* prohibits the unreasonable search and seizure of persons and property, and requires that warrants for search or arrest be specific as to the place to be searched and the persons or things to be seized.

The *Fifth Amendment* provides that a person accused of a crime may not be tried twice for the same offense, meaning no *double jeopardy;* that he or she may not be compelled to be a witness against himself or herself, meaning no *self-incrimination;* and that no person may "be deprived of life, liberty, or property, without *due process of law,*" meaning proper legal procedures. It further provides that the government may take private property for public use, that is, exercise the power of *eminent domain,* but the government must pay just compensation.

The *Sixth Amendment* gives an accused person in a criminal case certain basic rights: to a speedy and public trial, an impartial jury, defense counsel; and to know the charges, confront hostile witnesses, and obtain friendly witnesses.

The *Seventh Amendment* guarantees a jury trial in most civil cases.

The *Eighth Amendment* prohibits excessive fines and bails and cruel and unusual punishments.

The *Ninth Amendment* states that the rights of the people enumerated in the first eight amendments shall not be construed to deny their other rights.

The *Tenth Amendment* declares that all powers not prohibited to the states or given to the federal government are reserved to the states or the people.

DUE PROCESS CLAUSE: THE FIFTH AND FOURTEENTH AMENDMENTS

The Fifth Amendment prohibits the federal government, and the Fourteenth Amendment prohibits the states, from depriving any person of "life, liberty, or property without due process of law." The due process clause serves to protect the people's civil liberties and property rights. Many federal and state laws have been challenged in the courts for denying due process.

RIGHTS AND LIBERTIES IMPLY DUTIES

Our rights and liberties as Americans carry with them certain duties. Freedom of speech implies the duty to speak honestly and with a full knowledge of the facts. Freedom of religion implies the duty to respect the freedom of others whose religion differs from our own. The right to vote implies the duty to know the candidates and the issues. The right to trial by jury implies the duty to respond willingly when called for jury service.

INDIVIDUAL RIGHTS vs. THE NEEDS OF SOCIETY

Democratic peoples constantly face the problem of adjusting the rights of the individual to the needs of society. What is the correct balance between individual freedom and governmental restraint in the public interest? May individuals exercise freedom of speech even if their words cause a riot? May they exercise freedom of the press even if their writings obstruct the nation's war effort? Such questions arising out of specific cases have been answered by the Supreme Court.

In general, the Court has held that *individual rights are not absolute but relative,* depending upon specific circumstances: what, where, when, and how.

SELECTED CASES INVOLVING RIGHTS AND LIBERTIES

1. Freedom of Speech and Press

a. Schenck vs. United States (1919)—Issue: Freedom of the Press. Charles Schenck, general secretary of the Socialist party, published pamphlets urging World War I draftees to resist conscription. Convicted of obstructing the war effort—a violation of the 1917 *Federal Espionage Act*—Schenck appealed the case, claiming that the law violated freedom of the press. Justice

Oliver Wendell Holmes, speaking for a unanimous Supreme Court, held that "free speech would not protect a man falsely shouting fire in a theater and causing a panic" and that Schenck's writings in wartime created a "clear and present danger" to the American government and people. Schenck's conviction was upheld.

The "clear-and-present-danger" doctrine, herein stated, became the yardstick for later cases involving the freedoms protected by the First Amendment.

b. Dennis vs. United States (1951)—Issue: Freedom of Speech. *Eugene Dennis* and ten other American Communist party leaders were charged with violating the *Smith Act*. This 1940 federal law prohibited teaching or advocating "the overthrow or destruction of any government in the United States by force or violence." Found guilty by a District Court jury, the Communist party leaders appealed to the Supreme Court. They claimed that the Smith Act violated their right of free speech. By 6 to 2, the Court upheld the law.

For the majority, Chief Justice Fred Vinson wrote that, in this era of the Cold War struggle between Russia and the United States, the American Communist leaders were not merely explaining "an abstract doctrine" of overthrowing the government by force and violence but were seeking to incite people to such action and consequently constituted a "clear and present danger." In his dissent, Justice *William Douglas* pointed out that the Communist leaders were not charged with any overt acts, and accused the Court majority of misusing the "clear-and-present-danger" yardstick.

2. Freedom of Religion and Separation of Church and State

a. Prince vs. Massachusetts (1944)—Issue: Freedom of Religion. *Sarah Prince*, a Jehovah's Witness, permitted her nine-year-old legal ward to sell the sect's magazine on the streets. Convicted of violating a Massachusetts law that prohibited a guardian from allowing such child labor, Prince appealed the case eventually to the Supreme Court, claiming that the law interfered with freedom of religion. The Supreme Court decided that the law was a proper exercise of the state's police powers and upheld the conviction.

Delivering the opinion of the Court, Justice *Wiley Rutledge* explained that "a democratic society rests, for its continuance, upon the healthy well-rounded growth of young people" and therefore the states may legislate against evils such as "the crippling effects of child employment, especially in public places."

b. Engel vs. Vitale (1962)—Issue: Separation of Church and State. *Steven Engel* and four other parents, representing various religious views, sued to stop the New Hyde Park, New York, school board from requiring their children to recite a short, nondenominational prayer. The parents claimed that, by the so-called "Regents' Prayer," New York State was "establishing" a religion. For the school board, *William Vitale* replied that the prayer itself was a generalized statement affirming dependence upon God, and that the children could participate or abstain—as they wished—during the prayer recital. The Supreme Court, by 6 to 1, held the "Regents' Prayer" unconstitutional.

Speaking for the majority, Justice *Hugo Black* said that the "Regents'

Prayer" was a religious activity sponsored by New York State and that while not "a total establishment of one particular religious sect to the exclusion of all others," it was a dangerous step in violation of the First Amendment. Justice *Potter Stewart,* the lone dissenter, pointed out that New York State had not "interfered with the free exercise of anybody's religion," that our government has invoked the name of God in many cases—the pledge of allegiance, the Star-Spangled Banner, the imprint on our coins—and that the "Regents' Prayer" should have been upheld.

    c. Robinson vs. Dicenso (1971)—Issue: Separation of Church and State. To attract competent teachers to religious and other private elementary schools, the Rhode Island legislature enacted the *Salary Supplement Act.* It provided that the state could add a 15 percent supplement to the salaries of parochial school teachers who taught nonreligious subjects and who utilized "only teaching materials which are used in the public schools." To challenge this law, a suit was instituted against the Associate State Commissioner of Education, *William P. Robinson,* and eventually reached the Supreme Court. By 8 to 1, the Court held the Rhode Island law a violation of the First Amendment and therefore invalid.

    For the majority, Chief Justice *Warren Burger* pointed out that although previous Court decisions since 1947 had upheld indirect government aid to parochial schools—such as bus transportation, school lunches, and secular textbooks—this supplemental salary law involved "excessive entanglement." It would, for example, require the state to keep the parochial schools under surveillance "to insure that state aid supports only secular education." It would therefore breach the wall of separation between church and state.

3. Rights of Accused Persons

    a. Gideon vs. Wainwright (1963)—Issue: Due Process of Law and Right to Counsel. *Clarence Gideon,* charged with burglary, was tried in a Florida state court. Too poor to afford a lawyer, Gideon requested free legal counsel, but the state refused his request on the ground that he was not being tried for a capital offense punishable by death. Found guilty and imprisoned, Gideon appealed to the Supreme Court, which unanimously overturned his conviction.

    With Justice *Hugo Black* delivering the opinion, the Court held that Florida had denied Gideon his "due process" under the Fourteenth Amendment which, the Court reasoned, requires the state to fulfill the Sixth Amendment guarantee of "assistance of counsel" even in noncapital cases. Later assisted by a lawyer in a new trial in Florida, Gideon was acquitted of the original burglary charge.

    b. Escobedo vs. Illinois (1964)—Issue: Self-Incrimination and Right to Counsel. *Danny Escobedo* was arrested as a murder suspect. The police told him that they had a "pretty tight" case and subjected him to a continuous barrage of questioning. The police refused Escobedo's repeated demands to see his lawyer and failed to inform him that he had a right to remain silent. Escobedo eventually made incriminating statements that were used against him in state court to secure a verdict of "guilty." Escobedo appealed the case, and the Supreme Court, by 5 to 4, reversed the conviction.

Delivering the majority opinion for the Court, Justice *Arthur Goldberg* explained that the police, while interrogating the accused, had denied him his Constitutional rights to speak to his counsel and to be informed of his privilege against self-incrimination. The dissenting Justices held that the ruling was "wholly unworkable" and would cripple law enforcement.

   c. Miranda vs. Arizona (1966)—Issue: Self-Incrimination and Right to Counsel. *Ernesto Miranda* was questioned by the police about the kidnapping and assaulting of a young woman. Placed in a police lineup, Miranda was identified by the victim, whereupon he confessed his guilt. His confession was used in court and helped to convict him. This case was appealed on the ground that the police had denied the suspect his Constitutional protection against self-incrimination. In a 5 to 4 decision, the Court expanded the Escobedo Case doctrine and overturned the conviction.

Chief Justice *Earl Warren* wrote the majority opinion that, before questioning, the police must inform suspects of their rights to remain silent and to legal counsel, must offer to provide counsel if the suspects are indigent, and must warn them that their remarks may be used against them. The dissenting judges attacked the majority for complicating the job of law enforcement and enabling criminals to gain freedom on technicalities. In a second trial, Miranda was convicted by a jury after his common-law wife testified that he had told her of his guilt.

——————— MULTIPLE-CHOICE QUESTIONS ———————

1. Congress is empowered by the Constitution to establish "inferior courts," meaning courts that (a) hear cases only of persons with low incomes (b) have no appellate jurisdiction (c) do not provide for trial by jury (d) are below the Supreme Court.

2. The framers of the Constitution provided long terms for judges of the Supreme Court in order to (a) save expenses incurred by frequent changes in office (b) enable judges to acquire skill in trying cases (c) reward political followers with secure jobs (d) make it easier for judges to render decisions without political interference.

3. The number of Justices on the Supreme Court is determined by (a) its own membership (b) a law of Congress (c) a Constitutional provision (d) the President.

4. Supreme Court judges are (a) elected by the people (b) chosen by Congress in a joint session (c) nominated by the President (d) chosen by the electoral college.

5. A Supreme Court decision to declare an act of Congress unconstitutional requires (a) at least a simple majority vote (b) at least a two-thirds vote (c) at least a three-fourth vote (d) a unanimous vote.

6. According to the Constitution, which of these actions constitutes treason? (a) selling one's vote for money (b) giving aid and comfort to the enemy (c) refusing to bear arms in defense of one's country (d) working for an international organization.

7. In which instance would the Supreme Court have original jurisdiction? (a) New York State suing New Jersey over navigation on the Hudson River (b) the robbing of a national bank (c) violation by a citizen of the federal income-tax law (d) violation of a citizen's civil rights.

8. What is the role of the Supreme Court in the legislative process? (a) Congress must receive an advisory opinion from the Court before passing a bill (b) A citizen does not have to obey a law until the Court pronounces it Constitutional (c) The Court deals with legislation only when acting on a case (d) The Court may act on the constitutionality only of laws affecting states.

9. The power of the Supreme Court to declare acts of Congress unconstitutional was (a) assumed by the Court itself (b) granted by President Washington (c) granted by Congress in 1789 (d) secured by a Constitutional amendment.

10. The term *judicial review* refers to the (a) review of court decisions by the President (b) confirmation of judicial appointments by the Senate (c) requirement for a unanimous vote in Supreme Court decisions (d) power of the Supreme Court to decide the constitutionality of laws.

11. "The Supreme Court is not so much a court of justice as America's ultimate lawmaking body." This statement is most concerned with the power of the Supreme Court to (a) exercise judicial review (b) exercise original jurisdiction (c) hear cases without a jury (d) have the Chief Justice preside at Presidential impeachment trials.

12. A lawyer would probably seek a writ of habeas corpus for a person who has been (a) charged with a crime and who cannot afford bail (b) imprisoned without being charged with a crime (c) tried and convicted (d) tried twice for the same crime.

13. In 1920 a person committed a murder in State X. In 1921 the penalty for murder in State X was changed from life imprisonment to death. In 1922 this person was convicted of this crime in a state court and sentenced to death. On what Constitutional grounds might the person appeal to a federal court? (a) "due process of law"—Fourteenth Amendment (b) double jeopardy (c) bill of attainder (d) *ex post facto.*

14. Most of the federal Bill of Rights now applies also to the states because of the (a) due process of law clause—Fifth Amendment (b) reserved powers—Tenth Amendment (c) due process of law clause—Fourteenth Amendment (d) no voting discrimination based on race or color—Fifteenth Amendment.

15. The need for a warrant to conduct a lawful search is an indication that (a) the crime rate is increasing in the United States (b) the person about to be searched is really innocent (c) individuals are protected against government power (d) there is an excessive concern for the rights of criminals.

16. Most criminal trials take place in state courts rather than federal courts because (a) few crimes are a threat to the national security (b) most crimes involve a violation of state laws (c) only political crimes are tried in federal courts (d) state courts have more trial facilities available.

17. The Constitution prohibits the passage of a bill of attainder. The effect of this provision is that a citizen is guaranteed (a) a trial (b) the right to vote (c) the right to bear arms (d) freedom of religion.

18. Which part of the Constitution has been the basis of controversies over federal censorship and federal aid to religious schools? (a) Preamble (b) First Amendment (c) Thirteenth Amendment (d) Power denied to Congress.

19. The "clear and present danger" rule for cases involving freedom of speech was first stated in (a) the original Constitution (b) the Bill of Rights (c) an opinion written by John Marshall (d) an opinion written by Oliver Wendell Holmes.

20. ". . . nor shall any state deprive any person of life, liberty, or property, without due process of law . . . " is quoted from the (a) Northwest Ordinance (b) Preamble to the Constitution (c) First Amendment (d) Fourteenth Amendment.

21. The Constitutional provision ". . . nor shall [any person] be compelled in any criminal case to be a witness against himself . . . " protects against (a) a bill of attainder (b) cruel and unusual punishment (c) double jeopardy (d) self-incrimination.

22. The right of the government to take private property for public use, providing just compensation is made, is known as (a) bill of attainder (b) eminent domain (c) habeas corpus (d) *ex post facto.*

23. The Constitution encouraged the rise of capitalism by (a) establishing an economic policy of laissez-faire (b) providing for the protection of private property (c) guaranteeing the formation of labor unions (d) prohibiting Federal Government regulation of industry.

24. When a judge tells an accused person that he or she is charged with armed robbery and that he or she may have legal counsel and a jury trial, the accused is being (a) indicted by a grand jury (b) denied due process of law (c) granted a writ of habeas corpus (d) informed of his or her Constitutional rights.

25. The "double jeopardy" clause of the Constitution protects the legal rights of the individual by (a) requiring the testimony of two witnesses to the same criminal act in order to convict the defendant (b) prohibiting the placing of legal penalties on innocent members of a criminal's family (c) exempting a person from having to testify without adequate counsel (d) freeing an acquitted defendant from facing another trial based on the identical criminal charge.

26. Which conclusion can be drawn from the statement, "Peace demonstrations may be regulated by local ordinances"? (a) Freedom of assembly is no longer a right of Americans. (b) Freedoms guaranteed by the Bill of Rights have been limited by judicial action. (c) "Freedom" is a relative rather than an absolute right. (d) Police powers of local governments are too strong.

27. "In the United States, reporters have an obligation to publish all newsworthy information. Government has an obligation to protect national security." This conflict demonstrates that (a) the First Amendment does not apply to the mass media (b) there is a delicate balance between freedom and restraint (c) news coverage should be subject to government regulation (d) the public has the right to be informed.

28. The federal Bill of Rights provides that (a) Congress shall not prohibit the free exercise of religion (b) the writ of habeas corpus shall not be suspended (c) Congress must guarantee each state a republican form of government (d) no citizen may be deprived of the right to vote.

29. A decision of the Supreme Court declaring a law unconstitutional can be reversed by (a) a Presidential veto (b) a vote of the legislatures of three-fourths of the states (c) an amendment to the Constitution (d) a two-thirds vote of Congress.

30. The practice of a trial before a jury of one's peers is based primarily on the assumption that (a) peer groups have a better understanding of the legal process than do appointed judges (b) having a background similar to that of the accused helps in rendering fair decisions (c) trials can be conducted faster if the jury is carefully selected (d) decisions reached by peer groups are less likely to be overturned by higher courts.

31. Most amendments to the Constitution were designed to provide for (a) limitations on government expenditures (b) protection of personal rights (c) an increase in foreign aid (d) a strengthening of the legislative branch.

32. Decisions by the Supreme Court calling for approximately equal legislative districts to implement the "one person, one vote" principle have resulted in (a) the end of gerrymandering (b) more large-city riots (c) a decrease in the influence of rural residents (d) the adoption of unicameral legislatures by many of the states.

33. Which procedure is currently followed in the United States when an accused person cannot afford to hire a defense lawyer? (a) Law schools send an outstanding student to defend the individual. (b) The individual must depend on his or her own knowledge of the law. (c) The individual can ask that the lawyer serve without pay. (d) The court must provide counsel for the individual.

34. Under Chief Justice John Marshall, the Supreme Court (a) supported the doctrine of states' rights (b) strengthened the federal government at the expense of the states (c) strengthened Court principles established under previous Chief Justices (d) supported Thomas Jefferson's views on the division of powers.

35. The Warren Court handed down important decisions on all of the following issues *except* (a) segregation in public schools (b) rights of accused persons in criminal cases (c) legislative reapportionment (d) Presidential power to withhold from Congress tapes of White House discussions.

36. In *Engel vs. Vitale,* the Warren Court held that the New York State "Regents' Prayer" was (a) approved by the three major religious groups and therefore Constitutional (b) too general a statement to have any meaning (c) a dangerous step toward state religious activity and therefore unconstitutional (d) not to be printed in a magazine and sold on the streets.

37. One criticism that some law-enforcement officers have leveled at Warren Court decisions is concerned with the (a) right of a defendant to counsel in pretrial questioning (b) expansion of federal police power (c) lenient attitude toward civil rights demonstrators (d) elimination of capital punishment for major crimes.

38. Which statement about the Supreme Court is *best* classified as an opinion? (a) Supreme Court decisions are responsible for the recent decline in law and order. (b) Supreme Court decisions have affected the apportionment of state legislatures. (c) A dissenting view in one Supreme Court can become the majority view of a later Court. (d) The Supreme Court has broadened the interpretation of the "equal protection of the laws" clause.

DISCUSSION ANALYSIS QUESTIONS:
_____ RIGHTS OF ACCUSED PERSONS _____

Speakers *A, B, C,* and *D* have been accused of violating a law, and they are attempting to protect their rights. Base your answers to the following questions on their statements and on your knowledge of the Constitution and Supreme Court decisions.

Speaker A: I was found guilty of a serious crime in a federal district court. My conviction was based largely on the testimony of anonymous witnesses whose identities were concealed by the prosecution so as "to insure their safety."

Speaker B: I was indicted in a state court for the crime of murder. After the trial the jury was unable to reach a verdict. As a result, I was retried for the same offense.

Speaker C: I was arrested on suspicion of arson and questioned by the police for several days. During that time I confessed in order to get some rest. The police never told me I had a right to call a lawyer, but I wouldn't have been able to pay one, anyway.

Speaker D: I was arrested for giving a talk on a street corner. The police said I was inciting to riot. A police judge convicted me on the grounds that I was creating a "clear and present danger." I maintained that my freedom of speech was violated.

1. Which speaker is trying to plead double jeopardy? (a) *A* (b) *B* (c) *C* (d) *D*.
2. Will the plea of double jeopardy, in this case, be (a) upheld by the state court (b) denied by the state court (c) heard by the Supreme Court (d) used to compel the jury to reconsider the case?
3. The right of the accused to confront his or her accusers has been violated in the case of Speaker (a) *A* (b) *B* (c) *C* (d) *D*.
4. The Constitutional provision that a person shall not be compelled to be a witness against himself has been violated in the case of Speaker (a) *A* (b) *B* (c) *C* (d) *D*.
5. In cases similar to that of Speaker *C,* the Supreme Court has ruled that the accused (a) may not break the continuity of questioning by confessing (b) has a right to refuse to answer questions unless a lawyer, supplied by the state if necessary, is present (c) should not have been arrested solely on suspicion of arson (d) should have been furnished with a public defender after confessing.
6. A Supreme Court case similar to that of Speaker *C* was (a) *Escobedo vs. Illinois* (b) *Schenck vs. United States* (c) *Dennis vs. United States* (d) *Prince vs. Massachusetts.*
7. In previous cases like that of Speaker *D,* the Supreme Court has ruled that (a) the accused cannot plead the First Amendment when charged with violating local laws (b) the accused should have been tried in a federal court on the riot charge (c) freedom of speech does not include the right to endanger public safety (d) freedom of speech does not include the right to make speeches in public in support of a religious belief.
8. In which case did the Supreme Court decide that the state must provide impoverished accused persons with a lawyer—even in noncapital charges? (a) *West Virginia State Board of Education vs. Barnette* (b) *Bakke* (c) *Prince vs. Massachusetts* (d) *Gideon vs. Wainwright.*
9. The lawyer for Speaker *A* would appeal *A's* conviction to (a) another federal district court (b) a federal circuit court (c) the state court of appeals (d) the local bar association.

—————————— **ESSAY QUESTIONS** ——————————

1. *(a)* For an imaginary or a real case involving the Constitution, explain the *two* conflicting points of view regarding the Constitutional issue. *(b)* Trace the case through the federal court system to explain the roles of the district court, the circuit court, and the Supreme Court.
2. *(a)* Explain how the power of judicial review was established by the Supreme Court. *(b)* Discuss *one* reason *for* limiting the power of the Supreme Court and *one* reason *against* limiting its power. *(c)* Evaluate *one* proposal for limiting the power of the Supreme Court.

3. The Supreme Court has often been at the center of controversy. For any *one* of the following Supreme Court eras *(a)* prove the preceding statement to be true and *(b)* evaluate the impact of the decision(s) of the Court upon American life: (1) Marshall Court (2) Warren Court (3) Burger Court.

4. *(a)* Describe the historical circumstances under which the Bill of Rights became a part of the Constitution. *(b)* Several amendments in the federal Bill of Rights safeguard the rights of individuals before the courts. Give *three* provisions of these amendments relating to court procedures and show how *each* provision protects the individual against an unjust practice followed in totalitarian countries.

5. At times the rights of the individual may conflict with the needs of society. *(a)* What is the attitude toward such conflict in (1) a totalitarian society (2) a democratic society? *(b)* Select any *one* Supreme Court case involving either freedom of speech, freedom of the press, freedom of religion, or the rights of accused persons. For the case you have selected (1) show that it illustrates a conflict between the individual and society, (2) state the Supreme Court decision in the case, and (3) explain why you agree or disagree with the decision.

6. For *each* of the following cases *(a)* identify a Constitutional and/or legal issue involved. *(b)* Identify *two* opposing sides in the case and develop a legal argument for each side. (Each argument must refer to specific sections of the Constitution or laws or previous legal decisions. You need not cite specific laws or legal decisions by name.) *(c)* Indicate briefly which side you believe has the greater merit.
(1) Under a city ordinance, a radical political party is denied a permit to conduct a rally.
(2) A student charged with disruptive behavior is expelled from a public school without a hearing.

7. Agree or disagree with *each* of the following statements and present *two* arguments to support your point of view. *(a)* Trials in district courts should be decided by a panel of judges rather than by a jury. *(b)* The Supreme Court should follow a philosophy of judicial activism rather than judicial restraint. *(c)* In today's political climate, if the Bill of Rights had to be submitted to the states for ratification, it would be defeated.

PART 7. The Constitution Is a Living and Flexible Document

In 1787, when the Constitution was written, the United States consisted of 13 states with a population of 4 million people, over 90 percent occupied in agriculture. As yet unknown were the giant machines, large factories, huge cities, and rapid means of transportation and communication that exist today. How has it been possible for this Constitution, drawn up in a small, simple agricultural society, to function in today's huge, complex industrial civilization?

Our Constitution is living and flexible, able to redirect and expand the powers of government to serve the needs of the nation and to surmount periods of great crisis.

The flexibility of our Constitution has been based upon (1) its elastic clause and other general or vague terminology, (2) judicial interpretation by the Supreme Court, (3) the adoption of amendments, and (4) the growth of governmental traditions and practices, called the unwritten Constitution.

GENERAL TERMINOLOGY IN THE CONSTITUTION

1. Elastic Clause. By the elastic clause, Congress received the power to pass all laws "necessary and proper" for its delegated powers. Interpreting the term "necessary and proper" in its broadest sense, Congress has utilized implied powers and has been able to keep pace with the changing times.

2. Other Terminology Susceptible to Reinterpretation. Among its delegated powers, Congress may collect taxes for the "general welfare" and may "regulate commerce . . . among the several states." As our society has evolved, Congress has accepted new meanings for such vague terms so as to deal with current problems. In the amendments, among the terms that have changed meaning with the times are "due process of law," "impartial jury," and "equal protection of the laws."

JUDICIAL INTERPRETATION

The Supreme Court has played a major role in assuring flexibility in the Constitution. (a) By the decisions of John Marshall, the Supreme Court established the precedents of *judicial review* of federal and state laws, *loose construction* of the Constitution, and *broad interpretation* of the interstate commerce clause. (b) Over the years, the Supreme Court has proved willing to deliver decisions reflecting more modern interpretations of the Constitution's vague terminology.

LAW COMPARED WITH AMENDMENT

1. Law. A federal law must be based upon a power granted or implied in the Constitution. For example, acting on a granted power, Congress authorized district and circuit courts; acting on an implied power, Congress established the National Bank.

2. Amendment. To change the Constitution an amendment is necessary. (a) Some amendments add to or subtract from the existing constitutional powers of the federal government. For example, the Sixteenth Amendment gave Congress the added power to levy income taxes. (b) Other amendments limit the powers of the states. For example, the Fourteenth Amendment prohibited the states from denying any person the equal protection of the laws. (c) Still other amendments alter the election processes or the federal government structure. For example, the Seventeenth Amendment transferred the power to elect United States Senators from the state legislatures to the people.

PROCESS OF AMENDING THE CONSTITUTION

A Constitutional amendment must be proposed and ratified as follows:

PROPOSED BY	RATIFIED BY
1. A two-thirds vote of each house of Congress.	1. The legislatures of three-fourths of the states.
or	*or*
2. A national convention called by Congress upon the request of two-thirds of the states. (This method has never been used.)	2. Special conventions called by three-fourths of the states. (This method has been used only once—for the Twenty-First Amendment.)

EVALUATION OF THE PROCESS OF AMENDMENT

1. Merits. *(a)* By requiring the approval of many legislatures, the amending process may prevent hasty and ill-considered changes in the Constitution. *(b)* By requiring an "extraordinary" majority, the amending process may prevent any "temporary" majority, arising out of momentary excitement, from tampering with our governmental system and basic civil liberties. *(c)* Members of special state conventions called to ratify a proposed amendment are elected by the voters on that single issue. The state convention, a method used only once, reflects public opinion.

2. Criticisms. *(a)* The amending process, necessitating action by many legislative bodies, may be time-consuming. *(b)* Since the amending process requires far more than a simple majority, few amendments are passed, and the process may thwart the will of the people. *(c)* State legislators, empowered to ratify proposed amendments, may have been elected on other issues. Lacking a formal expression of the public will, they may vote their personal preference.

BRIEF SUMMARY OF AMENDMENTS

First Ten Amendments (1791). The first ten amendments, listing the rights and liberties of the people, are known as the Bill of Rights.
Background. Check the Index for Bill of Rights.

Eleventh Amendment (1798). Federal courts shall have no power to hear suits against a state by a citizen of another state or of a foreign country.
Background. In *Chisholm vs. Georgia* (1793), the Supreme Court affirmed the right of a South Carolina citizen to sue the State of Georgia without the state's consent. Georgia denied the authority of the court in this matter. To protect state sovereignty, the states secured adoption of the Eleventh Amendment.

Twelfth Amendment (1804). Electors (members of the electoral college) shall cast separate ballots for President and Vice President.
   Background. Check the Index for Thomas Jefferson and the election of 1800.

Thirteenth Amendment (1865). No slavery shall exist within the United States.
   Background. During the Civil War, President Lincoln issued the Emancipation Proclamation (1863) declaring free the slaves in the states still in rebellion. The Proclamation did not apply to slaves in Confederate territories occupied by Union armies and in border slave states loyal to the Union. This first Civil War amendment prohibited slavery throughout the country.

Fourteenth Amendment (1868). *(a)* All persons born or naturalized in the United States are citizens of the United States and of their state. *(b)* No state shall abridge the privileges of citizens, or deprive "any person of life, liberty, or property without due process of law," or deny to any person "equal protection of the laws." *(c)* Any state unfairly denying its male citizens the right to vote shall have its representation in the House of Representatives proportionately reduced. *(d)* Leading Confederate officials shall be disqualified from holding any federal or state office. *(e)* The Confederate debt shall be void.
   Background. This second Civil War amendment, passed during the Reconstruction Era, was intended to prevent states from infringing upon the rights of blacks and to punish leaders and bondholders of the Confederacy.

Fifteenth Amendment (1870). The right of citizens to vote "shall not be abridged by the United States or any state on account of race, color, or previous condition of servitude."
   Background. This third Civil War amendment was intended to assure the voting rights of blacks.

Sixteenth Amendment (1913). Congress shall have the power to levy a tax on incomes.
   Background. To supplement federal revenue from tariffs, Congress in 1894 authorized a 2 percent tax on certain incomes. In *Pollock vs. The Farmers' Loan and Trust Company* (1895), the Supreme Court held the income tax to be a direct tax not levied among the states in proportion to population and therefore unconstitutional. This amendment overcame the Supreme Court ruling.

Seventeenth Amendment (1913). Senators shall be elected directly by the people.
   Background. The Seventeenth Amendment ended the election of Senators by state legislatures. It was a democratic reform urged by the Progressive movement.

Eighteenth Amendment (1919). The manufacture, sale, or transportation of intoxicating beverages is prohibited.
   Background. Check the Index for Prohibition.

Nineteenth Amendment (1920). The right of citizens to vote shall not be denied by the United States or by any state on account of sex.

Background. Check the Index for Woman suffrage.

Twentieth Amendment (1933). Congress shall meet annually on January 3, and the President shall take office on January 20 following the election.

Background. This amendment recognized advances in communication and transportation by moving up the dates for taking office. Previously, the new Congress, elected in November, did not meet until 13 months later. The old Congress, which met in December immediately following the election, contained some defeated Congress members, called *lame ducks*. The "lame duck" Congress rarely was a productive legislature. Also, before this amendment, the President waited an additional six weeks before taking office on March 4.

Twenty-First Amendment (1933). The Eighteenth (Prohibition) Amendment is repealed.

Background. Check the Index for Prohibition.

Twenty-Second Amendment (1951). No person shall be elected President for more than two terms.

Background. Check the Index for Two-term tradition.

Twenty-Third Amendment (1961). Residents of the District of Columbia shall have the right to vote for the President. The District's electoral vote shall be no greater than that of the least populous state (currently Alaska with three electoral votes).

Background. Since the District of Columbia is not a state and has no representation in Congress, its residents previously had no vote in Presidential elections.

Twenty-Fourth Amendment (1964). The right of citizens to vote in primaries and general elections for federal officials—President, Vice President, Senators, and Representatives—shall not be denied by the United States or by any state because of failure to pay a poll tax.

Background. Check the Index for Poll tax.

Twenty-Fifth Amendment (1967). In case the office of Vice President is vacant, the President shall select a new Vice President subject to Congressional approval. In case of Presidential disability, the Vice President may serve as Acting President until the President is able to resume the duties of office.

Background. Check the Index for Presidential disability and succession.

Twenty-Sixth Amendment (1971). The right of citizens 18 years or older to vote shall not be denied by the United States or by any state on account of age.

Background. The Supreme Court ruled that a 1970 federal law granting the vote to 18-year-olds was valid for federal elections but not state and local elections. This amendment gave 18-year-olds the vote in all elections.

In which case, who'd be in charge?

Alexander in The Philadelphia Bulletin

THE UNWRITTEN CONSTITUTION

The "unwritten Constitution" consists of American governmental practices and institutions not specifically set down in the Constitution but based upon customs and traditions that may be changed or broken relatively easily. Examples of the "unwritten Constitution" are (1) judicial review by the Supreme Court, (2) the committee system in Congress, (3) the Cabinet as an advisory group to the President, (4) pledges by Presidential electors to vote for specific candidates, and (5) political parties.

INDIVIDUAL AND GROUP INFLUENCE UPON THE GOVERNMENT

INFLUENCE THROUGH POLITICAL PARTIES

1. Purpose. Although not mentioned in the Constitution, political parties appeared as early as George Washington's first administration. In a democracy a political party arises when people with similar interests and ideas band together to advance their program by peacefully influencing and gaining control of the government.

2. Two-Party System Today. Traditionally, the United States has had a *two-party system*. The two major parties today are the Democrats and the Republicans. Although both parties have supporters from all social, ethnic, and economic backgrounds, each party has traditionally been identified with certain segments of our population. Also the two parties have differed, sometimes slightly and sometimes considerably, on broad economic and Constitutional principles.

a. The Republican Party. This party has drawn strong support from business leaders and well-to-do farmers. Today's Republicans favor less federal involvement in the economy, more states' rights, and a less powerful central government.

b. The Democratic Party. This party has drawn strong support from minority groups, workers, and poor farmers. Today's Democrats favor greater federal involvement in economic matters, fewer states' rights, and a more powerful central government.

c. "Broad-Spectrum" Parties. Since control of the government depends upon gaining the support of a majority of the American electorate, our major parties today usually avoid narrow regional or class appeals. Each is a *broad-spectrum* party, containing advocates of divergent political views—liberal, moderate, and conservative. Each party, however, usually adopts moderate positions so as to gain the widest possible public support.

d. Factional or Intraparty Strife. With each of our major political parties including a broad spectrum of political views, each party has been torn by bitter factional strife. Conservative Republicans oppose liberal Republicans; conservative Democrats oppose liberal Democrats. Such divisions often surface during Presidential election years. Each faction struggles to secure the party's Presidential nomination for its candidate. After the candidate is nominated, the party divisions may be glossed over in a "unity appeal," or the defeated faction may "sit on its hands," extending little assistance to the party candidate, or the defeated faction may even run its own candidate on a third-party ticket. (For examples, check the Index for Third-party candidates.)

3. Role of Minor or "Third" Parties. With one exception, minor or "third" parties have attracted little support from the American electorate. Such parties usually have advocated limited objectives, have appealed to limited groups—economic, regional, or racial—and sometimes have revolved around a single individual. Usually they have been short-lived. *(a)* The Free-Soil party before the Civil War opposed the extension of slavery. *(b)* The Populist party of the 1890s appealed chiefly to farmers with a program calling for cheap money. *(c)* The Socialist party, created in 1900, advocated many social and economic reforms but appealed only to a relatively small number of voters. Its best-known leaders were its Presidential candidates: Eugene V. Debs (1900 to 1920) and Norman Thomas (1928 to 1948). *(d)* The American Independent party in 1968 ran George Wallace, who advocated segregation and states' rights.

The Republican party, which started in 1854, has been the only minor party to become a major party. Its initial success was due, in part, to its broad appeal—not only to antislavery groups, but also to business leaders, farmers, western settlers, and supporters of a strong national government.

Minor parties contributed to our government, chiefly by presenting the people with new ideas, such as the income tax, direct election of Senators, and Social Security. In time the major parties enacted into law such new ideas as were practicable and in keeping with American tradition.

4. Services of Political Parties. Political parties are essential to American democracy. They hold conventions, draw up political platforms, reconcile conflicting interests, nominate candidates for public office, and conduct campaigns. Thus they crystallize campaign issues, educate the public, and offer the voters a choice of ideas and candidates. Parties also keep check on each other, since each is eager to uncover and publicize the other's mistakes.

5. Dangers of Political Parties

a. Dependence Upon Large Contributors. Parties raise funds chiefly from well-to-do persons and organizations. Such contributors may want favors in return: appointments to office or passage of special legislation. By various laws, the federal government regulates contributions to reduce the political influence of large donors. The 1974 Federal Campaign Reform Act provides for extensive federal funding of Presidential elections but leaves the funding of Congressional races entirely to private contributors. (Check the Index for Campaign finances.)

b. Partisanship. With the party out of power seeking to unseat the party in control of the government, the "outs" often denounce the "ins" unfairly. They may oppose worthwhile measures, raise irrelevant issues, and seek partisan advantage at the expense of the public welfare.

c. Party Machines. Especially on the local level, political parties may be controlled undemocratically by a small group of insiders, called a *party machine.* These insiders are professional politicians who devote their lives to politics, usually as a means of earning a living. They are generally led by a *party boss.* The political machine remains in power as long as it is able to crush opposition, control votes, and win elections. Party machines, infamous for graft, corruption, and disregard of public welfare, have included the *Pendergast Machine* in Missouri, the *Vare Machine* in Pennsylvania, and the *Tweed Ring,* which controlled Tammany Hall in New York City.

d. Public Apathy. Average citizens, having little contact with or knowledge of political parties, generally restrict their political activities to reading a newspaper and to voting in general elections. They remain indifferent, even for long periods, to rule by party machine. Only when machine rule becomes flagrant and a fighting reform leader appears may average citizens become aroused. They may then seek to awaken the community to go to the polls and "throw the rascals out."

6. The People and Political Parties. Political parties have been called a bridge between the people and their government. The more the people are involved with political parties, the greater is their influence on the government; and, conversely, the less involved politically, the less influence they exert. In a democracy, the kind of government the people get depends, in considerable measure, upon their own political involvement.

INFLUENCE THROUGH VOTING

1. Democracy and the Right to Vote

Democratically minded peoples historically have struggled to extend the suffrage to more citizens and to remove unfair restrictions upon voting. Over the years Americans have achieved much: the states eliminated property and religious qualifications for voting; Constitutional amendments guaranteed the vote to all citizens regardless of race, color, or sex, and to 18-year-olds; amendments also provided for the direct election of Senators and outlawed the poll tax in federal elections; political parties and tradition turned the electoral college into a "rubber stamp"; and the Supreme Court ordered legislative reapportionment to provide more equitable districts reflecting the "one-citizen, one-vote" principle.

Armed with the ballot and offered a choice of candidates in honest elections, American citizens can place in public office those candidates who they hope will best further the public interest. American citizens, further, can scrutinize the doings of their elected officials and subsequently reelect those who have performed satisfactorily and retire from public life those whose performances have been disappointing. Through the ballot, the American people can exercise their greatest influence upon their government.

2. American Voting Patterns

Despite the importance of the ballot, millions of Americans fail to vote. *(a) In Presidential Elections.* The greatest number of voters turn out for Presidential elections, but the percentage of total voting population voting in Presidential elections in recent years has been falling—from 63 percent in 1960 to 53 percent in 1984. *(b) In Congressional Elections.* Fewer citizens vote in Congressional elections. In a Presidential election year, about 5 percent of those who go to the polls and vote for President do not vote for members of Congress. In a non-Presidential or an off-year election, the number going to the polls has dropped below 40 percent. *(c) In State and Local Elections.* Still fewer citizens vote in purely state and local elections.

3. Nonvoting: Reasons and Remedies

a. Deliberate Obstructions of the Right to Vote. Especially in the South, and before the 1960s, blacks and poor whites were kept from voting by poll taxes, unfair literacy tests, and threats of economic reprisals and physical violence.

Remedies. In 1964 the Twenty-Fourth Amendment prohibited the poll tax in federal elections; in 1970 the Voting Rights Act suspended literacy tests across the nation as a qualification for voting.

b. Residency Requirements. Voters in all states had to satisfy state residency requirements, usually one year before election time. This requirement disenfranchised many citizens who had moved from one state to another. Also disenfranchised were citizens who had moved within a state and could not meet the county and district residency requirements.

Remedy. The 1970 Federal Voting Rights Act set a 30-day state residency requirement for voting in federal elections. Many states have adopted this requirement for state and local elections, in part to avoid the need of keeping two sets of voter registration records.

c. Personal Reasons. (1) Aged citizens were infirm or ill, (2) small storekeepers feared the loss of business and workers feared a deduction in wages for the time spent in voting, (3) homemakers were busy with young children and housekeeping chores, and (4) college students, vacationers, and traveling businesspeople were away from home.

Suggested Remedies. Political scientists have suggested making election day a national holiday so that storekeepers and workers would not have to go to work; simplifying absentee ballot procedures so that sick persons, travelers, and college students away from home could vote by mail; and providing babysitters so that busy homemakers could get to the polls.

d. Disinterest. Some 10 percent of the potential voters have claimed that they have no interest in the government, find no candidates worth voting for, and are "fed up with politics." With the enfranchisement of 18-to-20-year-olds, the number of nonvoters increased significantly.

Possible Remedy: Compulsory Voting? Belgium and Australia have a system of compulsory voting under which citizens who fail to perform this civic duty must pay a fine. Should the United States adopt compulsory voting?

INFLUENCE OF THE MASS MEDIA

1. Mass Media and the Government. In the long run, democratic government must respond to the "will of the people." Elected officials eventually will not be reelected if, on major issues, they continually resist public opinion. Consequently, government leaders are concerned with the molders of public opinion—notably the mass media.

The mass media serve to interest, inform, and influence the American people in regard to their government. The mass media also keep a critical watch and report upon the activities of governmental leaders.

2. Mass Media and the Individual. Individuals may influence newspapers by writing letters to the editor. Many such letters are printed by the paper and help indicate the community's thoughts and emotions. Individuals who are displeased with one newspaper may switch to another. If enough people stop reading any given newspaper, its circulation will drop and its sale of advertising space—its chief source of revenue—will fall off, thereby compelling the paper to rethink its policies or go out of business. The ability of readers to switch from one paper to another, however, is limited because many communities have only one newspaper.

INFLUENCE THROUGH OTHER METHODS

Individuals and groups may attempt to influence the government by (1) writing letters and sending petitions to the President, the members of Congress, and other governmental officials, (2) themselves lobbying or employing lobbyists, (3) demonstrating peacefully by means of picketing, marches, rallies, and mass turnouts at government hearings, and (4) deliberately violating laws that they consider "immoral."

———————— MULTIPLE-CHOICE QUESTIONS ————————

1. Flexibility is provided in the Constitution by the (a) Preamble and Bill of Rights (b) amending process and elastic clause (c) division of federal and state powers (d) electoral college system and enumerated powers of Congress.

2. Loose construction of the elastic clause has contributed to the fact that (a) a committee system has developed in Congress (b) the Constitution has met the needs of changing times (c) the principle of checks and balances is generally accepted (d) gerrymandering has become an established practice.

3. In authorizing a space-exploration program, Congress used (a) an implied power (b) a police power (c) a concurrent power (d) a delegated power.

4. The process of amending the Constitution requires much more than a simple majority. This statement could be used to prove that (a) laws are more important than amendments (b) the Framers did not understand the meaning of democracy (c) true democracy sometimes requires a check upon hasty and ill-considered action by any simple majority (d) methods other than amendment are more desirable to achieve flexibility in our federal government.

5. The Constitution provides that amendments may be proposed by (a) Congress (b) the President (c) the governors of the states (d) state conventions.

6. An amendment to the Constitution needs to be ratified by (a) the President and Congress (b) a majority of the Supreme Court Justices (c) legislatures or conventions in three-fourths of the states (d) a majority of the eligible voters.

7. Which has changed from "unwritten" to written Constitution? (a) provision for a President's Cabinet (b) provision for the committee system in Congress (c) formation of political parties (d) limits on the number of terms for any one President.

8. The reason that an amendment was necessary to levy a federal income tax is that (a) the people opposed federal taxation (b) it was a type of tax that had never been used (c) the states were already using this type of taxation (d) it was a direct tax not apportioned according to population.

9. Which one of the following would require a Constitutional amendment? (a) eliminating the electoral college system (b) raising the minimum wage (c) increasing the number of Supreme Court Justices (d) terminating American membership in the United Nations.

10. Of the Constitutional amendments adopted since the Civil War, the largest number have dealt with the (a) prohibition of intoxicating beverages (b) succession to the Presidency (c) voting rights of American citizens (d) federal powers to levy taxes.

11. Citizens living in the District of Columbia (a) elect voting representatives to Congress (b) do not pay personal income taxes (c) are ineligible for civil service positions (d) vote for Presidential electors.

12. Since the adoption of the Twentieth Amendment, Congress convenes every year on (a) December 10 (b) January 3 (c) January 20 (d) March 4.

13. Which is no longer a provision of the Constitution? (a) Three-Fifths Compromise (b) Connecticut Compromise (c) election of the President by electors (d) prohibition of export taxes.

14. That Presidential electors vote separately for President and Vice President was provided in (a) the original Constitution (b) the Presidential Succession Act of 1947 (c) a Supreme Court decision (d) an amendment to the Constitution.

15. The amendment to the Constitution giving 18-year-olds the right to vote restricted the (a) reserved powers of the states (b) delegated powers of Congress (c) powers assumed by the Supreme Court (d) powers retained by the people.

16. A practice that has become a part of our "unwritten Constitution" is (a) the convention method of nominating Presidential candidates (b) Senate approval of Presidential appointments (c) the order of succession to the Presidency (d) the President's power to negotiate treaties.

17. The President makes use of the "unwritten Constitution" when (a) vetoing a Congressional bill (b) appointing an ambassador to a foreign country (c) calling a special session of Congress (d) summoning the Cabinet.

18. The practice that Presidential electors vote for the candidate nominated by their political party is based upon (a) the Constitution of the United States (b) custom and tradition (c) a law of Congress (d) a decision of the Supreme Court.

19. The primary reason for the development of political party organizations in the United States was the (a) outline for their structure in the Constitution (b) need for some structure for groups with common political interests (c) formation of political organizations by state militia units after the Revolutionary War (d) controversy over the selection of the person to succeed George Washington as President.

20. Why have relatively few amendments been added to the Constitution? (a) Necessary changes have been brought about through a broad interpretation of the Constitution. (b) The sole initiative for the amending process resides in the federal government. (c) The federal government has restricted state activity in the amending process. (d) The need for changes has been met by the states.

21. Which statement *most* accurately describes the history of political parties? (a) The victorious party in the national election always controls the three branches of government. (b) The same political parties have remained in existence throughout our history. (c) Within each major party, there is a wide variety of political opinion. (d) Third parties have not been needed since the major parties have shown sufficient flexibility in dealing with controversial issues.

22. Which is a result of the fact that, in our political system, each major party must appeal to a wide variety of viewpoints? (a) Positions taken by major parties on issues usually are compromises. (b) Elections are likely to produce sharp disagreement on major issues. (c) Minority parties are likely to succeed in national elections. (d) Minority groups have too much influence on national nominating conventions.

23. Each of our major political parties has usually (a) eliminated differences among its members (b) financed its activities without difficulty (c) represented a cross section of interest groups (d) differed radically from its opposition party on basic principles.

24. Members of a political party are given a ballot on which they may choose a candidate from among three members of that party—A, B, or C. This situation is typical of (a) an uncontested election (b) a machine-controlled district (c) a primary election (d) a gerrymandered district.

25. The *most* important reason why a person should enroll in a political party is to be able to (a) help influence the choice of party candidates and policies (b) attend party rallies and dinners (c) vote in local elections (d) petition the state legislature.

26. Which is the *most* valid statement regarding minor political parties in the United States? (a) They usually have evolved into major parties. (b) They usually have been started by wealthy individuals who have desired political power. (c) They have presented new ideas, some of which have been adopted by our major parties. (d) They have served no useful function in our society.

27. The federal government has acted to increase the number of citizens who vote in Presidential elections by all of the following *except* (a) prohibiting a poll tax (b) setting a 30-day residency requirement (c) suspending literacy tests as a voting qualification (d) placing a penalty tax upon any qualified citizen who failed to vote.

28. Voters in the United States have the *most* direct voice in the selection of (a) the President (b) their United States Senator (c) the Chief Justice of the United States Supreme Court (d) their local postmaster.

29. "Without our two great political parties cutting across economic and geographic interests, democracy as we know it could never have been made to function." This statement probably means that (a) political parties in the United States tend to represent sectional interests (b) each political party appeals to a different social class (c) there is no significant difference between the Democratic and Republican parties (d) an important feature of our political system is the broadly based appeal of the two political parties.

30. "An informed public depends on accurate and open reporting by the news media. . . . The press therefore acts as an agent of the public at large." The quotation supports the idea that the news media have a responsibility to (a) report news in an objective fashion (b) create national agreement on controversial issues (c) eliminate editorials on controversial subjects (d) encourage public participation in news-gathering.

31. "Historically, in the United States, the extreme left and the extreme right fail and the center prevails." Which is the most valid interpretation of this statement? (a) Liberals have few supporters within the United States. (b) Progress is by its nature a revolutionary change. (c) Conservatives have the greatest strength within United States society. (d) Political and economic moderates have had the greatest influence in the United States.

———————————————— ESSAY QUESTIONS ————————————————

1. For 200 years the Constitution has been able to survive in a rapidly changing civilization. Giving *one* specific example for *each,* show how the original Constitution has been expanded by the following: *(a)* amendments *(b)* implied powers *(c)* custom and usage.

2. The United States Constitution is a living document. Describe a circumstance that led to the adoption of *one* amendment to the Constitution in each of the following periods: *(a)* 1789–1815 *(b)* 1860–1875 *(c)* 1900–1930 *(d)* 1930 to the present.

3. "The cure for the ills of democracy is not more democracy but more intelligence." *(a)* Give *one* argument for *or one* argument against this statement. *(b)* Discuss *two* attempts to cure the ills of democracy by more democracy.

4. Agree or disagree with each of the following statements and provide *two* arguments to support your opinion. *(a)* The general terminology used in the Constitution has turned out to be a blessing in disguise. *(b)* The method of amending the Constitution should be changed. *(c)* Citizens could improve the workings of our democracy if they involved themselves actively in political party affairs. *(d)* Third-party movements have been an important factor in the democratic process.

5. Over the years government in the United States has become more truly representative of all the people. *(a)* Show how *each* of the following has furthered this goal: (1) an amendment to the Constitution (2) a decision of the Supreme Court (3) a state or federal law (4) an action within political parties. *(b)* Describe *two* proposals that could lead to increased participation by citizens in government.

6. Present *two* arguments for or *two* arguments against *each* of the following possible amendments to the Constitution: *(a)* a ban on abortion *(b)* repeal of the right to keep and bear arms *(c)* requiring a balanced federal budget *(d)* allowing prayer in public schools *(e)* equal rights for women *(f)* a four-year term for members of the House of Representatives.

UNIT IV The Young Nation Tackles Its Many Problems

PART 1. The Federalists Guide the New Government

GEORGE WASHINGTON: OUR FIRST PRESIDENT

In our first Presidential election, George Washington received the vote of every elector. On April 30, 1789, he took the oath of office in the nation's temporary capital, New York City.

Washington, a dedicated man with a keen sense of duty, sought no personal power. He commanded the loyalty and service of outstanding patriots. With calm and farsighted judgment that rose above petty detail, Washington concentrated upon the larger view: the need to foster national unity, to assure a smoothly functioning administration, and to develop respect for the new government.

FIRST ACTS OF THE NEW GOVERNMENT

1. Judiciary Act of 1789. Washington signed the Judiciary Act of 1789 establishing district and circuit courts and specifying that the Supreme Court shall consist of six judges. Washington appointed the first Chief Justice, John Jay.

2. Bill of Rights. Washington urged Congress to give prompt attention to the matter of a federal bill of rights. Congress proposed a series of amendments and by 1791 the states ratified ten of them, constituting our Bill of Rights.

3. Formation of the First Cabinet. Washington appointed capable persons to the major offices in the new government. His closest assistants were Thomas Jefferson as secretary of state, Alexander Hamilton as secretary of the treasury, Henry Knox as secretary of war, and Edmund Randolph as attorney general. These four men, occasionally called together by Washington for advice, constituted the first Cabinet. The Cabinet officer who exercised the greatest influence on Washington's administration was Alexander Hamilton.

HAMILTON'S VIEWS

Hamilton was a brilliant thinker who possessed practical common sense and great foresight. A nationalist, Hamilton urged a strong central government and a loose interpretation of the Constitution. He feared the divisiveness of states' rights. Hamilton envisioned the development of the United States into an industrial nation and held that the success of the new government depended upon its securing the support of the aristocracies of birth, wealth, and ability. Such a successful government, Hamilton believed, would benefit the entire American citizenry.

156

HAMILTON'S FINANCIAL PROGRAM

The new government faced a most urgent problem: organizing its finances. Hamilton, in his reports on public credit and on manufacturing, urged Congress to enact the following program:

1. Payment of Debts. According to the Constitution, the new government assumed responsibility for all debts contracted by the central government during the Revolutionary War and Confederation periods. Hamilton recommended:

a. Full payment of the domestic debt—government bonds and certificates held by Americans. Hamilton proposed that this debt be "funded," meaning that all old bonds and certificates be exchanged for new bonds to be issued by the government.

b. Full payment of the foreign debt—loans extended by our Revolutionary War allies: France, Spain, and the Netherlands.

c. Assumption of state debts by the federal government, since these debts mainly were incurred in fighting the Revolutionary War.

Such repayments, Hamilton argued, would firmly establish the credit of the United States at home and abroad.

2. Excise Tax. To raise funds, Hamilton proposed an excise tax on various commodities, notably on distilled liquors.

3. Protective Tariff. Congress had already passed a tariff on imports. Hamilton urged that tariffs on manufactured goods be sharply increased to discourage the importation of such goods and to encourage American industry. Although Congress rejected Hamilton's proposal for a protective tariff, it raised rates slightly for revenue purposes.

4. Money Management. Hamilton urged the chartering of a *National Bank,* or Bank of the United States. This would be a private institution with a capital stock of $10 million, of which private investors would own 80 percent and the government 20 percent. The bank would serve as the government's financial agent, holding government moneys, assisting in tax collections, and selling government bonds. The bank also would issue bank notes, or paper money, but with a sufficient backing of specie (metals of gold and silver) to constitute a stable currency. The bank finally would provide loans for manufacturing and other business ventures and facilitate financial transactions throughout the nation.

5. Overall Objectives. Hamilton's program—to establish the national credit, encourage manufacturing, and provide a sound currency—favored persons of wealth and enterprise: creditors, merchants, and manufacturers. By giving these groups an economic stake in the new government, Hamilton believed that he was assuring its success.

ADOPTION OF HAMILTON'S PROGRAM DESPITE BITTER OPPOSITION

1. Repayment of the Domestic Debt. Speculators had purchased government bonds and certificates from their original owners at prices far below face value. The original owners now protested that repaying the domestic debt in full would enrich the speculators. Hamilton argued that the measure was necessary to establish the nation's credit. Hamilton won, and in 1790 Congress passed the Funding Bill.

2. Assumption of State Debts. Hamilton's opponents argued that this proposal was unfair to those states, chiefly in the South, that themselves had paid off their indebtedness. Hamilton won adoption of the proposal by logrolling. In exchange for southern votes, he promised to support the establishment of the nation's permanent capital in the South—on the banks of the Potomac River between Maryland and Virginia. (This site became the national capital—Washington, in the District of Columbia.)

3. Excise Taxes. Congress passed Hamilton's excise taxes. The excise tax on whisky chiefly affected farmers on the western frontier. For shipment to the East, they were converting much of their bulky, low-priced grain into less bulky and higher-priced liquor.

Farmers in western Pennsylvania refused to pay the whisky tax. In 1794 a group of these farmers put up armed resistance against federal tax collectors, an incident called the *Whisky Rebellion.* Hamilton prevailed upon Washington to recruit 15,000 troops and to crush the rebels. This action, contrasting with the inaction of the Confederation during Shays' Rebellion, demonstrated the power of the new government.

4. Bank of the United States. Opponents of the bank argued for a strict interpretation of the Constitution. Thomas Jefferson pointed out that Congress was not specifically granted the power to establish a National Bank. Hamilton replied that the bank was "necessary and proper" for carrying out the delegated power to "coin money" and "regulate the value thereof." Hamilton's loose interpretation was accepted by George Washington, who signed the bill chartering the bank.

RISE OF POLITICAL PARTIES

The bitter struggle over financial matters resulted in the formation of two political parties:

1. Federalists. The Federalists were led by John Adams and Alexander Hamilton. (The Federalists are considered the forebears of the mid-19th-century Whig party and of our present-day Republican party.)

COMPARISON OF FEDERALIST AND DEMOCRATIC-REPUBLICAN PARTIES

FEDERALIST PARTY	DEMOCRATIC-REPUBLICAN PARTY
1. Consisted of the upper classes of well-to-do people: merchants, manufacturers, bankers, and large landowners.	1. Consisted of the lower classes of common people: farmers, small shopkeepers, and city workers.
2. Was strongest in the North, especially in New England.	2. Was strongest in the South and West.
3. Believed in government by and for the "rich, well-born, and able," distrusted the common people, and feared what Federalists termed the "excesses of democracy."	3. Believed in government by capable leaders, emphasized that government should work in the interests of the common people, and strongly advocated democratic principles.
4. Favored a strong central government and consequently urged a loose interpretation of the Constitution.	4. Favored states' rights and consequently urged a strict interpretation of the Constitution.
5. Supported Hamilton's financial program as beneficial to the economic interests of the party's supporters.	5. Opposed Hamilton's financial program as harmful to the economic interests of the party's supporters.
6. In foreign affairs, tended to favor Britain, whose government was dominated by the upper classes.	6. In foreign affairs, tended to favor France, whose people had revolted in 1789 for liberty and equality.

2. Democratic-Republicans. The Anti-Federalists were led by James Madison and Thomas Jefferson. The Anti-Federalists were also known as the Democratic-Republicans. (From this party evolved our present-day Democratic party.)

FRENCH REVOLUTION OF 1789 STIRS AMERICA

Washington's inauguration coincided with the beginning of a 25-year period of revolution and warfare in Europe. In 1789 began the French Revolution, which led to the Reign of Terror—a short period of brutal suppression of all persons considered enemies of the revolution—and to an armed struggle between revolutionary France and a coalition of conservative European nations: Austria, Prussia, and Great Britain. In 1799 France fell under the rule of the ambitious Napoleon Bonaparte, and until 1815 Europe experienced almost continuous warfare. The prize was the domination of Europe. The chief contestants were France and Britain.

American public opinion quickly divided in regard to the early phase of the French Revolution and the outbreak of war in Europe.

1. The Democratic-Republicans sympathized with the French Revolution, arguing that the French were fighting for democracy, and pointing to similarities between the French and American revolutions. The French had (a) overthrown

the authority of their king, (b) issued the Declaration of the Rights of Man, and (c) proclaimed their democratic ideals as "liberty, equality, and fraternity."

2. The Federalists were unsympathetic to the French Revolution, pointing to the Reign of Terror as evidence of the "excesses of democracy." In the wars between Britain and France, the Federalists generally sympathized with Britain.

WASHINGTON'S PROCLAMATION OF NEUTRALITY (1793)

President Washington deplored the violent division of American public opinion regarding the European war. He also feared that, in accordance with the 1778 Franco-American treaty of alliance, the French republic would call for American military assistance, especially the use of American ports to outfit expeditions against British ships and colonies.

President Washington believed that for the young nation to become involved in the European war would be suicidal. His views were supported by Hamilton and Jefferson, both of whom urged neutrality. Hamilton further argued that the treaty of 1778 was no longer valid as we had signed it with the French monarchy, not with the French Republic. Washington did not declare the treaty invalid but instead issued a *Proclamation of Neutrality*. He declared America to be neutral and urged Americans to be impartial toward the warring nations.

"CITIZEN" GENÊT AFFAIR (1793)

The French Ambassador to the United States, "Citizen" Edmond Genêt, played upon the pro-French sentiments of many American citizens. Defying Washington's Proclamation of Neutrality, he outfitted privateers (privately owned armed ships) in American harbors and commissioned them to raid British ships and colonies.

Fearing that Genêt would involve the United States in a war against Great Britain, Washington ordered Genêt to halt his activities and, when this order was ignored, demanded Genêt's recall by the French government. Washington thus halted an attempt to breach our neutrality.

JAY TREATY WITH BRITAIN (1794–1795)

1. Background. To keep supplies from France, Britain ordered its powerful navy to seize American merchant ships bound for French ports. Such seizures violated the principle of *freedom of the seas,* the right of a neutral nation to trade with belligerents in goods not intended for war use. The British also impressed American sailors into the British navy. Anti-British sentiment in the United States was further aroused because the British still held posts in the Northwest Territory and because the Americans believed that the British were encouraging the Indians to raid American frontier settlements. Washington sent John Jay to London to settle the outstanding issues.

2. Provisions. Britain, confident that the United States would not go to war, made few concessions. The resulting *Jay Treaty* provided that *(a)* Great Britain withdraw its troops from the American Northwest, and *(b)* arbitration commissions settle financial claims of Americans against Britain and of the British against the United States.

3. American Reaction to the Treaty. The treaty's terms further aroused American resentment. The treaty *(a)* did not provide for freedom of the seas, and *(b)* did not pledge Britain to halt the seizure of American ships or the impressment of American sailors. The treaty secured minimal Senate ratification only through the full influence of Hamilton and Washington. In spite of its failings, the Jay Treaty meant peace with Britain.

PINCKNEY TREATY WITH SPAIN (1795)

Spain was alarmed by the Jay Treaty because it feared a secret Anglo-American alliance to seize the Spanish territories of Florida and Louisiana. Spain therefore negotiated outstanding problems with the United States.

The resulting *Pinckney Treaty* (1) established the Mississippi as the western boundary and the 31st parallel as the southern boundary of the United States (see map, page 52), and (2) guaranteed Americans free navigation of the entire Mississippi and the *right of deposit* at New Orleans—the right to transfer goods from riverboats to oceangoing ships without payment of a Spanish tariff. Because the Mississippi River and the port of New Orleans were economically vital to our western farmers, the Pinckney Treaty was an American triumph.

WASHINGTON'S FAREWELL ADDRESS (1796)

Prior to his retirement as President, George Washington gave advice to the new nation by his *Farewell Address*. In foreign affairs, Washington urged developing commercial relations with all nations but avoiding political entanglements. He stated, "It is our true policy to steer clear of permanent alliances with any portion of the foreign world." He added, however, that the United States could "safely trust to temporary alliances for extraordinary emergencies."

The Farewell Address urged a policy of noninvolvement, not isolation—a significant but subtle distinction. In practical effect, Washington's words strongly influenced the United States toward remaining politically aloof from the rest of the world by following a foreign policy of isolation. In the early days of the republic, isolation was advocated on the grounds that the United States (1) to a large extent was not concerned with Europe's quarrels, (2) was separated from Europe by 3000 miles of Atlantic Ocean, requiring a trip of several weeks, (3) lacked military and naval power, (4) might lose its independence if defeated in a war, (5) was internally divided on foreign policy so that any alliance would endanger national unity, and (6) should devote its energies to developing its economy and solving its domestic problems.

PRESIDENTIAL ELECTION OF 1796

1. Washington Retires. In 1796 George Washington announced his retirement. Washington was tired of the cares of public office and of the bitter criticisms hurled at him by the Democratic-Republicans. In his Farewell Address, Washington also warned that excessive political partisanship endangered the well-being of the nation.

Washington's refusal to run for a third term established the two-term precedent and the principle that no one person is indispensable to the republic. He returned to his home at Mount Vernon, Virginia, where he died a few years afterward.

2. Adams Wins the Election. John Adams, the Federalist candidate, defeated Thomas Jefferson, the Democratic-Republican candidate, by the close electoral vote of 71 to 68. The Federalist electors, however, split their second-place votes, and Jefferson, with the second largest number of votes in the electoral college, became Vice President. This election marked the only time that candidates running on opposing party tickets were elected President and Vice President. (A repetition was barred by the Twelfth Amendment, requiring separate ballots for President and Vice President.)

ADAMS FACES DIFFICULTIES WITH FRANCE (1797–1801)

1. French Hostility. French resentment at American foreign policy created serious problems for President Adams. The French government had been enraged by *(a)* Washington's Proclamation of Neutrality and *(b)* Senate ratification of the Jay Treaty. French warships and privateers attacked and seized American merchant ships. Anti-French sentiment developed in the United States, and many Federalists demanded war.

2. XYZ Affair (1797). Seeking peace, President Adams sent a special negotiating mission to Paris. The delegation was insulted by French agents who demanded that, before talks begin, the Americans pay a large bribe. Adams, enraged, reported the episode to Congress, identifying the French agents only as X, Y, and Z. Hence the incident became known as the *XYZ Affair*. American public opinion became strongly anti-French, as illustrated by the slogan, "Millions for defense, but not one cent for tribute."

3. Undeclared Naval Warfare (1798–1800). Congress voted large military funds, especially to build up the navy, and in 1798 established a Cabinet-level Navy Department. American warships and privateers engaged in an undeclared naval war with France, capturing about 100 French vessels.

Although Hamilton wanted to expand the war, Adams steadfastly desired peace. In 1800 Adams sent a second mission to France, now controlled by Napoleon Bonaparte. Both countries agreed to end the naval conflict and to cancel the 1778 treaty of alliance. Adams lost popularity with pro-war Federalists at home, but he had succeeded in ending the troublesome French treaty and in restoring the peace.

ALIEN AND SEDITION ACTS (1798)

While the crisis with France was at its height, Federalist partisans in Congress secured the passage of the *Alien and Sedition Acts*. Although the Federalists claimed that the laws were meant to protect the United States against alien agitators, many Americans held that the chief purpose of the laws was to weaken the Democratic-Republican party.

1. Naturalization Act. This act increased from five to 14 years the time required for immigrants to become American citizens. The Federalists lengthened the naturalization process since most immigrants, upon becoming citizens, voted for Democratic-Republican candidates.

2. Alien Acts. The first aliens act empowered the President to deport any alien whom he considered dangerous to the United States. The second aliens act authorized detention of enemy aliens in time of war. Although not used by Adams, these two laws caused some aliens to leave the country and caused others to refrain from speaking out against the Federalists.

3. Sedition Act. This act provided fines and imprisonment for any person who uttered or wrote "false, scandalous, and malicious" statements against Congress or the President. Even Hamilton disapproved of this law, and many people considered it a violation of the First Amendment. Nevertheless, the Sedition Act was used to bring to trial and convict ten Democratic-Republican printers and editors.

VIRGINIA AND KENTUCKY RESOLUTIONS (1798–1799)

Instead of weakening the Democratic-Republican party, the Alien and Sedition Acts actually strengthened it. Many people felt that the Federalist party threatened their civil liberties.

At the urging of Madison and Jefferson, the state legislatures of Virginia and Kentucky passed resolutions condemning these acts as unconstitutional. The Virginia and Kentucky Resolutions asserted that (1) the federal government was created by the states to serve as their agent, and (2) state legislatures could declare laws of Congress unconstitutional and therefore null and void. These resolutions constituted the first formal expression of states' rights and nullification.

Madison and Jefferson intended these resolutions primarily as campaign documents for the 1800 Presidential election. Nevertheless, the issue of *states' rights* and *nullification* was to plague the United States until the supremacy of the federal government was established by the Civil War.

SUMMARY OF THE FEDERALIST ERA (1789–1801)

In the election of 1800, the Federalists lost control of the executive and legislative branches of the government. (However, Federalist judges, appointed for life, remained in office and for many years dominated the Supreme Court. The most important of these was Chief Justice John Marshall.) Never again to win a national election, the Federalist party—but not its ideas—slowly disappeared from American life.

1. Federalist Achievements. During their 12 years in power, the Federalists had *(a)* fostered the loose interpretation of the Constitution and developed a workable system of government, *(b)* established the nation's credit and spurred economic prosperity, *(c)* created a court system, *(d)* demonstrated the ability of the government to enforce laws, *(e)* admitted three states to the Union, and *(f)* kept the nation from war and instituted a foreign policy of isolation.

2. Reasons for the Federalist Downfall. The major causes for the defeat of the Federalists were the following: *(a)* the spread of democratic ideals throughout the nation, especially in the West, *(b)* the growing realization that the Federalist party distrusted the common people, *(c)* widespread opposition to Federalist economic measures, *(d)* opposition to the Federalists' pro-English foreign policy, *(e)* bitter intraparty rivalry between Adams and Hamilton, and *(f)* public opposition to the Alien and Sedition Acts.

———————— MULTIPLE-CHOICE QUESTIONS ————————

1. President George Washington established a Cabinet to (a) help execute the laws of Congress (b) imitate the British Cabinet system (c) enforce the Bill of Rights (d) obtain the advice of a group of persons in whom he had confidence.
2. Alexander Hamilton based much of his financial program on his belief that (a) the success of the new government required the support of the propertied classes (b) the states should be discouraged from depending on the federal government (c) speculation in government securities had to be prevented (d) land was the most important source of wealth.
3. The *least* controversial of Hamilton's financial proposals was that the national government (a) assume the states' debts (b) pay its debt to foreign investors (c) levy the whisky tax (d) establish a National Bank.
4. Which powers did Congress use to charter the Bank of the United States in 1791? (a) concurrent powers (b) unlimited powers (c) implied powers (d) reserved powers.
5. On which issue were Alexander Hamilton and Thomas Jefferson in closest agreement? (a) establishing a National Bank (b) locating the national capital in the South (c) supporting Britain in its war with France (d) favoring manufacturing over farming.
6. Which was a result of Alexander Hamilton's financial policies? (a) issuing of cheap currency (b) extending participation in government to the people (c) strengthening the credit of the national government (d) defaulting on the nation's foreign debts.
7. The suppression of the Whisky Rebellion (a) constituted the first conflict between

the North and the South (b) limited the power of the states to nullify federal laws (c) violated the principle of "no taxation without representation" (d) illustrated the power of the federal government.

8. Political parties appeared in the United States shortly after the adoption of the Constitution because (a) Washington disliked Jefferson (b) the Constitution provides for the two-party system (c) Great Britain had a two-party system (d) differences arose over political and economic issues.

9. In his Farewell Address, Washington warned the United States against (a) expansion west of the Mississippi (b) the imperialistic ideas of Napoleon (c) permanent alliances with foreign nations (d) quarrels with Britain over commerce.

10. A person who favored George Washington's ideas on foreign policy would be most likely to object to United States (a) recognition of the Soviet Union (b) trade with Common Market nations (c) membership in the North Atlantic Treaty Organization (d) participation in international scientific conferences.

11. Which was a provision of the treaty ending the American Revolution that was *not* carried out by Great Britain until after the Jay Treaty? (a) evacuation of British troops from United States soil (b) determination of the western boundary of the United States (c) freedom of the seas for American merchant ships (d) sharing of the Newfoundland fisheries with the United States.

12. The *chief* goal of President George Washington's foreign policy was to (a) persuade Spain to grant independence to its American colonies (b) maintain the neutrality of the United States (c) prohibit United States commercial contacts with Europe (d) extend the boundaries of the United States beyond the Mississippi River.

13. President Washington's reason for issuing the Proclamation of Neutrality was to (a) fulfill our obligations to France (b) protect our interests in the Caribbean (c) safeguard our newly won independence (d) unify the country on foreign policy.

14. The Jay Treaty was criticized by Americans for its failure to provide for (a) arbitration as a method of settling disputes (b) British withdrawal of troops in the Northwest (c) the prevention of impressment (d) trade with the British East Indies.

15. "The great rule of conduct for the United States in relation to foreign nations is, in extending commercial relations, to have as little political connection with them as possible." This quotation is most closely associated with which concept? (a) militarism (b) intervention (c) nonrecognition (d) nonalignment.

16. The Pinckney Treaty directly benefited (a) New England merchants (b) farmers in the Ohio Valley (c) southern plantation owners (d) shipping interests on the Atlantic coast.

17. The XYZ Affair showed that (a) Americans would not tolerate French seizure of Louisiana (b) Americans were developing a sense of national pride (c) our government was pursuing a policy of aggression (d) our government was still bound to its alliance with France.

18. Which would probably promote the *greatest* cooperation among the people of a nation? (a) the election of a new national leader (b) a threat to national security from an outside force (c) the discovery of a new product that will improve the nation's economy (d) the decision to join an international peacekeeping organization.

19. The Alien and Sedition Acts (a) eased naturalization procedures for aliens (b) were supported by the Democratic-Republicans (c) were used to silence opposition to the Federalist administration (d) had widespread public support.

20. According to the doctrine of nullification, the right to determine the constitutionality of an act of Congress resides in (a) Congress itself (b) the states (c) the United States Supreme Court only (d) the executive branch of the federal government.

21. The Democratic-Republican party used the Alien and Sedition Acts to (a) unite the country for possible war against Great Britain (b) advance arguments for a strong central government (c) indicate approval for war against France (d) influence voters against the Federalists.
22. Which statement about the Virginia and Kentucky Resolutions is true? (a) They supported the Alien and Sedition Acts. (b) They aimed to prevent sectionalism. (c) They reflected the views of most Federalists. (d) They contributed to the defeat of the Federalists in 1800.
23. Which was a major contribution by the Federalist party to the United States? (a) strengthening of the central government (b) aid to France (c) the states' rights theory (d) a decentralized banking system.

─────────────── **ESSAY QUESTIONS** ───────────────

1. President Herbert Hoover said, "The true eulogy of Washington is this mighty nation." *(a)* Describe *two* services of George Washington to the government of the United States. *(b)* State *one* outstanding trait that fitted him to be a leader of democracy.
2. "As Hamilton's measures were debated in Congress, the country gradually divided into two parties, each with its own program." *(a)* Mention the *two* parties referred to in the quotation and give the names of *two* prominent leaders of each party. *(b)* State *three* essential differences in the principles advocated by these two parties.
3. It has been said that the principles of Hamilton and Jefferson are still very much alive. *(a)* Discuss briefly a difference of opinion between Hamilton and Jefferson concerning *two* of the following issues of their day: federal taxation, protective tariff, national control of banking, national debt. *(b)* Select *two* issues listed in part *(a)* and show why *each* has been an important problem in the United States during the 20th century.
4. *(a)* For the Alien and Sedition Acts, show that their actual result differed from the intended purpose of their sponsors. *(b)* Provide the same analysis for the Virginia and Kentucky Resolutions. *(c)* State *one* important conclusion that you can draw from your discussion of these documents.
5. Although the Federalist party compiled a record of considerable achievement while in power, it lost the election of 1800 and thereafter disappeared as a political party. *(a)* Discuss *three* achievements of the Federalist party. *(b)* Discuss *two* factors that led to the downfall of the Federalist party.

PART 2. The Democratic-Republicans Take Control

ELECTION OF 1800

Thomas Jefferson and Aaron Burr, meant to be respectively the Presidential and Vice Presidential candidates of the Democratic-Republican party, defeated the Federalist contenders. Victory in the election, however, did not assure Jefferson the Presidency. According to the original Constitution, each elector was to cast two ballots unmarked as to office. The candidate with the largest number of votes became President; the candidate with the second largest number of votes became Vice President. As each Democratic-Republican elector gave one vote to each of the party's candidates, Jefferson and Burr were tied in electoral votes, and the election was thrown into the House of Representatives. This was not the House elected in 1800 but the Federalist "lame duck" House chosen in 1798. Disliking Jefferson, many Federalists backed Burr, and the vote in the House was deadlocked for 35 ballots. On the thirty-sixth ballot, a number of Federalists abstained from voting and ensured Jefferson's election. These Federalists were influenced by Hamilton, who considered Burr a scoundrel. Although Hamilton disagreed with Jefferson on most political issues, Hamilton believed him to be an honorable person. One result of this election was the adoption of the Twelfth Amendment, requiring separate ballots for President and Vice President.

JEFFERSON'S VIEWS

Thomas Jefferson, third President of the United States, was a man of deep and abiding faith in the common people. Considering democracy the ideal form of government, he held that democracy could function best in an agricultural society of small, independent farmers. He favored popular education and careful protection of civil liberties. Jefferson disliked pomp and ceremony in government, preferring simplicity. He believed in strictly limiting the role of government. Although he urged a strict interpretation of the Constitution in opposing the National Bank, Jefferson was not doctrinaire and supported a loose interpretation when he believed that the national welfare required it, as in the the purchase of Louisiana. Of his many achievements, Jefferson wished future generations of Americans to remember him for these three: (1) the Declaration of Independence, (2) the Virginia Statute of Religious Freedom, and (3) the founding of the University of Virginia—none associated with his Presidency.

Jefferson viewed his election as the triumph of the common citizen over the propertied and aristocratic classes and proclaimed it the *Revolution of 1800.*

JEFFERSON AS PRESIDENT (1801–1809)

1. Reverses Some Federalist Policies. Jefferson *(a)* secured Congressional repeal of the excise tax on whisky, *(b)* curtailed army and navy expenditures and, with the assistance of Secretary of the Treasury *Albert Gallatin,* reduced the national debt, *(c)* secured repeal of the Naturalization Act, thereby restoring the previous five-year waiting period for citizenship; permitted the Alien and Sedition Acts to expire; and pardoned persons still imprisoned under the Sedition Act, *(d)* replaced some Federalist officeholders with Democratic-Republicans, and *(e)* secured repeal of the Judiciary Act of 1801, by which the Federalists had created new circuit courts. The Democratic-Republicans thusly removed those Federalist judges whom Adams had appointed near the end of his term, supposedly up to midnight of his last day in office—the so-called *midnight judges.*

2. Continues Other Federalist Policies. *(a)* Except for repealing the whisky tax, Jefferson continued Hamilton's financial program. Jefferson continued the full repayment of the domestic debt, including the assumed debt of the states, and he permitted the National Bank to operate undisturbed. *(b)* In his inaugural address, Jefferson reaffirmed Washington's foreign policy of nonalignment. Jefferson urged the United States to seek "peace, commerce, and honest friendship with all nations, entangling alliances with none." *(c)* When the needs of western settlers led him to purchase Louisiana, Jefferson moved toward the Federalist view of loose construction of the Constitution.

PURCHASE OF LOUISIANA (1803)

1. Importance of the Mississippi River and New Orleans. In the early 19th century, the settlers west of the Appalachian Mountains found it difficult to send their bulky agricultural produce overland to eastern markets and seaports. Instead, they depended for transportation upon the Mississippi River and the port of New Orleans. By the Pinckney Treaty with Spain (1795), the Americans had gained the right of deposit at New Orleans.

2. Napoleon and the Louisiana Territory. In 1800 Napoleon Bonaparte of France secretly secured the vast Louisiana Territory from Spain. In 1802 the right of deposit at New Orleans was suspended. This action enraged the western settlers and gave new weight to Jefferson's opinion that the foreign nation possessing New Orleans "is our natural and habitual enemy." Jefferson quickly instructed Robert Livingston and James Monroe to negotiate with France for the purchase of New Orleans. Napoleon meanwhile decided to sell the entire territory. He *(a)* needed money to carry on his war against Britain, *(b)* could not defend the territory while the British navy controlled the seas, and *(c)* had abandoned plans for an American empire—in part because his armies had been unable to suppress a black slave revolt on Hispaniola led by *Toussaint-Louverture.* Livingston and Monroe readily agreed to a purchase price of $15 million.

3. Constitutional Problem. Jefferson was disturbed by the agreement, for the Constitution did not specifically give the federal government the power to purchase territory. A "strict" interpreter of the Constitution, Jefferson suggested a Constitutional amendment to provide the necessary power. He was warned, however, that delay might lead Napoleon to withdraw his offer. Jefferson consequently agreed to purchase Louisiana under the Presidential power to make treaties, thus adopting a loose interpretation of the Constitution.

4. Exploration of the Territory. The entire nation was eager to learn of the resources and possibilities of the new territory. Jefferson arranged several journeys of exploration. In 1804 *Meriwether Lewis* and *William Clark* started out from St. Louis, went up the Missouri River and across the Rocky Mountains, and reached the Columbia River in the Oregon Territory and then the Pacific Ocean. In 1805 *Zebulon Pike* led an expedition up the Mississippi to look for its source.

Louisiana Territory and Explorations 1804–1806

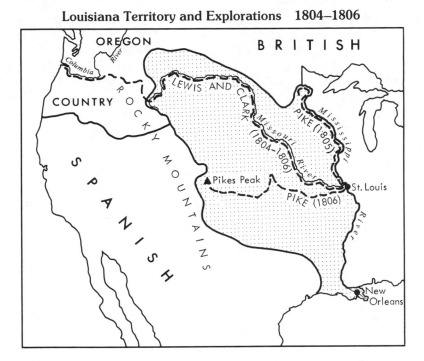

In 1806 Pike led another expedition to the Rockies in what is today Colorado. Lewis and Clark, as well as Pike, issued optimistic reports and thereby encouraged settlers.

5. Significance. The purchase of Louisiana *(a)* almost doubled the area and greatly increased the wealth of the United States, *(b)* gave the United States control of the entire Mississippi, *(c)* removed French influence in North America, *(d)* established a precedent for future purchases of territory, and *(e)* moved the Democratic-Republicans toward a loose interpretation of the Constitution.

NAPOLEONIC WARS: FRANCE AGAINST GREAT BRITAIN

In 1803 France and Britain renewed their conflict, and for the next 12 years they struggled for control of Europe. While, at first, France held supremacy on land, Britain dominated the seas. Their struggle is often referred to as the battle of "the tiger against the shark."

1. Economic Warfare. While military action was temporarily stalemated, the two countries endeavored to strike at each other economically. Napoleon issued the *Berlin* and *Milan Decrees* (1806–1807) restricting neutral trade with Britain. The British government issued *Orders in Council* (1806–1807) restricting neutral trade with the French-held continent. Since Britain had the stronger navy, its blockade of the European continent was far more successful than France's blockade of the British Isles.

2. Effect Upon the United States. The neutral United States was adversely affected by these blockades. The American merchant marine had grown greatly, and many American shippers carried on a prosperous but risky trade with wartime Europe. If only one out of every three ships carrying foodstuffs and raw materials got through the blockades, its profits more than made up for the losses of ships caught. The greater damage to American commerce was inflicted by the British, who, in addition to seizing many American ships, impressed several thousand American sailors into British service, claiming that they were deserters from the British navy.

3. *Chesapeake-Leopard* Affair (1807). Off the Virginia coast the captain of the *Leopard,* a British warship, demanded to search the American navy vessel *Chesapeake.* When the captain of the *Chesapeake* refused, the British fired on the *Chesapeake,* boarded it, and took off four sailors as deserters. Three were American citizens. This indignity inflamed the American public to demand that Jefferson take retaliatory action.

EMBARGO ACT (1807–1809)

To avoid war, Jefferson secured from Congress the *Embargo Act* (1807). It forbade American ships to sail to foreign ports and prohibited American exports to all foreign countries. Jefferson believed that by depriving Britain and France of our foodstuffs and raw materials, the United States could compel these nations to change their policies toward American shipping. The warring nations, however, were not sufficiently distressed by the Embargo Act's "peaceable coercion."

In the maritime New England states, meanwhile, the embargo caused considerable economic hardship, almost completely destroying the region's commerce and causing widespread unemployment. Jefferson and the embargo were roundly condemned by New England Federalists. The agricultural sections— South and West—were also somewhat hurt as they lost foreign markets for their farm produce. In 1809, near the end of his second term, Jefferson signed the *Non-Intercourse Act,* repealing the Embargo Act but continuing the prohibition on trade with Britain and France.

MADISON AND THE DRIFT TO WAR (1809–1812)

1. Efforts for Peace. James Madison, who succeeded Jefferson as President, tried for three years to protect American shipping by diplomatic negotiations, but he was unsuccessful. Meanwhile, the war spirit in America grew stronger.

2. "War Hawks." In 1810 southern and western voters elected to Congress a group of Democratic-Republicans called the "War Hawks." Led by John Calhoun of South Carolina and Henry Clay of Kentucky, they demanded war against Britain to acquire Canada and against Britain's ally, Spain, to acquire

Florida. These acquisitions, they argued, would remove European powers from American borders and would open new lands for liberty-loving Americans.

In 1812 Madison surrendered to the war spirit and asked Congress for a declaration of war against Britain.

CAUSES OF THE WAR OF 1812

The major causes of this war were: (1) Britain's seizure of American ships and impressment of American sailors. (2) American resentment of Britain, dating back to Revolutionary days. (3) American belief, probably correct, that the British in Canada were arming the Indians and inciting them to raid American settlements. (4) American ambitions to annex Canada and Florida.

Historical Analysis. *Which was the primary cause of the War of 1812—maritime rights or territorial expansion?* Historians have long debated this issue.

Maritime Rights. Historians supporting this point of view claim that "the impressment issue was the rock that wrecked the last hope of peace." They point out that the diplomacy preceding the war dealt with maritime rights and that Madison's war message to Congress emphasized impressment of American sailors and seizure of American ships— both violations of our right as a neutral nation to freedom of the seas.

Territorial Expansion. Historians supporting this point of view claim that "without the peculiar grievances and ambitions of the West, there would have been no war." The "War Hawks" wanted to end Indian raids and to annex Canada and Florida. These historians point to the Congressional vote favoring war—by little more than a majority— showing that the Northeast, most directly concerned with maritime rights, was mainly opposed to the war and refused government requests for soldiers and money, whereas the South and West, most strongly for territorial expansion, were wholeheartedly in favor of the war. They also quote John Randolph, a Virginia Representative opposed to the war, who charged in a House speech that "agrarian cupidity [greed], not maritime rights, urges the war."

MILITARY EVENTS OF THE WAR (1812–1815)

(1) American attempts to invade Canada all proved unsuccessful. (2) British attempts to invade the United States from Canada were thwarted when British naval squadrons were defeated by Captain Oliver Perry on Lake Erie and by Captain Thomas Macdonough on Lake Champlain. Perry reported his victory with the message, "We have met the enemy and they are ours." (3) On the high seas, American privateers and naval vessels—notably the warships *Constitution* (nicknamed "Old Ironsides") and *United States*—at first won great victories. In time, however, the British navy asserted its superiority and instituted a tight block-

The War of 1812

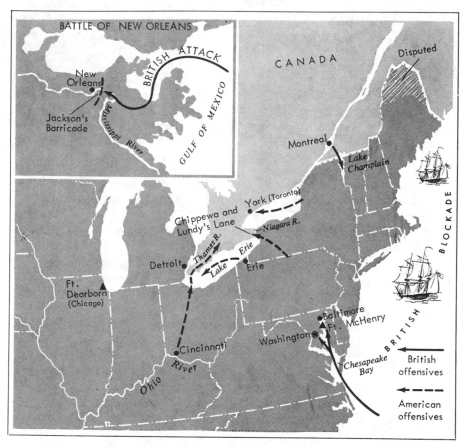

ade of the American coast. (4) The British invaded the Chesapeake Bay area, captured Washington, D.C., burned many government buildings, and then advanced on Fort McHenry at Baltimore. Fort McHenry withstood the British bombardment, inspiring Francis Scott Key—held prisoner on a British ship—to write *The Star-Spangled Banner.* (5) The British attempted an invasion of the American Southwest but were decisively defeated at New Orleans. Andrew Jackson, the American commander, overnight became a national hero. (With modern methods of communication, this battle would not have been fought, since a peace treaty had already been signed in Europe.)

TREATY OF GHENT

In December 1814, at Ghent, Belgium, negotiators signed a treaty of peace that reestablished the prewar boundaries of the United States. The treaty did not mention the seizure of American ships and the impressment of American sailors. However, with the European war over, these issues were no longer crucial.

RESULTS OF THE WAR OF 1812

1. Strengthening Isolation. Americans had been directed toward isolation by the foreign policies of both Washington and Jefferson. After the War of 1812, Americans turned still more sharply away from Europe's affairs and concentrated upon domestic problems.

2. Spurring Westward Migration. Having lost maritime jobs, some New Englanders migrated westward. Their travels and settlements were safer since several war battles had destroyed hostile Indian forces.

3. Encouraging American Industry. With the war cutting off British imports, Americans met the need for goods by increasing domestic manufactures. Also, since the war made shipbuilding and foreign commerce unprofitable, investors placed their capital in industrial establishments, chiefly New England textile mills.

4. Ending the Federalist Party. The Federalists, who had retained political power in the New England states, disapproved of the war, bitterly calling it "Mr. Madison's War." The New England states refused to honor federal requests for financial assistance and troops.

In 1814 the leading Federalists held the *Hartford Convention.* Advocating states' rights and nullification, they demanded that the Constitution be amended to require a two-thirds vote of Congress to admit new states and declare war; further, they hinted at secession. (The Federalist arguments were similar to the Democratic-Republican statements in the Virginia and Kentucky Resolutions. Check the Index.)

Soon after the Hartford Convention, the nation learned of Jackson's triumph at New Orleans and of the signing of the Treaty of Ghent. In public opinion, the Federalists were associated with treason and thereafter the Federalist party went out of existence.

5. Inspiring American Nationalism. Rejoicing in their military achievements, Americans felt greater pride in their country. The War of 1812, therefore, is often called the "Second War for American Independence."

————————— **MULTIPLE-CHOICE QUESTIONS** —————————

1. A direct result of the election of 1800 was the (a) settlement of differences with France and Britain (b) charter for the first Bank of the United States (c) provision for separate ballots in the electoral college for President and Vice President (d) split in the Democratic-Republican party.

2. The election of 1800 has sometimes been referred to as a revolution because (a) the Western farmers were in armed rebellion (b) Aaron Burr was tried for treason (c) the Twelfth Amendment was added to the Constitution (d) the incoming administration was more sympathetic to agricultural than to commercial interests.

3. Which characteristic of our country today may be considered a fulfillment of one of Jefferson's principles? (a) an industrialized society (b) popular elections (c) a large public debt (d) a strong central government.

4. On which issue did Thomas Jefferson reverse his opinion of strict construction of the Constitution? (a) the Bank of the United States (b) the purchase of the Louisiana Territory (c) the moving of the capital to Washington, D.C. (d) the appointment of the "midnight judges."

5. "The moment France takes possession of New Orleans, we must marry ourselves to the British fleet and nation." This argument influenced the United States to (a) enter into a treaty of alliance with Spain (b) purchase the Louisiana Territory from France (c) wage a naval war against France (d) adopt neutrality legislation.

6. The primary reason for our purchase of the Louisiana Territory was to provide (a) people on the frontier with unrestricted use of the Mississippi River (b) Napoleon with money in return for French assistance during the American Revolution (c) New England manufacturers with a source of cheap raw materials (d) land for Indian reservations.

7. Which was a direct result of the purchase of the Louisiana Territory? (a) an amendment to the Constitution permitting the federal government to purchase land (b) the opening of a vast region for fur trading and farming (c) the loss of Canada by France (d) the elimination of Spain from the North American continent.

8. Which economic group was most severely harmed by the Embargo Act of 1807? (a) New England shippers (b) southern cotton growers (c) frontier farmers (d) northern factory workers.

9. The Embargo and Non-Intercourse Acts illustrate the (a) unsuccessful attempt of the United States to isolate itself from a European conflict (b) success of the United States in obtaining recognition of its neutral rights (c) confiscation of British investments in America (d) overwhelming support given by Congress to President Jefferson's policy.

10. The United States reacted strongly to interference with its commerce on the open seas chiefly because such interference (a) limited its naval power (b) hurt its balance of payments (c) violated its rights as a nation (d) threatened its friendship with France.

11. During the administrations of Presidents Jefferson and Madison, the expression "British man-stealing" referred to (a) the sale of African slaves in British West Indian ports (b) the practice of forcibly enlisting United States sailors into the British Navy (c) Britain's incitement of Indian raids against frontier settlements (d) Britain's refusal to help the United States combat drug traffic.

12. Which was the *main* reason why the United States declared war on Great Britain rather than on France in 1812? (a) France had aided the United States during the American Revolution. (b) France's democratic revolutionary principles were similar to those of the United States. (c) New England merchants wanted revenge for shipping losses. (d) The "War Hawks" favored the conquest of Canada.

13. The United States government had difficulty financing the War of 1812 because (a) western farmers refused to pay excise taxes (b) the revenue tariff had been repealed (c) New Englanders refused to lend money to the federal government (d) the internal improvements program had drained the federal treasury.

14. Francis Scott Key was inspired to write *The Star-Spangled Banner* by the (a) American victory at New Orleans (b) defense of Baltimore (c) triumphs of *Old Ironsides* (d) signing of the Treaty of Ghent.

15. The Treaty of Ghent failed to prevent the Battle of New Orleans because (a) the United States was determined to destroy the British navy (b) the "War Hawks"

continued to be important (c) Madison was eager to win a military reputation (d) communication at that time was slow.

16. One reason why the United States was able to maintain its independence in *both* the Revolutionary War and the War of 1812 was that (a) American troops were better trained than British troops (b) American troops had the support of Indians in the Northwest Territory (c) Great Britain was fighting other enemies (d) the British navy avoided battles with American ships.

17. An important result of the War of 1812 was that it (a) strengthened the Federalist party (b) introduced ironclad naval vessels (c) marked the end of the American policy of isolation (d) encouraged manufacturing in New England.

18. Two Americans, known as "War Hawks," who were eager for war in 1812 were (a) Jackson and Madison (b) Webster and Clinton (c) Calhoun and Clay (d) Burr and John Quincy Adams.

19. Which of the following events occurred last? (a) adoption of the federal Bill of Rights (b) Hartford Convention (c) election of James Madison as President (d) Whisky Rebellion.

——————————————— **ESSAY QUESTIONS** ———————————————

1. *(a)* State *two* fundamental principles of the Democratic-Republican party under the leadership of Thomas Jefferson. *(b)* Show, by using a specific illustration, how Jefferson modified *one* fundamental principle of his party. *(c)* Describe *two* ways in which Jefferson's interests went far beyond political affairs. *(d)* In which of our two major parties would Jefferson probably feel more at home today? Present *one* argument to defend your opinion.

2. The United States from 1789 to 1815 was in a position similar to new African and Asian nations after 1945. *(a)* Prove this statement by discussing *two* similarities. *(b)* Why do newly emerging nations tend to favor a policy of nonalignment? *(c)* What is the distinction between nonalignment and isolation? *(d)* Give *one* argument for or against a United States policy of isolation today.

3. Some historians claim that the War of 1812 was "rash and unnecessary" for the United States. *(a)* Evaluate *two* causes of the war to show whether or not each supports the claim of "rash and unnecessary." *(b)* Discuss *two* results of the war to show whether or not each benefited the United States.

4. During the early history of our national government, its authority was frequently challenged. *(a)* Show how the authority of the national government was challenged by organized opposition within the United States on *two* occasions between 1790 and 1815. *(b)* Give a result of each controversy.

UNIT V   The Nation Is Torn Between Nationalism and Sectionalism

PART 1.   The War of 1812 Is Followed by a Temporary Upsurge of Nationalism

NATIONALISM IN AMERICA

Although some nationalistic and patriotic feeling was evident early in our history, this feeling gained strong momentum in the years immediately following the War of 1812. As nationalism briefly became dominant over sectionalism (check the Index), most Americans (1) were proud to be known as Americans, rather than as residents of a state or section, (2) gave primary loyalty to the nation, rather than to a state or section, (3) favored extending the powers of the central government, and (4) considered problems from a national, rather than from a sectional, viewpoint.

ECONOMIC LEGISLATION AND NATIONALISM

By 1815 the Democratic-Republicans in control of the government were considering problems not as representatives of the agricultural South and West, but from the viewpoint of national interest. Discarding their previous positions, the Democratic-Republicans adopted Federalist ideas in enacting the following legislation:

1. Second National Bank. Following 1811, when the charter of the first National Bank expired, the United States experienced financial disorder. State banks, although numerous, could not provide a uniform national currency. In addition, they could not provide a sound currency, since they often lacked adequate specie reserves for their paper money. Finally, the state banks could not provide a safe depository for federal funds.

In 1816 Congress passed and President Madison signed a law chartering the second Bank of the United States. Although Democratic-Republicans previously had opposed such a bank as unconstitutional, they now supported it in the national interest.

2. Protective Tariff of 1816. Previously, the United States had maintained a revenue tariff—designed chiefly to provide income for the government rather than to protect American industries from competition by low-priced foreign imports. In spite of the lack of protection, American "infant industries," such as New England textile mills and Pennsylvania iron smelters, had prospered before and during the War of 1812, when competition from abroad declined sharply. After the War of 1812, American manufacturers faced renewed competition, as the British planned the deliberate "dumping" of low-priced goods to stifle the new industries. To counter this threat, Congress members from all sections approved the Tariff of 1816 with its protective rates. Although consumers would

176

have to pay more for American-made goods, the Democratic-Republicans agreed, as Jefferson stated, that manufactures were "necessary to our independence."

3. Internal Improvements at Federal Expense. In 1806 Congress had approved the construction of the *National* or *Cumberland Road* extending from Cumberland, Maryland, westward across the Appalachian Mountains to Wheeling on the Ohio River. Congress, however, appropriated limited funds, and construction lagged. By 1815 only 20 miles had been completed.

The war years demonstrated that our internal transportation system was inadequate for national needs. In 1816 Congress voted substantial new funds, and, within two years, the Cumberland Road was extended an additional 110 miles to reach Wheeling. Supporters of the Cumberland Road argued that since the road would help bind the nation together, its cost should be borne by the federal government.

POLITICAL AFFAIRS AND NATIONALISM: THE ERA OF GOOD FEELING

The years 1817–1823, marked by an absence of open political strife, are called the *Era of Good Feeling.* The Federalists disappeared as a national political party following their overwhelming defeat in the 1816 election. James Monroe, the victorious Democratic-Republican candidate, was hailed throughout the country, even in New England. In 1820 Monroe was reelected, receiving all the electoral votes but one. Having adopted many Federalist ideas, the Democratic-Republicans, as the only major political party, reflected national unity. Below the surface, however, bitter sectional strife was brewing, and the Democratic-Republican party split apart following the 1824 Presidential election.

FOREIGN AFFAIRS AND NATIONALISM

With the American people strongly nationalistic, the nation's leaders were able to conduct a vigorous foreign policy. In turn, their capable handling of foreign affairs furthered American nationalism.

1. Rush-Bagot Agreement (1817). The United States and Great Britain agreed to naval disarmament on the Great Lakes. Later, this agreement was extended to provide for disarmament along the land border between the United States and Canada. Today, the entire 3000-mile United States–Canadian border remains unfortified. The Rush-Bagot Agreement was significant because it (*a*) treated the United States and Britain as equals, (*b*) demonstrated mutual trust and understanding, and (*c*) provided an early example of disarmament.

2. Convention of 1818. This treaty fixed the boundary line between the United States and Canada at the 49th parallel of latitude from Lake of the Woods (in northern Minnesota) to the Rocky Mountains. This line became known as the *Treaty Line of 1818.* The treaty also provided that the United States and Britain jointly occupy the Oregon Country.

3. Purchase of Florida (1819)

a. Spanish-Owned Florida: A Trouble Spot. In the hands of Spain, Florida housed pirates, smugglers, runaway slaves, and Seminole Indians. With the Spanish authorities too weak to restrain them, the Indians raided American settlements in the Southeast and then retreated to safety across the international border to Florida.

In 1818 Andrew Jackson led an American military force into Florida, crushed the Seminole Indians, and captured two Spanish forts. Spain, having already lost west Florida to the United States, now realized that unless it sold the rest of Florida it might lose the territory by force.

b. Adams-Onís Treaty. Secretary of State John Quincy Adams and Spanish minister Luis de Onís agreed that Spain sell Florida to the United States for $5 million. Also called the *Transcontinental Treaty,* the Adams-Onís agreement provided that the United States give up claims to Texas and that Spain accept the 42nd parallel as the boundary between Spain's rebellious colony of Mexico and the Oregon Country.

Although the South gained the most, the entire country, motivated by nationalism, supported the purchase of Florida.

4. Monroe Doctrine (1823)

a. Latin American Independence. While Spain was entangled in the Napoleonic Wars, the Spanish colonists in Latin America revolted and began a series of wars for independence. (Brazil, meanwhile, threw off the rule of Portugal.) Spanish attempts to retain control were defeated by the colonists under the leadership of *José de San Martín, Bernardo O'Higgins,* and "the George Washington of South America," *Simón Bolívar.*

The United States hailed Latin American independence because (1) the American Revolution against Britain had helped inspire the Latin American colonists, (2) the United States preferred having weak independent republics to the south instead of the more powerful monarchical Spain, and (3) American merchants and shippers had built up a profitable trade with the independent Latin American countries. Such trade had previously been barred by Spain, whose mercantilist regulations required its colonies to trade only with it.

b. Immediate Causes for Issuing the Doctrine. In 1823 President Monroe was faced with two threats of foreign intervention in the Western Hemisphere. (1) A reactionary European alliance of Austria, Prussia, France, and Russia—all opposed to revolution anywhere—was rumored planning to reconquer Latin America for Spain. (2) Russian expansion southward from Alaska into Oregon and California constituted a threat to ultimate American expansion to the Pacific.

c. Rejection of the British Proposal for a Joint Declaration. Britain too opposed the restoration of Spanish control in Latin America, since British merchants also had built up a profitable trade with the new nations. *George Canning,* the British foreign minister, proposed that Britain and the United States issue a joint declaration warning Europe against any attempt to deny independence to Latin America.

John Quincy Adams, the American secretary of state, vigorously opposed a joint declaration. He insisted that we act alone, as befits a proud, independent, nationalistic people. Adams did not want the United States to appear as a tiny boat coming "in the wake of the British man-of-war." Adams' point of view and much of his phrasing were accepted by Monroe. In his annual message to Congress, Monroe included a statement of Presidential foreign policy that became known as the *Monroe Doctrine.*

d. Basic Ideas of the Doctrine. (1) The Western Hemisphere was closed to further European colonization. (2) The United States would not interfere with the existing colonies of any European power. (3) The United States would not interfere in the internal affairs of any European power. (4) Any attempt by European powers to intervene in the Western Hemisphere would be regarded as "dangerous to our peace and safety." (This final statement did not commit the United States to a definite course of action in case of European intervention. Instead, it left the American response up to the discretion of the President.)

e. Significance and Some Results. The American people approved of the Monroe Doctrine for (1) expressing the prevailing spirit of American nationalism, (2) evidencing America's importance in world affairs, and (3) attempting to isolate the entire Western Hemisphere from European affairs. Latin Americans generally welcomed the Monroe Doctrine as a friendly offer of assistance.

The Russians in 1824 agreed to halt their expansion by accepting the 54° 40′ parallel as the southern boundary of Alaska. The European alliance did not pursue its rumored plans for reconquest of Latin America. Its primary consideration was probably the power of Britain and the British navy. At that time, the United States hardly had the power to enforce the Monroe Doctrine. By 1862–1867, however, when the Doctrine was challenged for the first time, the United States had grown powerful enough to uphold it against France in the Maximilian Affair. (Check the Index.) To this day the Monroe Doctrine survives as a cornerstone of American foreign policy.

THE SUPREME COURT AND NATIONALISM

1. Role of John Marshall. (For Marshall's background and views, check the Index.) While serving as Chief Justice of the Supreme Court, John Marshall reflected and strengthened the spirit of American nationalism by his decisions speaking for the Court majorities, as follows:

2. Major Cases

a. Marbury vs. Madison (1803). Marshall assumed for the Supreme Court the power of judicial review. For details of this case, check the Index.

b. Dartmouth College vs. Woodward (1819)

(1) *Issue.* Without the consent of the trustees (governing body) of Dartmouth College, a New Hampshire law revised the college's original charter of

incorporation and placed the college under state control. The trustees objected and sued William Woodward to recover possession of the college records.

(2) *Decision.* Speaking for a 6-to-1 Court majority, Marshall held: (a) Dartmouth's charter was a contract protected by the Constitutional provision that states may not pass any "law impairing the obligation of contracts." This part of the decision assured not only colleges, but also business interests, that charters, once granted, were fixed and not changeable according to the fancy of state legislatures. (b) The state law revising the Dartmouth charter was therefore unconstitutional. Marshall thus expanded the Supreme Court's power of judicial review to invalidate a state law.

c. McCulloch vs. Maryland (1819)

(1) *Issue.* Maryland's legislators, hostile toward the federally chartered Bank of the United States, placed a heavy tax upon the bank's Baltimore branch. James McCulloch, a bank official, refused to pay the tax.

(2) *Decision.* Speaking for a unanimous Court, Marshall declared the Maryland bank tax unconstitutional. He (a) denied the power of a state to tax an agency chartered by the federal government, declaring that "the power to tax involves the power to destroy," and (b) upheld the constitutionality of the United States Bank, thus supporting the doctrines of loose construction and implied powers.

d. Gibbons vs. Ogden (1824)

(1) *Issue.* Aaron Ogden, operating under a New York State monopoly grant, ran a ferry on the Hudson River between New York and New Jersey. Thomas Gibbons ran a competing line under a federal license. Ogden sued to halt Gibbons.

(2) *Decision.* The Supreme Court unanimously declared that New York's grant of a Hudson River monopoly to Ogden was invalid. Marshall held that this grant violated the Constitution's delegation of interstate commerce to federal control. Further, he defined commerce in the broadest possible terms. Marshall thus prepared the way for federal regulation of railroads, buses, airlines, radio and television broadcasting, business organizations, and labor unions—when engaged in interstate commerce.

THE WEST AND NATIONALISM

1. Routes to the West

a. *Early Turnpikes and Public Roads.* (1) Even before the War of 1812, western settlers were traveling a privately built toll road linking Philadelphia to Lancaster—the *Lancaster Turnpike.* These settlers then crossed the Appalachian Mountains and reached Pittsburgh by taking the *Pennsylvania State Road.* This road had been built by a private company and financed in part by the state. At Pittsburgh they transferred to flatboats and traveled down the Ohio River. (2) Settlers also crossed the Appalachians by following the *National* or *Cumberland*

Major Roads and Waterways to the West

Road. In 1818 this road, which started at Cumberland, Maryland, reached Wheeling on the Ohio River. By 1852 the road was extended to Vandalia in Illinois. This road was financed partly by federal funds derived from the sale of land. (3) Farther to the south, settlers traversed Appalachian mountain passes by following state roads such as the *Wilderness Road.* This road went through the *Cumberland Gap,* an often-traveled mountain pass running from North Carolina into Tennessee and Kentucky.

   b. Steamboats. In 1807 Robert Fulton built the *Clermont,* the first successful steamboat, thereby making river transportation quicker and cheaper. By the 1820s steamboats carrying settlers and cargoes were plying the Mississippi and Ohio Rivers. Cincinnati and Louisville on the Ohio and St. Louis on the Mississippi became thriving river cities. New Orleans, at the mouth of the Mississippi, became a major commercial center.

   c. Canals. The Erie Canal, financed by New York State under Governor De Witt Clinton and completed in 1825, proved an immediate success. Settlers going west from New York City could travel up the Hudson River to Albany, and then westward on the Erie Canal to Buffalo on Lake Erie. With this all-water route between the Great Lakes and the Atlantic Ocean, western farmers could ship their produce eastward at greatly reduced cost—as much as 85 percent less than before. Cities on the Great Lakes—such as Rochester, Buffalo, and Cleveland—

prospered from trade in grain, hides, iron ore, and lumber. New York City, at the junction of the Hudson River and the Atlantic Ocean, became the nation's leading commercial center.

The success of the Erie Canal spurred an era of canal building, notably by (1) Philadelphia, which wanted to partake of the western trade, and (2) Ohio and Indiana, which built canals to connect Lake Erie with the Ohio River and its tributaries.

2. The Growing Frontier Population Is Nationalist. After the War of 1812 many people—from the eastern seaboard and from Europe—migrated to the western frontier. Between 1810 and 1820 the number of settlers west of the Appalachian Mountains more than doubled. Between 1816 and 1821 five western territories achieved sufficient population to be admitted to the Union as states.

The western settlers, being migrants, possessed little attachment to a state or section but were strongly nationalist. Loyal to the nation, they looked to the federal government for (a) cheap land, (b) internal improvement of roads and canals, and (c) protection against the Indians. (For a further discussion of the frontier, check the Index.)

3. Clay's American System. Henry Clay, representative to Congress from the then western state of Kentucky, urged making the nation economically self-sufficient by a plan that in 1824 he named the *American System*. Clay proposed that (a) the West and South support a protective tariff and a national bank to aid industry in the North, and (b) the North support a federal program of roads and canals to unite the country. Clay argued that all sections would benefit as the West and South would exchange their agricultural produce for the manufactured goods of the North. Clay's American System never came into being, since by the mid-1820s the country's nationalist outlook was retreating before the rise of sectional loyalties.

—————————— MULTIPLE-CHOICE QUESTIONS ——————————

1. The War of 1812 resulted in the (a) growth of American nationalism (b) postponement of the Industrial Revolution in the United States (c) increase in the prestige of the Federalist party (d) decline of British naval power.
2. Which statement about nationalism is most accurate? (a) It prevents the rise of militarism. (b) It preserves the ethnic identities of different groups within a country. (c) It is an idea that can be used to unite people. (d) It encourages diversity of thinking within national states.
3. Nationalism is most likely to develop in areas where people have (a) strong local traditions (b) a common language and system of laws (c) little contact with the outside world (d) an economy based on subsistence agriculture.
4. The nationalism of the Era of Good Feeling is most clearly evident in the (a) widespread support for the Tariff of 1816 (b) appointment of John Marshall to

the Supreme Court (c) widespread support for the Hartford Convention (d) refusal of President Monroe to purchase Florida.

5. Which illustrates the spirit of aggressive expansionism in the United States following the War of 1812? (a) ratification of the Treaty of Ghent (b) negotiation of the Rush-Bagot Agreement (c) Andrew Jackson's action in the Florida Territory (d) John Quincy Adams' role in the issuance of the Monroe Doctrine.

6. Spain sold Florida to the United States because Spain was (a) so ordered by Napoleon (b) in great need of funds (c) unable to control the Seminole Indians (d) afraid of losing the territory by force.

7. Which man was not a revolutionary leader of the Spanish colonies in Latin America? (a) Luis de Onís (b) Simón Bolívar (c) Bernardo O'Higgins (d) José de San Martín.

8. A fundamental reason for the issuance of the Monroe Doctrine was the belief that (a) it would justify increasing United States military forces (b) it would eliminate the threat of impending civil war (c) the policy of noninvolvement in European affairs no longer appealed to the American people (d) the defense of the United States depended upon limiting European influence in this hemisphere.

9. The original Monroe Doctrine was part of (a) an act of Congress (b) a treaty with Britain (c) a Presidential message to Congress (d) an agreement with Latin America.

10. One purpose of the Monroe Doctrine in 1823 was to curb (a) Asian expansion in South America (b) Russian expansion in North America (c) British control over Canada (d) the ambitions of Napoleon in Latin America.

11. The Monroe Doctrine declared that (a) the Western Hemisphere was no longer open to further European colonization (b) no European country could own territory in Latin America (c) there could be no trade agreements between Latin America and Britain (d) Spain should give up its possessions in the Western Hemisphere.

12. The reactionary alliance of European nations did not seriously threaten the Monroe Doctrine because (a) the United States was a great world power (b) Spain was willing to give up its colonies (c) Great Britain supported independence for Latin America (d) Russia had no interest in American affairs.

13. The Monroe Doctrine was (a) a continuation of Washington's foreign policy (b) a reversal of Washington's policy (c) a concession to the Federalists (d) an attempt to open new territory to slavery.

14. One reason why Great Britain supported the Monroe Doctrine in 1823 was that it (a) had declared war on Spain (b) wished to support the reactionary European alliance (c) had a profitable trade with the Latin American countries (d) followed a policy of supporting democratic revolutions.

15. In Marbury vs. Madison, the Supreme Court (a) decided the election of 1800 (b) approved the Monroe Doctrine (c) blamed the War of 1812 upon Madison (d) assumed the power of judicial review.

16. In McCulloch vs. Maryland, the Supreme Court (a) rejected loose construction of the Constitution (b) denied the power of the state to tax a federal agency (c) ordered Maryland to cede territory for the nation's capital (d) upheld the election of McCulloch as Maryland's governor.

17. In Gibbons vs. Ogden, the Supreme Court expanded the meaning of (a) civil rights (b) eminent domain (c) corporate monopoly (d) interstate commerce.

18. In Dartmouth College vs. Woodward, the Supreme Court (a) approved loans for educational purposes by the second National Bank (b) limited the taxing power of the states (c) assured corporations that their state charters could not be changed arbitrarily (d) awarded Dartmouth College a federal land grant.

19. The decisions of Chief Justice John Marshall (a) increased the power of the federal government (b) established a strict interpretation of the Constitution (c) strengthened the President's power at the expense of Congress (d) decreased the importance of the Supreme Court.
20. The invention that "made the Mississippi River flow upstream" most probably refers to the (a) railroad (b) covered wagon (c) steamboat (d) river barge.
21. Which one of the following statements regarding the Erie Canal is *true?* It (a) was financed by the federal government (b) lowered the cost of transporting western farm products to the East (c) enhanced the position of Boston as a major commercial center (d) discouraged canal building in the midwest.
22. Clay's American System was a plan to (a) develop national self-sufficiency through tariff laws and internal improvements (b) drive subversives from the government (c) free the remaining North American colonies held by European powers (d) teach American history in public schools.

—————————————— **ESSAY QUESTIONS** ——————————————

1. (a) Explain the meaning of the term "nationalism." (b) Discuss *two* reasons why nationalism developed in the United States after the War of 1812. (c) Describe *two* developments during this period that illustrate the growth of nationalism.
2. (a) Name *three* leaders during the Era of Good Feeling (1817–1823). (b) Describe *one* important event in the career of each leader that illustrates nationalism.
3. (a) Discuss *two* reasons why the United States in the 1820s opposed the restoration of Spanish control in Latin America. (b) Why did John Quincy Adams advise against a joint declaration with England? (c) State *two* provisions of the Monroe Doctrine. (d) Is the Monroe Doctrine still valid today? Present *one* argument to support your opinion.
4. As Chief Justice, John Marshall molded the Supreme Court so that it has played a major role in shaping American institutions. For each of *three* cases decided while Marshall was Chief Justice, (a) state *one* principle that the Supreme Court established, and (b) show why this principle is important in the United States today.

PART 2. The Jacksonian Era Furthers Democratic Reforms

POLITICAL DISPUTES, 1824–1828

By 1824 the Era of Good Feeling was over, and sectional disputes brought the nation upon a lengthy *Era of Hard Feeling.*

1. Presidential Election of 1824. The four Presidential candidates—each a Democratic-Republican and each a sectional favorite—were John Quincy Adams of the North, William H. Crawford of the South, and Henry Clay and Andrew Jackson, both of the West. With the people generally voting along sectional lines, no candidate received a majority in the electoral college. The House of Representatives therefore acted to select a President from the top three candidates in electoral votes: respectively, Jackson, Adams, and Crawford.

Since Adams advocated strong nationalist policies similar to Clay's American System, Clay, who had run fourth in the electoral college, threw his political support to Adams, who was second. Although Jackson had been the front-runner, the House chose Adams as President. When Adams appointed Clay as secretary of state, Jackson's supporters bitterly denounced the two as politicians engaged in a "corrupt bargain."

2. Revival of the Two-Party System. Embittered by the sectional and personal animosities of the 1824 election, the Democratic-Republicans split into two opposing parties:

a. National Republicans, Later Called Whigs. Led by Clay, Adams, and later by Daniel Webster, the National Republicans sought mass support but derived their strength chiefly from the well-established propertied classes: bankers, merchants, manufacturers, and large landowners. Since the National Republicans stood for a strong federal government, a national bank, and a protective tariff, and favored the interests of business, they resembled Hamilton's Federalist party.

b. Democrats. Led by Jackson and Martin Van Buren, the Democrats appealed chiefly to small farmers, newly emerging business leaders, and city workers. Since the Democrats generally opposed an all-powerful federal government, urged greater democracy, and claimed to represent the common people, they conformed to major Jeffersonian ideals.

3. Presidential Election of 1828. In a campaign devoid of a serious discussion of issues but marked by personal abuse and mudslinging, Jackson defeated Adams. Jackson's election has been called a sectional victory, for he lost New England but overwhelmingly carried the South and West. Jackson, who came from Tennessee, was the first President from a state west of the Appalachian Mountains.

JACKSON'S ELECTION—THE REVOLUTION OF 1828

Jackson's election was viewed as a victory of the common people—small farmers and city workers—over the aristocracy of money, factory, and land. Jackson was the first President to come from a poor family and to have received little formal education. He had risen in the world through his own efforts. "Old Hickory," Jackson's nickname, aroused visions of a tough Indian fighter and frontier military hero. Since Jackson opposed special privilege and campaigned as the champion of the people, his election is often referred to as the *Revolution of 1828.*

Breaking with the traditions set by previous Presidents, Jackson kept his inauguration informal. He walked to his inaugural ceremonies and, after taking the oath of office, went to the White House, where his noisy supporters cheered at a crowded public reception.

In another break with tradition, Jackson in his early Presidential years rarely held Cabinet meetings. He relied for advice upon a group of close friends whom his opponents dubbed the Kitchen Cabinet. Its leading figures included newspaper editors, a speech writer, and a political leader who was also secretary of state, Martin Van Buren.

JACKSON: A COMPLEX MAN

The common person's view of Jackson was in some ways far too simple. Although Jackson was born in poverty, he amassed considerable wealth, owned a large Tennessee plantation with many slaves, and raced fine horses. Although he had little formal education, Jackson learned to read and write at an early age, became a lawyer and judge, and maintained an extensive personal library. Although he grew up on the western frontier, by the time of his election Jackson possessed the manners, dignity, and bearing of a cultured person.

JACKSONIAN DEMOCRACY

The growing democratic ideas and practices that accompanied Andrew Jackson's leadership in American life are together called *Jacksonian democracy*. Jackson himself brought about certain democratic advances. Other advances were encouraged by that era's democratic atmosphere.

POLITICAL ASPECTS OF THE JACKSONIAN ERA

1. Democracy in the States. By 1828 most states had (a) removed property and religious qualifications for officeholding and voting, (b) increased the number of elected rather than appointed state and local officials, and (c) given the people a greater check upon elected officials by shortening their terms of office.

2. Democracy in Presidential Elections. (a) Beginning with the 1832 election, major Presidential candidates, instead of being named by a caucus of a few party leaders, were named by a larger number of active party members

JACKSONIAN DEMOCRACY COMPARED WITH JEFFERSONIAN DEMOCRACY

Jefferson	Jackson
1. Believed that capable, well-educated leaders should govern in the people's interests.	1. Believed that the people themselves should manage governmental affairs.
2. Reflected chiefly an agricultural society.	2. Reflected an agricultural as well as a rising industrial society.
3. Limited democracy chiefly to its political aspects.	3. Expanded democracy from its political aspects to include social and economic aspects.

at nominating conventions. (b) By 1832 the Presidential electors in all but one state were chosen not by state legislatures, but directly by the voters.

3. Democratic View of the Presidency. Jackson held that the President, the only nationally chosen official, was the servant of the people, elected to further their interests and protect their rights. To achieve these purposes, Jackson used his powers vigorously. (a) He employed the veto more often than all the preceding Presidents together. (b) He prepared to use force when South Carolina challenged the authority of the federal government regarding the 1832 tariff (check the Index). (c) He refused to enforce John Marshall's Supreme Court decision prohibiting Georgia from seizing Cherokee Indian lands. Jackson argued that the decision was contrary to the people's interests.

Jackson's enemies referred to him as *King Veto* and *King Andrew I.* They called themselves *Whigs* as had the 18th-century opponents of monarchical power in Britain. To the ordinary people, however, Jackson remained both a valiant hero and a democratic servant.

4. Spoils System. Jackson was the first President to employ the spoils system widely. He filled some 20 percent of federal positions with "deserving" members of his own party, replacing the former officeholders. A Jacksonian supporter coined the phrase, "To the victor belong the spoils."

Rotation in office, Jackson believed, was democratic because (a) it prevented a permanent class of officeholders from becoming an aristocracy, and (b) "the duties of public office are so plain and simple that men of intelligence may readily qualify themselves for their performance."

ECONOMIC ASPECTS OF THE JACKSONIAN ERA

1. Cheap Land. Throughout the early years of the United States, Westerners demanded cheap land. In 1820 settlers had been permitted to purchase as little as 80 acres at $1.25 per acre. However, many settlers considered even this price too high. Often, they merely occupied public land as *squatters.* The *preemption laws,* originating during the Jacksonian Era, gave squatters first right to buy the lands they had occupied and farmed.

2. Growth of Trade Unions. During the Jacksonian Era, the trade union movement spread to several large cities, and there briefly existed a National Trades Union. Subsequently, in 1842, the courts for the first time held trade unions and strikes legal. Workers also engaged in politics to further their economic interests. Nevertheless, the labor movement remained weak until well after the Civil War.

SOCIAL ASPECTS OF THE JACKSONIAN ERA

With the political reforms of the Age of Jackson came a growing spirit of social reform. Motivated by humanitarianism, social reformers felt a deep concern for the welfare of the ordinary people and acted to improve conditions. Movements arose to secure (1) women's rights, (2) the abolition of slavery, (3) the prohibition of intoxicating liquors, (4) better care of the insane and other unfortunates, and (5) free public education. (For a detailed discussion of social reform, check the Index.)

CULTURAL DEVELOPMENTS IN EARLY AMERICA

ARCHITECTURE

Americans won their independence from Britain politically and then moved to express their independence of Britain architecturally by rejecting the Georgian style. American architects turned to the past for inspiration and models, but adapted them to express American sentiments—such as individual freedom, republican dignity, and national pride.

1. The New Classicism (To the 1840s). Classicism refers to the cultural movement inspired by the civilizations of ancient Greece and Rome—the classical era of European history. In architecture, classical buildings employed the forms and shapes used by the ancient Greeks and Romans and expressed the classical ideals of emotional restraint, formality, symmetry, dignity, and grandeur.

a. Roman Revival: The Federal Style. During the early years of the young republic, as the federal government was established, the new classicism in architecture looked mainly to ancient Rome. The *Roman Revival* consequently became known as the *Federal style.*

Thomas Jefferson—author, national leader, politician, scientist, educator, and architect—was the leading advocate of the Roman Revival. This architectural style, he believed, best expressed American ideals as he had stated them in the Declaration of Independence, and best symbolized the American republic as successor to the ancient Roman republic. In remodeling *Monticello,* his home in Virginia, Jefferson utilized Roman shapes to convey a sense of pride and dignity. Jefferson also used the Federal style in designing two major public buildings: the *Virginia State Capitol* at Richmond and the *central library,* or *Rotunda,* at the University of Virginia—which institution Jefferson had founded.

b. Greek Revival. By the 1820s, the new classicism had shifted its emphasis from Roman to Greek architectural styles. Americans were reminded by the career of Napoleon Bonaparte, who had overthrown the French republic, that the Roman republic also had ended in a despotic empire. Americans furthermore sympathized with the Greek people, who were then struggling for independence against Turkey, and recalled that ancient Greece had been the original home of democracy. Although the Roman and Greek styles had certain similarities, Greek Revival was more severe. Many American cities established in this era adopted Greek names—such as Athens, Ithaca, and Homer—and usually constructed their public buildings in the Greek Revival style.

SCULPTURE

After the War for Independence, Americans turned to sculpture to commemorate their victory and honor their heroes. As American sculptors received training—some in Italy, others in the United States—they secured commissions from governmental bodies for works dealing with Revolutionary War leaders; democratic virtues, such as justice and wisdom; state and local celebrities; and citizens who gave their lives in their country's wars. Sculptors also attempted other works, including scenes of American life.

The early American sculptors chiefly imitated the classical works of ancient Greece and Rome. Two outstanding works portray George Washington in the classical tradition. *William Rush* (1756–1833) shows Washington dressed in the garb of a Roman general. *Horatio Greenough* (1805–1852) sculpted Washington as seated on a throne with his body naked to the waist and draped below—in the manner of a Greek statue of the god Zeus.

PAINTING

With the end of the American Revolution, American painters increasingly traveled to Europe to observe the great original works of European art and to receive instruction in European painting techniques. When they returned home American artists applied their knowledge in the painting of American personalities, scenes, and wildlife.

Two outstanding artists of this era who studied abroad were the following:

Charles Willson Peale (1741–1827), a strong believer in freedom, served with the American forces in the Revolutionary War. He painted portraits of American leaders, including Washington and Lafayette. At Valley Forge, Peale made miniature portraits of the soldiers for them to send home. In addition to portraits, Peale painted realistic, everyday scenes.

Also a naturalist and taxidermist interested in wildlife, Peale stuffed and mounted the skins of many wild animals. In Philadelphia he organized one of America's first museums displaying his collections of natural history and his portraits of great American leaders. To commemorate the museum, Peale at age 81 painted a canvas entitled *Peale in His Museum*.

Gilbert Stuart (1755–1828) specialized in portraits only, depicted face and head to the exclusion of all other details, and probed for fundamental character. In America, Stuart executed nearly 1000 commissions, including portraits of our first six Presidents. Stuart is best known for his portrait of George Washington. Stuart shows Washington as strong, dignified, and humane. This portrait has become the nationally accepted likeness and the basis of the imprint on the $1 bill.

LITERATURE

Two outstanding writers in the early 19th century, who drew inspiration from the American environment, were the following:

(1) Washington Irving (1783–1859) wrote of the early Dutch settlers in his

satirical *Knickerbocker's History of New York.* He also related the folklore of the Hudson River Valley in his *Legend of Sleepy Hollow* and *Rip van Winkle.*

(2) *James Fenimore Cooper* (1789–1851) wrote adventure stories detailing the exploits of a frontier hero, Natty Bumppo. *The Deerslayer* and *The Last of the Mohicans* are two of the five Natty Bumppo novels, which together are known as the *Leatherstocking Tales.*

NEWSPAPERS

In the early republic, newspapers grew in number. By the 1830s they totaled about 1200. They presented much advertising, set like today's classified ads. The papers became vehicles for political parties and often engaged in strongly worded debate. The functions of editor and printer began to be separated, and the editor rose in esteem as the author of newspaper policy.

SCIENCE

In the early republic, Americans emphasized practical science and relied upon Europeans for progress in pure science. *Pure* or *basic scientists* sought knowledge for its own sake. *Practical* or *applied scientists* were concerned with solving everyday, down-to-earth problems. The following were American practical scientists: *Eli Whitney* invented the cotton gin (1793), providing an inexpensive method of separating the cotton seeds from the fibers. Whitney in 1798 began the mass production of guns by assembling them out of interchangeable parts. *Peter Cooper* built *Tom Thumb,* a locomotive that in 1830 traversed the 14 miles of track of America's first railroad, the *Baltimore and Ohio.* This event spurred an era of building railroad track mileage to bind the nation together. *Cyrus McCormick* invented the reaper (1831), which cut grain many times faster than the hand-held scythe. The reaper was of great value to farmers burdened by the lack of farm workers.

Americans became known for their originality, resourcefulness, and inventiveness—traits encompassed by the term "Yankee ingenuity."

PART 3. Sectional Interests Arise and Battle Nationalism

MEANING OF SECTIONALISM

In the 1820s nationalism gave way to a growing spirit of sectionalism. Americans now (1) gave their primary loyalty to their state or region, rather than to the entire nation, and (2) considered problems from a sectional rather than a national point of view.

Southerners sought to protect their sectional interests by supporting states' rights and opposing federal power. Northeasterners and Westerners argued that what was good for their section was good for the nation and sought to further their interests by using federal power. The struggle between sectionalism and nationalism eventually resulted in the Civil War and, ultimately, in the triumph of nationalism.

ECONOMIC BASIS OF SECTIONALISM: REGIONAL SPECIALIZATION

1. Industrial Northeast. Consisting of New England and the Middle Atlantic states, the Northeast pursued shipping, fishing, lumbering, and farming— and industrialized significantly. Industrialization highlights included the following: (a) *Samuel Slater,* an immigrant from England, in 1790 in Rhode Island, constructed the nation's first cotton-spinning mill. Since Britain forbade textile workers to emigrate, Slater had left in disguise and built his machines in America from memory. Slater became known as "the father of the American factory system." (b) *Francis Cabot Lowell,* an inventor and wealthy Boston merchant, in 1813 in Massachusetts built the nation's first textile factory to combine all steps from raw material to finished product—processing the raw cotton, spinning thread, and weaving cloth.

By the 1830s, the Northeast contained a powerful class of industrial capitalists and was the nation's manufacturing region. Its leading industrial state was Massachusetts. The Northeast's chief manufactures were textiles, leather goods, iron implements, utensils, and machinery.

Industrialization in the Northeast was aided by the following: (a) Shipbuilding and foreign commerce had declined during the War of 1812 era, and workers and capital were available for the new industries. (b) Waterpower was available from swift-flowing streams, and steampower from Appalachian coal. (c) Factory hands could easily be recruited from farm families discouraged by New England's rocky soil, as well as from immigrants. (d) As the nation's banking center, the Northeast possessed investment capital. (e) The South and the West represented a growing market for the Northeast's manufactured goods.

2. Plantation South. Consisting of the south Atlantic and southwestern states, the South contained many small subsistence farmers but was dominated by a small number of wealthy and influential plantation owners. They were planter capitalists whose money was invested in land and slaves. They raised cash crops for the market: tobacco, rice, sugar, and, most important, cotton. From 1790 to 1826 cotton production increased from 2 million to 330 million pounds annually.

King Cotton's rise was aided by the following: (a) Cheap, fertile land was plentiful. As the soil became exhausted by the continuous cultivation of a single crop, planters gradually moved from the south Atlantic states into the fertile lands of the Southwest. (b) The cotton gin, invented by Eli Whitney in 1793, provided a simple and inexpensive method of separating the cotton fiber from the seed. It replaced the costly and time-consuming practice of doing the job by hand. (c)

Cotton-growing was a simple and year-round activity. Black slaves could therefore be trained easily and kept occupied continuously. (*d*) Northeastern and English factories provided a growing market for the South's raw cotton.

3. Small-Farm West. Consisting of the central and northwestern states, the West emphasized agriculture on the small, family-size farm. Western settlers raised great amounts of wheat, rye, corn, and meat. In producing abundant harvests, Westerners were aided by the following: (*a*) Fertile lands were plentiful. (*b*) The federal government sold the western lands at very liberal prices—after 1820 at $1.25 per acre. (*c*) Free landowners worked hard on their own farms, seeking larger crops so as to better their economic status. (*d*) Northeastern and English cities represented an ever-growing demand for foodstuffs.

SECTIONAL DISPUTES

1. Protective Tariff. The Northeast strongly favored a protective tariff to protect factory owners and workers against foreign competition. The South opposed a protective tariff because it would raise the price of manufactured goods. The planters also feared that Britain might retaliate against an American protective tariff by curtailing purchases of southern cotton. The West generally supported the North on this issue. Although farmers in the West disliked the higher prices on manufactures, they wanted a prosperous market in the Northeast for their foodstuffs.

2. Second Bank of the United States. The Northeast strongly supported the bank, since manufacturers and bankers benefited from available investment capital and stable currency. The South and the West both opposed the bank. Planters, farmers, and debtors generally preferred state banks, since these would bring easy credit, cheap money, and high agricultural prices.

3. Internal Improvements at Federal Expense. The West favored such projects. Farmers needed roads and canals to send their agricultural products to Northeast markets and seaports. The South opposed these federal expenses. Planters had satisfactory water routes to Northeast and British markets and had little need of routes to the West. The Northeast generally supported the West on this issue. Manufacturers desired improved routes to western markets. However, many Northeasterners preferred internal improvements through private enterprise or at the expense of the states.

4. Liberal Land Policy. The West strongly favored cheap land. Farmers wanted to acquire more land. Also, they wanted to attract new settlers, form new states, and increase the influence of the West in the federal government. The Northeast opposed a liberal land policy. Manufacturers feared the loss of factory workers to the West. Northeasterners also feared a drop in the value of their land and a decrease in influence in the federal government. The South was divided on this issue. Planters wanted cheap lands in the Southwest and yet feared that growth in the West would reduce the South's influence in the federal government.

5. Territorial Expansion to the Southwest. The South favored annexing Texas and acquiring land from Mexico. Southern planters wanted to secure more slave states and to replace lands exhausted by continuous cotton cultivation. The Northeast opposed territorial expansion to the Southwest. Northeasterners feared that this would mean new slave states, which would reduce the Northeast's influence in the federal government. The West generally supported the South on this issue. Although Westerners opposed the extension of slavery, they wanted additional sources of cheap fertile land.

6. Expansion of Slavery. The South favored the expansion of slavery into new territories. The southern economy was tied to slavery, and Southerners were eager to increase the number of slave states. The Northeast and most of the West utilized free labor. They considered slavery morally wrong and opposed its expansion.

TARIFF DISPUTE

THE SOUTH AND THE TARIFF (1816 AND 1824)

In 1816, America's first protective tariff was supported by all sections, including the South. This region had visions of becoming industrialized. In 1824, however, the South vigorously but unsuccessfully opposed an increase in tariff rates. Southern Congress members, realizing that the South was to remain agricultural, argued that the tariff raised the price of manufactured goods and caused foreign countries to cut back their purchases of southern cotton.

TARIFF OF ABOMINATIONS (1828)

In 1828 members of Congress from the West and Northeast secured passage of a tariff that provided extremely high rates on imports of raw materials and manufactured goods. Southerners called the law hateful, a *Tariff of Abominations.*

SOUTH CAROLINA EXPOSITION AND PROTEST (1828)

South Carolina planters, adversely affected by the depletion of their land and by the increased competition from rich cotton land in the Southwest, blamed the decline in their prosperity on the tariff. John Calhoun of South Carolina, the leading champion of the South, protested the 1828 tariff and secretly wrote the *South Carolina Exposition and Protest.* This document, patterned after the Virginia and Kentucky Resolutions (check the Index), presented the states' rights doctrine: (1) The federal government was created by a compact among the states to serve as their agent. (2) State conventions have the power to declare laws of Congress, such as a tariff law, unconstitutional. (3) Laws so declared unconstitutional are null and void. Calhoun also argued that, as a last resort, a state could terminate its compact with the other states and secede from the Union.

WEBSTER-HAYNE DEBATE (1830)

The controversy over the nature of the federal Union erupted in the Senate. Robert Y. Hayne, Senator of South Carolina, presented the states' rights argument, closely paralleling the *Exposition and Protest.* Daniel Webster of Massachusetts, the leading northern orator, answered Hayne in a speech often considered the greatest ever delivered in the Senate. Webster presented the nationalist point of view: (1) The Constitution and the federal government were created by the people, not by the states. (2) The proper agency for determining the constitutionality of laws is the Supreme Court, not the individual states. (3) No state has the right to nullify a federal law or secede from the Union; otherwise the Union would be an absurdity, a "rope of sand." Webster concluded dramatically with the words, "Liberty and Union, now and forever, one and inseparable."

ATTITUDE OF THE WEST (STATED IN 1830)

At the 1830 Jefferson Day dinner, attended by the leaders of the Democratic party, President Andrew Jackson aligned the West with the Northeast against the South on the issue of nullification. Looking directly at Vice President Calhoun, Jackson proposed a toast, "Our Federal Union! it must be preserved!" For the South, Calhoun offered a counter-toast, "The Union, next to our liberty, most dear."

NULLIFICATION BY SOUTH CAROLINA (1832)

In 1832 a new tariff law provided only modestly lower rates than the Tariff of Abominations. South Carolina thereupon passed an *Ordinance of Nullification,* voiding the 1832 tariff and threatening secession if the federal government attempted to collect tariff duties within South Carolina.

Jackson accepted the challenge. He warned that nullification is "incompatible with the existence of the Union" and asked Congress to pass a *Force Bill* empowering him to enforce the nation's tariff law in South Carolina by utilizing the army and navy if necessary.

COMPROMISE TARIFF (1833)

South Carolina did not receive support from the other southern states, and all sections seemed eager to avoid an armed clash. Henry Clay introduced a Compromise Tariff, which provided for a gradual reduction of rates over a ten-year period to the level of the Tariff of 1816. Congress passed the Compromise Tariff and on the same day passed Jackson's Force Bill. South Carolina withdrew its Ordinance of Nullification, thus making it unnecessary for Jackson to employ armed might. South Carolina, however, reasserted its right to void federal laws by nullifying the Force Bill.

The compromise settled the tariff dispute, but did nothing to resolve the more basic issue of states' rights and nullification.

BANK DISPUTE

SECOND BANK OF THE UNITED STATES

1. Organization. Chartered in 1816 by a nationalist-minded Congress, the second Bank of the United States was a private, profit-making corporation. Four-fifths of its stock was held by private investors and one-fifth by the federal government, which also appointed five of the bank's 25 directors. Under Nicholas Biddle, its best-known president, the bank prospered and, by 1830, maintained some 29 branches throughout the country.

2. Services. The bank (a) served as the official depository for government funds and sold government bonds, (b) held private deposits of money and provided loans for business purposes, (c) issued paper banknotes, which constituted a sound national currency, and (d) restrained state banks from overissuing banknotes in relation to their specie (metal) reserve. State banks were restrained by the knowledge that if they overissued, the United States Bank would accumulate their paper notes and demand specie, thereby forcing them into financial disaster.

THE NORTHEAST FAVORS THE BANK

Northeastern manufacturers as well as business and financial interests generally approved the bank because it (1) paid dividends on the bank stock they owned, (2) provided business loans, (3) held deposits of their surplus funds, and (4) maintained a sound currency.

THE WEST AND SOUTH OPPOSE THE BANK

In the West and South, state banks, small-business executives, farmers, planters, and debtors generally opposed the bank. (1) It prevented state banks from issuing large quantities of banknotes, which would cheapen the value of money, lower interest rates, inflate farm prices, and ease the payment of debts. (2) The bank refused many loans to small-business executives and farmers who could not provide adequate collateral guaranteeing repayment.

OTHER CRITICISMS OF THE BANK

1. On "Hard-Money" Grounds. Some Americans, including President Jackson, opposed all paper banknotes. They expected that the destruction of the bank would lead to the exclusive use of hard money—gold and silver—

thereby protecting the working classes from being "cheated" by changes in the value of paper money.

2. On Political and Social Grounds. (a) By paying dividends, the bank enriched a few hundred wealthy Northeastern and foreign stockholders. (b) Its opponents claimed that the bank was illegal, since the Constitution did not specifically authorize such a bank. (c) The bank engaged in politics by supporting candidates for office, making loans to members of Congress, and retaining Senator Daniel Webster of Massachusetts as its attorney. (d) Opponents of the bank argued that it enabled a few private individuals, the bank's officers and directors, to exercise a monopoly over the nation's credit and currency. By virtue of its vast economic power, the bank represented a challenge to the authority of the government. The bank's enemies nicknamed it the "octopus" and the "monster."

THE BANK AND THE ELECTION OF 1832

Jackson's enemies, aware of his hostility to the bank, acted to make the bank the leading issue of the 1832 election. Nicholas Biddle, president of the bank, following the advice of Clay and Webster, requested a new charter of Congress although the old charter was good for four more years. When Congress passed the recharter bill, Jackson vetoed the bill and denounced the aristocracy of money. Jackson rallied the common people to his support. He won an overwhelming victory in the election, receiving 219 electoral votes to 49 for the National Republican candidate, Henry Clay.

WILDCAT BANKS

Jackson interpreted his reelection as a mandate from the people to destroy the bank. He ordered government funds withdrawn and placed in state banks, which Jackson's enemies named *pet banks*. The withdrawal of government funds crippled the second Bank of the United States.

With the second National Bank enfeebled, state banks, especially in the West, engaged in imprudent banking practices. Nicknamed *wildcat banks,* they (1) made unwise loans, many of which were not secured by adequate collateral and were used for speculation in land, and (2) printed far more paper money than was justified by their reserves of specie. Alarmed by these practices, Jackson in 1836 issued the *Specie Circular.* He instructed federal land agents to accept payment for public lands only in gold or silver.

PANIC OF 1837 AND ITS EFFECTS

Soon after Jackson ended his second term, the nation experienced a financial crisis known as the *Panic of 1837*.

1. Causes. Jackson's Specie Circular was the immediate cause of the panic. State banks, unable to meet the demand for specie, closed their doors, thus bringing on the panic. Other causes of the panic were: (a) Wildcat banks had made loans to land speculators, who hoped to resell the land at a higher price. The speculators, however, found no purchasers and were unable to repay their loans. The banks were left with large, uncollectable debts. (*b*) Western states, in particular, had recklessly floated bond issues to finance construction of turnpikes and canals that proved to be unnecessary and unprofitable. Many investors in such projects lost all that they had invested.

2. Independent Treasury System. Martin Van Buren, Jackson's friend and successor as President, did little to ease the panic and the ensuing depression. However, to safeguard government funds, he influenced Congress to pass the *Independent Treasury Act*. The act empowered the government to establish depositories in various cities and to keep its funds in its own safety vaults.

3. Election of 1840. Blamed for the panic and depression, Van Buren was swept from office in the election of 1840. The Whigs won easily following a campaign marked by ballyhoo and slogans such as "Van, Van is a used-up man," and "Tippecanoe and Tyler too." General William Henry Harrison, victor over the Indians at the 1811 Battle of Tippecanoe, became President, and John Tyler became Vice President.

SIGNIFICANCE OF THE WAR AGAINST THE BANK

The destruction of the second Bank of the United States was a sectional victory for the West and South over the Northeast. To Jackson's supporters, it was also a victory of democracy—of the common people over a powerful economic monopoly. Jackson, a hard-money advocate, found "defeat in victory" as cheap paper money and inflation followed his triumph over the bank. Jackson's war against the bank left the American people with a heritage of distrust for any central bank.

For over three-quarters of a century, the United States had no centralized banking system. When in 1913 Congress established a national banking system— the *Federal Reserve* (check the Index)—every effort was made to gain the advantages of sound banking practices without the disadvantages of concentrating banking power in the hands of a few private individuals.

———————————— **MULTIPLE-CHOICE QUESTIONS** ————————————

1. The term "corrupt bargain" was applied most directly to (a) Jackson's use of the spoils system (b) Adams' appointment of Clay as secretary of state (c) Jackson's use of his "Kitchen Cabinet" (d) Van Buren's election as President.
2. Which contributed to the election of Andrew Jackson in 1828? (a) Voters were tired of the Federalist party. (b) Voters wanted to register a protest against John Marshall's decisions. (c) The importance of the West in national elections had increased. (d) Andrew Jackson advocated the spoils system.
3. During the first half of the 19th century, the right to vote was most generally extended by (a) lowering the voting age (b) removing property qualifications (c) outlawing poll taxes (d) amending the federal Constitution.

4. Which two groups most strongly supported Jacksonian democracy? (a) creditors and urban workers (b) supporters of the Bank of the United States and western farmers (c) New England shipbuilders and southern plantation owners (d) small farmers and proprietors of small businesses.

5. Andrew Jackson believed that the President should (a) observe strict limits on the Constitution (b) follow the lead of Congress in all matters (c) carry out policies advocated by his party's leaders (d) act as defender of the people.

6. Two achievements of the Jacksonian Era were (a) rotation in public office and further widening of the suffrage (b) promotion of central banking and expansion of states' rights (c) encouragement of states' rights and active involvement in foreign affairs (d) the limitation of Presidential powers and the growth of nationalism.

7. During 1830 to 1860, which is the best example of a minority that exercised great political power within a section? (a) planter class in the South (b) unionized workers in northern cities (c) farmers in the Northeast (d) shipbuilders in New England.

8. Which was a major cause of the rapid industrialization of New York and New England during the period 1800 to 1850? (a) Water power and investment capital were available. (b) The Northeast was close to the cotton-growing areas of the country. (c) The cost of shipping raw materials to Europe for manufacture was prohibitive. (d) The Northeast had a large supply of highly skilled laborers.

9. A major reason why people migrated to the western part of the United States during the 19th century was because that part of the country (a) provided an abundance of cheap labor (b) guaranteed protection from violence (c) protected the right of landowners to own slaves (d) offered increased opportunities for social mobility.

10. Which of the following would probably have received support from both a New England factory owner and a western farmer? (a) a liberal land policy (b) a national banking system (c) restrictions on immigration (d) a national program of building roads and canals.

11. Before the Civil War, the South objected to high tariffs because they (a) kept the price of cotton low (b) increased the cost of slaves (c) increased the prices of manufactured goods (d) helped western farmers at the planters' expense.

12. Andrew Jackson *most* clearly demonstrated the Westerner's point of view in his (a) request for passage of the Force Bill (b) selection of his successor to the Presidency (c) attitude toward the Bank of the United States (d) acceptance of advice from his "Kitchen Cabinet."

13. The history of the tariff to 1860 shows that (a) President Jackson supported the South on the tariff (b) the North consistently opposed a protective tariff (c) the tariff issue contributed to the conflict between North and South over states' rights (d) the tariff restored American industry destroyed during the War of 1812.

14. According to the *South Carolina Exposition and Protest,* a federal law could be nullified by a state because the federal government was (a) dependent on the states for taxes (b) created by the states (c) composed of people elected or appointed from the states (d) limited in its power by the Bill of Rights.

15. According to the doctrine of nullification, the right to determine the constitutionality of an act of Congress resides in (a) Congress itself (b) the states (c) the United States Supreme Court only (d) the executive branch of the federal government.

16. President Jackson's action in the nullification controversy (a) antagonized the North (b) brought on the Panic of 1837 (c) won him the support of Calhoun (d) strengthened the power of the national government.

17. President Jackson claimed that the Bank of the United States (a) was supported by the plantation aristocracy (b) was responsible for the Panic of 1837

(c) discriminated against the farmer and small business owners (d) had become unprofitable.

18. Which action by President Jackson led to the Specie Circular? (a) accepting the Compromise Tariff of 1833 (b) vetoing the recharter bill for the second Bank of the United States (c) advocating the spoils system (d) supporting the seizure of Cherokee lands by Georgia.

19. An important cause of the Panic of 1837 was the (a) end of the frontier (b) shortage of paper money (c) building of the Erie Canal (d) speculation in western lands.

20. Westerners opposed the Bank of the United States because they (a) feared inflation (b) believed that the bank favored the debtor class (c) were forbidden to borrow money from it (d) believed that Easterners received most of the benefits.

21. One immediate effect of President Jackson's Specie Circular was to increase the (a) sale of public lands (b) demand for hard money (c) value of paper currency (d) general prosperity of the country.

———— IDENTIFICATION QUESTIONS: WHO AM I? ————

John Quincy Adams	William Henry Harrison	John Tyler
Nicholas Biddle	Robert Hayne	Martin Van Buren
John C. Calhoun	Francis Cabot Lowell	Daniel Webster
Henry Clay	Samuel Slater	Eli Whitney

1. In a Senate debate, I presented the nationalist viewpoint on the Constitution and called for "Liberty and Union."
2. I benefited from economic discontent to win the 1840 Presidential election.
3. A leading champion of the planter aristocracy, I wrote the *South Carolina Exposition and Protest.*
4. An immigrant from England, I built the first cotton-spinning mill in the United States.
5. After serving as Secretary of State under James Monroe, I won the Presidency in the bitterly contested election of 1824.
6. A Connecticut Yankee, I invented the cotton gin and later pioneered the mass production of guns.
7. A Westerner and Whig leader, I proposed the Compromise Tariff of 1833.
8. As president of the second National Bank, I bitterly opposed Andrew Jackson.
9. After succeeding Andrew Jackson as President in 1837, I proposed an independent treasury system.

———————— ESSAY QUESTIONS ————————

1. Both the election of Thomas Jefferson in 1800 and the election of Andrew Jackson in 1828 have been called revolutions. (a) Give *two* specific facts to show the extent to which the election of 1800 might be called a revolution. (b) Give *two* specific facts to show the extent to which the election of 1828 might be called a revolution. (c) Give *one* specific fact to show the difference between these revolutions.

2. The period in American history between the War of 1812 and the Civil War saw first nationalism and then sectionalism. For this period, discuss *one* factor that contributed to the development of nationalism, and *two* factors that contributed to the development of sectionalism.

3. During the Jacksonian Era there were conflicting currents of nationalism and sectionalism, as well as a trend toward democracy. (*a*) Including specific illustrations, explain *two* controversies created by the conflict between nationalism and sectionalism during the Jacksonian Period. (*b*) Show *two* different ways in which democracy was extended during the Jacksonian Era.

4. Some historians have described the administration of Andrew Jackson as "the Reign of King Andrew" and others as "the Era of Jacksonian Democracy." For *each* expression, discuss *two* examples to justify its use as a description of the era in which Jackson was President.

5. The doctrine of states' rights was not limited to any one section of the country. Prove this statement by describing *one* instance of the formal assertion of states' rights in each of *two* different sections before 1860.

PART 4. The Young Nation Expands Across the Continent

MANIFEST DESTINY

Americans were a restless, migratory people, satisfied temporarily by the relatively easy acquisitions of the Louisiana Purchase and Florida (check the Index). By the 1840s, Americans had again become expansion-minded. They believed that their country had a "divine mission"—that it was destined to spread to the Pacific coast, or perhaps over the entire North American continent. This belief became known as *manifest destiny*.

Manifest destiny was promoted by (1) land-hungry Americans who eyed tracts of rich but sparsely settled lands, (2) patriots who feared British designs upon such lands, (3) eastern merchants whose ships trading with Asia needed ports on the Pacific coast, (4) democratic-minded people who believed that American territorial growth meant the spreading of freedom, and (5) nationalists who sought American greatness.

EVENTS IN TEXAS

1. Americans in Texas. Americans were invited by newly independent Mexico in 1821 to settle in its northern province of Texas. Stephen Austin led the first group of land-hungry Americans. Others soon followed. By 1835 some 30,000 whites with 5000 black slaves—all from the United States—resided in Texas. In the 1830s friction developed between the Mexican government and the American settlers, as Mexico attempted to (*a*) halt further American immigration into Texas, (*b*) free the black slaves, and (*c*) deprive Texas of local self-government.

2. Texas Revolution (1836). Claiming a parallel with the American Revolution against Britain, the Texans rebelled for independence. At the Alamo, a fortified church mission at San Antonio, a small Texan force was besieged and annihilated by a Mexican army under General Santa Anna. Inflamed by the bloody massacre of the Alamo defenders, Texans raised the battle cry, "Remember the Alamo!" Led by *Sam Houston,* the Texans won a great victory at the Battle of San Jacinto, capturing Santa Anna and driving his troops out of Texas. The settlers proclaimed the Republic of Texas—the Lone Star Republic. They elected Sam Houston as president and requested annexation by the United States.

ANNEXATION OF TEXAS

1. Delayed by Sectional Rivalry. While Southerners favored the annexation of Texas, Northeasterners opposed it. Northeasterners feared (a) the extension of slave territory, (b) increased southern membership in the House of Representatives, (c) increased southern membership in the Senate, especially if Texas were divided into several states, and (d) the possibility of war with Mexico. For nine years, opposition from the Northeast delayed any treaty for the annexation of Texas.

2. Achieved by Joint Resolution (1845). In the 1844 Presidential election, *James K. Polk* of Tennessee, the Democratic candidate, demanded the

Area disputed between the United States and Mexico

Annexation of Texas 1845

"reannexation of Texas," arguing that Texas had been part of the original Louisiana Purchase. Henry Clay, the Whig candidate, straddled the issue. Polk narrowly won the election. In 1845, just before Polk took office, Congress admitted Texas to the Union by means of a joint resolution. (Whereas a treaty requires a two-thirds vote in the Senate, a joint resolution requires only a majority vote, but in each house.)

WAR WITH MEXICO (1846–1848)

1. Causes. Mexican patriots resented the American (a) annexation of Texas, (b) claim that the southern boundary of Texas was the Rio Grande, rather than the Nueces River (see map, page 201), and (c) ambition to acquire additional Mexican territory. The Mexican government, in debt to a number of American citizens, was incompetent and unstable. Bowing to public opinion, the Mexican government refused to receive the American negotiator, John Slidell, and refused to consider his proposal to settle outstanding issues peacefully.

The Mexican War   1846–1848

Meanwhile, Mexican and United States troops entered the disputed area between the Rio Grande and the Nueces River, and in 1846 fought a minor battle.

President Polk, infuriated, informed Congress that "Mexico has invaded our territory and shed American blood upon American soil." Polk secured an overwhelming declaration of war. Members of Congress from the South and West voted for the declaration, and their constituents welcomed the war. Most members of Congress from the Northeast voted for the declaration, but many people in the Northeast condemned the war as an imperialist plot against a weak neighbor to seize land and extend slavery.

2. Military Events. American volunteer armies soon demonstrated their military superiority. General Zachary Taylor ("Old Rough and Ready") won victory after victory in northern Mexico. General Winfield Scott captured Vera Cruz and Mexico City, the capital. Colonel Stephen Kearny occupied New Mexico and advanced on California. In California, Captain John C. Frémont led American settlers to drive out the Mexican authorities and establish the temporary California (Bear Flag) Republic. Mexico's defeat was complete.

3. Treaty of Guadalupe Hidalgo (1848). Mexico (a) accepted the Rio Grande as the southern boundary of Texas, and (b) gave up California and the province of New Mexico, together called the *Mexican Cession*. (This area was eventually carved up into five states and parts of two others.) The United States agreed to pay Mexico $15 million and to assume the claims of American citizens against the Mexican government. (The terms of the treaty closely paralleled the American proposals that Mexico had refused to hear before the war.)

GADSDEN PURCHASE (1853)

Five years after purchasing the Mexican Cession for $15 million, the United States paid Mexico $10 million for a small strip of land in southern Arizona and New Mexico. James Gadsden, American minister to Mexico, negotiated the agreement, and this land is called the *Gadsden Purchase*. It provided a favorable railroad route into California. Many Americans felt, however, that the large sum paid for this territory was "conscience money."

> **Historical Analysis.** *Which country bears primary responsibility for the Mexican War—the United States or Mexico?*
>
> **United States.** Americans believed in manifest destiny and sought territorial expansion. Southerners especially wanted more territory for slave states. President Polk seized upon a minor clash as an excuse for war, and his statement that American blood had been shed upon American soil was in error, for the clash took place upon disputed soil. By the excessive sum paid for the Gadsden Purchase, the American government tacitly was admitting that it had wronged Mexico and was now paying "conscience money."
>
> **Mexico.** Mexico lacked the population to settle and lacked the military power to control its extensive but relatively empty northwest

lands. This rich, fertile area remained mainly unutilized. Mexico's government was unstable and easily swayed by anti-American public opinion. This government was unable or unwilling to listen to the reasonable proposals carried by envoy Slidell. The refusal to negotiate peacefully over existing differences with the United States made war inevitable.

EXPANSION TO THE NORTH

MAINE BOUNDARY DISPUTE

The United States and Britain both claimed a territory of 12,000 square miles lying between Maine in the United States and New Brunswick in Canada. Secretary of State Daniel Webster and British envoy Lord Ashburton negotiated a compromise boundary. The *Webster-Ashburton Treaty* of 1842 granted Canada 5000 square miles and the United States 7000 square miles.

OREGON DISPUTE

1. Conflicting Claims. The United States and Britain both claimed the Oregon Country, a huge area extending from the Rockies westward to the Pacific and from the latitude of 42° northward to 54° 40'. British claims were based upon the (a) 16th-century voyage of Sir Francis Drake, (b) 18th-century explorations of captains Cook and Vancouver, and (c) subsequent fur-trading activities of the Hudson's Bay Company. American claims rested upon the (a) 1792 discovery

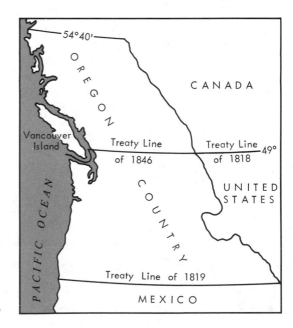

Oregon Country

Territorial Growth of the United States   1783–1853

OREGON COUNTRY 1846

1842

1818

LOUISIANA PURCHASE 1803

MEXICAN CESSION 1848

UNITED STATES 1783

ANNEXATION OF TEXAS 1845

1795

GADSDEN PURCHASE 1853

1813

1810

FLORIDA

1819

of the Columbia River by Captain Robert Gray, (b) 1804–1806 explorations of Lewis and Clark, who after traversing the Louisiana Territory northward crossed the Rocky Mountains and descended the Columbia River to the Pacific, (c) subsequent fur-trading activities of the American Fur Company, owned by John Jacob Astor, and (d) 5000 Americans who had settled in the territory by 1845, many seeking the good climate and fertile land as reported by the American missionary to the Indians, *Marcus Whitman.* For many years the United States and Britain jointly occupied the territory.

2. Peaceful Settlement of the Dispute. In the Presidential campaign of 1844, James K. Polk demanded the "reoccupation of Oregon." His supporters chanted the slogan, "Fifty-four forty or fight." When he achieved the Presidency, however, Polk decided to compromise on the Oregon issue. In 1846 the United States and Britain agreed to divide the Oregon Country at the 49th parallel. This agreement extended the Line of 1818 between the United States and Canada westward to the Pacific.

———— READING INTERPRETATION QUESTIONS ————

"What is the territory, Mr. President, which you propose to wrest from Mexico? It is consecrated to the heart of the Mexican by many a well-fought battle with his old Castilian master. His Bunker Hills, and Saratogas, and Yorktowns are there, and shall he surrender that consecrated home of his affection to the Anglo-Saxon invaders? What do we want with it? The Senator from Michigan says he must have this. Why, my Christian brother, on what principle of justice?" (From an 1847 speech by a United States Senator)

1. The parallel between the United States and Mexico which the speaker indicated was that both (a) were Anglo-Saxon countries (b) disliked Britain (c) had a revolutionary heritage (d) were overcrowded.
2. With which position would the speaker most likely have agreed? (a) The United States should pressure Britain out of Texas. (b) The pursuit of a policy of manifest destiny is unfair. (c) The annexation of Texas is justified because most of its people are settlers from the United States. (d) The extension of United States democracy to parts of Mexico is divinely intended.
3. In referring to Mexico's "old Castilian master," the speaker means the (a) Aztecs (b) French (c) Spaniards (d) Canadians.
4. The speaker's reference to Saratoga and Yorktown meant that (a) Mexicans fought on the side of the Americans in these battles (b) There are towns in Mexico with these names (c) in winning independence Mexicans fought battles similar in significance to these American victories (d) French aid was instrumental in achieving Mexican independence.
5. This speech probably best represented the views of a (a) Mississippi cotton planter (b) Texas rancher (c) Massachusetts factory worker (d) Michigan lumberjack.

——————— MODIFIED TRUE-FALSE QUESTIONS ———————

1. The belief of most Americans in the first half of the 19th century that the United States would expand to the Pacific coast was known as *imperialism.*
2. Americans migrated to Mexico's northern province of Texas in order to get *cheap land.*
3. The battle at the Alamo resulted in a military victory for the *Texans.*
4. *John C. Frémont* was elected President of the Lone Star Republic.
5. The section of the United States most opposed to the annexation of Texas was the *West.*
6. Texas was admitted to the Union by means of *a treaty.*
7. The Americans claimed that the southern boundary of Texas was the *Rio Grande.*
8. The American President who asked for a declaration of war against Mexico was *Andrew Jackson.*
9. An important result of the Mexican War was the annexation of *California.*
10. The Gadsden Purchase provided a railroad route into *Oregon.*
11. An American missionary who helped settle the Oregon Country was *Marcus Whitman.*
12. The Webster-Ashburton Treaty settled our dispute with Great Britain over the *Newfoundland fisheries.*
13. American claims to the Oregon Country were based partly on the explorations of *Lewis and Clark.*
14. British claims to the Oregon Country were based partly on the fur-trading activities of the *American Fur Company.*
15. The Oregon boundary dispute was settled by dividing the land at the *54° 40′ parallel.*

——————————————— **ESSAY QUESTIONS** ———————————————

1. (*a*) What were the boundaries of the United States in 1789? (*b*) Mention *three* additions of territory to the United States between 1789 and 1860. (*c*) Show how *each* of these territories was acquired.
2. (*a*) Discuss *two* reasons why New England opposed the annexation of Texas.
   (*b*) Discuss *one* reason why James K. Polk felt justified in demanding the annexation of Texas.
3. (*a*) Explain *two* arguments used by Americans who opposed the Mexican War.
   (*b*) Explain *two* arguments of Americans who favored the Mexican War. (*c*) State *two* provisions of the treaty of peace ending the Mexican War. (*d*) Which nation—the United States or Mexico—bears the primary responsibility for the Mexican War? Present one argument to support your opinion.
4. (*a*) Name *four* foreign nations that once owned part of the present territory of the United States. (*b*) Show how each of *two* of these nations lost its territory.

PART 5. Slavery and Sectional Crisis Lead to Civil War

SLAVERY IN COLONIAL TIMES

(Check the Index.)

BLACKS AND THE REVOLUTIONARY WAR ERA

1. The Declaration of Independence (1776). In regard to slavery, the Declaration was silent. Jefferson's original statement condemning the slave trade and slavery was removed by the Continental Congress. Since the Declaration required unanimous approval by Congress, the removal of any condemnation of slavery secured the support of New England, whose shipowners engaged in the slave trade, and of the South, whose plantation owners used slave workers.

2. Military Matters. In 1770 Crispus Attucks, a black, was one of five men killed when British soldiers fired upon a hostile crowd—an event the colonists called the Boston Massacre. During the Revolutionary War, of some 300,000 American soldiers, 5000 were blacks. Best known were two Bunker Hill battle heroes, Peter Salem and Salem Poor.

EARLIEST STEPS AGAINST SLAVERY

Many leading Southerners disapproved of slavery. Washington and Jefferson, both planters, left wills freeing their slaves. They considered slavery immoral and a danger to the South's ultimate welfare.

In the North slavery was economically unprofitable. Northern farmers owned small, family-operated farms where little work could be done during the severe winter months. Factory owners considered slave labor less efficient than wage labor. By 1804 all the states in the North were committed to the abolition of slavery.

Southerners and Northerners favoring the transport of free blacks back to West Africa founded in 1817 the *American Colonization Society*. Although few blacks were willing to return to their ancestral continent, the society in the 1820s founded the West African nation of Liberia.

Congress in 1787 enacted the Northwest Ordinance (check the Index), which closed that area to slavery. In 1808, the first year permitted by the Constitution, Congress prohibited the importing of slaves. This law was enforced inadequately, and the slave trade continued illegally.

COTTON GIN AND SLAVERY

The cotton gin, a machine invented in 1793 by Eli Whitney, provided an efficient method of separating the cotton seeds from the fibers. With cotton production now extremely profitable, southern plantations grew rapidly and increasingly became dependent upon slave labor. Thus, while slavery declined elsewhere, it fastened its hold upon the economy of the South and later the Southwest.

MISSOURI COMPROMISE (1820)

1. Issues. The Missouri Territory, part of the Louisiana Purchase, applied for admission into the Union as a slave state. Missouri's admission would have upset the balance of 11 free and 11 slave states and would have given the South control of the Senate. The North, by reason of its larger population, already controlled the House of Representatives. Representative James Tallmadge of New York proposed that Congress abolish slavery in Missouri. He thereby set off a bitter sectional debate as to whether Congress had the right to prohibit slavery in a territory or in a state. Both North and South argued vehemently, and Thomas Jefferson wrote that the slavery issue filled him with terror, "like a firebell in the night."

2. Compromise. Henry Clay devised the *Missouri Compromise:* (a) Maine was separated from Massachusetts and entered the Union as a free state, (b) Missouri entered as a slave state, and (c) all other territory in the Louisiana Purchase north of the 36° 30′ parallel was closed to slavery. The Compromise thus left far less territory open to slavery than it closed to slavery.

ABOLITIONIST MOVEMENT

1. Antislavery Arguments. Abolitionist societies, arising in the 1830s during the era of Jacksonian democracy, were concerned with ending slavery. Most abolitionists demanded the immediate freeing of the slaves without compensation to their masters. The abolitionists argued that slavery (a) was morally

Missouri Compromise   1820

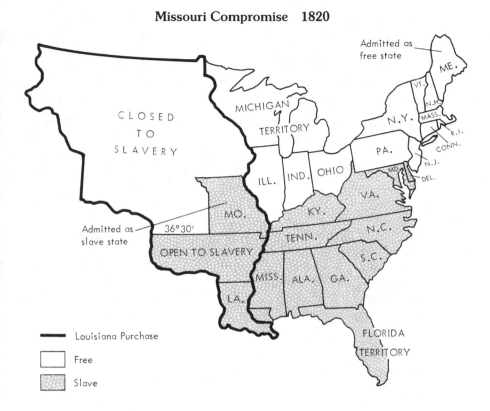

Admitted as free state

ME.

VT.

N.H.

N.Y.   MASS.

R.I.

CONN.

MICHIGAN

TERRITORY

CLOSED
TO
SLAVERY

PA.

N.J.

ILL.   IND.   OHIO

MD.

DEL.

VA.

MO.

KY.

Admitted as slave state   36°30'

TENN.

N.C.

OPEN TO SLAVERY

S.C.

MISS.   ALA.   GA.

LA.

FLORIDA
TERRITORY

━━━ Louisiana Purchase

☐ Free

▨ Slave

wrong—that no person had the right to hold another in bondage, (b) transgressed religious teachings and violated the ethics of the Bible, (c) resulted in cruel and inhuman treatment of slaves and their families, (d) degraded slave owners, and (e) violated democracy—the equality and the unalienable rights of all persons as stated in the Declaration of Independence.

2. Abolitionist Activities. To sway public opinion, the abolitionists conducted meetings and published newspapers. Theodore Parker, a Boston preacher, lectured and wrote against slavery, as did the orator Wendell Phillips, and the authors James Russell Lowell, John Greenleaf Whittier, and Ralph Waldo Emerson. A former slave, *Frederick Douglass,* edited an abolitionist newspaper in Rochester, New York. In Boston, *William Lloyd Garrison,* the best-known abolitionist, published the leading antislavery newspaper, the *Liberator.* Militant and uncompromising, Garrison condemned the Constitution, because it permitted slavery, as "an agreement with hell."

Moderate abolitionists entered politics by founding the Liberty party. In 1840, it ran its first Presidential candidate—a former southern slaveholder, James G. Birney. (In 1844 the Liberty party unintentionally helped defeat Clay and assured the election of James K. Polk.)

The abolitionists also organized a network of secret stations by which runaway slaves were smuggled out of the South to freedom in the North and Canada—a network called the *underground railroad*. By 1860 some 50,000 slaves were estimated to have escaped to freedom via the underground railroad. A leading worker on this "freedom road" was a former slave, *Harriet Tubman*.

The abolitionist movement, however, lacked realistic plans for ending slavery and for improving the life of blacks once they were free.

3. Limited Following Even in the North. In the 1830s the abolitionists in the North were treated roughly. Their meetings were heckled, their newspapers seized, and their leaders set upon violently. In Boston in 1835, Garrison was attacked by a mob and dragged through the streets. In Illinois in 1837, Elijah Lovejoy, an abolitionist editor, was attacked and murdered.

Most Northerners (a) considered the abolitionists as irresponsible fanatics, (b) believed that the South should solve the problem of slavery in its own way, (c) were anxious not to disturb their profitable business relations with the South, and (d) feared that freed blacks would come North and compete for jobs.

As time went on, however, many Northerners accepted the argument that slavery was morally wrong and had to be abolished. They hoped that the United States would follow the British example. In 1833 Great Britain had freed the slaves throughout its empire peacefully, and it had granted compensation to the slave owners.

THE SOUTH AND SLAVERY

1. Extent of Slavery. By 1860 the South held almost 4 million blacks as slaves. Of the southern white families, (a) 80 percent (poor whites, small farmers, and many city dwellers) owned no slaves, (b) 19 percent (mostly small farmers) owned a few slaves, usually five or fewer, and (c) 1 percent (large planters) owned 50 or more. These large planters possessed great estates, lived in splendid mansions, and dominated the South socially, economically, and politically.

Psychologically, the nonslave-owning lower classes may have had an interest in maintaining slavery because they could (a) look down upon the slaves as inferior beings, and (b) hope to rise in status by acquiring slaves.

2. Treatment of Slaves. The South's treatment of blacks varied from urban to rural areas, from small farms to large plantations, and according to the character of the white owner. Although cruel treatment existed, especially in the breaking up of black families, physical brutality was not the rule. Most slaves received adequate food, clothing, and shelter. Since a male field hand by 1860 was worth between $1200 and $1800, slaves represented valuable property to be conserved and utilized, not wantonly harmed.

3. Black Resistance. Considerable discontent existed among the slaves. Some ran away, some engaged in deliberate slowdowns or sabotage at work, and some undertook revolts. The fear of slave uprisings haunted southern whites. In 1822 Denmark Vesey, a free black, planned a slave revolt in South Carolina. In

1831 Nat Turner, a slave, led a bloody insurrection in Virginia. These and other resistance efforts were sternly suppressed.

4. Proslavery Arguments. Southern whites defended slavery, not as a necessary evil, but as a positive good. They argued that slavery (a) had existed through the ages and had provided the economic basis of the great civilizations of ancient Greece and Rome, (b) was sanctioned by the Bible, (c) assured continued cotton production and southern prosperity, (d) meant a better life for blacks in the South than in Africa, and (e) provided blacks with better treatment and more security than the North granted its free factory workers. Furthermore, southern whites insisted that blacks were mentally inferior and, if freed, would endanger the lives of southern whites and would be incapable of caring for themselves.

SLAVERY AND THE MEXICAN CESSION

At the start of the Mexican War in 1846, Representative *David Wilmot* of Pennsylvania introduced a resolution to prohibit slavery in any territory taken from Mexico. The *Wilmot Proviso* passed in the House but met defeat in the Senate. In 1848 the United States acquired the Mexican Cession, and the North and South resumed the struggle over the status of slavery in federal territory.

In 1848 settlers discovered gold in California, part of the Mexican Cession. The "Forty-Niners," as the incoming fortune hunters were called, soon increased the territory's population to 100,000. Californians drew up a constitution prohibiting slavery and applied for admission to the Union.

COMPROMISE OF 1850

1. The Issue. Congress now faced the problem of the status of slavery in California and in the rest of the newly acquired territory. In Congress and throughout the country, Northerners and Southerners debated bitterly regarding the extension of slavery. Finally, Henry Clay, the "Great Compromiser," proposed an all-inclusive plan.

Clay's compromise was denounced by extremists on both sides. Senator John Calhoun of South Carolina, ill and near death, had another Southerner read his speech opposing the compromise. Senator William H. Seward of New York cited a "higher law" than the Constitution in opposing the extension of slavery and the compromise.

Clay's compromise was supported by moderate Northerners, especially Senator Stephen A. Douglas of Illinois and Senator Daniel Webster of Massachusetts. In his Seventh of March speech, Webster declared that he spoke "not as a northern man, but as an American" who sought "the preservation of the Union." Webster argued that a law to prohibit slavery was unnecessary since the acquired territory was not suited for slavery because of its soil and climate. The compromise—really a series of five separate bills—was easily approved.

Compromise of 1850

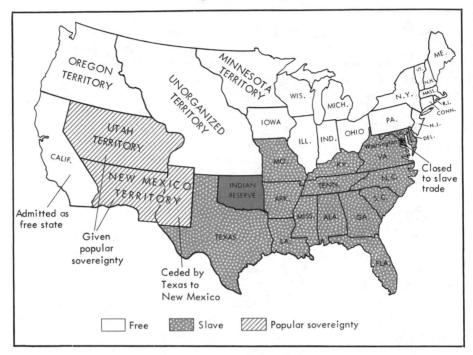

OREGON TERRITORY

UNORGANIZED TERRITORY

MINNESOTA TERRITORY

WIS.

MICH.

ME.

VT.

N.H.

N.Y.

MASS.

R.I.

CONN.

IOWA

PA.

N.J.

ILL. IND. OHIO

DEL.

UTAH TERRITORY

Washington

CALIF.

MO.

KY.

VA.

NEW MEXICO TERRITORY

INDIAN RESERVE

TENN

N.C.

Closed to slave trade

ARK

S.C.

Admitted as free state

MISS. ALA GA

Given popular sovereignty

TEXAS

LA

Ceded by Texas to New Mexico

FLA

☐ Free   ▨ Slave   ▨ Popular sovereignty

2. Provisions of the Compromise. (*a*) California was admitted as a free state. (*b*) The rest of the Mexican Cession was divided into the territories of New Mexico and Utah and was to follow the principle of *popular,* or *squatter, sovereignty.* This principle permitted the territorial inhabitants themselves to decide whether or not they wanted slavery. (*c*) Texas was given $10 million in exchange for a strip of land, most of which was assigned to New Mexico. (*d*) Slave trade, but not slavery, was prohibited in the District of Columbia. (*e*) A strict fugitive slave law was adopted to make it easier for Southerners to recover runaway slaves found in the North.

The Compromise of 1850, many moderate white Americans hoped, would finally settle the slavery issue—but it was not to be so.

FURTHER GROWTH OF ANTISLAVERY FEELING IN THE NORTH

1. The Fugitive Slave Law (1850). This law, with its harsh treatment of suspected runaway slaves, aroused northern resentment. The law authorized federal commissioners to try black suspects without allowing them to testify and without a jury. The commissioner received a double fee if he ruled the suspect a runaway slave rather than a free black. To obstruct the Fugitive Slave Law, many northern legislatures passed *personal liberty laws.* These laws prohibited state officials from cooperating in the capture of runaway slaves.

2. Harriet Beecher Stowe. Mrs. Stowe, an abolitionist and underground railroad worker, in 1852 wrote *Uncle Tom's Cabin*. This book, with its dramatic picture of black suffering in the South, swayed northern sympathies. Later, during the Civil War, Abraham Lincoln supposedly called Mrs. Stowe "the little woman who wrote the book that made this great war."

3. Horace Greeley. The founder of the influential New York *Tribune* aroused northern opinion by his vigorous antislavery newspaper editorials.

KANSAS-NEBRASKA ACT (1854)

1. Provisions. Stephen A. Douglas of Illinois secured passage of a bill that repealed the Missouri Compromise and, in its place, (a) divided the remaining land of the Louisiana Purchase into the territories of Kansas and Nebraska, and (b) authorized the people in these territories to determine the status of slavery according to popular sovereignty.

Status of Slavery in the West After the Kansas-Nebraska Act   1854

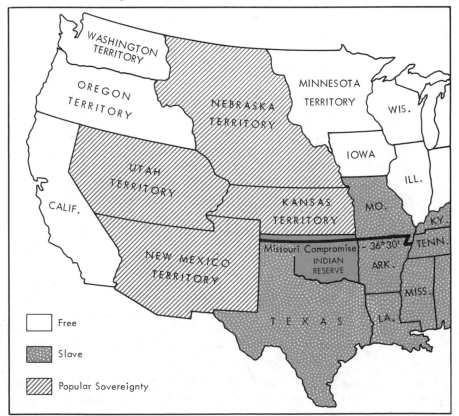

Free

Slave

Popular Sovereignty

2. Douglas' Motives. Although not definitely known, Douglas' motives were assumed to include a (a) belief in popular sovereignty as a democratic way to resolve the issue of slavery in federal territories, (b) belief that Kansas and Nebraska, by reason of soil and climate, were unfit for a slave economy, (c) desire for southern support for his Presidential ambitions, and (d) desire to populate the Kansas area so as to spur the building of the transcontinental railroad out of Chicago in his home state.

3. "Bleeding Kansas." Slaveowners, especially from Missouri, and abolitionists, chiefly from New England, hurried to Kansas, each group seeking to gain control of the territory. These proslavery and antislavery groups resorted to armed violence and began a small-scale civil war. Missouri "border ruffians" attacked free-soil settlements. Abolitionist bands, notably one led by *John Brown,* raided proslavery centers. "Bleeding Kansas" provided reports that kept sectional passions inflamed throughout the country.

FORMATION OF THE REPUBLICAN PARTY (1854)

Northern antislavery groups were shocked by the passage of the Kansas-Nebraska Act. Displeased by the wavering stand on slavery of both the Whig and Democratic parties, antislavery political leaders, meeting in Wisconsin and Michigan, created the present-day Republican party. They pledged to (1) oppose the extension of slavery into new territory, and (2) repeal the Fugitive Slave Law and the Kansas-Nebraska Act.

PRESIDENTIAL ELECTION OF 1856

As their first Presidential candidate, the Republicans in 1856 nominated the famed western explorer and opponent of slavery, *John C. Frémont.* The Democrats, again seeking to evade the slavery issue, nominated a Pennsylvanian with southern sympathies, James Buchanan. (The American, or Know-Nothing, party [check the Index], a short-lived third party that was anti-Catholic and anti-immigrant, also ran a candidate.) The Whig party had disintegrated.

Frémont carried 11 northern states, but Buchanan triumphed in the South as well as in five other northern states and easily won the election.

DRED SCOTT CASE

1. Issue. *Dred Scott,* a black slave, had been taken by his master into the Minnesota region, which according to the Missouri Compromise was free territory. He was then brought back to Missouri, a slave state. To create a test case, the abolitionists had Dred Scott sue for his freedom on the grounds that his residence in free territory had made him a free man.

2. Supreme Court Decision (1857). The Supreme Court ruled against Scott. Chief Justice *Roger B. Taney* began the majority opinion by stating that a black could not be a citizen and that Scott therefore could not bring suit in a federal court. Taney then went beyond this point to comment on the issue of slavery in federal territories, hoping to end the slavery controversy by a judicial statement. His further conclusions were labeled by antislavery leaders as *obiter dicta* (Latin for "some things said in passing") and therefore not legally binding. Taney stated that (*a*) slaves were property, (*b*) Congress may not deprive any person of the right to take property into federal territories, and (*c*) the Missouri Compromise, which prohibited slavery in part of the Louisiana Territory, was unconstitutional.

The dissenting opinions in the Dred Scott case pointed out that free blacks were considered citizens in some states and that the Constitution granted Congress the power to make "all needful rules and regulations" for federal territories.

The Dred Scott decision was applauded by the South but denounced by the North. It increased sectional ill will.

LINCOLN-DOUGLAS DEBATES (1858)

Abraham Lincoln, a Republican relatively unknown nationally, contested for the Senate seat from Illinois with the Democratic incumbent, the "Little Giant," Stephen A. Douglas. They engaged in a series of seven remarkable debates. In Freeport, Lincoln forced Douglas to state his view on slavery in the territories. Douglas said that the Dred Scott decision made slavery legal in the territories in theory, but the people of a territory could keep slaves out in practice. Douglas was narrowly reelected Senator, but his *Freeport Doctrine* cost him southern support for the Presidency in 1860. Abraham Lincoln meanwhile became known throughout the North.

JOHN BROWN'S RAID (1859)

John Brown, a fanatical abolitionist, led a band of some 20 men in a raid against the federal arsenal at *Harpers Ferry* in Virginia. Brown hoped to secure guns, arm the nearby blacks, and lead a slave rebellion. He was caught by federal troops, tried for treason against Virginia, found guilty, and hanged. In the North generally, Brown was honored for having sacrificed his life for human liberty. In the South, Brown was despised as a dangerous criminal.

PRESIDENTIAL ELECTION OF 1860

1. Issues and Candidates

a. The Democratic party, unable to agree on a platform or a candidate, split into two parts. The northern Democrats stood for popular sovereignty and nominated Stephen A. Douglas. The southern Democrats demanded enforcement of the Dred Scott decision and chose John C. Breckinridge.

b. The Republican party opposed the extension of slavery to the territories but promised not to interfere with slavery in the states. The Republicans also appealed to northern business leaders and western settlers by pledging a protective tariff, federal aid for internal improvements, a transcontinental railroad, and free homestead farms. In selecting a candidate, the Republicans passed over the extremist William H. Seward, who saw the struggle over slavery as an "irrepressible conflict." They nominated, instead, the more moderate Abraham Lincoln.

    c. The Constitutional Union party, a third party, affirmed its support of the Union and nominated John Bell.

    2. Results. Lincoln polled only 40 percent of the total popular vote but carried the North and West solidly. He won the election with a decisive majority in the electoral college.

THE SOUTH SECEDES

    1. Southern Reaction to the Election. Southern leaders were outraged by the election of Lincoln, whom they called a "black Republican." Many Southerners ignored the facts that (*a*) the Republicans controlled neither the Senate nor the House of Representatives, and (*b*) prosouthern judges dominated the Supreme Court.

    2. Confederate States of America. In December 1860, South Carolina seceded from the Union and was soon followed by six other southern states. In February 1861, the secessionist leaders met at Montgomery, Alabama, established the *Confederate States of America,* and selected as president *Jefferson*

The Divided Nation: The Union and the Confederacy

Davis. The Confederacy hastened military preparations in case it would have to use force to defend its independence.

THE FEDERAL GOVERNMENT AND THE CHALLENGE OF SECESSION

1. Buchanan's Inaction. In office until March 4, 1861, President Buchanan behaved cautiously and ineffectively. He said that states had no right to secede, but he added that the federal government had no right to use force against secession. Buchanan urged compromise but took no decisive action to preserve the Union.

2. Lincoln Takes Office. In his Inaugural Address, Lincoln was both conciliatory and firm. He pledged not to interfere with slavery in the states where it existed, and he promised to enforce federal regulations, including the Fugitive Slave Law. However, he labeled secession as illegal and emphasized his solemn oath to "preserve, protect, and defend" the Constitution. He warned, "In your hands, my dissatisfied countrymen, and not in mine, is the momentous issue of civil war."

In April 1861, Lincoln notified southern authorities that unarmed ships would carry food to the federal troops at Fort Sumter in the harbor of Charleston, South Carolina. Nevertheless, southern guns bombarded the fort and compelled its surrender. The Civil War had begun.

Historical Analysis. *Was slavery the most important cause of the Civil War?*

Yes. Slavery (1) presented a dramatic moral issue, since it dealt with human beings and involved individual freedom and democratic ideals, (2) distinguished the South from the North most clearly, and (3) was at the heart of most major issues dividing the two sections.

No. (1) The overwhelming majority of Southerners did not own slaves, (2) most Northerners were not abolitionists, (3) Lincoln and the Republicans did not threaten slavery where it already existed, and (4) four slave states remained loyal to the Union.

OTHER CAUSES OF THE CIVIL WAR

1. Economic Differences. Because of geographical conditions, the South had become agricultural and the North industrial. These economic differences led to bitter sectional rivalry on such issues as slavery and the protective tariff. The aristocratic southern planters were determined to resist domination by the northern industrialists and to advance the interests of the South's agrarian economy.

2. Nature of the Federal Union. The South insisted that the federal Union was created by the states and that any state had the right to secede. The

North insisted that the Union was created by the people and was indivisible, and that no state had the right to secede. Lincoln proclaimed that the primary object of the war was not to abolish slavery, but to preserve the Union.

3. Control of the Central Government. To secure control of the central government, both the North and the South had sought the support of new territories. Consequently, the South favored and the North opposed the extension of slavery into the western territories. In time, most of the West became tied economically to the North by a network of railroads and a mutually profitable exchange of foodstuffs for manufactured goods. Southerners increasingly realized that (a) most western lands were not suitable for cotton culture, (b) the South was losing the battle for western support, and (c) the South would remain a minority section in the Union.

4. Differences in Civilization. The South had developed a static civilization, dominated by a small aristocracy of influential planter families. Northern civilization was more democratic and dynamic. The clash of civilizations made understanding of each other's point of view difficult.

5. Fanaticism. Extremists on both sides sought to exaggerate differences. Northern abolitionists projected unfair stereotypes of southern slaveowners.

Southern secessionists did likewise with respect to northern free-soilers and Republicans. In the crucial decade of the 1850s, the nation lacked leaders able to move the sections toward compromise and peaceful solutions. Instead, hysteria and emotion mounted, and the "blundering generation" went to war.

CONCLUSION

No single cause brought about the Civil War. Rather, it resulted from the interrelationship of many complex factors. The causes of the Civil War remain a subject of intense historical research, revision, and debate.

———————— MULTIPLE-CHOICE QUESTIONS ————————

1. "If you put a chain around the neck of a slave, the other end fastens itself around your own." This statement refers to the idea that (a) absentee ownership of plantations was not wise (b) slavery was an economically costly institution (c) slavery degraded both owner and slave (d) slaves accompanied settlers going West.

2. The Declaration of Independence, as finally adopted (a) vigorously condemned slavery (b) was silent regarding slavery (c) recognized the need of southern planters for slave labor (d) offered independence to blacks who volunteered to fight against the British troops.

3. Which is the *most* valid statement concerning slavery in the 19th-century United States? (a) Although slaves deeply resented their status, they did not openly protest. (b) There were individual protests and collective rebellions by slaves. (c) Many laws were enacted to protect the slaves from cruel treatment. (d) Most slaves accepted their status and did not want to obtain their freedom.

4. Which was a result of the other three? (a) strong southern support of slavery (b) invention of the cotton gin (c) Industrial Revolution in England (d) abundant supply of good land in this country.

5. The territorial expansion of the United States before the Civil War became a matter for furious political debate because (a) the South would not send troops to acquire free territory (b) Northerners were opposed to any expansion (c) additional states would tend to upset the sectional balance in the Senate (d) no new territory could be admitted until the Texas controversy was settled.

6. In 1860, 19 million bushels of corn went east over the railroads while 4.8 million bushels went south over the Mississippi-Ohio River system. This statement helps to explain the (a) victory of canals over railroads (b) sympathy of the West for the South in the secession movement (c) dislike of southern cotton farmers for the West (d) support given the North by the West in the Civil War.

7. The Missouri Compromise established the 36° 30′ parallel as the boundary between free and slave territories in (a) the Louisiana Purchase only (b) the Northwest Territory only (c) all land west of the Mississippi (d) the entire United States.

8. Many Northerners took serious issue with the abolitionists for (a) attacking slavery as a moral issue (b) writing books about slavery that were sometimes inaccurate (c) demanding the immediate freeing of all slaves (d) advocating that factory owners employ fugitive slaves.

9. Henry Clay is classified as both (a) a Whig leader and a victorious general (b) a "War Hawk" and a "Great Compromiser" (c) a member of the Virginia dynasty and a Presidential nominee (d) an ambassador to France and a secretary of state.

10. In the Compromise of 1850, the South regarded as its main concession to the North the provision concerning (a) fugitive slaves (b) the admission of California (c) slavery in New Mexico (d) the state of Texas.

11. Which is an expression of states' rights by the northern states? (a) personal liberty laws (b) Kansas-Nebraska Act (c) Fugitive Slave Law (d) Compromise of 1850.

12. Stephen A. Douglas sponsored the Kansas-Nebraska Act because he (a) was a Senator from a slave state (b) opposed popular sovereignty (c) wanted to hasten the building of a railroad through Kansas (d) expected to be appointed to the Supreme Court.

13. One direct result of the passage of the Kansas-Nebraska Act was the (a) beginning of the abolitionist movement (b) migration of settlers out of the Kansas and Nebraska territories (c) formation of the Republican party (d) organization of the first underground railroad.

14. In 1857 which act of Congress was declared unconstitutional by the Supreme Court in the Dred Scott decision? (a) the Fugitive Slave Law (b) the admission of California (c) the Missouri Compromise (d) the Kansas-Nebraska Act.

15. The significance of the Dred Scott decision was that (a) Congress could not prohibit slavery in the territories (b) only Congress could prohibit slavery in any part of the United States (c) the people of a territory, by popular sovereignty, could outlaw slavery (d) the Fugitive Slave Law was severely weakened.

16. A significant result of the Lincoln-Douglas debates was that (a) Douglas failed to be reelected Senator (b) the Missouri Compromise was repealed (c) Lincoln supported the doctrine of popular sovereignty (d) Douglas lost the support of the South for the Presidency.

17. The chief reason for the opposition of the South to the election of Abraham Lincoln in 1860 was his (a) resistance to secession (b) demand for the immediate abolition of slavery (c) hostility to the extension of slavery (d) insistence on equal education for blacks and whites.

18. As a result of the election of 1860, Lincoln was a "minority" President. This means that he (a) received less than 50 percent of the popular vote (b) received less than 50 percent of the electoral vote (c) was elected by running on the tickets of two parties (d) was elected by the House of Representatives.

19. Which was a *major* cause for the secession of the southern states? (a) northern demands that slave states get out of the Union (b) failure of Congress to support the principle of popular sovereignty in the territories (c) President Buchanan's forceful attack on the doctrine of nullification and secession (d) belief that southern interests could be better advanced outside the federal Union.

——————————————— MATCHING QUESTIONS ———————————————

Column A

1. Editor of the *Liberator*
2. Senate advocate of Kansas-Nebraska Act
3. President of the Confederacy
4. Editor of New York *Tribune*
5. President of the United States when seven southern states seceded
6. Leader of raid at Harpers Ferry
7. Author of *Uncle Tom's Cabin*
8. Black abolitionist editor
9. Black leader of insurrection
10. Chief Justice of Supreme Court in Dred Scott case

Column B

a. John Brown
b. James Buchanan
c. Jefferson Davis
d. Stephen A. Douglas
e. Frederick Douglass
f. William Lloyd Garrison
g. Horace Greeley
h. Abraham Lincoln
i. Harriet Beecher Stowe
j. Roger B. Taney
k. Harriet Tubman
l. Nat Turner
m. David Wilmot

——————————————— ESSAY QUESTIONS ———————————————

1. (a) Describe *two* economic differences and *one* difference in political views between the North and the South before 1860. (b) Discuss *two* factors that have helped to break down sectional differences within the United States since then.

2. Democracy is a series of compromises. (a) Mention *three* important compromises in our history. (b) For each of *two* of these compromises, state the main issue and give the major provisions.

3. Show how the North and the South, from 1820 to 1860, differed bitterly in regard to *each* of the following: (a) tariffs (b) westward expansion (c) states' rights theory of government (d) *Uncle Tom's Cabin* (e) Dred Scott decision.

4. Students of American history continue to argue about the fundamental causes of the Civil War. (a) State briefly *three* fundamental causes for the Civil War that have been advanced by historians. (b) For *each* cause stated, discuss *one* argument for agreeing and *one* argument for disagreeing with the conclusion that this factor brought on the war.

PART 6. The Civil War Marks the Triumph of Nationalism

COMPARISON OF THE NORTH AND THE SOUTH

Many historians hold that the leaders of the South risked civil war because they underestimated the strength and tenacity of the North while overestimating their own power.

ADVANTAGES OF THE NORTH

1. The North retained control of more than two-thirds of the states. These included 19 free states and 4 slaveholding border states: Delaware, Maryland, Kentucky, and Missouri. The North also retained the northwestern part of Virginia, whose pro-Union inhabitants in 1863 formed the state of West Virginia. However, strong prosouthern sentiment existed in the four border states and in the southern parts of Ohio, Indiana, and Illinois.

2. The North's population totaled 22 million, as compared with the South's 9 million, of whom almost 4 million were slaves.

3. Northern manufacturing represented over 90 percent of the country's industry. The North had abundant textile factories, iron and steel mills, and armament plants. The South had few factories and had to depend largely upon imports for manufactured goods.

4. The North contained over 20,000 miles of railroad, more than double the South's railroad facilities.

5. The North possessed more than three-fourths of the nation's financial resources. Being short of capital, the South had great difficulty in financing the war.

6. The North maintained control of the navy and merchant marine.

ADVANTAGES OF THE SOUTH

1. The South consisted of a geographically compact group of 11 states. The seven states that had seceded following Lincoln's election were joined, with the outbreak of hostilities, by four border states: Arkansas, Tennessee, North Carolina, and Virginia. However, the South contained some areas of pro-Union sentiment.

2. Southerners were fighting essentially a defensive war, held the interior, or shorter, lines of communication, and knew their own terrain.

3. The South retained the loyalty of outstanding military commanders, notably *Thomas J. ("Stonewall") Jackson* and *Robert E. Lee.*

4. Southerners were accustomed to an outdoor life of riding and hunting. They were therefore better prepared than northern factory workers and shopkeepers for hardships as soldiers.

5. The South had many friends in Britain and France who favored the southern aristocracy. These nations also depended on imports of southern cotton. Southern leaders therefore expected Britain and France to rally to their support.

MILITARY ASPECTS OF THE WAR

WAR ON LAND

1. Stalemate in the East (1861–1862). Moving southward toward the Confederate capital of Richmond, Virginia, a Union army in 1861 met defeat in the first major engagement of the war, in Virginia at *Bull Run.* For the next three years in the East, the Union's *Army of the Potomac* confronted the Confederacy's *Army of Northern Virginia.* Military action took place mainly on southern soil as Confederate forces repeatedly repulsed Union offensives.

The North was twice invaded by Confederate armies under General Robert E. Lee. Union forces repulsed these invasions in bloody battles—in 1862 in Maryland at *Antietam* and in 1863 in Pennsylvania at *Gettysburg.* The Union victory at Gettysburg, achieved by General *George Meade,* was the turning point of the war.

2. Northern Victories in the West (1862–1863). General *Ulysses S. Grant* led Union forces to victories on the western front. In 1862 he captured *Fort Donelson* in western Tennessee, gaining his nickname of "Unconditional

The Civil War: Union Victories in the West and on the Mississippi; Sherman's March to the Sea

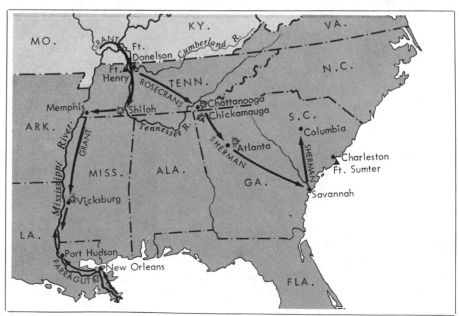

The Civil War: Major Battles in the North and the East; Union Victory at Appomattox

Surrender," and repulsed Confederate troops at *Shiloh*. Moving southward into Mississippi in 1863, Grant established Union control of the lower Mississippi River by capturing the Confederate fortress at *Vicksburg*.

3. Final Phase (1864–1865). Grant received command of all Union forces in 1864, and General *William T. Sherman* was placed in charge of the Union army in the West. Sherman captured *Atlanta*, in western Georgia, and started on a 300-mile "march through Georgia" to the coastal city of *Savannah*, devastating the Confederate countryside. Grant meanwhile led the Union forces in Virginia and launched a relentless attack against Lee's army. In April 1865, after 11 months of fighting, Grant captured Richmond. Lee realized that the war was lost and surrendered to Grant at the small Virginia town of *Appomattox Court House*. Grant generously permitted the Confederate soldiers to keep their horses "for the spring plowing" and announced, "The rebels are our countrymen again."

NAVAL WAR

1. Blockade of Southern Ports. Northern strategy called for a coastal blockade of the South to prevent the export of cotton and the import of goods for the southern war effort. Within two years the blockade reduced southern cotton exports from $200 million to $4 million.

2. *Monitor* vs. *Merrimac*: First Ironclad Ships. To break the blockade, the South put iron plates on a wooden frigate, the *Merrimac,* and sent it against the Union fleet. The *Merrimac* easily destroyed two wooden vessels before encountering the ironclad *Monitor.* Designed by *John Ericsson,* the *Monitor* was described as a cheese box on a raft. The *Monitor* battled the *Merrimac* for hours, until the *Merrimac* withdrew, thus enabling the North to maintain the blockade. These first ironclad ships revealed such superiority in battle that they forecast the doom of wooden fleets.

3. Control of the Mississippi River. In 1862 Admiral *David G. Farragut* led a Union naval force into the mouth of the Mississippi and captured New Orleans. Farragut's victory, together with Grant's success at Vicksburg in 1863, gave the North complete control of the Mississippi, thereby splitting the Confederacy.

4. Confederate Attacks on Northern Merchant Ships. The Confederacy was able to harass northern commerce on the seas chiefly because of British aid. In violation of its neutrality, Britain built several warships for the South, the most famous being the *Florida* and the *Alabama.* Southern sea raiders sank many northern merchant ships and brought about a decline of the American merchant marine. Though costly, these southern raids little affected the outcome of the war.

FOREIGN AFFAIRS DURING THE WAR

RELATIONS WITH GREAT BRITAIN

The North and the South both realized that Britain's industrial and naval power could tip the scales in the American Civil War. The North sought to keep Britain neutral, while the South worked for active British intervention.

SHARPLY DIVIDED SYMPATHIES IN BRITAIN

The British middle and working classes opposed the South because it supported slavery, and favored the North, which was considered more democratic. Sympathy for the Union increased sharply in Britain after Lincoln issued the Emancipation Proclamation, freeing the slaves in the Confederate territories.

The British upper classes, including most government leaders, favored the

South because it (1) was dominated by the aristocracy, (2) maintained class distinctions, and (3) supported free trade with Britain. British officials, furthermore, anticipated an advantage for Britain if the United States split into two contending nations in place of one united country.

REASONS FOR BRITAIN'S NEUTRALITY

In spite of the sympathy of British leaders for the South, Britain remained neutral. (1) The London government feared intensifying the sharp divisions within British public opinion. (2) In the early years of the war, British textile manufacturers had no need to import southern cotton since they held large cotton surpluses. (3) The British populace depended upon the North for imports of wheat. (These considerations of imports are often called "the battle of cotton versus wheat.") (4) In 1863 British military experts predicted that the South would lose the war.

WARTIME CONTROVERSIES BETWEEN THE UNITED STATES AND GREAT BRITAIN

1. *Trent* Affair (1861). A United States naval vessel stopped the British steamship *Trent* and took off two European-bound Confederate agents, *James Mason* and *John Slidell.* The British government demanded the release of the two agents, claimed that the North had violated Britain's rights as a neutral, and threatened war. President Lincoln and Secretary of State William Seward both realized that Great Britain had to be prevented from intervening in the war. The Union government released Mason and Slidell.

2. British-Built Warships for the Confederacy. British shipyards built several warships for the Confederacy, notably the *Florida* and the *Alabama,* which preyed upon northern merchant ships. By turning these cruisers over to the Confederacy, Britain violated its obligations as a neutral. Charles Francis Adams, the American minister to Great Britain, repeatedly protested until the British finally halted any further building of ships for the southern navy.

After the war the United States demanded reparations from Britain for the damage caused by the *Alabama* and other British-built cruisers. In 1871 the two nations agreed to a peaceful settlement of the *Alabama claims.* In 1872 the United States was awarded $15 million by an international court of arbitration.

RELATIONS WITH FRANCE

PROSOUTHERN POLICIES

The French upper classes and government favored the South. A French banking firm raised several million dollars for the South by selling Confederate bonds in Europe. Napoleon III, the French Emperor, believed that a southern victory would weaken the Monroe Doctrine and permit him to extend French influence into Mexico.

MAXIMILIAN AFFAIR (1862–1867)

In 1862 Napoleon sent an army into Mexico and established a French protectorate under the puppet Emperor *Maximilian*. Secretary of State Seward protested immediately, but the United States could take no action until the end of the Civil War. Thereafter, the United States stationed a large force at the Mexican border and again demanded that Napoleon withdraw his troops. Napoleon did so in 1867, but Maximilian chose to remain. He was soon captured and executed by Mexican troops under the command of their President, *Benito Juarez*.

The *Maximilian Affair* demonstrated the ability and determination of the United States to enforce the Monroe Doctrine.

RELATIONS WITH RUSSIA

PRONORTHERN POLICIES

Russia, desiring a strong United States as a balance against British power, favored the northern cause. Czar Alexander II, furthermore, applauded the North's antislavery sentiment, since in 1861 he had emancipated (freed) the Russian serfs. In 1863 Russian fleets visited New York City and San Francisco—visits interpreted as friendly gestures to the North and as stern warnings to Britain and France to refrain from assisting the South.

PURCHASE OF ALASKA (1867)

For several years Russia had proposed selling Alaska to the United States. In 1867, in part out of gratitude for Russia's friendship during the Civil War, Secretary of State Seward agreed to buy Alaska. (Check the Index.)

THE HOME FRONT

RECRUITING FOR MILITARY SERVICE

1. In the South. At first, Confederate armies consisted of volunteers. After the initial enthusiasm had worn off, the South in 1862 instituted a conscription, or draft. It provided many occupational exemptions, such as for slave overseers, and permitted conscripts to escape service by hiring substitutes. The draft law aroused considerable opposition. The lower classes protested a "rich man's war and a poor man's fight." In total, the Confederacy placed under arms approximately one million persons.

2. In the North. Originally, Union army ranks were also filled by volunteers. When enlistments fell off, the northern governments—federal, state, and local—encouraged volunteers to enlist by offering cash bounties. The bounty system spurred enlistments but also led to *bounty-jumping:* dishonest individuals would enlist, receive their bounties, desert, and reenlist elsewhere to secure additional bounties.

In 1863 the North, too, passed a draft law, which allowed draftees to avoid service by hiring substitutes or by paying $300 to the government. Many poor people resented the draft, and riots broke out, most notably in New York City. In total, the Union recruited approximately 2 million persons, twice the number of Confederate soldiers.

FINANCING THE WAR

1. In the South. Since its wealth consisted chiefly of slaves and land, the South had great difficulty in raising money. The Confederate government (a) levied excise taxes, (b) sold bonds to its people, and (c) issued tremendous quantities of paper money without specie backing. As southern military prospects declined, the value of Confederate paper money fell sharply. The South sought loans in Europe, but had little success. European bankers generally doubted the South's ability to repay loans, since the northern blockade prevented the export of southern cotton and tobacco.

2. In the North. The prosperous North raised money more easily, as follows: (a) Imposed high excise taxes and a modest income tax—the first in American history. (b) Passed the *Morrill Tariff Act* (1861), which raised import duties and yielded considerable revenue while giving northern manufacturers protection against foreign competition. (c) Issued $450 million in paper money called *greenbacks*. (Since they were backed by the people's confidence in the government, not by specie, the greenbacks fluctuated in purchasing power with the North's changing military prospects.) (d) Sold government bonds to banks and individuals. (e) Passed the *National Banking Act* (1863), permitting banks to secure national charters, requiring them to purchase government bonds, and authorizing them to use the bonds as backing for paper banknotes. This law thusly provided a national currency and also helped boost the sale of bonds to finance the war.

POLITICAL MATTERS

1. In the South. *Jefferson Davis,* Confederate president, appointed an undistinguished cabinet and himself lacked qualities of leadership. He proved inflexible, intolerant of criticism, and unable to arouse public enthusiasm. Davis faced attack by personal enemies and political opponents—the more so as the Confederacy moved closer to defeat.

2. In the North

a. Expansion of Presidential Powers. Lincoln used his Presidential powers extensively. He was often accused of acting dictatorially, as he stretched his authority, sometimes beyond Constitutional limits. In the first months of the war, before Congress convened, Lincoln expanded the regular army, called for army volunteers, and spent federal funds not yet appropriated—explaining that when Congress met, it would approve these actions. Stretching his war powers as commander in chief, Lincoln ordered a naval blockade of southern ports and substituted martial law for civil law in various states, thereby suspending the writ of habeas corpus and imprisoning southern sympathizers. Lincoln reasoned that rather than let the government fall into ruin, he had availed himself of the "broader powers conferred by the Constitution in cases of insurrection" so as to save the Constitution "with all its blessings for the present age and posterity."

b. The Peace Democrats. These were northern inhabitants whose enemies called them *Copperheads* (after a venomous snake) because they sympathized with the South and urged that the South be allowed to secede. Lincoln exiled their leader, Ohio Congress member Clement L. Vallandigham, to the Confederacy. Also in regions inhabited by Confederate sympathizers, Lincoln ordered that certain cases of obstructing the war effort be tried by military courts. (In 1866, in the case *ex parte Milligan*, the Supreme Court ruled Lincoln's action unconstitutional. It held that martial law could not be imposed on civilians in areas remote from the war and where civil courts were still operating.)

c. The Emancipation Proclamation (1863). After the Union success at the Battle of Antietam and in response to northern public opinion, Lincoln issued the *Emancipation Proclamation.* It declared free all slaves in areas under Confederate control so that, in its immediate impact, it freed no slaves. This unprecedented declaration was based upon Lincoln's power as commander in chief and was designed to weaken the southern war effort by encouraging blacks to flee the Confederacy.

Blacks worked the southern farms and plantations and performed many noncombat army tasks, thus releasing the whites for battle duty. The Emancipation Proclamation inspired the northern populace, won support abroad for the Union, was a step toward ending all slavery as achieved by the Thirteenth Amendment, and earned Lincoln the title of *Great Emancipator.*

d. Election of 1864. The Republicans renominated Lincoln. To broaden their support, the Republicans assumed the name Union party and chose as their Vice Presidential candidate a pro-Union Democrat, *Andrew Johnson* of Tennessee. The Republican platform urged the North to continue the struggle to victory. The Democrats adopted a platform calling the war a failure and urging an armistice. This platform, however, was repudiated by the Democratic Presidential candidate, General *George B. McClellan.*

Lincoln at first feared he would lose the election, but a series of northern victories in 1864 gained him decisive public support. Lincoln received 55 percent of the popular vote and an overwhelming electoral college majority.

LINCOLN'S PLACE IN HISTORY

LINCOLN: THE NATION'S LEADER

In March 1861, when Lincoln was inaugurated, he was little known to his fellow Americans. Today, he ranks as one of the greatest of all Americans. His claim to greatness rests on his leadership during four long, hard years of civil war. With courage, dignity, and humility, he carried the nation's many burdens. Without hate, he kept steadfastly to his primary purpose—the preservation of the Union. Despite his exercise of almost dictatorial wartime powers, he maintained an unwavering faith in the superiority of the democratic way of life. At all times, he remained close to the people.

LINCOLN'S PHILOSOPHY

1. Democracy. In a letter, Lincoln gave a simple yet eloquent definition of democracy: "As I would not be a slave, so I would not be a master. This expresses my idea of democracy." In his debates with Douglas, although disclaiming any intention of introducing social equality between the races, Lincoln insisted that the black is the equal of any person as regards "life, liberty, and the pursuit of happiness. . . . "

In the *Gettysburg Address* (1863), Lincoln declared that the United States had been "conceived in liberty and dedicated to the proposition that all men are created equal," and he urged Americans to "highly resolve" that "government of the people, by the people, for the people, shall not perish from the earth."

2. The Union. Accepting the Republican nomination for the Senate in 1858, Lincoln warned, "A house divided against itself cannot stand. I believe that this government cannot endure permanently half slave and half free." In his *First Inaugural Address* (1861), Lincoln appealed to the South to remember the historic ties that had held the Union together and to refrain from seceding.

3. Reuniting the Nation. When Lincoln began his second term, the war was nearing its conclusion. In his *Second Inaugural Address* (1865), Lincoln looked forward and said, "With malice toward none; with charity for all; with firmness in the right, as God gives us to see the right, let us strive on to finish the work we are in; to bind up the nation's wounds."

LINCOLN'S ASSASSINATION (APRIL 1865)

Lincoln did not live to carry into effect his humane plans for binding up the nation's wounds and achieving a lasting peace. Shortly after the war's end, he was assassinated at Ford's Theater in Washington, D.C., by a fanatical Confederate sympathizer, John Wilkes Booth. The death of Abraham Lincoln removed the one person who might have reunited the nation without further bitterness.

———————— MAP QUESTIONS ————————

For each state described below, write *both* its name and the *letter* indicating its location on the map.

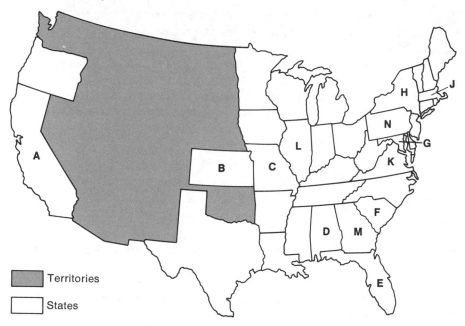

1. By the Compromise of 1820, this state was admitted to the Union as a slave state.
2. This state was the first to secede from the Union.
3. At Appomattox Court House, in this state, General Lee surrendered to General Grant, thereby ending the Civil War.
4. According to the Compromise of 1850, this state entered the Union as a free state.
5. The bloody and decisive Battle of Gettysburg was fought in this state.
6. During the Civil War, keeping this border state in the Union was necessary to prevent the isolation of Washington, D.C., from the northern states.
7. General William Sherman's march to the sea devastated this state.
8. Formerly part of a territory granted popular sovereignty by a law sponsored by Stephen A. Douglas, this state was admitted to the Union in 1861.
9. In 1858 Lincoln and Douglas engaged in a series of debates while seeking the Senate seat from this state.
10. In this state was located the first Confederate capital.

———————— MULTIPLE-CHOICE QUESTIONS ————————

1. A primary source for the study of the Civil War is (a) an American history textbook (b) *The Dictionary of American History* (c) *Abraham Lincoln: The War Years,* by Carl Sandburg (d) *The Blue and the Gray, The Story of the Civil War As Told by Participants,* edited by Henry Steele Commager.

2. The chief purpose of the northern blockade during the Civil War was to prevent (a) British volunteers from reaching the South (b) Confederate officials from escaping to Europe (c) the South from exporting cotton (d) the French navy from aiding the South.

3. The Emancipation Proclamation was (a) a law of Congress (b) an amendment to the Constitution (c) a Presidential order (d) a joint resolution of Congress.

4. During the Civil War, which action posed the greatest threat to civil liberties? (a) seizure of Mason and Slidell from the *Trent* (b) suspension of the writ of habeas corpus by President Lincoln (c) use of conscription to secure troops for the armed forces (d) nomination of General McClellan for the Presidency.

5. Which group in Britain showed the most sympathy for the Union during the Civil War? (a) large landowners (b) governing classes (c) factory workers (d) merchants.

6. The chief reason why the British commercial class supported the Confederacy in the Civil War was that the South was (a) fighting for the preservation of its social structure (b) more likely to win the war (c) more likely to repay debts to British citizens (d) more likely to provide favorable tariff conditions for British goods.

7. Britain did not recognize the Confederacy during the Civil War because (a) Britain needed northern wheat (b) Britain never had much trade with the South (c) Britain needed northern manufactures (d) Russia favored the South.

8. Which dispute involved the United States and France? (a) Florida boundary dispute (b) *Alabama* claims (c) *Trent* Affair (d) Maximilian Affair.

9. Our demand that French forces be removed from Mexico after the Civil War is an example of our enforcement of (a) the Constitution (b) the Monroe Doctrine (c) Washington's Proclamation of Neutrality (d) Clay's American System.

10. The main objection to the North's draft law was that it was (a) unconstitutional because it violated civil rights (b) unnecessary because there were so many volunteers (c) unfair because it provided loopholes for persons of wealth (d) discriminatory because it applied only to New Englanders.

11. Which advantage did the North *lack* in fighting the Civil War? (a) large population (b) more industry (c) greater financial resources (d) interior lines of communications in a defensive war.

12. In financing the Civil War, which method did the North *not* employ? (a) higher excise taxes (b) increased price of western lands (c) issuance of greenbacks (d) selling bonds to national banks.

13. Lincoln's secretary of state, later responsible for the purchase of Alaska, was (a) John Q. Adams (b) William H. Seward (c) William T. Sherman (d) John W. Booth.

14. The designer of the Union's ironclad ship, the *Monitor,* was (a) John Ericsson (b) David G. Farragut (c) James Mason (d) Clement Vallandigham.

———————————— ESSAY QUESTIONS ————————————

1. Discuss *two* reasons to support *each* of the following statements: (*a*) The campaign to win the Senate seat from Illinois made Abraham Lincoln a national figure. (*b*) Abraham Lincoln made bold use of his Presidential powers. (*c*) Lincoln's public addresses deserve the praise they have received. (*d*) Abraham Lincoln's views on slavery were moderate in comparison with the views of other antislavery leaders of the period.

2. Giving *two* reasons, discuss which item in each of the following pairs did more to win the Civil War for the North: (a) the McCormick reaper or the skill of the Union generals, (b) the blockade of southern ports or the attitude of foreign powers, (c) the leadership of President Lincoln or the superior resources of the North.

3. In regard to the Civil War, discuss (a) *two* ways in which writers helped bring about the Civil War, (b) *two* reasons why the South seceded from the Union, (c) *two* problems faced by the Union in conducting the Civil War, (d) *two* problems faced by the Confederacy in conducting the Civil War.

4. Southern leaders risked civil war because they underestimated the North's strength and overestimated the South's power. (a) Describe *two* evidences of the North's strength. (b) Describe *two* evidences of the South's power. (c) Do you agree or disagree with the introductory statement? Present *one* argument to support your point of view.

PART 7. An Embittered South Is Brought Back Into the Union

RECONSTRUCTION: MEANING AND PROBLEMS

The term *reconstruction* refers to the years from 1865 to 1877 when the American people reestablished the southern states as an integral part of the Union. In so doing, Americans had to answer the following questions:

1. What conditions should be placed upon the southern states before permitting them to return to the Union and to assume their former rights?

2. Which branch of the federal government—executive or legislative—should determine the conditions for the return of the southern states?

3. What political, economic, and social rights should be granted to blacks, and how should these rights be enforced?

LINCOLN'S PLAN OF RECONSTRUCTION

Abraham Lincoln believed that (1) the southern states had never seceded, since no state could legally leave the Union, (2) the rebellion against the federal government was the work of individual Southerners, (3) reconstruction was a task for the President because of his Constitutional power to pardon acts against the government, and (4) reconstruction should be lenient, seeking primarily to regain the South's loyalty to the Union.

In 1863 Lincoln proposed that (1) all Southerners (except high Confederate military and government leaders) be pardoned upon taking an oath of allegiance to the Union, and (2) when 10 percent of the voters in a state took this oath of allegiance, they be permitted to form a legal state government. These generous provisions for political reconstruction became known as Lincoln's *10 percent plan.*

JOHNSON RETAINS LINCOLN'S VIEWS ON RECONSTRUCTION

Andrew Johnson, thrust into the Presidency in 1865 by Lincoln's assassination, was a pro-Union Tennessee Democrat. He had been placed on the 1864 ticket with Lincoln in order to attract votes and emphasize national unity. Johnson lacked Lincoln's prestige with the people and Lincoln's influence with the Republican party. Although courageous, Johnson was also stubborn and tactless.

As President, Johnson essentially continued Lincoln's conciliatory reconstruction plan. He offered pardons to most Southerners who pledged allegiance to the Union and who agreed to the abolition of slavery. He accepted the government of every southern state that disowned its act of secession, repudiated the Confederate debt, and ratified the Thirteenth Amendment prohibiting slavery. By early 1866 white Southerners had reestablished all their state governments and had elected Senators and Representatives, including some prominent ex-Confederates, to the federal Congress.

CONGRESS, UNDER RADICAL REPUBLICAN LEADERSHIP, OPPOSES JOHNSON

The Congresses that met in December 1865 and for several years thereafter were dominated by the *Radical Republicans,* a powerful group led by Senator *Charles Sumner* and Representative *Thaddeus Stevens.* At the urging of the Radical Republicans, Congress refused to recognize the leniently reconstructed southern governments or to seat their delegates. The Radical Republicans condemned the entire Lincoln-Johnson reconstruction program for:

1. Infringing Upon the Powers of Congress. The Radical Republicans claimed that the southern states had in fact seceded. They had committed "suicide" and were "conquered provinces." Since only Congress had the power to admit a state into the Union, the Radical Republicans insisted that Congress had the sole power to determine the conditions for southern readmission.

2. Being Too Lenient. The Radical Republicans argued that the South had to be treated harshly and be severely punished so as to deter any future challenge to federal authority.

3. Endangering Republican Influence. In the leniently reconstructed southern states, the Democrats, including former Confederate leaders, regained control. They prevented blacks from voting, thereby depriving Republicans of their largest potential block of southern votes. The Radical Republicans feared that southern and northern Democrats together would gain control of Congress.

4. Abandoning the Blacks. In the leniently reconstructed southern states, the blacks were regulated by state laws called *Black Codes.* Most of the codes, although they listed certain black privileges, denied blacks the right to bear arms, serve on juries, and hold public office. Furthermore, unemployed blacks might be sentenced to work as "apprentices" to white masters—remindful of pre-Civil War days. The blacks, the Radical Republicans insisted, needed protection.

CONGRESSIONAL RECONSTRUCTION

1. Civil Rights Act of 1866. Passed over Johnson's veto, this act sought to weaken the Black Codes. The law gave blacks equal rights with whites and authorized the use of federal troops for its enforcement.

2. Freedmen's Bureau Act of 1866. Also passed over Johnson's veto, the act extended the life of this federal agency. Staffed chiefly by Radical Republican supporters, the Freedmen's Bureau provided the newly freed blacks with food, clothing, and schooling; found them work; and protected their civil rights. This law permitted the bureau to use military force when necessary.

3. Fourteenth Amendment. Proposed in 1866, this amendment (a) made blacks citizens both of the United States and of the state in which they resided, (b) provided that no state may "deprive any person of life, liberty, or property without due process of law," or "deny to any person . . . equal protection of the laws," (c) called for a reduction in the Congressional representation of a state that deprived any of its male citizens of the right to vote (this provision has never been used), (d) declared the Confederate debt void, and (e) disqualified most former Confederate leaders from holding office unless pardoned by Congress.

As every southern state except Tennessee refused to ratify the Fourteenth Amendment, the Radical Republicans became further enraged and pressed on with more stringent reconstruction measures.

4. First Reconstruction Act. Passed in 1867 over Johnson's veto, this act, as well as later supplementary measures, rejected as illegal all the reconstructed southern governments except Tennessee. The legislation divided the South into five military districts, each under a military governor commanding federal troops. To remove military rule and be readmitted into the Union, the states had to meet certain conditions: (a) Each state had to conduct an election, open to blacks and whites, for delegates to a constitutional convention. (b) Each new state constitution had to guarantee black suffrage and receive the approval of the voters, as well as of Congress. (c) The state legislature elected under the new constitution had to ratify the Fourteenth Amendment. An additional requirement, placed upon the four southern states that had not met these demands by 1869, was ratification of the Fifteenth Amendment prohibiting any state from denying black suffrage.

In 1870 the last of the southern states was readmitted by Congress into the Union. Nevertheless, federal troops, operating under the *Force Acts* (1870 and 1871), remained in the South to protect the rights of blacks and to support the state governments formed under Congressional reconstruction.

IMPEACHMENT OF JOHNSON

1. Tenure of Office Act (1867). Infuriated by Johnson's vetoes and by his public statements denouncing Congressional reconstruction, the Radical Republicans determined to find cause for removing him from office. Again over Johnson's veto, Congress passed the *Tenure of Office Act.* It forbade the President from discharging important government officials without the consent of the Senate. To test the constitutionality of this law and to rid himself of a Radical Republican Lincoln appointee, Johnson removed from office his secretary of war, Edwin M. Stanton.

2. Failure of the Impeachment. Led by Thaddeus Stevens, the House of Representatives quickly impeached Johnson on grounds of "high crimes and misdemeanors." The House bill of particulars, however, was repetitious, vague, and muddled. With Supreme Court Chief Justice Salmon Chase presiding, the Senate sat as the jury and heard the evidence. As seven Republican Senators voted with the Democrats, the Radical Republicans failed by one vote to secure the two-thirds majority necessary for conviction.

3. Significance. Johnson's acquittal upheld the American principle of Presidential independence of Congress. Johnson's conviction might have started a precedent that the President is responsible to Congress—akin to the British system, in which a prime minister may be forced to resign by Parliament.

Johnson's view of the Tenure of Office Act was upheld in 1887 when President Grover Cleveland secured its repeal and again in 1926 when the Supreme Court affirmed the President's unrestricted power to dismiss Cabinet officials.

Johnson remained as President until March 1869, the end of his term. He was succeeded by General Ulysses S. Grant, who had won the 1868 election—strongly in electoral vote but barely in popular vote—as the candidate of the Radical Republicans.

RECONSTRUCTION GOVERNMENTS OF THE SOUTHERN STATES

1. Controlling Political Groups. With the former Confederate leaders barred from office, the southern state governments during Congressional reconstruction fell into the hands of:

a. Carpetbaggers. Some Northerners went South after the Civil War. Since many of them carried their belongings in a traveling bag of carpeting material, southern whites contemptuously named them *carpetbaggers.* The carpetbaggers had mixed motives. Some were eager to help blacks adjust to freedom. Others sought to further their own fortunes through business and politics. During reconstruction carpetbaggers dominated the southern state governments.

b. Scalawags. Some southern whites, many of them pro-Union during the Civil War, cooperated with the carpetbaggers. These southern whites were labeled by the other Southerners as rascals, or *scalawags.*

c. Blacks. Southern blacks, who had been enfranchised by the Fifteenth Amendment, were mostly illiterate and inexperienced. Together with some whites, the blacks provided the votes to elect "carpetbag governments." Blacks, some educated and capable, held a number of public offices, but they never controlled any southern state government.

2. Criticism of the Reconstruction Governments. The "carpetbag governments" were marked by graft and corruption, wild spending, heavy taxation, and tremendous increases in the public debt. These governments nevertheless remained in power, protected by federal troops. Southern whites referred to Congressional reconstruction as a "tragic era" and a "crime."

3. Defense of the Reconstruction Governments. The "carpetbag governments" (a) framed liberal constitutions that guaranteed civil liberties, provided universal male suffrage, reapportioned legislative districts fairly according to population, and abolished imprisonment for debt, (b) began to rebuild the South—devastated by war losses, property destruction, and currency inflation—by constructing public buildings and roads, and by extending grants to railroads, (c) introduced free, compulsory public education for all children, and (d) were no more guilty of graft and corruption than governments elsewhere in the nation. (In New York City the *Tweed Ring* defrauded taxpayers of millions of dollars. In Washington the Grant administration, 1869–1877, was honeycombed with dishonesty.)

FACTORS ENABLING SOUTHERN WHITES TO REGAIN CONTROL OF THEIR STATE GOVERNMENTS

1. Ku Klux Klan. Southern whites organized secret societies, most notably the *Knights of the White Camelia* and the *Ku Klux Klan*. These organizations operated to drive out the carpetbaggers, to frighten the scalawags, and to intimidate blacks. Klan members, wearing weird, white-hooded robes, threatened blacks, burned their homes, flogged them, and sometimes lynched them. Increasingly terrorized, blacks refrained from exercising their voting and other rights. Klan activities were subdued but never completely suppressed by federal forces acting under the Force Acts.

2. Increased Number of Southern White Voters. Each year new white voters came of age. Furthermore, in 1872, 160,000 former Confederates regained their political rights as Congress passed the *Amnesty Act*.

3. Waning Northern Interest in the Problems of Blacks. Disappointed with the carpetbag governments, Northerners grew weary of reconstruction. Industrialists seeking business in the South wanted an end to social and political turmoil. Reformers turned from the crusade for black equality to other issues: curtailing the abuses of big business, securing civil service reform, and aiding the farmer.

End of Reconstruction

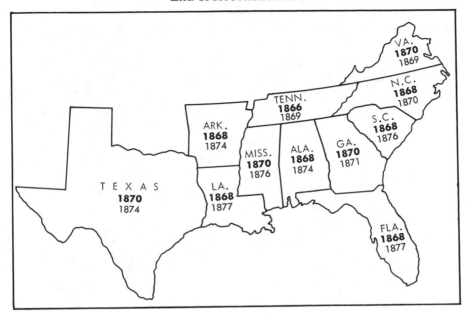

(Dates in boldface indicate readmission to the Union. Dates in lightface indicate end of carpetbag governments.)

Northerners came to believe that the South could not be coerced into changing its traditional attitude toward blacks and that Southerners themselves should work out the problems of race relations. In North and South, leaders sought genuine reconciliation, even at the expense of black rights.

4. Presidential Election of 1876. The Democrats nominated Governor *Samuel J. Tilden* of New York to run for President against the Republican nominee, Governor *Rutherford B. Hayes* of Ohio. After a bitter contest, Tilden received 184 electoral votes, Hayes received 165, and both candidates claimed the remaining 20 votes—one from Oregon and 19 from Louisiana, Florida, and South Carolina, the last three southern states still under carpetbag rule. Congress established an electoral commission of eight Republicans and seven Democrats to assign the disputed votes. The commission, by an 8-to-7 decision, gave all 20 votes to Hayes. Despite Tilden's popular majority of 265,000, Hayes became President by an electoral vote of 185 to 184.

Hayes and his supporters calmed the Democratic opposition by promising to (a) provide federal funds for internal improvements in the South, (b) assign a Cabinet post to a Southerner, and (c) remove all federal troops from the South. In 1877, soon after taking office, Hayes withdrew the troops, whereupon the remaining carpetbag governments collapsed. Reconstruction was over.

Historical Analysis. *Which predominated during the recon-struction era—its harsh or lenient aspects?*

Harsh Aspects. Southern whites suffered the evils of carpetbag government and military occupation. They resented the use of blacks in the occupation troops. Southern states were compelled to ratify the Fourteenth Amendment and give the illiterate, newly freed blacks equal political and civil rights while experienced white leaders were barred from office. Some historians believe that Southerners resented the era of reconstruction even more than they did the Civil War. Southerners retained a legacy of bitterness toward the North and toward blacks.

Lenient Aspects. Most southern whites regained their political rights immediately by merely taking an oath of loyalty. Most Confederate leaders were pardoned within seven years, a short period. No Confederate leader was tried or executed for treason. Except for the loss of slaves, southern whites were not subjected to economic penalties. They were not forced to pay reparations for war damages or to give up plantation lands for distribution to poor whites and landless blacks. Southern whites experienced military rule and carpetbag government for a short time—depending on the state, from two to ten years. Thereafter, they circumvented the Fourteenth and Fifteenth Amendments and placed blacks in a subordinate status. Some historians maintain that vanquished rebels have rarely been treated so mildly.

LASTING RESULTS OF THE CIVIL WAR AND RECONSTRUCTION

ABOLITION OF SLAVERY AND CONSTITUTIONAL GUARANTEE OF BLACKS' RIGHTS

In 1863 the *Emancipation Proclamation* freed the slaves in the states in rebellion, but not in the border states loyal to the Union or in Confederate territory occupied by Union forces. In 1865 the Thirteenth Amendment completely abolished slavery. In 1868 the Fourteenth Amendment guaranteed the former slaves the status of citizens and equal protection of the laws. In 1870 the Fifteenth Amendment proclaimed their right to vote.

DISCRIMINATION AGAINST BLACKS IN THE SOUTH

By 1900 southern whites had found ways to evade the Fourteenth and Fifteenth Amendments: (1) Southern states required a poll tax, which discouraged blacks, mostly poor, from voting. (2) Southern states established difficult and unfair literacy requirements, which barred blacks, mostly little educated, from voting. (3) Some states enacted a *grandfather clause,* exempting from literacy requirements persons whose grandfathers had been eligible to vote before the Civil War. Since blacks had then been slaves and ineligible to vote, this exemption benefited only the whites. (4) The Democratic party denied membership to blacks and thus kept them from voting in party primaries. This had the effect of disenfranchising blacks, since, in the South, the Democratic nomination was equivalent to election. (5) Southern states enacted segregation, or Jim Crow, laws. These laws kept blacks separated from whites in such public places as railroads, hotels, restaurants, beaches, and schools. Facilities provided for blacks were usually inferior to those for whites. (6) Southern states barred black city workers from labor unions and relegated them to the lowest paying occupations. (For subsequent efforts to gain for blacks full rights as American citizens, check the Index.)

BEGINNINGS OF EDUCATION FOR BLACKS IN THE SOUTH

Formal schooling for blacks in the South started with the Freedmen's Bureau. This federal agency had spent over $5 million by 1870 to teach blacks to read and write. Furthermore, it cooperated with northern philanthropists in establishing schools of higher learning for blacks: *Howard University, Hampton Institute,* and *Fisk University.* In 1881 the *Tuskegee Institute* for vocational training for blacks began instruction under the leadership of the black educator *Booker T. Washington.* (To the early 20th century, Washington was the outstanding black leader. He advised black people to emphasize economic progress and temporarily to accept social segregation and political discrimination, confident that they would progress in these areas through *gradualism.*)

Blacks as well as whites were guaranteed free compulsory public education by the reconstruction constitutions of southern states. However, after the southern whites regained control, blacks received schooling that was segregated and inferior. (For Supreme Court decisions regarding segregation in public schools, check the Index.)

SUPREMACY OF THE FEDERAL GOVERNMENT

The Civil War and the reconstruction era marked the triumph of nationalism over sectionalism. Since that time no state has threatened to secede. The United States emerged as one nation, indivisible and indissoluble. Further, by the Fourteenth and Fifteenth Amendments, Congress and the Supreme Court gained the power to challenge state activities denying "due process" and "equal protection of the laws."

EXPANSION OF PRESIDENTIAL POWERS IN WARTIME

By expending funds not yet appropriated by Congress, suspending habeas corpus, and issuing an executive order declaring some slaves free, Lincoln exercised powers never before used by an American President. Such expansion of Presidential powers was inevitable because a modern war demands vigorous leadership, and this can come only from the nation's chief executive, the President.

THE "SOLID SOUTH"

Southern whites resented the Republican party because Republicans had controlled the federal government during the Civil War and the reconstruction era. Therefore, the South developed a tradition of voting almost solidly Democratic in local, state, and national elections.

The first crack in the "Solid South" appeared in the Presidential election of 1928. Four southern states voted for the Republican candidate, Herbert Hoover. They rejected Alfred E. Smith, the Democratic nominee, because he opposed prohibition and was a Roman Catholic. Since 1948 various southern states have denied support to Democratic Presidential candidates, in part because each strongly supported civil rights for blacks. In the 1960s southern voters began electing a noticeable number of Republicans to Congress and to state offices. In 1972, the 11 states of the Old Confederacy all went to Richard Nixon, the Republican Presidential candidate. Seemingly, the South has abandoned its 100-year-old legacy of voting solidly Democratic.

DEVELOPMENTS IN THE SOUTHERN ECONOMY

1. Physical and Economic Devastation. The South was physically ruined by the war. Its lands were devastated, its railroads demolished, and its cities ravaged by the military campaigns waged on its soil. The southern economy was destroyed as the war (a) kept southern cotton from northern and European markets, (b) exhausted southern wealth for war needs, and (c) resulted in freeing the slaves without payment to the former owners.

2. Revival of Southern Agriculture

a. Sharecropping. After the Civil War, southern plantation owners had land but no labor, and the newly freed slaves had no land but needed work. This situation led to the rise of *sharecropping*. The plantation owner (often a merchant who had bought the plantation from the prewar owner) provided the sharecropper—black or poor white—with a few acres of land and perhaps a cabin, a mule, and tools. In exchange, the plantation owner received a 50 percent or larger share of the crop. Often the sharecropper also pledged a share of the crop to the local merchant for credit to buy foodstuffs, seeds, and tools.

Sharecropping resulted in a standard of living and farm productivity that were extremely low. The sharecropper had a meager knowledge of farming techniques, worked with crude equipment, employed little or no fertilizer, and depleted the soil of its minerals by continuous planting of a single cash crop, such as tobacco or cotton. Owing the plantation owner and merchant a large portion of the crop, the sharecropper was entrapped in debt and practically bound to the land.

b. Diversified Agriculture. To end dependence upon a single crop and to halt soil depletion, southern farmers near the end of the 19th century turned to diversified agriculture. Today, the South raises varied crops, including fruits, vegetables, soybeans, and peanuts.

3. Development of Industry: The "New South." Learning from their experience in the Civil War, Southerners realized the importance of establishing industries. The South had cheap labor, a plentiful water supply, valuable minerals, and agricultural products. Iron and coal gave rise to steel mills; tobacco to cigarette factories; cotton to textile mills; timber to paper mills and furniture plants; oil to refineries and chemical works. Despite low wages and poor working conditions, Southerners left the countryside and flocked to the new factory towns. Birmingham, Alabama, developed into a steel center and became known as the *Pittsburgh of the South*.

Although the industrial growth of the South lagged behind that of the rest of the nation, in 1900 southern manufacturing output was four times the pre-Civil War level. To describe the industrialization of the South, historians use the term the *New South*.

EFFECTS OF THE WAR ON THE NORTH

1. Economic Prosperity. During the Civil War, northern industrialists operated their factories at full capacity and even built new factories to meet the unprecedented demand. They overcame labor shortages by rapidly introducing new machinery. Given impetus by the war years, captains of industry soon created tremendous empires in meat packing, flour milling, oil refining, and steel production. The United States entered an age of business consolidation.

2. Republican Control. The Republican party, largely favorable to northern business interests, dominated the federal government. Republican legislators furthered business interests by such measures as the *Morrill Tariff Act* (1861), which sharply raised import duties; the *National Banking Act* (1863), which set up a system of nationally chartered banks; and various laws providing land grants to railroads. For many years after the Civil War, the Republicans retained control of the government.

EFFECTS OF THE WAR ON THE WEST

Western farmers prospered as the war increased the demand for foodstuffs. To overcome labor shortages, farmers purchased farm machinery, especially more efficient plows and reapers. Western agriculture was furthered by Congressional acts such as the *Homestead Act* (1862), which gave 160 acres free to any head of a family who cultivated the land for five years; the *Morrill Act* (1862), which encouraged agricultural education by providing for the establishment of land-grant colleges; and land grants for transcontinental railroads. Free homesteads and improved transportation, in addition to the West's natural resources, attracted many Easterners and immigrants after the Civil War, and the western population increased rapidly.

CULTURAL DEVELOPMENTS IN 19TH-CENTURY AMERICA

ARCHITECTURE

1. Romanticism. In the 1840s American architects rebelled against the classical tradition with its emphasis on symmetry, formality, restraint, and dignity. Instead, they favored romanticism, a style that proposed irregularity, informality, exuberance, and imagination. Americans now held that, in architecture, romanticism would best express the growing spirit of democracy.

    a. **Gothic Revival.** Architects working in the Romantic style first looked to medieval European cathedrals built in the *Gothic style.* An outstanding building in the 19th-century *Gothic Revival style* is *St. Patrick's Cathedral,* on Fifth Avenue in New York City.

    b. **Romanesque Revival.** In the post-Civil War era, romanticism in architecture began emphasizing another medieval European style called *Romanesque.* In America, the Romanesque style became associated with the architect *Henry Hunt Richardson* (1838–1886).

Although Richardson borrowed ideas from other styles, he used the Romanesque style to express the buoyant energy and massive strength of America. Richardson's use of Romanesque features is seen in a number of buildings, including the *New York State Capitol* at Albany and *Trinity Church* in Boston.

2. Diverse Styles. In the post-Civil War era, American industrialists and financiers amassed tremendous fortunes. When they toured Europe, they admired the villas, chateaux, and mansions of the European nobility. The "new rich" Americans desired similar dwellings and commissioned the services of several Eastern architectural firms. Notable among these was the firm of *McKim, Mead, and White.* This firm was eclectic—that is, willing to utilize any past styles such as Italian Renaissance, colonial Georgian, and classical Roman and Greek Revival. McKim, Mead, and White built private homes for the wealthy and also a number of outstanding public buildings.

SCULPTURE

After the Civil War, a number of American sculptors turned from classicism to an "American" style of detailed realism. This style suited the growing interest in sculpting Civil War military and civilian figures and scenes of American life.

PAINTING

1. Landscapes and the Hudson River School. By the mid-19th century, landscape painting had acquired great popular appeal. For its many admirers, landscape painting expressed a romantic love of nature, a religious awe of the Almighty's creations, a scientific interest in natural history, resentment against society's growing industrialization and urbanization, and patriotic pride in the beauty of the American countryside.

One group of painters detailing scenes of the American landscape became primarily associated with the Catskill Mountains and the Hudson Valley. They are known as the *Hudson River School*. *Thomas Cole* (1801–1848), the leader of this school, is known for his painting of a bend in the Connecticut River—a work called *The Oxbow*.

2. Painting of Birds. *John J. Audubon* (1785–1851) came to America at the age of 18 and later settled on the Kentucky frontier. There he pursued his passion for painting the birds of America in their natural habitats. As an ornithologist, or bird specialist, Audubon achieved detailed accuracy. As an artist, he produced colorful and dramatic drawings. Between 1827 and 1839, Audubon published a four-volume *Birds of America* accompanied by a five-volume explanatory text, the *Ornithological Biography*. Audubon's work won him fame, fortune, and prestige.

3. Recording the American Scene With Realism. *Winslow Homer* (1836–1910) rejected the public's demand for sentimentality but painted with realism. During the Civil War, Homer served as an artist-correspondent with the Union forces and later painted several powerful war pictures, such as *Prisoners From the Front*. Homer won artistic acclaim but his paintings sold slowly. In 1883, Homer moved to Maine where he portrayed nature—the ocean and the rockbound coast—in conflict with the fisher folk. Among his vivid seascapes are *The Lifeline* and *The Herring Net*. Homer again won artistic acclaim but this time coupled with public realization of his talent and demand for his works.

LITERATURE

1. Historians. (a) *William H. Prescott* (1796–1859) detailed the impact of Spain upon the New World in his works *History of the Conquest of Mexico* and *History of the Conquest of Peru*. (b) *George Bancroft* compiled a ten-volume *History of the United States,* from the discovery of the New World to the Presidency of George Washington. Bancroft extolled American democracy and patriotism.

2. Essayists for Individualism. (a) *Ralph Waldo Emerson* (1803–1882), in essays "Self-Reliance," "Experience," and "Fate," expounded on the worth and dignity of the individual. In his essay "Civilization," Emerson claimed that "the true test of civilization is, not the census, nor the size of cities, nor the crops—no, but the kind of man the country turns out." In his poem "Concord Hymn," Emerson honored the "embattled farmers" who in 1775 "fired the shot heard around the world." (b) *Henry David Thoreau* (1817–1862) wrote the autobiographical work *Walden*. In it Thoreau described the two years he spent living in the woods, seeking to live in accordance with his values as an individual. In his essay on "Civil Disobedience," Thoreau insisted that, in case of a conflict between the individual's conscience and the government's dictates, the individual must follow his or her conscience.

3. Writers Against Slavery and for Democracy. (a) *John Greenleaf Whittier* (1807–1892) hated slavery and wrote many abolitionist poems. (b) *James Russell Lowell* (1819–1891) condemned the Mexican War and slavery in his poems collected as the *Biglow Papers*. (c) *Walt Whitman* (1819–1892) wrote poems in praise of democracy and individualism that were collected together as *Leaves of Grass*. He honored the fallen Abraham Lincoln in the inspiring poem "O Captain! My Captain."

4. Writers of Distinctive Works. (a) *Edgar Allan Poe* (1809–1849) wrote highly rhythmic poems such as "The Raven" and "Annabel Lee." He also perfected the detective story and short story of mystery and horror such as "The Murders in the Rue Morgue" and "The Fall of the House of Usher." (b) *Herman Melville* (1819–1891) wrote the novel *Moby Dick*. On the surface it is an adventure story of whaling but, for most literary critics, it is an allegory symbolizing the struggle of humanity against the brute forces of nature.

NEWSPAPERS

1. The Penny Press. In 1833 *Benjamin Day* launched the first successful penny newspaper, the New York *Sun*. Less expensive than other papers, the *Sun* also serialized popular stories and presented news in a lively manner. The *Sun* expanded its circulation, increased its sale of advertising space, and became a very profitable enterprise.

Day's example was followed by other editors. (a) *James Gordon Bennett* in 1835 founded the New York *Herald*. He presented "spicy" news of sports, society, and crime; he did not wait for the stories to come to him but started the practice of employing staff reporters to go out and get the news. (b) *Horace Greeley* in 1841 founded the New York *Tribune*. A liberal reformer, Greeley supported abolition, labor unions, prohibition of intoxicating beverages, and westward expansion, advising "Go west, young man." His vigorous antislavery editorials greatly influenced northern public opinion. (c) *Henry Raymond* in 1851 founded *The New York Times*. He set standards of well-balanced and accurately written news stories. During the Civil War, Raymond was a leading advocate of the Lincoln administration.

2. Inventions Affect the Press. Samuel F. B. Morse's telegraph (1844) and Alexander Graham Bell's telephone (1876) simplified newsgathering. Richard Hoe's rotary press (1847) speeded the printing process and reduced the cost of newspapers. Ottmar Mergenthaler's linotype machine (1884) eliminated the hand-setting of newspaper type and made possible the mass-circulation newspaper.

SCIENCE

Americans continued to excel in applied science: (1) *Samuel F. B. Morse* (1791–1872) demonstrated the first long-distance telegraph and devised the Morse code. (2) *Joseph Henry* (1797–1878), a physicist, used his understanding of electromagnetism for practical purposes. He insulated wire so that it could be easily wound about an electromagnet, thereby strengthening it. He also devised an electric motor and an electromagnetic relay to amplify electric impulses sent through wire. (3) *William Morton* (1819–1868), a dentist, pioneered the use of ether as an anesthetic during surgery. (4) *Alexander Graham Bell* (1847–1922) invented the telephone. (5) *Thomas Alva Edison* (1847–1931) invented the phonograph, electric light bulb, and later motion picture machine. (6) *Luther Burbank* (1849–1926), a horticulturist and plant breeder, raised new and improved varieties of fruit such as the *plumcot* and of vegetables such as the Burbank or *Idaho potato.*

LITHOGRAPHY

Invented in the late 1700s, the lithographic printing process reproduces images from flat surfaces, usually metal plates. Lithography makes it possible to reproduce on paper or other materials works of art in quantity and at low cost.

Beginning in the 1830s in New York City, *Nathaniel Currier* (1813–1888), later joined by *James M. Ives* (1824–1895), produced and sold lithographic prints. The inexpensive Currier and Ives lithographic reproductions were enjoyed by millions of people. Thousands of catalog items depicted wide-ranging aspects of American life, among them notable people, farm scenes, the frontier, sporting events, natural disasters, patriotic themes, leisure activities, and transportation. Well-known Currier and Ives prints are *Home for Thanksgiving, Western Frontier Home,* and *Hudson River Craft.*

PHOTOGRAPHY

Invented in 1839, photography made it possible to record exactly the way people, buildings, and landscapes looked. *Matthew Brady* (1823–1896), born in New York State, was a skilled portrait photographer by 1850. In 1861 Brady conceived the idea of producing a photographic record of the Civil War. With assistants, he accompanied the Union armies and supervised the making of thousands of pictures. This photographic history of places, events, and people during the war won Brady great fame. Among Brady's best-known photographs are the *Ruins of Richmond, Virginia,* and the portrait of Lincoln, which is reproduced on our five-dollar bill.

MUSIC

By the 19th century, Americans had made original contributions in two musical areas. (1) Folk Music. Often created by unknown musicians, folk music has stirred Americans to listen, dance, march, and sing. Lively folk music such as

"Turkey in the Straw" has animated countless participants and callers at square dances. Folk songs have arisen out of wars, such as the Civil War marching song "John Brown's Body." Folk songs identified with work include "Pick a Bale of Cotton," "The Last Roundup," and "I've Been Working on the Railroad." (2) Spirituals. Originated by southern black slaves, spirituals are a type of folk song. They reflect, in varying degrees, African rhythms, plantation life, deep religious faith, anguish over slavery, and hope for the future. Well-known spirituals include "Go Down, Moses," and "Nobody Knows the Trouble I've Seen." Closely related to spirituals are the folk songs of *Stephen Foster* (1826–1864), including "Oh! Susanna" and "My Old Kentucky Home."

———————————— MULTIPLE-CHOICE QUESTIONS ————————————

1. President Lincoln's plan for reconstruction was based on the theory that the Confederate states (a) were to be treated as territories (b) could be readmitted to the Union by Congress only (c) had never actually left the Union (d) were to be occupied by Union forces for a period of 20 years.
2. The Radical Republicans in Congress after the Civil War (a) favored Lincoln's ideas on southern reconstruction (b) passed the Black Codes (c) regarded the southern states as conquered territories (d) voted against the Tenure of Office Act.
3. The purpose of the Black Codes was to (a) aid the carpetbaggers (b) grant suffrage to blacks (c) prevent exploitation of blacks (d) restrict the civil rights of blacks.
4. An important objective of Congressional reconstruction was to (a) destroy the economy of the South (b) maintain Republican domination of the national government (c) restore pre-Civil War conditions in the South (d) pardon southern leaders for Civil War activities.
5. Which development was the result of the other three? (a) activities of the carpetbaggers and scalawags (b) formation of the "Solid South" (c) passage of the reconstruction acts (d) ratification of the Fourteenth Amendment.
6. During reconstruction, which branch of the national government attempted to achieve supremacy over another? (a) judicial over legislative (b) executive over judicial (c) legislative over executive (d) legislative over judicial.
7. President Andrew Johnson's view of the Tenure of Office Act was (a) similar to views of the Radical Republicans (b) upheld years later by the Supreme Court (c) not involved in Johnson's impeachment (d) important in the development of southern sharecropping.
8. The impeachment case against President Andrew Johnson was tried in the (a) House of Representatives (b) Court of Appeals for the District of Columbia (c) United States Supreme Court (d) United States Senate.
9. Thaddeus Stevens was the (a) Radical Republican leader in the House of Representatives (b) Radical Republican leader in the Senate (c) Chief Justice of the Supreme Court (d) secretary of war under President Andrew Johnson.
10. In the Presidential election of 1876, (a) three southern states each submitted two sets of electoral votes (b) a third party was influential in the outcome (c) the Republican party returned to power for the first time since 1860 (d) the stationing of federal troops in the South had no political effect.
11. An important result of the Civil War was that it (a) discouraged banks from securing national charters (b) strengthened our ties with Great Britain (c) helped make in-

dustry rather than agriculture the basis of our economy (d) established equality for blacks in the South.

12. Sharecropping in the post-Civil War South meant that (a) southern planters exchanged crops for northern manufactured goods (b) more than one crop shared the land on a plantation (c) former slaves formed cooperatives to share the costs of buying farms (d) impoverished planters and former slaves supplied each other's need for land and labor.

13. In the South, near the end of the 19th century, (a) cotton growing was abandoned (b) sharecropping disappeared (c) the size of the plantations was increased (d) agriculture became diversified.

14. Which was *not* a method used to keep blacks from voting? (a) Fifteenth Amendment (b) poll tax (c) literacy test (d) activities of the Ku Klux Klan.

15. The existence of such groups as the Ku Klux Klan and the Knights of the White Camelia shows that (a) some groups feel compelled to resort to extremism in pursuit of goals (b) constitutions do not generally support the principle of equal rights (c) most radical groups are founded by aliens (d) radical groups have found widespread public acceptance.

16. The term "New South" refers to all of the following *except* (a) tobacco-processing plants (b) furniture factories (c) textile mills (d) cotton plantations.

17. Which section of the United States was most directly affected by the Homestead Act? (a) South (b) New England (c) West (d) Central Atlantic states.

18. Booker T. Washington was (a) a black educator who urged vocational training (b) a former Confederate leader elected governor of Alabama (c) a northern capitalist who built the southern steel industry (d) a carpetbagger active in Louisiana reconstruction politics.

19. Which was *not* a result of the Civil War? (a) abolition of slavery (b) end of Jim Crow laws (c) supremacy of the federal government (d) prosperity in the industrial North.

———————————————— **ESSAY QUESTIONS** ————————————————

1. (*a*) Discuss *two* reasons why Congress rejected President Lincoln's plan for readmission of the southern states. (*b*) Describe *one* social result and *one* political result that the reconstruction period brought about in the South. (*c*) Discuss *two* important economic changes in the South since the Civil War.

2. The extension of democracy, the unification of the nation, and disputes between the President and Congress over the use of power have often been important national issues. For the period of the Civil War and reconstruction, give specific evidence to show that *each* of these three issues was present.

3. War inevitably has far-reaching effects upon a nation. Show how the Civil War and reconstruction affected *each* of the following: (*a*) the powers of the states (*b*) American industry (*c*) blacks (*d*) the powers of the President (*e*) the economy of the South.

4. Southern whites as well as blacks have condemned Congressional reconstruction, but for vastly different reasons. (*a*) Explain *two* reasons why southern whites have condemned Congressional reconstruction. (*b*) Explain *two* reasons why black leaders have condemned Congressional reconstruction. (*c*) Briefly evaluate Congressional reconstruction as harsh or lenient, and give *two* reasons to support your evaluation.

The United States Changes From an Agricultural to an Industrial Society

PART 1. The Frontier Influences American Development

THE FRONTIER: DEFINITION

The *frontier* in American history refers to the farthermost region of settlement—an imaginary line dividing civilization from wilderness. The United States Census Bureau defined the frontier as that area having less than six but more than two persons per square mile.

For almost 300 years, from colonial times to the end of the 19th century, the frontier was part of the American environment. In 1650 the frontier ran along the Atlantic coast. By 1750 it spread to the foothills of the Appalachian Mountains. By 1840 it reached the Mississippi River. By 1890 the West was sufficiently populated for the Census Bureau to consider the frontier as closed.

REASONS FOR WESTWARD MIGRATION

1. Adventure. The West, with its Indians, wild animals, rugged country, and unexplored regions, attracted people who sought the thrill of adventure and discovery.

2. Improvement of Economic Conditions. Eastern farmers and city workers considered the West as the land of opportunity. They went west looking for fertile land, fur-bearing animals, timber, and precious minerals such as gold, silver, copper, and iron. Southern planters, having exhausted the soil by the continuous growing of cotton, looked to the Southwest for new fertile land.

3. Greater Social and Political Democracy. In the more settled eastern states, the lower classes became sharply divided from the upper classes and found it difficult to improve their social status. They also resented the slow pace at which state governments extended democratic rights. Many poorer Americans therefore migrated to the West, where they faced less rigid class distinctions and less opposition to the extension of democracy.

PEAK PERIODS OF WESTWARD MIGRATION

1. After the American Revolution. Farmers and workers along the Atlantic seaboard suffered postwar economic distress. With the British prohibition of westward migration removed, settlers moved west. The population influx soon enabled three new states to enter the Union—Kentucky, Tennessee, and Ohio.

2. After the War of 1812. Many New Englanders lost their jobs as the shipping industry declined. Europeans meanwhile fled the poverty and autocracy of the post-Napoleonic Era. With the Indian menace lessened by Indian defeats during the war, settlers went southwest to Mississippi and Alabama, and northwest to Indiana and Illinois.

3. During the Era of Manifest Destiny

a. Mormons in Utah. The *Mormons,* or *Latter-Day Saints,* were a religious sect founded in 1830 in upstate New York by the prophet *Joseph Smith.* The Mormons differed from other Christian sects in that they accepted the religious revelation and prophecy as stated in the *Book of Mormon.* Subjected to persecution in the East, the Mormons continually fled, migrating westward. In 1844 Joseph Smith was murdered in Illinois by an anti-Mormon mob.

Brigham Young, a strong-willed leader, assumed control. Determined to be free of further persecution, Young in 1847 led the Mormons far into the unpopulated West to the Great Salt Lake Valley in Utah. (This territory was part of the Mexican Cession soon to be acquired by the United States.)

Despite Utah's inhospitable mountains and deserts, the Mormon settlers survived and prospered. They built irrigation systems, transformed desert land into good farmland, founded Salt Lake City, and sold supplies to migrants traveling the northern route to California.

b. Fortune Hunters. The 1848 discovery of gold in California brought on a westward gold rush. California's population soared with the influx of fortune hunters, called the forty-niners. Ten years later, discoveries of gold at *Pikes Peak* in Colorado and of gold and silver in the *Comstock Lode* in Nevada set off new stampedes of fortune seekers.

4. After the Civil War

a. Farmers. War veterans were restless for new homes. Farmers desired more fertile lands. Europeans responded to the advertising campaigns of steamship companies seeking passengers. Europeans as well as Easterners answered advertisements by transcontinental railroads seeking to sell lands granted them by the federal and state governments. Settlers were further encouraged by the offer of free federal land under the Homestead Act of 1862. (Check the Index.) The westward movement was also helped as the federal government sent troops to subdue the Plains Indians.

b. Miners. Another gold rush occurred in 1875, when gold was discovered in the Black Hills of South Dakota. However, mining in the West was changing, and the individual prospector soon disappeared. By the 1880s big business companies had taken over, buying up claims, systematizing exploration, and introducing the latest mining processes and machinery. These corporations ended the romantic era of the mining frontier.

LAST FRONTIER: THE GREAT PLAINS

LOCATION AND CHARACTERISTICS

The Great Plains are a region over 500 miles wide, extending from the first tier of states west of the Mississippi to the foothills of the Rocky Mountains. The soil is fertile and suitable for grazing animals and growing wheat. The Great Plains are generally level and treeless, and receive little rainfall.

RAILROADS CROSS THE GREAT PLAINS

In 1869 the *Union Pacific* and the *Central Pacific Railroad* came together at Promontory Point, Utah, to complete the first transcontinental railroad. By the 1890s American railroad builders had completed four more transcontinental railroads. The railroads were the fastest and most convenient means of reaching the Great Plains and the Far West.

INDIAN PROBLEM

1. Indian Hostility to Whites. The Plains Indians, such as the Comanches, Cheyennes, and Sioux, were nomadic, horse-riding peoples. From the buffalo, which roamed the Plains in huge herds, the Indians secured food, clothing, and shelter.

The Plains Indians resented the whites: (*a*) settlers took Indian lands, (*b*) hunters wantonly killed the buffalo for pelts and for sport, (*c*) communities upset the traditional migratory paths of buffalo herds, and (*d*) traders and government officials cheated and robbed the Indians, and broke promises.

2. Indian Wars (To About 1890). For over 25 years the Plains Indians battled wagon trains, settlers, and federal troops in savage guerrilla warfare. In 1876, after gold-seeking fortune hunters invaded an area in South Dakota assigned to the Indians, the Sioux, led by *Sitting Bull,* overwhelmed General *George A. Custer* in his "last stand" at the Battle of Little Big Horn. Despite this and lesser victories, the Indian cause was doomed. The Indians lacked manpower, organization, equipment, and—with the extermination of the buffalo herds—food. The last battle—the Indians call it a massacre—took place in 1890 when federal troops wiped out a Sioux band under Chief *Big Foot* at *Wounded Knee* (South Dakota).

3. Indian Reservations. By the 1880s most Indians were confined to specific, usually undesirable, lands called *reservations.* No longer a free people, they received from the federal government food, clothing, and shelter and were treated as legal dependents or *wards.* Their very existence was under the control of federal Indian agents, many of whom were corrupt and unsympathetic to Indian needs. (For background on more humane treatment of the Indian, check the Index.)

CATTLE KINGDOM (TO THE LATE 1880s)

1. The Long Drive. In the late 1860s Texas ranchers became aware that their cattle, worth $4 a head in Texas, were worth $40 a head in Chicago. Cowboys began the *long drive* northward—more than a thousand miles—to deliver the cattle to the nearest railroad towns, located mostly in Kansas. They fed the moving herds on the *open range,* which was being rapidly depleted of its native buffalo herds. They fought stampedes, Indians, rustlers, and farmers. Ranchers who completed successful drives made great profits.

2. Collapse (By the Late 1880s). Greedily, ranchers sent so many cattle herds northward that they overgrazed the open range and oversupplied the market, driving beef prices sharply downward. In addition, farmers, arriving in increasing numbers, fenced in parts of the open range and thus reduced the grazing lands. Cattle owners fought bitter range wars with farmers but to no avail. Also, from 1885 to 1887 natural disasters struck as severe winters and dry summers destroyed entire herds. The cattle kingdom—romanticized in American song and story—came to an end.

Big-business operators took over the cattle industry. They raised herds on fenced-in ranches, improved quality by better breeding, and moved the cattle to market on railroad lines that had been extended southward.

THE FARMER ON THE GREAT PLAINS (TO ABOUT 1900)

1. Factors Encouraging Settlement. (a) *Fertile Soil.* Farmers realized that the Great Plains, long considered the "Great American Desert," were fertile and were capable of producing abundant harvests. (b) *Good Transportation.* Railroads provided easy and relatively inexpensive access to the region, brought machinery and other manufactured goods from eastern suppliers, and carried farm products to eastern markets. (c) *Homestead Act* (1862). This act offered a free 160-acre farm to any settler who would cultivate it for five years. However, less than one out of every five settlers secured free homesteads, and these homesteads were usually the less desirable lands. Most settlers were compelled to buy the more desirable lands that were granted to railroads or to the states, or that were acquired, often fraudulently, by land speculators.

2. Science and Invention Aid Settlement. (a) Since the Great Plains were treeless, farmers lacked lumber with which to build fences. They therefore welcomed the introduction of barbed wire. (b) Since the Great Plains lacked sufficient rainfall, farmers pumped up water from far below the surface by employing windmills. Also, they devised dry farming techniques: plowing deep for subsurface moisture and pulverizing the soil to retard evaporation. (c) Since the winters on the Great Plains were severe, farmers planted new, hardier strains of winter wheat. (d) Since the Great Plains soil was tough, farmers utilized James Oliver's inexpensive and efficient invention, the chilled-iron plow. Increasingly, Great Plains farmers used machines—grain drills for seeding, as well as reapers, harvesters, and threshers. Improved farm machinery paved the way for large-scale farming.

3. Effects of Settlement. European immigrants—Swedes, Norwegians, Danes, Germans, and Irish—together with Americans from the East and the Midwest, occupied the Great Plains. In three decades (1870–1900) they almost tripled the number of American farms. By 1890 they had brought to an end an environmental factor that for almost 300 years had influenced American life: the frontier.

THE FRONTIER IN AMERICAN HISTORY

INFLUENCE OF THE FRONTIER

Frederick Jackson Turner, an American historian, born in 1861 on the Wisconsin agricultural frontier, wrote the perceptive essay *The Significance of the Frontier in American History.* Turner stated: "The true point of view in the history of this nation is not the Atlantic coast, it is the Great West." He argued that the frontier was the chief influence in shaping a distinctive American way of life.

1. Social Equality. The frontier offered free or cheap land, so that no person had to work for another. The individual's survival and progress on the frontier depended on the ability to hunt, fight, and farm. Frontier conditions prevented the rise of class distinctions and promoted the ideal of equality. The West judged people not by ancestors, race, religion, or national origin, but by deeds.

2. Growth of Political Democracy. The frontier settlers believed in political equality, hated special privilege, considered the government as their servant, and insisted that it carry out the wishes of the people. The West originated such democratic reforms as universal manhood suffrage, woman suffrage, direct election of Senators, and the secret ballot. Turner claimed that democracy in the United States resulted from frontier conditions.

3. Nationalism. The frontier settlers were nationalistic because they depended on the federal government for cheap land, acquisition of new territories, and protection against the Indians.

4. Faith in the Future. Inspired by the resources of the West, frontier dwellers looked to the future optimistically. This optimism was reflected in the boast that "the difficult we do immediately, the impossible takes a little longer."

5. Economic Independence. The frontier reduced America's economic dependence upon Europe by (a) providing raw materials and foodstuffs for the industrial cities, (b) providing a market for goods manufactured in the East, and (c) serving as a place for investment of surplus capital. Such economic independence enabled 19th-century America to follow a policy of isolation.

6. Safety Valve for Factory Workers. Knowing that workers could leave their jobs and migrate westward, employers in the East offered good wages and working conditions. Labor in the 19th century seldom sought the protection of unions. Workers had a simpler solution to their problems: going to the frontier—the "safety valve."

7. Invention. The frontier encouraged the invention of new machinery. Westward migration threatened to drain the labor market in the East. So factory owners turned to new labor-saving machines. Labor was also scarce in the West. Farmers eagerly utilized new farm machinery.

8. Wasteful Agriculture. Since land was so easily available, frontier settlers were not mindful of the need for conservation of soil and forests. They cut down trees senselessly and cultivated the land unwisely, destroying its fertility.

EFFECTS OF THE CLOSE OF THE FRONTIER: AFTER 1890

Turner stated that the close of the frontier, ending the era of cheap or free land, caused many of the problems that face us today.

1. Labor. Discontented factory workers no longer had the "safety valve" of easily available land in the West. These workers therefore remained in the industrial East and turned to labor unions to improve their conditions. The struggle between capital and labor now intensified.

2. Immigration. Immigrants could no longer easily acquire farms. Many now crowded into the cities and competed for jobs in the factories. American workers and others began to demand restrictions upon immigration.

3. Conservation. With the close of the frontier, Americans awakened to the need for conservation. Farmers, timber and mining companies, and government agencies acted to conserve the nation's soil, water, timber, and other natural resources. (Check the Index.)

4. Imperialism. American capitalists, who had looked to the frontier for raw materials, markets, and investment opportunities, now began to look elsewhere. The United States embarked on a program of imperialism in the Caribbean, Central and South America, and the Far East.

Historical Analysis. *What criticisms have been voiced against Turner's frontier theory?*

Many historians believe that Turner exaggerated the importance of the frontier. They claim that Turner ignored the following facts: (1) American democracy was fostered by our democratic heritage from Britain and by the demands of workers in the industrial East for a voice in government. (2) Britain developed a democratic form of government without the existence of a frontier. (3) The southwestern frontier, settled by cotton planters, developed neither democracy nor nationalism. (4) The frontier did not serve as a "safety valve" for many eastern factory workers. They lacked knowledge of farming and lacked the funds to transport their families and to equip farms in the West. (5) The frontier itself was the result of industrial expansion in Europe and in the north-eastern United States. The demand from industrial areas for raw materials and agricultural produce encouraged western settlement. (6) Despite the frontier, 19th-century America was never economically in-dependent. It always depended on Europe for markets for its agricultural produce and for capital with which to build up American industry.

Most historians agree that many factors, including (1) European ideals and influences, (2) industrialism and the factory system, and (3) agriculture and the frontier—all have helped shape modern America.

——————————— MULTIPLE-CHOICE QUESTIONS ———————————

1. What is the best definition for the term "American frontier"? (a) a fixed boundary line (b) the Atlantic or Pacific coastline (c) a shifting area where pioneer settlement ended (d) the dividing line between French and English settlements.

2. Which one of the following characterizes *all* movements to the frontier? (a) search for religious freedom (b) greed (c) escape from political persecution (d) hardship.

3. The migration of the Mormons to Utah was (a) led by Brigham Young (b) led by Joseph Smith (c) authorized by the Mexican government (d) spurred by the discovery of gold in Utah.

4. "Long drive" and "range wars" are terms most closely associated with the (a) Indian Wars (b) forty-niners (c) cattle kingdom (d) building of the Union Pacific Railroad.

5. The major purpose of the Homestead Act of 1862 was to (a) create future slave states (b) raise revenue for the federal government (c) encourage settlement of public lands for farming (d) provide railroad companies with new land to sell.

6. The policy of the federal government toward the Indians in the period immediately following the Civil War was to (a) move them to reservations (b) drive them from the country (c) require Indian children to attend public school (d) grant Indians full citizenship.

7. What is the generally accepted date for the disappearance of the frontier in Ameri-can history? (a) 1860 (b) 1890 (c) 1910 (d) 1940.

8. Frederick Jackson Turner contributed *most* to American history by (a) discovering the frontier (b) distinguishing between the mining and agricultural frontiers (c) making the frontier central to an interpretation of the American experience (d) explaining how the frontier brought about the Civil War.

9. The government's land policy in the West before 1890 did *not* (a) promote wise use of the land (b) lead to the building of railroads (c) permit most settlers to own their own farms (d) encourage settlers to develop a spirit of independence.

10. The western frontier contributed to American democracy by (a) establishing the first public elementary schools (b) serving as a symbol of economic opportunity and po-litical equality (c) supporting the establishment of Indian reservations (d) opposing government involvement in internal improvements.

11. Which one of the following was first adopted in the United States on the western frontier? (a) elementary education (b) the town meeting (c) the granting of suffrage to women (d) separation of church and state.

12. An important influence of the expanding frontier on American life was that it *decreased* (a) our dependence on Europe (b) the growth of nationalism (c) our concern over the slavery controversy (d) our interest in manufacturing.

13. The disappearance of the frontier (a) brought new social and economic problems to the United States (b) decreased American investments abroad (c) discouraged American workers from joining unions (d) made conservation unnecessary.

14. Which characteristic of the American frontier is still an important part of American life? (a) established churches in some states (b) self-sufficient farming (c) a predominantly industrial economy (d) absence of a rigid class system.

———————— **READING INTERPRETATION QUESTIONS** ————————

. . . American social development has been continually beginning over again on the frontier. This perennial rebirth, this fluidity of American life, this expansion westward with its new opportunities, its continuous touch with the simplicity of primitive society, furnish the forces dominating American character. The true point of view in the history of this nation is not the Atlantic coast, it is the Great West. The frontier is the line of most rapid and effective Americanization. The wilderness masters the colonists. Frederick Jackson Turner, *The Significance of the Frontier in American History,* 1893

1. According to Turner, the culture of the United States was primarily the result of the (a) dependence of each generation upon its predecessors (b) western settler's experience in adjusting to new surroundings (c) pioneer's ability to maintain contact with the settled areas back east (d) influence of the frontier in making settlers more like Easterners.

2. In this statement Turner describes the frontier not only as an area but also as a (a) process of developing culture (b) preserver of traditions (c) solution to European problems (d) developer of economic systems.

3. Which characteristic of the West as described by Turner is most applicable to contemporary society in the United States? (a) simplicity of life (b) westward expansion (c) new opportunities (d) frontier environment.

———————————— **ESSAY QUESTIONS** ————————————

1. "Go west, young man" has been important advice for the American people. (*a*) Show *two* different ways in which the westward movement affected life in the Eastern seaboard states. (*b*) Describe *three* effects of the closing of the frontier upon American life. (*c*) What is meant by the statement that there are still frontiers in American life?

2. Giving *one* specific fact, show how each of the following was *either* a cause *or* a result of the westward movement in the 19th century: (*a*) growth of democracy (*b*) internal improvements (*c*) immigration from Europe (*d*) nationalism (*e*) growth of labor unions (*f*) development of industry (*g*) conservation movement.

3. The expanding frontier has influenced our nation in several ways. Present *two* facts to prove that *each* of the following statements applies to the history of our nation: (*a*) The expanding frontier has helped the growth of democracy. (*b*) The expanding frontier has led to conflicts. (*c*) The expanding frontier has helped the nation to achieve greater economic self-sufficiency.

4. (a) Give the provisions of the Homestead Act (1862). (b) Describe an effect of the Homestead Act on each of the following: (a) agriculture in the East (b) immigration (c) the Indian (d) the cattle industry.

PART 2. Farmers Struggle for an Increased Share of the National Income

THE AGRICULTURAL REVOLUTION

BEFORE THE AGRICULTURAL REVOLUTION: COLONIAL FARMERS

The colonial farmers employed primitive implements and methods. They had only a few simple tools: the rake, hoe, scythe, and wooden plow. They cultivated their farms inefficiently because they (1) had little knowledge of proper soil care, and (2) could secure additional land at low cost. Although they worked long hours, usually at exhausting manual tasks, their harvests remained relatively small; productivity, or output per worker, was low.

AGRICULTURAL REVOLUTION: BRIEF DESCRIPTION

1. Meaning. The term *agricultural revolution* refers to the change from primitive to modern farming methods: the use of farm machinery and scientific agriculture. In the United States, the agricultural revolution began early in the 19th century and continues, at a rapid pace, to this very day.

2. Farm Machinery

a. The Metal Plow. For centuries, the farmer's basic tool had been the wooden plow. *Charles Newbold* in 1797 invented a cast-iron plow; *Jethro Wood* in 1814 improved upon the cast-iron plow; *John Deere* in 1837 invented the self-cleaning steel plow; and *James Oliver* in 1877 perfected a chilled-iron plow. These metal plows turned the soil more easily and more deeply.

b. Other Farm Equipment. Cyrus McCormick in 1831 invented a reaper. It cut grain many times faster than a scythe. Other agricultural inventions included the thresher to separate grain from the stalk; the harvester to cut and bind the grain; the combine to cut, thresh, and sack the grain; and the tractor to pull equipment through the field.

3. Scientific Agriculture. Research into agricultural problems led to (a) the rotation of crops and the use of artificial fertilizer to renew soil fertility, (b) contour plowing to prevent soil erosion, (c) the drainage of swamps and the irrigation of dry land to provide land suitable for crops, (d) insecticides and germicides to combat insect pests and plant diseases, (e) breeding of plants and animals to produce better offspring, (f) new uses for agricultural products, and (g) processing of canned, frozen, and powdered foods.

SPREAD OF AGRICULTURAL KNOWLEDGE

1. Private Efforts. Agricultural societies, fairs, and journals served to pass new agricultural knowledge on to the American farmer. In 1860 over 900 agricultural societies existed in the United States.

2. Governmental Efforts

a. The *Morrill Act* (1862) offered federal land grants to states to endow colleges with the object to teaching "agriculture and the mechanic arts." Eventually, the states received some 12 million acres and used the income from selling or renting the land to develop outstanding land-grant colleges (check the Index).

b. Subsequent federal laws provided funds for (1) agricultural experiment stations affiliated with the land-grant colleges (*Hatch Act,* 1887), (2) county agents to bring agricultural information directly to the farmer (*Smith-Lever Act,* 1914), and (3) high school courses in agriculture (*Smith-Hughes Act,* 1917).

c. In 1862 Congress created the *Department of Agriculture.* In 1889 the department was elevated to Cabinet status. The department conducts research projects; provides marketing services; and publishes periodicals, pamphlets, and bulletins.

EFFECTS OF THE AGRICULTURAL REVOLUTION

1. Proportional Decrease in Farm Population. Compared to the entire nation, our farm population decreased from 80 percent in 1860 to 40 percent in 1900. Nevertheless, farmers produced enough to feed our growing population and, in addition, provided surpluses for export.

2. Increased Production. Farmers increased their output tremendously, in terms of both output per worker and total output. From 1860 to 1900, cotton production rose almost threefold and wheat production fourfold.

3. Increased Mechanization. As machines took over the heavy, backbreaking tasks, farmers' work became less wearisome, but they had to learn the mechanical skills of operating and maintaining their machines.

4. End of Farm Isolation. With the invention of the telephone and the automobile, farmers came into closer contact with the outside world.

5. Shift From Self-Sufficient to Commercial Farming. Until the mid-19th century, many farmers were self-sufficient. After the Civil War, farmers became less self-sufficient and more commercial. They raised large quantities of a few staple crops, such as corn and wheat, and sold these crops in domestic and world markets.

6. Business Problems Facing Commercial Farmers. (a) *Credit.* Farmers often needed long-term loans to purchase land, livestock, and machinery, and short-term loans to sustain them until harvest time. (b) *Labor.* Farmers employed full-time hired hands and, at peak seasons, migratory labor. (c) *Production.* Farmers sought maximum harvests at minimum cost. Since they hired workers and used expensive machinery, farmers achieved greater efficiency by operating large farms. (d) *Prices.* Farmers experienced good or bad times depending upon the price their products commanded in the marketplace. (e) *Supplies.* Farmers relied upon industry for manufactured goods and upon other farmers for foodstuffs.

AMERICAN AGRICULTURE FROM THE CIVIL WAR TO WORLD WAR I

AGRICULTURAL PROSPERITY DURING THE CIVIL WAR

Northern and western farmers experienced heavy demand for foodstuffs for the Union armed forces and for the thriving industrial cities. Farmers cultivated increased acreage, employed more machines, and enjoyed relatively high agricultural prices.

COMPLAINTS OF FARMERS AFTER THE CIVIL WAR

1. Low Agricultural Prices. The demand for agricultural produce declined and prices fell. American farmers also faced increased competition in world markets from newly plowed lands in Argentina, Australia, and Canada. Nevertheless, American farmers continued to expand their output.

Wheat farmers, who in 1866 received more than $1.50 per bushel, in 1894 received less than $.70. Corn and cotton farmers suffered similar sharp price declines. With low prices, farmers had great difficulty earning a living.

2. Insufficient and Expensive Credit. Since farmers were considered poor credit risks, banks were reluctant to grant them loans. Despite state laws prohibiting usury, farmers often had to pay excessive interest rates, up to 25 percent per year. Farmers unable to meet mortgage payments lost their homes and farms.

3. High Rates Charged by Others. Farmers complained that they received only about half the price that city consumers paid for agricultural produce. Farmers blamed this situation on the high rates charged by grain storage elevators, packinghouses, insurance companies, wholesale distributors, and especially the railroads. Since each railroad had a virtual monopoly over the transportation of crops from the small farm towns along its tracks, farmers endured poor service and exorbitant rates. The rule that guided railroads in determining their rates was "what the traffic will bear."

4. High Industrial Prices. While farmers received low agricultural prices, they paid dearly for manufactured goods. The farmers blamed high industrial prices upon (a) high tariff rates, which kept out many foreign goods and protected American manufacturers from foreign competition, and (b) the growth of business monopoly, which curtailed domestic competition.

AGRARIAN CRUSADE (1865–1900)

To improve their economic conditions, farmers undertook an *Agrarian Crusade*. They joined in organizations—the Grange, the Greenback-Labor party, and the Populist party—to demand help from the states and from the federal government. These movements signaled the beginning of a significant change in American economic beliefs: (1) away from *laissez-faire*—that the government should not interfere in economic matters, and (2) toward government responsibility for the economic well-being of the people. (For *laissez-faire*, check the Index.)

GRANGER MOVEMENT

1. Granger Laws. The Patrons of Husbandry, or *National Grange*, founded by *Oliver H. Kelley* in 1867, was an organization of local farmers' clubs. As farmers became discontented with their economic conditions, they joined their local Granges, and became active in state politics. Farmers elected Granger candidates to state legislatures, and several midwestern states passed *Granger laws*— regulating the rates and practices of grain elevators and railroads. However, in the case of *Wabash vs. Illinois* (1886), the Supreme Court ruled that, since railroads were engaged in interstate commerce, they were not subject to regulation by the states.

2. Granger Cooperatives. To eliminate the profits of others, the Grangers established *cooperatives,* or "*co-ops.*" Owned and operated by the farmers, these organizations were to do the work of grading, packing, selling, and shipping crops, and buying farm equipment and other necessities. The profits that the cooperatives earned were to be distributed to their farmer owners. These early "co-ops" failed, in part because of insufficient capital and inexperienced management.

3. Lasting Contributions. The Grange (a) taught farmers to work together to solve their common problems, (b) hastened federal railroad regulation, which started in 1887 with the Interstate Commerce Act (check the Index), (c) stimulated the development of mail-order houses, such as Montgomery Ward and Sears Roebuck, to compete with local merchants, (d) paved the way for the successful present-day farm cooperatives (check the Index), and (e) still serves rural communities today by providing social activities—meetings, lectures, picnics—and by lobbying for farmers.

FARMERS DEMAND CHEAP MONEY, OR INFLATION

Farmers generally were debtors who raised and sold crops. Their economic well-being reflected the amount of their debt—a fixed sum—and the price of their crops—a varying figure. Farmers wanted the prices they received to be high, which meant that money would have a low value as measured by its purchasing power. Money whose purchasing power is falling or low is known as cheap money. Because cheap money means high prices, it eases the debt burden in an economy of inflation.

To arrest the downward trend in agricultural prices after the Civil War, farmers demanded cheap money—to increase prices and ease the repayment of debts. For example, if wheat sold at $1 per bushel, a farmer would need 5000 bushels to pay off a $5000 mortgage. However, at an inflated price of $2 per bushel, the farmer would need only 2500 bushels—half the amount—to pay off the same debt. True, the farmer would have to pay more for manufactured goods, but would benefit overall. Furthermore, cheap money would help debtors by making available more funds for loans.

(Cheap money would hurt creditors—people who lent money—since the purchasing power of the money repaid would be less than the purchasing power of the money lent, although the fixed amount would be the same. Creditors favor sound or dear money.)

Since cheap money could be attained by having the government increase the amount of currency in circulation, the farmers supported movements for the printing of greenbacks and the coinage of silver.

GREENBACK MOVEMENT

1. Greenbacks and Inflation. During the Civil War the federal government placed into circulation more than $400 million in *greenbacks*. This was paper money supported by confidence in the government but without metallic, or specie, backing. Following the war the government started to recall the greenbacks, and money became scarcer. Farmers protested that the government was hastening the decline of agricultural prices.

2. Specie Resumption Act (1875). In spite of the farmers' protests, Congress passed the Specie Resumption Act. The act (a) fixed the amount of greenbacks in circulation at $346 million, and (b) made greenbacks redeemable in gold. This latter provision, raising greenbacks to the value of gold-backed money, continued the trend toward deflation and lower prices.

3. Greenback-Labor Party. In their fight for cheap money, farmers joined the *Greenback-Labor party*. They demanded repeal of the Specie Resumption Act and urged the issuance of more greenbacks. Although the party attracted over a million votes in the Congressional elections of 1878, it declined soon afterward. Farmers next concentrated on the silver movement.

SILVER MOVEMENT

1. Crime of '73. For years the federal government used two metals, silver and gold, for coinage—a monetary practice called *bimetallism*. The government set the ratio between silver and gold at 16 to 1; that is, the government considered 16 ounces of silver to be worth 1 ounce of gold. Since private silversmiths needed silver for commercial use and offered a slightly higher price, the government received very little silver for coinage. So Congress passed the *Coinage Act* in 1873, ending the coinage of silver money, that is, *demonetizing* silver. Shortly afterward, miners discovered rich deposits of silver at the Comstock Lode in Nevada and in Colorado, so that the market price of silver fell sharply. Silver interests now wanted to sell their silver to the government and vigorously denounced the demonetization of silver as the *"Crime of '73."*

2. Silver Purchase Acts (1878, 1890). Silver interests demanded that the government resume the coinage of silver at the ratio of 16 to 1, and their demand received the support of the nation's farmers. The farmers reasoned that the coinage of silver would increase the amount of money in circulation and thus cheapen the value of money. The political alliance of farmers and silver interests mustered sufficient strength in Congress to pass two acts, in 1878 and 1890, for the government to purchase limited quantities of silver to be used to support issuance of additional currency. Although these laws increased the amount of available currency, they did not halt the decline of agricultural prices.

3. Effects of Silver Purchases on Currency. So much silver was now being mined that its value rapidly declined. Private individuals now found it advantageous to present silver-backed paper money to the government to be redeemed in gold. By 1893 these redemptions had reduced the government's gold reserves to a bare minimum. Many people believed that the Treasury would soon be unable to redeem silver currency for gold and that the nation would have to go off the gold standard.

CLEVELAND PROTECTS THE GOLD STANDARD

In 1893 the United States suffered a severe depression. President Grover Cleveland, a conservative eastern Democrat, blamed the depression as well as gold reserve losses upon a single cause: the government's purchase of silver. He claimed that, by paying out gold for silver, the nation had drained its gold reserve and that this had caused the depression. Cleveland (1) secured Congressional repeal of the 1890 silver purchase act, and (2) authorized the Treasury to obtain gold by selling bonds. He permitted the largest sale of bonds to be handled directly through the Wall Street banking firm of J. Pierpont Morgan.

Cleveland's actions preserved the gold standard but did little to improve economic conditions. Cleveland was hailed by banking and business interests, which opposed inflation and favored sound money. He was condemned by the silver interests and farmers as a "tool of Wall Street."

POPULIST PARTY: A THIRD-PARTY MOVEMENT

1. Origin. Farmers came to believe that eastern industrialists and bankers controlled both the Democratic and Republican parties. Exhorted by agrarian orators to "raise less corn and more hell," farmers in the 1880s established politically minded *Farmers' Alliances* that evolved into the *People's* or *Populist party.*

2. Program. Meeting at Omaha, Nebraska, in 1892, the Populists adopted the following program: (a) Free and unlimited coinage of silver at the ratio of 16 to 1. Populists expected this proposal to increase the amount of money in circulation from $20 to at least $50 per person. (b) A graduated income tax. Such a tax would bear more heavily on wealthy persons than on farmers and workers, and would provide the federal government with a source of revenue to replace the tariff. (c) Government ownership of telephone, telegraph, and railroad systems. Farmers looked to government ownership as a remedy for the abuses of private enterprise in the communication and transportation industries. (d) The secret ballot and direct election of Senators. These proposals would provide greater democracy.

To achieve a farmer-labor alliance, the Populists also endorsed prolabor planks: shorter working hours and restrictions on immigration.

3. Early Vote-Getting Successes. In the 1892 Presidential election, the Populist candidate, General James B. Weaver, received more than one million popular votes and 22 electoral votes, all from western states. In the 1894 Congressional elections, the Populists increased their voting strength. Elated, they looked forward confidently to the 1896 Presidential election.

ELECTION OF 1896

1. Candidates

a. William Jennings Bryan. Farmers and silver interests gained control of the Democratic convention. They cheered William Jennings Bryan, the "silver-tongued orator" from Nebraska who delivered an emotional attack upon the gold standard in his famous "Cross of Gold" speech, concluding: "You shall not crucify mankind upon a cross of gold." Bryan became the Democratic candidate for President. He also won the Populist nomination.

b. William McKinley. Conservative eastern business and banking interests controlled the Republican convention. They nominated the astute Ohioan William McKinley, who opposed free silver, supported the gold standard, and advocated high protective tariffs.

2. The Campaign. Traveling extensively and speaking frequently, Bryan demanded reforms to help the farmer and to provide social and economic justice. McKinley, content to issue carefully prepared campaign statements, stayed home. His campaign was managed by the wealthy Ohio industrialist and banker *Marcus A. Hanna.* Hanna raised large campaign contributions, some ten times the amount available to Bryan. Hanna's business associates warned their workers and mortgagors that they would lose their jobs and farms if Bryan was elected. McKinley also benefited from the almost unanimous support of the press, which ridiculed Bryan as a radical, irresponsible "boy orator."

The election offered clear-cut issues: McKinley stood for the gold standard, high tariffs, and noninterference by the government with business. Bryan stood for free coinage of silver, lower tariffs, and government responsibility for the economic well-being of the people. McKinley drew his greatest support from bankers and industrialists; Bryan, from silver miners and farmers. McKinley's strength lay in the North and the East; Bryan's, in the South and the West.

3. Results. McKinley carried all industrial states and some older agrarian states. With 271 electoral votes to Bryan's 176, McKinley won the election.

Shortly afterward, the Populist party disappeared. Some Populist goals emerged later in the progressive movement. (Check the Index.)

TEMPORARY AGRICULTURAL PROSPERITY

Unexpectedly, after 1896, American farmers entered upon better times. (1) New goldfields were discovered in South Africa, Australia, and Alaska, and methods of gold mining were improved. The considerable increase in the supply of gold permitted an increase in the amount of money in circulation. (2) Crop failures in Europe and India led to increased foreign demand for American agricultural products. (3) Heavy immigration to the United States increased the domestic market for farm products.

Farmers, cheered by rising agricultural prices, abandoned their interest in free silver. They offered little opposition when Congress passed the *Gold Standard Act* (1900). This act declared that the United States was on the gold standard and made all paper money redeemable in gold.

Farmers considered the pre-World War I years from 1900 to 1914 as the *golden age of American agriculture.*

AGRICULTURE FROM WORLD WAR I TO THE PRESENT

WORLD WAR I AND AGRICULTURE

1. Immediate Effect: Favorable. During World War I, farmers experienced a tremendous demand for agricultural produce for domestic, military, and export use. They enjoyed high prices; for example, wheat, which had sold for less than $.70 per bushel in 1894, now sold at over $2.

2. Long-Range Effect: Unfavorable. To meet the increased demand, farmers increased output by purchasing more land and more farm machinery, paying inflated wartime prices. Since most farmers lacked funds, they borrowed money, often at high interest rates. After the war, demand returned to prewar levels, and prices fell. Desperate, farmers could not afford to allow their land and machines to lie idle, so they continued to produce huge surpluses that drove farm prices still farther downward.

DEVELOPMENTS AFTER WORLD WAR I

1. Cooperative Movement. Farmers again turned to cooperatives. *Marketing co-ops* graded, stored, packed, sold, and shipped the produce of their members. *Purchasing co-ops* bought supplies for resale to members. Co-ops distributed their profits to their members. They benefited from federal and state laws offering them low-cost loans and special tax exemptions. Today, with a membership of several million, co-ops are an essential aspect of American agriculture.

2. Farm Bloc. Members of Congress from farm states, Democrats as well as Republicans, joined together as the *farm bloc* to help the farmers. During the 1920s the farm bloc secured laws providing low-interest farm loans and exempting cooperatives from prosecution as monopolies.

3. Agricultural Marketing Act (1929). To deal with farm surpluses, President *Herbert Hoover* requested Congress to pass the Agricultural Marketing Act. It created a *Federal Farm Board* with $500 million to lend to farm organizations. They would purchase and store surplus agricultural products until the surpluses could be resold in time of scarcity. The act failed because it did not limit production and did not increase the market for farm produce. Soon the Federal Farm Board exhausted its funds.

4. Farmers and the Great Depression (Starting in 1929). With the 1929 Depression, farmers were especially hard hit. From 1929 to 1932 wheat fell from $1.00 to $.38 a bushel; cotton fell from $.16 to $.06 a pound; average cash income per farmer fell about 70 percent. Farmers could not keep up their mortgage payments or buy the necessities of life. Nebraska farmers burned their low-priced corn as fuel. Iowa and Minnesota farmers forcibly prevented mortgage foreclosures. Angry and desperate, farmers demanded federal action.

THE NEW DEAL AND THE PROBLEM OF FARM SURPLUSES

Promising the nation a New Deal, Franklin D. Roosevelt, the Democratic candidate, overwhelmingly defeated the incumbent, Herbert Hoover, in the 1932 Presidential election. Having received widespread farm support, Roosevelt involved the federal government actively in assisting the farmer.

1. Agricultural Adjustment Act (1933). The AAA of 1933 sought to raise agricultural prices in relation to industrial prices so that farmers would regain the purchasing power they had enjoyed in the prosperous 1909–1914 years. This level of farm prices was called *parity*. If, for example, the price of wheat and the price level of industrial goods were both four times their 1909–1914 average, then wheat was said to be selling at *100 percent of parity.* However, if the price of wheat had only tripled while the price level of industrial goods had quadrupled, then wheat was said to be selling at *75 percent of parity.*

The law tried to raise farm prices by reducing acreage under cultivation and thereby preventing the production of surpluses. It provided for (a) *voluntary curtailment* of production of basic commodities, such as tobacco, corn, cotton, and wheat; (b) *cash bounties,* or *bonus payments,* to those farmers who left a percentage of their land idle; and (c) *processing taxes*—levied on wheat millers, cotton spinners, and meatpackers—to raise funds for bonus payments.

In 1936 the Supreme Court declared the AAA unconstitutional, one reason being that agriculture was an intrastate activity and not subject to federal regulation.

2. Soil Conservation and Domestic Allotment Act (1936). To replace the defunct AAA, Congress passed the SCDAA. It provided that farmers be paid a bounty for planting part of their land with soil-conserving crops such as clover and alfalfa. Indirectly, this law worked to curtail production of basic agricultural crops. The Supreme Court held that soil conservation was a legitimate federal power and declared the SCDAA constitutional.

3. Agricultural Adjustment Act (1938) Drawing upon its experience with the two previous laws, the New Deal enacted the extensive AAA of 1938.

a. The government established *acreage quotas* for basic commodities, and paid the farmers bounties for planting soil-conserving crops on acreage withheld from production.

b. If, despite acreage quotas, farmers raised surplus crops, the government, with the consent of two-thirds of the farmers concerned, could establish *marketing quotas.* These quotas limited the amount that the farmers could sell.

c. Farmers stored surplus crops under government seal. With the crops in storage as security, the government granted farmers *commodity loans.* The government set the loan value for each commodity at slightly below parity. In good harvest years, to prevent falling prices, farmers placed surplus crops in storage and accepted commodity loans. In bad harvest years, they could take advantage of rising prices by taking surpluses out of storage, selling the commodities, and paying off the loans. This idea was called the *ever-normal granary plan.*

d. Also to bring prices up to the 1909–1914 levels, the government gave the farmers direct subsidies, called *parity payments.*

Historical Analysis. *What is a reasonable evaluation of the New Deal's farm-surplus laws?*

In Favor. (1) Farmers secured higher prices. Between 1932 and 1940 farm income rose from less than $5 billion to over $9 billion. (2) Farmers enjoyed a fairer share of the national income. From 1932 to 1936 the parity ratio of agricultural to industrial prices rose from 55 to 90. (3) The nation's economy improved, as farmers now had the money to purchase more manufactured goods. (4) Soil conservation was widely practiced. (5) Farmers were able to adjust production to demand. (6) Farmers regained confidence in the federal government.

Against. (1) Consumers had to pay higher prices. (2) Agricultural prices above world levels caused American farmers to lose foreign markets. (3) Taxpayers were burdened with the cost of financing government spending for agriculture. (4) The farm laws proved unable to decrease output sufficiently. Even though farmers cultivated less land, they were able to increase total output by retiring least fertile lands from cultivation, practicing intensive farming, and using more fertilizer. From 1930 to 1940 wheat productivity rose from 11 to 15 bushels per acre. (5) The laws brought little benefit to tenant farmers, sharecroppers, and migratory workers. Some tenant farmers and sharecroppers were driven off their farms by the landowners, who wanted to withdraw land from production and thus qualify for bounties. (6) The laws tried to curtail agricultural production when many people throughout the world were hungry.

OTHER NEW DEAL FARM MEASURES

1. Credit. The *Farm Credit Administration* furnished long-term, low-interest loans to farmers to refinance existing mortgages.

2. Electrification. The *Rural Electrification Administration* (REA) provided low-interest loans for cooperatives to supply electricity to rural areas not served by private utilities. The REA enabled many farm families to enjoy modern electrical appliances.

3. Aid to Tenants and Other Poor Farmers

a. Disadvantages of Tenancy. Tenant farmers and sharecroppers comprised over 40 percent of our farm population in the early 1930s. They constituted most of the rural poor. Tenants and sharecroppers (1) received the least fertile lands to farm, (2) took poor care of the property since it was not theirs, (3) earned extremely low incomes, often less than $250 in cash per year, and (4) worked their children on the farms instead of sending them to school.

b. Federal Aid. The *Farm Security Administration* (FSA) assisted needy farm families. It provided loans to sharecroppers, tenant farmers, and farm laborers for the purchase of land, equipment, and supplies. Loans were made for up to 40 years and at the low interest rate of 3 percent. In 1946 the FSA was replaced by a new agency, the *Farmers Home Administration*.

c. Results. Tenancy and sharecropping were reduced by (a) these government efforts, (b) the flight of poorer farmers to the city, and (c) farm prosperity during World War II. Of our farm population in 1969, sharecroppers and tenant farmers comprised 13 percent, a sharp decrease from the 1930s.

AGRICULTURE DURING WORLD WAR II AND AFTERWARD

With World War II, American farmers again enjoyed a period of prosperity. The demand for farm produce increased, and prices rose to new highs. To stimulate production, the government (a) removed all restrictions on output and (b) gave special draft deferments to farmers and farm laborers.

After the war, foodstuffs from the United States helped feed the war-torn countries of the world, and demand for American farm goods remained high. In 1949, however, as relief needs overseas tapered off, agricultural prices turned downward.

A series of laws—providing acreage quotas, marketing quotas, price supports through commodity loans, and transfer of substantial acreage from commercial production to conservation uses—all proved ineffective. From 1947 to 1960 farmers' total income fell from $17 billion to $11 billion, a decrease of 35 percent. Despite government programs, farmers still produced surpluses as they offset decreased acreage by increased productivity per acre.

AGRICULTURE: THE TECHNOLOGICAL SPEEDUP (1940–1970)

The agricultural revolution has changed American farming, but since World War II at a quicker pace than ever before. Farmers have utilized the latest technological advances: complex machines, improved fertilizers, pesticides, weed-killers, and better seed varieties. The record from 1940 to 1970 was startling:

1. Increase in Productivity per Acre. The per acre output of wheat increased from 15 to 30 bushels, of cotton from 262 to 454 pounds. Overall crop production per acre rose 66 percent. This sharply increased output per acre has been called the *green revolution*.

2. Increase in Output per Worker. The number of worker-hours needed to produce one bale of cotton fell from 200 to 47. Whereas one farmer used to produce enough goods to meet the needs of 12 other persons, one farmer now met the needs of 47.

3. Decrease in Farm Population. The ratio of farm population to total population decreased from 23 to 5 percent. Some 21 million people left agriculture. These were mostly (a) poor farmers who lacked sufficient land and capital and (b) farm laborers and migratory workers who were replaced by machines. Most of these people migrated to the cities.

4. Decrease in Number of Farms. The number of farms declined from 6.4 million to 2.9 million. The decrease was due to the abandonment of many subsistence farms and the merging of other farms.

5. Increase in Farm Size. The size of the average farm increased from 167 to over 373 acres. By using modern machines, the larger farm achieved greater efficiency. The worth of the average farm in land, livestock, equipment, and buildings rose from $7000 to $76,000.

6. Growing Importance of the Large Farm. Of total farm produce, the amount sold by (*a*) small, or subsistence, farms decreased to less than 10 percent, (*b*) medium-sized farms remained at about 50 percent, and (*c*) large farms increased to over 40 percent. Large commercial scientifically run farms are known as *factories in the field, corporate farms, agribusiness,* or *agricorporations.*

AGRICULTURE TODAY

1. Problems of Poverty and Hired Workers

a. Impoverished Farmers. The problems of American agriculture in the 1980s remained as serious as ever. Some 2.2 million farms were operating in 1985, down 700,000 in a decade. More than half of these farms had sales totaling under $20,000. While a small percentage of farmers earned high incomes from agriculture, hundreds of thousands of others earned more from off-farm jobs than they did from farming. Many farmers had incomes below the poverty line.

The government has assisted struggling farmers by (1) providing loans for them to expand their landholdings, (2) spurring rural communities to undertake job-creating projects such as constructing water systems, (3) encouraging new industries to locate in rural areas, and (4) granting funds for occupational retraining of farmers.

b. Hired Farm Workers. The number of hired farm workers declined sharply in the 1980s, from 2.6 million in 1975 to about 1.2 million in 1986. Approximately 200,000 of those were migratory workers. These workers travel from region to region and find employment chiefly on large commercial farms at peak

Smith, Las Vegas Sun/ROTHCO

periods such as harvesttime. Working only a few months a year and earning an average of under $5 an hour, they live in extreme poverty. Many migratory workers come from Mexico and Haiti or are *Chicanos* (Americans of Mexican descent).

Beginning in 1951, Congress permitted Mexican farm workers called *braceros* (laborers) to come to the United States on a temporary basis. Growers supported the *bracero* program because it increased the supply of people willing to work for low wages. Labor unions criticized the program because it increased the difficulty of organizing farm workers into unions. After 1962, temporary foreign farm workers became subject to United States minimum-wage laws, and in 1965 Congress ended the *bracero* program. However, growers continued to hire foreign workers. Under the Immigration Reform and Control Act of 1986, up to 350,000 foreign farm workers per year may enter the United States.

The first union to meet success in organizing farm workers was the *United Farm Workers* (UFW), an AFL-CIO affiliate led by *Cesar Chavez*. In 1965 the UFW called thousands of California farm workers, mainly *Chicanos,* out on strike. Rallying support from segments of the public, the UFW won contracts for improved wages and working conditions from major grape and lettuce growers. In 1977 Chavez reached agreements with the Teamsters Union to settle a jurisdictional struggle over representation of farm workers. The UFW and other unions have had little success in organizing farm workers outside of California. In the mid-1980s, the UFW represented slightly less than 10 percent of California's 200,000 farm workers. Nationwide, less than 1 percent of farm workers belonged to a labor union.

2. The Problem of Food Surpluses. Agriculture in the United States has been too successful for its own good. Each year farmers produce far more food than Americans consume. Since the 1930s, United States farm policy has had two chief aims: (*a*) finding an outlet for food surpluses, and (*b*) finding an acceptable means of bringing farm production down so that the supply of food is in line with the demand for food.

3. The 1970s: Farm Prosperity—For a Time. United States agriculture began a dizzy roller coaster ride in the 1970s. A sharp rise in world demand for food opened up new markets for farm products and brought prosperity to many farmers. The rise in world demand resulted from (*a*) crop failures in the Soviet Union in 1972 and in other parts of the world in 1974, (*b*) a 1971 devaluation of the United States dollar that made our products cheaper for foreign customers, (*c*) sharply rising populations in many developing countries, and (*d*) growing prosperity in traditional food-importing countries such as Japan. Exports of United States farm products shot up from $7.3 billion in 1970 to a peak of $43.3 billion in 1981. For a time in the mid-1970s, the prices that farmers received for their crops were quite high in relation to farmers' costs. Flush with prosperity, many farmers expanded their operations by borrowing money and buying new land. As a result, the cost of farmland rose sharply.

a. **The Farm Act of 1973.** The 1973 farm law started from the assumption that the problem of food surpluses had been solved. It sought to "unleash" farmers so that they could produce more food to meet the rising demand abroad. The act (1) reduced or eliminated many forms of price supports and other programs designed to hold down production, (2) did away with the New Deal approaches of parity price and complex farm regulations, and (3) protected farmers by assuring them a "floor" under their income based on "target prices" for basic crops such as wheat, corn, and cotton. If market prices should fall below the target prices, the government would make up the difference by crop loans or cash subsidies, limited to a maximum payment per farmer of $20,000. Critics warned that (1) if market prices fell sharply below target prices, the government would have to make large subsidy payments, and (2) farmers would lobby for ever higher target prices. The 1973 act unleashed farmers so successfully that production once again outstripped demand. By 1977 the country again had large crop surpluses.

b. **The Farm Act of 1977.** This act (1) raised target prices and provided that they be geared to production costs, (2) authorized the secretary of agriculture to offer special subsidies to farmers who agreed to take a percentage of their land out of production, and (3) established a grain-reserve system to store surplus crops on farms. Many farmers thought that the 1977 law did not go far enough. During the winter of 1977–1978, activist farmers drove parades of tractors through farm-belt cities and Washington, D.C., to demand higher benefits.

4. The 1980s: Crisis on the Farm. The hard times that began to affect some farmers in the late 1970s spread across the country in the 1980s. Farm exports declined sharply, to about $23 billion in 1985. The reasons for falling revenue included (*a*) a United States embargo on food exports to the Soviet Union after Soviet troops invaded Afghanistan in 1979, (*b*) a "green revolution" that enabled developing countries such as India and Thailand to step up food production dramatically, (*c*) growing competition from other food-exporting areas, especially Europe, Canada, Australia, and Argentina, and (*d*) an unfavorable exchange rate for the dollar that made our products more expensive in many countries. Although President Reagan responded to farmers' complaints by ending the embargo on sales to the Soviet Union in 1981, Soviet purchases remained far below previous levels.

With falling demand, the prices received by United States farmers also dropped. Farmers who had borrowed heavily in the prosperous 1970s often found themselves unable to keep up payments to banks and other lenders. Many farmers went bankrupt, losing their land and even their homes. The crisis touched many parts of the nation's economy, from manufacturers and dealers of farm equipment to grain traders to bankers to shopowners in farm communities. Efforts to solve farm problems through legislation made little headway.

a. **The Farm Act of 1981.** While the Reagan administration that took office in 1981 championed free enterprise, it soon ended its efforts to abolish farm subsidies. The Farm Act of 1981 was essentially a renewal of the 1977 act. The 1981 act (1) further raised target prices on major crops, (2) cut back on dairy price supports, and (3) revived a program of loans to sugar producers that had been suspended in 1978.

b. The Food Security Act of 1985. The 1985 act set the nation's farm policy on a sharply different course. Abandoning the traditional goal of keeping crop prices high, the act sought to lower crop prices in order to make United States farm exports more competitive on the world market. The 1985 act called for (1) sharp cuts in the loan rates for major crops, (2) a guarantee of minimum payments (up to $50,000) to help farmers who were hurt by falling prices, and (3) a freeze on target prices in 1986 and 1987 and slight reductions from 1988 to 1990. Since market prices are closely affected by interest rates for farm loans, the cuts in rates helped to lower the cost of food for buyers in the United States and other countries. Farmers were eligible to receive "deficiency payments" to make up the difference between market prices and target prices. In return, they had to accept restraints on the amount of land they kept in production. Other provisions of the 1985 act (4) sought to cut milk production and (5) created a new soil conservation program.

Supporters of the 1985 act argued that in the long run it would (1) help reduce government interference in free-market forces, (2) reduce production enough to let farmers' incomes rise to acceptable levels, and (3) encourage inefficient farmers to leave farming. Critics said that the law would (1) favor large farmers and farm corporations, (2) imperil the family farm that many see as the backbone of United States rural life, and (3) be extremely costly. So many farmers signed up for the support programs under the 1985 law that government farm expenditures in fiscal 1986 soared to a record $25.6 billion, significantly higher than predicted. With many farmers still suffering serious difficulties, a new battle opened in Congress over ways to resolve the farm crisis.

5. Sugar: A Special Case. One of the few major United States crops that has never been in surplus is sugar. Thanks to lobbying by sugar producers, the government sets a minimum United States sugar price and places strict quotas on sugar imports. The present sugar program has been in effect since 1981. Sugar producers praise it for (a) assuring a fair price for United States growers and (b) raising the price received by sugar-producing countries such as the Philippines, the Dominican Republic, and Australia, which have United States sugar quotas and thus can sell their sugar here at highly favorable prices. (Since 1981, United States sugar prices have hovered around 20 cents a pound, roughly four times the world price.) Critics say that the United States sugar program (a) forces the nation's consumers to pay an extra $3 billion a year in higher food prices and (b) reduces consumption of sugar by encouraging food processors to switch to cheaper products such as corn syrup and artificial sweeteners. Sugar production in the United States has been increasing, however, and some analysts say that the country could become a net exporter of sugar by 1990.

TIME-LINE QUESTIONS

On the time line the letters A–F represent time intervals as indicated. For *each* event listed below, select the letter that indicates the time interval within which the event occurred.

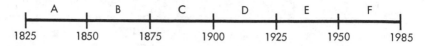

1. Migratory grape pickers in California gained recognition of their union.
2. An Agricultural Adjustment Act introduced acreage and marketing quotas.
3. Cyrus McCormick patented the mechanical reaper, which helped to revolutionize agriculture.
4. The Rural Electrification Administration was established to bring electricity to neglected farm areas.
5. Grover Cleveland purchased gold bullion and preserved the gold standard.
6. Farmers enjoyed prosperous years that later were used as the base period for determining parity prices.
7. The Morrill Act set up provisions for land-grant colleges.
8. The Supreme Court decision in *Wabash vs. Illinois* led the next year to federal regulation of railroads.
9. An Agricultural Act set a "floor" under farm income by establishing "target prices."
10. The National Grange was founded to organize farmers for political action.
11. The government sought to lower crop prices and make our farm exports more competitive on world markets.

MULTIPLE-CHOICE QUESTIONS

1. Which was a result of the agricultural revolution during the 19th century? (a) The size of the average farm declined. (b) Subsistence farming became more common. (c) The percentage of the population engaged in farming declined. (d) The cost of farm products rose more sharply than the cost of manufactured goods.
2. Following the Civil War, what effect did the decline of prices have upon western farmers? (a) It helped them by lowering the prices of manufactured goods. (b) It helped them by creating a greater demand for their crops. (c) It hurt them by forcing them to pay back a more valuable dollar than they had borrowed. (d) It had no important effect upon them.
3. The denunciation by farmers of the "Crime of '73" reflected their demand for (a) increased regulation of railroads (b) an increase in aid to land-grant colleges (c) federal regulation of wheat markets (d) higher prices through currency expansion.
4. During the late 19th century, western farmers demanded that Congress enact laws to (a) restrict farm production (b) maintain a gold standard (c) assure fair transportation rates and practices (d) tax agricultural exports to other nations.
5. A major problem confronting American farmers in the period 1865 to 1900 was (a) unavailability of agricultural machinery (b) severe inflation in the United States

(c) selling in world markets in competition with farmers of foreign countries
(d) limited amount of arable land.

6. In the 1890s, the Populist party supported (a) removal of immigration restrictions (b) abolition of income taxes (c) end of silver purchases by the Treasury (d) proposals to raise farm prices by increasing the amount of currency in circulation.

7. Which statement concerning the Populist party of the United States is most valid? (a) It obtained most of its support from the East. (b) It succeeded in getting its Presidential candidates elected in the 1890s. (c) It succeeded in influencing other political parties. (d) It failed to influence reforms in government.

8. From 1875 to 1885 American farmers increased the production of corn by almost 50 percent while the price per bushel of corn decreased from 42 cents to 32 cents. These data illustrate the economic concept of (a) inflation (b) bimetallism (c) supply and demand (d) parity pricing.

9. In an outline, one of these is a main topic and three are subtopics. Which is the main topic? (a) In 1890 Congress passed a silver purchase act. (b) Many farmers joined the Greenback and Populist parties. (c) The Grangers secured laws to check the power of the railroads. (d) Agrarian discontent has led to political action in our country.

10. During World War I, farmers helped create some of their later problems by (a) limiting production to raise prices (b) forming cooperatives to market their products (c) borrowing to expand production (d) urging the defeat of the Agricultural Marketing Act.

11. Which is characteristic of agriculture but *not* of industry? (a) There is widespread use of credit. (b) Advanced technology is used extensively. (c) It is difficult to adjust production to market demand. (d) Use of mass production techniques is common.

12. The 1920s saw the formation of the farm bloc, an organization of (a) members of Congress from the agricultural states (b) agricultural states in the Midwest (c) farmers wanting to start cooperatives (d) banks that held farm mortgages.

13. From 1920 to 1933 agriculture in the United States was generally characterized by (a) increased tenancy and the production of surplus crops (b) increased land ownership and an increase in farm population (c) much greater increases in farm prices than in farm labor costs (d) a vast expansion of foreign markets for farm products.

14. The New Deal attempted to solve the farm problem primarily by (a) purchasing one-half of all farm products (b) sponsoring the cooperative movement (c) increasing the tariff on farm products (d) inducing farmers to curtail production.

15. In applying the principle of parity to farm prices, the government tries to (a) fix prices on farm products (b) provide farmers a purchasing power equivalent to their spending power in a base period (c) establish price levels agreed upon at commodity exchanges (d) reduce imports from low-wage-paying nations.

16. In which area was the New Deal farm program *least* successful? (a) encouraging soil conservation (b) preventing farm surpluses (c) keeping farm surpluses from the market (d) giving stability to farm prices.

17. Which is *not* an economic trend in American agriculture today? (a) large farms (b) large investments in machinery (c) increased productivity per acre (d) increased percentage of farm workers in total population.

18. In the United States, agriculture has posed a persistent problem since the Civil War chiefly because (a) consumers have been buying fewer farm products (b) the federal government has done little to aid the farmer (c) there has been a technological revolution in farming (d) there generally has been insufficient money in circulation.

19. Which has been a result of the increased application of science and technology to farming? (a) rapid exhaustion of the soil (b) overall decline in farm prices (c) increased demand for farm laborers (d) replacement of small farmers by corporate farming.

20. The fact that political controversy often occurs when governments try to solve complex economic problems most clearly indicates that (a) proposed solutions to problems often generate new problems (b) government should not interfere in economic matters (c) major political parties hold fundamentally different philosophies (d) political and economic issues are not related.

——————— DISCUSSION ANALYSIS QUESTIONS ———————

Speakers A, B, C, and D are discussing the role of a political party in the Presidential election of 1896. Base your answers to the following questions on their statements and on your knowledge of American history.

Speaker A: The members of that political party are radical! Why, they would do away with capitalism!

Speaker B: No. They merely want more direct participation by the people in their government. Perhaps they are far ahead of their times!

Speaker C: Their candidate is a clever politician. A Democrat, he steals their thunder. Then they give him coalition support!

Speaker D: There are factors other than candidates that determine elections.

1. To which political party are the speakers referring? (a) Whig (b) Populist (c) Republican (d) Socialist.

2. The concern of Speaker A about capitalism is based on the fact that this party advocated (a) an income tax (b) bimetallism (c) a substantial increase in the tariff (d) government ownership and operation of railroads.

3. To which candidate does Speaker C refer as a "clever politician"? (a) William Jennings Bryan (b) Franklin D. Roosevelt (c) William McKinley (d) Marcus A. Hanna.

4. The reference by Speaker B to the members of this party being far ahead of their times is supported by (a) its victory in a Presidential election many years later (b) its victory in the following Congressional election (c) its prediction that the United States would adopt a policy of imperialism (d) the subsequent adoption of many of the reforms that it advocated.

5. When Speaker D mentions "factors . . . that determine elections," the reference is to the (a) advocacy of the forceful overthrow of government (b) assumption of political power by military leaders (c) control of the Supreme Court by extremists (d) power of pressure groups and vested interests.

————————————— ESSAY QUESTIONS —————————————

1. Citing *three* specific examples, explain the meaning of this statement: "The agricultural revolution had a decided effect on the economic self-sufficiency of the American farmer."

2. (a) Discuss briefly *two* major problems that farmers face because of the nature of their business. (b) Describe *two* attempts that were made by farmers before 1900 to solve their problems.

3. (a) Using *one* specific law dealing with agriculture, explain the effect of the law upon *each* of the following groups: (1) farmers (2) industrial workers (3) business executives (4) consumers (5) taxpayers. (b) On the basis of your answer to part (a) would you agree or disagree with the statement "When the farmer prospers, the nation prospers"? Defend your answer.

4. Use historical evidence to support *or* to refute *each* of the following statements: (a) The third-party movement in the West and South in the late 19th century took the form of agrarian revolt. (b) The conversion of American agriculture to a commercial basis has made the farmer a specialist. (c) Unlike the manufacturer, the farmer has no control over markets or prices. (d) Instead of benefiting from the technological revolution in agriculture since World War II, the small farmer has been its victim.

5. Discuss *each* of the following statements, giving *two* specific facts to support *or* refute each statement: (a) The Industrial Revolution has greatly influenced the life of the farmer. (b) Wars have had important effects on the farmer. (c) The farmer has always been a "rugged individualist" who has made few demands for assistance from the government. (d) The farm problem is an important political issue today. (e) The surplus of American farm products has been a factor in our foreign relations since World War II.

PART 3. The Government Helps Promote Conservation and Environmental Protection

WASTE: AN AMERICAN TRADITION

Blessed with an abundance of natural resources, Americans used them wastefully:

(1) Farmers and planters exhausted the soil's fertility. (2) Farmers cleared their lands by chopping down or burning trees wantonly. (3) Lumber companies leveled vast forests without reforesting. (4) By destroying trees whose roots had served to bind the soil, farmers and lumber companies invited floods and soil erosion. (5) Hunters depleted wildlife, almost completely destroying the vast herds of buffalo. (6) Oil drillers who struck successful wells burned the escaping natural gas. (7) Coal companies mined the richest seams and neglected the rest. (8) Cities and factories dumped sewage and wastes into nearby streams and lakes, thereby polluting the waters and killing the fish.

BEGINNINGS OF THE CONSERVATION MOVEMENT

In the late 19th century, as the frontier was drawing to a close, the American people became aware that the nation's resources were not limitless. Agricultural scientists, forestry experts, and nature lovers spurred public interest in conservation—the proper care and wise use of our natural resources.

1. In 1872 Congress designated the Yellowstone region, lying mostly in Wyoming, as our first national park. From this beginning evolved today's extensive

system of national monuments, historical sites, and parks, all administered by the *National Park Service.*

2. In 1891 Congress passed the Forest Reserve Act, permitting successive Presidents to set aside lands as *national forest reserves.*

THEODORE ROOSEVELT AND CONSERVATION

More than any other person, Theodore Roosevelt awakened the American people to the need for conservation. A nature lover, Roosevelt had lived in the West and had personally seen the waste and destruction of our natural resources. As President (1901–1909), Roosevelt promoted the following conservation measures:

1. Land Reserves. Roosevelt withdrew from sale millions of acres of forest land, coal land, and potential waterpower sites. These lands were to be kept from reckless exploitation and used wisely for the national welfare.

2. Newlands Reclamation Act (1902). This act provided that the federal government use the proceeds from the sale of lands in 16 western states to finance irrigation projects. It began a program of government construction of huge dams.

3. Forest Service. Congress strengthened the *Forest Service,* headed by Roosevelt's friend *Gifford Pinchot.* Using increased funds and expanded powers, Pinchot built the Forest Service into a major force for conservation. Forest Service rangers patrol the national forests, fight fires, and replant cutover areas.

4. Governors' Conference (1908). Roosevelt invited the state governors and other interested persons to a conference on conservation. The conference led to the establishment of 41 state conservation commissions and a *National Conservation Commission.*

OPPOSITION TO CONSERVATION

Theodore Roosevelt's conservation efforts aroused considerable opposition. Coal and lumber companies wanted to take over the government's land reserves. Private utility companies were hostile to the government's dam-building program because they feared competition from government hydroelectric power. Anti-conservationists hoped that, after Roosevelt retired, the public would again become apathetic about conservation.

NEW DEAL AND CONSERVATION

1. Background. In 1933 *Franklin D. Roosevelt* became President and faced (a) the Great Depression, with 13 million persons unemployed, and (b) a series of natural disasters: droughts, dust storms, and floods. A strong supporter of conservation, Roosevelt sponsored a dual-purpose program: to provide work for the unemployed and to protect our natural resources.

2. Major Undertakings

a. Civilian Conservation Corps. The CCC, from 1933 to 1942, provided employment for 2 million young people in conservation work. They constructed reservoirs, planted trees, cut forest trails, dug drainage ditches, fought plant diseases, and established forest-fire control systems.

b. Public Works Administration. The PWA, from 1933 to 1939, provided work for half a million unemployed persons on projects for hydroelectric power, sewage treatment, and flood control.

c. Soil Conservation. The New Deal farm laws (SCDAA of 1936 and AAA of 1938) granted bounties to farmers for planting soil-conserving crops. The Soil Conservation Service educated farmers in methods of preventing and halting soil erosion.

d. Multipurpose Dam Projects. The New Deal completed construction, begun during the Hoover administration, of the *Hoover (Boulder) Dam* on the Colorado River. This huge dam provides electric power, irrigation, and flood control. To utilize other waterpower sites, the New Deal built the *Bonneville Dam* and *Grand Coulee Dam* on the Columbia River, and established the *Tennessee Valley Authority* (TVA).

TVA: AN ALL-INCLUSIVE REGIONAL APPROACH

1. Background. The Tennessee River Valley, encompassing parts of seven states, was a region of impoverished farmers, eroded soil, cutover forests, and floods. Its rural areas had almost no electricity. But the region had the potential waterpower site in Alabama at *Muscle Shoals.*

During World War I the federal government began construction at Muscle Shoals of a project for producing nitrates and electricity. Completed in the 1920s, the project caused considerable dispute between public power and private power interests. Three times Congress passed bills providing for federal ownership and operation. The first bill was vetoed by President Coolidge; the second bill, by President Hoover. The third bill, in 1933, met with the hearty approval of President Roosevelt.

2. Organization and Services. The TVA is a government corporation empowered to plan for the "economic and social well-being of the people" in the Tennessee Valley. It represents a *regional approach* and, in many activities, TVA cooperates with various state and local agencies. Physically, TVA consists of a series of dams, reservoirs, nitrate factories, power plants, and electrical transmission lines.

A multipurpose project, the TVA (a) controls the Tennessee River to prevent floods and permit navigation, (b) encourages reforestation and soil conservation, (c) produces nitrates for fertilizer, (d) maintains agricultural experiment stations, and (e) generates electricity, originally by waterpower and later also by coal and nuclear power. The TVA sells its electricity primarily to municipal and cooperative utility companies that resell the electricity to the public, generally at rates below those of private utilities. TVA rates have been used to measure the fairness of private utility rates—that is, as a yardstick.

3. Achievements. The TVA greatly improved the standard of living of the Tennessee Valley people. Farmers diversified their crops, used more fertilizer for higher crop yields, and enjoyed rising incomes. Their homes were brightened by low-cost electricity. Foresters replanted cutover areas. Aluminum and chemical companies, attracted by plentiful low-cost electric power, established plants in the valley and created new jobs. During World War II the TVA produced nitrates for explosives and furnished electric power for the atomic bomb project at Oak Ridge, Tennessee.

4. Opposition. Private utility companies claimed that the TVA provided an unfair yardstick of rates because, as a government agency, it could secure loans at lower interest rates than private borrowers and it paid no federal income taxes. Also, TVA hydroelectric power was cheaper to produce than private utilities' steam-generated power.

Private utility companies tried to overturn the TVA by legal action. They failed, as the Supreme Court upheld the constitutionality of the TVA and its right to sell electricity. Political leaders fearful of "big government" also attacked the TVA. President Eisenhower called the TVA an example of "creeping socialism."

The TVA has weathered all opposition, but its opponents have proved sufficiently strong to prevent establishment of other all-inclusive regional projects on the Columbia, Missouri, and St. Lawrence rivers.

ST. LAWRENCE RIVER PROJECT

1. Background. Proposed early in the 20th century, this project called for the construction of (a) hydroelectric power dams on the St. Lawrence River, and (b) a seaway that would enable oceangoing vessels to sail from the Atlantic Ocean up the St. Lawrence and into the Great Lakes. The project met opposition. (a) Railroads feared the loss of freight business. (b) Private utilities feared competition from public power. (c) Atlantic coast ports feared loss of trade to ports on the Great Lakes. The project was urged by Canada but turned down repeatedly by Congress.

2. Construction of the Project (1954–1959). President Eisenhower recognized the importance of the St. Lawrence project for national defense and economic well-being, but he rejected an all-inclusive regional approach. He authorized New York State to proceed, with the Province of Ontario, in building dams for hydroelectric power. He secured Congressional approval for the United States to cooperate with Canada in building canals and locks for the seaway. By 1959 construction was completed on both the seaway and the power projects.

The seaway charges tolls to ships using its facilities. It has substantially increased the amount of cargo carried on the St. Lawrence River and the Great Lakes and facilitated the economic growth of the Great Lakes area. The New

York State Power Authority sells its St. Lawrence power to municipal and co-operative electric systems as well as to private manufacturing and utility companies.

FACTORS SPURRING POSTWAR PUBLIC INTEREST IN CONSERVATION

1. Postwar Prosperity. After World War II, affluent Americans had more time and money for recreational purposes. However, the number of campers overwhelmed the limited facilities of national and state parks.

2. Growing Population. From 1940 to 1980 the American population multiplied from 132 million to 227 million, an increase of over 70 percent. More people meant greater demands upon our shrinking natural resources.

3. Floods. Dwellers along the Mississippi and Missouri Rivers in the 1950s suffered severe floods, with much property damage and loss of life.

4. Water Pollution and Water Shortages. As cities and factories dumped sewage and industrial wastes into nearby waters, magnificent rivers and beautiful lakes became polluted, disease ridden, and ugly. People found beaches closed and fish dying out.

In the cities of the Northeast, a drought in the 1960s caused water shortages. The people were restricted in the use of water for washing cars, sprinkling lawns, and air-conditioning places of business.

5. Air Pollution. Exhaust fumes from automobiles and smoking chimneys of factories, apartment houses, and private homes polluted the urban air. Urban dwellers breathe this polluted air, often called *smog*. As a result, they suffer eye and nose irritations, and an increase in respiratory ailments and heart trouble.

6. Education. After World War II, conservationists redoubled their educational efforts. They encouraged schools to teach students about conservation, usually in biology, geography, or history. They produced specialized films and published popular articles and books. *Rachel Carson* wrote the book *Silent Spring,* warning that the irresponsible use of pesticides harms birds and other wildlife and contaminates our food supply.

In the 1960s, conservation, emphasizing the relationship of people to their surroundings, became known as *environmental protection.*

PRIVATE EFFORTS IN ENVIRONMENTAL PROTECTION

(1) Large-scale farmers employed the latest scientific methods of soil conservation. (2) Lumber companies managed their land as *tree farms,* with annual harvests and with replantings to assure future harvests. (3) Iron and steel companies, after almost exhausting deposits of high-grade iron ore, devised techniques for utilizing low-grade *taconite* ore. (4) Oil companies improved refining techniques to extract more usable products from crude petroleum. (5) Electric

utility companies, until recently dependent upon coal, gas, and oil to fuel their generators, turned to atomic energy. They were encouraged by the rising costs of conventional fuels and by technological advances reducing the costs of nuclear power.

NUCLEAR POWER ISSUE

In 1979 nuclear power received a severe setback because of an accident at the Three Mile Island (Pennsylvania) nuclear power plant. Although causing considerable damage to the plant, the accident seemingly caused negligible harm to people and the environment. Nevertheless, the accident aroused public concern and spurred mass antinuclear demonstrations. Opponents charged that nuclear power was not safe, endangered the environment, and lacked facilities for the proper disposal of nuclear waste materials. Nuclear advocates denied these charges, insisting that nuclear power posed less danger to people and the environment than burning coal and causing air pollution, and that scientists had solved the problem of nuclear waste disposal. President Carter asserted that, for the foreseeable future, the United States could not "abandon the nuclear supply of energy." This view was upheld by the President's commission investigating the Three Mile Island accident. After recommending improvements in plant licensing procedures and safety standards, the commission concluded that, by keeping nuclear risks "within tolerable limits," the country could if it wished continue to develop nuclear power.

A second setback to nuclear power came in 1986, when an explosion at the Soviet Union's Chernobyl nuclear power plant released massive amounts of radiation that spread to many European countries and contaminated food supplies for a time. Experts said that the Chernobyl disaster was the most serious nuclear

Reprinted by permission of United Feature Syndicate, Inc.

accident to have occurred anywhere in the world up to that time. A Gallup poll after Chernobyl found that 59 percent of the Americans who were questioned disapproved of building more nuclear power plants. Some 41 percent had expressed a similar opinion after the Three Mile Island accident.

In the mid-1980s, the United States possessed 102 of the world's 374 operating nuclear power plants. Nuclear power provided about 16 percent of the nation's electricity. However, construction of nuclear plants had fallen off dramatically, accelerating a trend that had begun even before Three Mile Island. The principal reasons included (1) sharply higher construction costs for nuclear plants, (2) lower costs for competing fuels such as oil and coal, (3) regulatory delays of years in securing operating licenses, and (4) persistent concerns over the risks of a nuclear accident.

STATE AND CITY EFFORTS IN ENVIRONMENTAL PROTECTION

Many states and cities undertook conservation activities: expanding parks, playgrounds, and wildlife preserves; encouraging good forestry; building sewage-treatment plants; and combating air pollution. Specific illustrations include the following: (1) California insisted that all new cars sold in the state contain exhaust-control devices. (2) New York City, to reduce air pollution, required soot-control devices on chimneys and ordered refuse compressors, not incinerators, installed in new buildings. (3) Pennsylvania, Illinois, Florida, and California all provided stiff fines for polluters. (4) Oregon and other states placed a deposit on all beverage bottles and cans so as to spur consumers not to litter but to return the empty containers.

FEDERAL EFFORTS IN ENVIRONMENTAL PROTECTION

1. Environmental Protection Laws. (a) The *Wilderness Act* (1964) established a National Wilderness Preservation System of 9 million acres of national forest lands to preserve "an enduring resource of wilderness" as recreational sites for public enjoyment. (b) The *Highway Beautification Act* (1965) assigned federal funds for the removal of billboards and junkyards from alongside interstate and primary highways. (c) The *Water Quality Act* (1965) and the *Clean Rivers Restoration Act* (1966) empowered the government to set standards of water quality and provided funds to construct sewage treatment plants and to combat water pollution. (d) The *Resource Recovery Act* (1970) provided funds for states and cities to build solid-waste disposal systems and to develop methods of recycling salvageable materials such as aluminum cans. (e) The *Clean Air Act* (1970) required the automobile industry to develop an engine that would eliminate 90 percent of noxious auto fumes.

2. New Agencies. (a) The *Council on Environmental Quality,* within the Executive Office, advises the President, and (b) the *Environmental Protection Agency* (EPA) enforces laws regarding conservation and environment.

ENVIRONMENTAL PROTECTION: BENEFITS AND COSTS

With the 1973 Arab oil embargo against the United States, Americans became aware of their energy crisis. They began to reconsider environmental protection, realizing that it brought benefits but also involved costs. They asked questions: (1) Which goal should the nation seek first—energy self-sufficiency or environmental protection? (2) Which standards should environmental protection seek—"absolute" or "reasonable"? These problems are illustrated as follows:

1. Alaska Pipeline. With the 1968 discovery of oil in the Prudhoe Bay area of Alaska's North Slope, oil companies planned an 800-mile pipeline to bring the oil southward to Alaska's ice-free port at Valdez. The pipeline was delayed for several years by conservation groups—notably the *Sierra Club* and the *Environmental Defense Fund*—which brought court suits claiming that the pipeline would damage the Alaskan environment. In 1973 Congress overwhelmingly approved legislation authorizing construction of the pipeline by private enterprise and banning lawsuits against the pipeline on environmental grounds. Congress thus expressed its view of American priorities: The need for Alaskan oil outweighed possible damage to the Alaskan environment. (In 1977 the pipeline was completed.)

2. Strip-Mining of Coal. Private utility companies have looked to our Western lands—both government reserves and private holdings—for clean, low-sulfur coal that can be dug out by surface, or strip-mining. Conservation groups claimed that strip-mining will scar the land permanently unless costly standards are imposed for restoring the mined land to good condition. In 1974 Congress enacted a strip-mining bill that imposed strict environmental safeguards. By a pocket veto, President Ford withheld his approval, claiming that the measure would reduce coal production "when the nation can ill afford significant losses from this critical energy source."

In 1977 Congress enacted another strip-mining bill that (a) required coal companies to restore strip-mined land to its original shape, to replant grass and trees, and to prevent the pollution of nearby waters, and (b) placed a tonnage fee on both strip-mined and underground coal to provide funds for restoring land left damaged by previous strip-mining. In signing this bill, President Carter claimed that it would encourage the "production of coal and also assuage the fears that the beautiful areas where coal is produced were being destroyed."

At first, the 1977 law met strong criticism. Many coal operators argued that the law was an unconstitutional infringement on their property rights. The focus of debate shifted in the 1980s, however, when the Reagan administration softened its enforcement of strip-mining rules as part of a general trend to deregulation. Then the environmentalists complained. They argued that the government was failing to enforce the law, and that thousands of strip mines were avoiding environmental regulations altogether.

3. Auto Exhaust Fumes. Automobile manufacturing companies were granted several delays in meeting auto exhaust standards set by the 1970 Clean

Air Act and intended to be achieved by 1975. The auto manufacturers claimed that these standards were unrealistic, could not be met over so short a time, would raise the cost of cars, and would impair auto operating efficiency. The Public Interest Research Group, a Ralph Nader organization, attacked the postponements and accused the auto manufacturers of "environmental blackmail."

THE COMPREHENSIVE NATIONAL ENERGY ACT OF 1978

In 1977 President Carter asked Congress to enact a comprehensive energy bill as necessary for the nation's well-being and as the "moral equivalent of war."

After 18 months of deliberation, Congress enacted a bill that bore only a faint resemblance to Carter's original proposals. Its major provisions were to: (1) permit the price of newly discovered natural gas to rise gradually until controls were removed in 1985, (2) require new electric utility plants to install boilers using coal—not oil or gas, (3) require existing electric utility plants using oil or gas to switch to coal by 1990, (4) provide tax benefits to business firms and homeowners who save energy by use of insulation and solar energy equipment, (5) require manufacturers of household appliances to meet fuel efficiency standards, (6) tax gas-guzzling cars beginning with the 1980 models.

What were the results of this legislation? (1) Natural gas prices rose, bringing higher bills for consumers but also spurring increased exploration for and production of natural gas. (2) Electric utility rates rose, partly because power companies expended large sums to convert their facilities from oil and gas to coal. (3) The greater use of coal intensified the problem of air pollution. (4) The increased use of natural gas and coal was a factor enabling the United States to limit its imports of oil.

FURTHER CARTER ENERGY PROPOSALS

By 1979 the United States depended upon imports for 50 percent of its oil needs. The United States consequently was severely affected when revolution in Iran sharply curtailed that country's oil exports and when the OPEC cartel raised oil prices by about 60 percent above the previous year's high levels.

To deal with the recurring energy crisis, President Carter proposed that Congress enact the following energy legislation: (1) Grant the President authority to institute gasoline rationing—if necessary. (2) Establish an Energy Security Corporation (ESC), with massive funds, to develop a synthetic fuel industry. The ESC will spur the production of "synfuels"—synthetic fuels made from such sources as coal, oil shale and tar sands, so as to replace 2.5 million barrels of imported oil per day by the year 1990. (3) Establish a Solar Bank to spur the use of solar power so as to provide 20 percent of our energy needs by the year 2000. (4) Establish an Energy Mobilization Board with broad powers to cut through red tape and override environmental and regulatory delays so as to speed key energy projects. (5) To provide the funds needed for some of the previous proposals, enact a "windfall-profits tax"—an additional levy on the extra profits that oil companies were expected to make in the 1980s when the government removed price controls on domestic oil and its price rises. This "windfall tax" was expected to provide a multibillion-dollar fund within ten years.

President Carter's proposals were subjected to considerable criticism: (1) The "synfuels" program would be in the hands of a government bureaucracy rather than under private initiative. The synthetic fuels so produced would be costly. (2) In speeding energy projects, the Energy Mobilization Board might override essential safeguards for the environment. (3) The "windfall-profits tax" would deprive oil companies of funds that could be used to uncover new energy supplies. (4) The major proposals set long-range goals; they do not deal with current energy problems.

In 1980 Congress enacted several of President Carter's energy proposals into law: (1) Authorizing the President to prepare a standby gasoline-rationing plan that could be put into operation in case of a gasoline shortage. (2) Placing a "windfall-profits tax" on the domestic oil companies, which tax is estimated to raise over $225 billion in ten years. (3) Establishing a Synthetic Fuels Corporation with a four-year, $20 billion fund for subsidies and loan guarantees to private industry to spur construction of synfuel plants.

Congress, however, rejected President Carter's proposal for an Energy Mobilization Board. This rejection reflected the strong opposition of states' rights advocates and environmentalists.

PROPER DISPOSAL OF TOXIC CHEMICAL WASTES

By 1980 the American people had been alerted to another public health and environmental problem—the inappropriate disposal of hazardous wastes. This problem received widespread publicity with reports of the health problems of persons living on or near an abandoned chemical dump site—the Love Canal area near Niagara Falls, New York. Subsequent studies indicated that, throughout the United States, thousands of abandoned and improperly maintained hazardous-waste dumps were leaking poisons into nearby land, air, and water, and endangering the health of nearby residents.

In 1980 Congress passed the *Waste Cleanup Act* (1) providing a five-year, $1.6 billion "superfund" to be raised mainly by excise taxes on chemicals, (2) authorizing federal agencies to contract for the removal and containment of chemical wastes, to protect water against contamination, and to relocate people from dangerous sites, and (3) instructing the government to sue companies responsible for the hazardous dumps and recover the funds spent for the cleanup and relocation programs.

When it became apparent that the problem of toxic wastes was even larger than had been thought, Congress passed a new "superfund" act in 1986. The act (1) expanded the funding of the program to $9 billion over the succeeding five years, (2) created a new tax on corporate earnings to help pay for the cleanup, (3) gave citizens new rights to sue dumpers for damages, (4) required dumpers to let communities know what they were dumping, and (5) ordered the

Environmental Protection Agency to complete the cleanup of a specified number of sites within five years. At the time the bill was passed, the EPA had resolved 650 short-term toxic emergencies and completed the cleanup of 13 waste sites, with more than 2000 sites yet to be inspected.

———————— MULTIPLE-CHOICE QUESTIONS ————————

1. Which of the following was most important in making Americans aware of the need to conserve their natural resources? (a) destruction caused by the Civil War (b) closing of the frontier (c) work of the Civilian Conservation Corps (d) enactment of immigration quotas.
2. Who was the first President to draw popular attention to the need for conservation? (a) Theodore Roosevelt (b) William Howard Taft (c) Herbert Hoover (d) Franklin D. Roosevelt.
3. Who is generally recognized as a pioneer of forest conservation in the United States? (a) Rachel Carson (b) Gerald Ford (c) Gifford Pinchot (d) Jimmy Carter.
4. A major stimulus for President Franklin D. Roosevelt's interest in conservation was his desire to (a) set aside more land as an oil reserve for the navy (b) find work for millions of unemployed young people (c) follow the tradition established by Theodore Roosevelt (d) reward the western states for their support in the election of 1932.
5. The federal government's concern for conservation is best illustrated by the (a) Homestead Act (b) Alaska pipeline (c) Three Mile Island accident (d) Tennessee Valley Authority.
6. The Tennessee Valley Authority has (a) tended to raise the standard of living in the region that it serves (b) established widespread irrigation projects (c) been declared unconstitutional (d) been ineffective in controlling floods.
7. The economic concept of the yardstick is most frequently associated with (a) minimum wages (b) income taxes (c) public utility rates (d) Social Security payments.
8. The St. Lawrence Seaway was built primarily to (a) increase trade between the United States and Canada (b) strengthen the defenses of the United States and Canada (c) increase the prestige of New York State (d) bring more world trade to the Great Lakes.
9. After World War II, the original interest in environmental problems came mainly from (a) corporations and business groups (b) the organized labor movement (c) the federal government (d) writers and private nonprofit organizations.
10. Which was not a factor in encouraging conservation after World War II? (a) rapid growth of the American population (b) need for fertile soil to increase cotton crop yields (c) pollution of rivers and lakes (d) increased number of automobiles.
11. By using atomic power, electric utilities further conservation because nuclear reactors (a) contain reusable lead shields (b) use nuclear fuels instead of coal and oil (c) make large dams unnecessary (d) are inexpensive to build and operate.
12. Recent federal environmental protection laws have been least concerned with (a) providing recreational sites (b) protecting the beauty of interstate highways (c) protecting the quality of our water and air (d) establishing regional planning authorities similar to the TVA.

13. One major conservation problem of the United States today is the result of (a) radiation in the atmosphere (b) air pollution from smoking chimneys and auto exhaust fumes (c) soil erosion from experiments with fertilizers (d) depletion of coal resources from the application of automation to mining.

14. Environmental protection groups opposed the Alaska pipeline on the ground that the (a) United States did not need the oil from Alaska's North Slope (b) Alaskan oil was of a poor quality (c) pipeline would damage the Alaskan natural habitat (d) pipeline would take too long to build.

15. President Carter's energy proposals did *not* include (a) developing synthetic fuels (b) using solar power (c) using more coal (d) importing more oil from the Middle East.

16. "We cannot long continue to utilize our natural resources merely to satisfy the ever-growing demands of the people of the United States for more luxuries, more conveniences, more, more, more!" The author of this statement would most probably favor (a) a reordering of national priorities (b) a dictatorship in the United States (c) increased United States aid to developing nations (d) a national program of birth control.

17. For an environmentalist, which is the most significant argument against offshore drilling for oil? (a) There is little need to take oil from the ocean waters. (b) Oil corporations are falsely advertising an oil shortage in order to expand their drilling operations. (c) The potential oil to be found is not worth the capital investment needed to extract it. (d) The possible harm to the balance of nature is more important than a gain in energy.

——————————— ESSAY QUESTIONS ———————————

1. (a) Discuss *two* reasons why the conservation of natural resources is more important today than it was 100 years ago. (b) Discuss briefly *two* ways in which the federal government or state governments have promoted conservation. (c) Explain *two* ways in which corporations and individuals can promote conservation.

2. (a) Describe *one* way in which the industrial development of the United States and one way in which the westward movement of the American people have affected our natural resources. (b) Explain *one* relationship between our natural resources and our leadership in world affairs.

3. Show the relation of *each* of the following to the conservation of natural resources: (a) Reclamation Act of 1902 (Newlands Act) (b) Governors' Conference of 1908 (c) Tennessee Valley Authority (d) Civilian Conservation Corps (e) one environmental protection proposal of President Carter.

4. The future development of the natural resources of the United States will come not so much from discovery as from advances in science and from skill in the utilization of our resources. (a) Why can we no longer depend upon discovery as a means of substantially increasing our supply of natural resources? (b) Indicate how each of *three* natural resources has been needlessly wasted. (c) Show how *each* method— advances in science, skill in utilization—has been or may be used to expand or conserve our supply of raw materials.

5. Environmental pollution is as much a result of what people do as it is a result of what they fail to do. Giving *two* specific evidences, show how the above statement applies to *each* of the following: (a) the producer (b) the consumer (c) the government.

PART 4. Big Business Becomes the Dominant Influence in Our Economy

GROWTH OF AMERICAN INDUSTRY

FACTORS ENCOURAGING INDUSTRIAL GROWTH (THE NEW NATION TO 1900)

1. Natural Resources. Nature endowed the United States with (a) an abundance of raw materials: coal, oil, iron, copper, gold, and silver, (b) fertile soil for raising foodstuffs, lumber, cotton, and tobacco, and (c) swift-running streams for waterpower.

2. The Constitution. (a) *Delegated Powers.* The Constitution gave the federal government certain delegated powers that could assist the growth of industry. These powers were: (1) coining money—to provide a stable and uniform currency for business transactions, (2) regulating interstate commerce—to legislate nationwide laws affecting industry, (3) levying tariffs on imports—to protect domestic industry against foreign competitors, and (4) establishing a system of patents—to encourage inventors. (b) *Restrictions on the States.* The Constitution forbade the states to (1) impair or alter the terms of a valid business contract and (2) tax imports entering or exports leaving the state, thus preventing barriers to the movement of goods and maintaining the United States as a nationwide "common market." (Check the Index.) (c) *Amendments.* The Fifth and Fourteenth Amendments to the Constitution provided that no person could be deprived of property without "due process of law." Thus protected against the arbitrary seizure of private property, American and foreign investors could provide capital for American industry.

3. Government Policies. From the Civil War era to the end of the 19th century, the government spurred the growth of business by (a) granting land and cash subsidies to railroad builders, (b) levying high tariffs to protect manufacturers, (c) fostering a uniform and stable currency, and (d) in most other matters, leaving business alone according to the policy of *laissez-faire* (check the Index).

4. Growing Population. Because of a high birthrate and considerable immigration, the American population in the 19th century almost doubled every 25 years—from 5 million in 1800 to 76 million in 1900. This huge increase provided industry with sufficient workers and expanding domestic markets.

5. New Sources of Power. (a) *Electricity.* In the 19th century, scientists developed the dynamo—a machine that converts mechanical energy into electric energy. At first, electricity was used mainly for communication—in the telegraph and the telephone. Later, it was used for lighting and for driving motors. (b) *Petroleum.* In 1859, in Pennsylvania, *Edwin Drake* drilled the first successful oil well. At first, oil was used for lubrication and lighting. Later, two petroleum products—gasoline and diesel oil—were used in the internal combustion engine, the basis of modern transportation.

6. Introduction of Machinery. The American people embraced the Industrial Revolution with its use of machinery and the factory system. Two leaders in this development were *Samuel Slater* and *Eli Whitney.* (For each, check the Index.)

7. American Inventors and Inventions. Americans displayed a genius for practical invention: (a) *Charles Goodyear*—the process of vulcanizing, or hardening, rubber, (b) *Elias Howe*—the first sewing machine, soon improved by *Isaac Singer,* (c) *Elisha Otis*—the safety elevator, (d) *Gordon McKay*—a machine for sewing shoes, (e) *Christopher Sholes* (with Carlos Glidden and Samuel Soule)—the modern typewriter, (f) *William Burroughs*—a key-operated calculating machine, and (g) *Thomas A. Edison*—the phonograph, the electric light bulb, and a motion picture machine.

8. Improved Means of Transportation and Communication

 *a. **Transportation.*** After *George Stephenson,* the English engineer, in 1829 demonstrated a successful steam locomotive, America turned to railroad building. By 1860 the United States had 30,000 miles of railroad track, almost all east of the Mississippi. Following the Civil War, America stepped up its railroad building. By 1900 the country had five transcontinental railroads and nearly 200,000 miles of track—more than the total trackage in all of Europe. Safety and comfort were increased by using iron and then steel in place of wood for rails and bridges, and by making heavier roadbeds. *George Pullman* invented the sleeping car, and *George Westinghouse* the air brake.

 Railroads helped the growth of industry by bringing foodstuffs to city markets, raw materials to factories, and manufactures to consumers.

 *b. **Communication.*** (1) In 1844 *Samuel F. B. Morse* proved the practicability of the telegraph. It was used extensively during the Civil War to send messages from the battlefront. To provide telegraph service nationally, several telegraph companies merged to form *Western Union.* (2) In 1876 *Alexander Graham Bell* exhibited a successful telephone. His work led to the formation of what is today the *American Telephone and Telegraph Company.*

 Rapid communications enabled businesspeople to direct their sales forces, contact customers, and take orders quickly and efficiently.

9. Effect of Wars. Industrialization in America was encouraged by wars. (a) Because the government needed war materials, industry prospered. (b) Because farmers and city workers had more money to spend, consumer goods were in greater demand. (c) Because the military services drained workers from factories and farms, industrialists and farmers turned to laborsaving machines.

 In particular, the growth of industry was promoted by the War of 1812 and the Civil War. (Check the Index.)

RESULTS OF INDUSTRIAL GROWTH

1. New Industrial Products and Services. Manufacturers replaced hand- and home-made products with machine- and factory-made products. Investors financed new industries to provide new services and goods: railroad transportation, telegraph and telephone communication, steel, and oil.

2. Higher Standard of Living. Our industrial economy produced a greater volume and variety of goods at lower cost than ever before. Americans purchased mass-produced goods through new outlets—mail order, department, and specialty stores—and enjoyed an ever-increasing array of material comforts.

3. Great Fortunes. Business leaders accumulated great wealth, exercised tremendous economic power, and exerted considerable influence upon the government. Some industrialists returned part of their fortunes to society by financing various philanthropies. (Check the Index.) In noteworthy instances, members of wealthy families devoted their lives to public service.

4. Growth of Cities. Many people flocked to the cities, some to find jobs, others to be near to urban society and culture. Cities faced many problems. (Check the Index.)

5. Increased World Trade and Imperialism. Manufacturers looked abroad for markets and raw materials. American trade with the rest of the world increased. Toward the end of the 19th century, the United States moved away from its policy of isolation and embarked on a policy of imperialism.

6. Serious Economic Problems. The growth of industry gave rise to major domestic problems: preventing monopoly, protecting consumers and small business owners, improving the living standards of workers, maintaining an effective banking system, levying fair taxes, and leveling out the business cycle.

CORPORATIONS AND BUSINESS CONSOLIDATION

DEFECTS OF THE OLD FORMS OF BUSINESS ORGANIZATION

Single proprietorships and *partnerships* proved inadequate in the post-Civil War era to meet the needs of large-scale business. Weaknesses were the (1) inability to raise large sums of money, (2) unlimited financial responsibility of the owners, extending even to their personal assets, for claims against the business, and (3) disruption of the business upon death of the owner or partner. To overcome these weaknesses, business leaders turned to another form of business organization, the *corporation.*

CORPORATION: MEANING

A corporation is a form of business organization created by the grant of a state *charter.* The corporation enables a group of individuals to operate as a single "artificial legal person." The corporation can sue and be sued, hire and fire, buy and sell, manufacture and trade.

ADVANTAGES OF INCORPORATION

1. Securing of Capital. By selling stocks and bonds to the public, the corporation can raise large sums of money. Stockholders are part owners of the corporation and share in the profits, paid to them as dividends. Bondholders are creditors who lend money to the corporation and receive interest. (To sell their securities, corporations had available a major market, the *New York Stock Exchange,* founded in 1792.)

2. Limited Liability. The personal assets of the part owners, or stockholders, cannot be seized in order to satisfy claims against the corporation. Even if the corporation goes bankrupt, the most the part owners can lose is the money they paid for the stock.

3. Transferability of Shares. Investors may withdraw from the corporation simply by selling their shares of stock.

4. Perpetual Life. The life of the corporation is not affected by the death of any of the part owners. The shares of deceased persons are transferable to their heirs, who thus become the new part owners.

DISADVANTAGES OF INCORPORATION

1. As a state-created entity, the corporation must make public its business and financial records by filing periodic reports.

2. As an "artificial legal person," the corporation is subject to taxes on its profits in addition to taxes paid by its individual part owners on their dividends. This is called "double taxation."

3. Most corporations are small, but the corporate form has made possible the growth of business giants. There is little personal contact between the large corporation and its workers and customers.

TURN TO MONOPOLY

Following the Civil War, business leaders moved to combine competing corporations in order to control prices, production, and sales territory. Such control would enable them to eliminate competition, thereby approaching full control, or *monopoly.* A company could then set high prices and thus increase its profits at the expense of consumers.

MONOPOLISTIC PRACTICES IN THE 19TH CENTURY: ILLEGAL TODAY

1. The *pool* was an agreement, usually secret, among competing companies to fix prices and output, and to divide sales territory. In the 1870s and 1880s

competing railroad lines often formed pools. By the Interstate Commerce Act (1887), railroad pools were declared illegal.

2. The *trust* was a more permanent consolidation than the pool. Stockholders of competing companies turned their stock over to a board of trustees and in exchange received trust certificates. In this way, the board of trustees gained full control and managed the member companies so as to eliminate competition. The Standard Oil Company (the forebear of several of today's leading oil companies) originated the trust arrangement and was imitated by other giant companies. After the passage of the Sherman Antitrust Act (1890), business leaders abandoned the trust and turned to other forms of consolidation.

The word "trust," however, remained part of our vocabulary, referring to any large and powerful business combination or corporation.

BUSINESS CONSOLIDATIONS TODAY: LEGAL WITHIN LIMITS

1. The *holding company* has sufficient voting stock in and thereby controls different companies, called subsidiaries. Some complex forms of the holding company have been declared illegal, but many holding companies legally exist today.

2. The *interlocking directorate* exists when one or more persons serve on the boards of directors of several companies. An interlocking directorate is legal unless it tends to lessen competition.

3. The *merger* is the consolidation of two companies into a single corporation. A merger is legal unless it causes an unreasonable restraint of trade. It is the most common form of business consolidation today. Giant corporations that have used the merger to branch out into unrelated fields are called *conglomerates.*

EXAMPLES OF BUSINESS CONSOLIDATION

1. Railroads. *Cornelius Vanderbilt* gained the nickname "Commodore" and a fortune in steamboating, and then turned to railroads. By 1869 he had combined a group of small lines into one railroad system running from New York City to Chicago—the *New York Central.* Vanderbilt improved the safety, comfort, and service of the railroad. However, he was disdainful of the public interest and of government regulations, once proclaiming, "What do I care for law? Hain't I got the power?"

James J. Hill, by a series of mergers to 1893, built a railroad from Minnesota westward to the Pacific coast—the *Great Northern Railroad.* Hill did not receive any federal land grants or cash subsidies. To attract settlers to Great Northern territory, Hill provided free transportation from the East, easy credit, and expert agricultural advice.

2. Oil. *John D. Rockefeller,* a food merchant, entered the oil-refining business and in 1870 formed the *Standard Oil Company of Ohio.* Rockefeller accumulated strong cash reserves, fought successful price wars, received secret railroad rebates on oil shipments, and, aided by the depression of 1873, ruthlessly drove out or bought out many competitors. By 1879 the Standard Oil Company controlled over 90 percent of the country's oil refineries. Rockefeller improved the quality of refined oil and distributed it efficiently.

In 1882 Rockefeller combined his many holdings into the *Standard Oil Trust,* but in 1890 it was ordered dissolved by the Ohio Supreme Court. Reorganized as a holding company, it was ordered dissolved in 1911 by the Supreme Court, which ruled that the 34 member companies had to function as separate units.

3. Steel. *Andrew Carnegie,* a railroad executive who foresaw the need to replace iron rails with steel ones, entered the steel business. He built a single company that owned iron ore deposits in the Mesabi Range near Lake Superior, steamships on the Great Lakes, and steel mills in Pittsburgh. Carnegie pioneered the use of the Bessemer process for making steel and improved its quality. He undersold and drove out competitors. By 1900 the *Carnegie Steel Company* produced one-fourth of the country's steel.

To reduce competition, other steel companies planned a huge monopoly to be created by the investment banker *J. Pierpont Morgan.* He bought out Carnegie's interests and in 1901 combined the various steel companies under a single holding company, the *United States Steel Corporation.* The first corporation in the United States worth over a billion dollars, it controlled 60 percent of the nation's steel production.

4. Other Industries. Business leaders who formed consolidations in other industries were: *Gustavus Swift* and *Philip D. Armour*—meat-packing; *Charles A. Pillsbury*—flour-milling; *James B. Duke*—cigarette-manufacturing; and *Andrew W. Mellon*—aluminum.

Historical Analysis. *What is the proper evaluation of post-Civil War business leaders?*

They have been both praised and condemned. For destroying small companies, charging high prices, exploiting workers, manipulating stock, and corrupting government officials, they have been called *robber barons.* For organizing new industries, providing better services, improving the quality of their products, supporting philanthropies, and hastening industrialization, they have been called *captains of industry.*

ADVANTAGES OF BIG BUSINESS

1. Mass Production. Giant corporations could produce goods in large quantities by applying mass production methods—the assembly line, division of labor, and standardization of parts. They could introduce the most modern machinery, purchase raw materials in large quantities at low prices, and utilize by-products. They could therefore offer the public new, improved, and less expensive products.

2. Wide Distribution. Large corporations could use large-scale advertising and distribute their products nationwide.

3. Efficient Management. Large corporations could hire the most capable executives, maintain costly research laboratories, and raise capital for expansion.

ABUSES BY BIG BUSINESS

1. Elimination of Competition. Large corporations could drive out small businesses by price wars and other methods of "cutthroat competition." The mere fact that large corporations could sell at lower prices and even offer superior products has had the effect of destroying small businesses.

2. Power Over Consumers. Once a large company achieved a degree of monopoly, it could force consumers to pay high prices and accept inferior quality.

3. Exploitation of Workers. By achieving control of the labor market in some communities, large companies could pay low wages and keep workers from forming unions.

4. Influence Over the Government. Unscrupulous business executives could bribe politicians and buy the votes of legislators. By their great concentration of wealth, large corporations could exercise great influence over government policy.

GOVERNMENT AND BIG BUSINESS

GOVERNMENT POLICIES TOWARD BUSINESS

1. Freedom From Government Regulations (To the End of the 19th Century). The government followed a policy of fostering but not regulating business. The government maintained protective tariffs and provided railroads with land subsidies but otherwise practiced the policy of leaving business alone—that is, *laissez-faire.*

Laissez-faire was advocated by the Scottish economist Adam Smith in his 1776 book *The Wealth of Nations.* Smith maintained that free competition would lower prices, increase the variety and the quality of goods, provide opportunities for new companies, and, in general, further the best interests of society.

2. Regulation in the Interests of Society (Since the End of the 19th Century). In the post-Civil War period, giant corporations arose and restrained the free competition that was supposed to regulate the economy automatically and thereby benefit society. Big business committed abuses threatening the public health and welfare, and harming the interests of farmers, laborers, and small business owners. An aroused people demanded government regulation of industry, a policy that was adopted gradually and that persists to this day.

RAILROADS: THE FIRST REGULATED INDUSTRY

1. Railroad Abuses

a. High Rates. (1) Each railroad, having a virtual monopoly over transportation in its territory, charged "what the traffic will bear." (2) Many railroads issued *watered stock* (stock in excess of the actual worth of the company) and charged high rates in order to pay dividends on their watered stock. (3) Railroads frequently entered into *pooling agreements* to divide business and raise rates that shippers had no choice but to pay.

b. Discrimination Regarding Rates. (1) Railroads granted rebates to large shippers but charged the full rate to small shippers—farmers and small-business owners. (2) Railroads charged lower rates for freight hauled between big cities, where they faced competing lines, than for freight hauled to or from rural areas, where they faced no competition. Thus, a long haul often cost less than a short haul.

c. Political Corruption. Railroads unduly influenced state and federal politics by bribing legislators, making campaign contributions to political parties, and granting free railroad passes to important people.

Farmers, small-business owners, and the general public protested these abuses. The Grange secured several state regulatory laws, but in 1886 the Supreme Court declared state regulations of interstate railroads unconstitutional in the case of *Wabash vs. Illinois*. (Check the Index.)

2. Beginning of Federal Regulations: Interstate Commerce Act (1887)

a. Provisions. This act prohibited railroads from (1) discriminating between persons by special rates or rebates, (2) charging more for a short haul than for a long haul, (3) entering into pooling agreements. It also (4) ordered a ten-day notice and public posting of new railroad rates, (5) declared that railroad rates should be "reasonable and just," and (6) established an enforcement agency, the *Interstate Commerce Commission* (ICC).

b. Weaknesses. The ICC originally was handicapped by (1) the vague language of the law, (2) the complexity of the railroad business, (3) the shortage of qualified personnel to work for the commission, and (4) its inability to enforce its decisions without appealing to the courts, which tended to be sympathetic toward the railroads.

c. Significance. The Interstate Commerce Act established the precedent of government regulation of private interstate business and paved the way for subsequent and stronger legislation.

3. Subsequent Regulation. The ICC was strengthened by (a) the *Elkins Act* (1903), enabling the ICC to punish shippers as well as railroads engaged in rebating, (b) the *Hepburn Act* (1906), empowering it to set maximum railroad rates, and (c) the *Physical Valuation Act* (1913), empowering it to determine the value of railroad property as a basis for setting fair rates.

To meet the emergency of World War I, the government operated the railroads, coordinating service and eliminating duplication.

The *Transportation Act* (*Esch-Cummins Act*) of 1920 returned the railroads to private operation. It also empowered the ICC to (a) fix minimum as well as maximum rates, and (b) approve railroad pools and consolidations. Since many railroads were in financial trouble, the ICC was now concerned with the welfare not only of the shippers but also of the railroads.

4. Railroads Today

a. Competition. Railroads no longer have a virtual monopoly, but face fierce competition from bus lines, trucking companies, and airlines. To meet such competition, railroads have requested that the ICC grant them greater flexibility in setting their rates. Also, railroads have improved their lines by using fast, low-cost diesel engines and flatcars for carrying loaded trailers "piggyback."

To cut costs, many railroads have obtained the ICC's permission to abandon unprofitable lines, chiefly short-run commuter hauls. To eliminate duplication and reduce costs, various railroads have secured the ICC's approval to merge. The New York Central and Pennsylvania railroads, with ICC approval, merged in 1968 but in 1970 declared bankruptcy. Other mergers proved successful.

b. Amtrak and Conrail. To assure service between heavily populated cities, mainly in the Northeast, Congress in the 1970s created and partly financed the *National Railroad Passenger Corporation,* or *Amtrak,* and the *Consolidated Rail Corporation,* or *Conrail.* The new railroads took over track of existing private lines. Amtrak, a passenger line, operated with significant deficits, necessitating considerable government financial assistance. Conrail, a freight line, became profitable, and the government in 1987 sold its stock for $1.6 billion to private investors.

c. Partial Deregulation. In 1980 Congress passed a *Rail Deregulation Act.* Its purposes were to lessen the control of the ICC over the railroads so as to allow them to compete more freely with other forms of transportation. The act empowered the railroads to (a) raise freight rates, within limits, without ICC approval, and (b) abandon routes and branch lines more easily with the ICC's authority restricted. Would such deregulation further railroad prosperity?

REGULATION OF BIG BUSINESS

1. Sherman Antitrust Act (1890)

a. Provisions. To deter monopolies and compel competition, this law (1) declared illegal "every contract, combination in the form of trust or otherwise, or conspiracy, in restraint of trade," and (2) provided that guilty corporations and individuals be subject to financial penalties—up to triple damages and that guilty combinations could be split up.

b. Weaknesses. In enforcing the law, the Department of Justice was handicapped by (1) the vague language of the law, (2) the ability of business leaders to use forms of combination other than the trust, (3) the lack of sufficient funds, personnel, and executive determination for enforcement, and (4) interpretations by the Supreme Court favoring big business. The Supreme Court held illegal only "unreasonable" restraint of trade, thereby establishing a loophole, called the *rule of reason.*

2. Theodore Roosevelt: "Trust Buster" (1901–1909). Theodore Roosevelt was the first President to vigorously enforce the Sherman Act. Roosevelt believed that the growth of big business was inevitable. He approved "good" trusts, but he sought to destroy "bad" trusts. Roosevelt instituted over 40 antitrust cases. His most famous victory was a 5-to-4 Supreme Court decision in 1904, ordering the breakup of the Northern Security Company, a railroad holding company that threatened to monopolize railroad service in the Northwest.

Roosevelt's successor, William Howard Taft, stepped up the government's trust-busting by instituting some 900 antitrust suits.

3. Publicity: Muckrakers. The trust-busting campaigns of Roosevelt and Taft were aided by a group of writers called *muckrakers.* To arouse the American people to demand reforms, they exposed the evils of big business.

The Jungle in particular aroused public opinion. In 1906 Congress began government protection of the consumer by passing two laws: (a) The *Meat Inspection Act* set sanitary regulations for meat packers and provided federal inspection of meat-packing plants. (b) The *Pure Food and Drug Act* forbade the manufacture, transportation, and sale of adulterated and poisonous foods and drugs.

MUCKRAKERS AND THEIR SUBJECTS

AUTHOR	MAJOR WORK	THEME
Ida M. Tarbell	*History of the Standard Oil Company*	Ruthless practices of a gigantic monopoly.
Frank Norris	*The Octopus*	Struggle of wheat farmers against the railroad.
Gustavus Myers	*History of the Great American Fortunes*	Corruption and exploitation by big business leaders.
Ray Stannard Baker	*Railroads on Trial*	Railroad evils and abuses.
Upton Sinclair	*The Jungle*	Disgusting practices of the meat-packing industry.

4. Woodrow Wilson and Business Regulation. Woodrow Wilson secured Congressional enactment of the following business reform laws:

a. Clayton Antitrust Act (1914). This law attempted to strengthen the Sherman Antitrust Act by listing specific illegal practices and combinations: (1) price discrimination toward purchasers, (2) "tie-in" contracts by which merchants could buy goods from a company only if they would not handle the products of that company's competitors, and (3) certain types of holding companies and interlocking directorates. The law declared these practices and combinations unlawful if they tended "to lessen competition or create a monopoly." This proviso limited the effectiveness of the Clayton Act. As with the Sherman Act, the Supreme Court held illegal only restraint of trade considered "unreasonable."

b. Federal Trade Commission Act (1914). This act established the *Federal Trade Commission* (FTC) to receive reports from and make investigations of business firms. The FTC enforces the Clayton Act's prohibitions of certain business practices and combats other unfair methods of competition—thereby providing protection for consumers.

The FTC has ruled the following practices as unfair: (1) misbranding and adulteration of goods, (2) false and misleading advertising, (3) spying and bribery to secure trade secrets, and (4) closely imitating a competitor's product. To halt such practices, the FTC issues *cease and desist* orders. FTC orders may be challenged by the firm involved and are subject to court review.

INDUSTRIAL GROWTH AND PROBLEMS SINCE WORLD WAR I

BUSINESS FOLLOWING WORLD WAR I: FROM "BOOM TO BUST"

1. Boom Conditions (To 1929)

a. Continued Growth of Big Business. Industrial leaders modernized their plants, utilized the newest production methods, and promoted business consolidations by forming mergers and holding companies. The government ignored these consolidations and failed to initiate new antitrust suits.

b. Age of the Automobile. Just prior to World War I, *Henry Ford* revolutionized the automobile industry by applying the techniques of mass production, especially the assembly line. Ford's production methods permitted the price of his cars to drop to moderate levels. After the war, many Americans considered a car a necessity, and auto production mounted rapidly.

The growth of the automobile industry had widespread effects. Automobile factories required raw materials: rubber, steel, aluminum, and plastics. The automobile fostered new enterprises—gasoline and repair stations, garages, and parking lots—and led to the construction of new and improved highways.

c. New Industries. These included (1) the chemical industry—spurred by the cutoff of German chemicals during the war and thereafter by high tariffs against chemical imports; (2) movies—first "silents" and then "talkies"; (3) the radio industry—made possible by the work of the Italian *Guglielmo Marconi,* with wireless telegraphy, and the American *Lee De Forest,* with the vacuum tube; (4) airplane travel in its earliest stage—evolving out of the first flight, in 1903, by *Wilbur* and *Orville Wright;* and (5) various electric-powered home appliances, such as refrigerators, vacuum cleaners, and toasters.

2. Bust: The Great Depression. In 1929 the American economy entered its most severe depression. By 1933 American business had reached its lowest ebb. Business bankruptcies, bank failures, mass unemployment, and even panic swept the country. This depression sapped the belief in a self-regulating economic system and strengthened the trend toward government regulation. (For details of this depression, check the Index.)

THE NEW DEAL AND BUSINESS

1. Background. In the 1932 Presidential election, Franklin D. Roosevelt, the Democratic candidate, ran against the incumbent, Herbert Hoover. The two men disagreed basically regarding the government's role in the economy. Roosevelt insisted that the government take firm steps to insure the nation's economic well-being. Hoover argued for only limited government interference in the economy. Hoover credited America's greatness to free enterprise and "rugged individualism." Roosevelt won the election overwhelmingly.

Pledging the American people a New Deal, Roosevelt summarized his goals as (a) *relief*—to assist distressed persons, (b) *recovery*—to lift the nation out of the depression, and (c) *reform*—to eliminate abuses in the economy.

The New Deal marked two significant changes in the relationship of the government to the economy: (a) By committing the government to an ever-increasing role in the economy, the New Deal completed the transition from laissez-faire to regulated capitalism. (b) By hiring many people to enforce complex economic laws and to staff numerous government agencies, the New Deal created a powerful *bureaucracy.*

2. National Industrial Recovery Act (1933). To aid the recovery of business, President Roosevelt secured Congressional passage of the *National Industrial Recovery Act* (NIRA). (a) *Provisions.* The NIRA (1) established the *National Recovery Administration* (NRA), (2) empowered the NRA to supervise industry in drawing up "codes of fair competition" providing for minimum wages, maximum hours, price-fixing, production controls, and fair methods of competition, and (3) exempted agreements made under the NIRA from the Sherman and Clayton Antitrust Acts. Thus the NIRA allowed monopolistic practices but kept them subject to government control. (b) *Business Response.* The NIRA was at first welcomed enthusiastically, but it soon drew much criticism. While small businesses complained that the codes favored the large corporations, large businesses complained about government "regimentation" and overregulation. (c) *Held Unconstitutional.* In 1935 the NIRA was declared unconstitutional by the

Supreme Court in the *Schechter Case.* The Court said that (1) the codes were illegal since they were laws not enacted by Congress, and (2) the federal government had no right to regulate intrastate commerce.

Subsequently, the Antitrust Division of the Department of Justice vigorously renewed enforcement of the Sherman and Clayton Acts.

BUSINESS AND WORLD WAR II (1939–1945)

1. "Miracle of Production." With the onset of World War II in 1939 and the fall of France to the Germans in 1940, Americans realized their military unpreparedness. Congress authorized tremendous expenditures for the production of military equipment. When the Japanese attacked Pearl Harbor in 1941, America was drawn actively into the war. American industrialists, displaying great managerial ability and drawing upon the pool of unemployed workers, fulfilled the nation's war needs. From 1940 to 1945 industry almost doubled the production of manufactured goods, thereby supplying our military forces and providing much equipment for our allies. American industry significantly helped win the war.

2. Increased Government Control. To mobilize American industry, the government established various agencies: (*a*) The *War Production Board* directed the conversion of industry to wartime production, granted essential industries priorities on raw materials, and spurred the construction of new factories. These new plants increased the production of aluminum, steel, airplanes, and ships, and initiated the production of synthetic rubber and of atomic research materials. (*b*) The *Office of Price Administration* combated inflation by setting price ceilings and by rationing scarce goods. (*c*) The *War Manpower Commission* directed labor to essential war industries. (*d*) The *War Labor Board* settled labor-management disputes.

3. Evaluation. Credit for America's "miracle of production" in World War II has been given to the managerial ability of private industry as well as to the centralized planning and controls exercised by government agencies. The American people regained their faith, severely shaken by the depression of 1929, in American industrial leadership.

BIG BUSINESS SINCE WORLD WAR II: RECENT TRENDS

1. Continued Economic Concentration. Corporations acted to improve their competitive position and diversify their activities by pursuing mergers. While permitting many mergers, the federal government continued to enforce the antitrust laws vigorously.

American companies that acquired or established subsidiaries in foreign countries became known as *multinational corporations.*

2. Continued Technological Progress

a. Electronics Industry and Automation. The electronics industry developed significant new products, such as high-fidelity sound reproduction equipment and television sets. Manufacturing and mining firms employed automatic devices to operate machines, a process called *automation*. It sped up production, lowered costs, and improved the quality of goods. To perform routine clerical and mathematical tasks, many firms employed "electronic brains" contained in computers.

b. Other Industries. Chemical manufacturers produced new synthetic fibers and plastics. Airlines employing modern jets provided faster, more comfortable service, and attracted many passengers. Drug companies developed radioactive isotopes to diagnose body ills. Public utilities built plants using the newest source of energy, atomic power.

3. Prosperity. To the mid-1970s, business prospered, profits rose, and production mounted. From 1950 to 1974 the *gross national product* (GNP), the total money value of goods produced and services rendered each year, increased almost sixfold. In terms of constant dollars (to eliminate the effect of inflation) with 1958 the base year, the GNP more than doubled. Industry provided jobs for more workers, and unemployment remained relatively low. Business downturns, or recessions, were comparatively short-lived and mild.

4. Economic Successes and Problems of the Reagan Administration. When the Reagan administration took office in 1981, the economy was stagnant and burdened by severe inflation, high interest rates, high unemployment, and falling labor productivity. To deal with these problems, the Reagan administration secured Congressional approval for the following measures: (*a*) federal outlays were cut so as to trim the budget deficit and reduce government borrowing—believed to be a prime factor in increasing the money supply and fostering inflation. (*b*) A 33-month tax-cut bill was designed to leave consumers with more money, which might be used to spur purchases and, to increase labor productivity, and to give industry tax incentives of faster depreciation, which might spur the purchase of more modern and efficient equipment.

Critics claimed that the budget cuts would bear most heavily upon the disadvantaged poor, and that the tax reductions would impede the efforts to balance the budget.

The Reagan administration was successful in reducing inflation and bringing interest rates down. The inflation rate dropped from 13.5 percent in 1980 to less than 3.2 percent in 1983. While the inflation rate rose slightly in succeeding years, it remained modest in comparison with the late 1970s.

In other ways, however, the Reagan program fell short of expectations. The unemployment rate rose above 10 percent in 1982, a level not seen since the Great Depression of the 1930s. By 1986 the unemployment rate was down to about 7 percent, but that was still high by the standards of the 1950s and 1960s.

Even more alarming to many people was a dramatic increase in federal budget deficits, caused in part by increased spending on such politically popular programs as Social Security, by a sharp rise in military spending, and by heavy interest payments on the soaring national debt. (Between 1980 and 1986, the national debt doubled, from $1 trillion to $2 trillion.) As concern over the high budget deficits mounted, President Reagan and Congress struggled to reach a solution. The President insisted that the way to bring down deficits was to cut domestic spending; he repeatedly rejected the idea of major tax increases (although accepting minor increases in 1982 and 1984). Congressional critics argued that the solution might have to include general tax increases. Deficits continued to rise even after Congress passed the *Gramm-Rudman-Hollings Act* of 1985, which set a timetable for gradually reducing budget deficits to zero by 1991. (Check the Index.) In 1986 Congress voted to slow down the President's military buildup as a cost-saving measure.

5. The Reagan Administration and Business. With specific reference to business, the Reagan administration adopted two major policies:

a. Less Government Regulation. President Reagan claimed that the "mass of regulations" imposed on small and large businesses added "one hundred billion dollars to the price of the things we buy." As part of his program to get the government "off our backs," Reagan planned to reform and eliminate regulations which were "unnecessary and unproductive or counterproductive." In doing so, he expanded and extended the process of deregulation begun under President Carter. President Reagan imposed a hiring freeze on federal employees, asked Cabinet members to postpone new regulations, instructed agency heads to review and rescind existing burdensome regulations, and had Vice President *George Bush* lead a Cabinet-level task force to seek regulatory relief. The administration eliminated regulations such as those requiring businesses to report fuel consumption, setting price controls on United States-produced oil, and limiting thermostat settings for business offices. It postponed deadlines on regulations such as those setting auto-fuel-economy standards and requiring automakers to install air bags. It eased environmental-protection rules and eliminated many regulations affecting the banking industry.

Reagan's efforts to lessen government regulation were criticized as deterring energy conservation, endangering the environment, and imperiling the health and safety of workers.

b. Less Restrictive Antitrust Policy. In contrast with previous administrations, the Reagan administration adopted a policy that was more lenient toward mergers. Reagan appointees concerned with antitrust policy stated that "bigness in business does not necessarily mean badness," and that business "success should not be automatically suspect." They indicated that the government would not challenge most "vertical" mergers, by which a manufacturer purchases a supplier, and would not challenge "conglomerate" mergers, by firms whose markets do not overlap. They declared that the antitrust laws would be used to spur competition and promote economic efficiency. However, the antitrust division of the Justice Department claimed it would vigorously prosecute "horizontal" mergers—by which a company acquires a direct competitor—and would seek jail terms for persons guilty of monopolistic price-fixing. (It should be noted that private parties—not the government—file over 95 percent of antitrust cases.)

The Reagan administration blocked some mergers and takeovers in industries such as steel and drilling equipment. It permitted other deals, often advising companies on how to fashion mergers that met the administration's antitrust standards. In 1986, after five years of using administrative guidelines to shape antitrust policy, the administration asked Congress to make sweeping changes in antitrust laws. It proposed five bills to carry out those changes, arguing that existing antitrust laws had harmed United States companies' efforts to meet foreign competition. While some of the proposed bills won strong bipartisan support, others stirred controversy.

Critics said President Reagan's antitrust policy (1) encouraged greater concentration of wealth and power, (2) reduced competition and lessened innovation, and (3) threatened the survival of many small businesses.

During President Reagan's first term, however, the Justice Department succeeded in breaking the telephone monopoly of the huge American Telephone and Telegraph Company (AT&T). In an antitrust case begun under President Ford, a federal judge in 1982 ordered AT&T to splinter into several smaller firms. The breakup led to vigorous competition in the residential and business telephone equipment industry and caused long-distance rates to fall. However, local rates and service charges rose sharply.

SOCIAL AND POLITICAL ROLES OF BUSINESS

Business executives increasingly showed concern not only for corporations and stockholders, but for all American society. A considerable number encouraged their corporations to provide grants to institutions of higher learning. They also supported retraining programs for displaced workers, participated in studies on the effects of automation, and advanced civil rights by hiring members of minority groups. Business leaders cooperated with the government to further economic and social progress. They realized that our capitalist economy must eliminate such problems as ignorance and poverty.

By 1980 corporations and business associations had established some 1750 *Political Action Committees* (PACs). Accepting funds from individuals, these PACs made contributions to political candidates whom they considered favoring business. (For labor's PAC, check the Index.)

CONSUMER PROTECTION

1. Role of Consumers. According to market economy theory, "consumers rule." They are the ultimate judges of the goods produced and the services offered. Every time consumers make purchases, they are voting in favor of the selected products and against competing choices. In contrast to the above description, many economists hold that "consumers are bewildered." They are bewildered by a barrage of advertising materials, by the complexity of materials and products, and by the fine print in warranties. In this state of bewilderment, consumers have made purchases forewarned only by the saying "Let the buyer beware."

2. Efforts at Consumer Protection

a. Private Action. (1) *Consumers Union* tests and rates products, which data are published in its monthly magazine, (2) *Better Business Bureaus* advise consumers regarding the reliability of local business concerns and investigate complaints, and (3) *Ralph Nader,* a lawyer and self-appointed crusader for consumers, has investigated various products and used publicity to spur government action.

b. Local and State Action. These governments have required honest weights and measures, the proper dating and grading of milk, and sanitary inspection of restaurants.

c. Early Federal Action. The first federal law to protect consumers was the *Pure Food and Drug Act* (1906). It was not strengthened for over 30 years. During the New Deal, Congress passed the *Food, Drug, and Cosmetic Act* (1938) empowering government agencies to (*a*) prevent adulteration, misbranding, and false advertising, (*b*) require manufacturers to list the ingredients of their products, (*c*) regulate cosmetics as well as food and drugs, and (*d*) require adequate testing of new drugs. The *Drug Industry Act* (1962) gave the Food and Drug Administration (FDA) more power over testing, advertising, and prescribing of new drugs. This law was passed amidst publicity caused by the FDA ban on the sale of a new sleeping pill, thalidomide, and the subsequent birth of deformed babies to European mothers who had taken thalidomide.

d. Recent Federal Action. The *Truth in Packaging Act* (1966) outlawed deceptive containers, required simple and easily read labels stating weight or volume, and set standards for such words as "small," "large," and "family-size." The government agency empowered to enforce this law was the Federal Trade Commission (FTC). The *Traffic Safety Act* (1966) created a National Traffic Safety Agency to establish and enforce minimum safety standards in the design and equipment of new automobiles. This law was passed after Ralph Nader published *Unsafe at Any Speed,* a book that attacked the automobile industry for emphasizing style, power, and speed while ignoring economy and safety. The *Meat Inspection Act* (1967) offered federal funds to the states to improve their inspection of intrastate meat packers. It empowered federal agents to inspect packing plants in states not complying with federal standards. The *Truth in Lending Act* (1968) required retailers and lenders to inform most consumers of the true cost of credit in dollars and in annual interest rates. The *Consumer Products Safety Act* (1972) created the Consumer Products Safety Commission to enforce safety standards for household items such as ladders, power tools, electric heaters, pressure cookers, and toys.

In 1976 the Supreme Court declared void—a violation of free speech—state regulations prohibiting pharmacists from advertising prescription drug prices. Subsequent Supreme Court and Federal Trade Commission rulings allowed other professionals—lawyers, engineers, dentists, and doctors—to advertise their services and fees.

——————————— MULTIPLE-CHOICE QUESTIONS ———————————

1. Which factor had *least* to do with the industrialization of the United States in the 19th century? (a) inventions (b) foreign demand for American manufactures (c) abundant natural resources (d) Constitutional protection of private property.

2. In the United States, which was a result of the Industrial Revolution? (a) elimination of class distinctions (b) movement of people from the cities to rural areas (c) fewer booms and busts in the business cycle (d) increased production of consumer goods.

3. The beginning of the "Age of Big Business" in the United States is associated with (a) the War of 1812 (b) the Civil War (c) World War I (d) World War II.

4. Because of the continuing Industrial Revolution, the industrialized nations of the world have been able to (a) raise their standards of living despite increases in population (b) eliminate periods of recession and depression (c) eradicate poverty and hunger among their peoples (d) resist demands to lower trade barriers.

5. Which statement concerning corporations is true? (a) They did not exist before the Civil War. (b) Small businesses seldom incorporate. (c) Businesses incorporate to secure discounts on large purchases. (d) Today, the corporation is the dominant form of business organization in manufacturing.

6. Company *Q* owns controlling shares of stock in companies *A, B, C,* and *D.* This is an example of a (a) pool (b) partnership (c) holding company (d) merger.

7. An important reason for the formation of trusts in the latter part of the 19th century was a desire to (a) escape federal regulation (b) eliminate competition (c) reduce prices (d) eliminate the use of rebates.

8. By which technique have most American business consolidations come about in recent years? (a) pooling agreement (b) merger (c) trust (d) trade association.

9. John D. Rockefeller's most significant contribution to business enterprise was his (a) elimination of competitive practices (b) introduction of assembly-line techniques (c) ethical approach to business (d) promotion of peaceful settlement of labor disputes.

10. Which pairs an industrial leader with his industry? (a) Vanderbilt—meat-packing (b) Carnegie—steel (c) Mellon—automobiles (d) Armour—railroads.

11. In the United States, which economic change contributed to the development of the other three? (a) formation of the Populist party (b) growth of the organized labor movement (c) large-scale industrial expansion (d) antitrust legislation.

12. Which statement concerning business enterprise in the United States is an opinion? (a) The corporation is an important form of business organization. (b) Some companies control all phases of production from the raw materials to the final sale of the product. (c) Monopolies tend to eliminate the need for price competition. (d) Large-scale producers in an industry offer better personal services than do small-scale producers.

13. Which policy toward business was generally followed by the federal government before 1880? (a) strict regulation (b) government ownership (c) laissez-faire (d) heavy taxation.

14. Which was the first industry to be regulated by the United States government? (a) railroads (b) hydroelectric power (c) telegraph communication (d) meat-packing.

15. The primary purpose of the Interstate Commerce Act was to (a) grant land to the railroads (b) regulate railroad rates (c) establish government ownership of railroads (d) supervise interstate truck and bus lines.

16. Before 1900 the Interstate Commerce Commission was handicapped by (a) the adoption of the Sherman Antitrust Act (b) the rise of the Populist party (c) court decisions (d) the establishment of the Federal Trade Commission.

17. The most important purpose of the Sherman Antitrust Act (1890) was to (a) encourage competition in business (b) improve relations between big business and the government (c) improve working conditions in factories (d) prevent business from becoming more powerful than labor.

18. An important effect of the Sherman Antitrust Act was that it (a) restored active competition (b) led to the passage of the Pure Food and Drug Act (c) corrected the weaknesses of the Clayton Antitrust Act (d) caused a change in the forms and techniques of business consolidation.

19. The attitude of Theodore Roosevelt toward business was that the federal government should (a) own public utilities (b) follow a policy of laissez-faire (c) eliminate bad business practices (d) leave the regulation of railroads to the states.

20. In applying the "rule of reason," the Supreme Court ruled that the most important consideration in antitrust cases was the (a) size of the business organization (b) number of stockholders (c) effect on competition (d) type of article manufactured.

21. The Clayton Antitrust Act strengthened the Sherman Antitrust Act by (a) forbidding corporate mergers (b) placing greater restrictions on labor unions (c) listing specific illegal methods of competition (d) prohibiting false advertising.

22. The term "muckraker" has been used to describe authors whose writings deal mainly with (a) criticizing the government's welfare policies (b) publicizing Constitutional issues relating to minority rights (c) advancing the cause of press freedom (d) exposing social conditions in need of reform.

23. Which action was hastened largely because public opinion was aroused by a contemporary novel? (a) ratification of the Sixteenth Amendment (b) establishment of the Interstate Commerce Commission (c) passage of the Sherman Antitrust Act (d) enactment of the Meat Inspection Act of 1906.

24. According to the Federal Trade Commission, which is an example of an unfair business practice? (a) creating a subsidiary corporation (b) lowering prices to meet competition (c) incorporating in one state and doing business in another (d) closely imitating goods sold by a competitor.

25. According to its supporters, one of the greatest contributions of the New Deal was that it (a) retained the principle of the balanced budget (b) weakened the power of the federal government (c) preserved the capitalistic system by making necessary reforms (d) prohibited speculation in corporate stocks and bonds.

26. Critics of the New Deal charge that it (a) created a powerful federal bureaucracy (b) weakened the power of the chief executive (c) failed to include labor legislation (d) promoted the ideas of laissez-faire.

27. The New Deal confirmed a change in American political thinking because it advanced the principle that (a) a public office is a public trust (b) government intervention in business should be kept to a minimum (c) the government should play a significant part in solving social and economic problems (d) the government should not become involved in building hydroelectric power plants.

28. The National Industrial Recovery Act was declared unconstitutional because (a) Congress has no right to regulate intrastate commerce (b) Congress has no right to regulate interstate commerce (c) no emergency existed (d) the act did not restore prosperity.

29. Since World War II, the railroads have asked the federal government for permission to (a) organize holding companies (b) engage in pooling (c) merge competing systems (d) combine with airlines.

30. "There are acres and acres of machines, and here and there you will find a worker standing at a master switchboard watching lights and dials that tell what is happening in each machine." This statement best describes (a) consolidation (b) monopoly (c) mass production (d) automation.

31. In the United States, the industry least influenced by automation is (a) domestic services (b) banking (c) baking (d) automobile production.

32. The gross national product (GNP) of the United States is a measure of the (a) total annual production of our mines and factories (b) increase in the number of people living in cities (c) extent to which natural resources have been used up (d) total money value of all the goods and services produced in a year.

33. The gross national product is a (a) means of estimating next year's national debt (b) barometer of the nation's economic growth (c) method of calculating the profits of large corporations (d) method for verifying the Consumer Price Index.

34. In order to interpret the significance of the gross national product (GNP), economists must take into consideration the (a) changes in price levels (b) interest charges on the national debt (c) total amount collected in taxes (d) type of economic system.

35. If a country's population increases at the same rate as its GNP, the net effect is to (a) nullify any per capita benefits from gains in production (b) decrease the standard of living of the population (c) increase the standard of living of the population (d) increase productivity because of a larger market.

36. The role of Ralph Nader in the consumer movement is most similar to the career of (a) John D. Rockefeller (b) Ida Tarbell (c) Woodrow Wilson (d) Thomas Edison.

37. Which statement regarding consumers is most valid? (a) Since consumers can always refuse to buy, they have no need of government protection. (b) Before World War II, the federal government had not passed any consumer protection laws. (c) Since World War II, the federal government has passed laws to require truth in packaging and in lending. (d) Federal safety standards for automobiles are unnecessary as long as the price of gasoline remains high.

38. Since the 1960s, the consumer movement has led to the (a) lowering of prices of major appliances (b) passage of antitrust legislation (c) decrease in the importance of the law of supply and demand (d) enactment of tougher safety requirements.

39. "Combinations in industry are the result of an . . . economic law which cannot be repealed by political legislation." The author of this quotation would probably favor which economic policy? (a) antitrust laws (b) laissez-faire (c) mercantilism (d) welfare state.

40. Which combination of factors has attempted to check the economic and political power of big business in the United States today? (a) many producers in basic industries, strict controls over monopolies, nationalization of the electrical power industry (b) unorganized workers, state labor laws, concentration of corporate ownership (c) competition of government corporations with private corporations, widespread stock ownership, pure competition (d) strong labor unions, antitrust laws, federal regulatory agencies.

————————————— ESSAY QUESTIONS —————————————

1. The United States now has the highest standard of living ever attained by any society. Giving *two* specific examples, explain how *each* of the following has helped to bring about this high standard of living: (*a*) labor supply (*b*) inventions (*c*) government policies (*d*) natural resources (*e*) a specific war.

2. The corporation has made possible the mass production that typifies American industry. (*a*) Explain *two* ways in which the corporation has promoted mass production. (*b*) Discuss briefly *two* reasons why small-scale production continues to exist. (*c*) Explain *two* ways in which mass production has affected the consumer.

3. The "captains of industry" played a major role in American economic development after the Civil War. (*a*) Show how *each* of the following factors contributed to the success of these industrial leaders: (1) use of natural resources (2) forms of business organization (3) the personal characteristics of these leaders. (*b*) Explain *two* effects of the activities of these leaders on the lives of the American people.

4. In 1887 the federal government began its efforts to regulate big business by the passage of the Interstate Commerce Act. (*a*) Discuss briefly *two* reasons why the federal government generally did not regulate business before then. (*b*) Show *two* ways in which the Interstate Commerce Commission has attempted to regulate big business. (*c*) Show *two* ways in which the increase in government control of business has directly affected the government itself. (*d*) Present *one* argument to explain why in the 1980s there has been a move to deregulate railroads.

5. Big business has occupied a significant place in the affairs of the United States for the past 100 years. (*a*) Discuss *two* reasons why the period after the Civil War was marked by great industrial expansion. (*b*) Discuss *two* specific problems created by the rise of big business. (*c*) Show how federal legislation has attempted to solve *each* of the problems given in answer to (*b*).

6. The policy of the federal government toward business has varied from one period to another. (*a*) Describe *two* ways in which the federal government aided the growth of business during the period 1865 to 1890. (*b*) Explain how *one* federal law passed during the 20th century attempted to regulate business. (*c*) Discuss *two* basic reasons for the change by the federal government from a policy of aiding the growth of business to a policy of regulating business. (*d*) Show *two* ways in which business has helped the United States assume a position of leadership in world affairs.

7. Give *one* reason to explain why you agree *or* disagree with *each* of the following statements: (*a*) The small-business owner must inevitably disappear. (*b*) The Sherman and Clayton Antitrust laws have proved effective. (*c*) Since consumers benefit from competition between corporations, consumers do not need the protection of the government. (*d*) Corporation executives today are showing concern for the overall welfare of American society.

PART 5. The Government Deals With the Business Cycle, Banking, and Taxation

BUSINESS CYCLE

PHASES OF THE BUSINESS CYCLE

(1) *Prosperity:* a large output of goods, extensive factory expansion, high prices and profits, easy bank credit, full employment, good wages, and a general feeling of optimism. (2) *Recession:* a falling off of demand for goods, decreased production, falling prices and profits, the calling in of bank loans, decreasing employment, falling wages, and a general feeling of caution. (3) *Depression:* low production, low prices, little or no profits, widespread business failures, few bank loans, heavy unemployment, low wages, and a general feeling of pessimism. (4) *Recovery:* increasing production, rising prices and profits, extension of bank loans, increasing employment, rising wages, and a general feeling of hopefulness.

CAUSES OF BUSINESS CONTRACTION

1. Overproduction. Factory owners and merchants overestimate demand and build up excessive inventories of goods. Eventually, retailers curtail orders, and factory owners reduce production, thereby causing a downturn in business.

2. Underconsumption. Workers and farmers find their incomes insufficient to purchase industry's output of goods. Eventually, this disproportion of industrial supply to consumer demand becomes too great, and the economy slows down.

3. Imbalance Between Savings and Investment. People who save part of their income instead of spending it all decrease the demand for consumer goods. These savings, invested in securities or deposited in banks, provide the capital essential for economic growth. Bank deposits may be invested in mortgage loans for the construction of homes and buildings, and in business loans for the purchase of materials and machinery. However, not all savings are invested, since banks may lack sufficient demand for loans. When a large proportion of savings is not invested, the total demand for goods falls off, and the economy turns downward.

4. Psychological Causes. When pessimism sets in, consumers refrain from buying, business leaders limit expansion, and bankers restrict loans. These responses cause the economy to worsen and pessimism to deepen.

Economists believe that recessions are not caused by any one factor but by the interaction of several factors. Many economists are convinced also that the business cycle can be controlled by intelligent human effort.

The Business Cycle 1905–1985

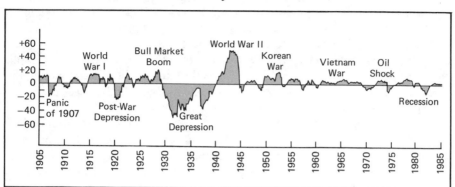

THE DEPRESSION OF 1929

1. Causes. (a) American industry overexpanded its production facilities. (b) Consumers lacked sufficient income to purchase the total output of industry. Farmers had low incomes following World War I because of the agricultural depression. Workers' wages failed to keep pace with increased productivity. (c) Bankers made unsound loans that ultimately resulted in bank failures wiping out the savings of many depositors. (d) "Get-rich-quick" speculators bid up the price of real estate and stocks to unrealistic levels. (e) International trade declined because World War I had hurt Europe's economy and had lessened Europe's ability to purchase goods. Also, high protective tariffs interfered with the flow of goods between countries. (f) The depression's immediate cause was the sharp stock market crash starting in October 1929.

2. Differences From Earlier Depressions. The 1929 depression was the most severe in American history because the United States (a) no longer had the frontier with its economic opportunities, (b) had become primarily industrial, and more Americans were affected by business variations, and (c) found the depression to be not limited but of worldwide extent.

3. Depth of the Depression. By 1932 production and prices were substantially down, stock prices had dropped 90 percent from their 1929 levels, business bankruptcies totaled over 32,000, bank failures numbered over 5,000, wages had been slashed, and over 12 million workers, or 25 percent of the labor force, were unemployed.

4. New Deal. In 1933 Franklin D. Roosevelt became President. His New Deal battled the depression with a series of approaches:

   a. Deficit Budgets and Public Works. Roosevelt incurred deficit budgets by heavy government borrowing. He used government funds to provide direct relief for the unemployed and to stimulate business and create jobs. The *Public Works Administration* let out contracts for massive programs of public works, which in turn stimulated other businesses. The *Works Progress Administration* spent government funds on such programs as statistical surveys, art and theater projects, and some construction work. By thus pumping funds into the economy, the New Deal attempted to invigorate business.

   b. Bank Reforms. The New Deal restored public confidence in the banks by insuring depositors' money in case of bank failure and by strengthening the powers of the Federal Reserve Board. To encourage loans for business purposes, the Federal Reserve followed a low-interest, easy-money policy.

   c. Investment Reforms. To restore investor confidence in the securities markets and thusly to stimulate the investment of capital essential for business growth, the New Deal established the Securities and Exchange Commission. It requires corporations offering new securities for sale to provide potential investors with full data regarding the corporation in a statement called a *prospectus.* The commission also regulates stock exchanges to prevent price manipulations and other fraudulent practices.

   d. Production Controls. To avoid overproduction, New Deal laws encouraged farmers to reduce output and temporarily suspended the antitrust laws so that businesses could establish production controls.

   e. Encouragement of Consumption. To promote mass purchasing power, the New Deal legislated minimum wage standards, encouraged the states to establish unemployment insurance systems, and fostered labor unions by guaranteeing collective bargaining.

   f. Optimism. Roosevelt instilled confidence into the people by asserting that the nation was basically sound. His optimism proved contagious.

   By 1939 people had regained confidence and the economy had achieved a partial recovery. Unemployment, however, although decreased, was still a substantial 17 percent of the labor force, over 8 million persons. The depression was not fully wiped out until the economy was spurred by national defense and World War II needs.

BUSINESS CYCLE SINCE WORLD WAR II

   1. Less Extreme Variations. The American people experienced several postwar recessions—mainly of short duration and comparatively mild. As measured by the gross national product (GNP), business activity recorded a pause or slight downward turn. The stock market fell, but there was no panic. Bank failures remained few. Unemployment rose, to around 7 percent.

   The 1973–1975 recession, however, was far more severe than earlier post-World War II economic downturns. It lasted the longest, the GNP drop was the sharpest, the stock market decline was the steepest, and unemployment climbed above 9 percent. This recession was complicated by strong inflation, caused in part by the quadrupling of oil prices by the Arab-dominated *Organization of Petroleum Exporting Countries* (OPEC). Some economists blamed the steepness of this "inflationary recession" upon the nation's rampant inflation.

2. Measures to Level Out Extremes of the Business Cycle

a. Nongovernmental Efforts. (1) Strong labor unions kept wage levels steady during periods of recession. They kept down unemployment by dividing the available work and by limiting the introduction of new machines. Unions also sought to assure workers 52 paychecks a year by securing the guaranteed annual wage. (2) Responsible business leaders geared their corporate policies to maintain steady employment and capital investment during recessions.

During prosperity both unions and management have been urged by the government to exercise restraint regarding wage and price increases.

b. Employment Act of 1946. This law affirmed the "policy and responsibility of the federal government to promote maximum employment, production, and purchasing power." It authorized the President to furnish Congress with economic reports covering current economic conditions and forseeable future trends, and including, if necessary, recommendations for federal action to halt any extreme swings in the business cycle. To assist the President, the law established a three-member *Council of Economic Advisers.*

c. Government Tax Policies. In periods of inflation, the government may move to reduce the purchasing power of individuals and corporations by raising excise taxes and income taxes. In periods of recession, the government may move to increase purchasing power by lowering excise and income taxes and by granting businesses a tax credit for buying new equipment.

d. Built-in or Automatic Stabilizers. Since 1933 the government has enacted significant laws to stabilize the economy once it turns downward. To maintain consumer purchasing power, these laws provide: unemployment insurance for laid-off workers, Social Security payments to retired workers, price supports for farmers, and minimum wages. Another built-in stabilizer is the Federal Deposit Insurance Corporation (FDIC). It now guarantees every depositor up to $100,000 per account in case of bank failure. FDIC protection helped restore confidence in our banking system and drastically reduced the number of bank failures.

e. Public Works Programs. During recession periods, the federal government and the states may increase the funds spent for public works. Such increased spending would pump more money into the economy and help reverse the cyclical downtrend.

f. Use of Federal Reserve Powers. The Federal Reserve used its bank and credit powers to prevent extremes in the business cycle.

BANKING (MONETARY POLICY)

FEDERAL RESERVE SYSTEM (THE FED)

Established by Congress in 1913 and strengthened during the 1930s, the Federal Reserve serves as our centralized banking system.

1. Purposes. The Federal Reserve (*a*) supervises banks and helps them serve the general public and the business community, (*b*) serves as the fiscal and banking agent of the federal government by holding government funds, selling government securities, and issuing currency (Federal Reserve Notes, which are our paper money), and (*c*) encourages the healthy growth of the national economy by acting to prevent business extremes: runaway prosperity and inflation, as well as serious recession and deflation.

2. Twelve Federal Reserve Banks. The United States is divided into 12 Federal Reserve Districts, each served by its own Federal Reserve Bank. Since the Federal Reserve banks do business not with individuals or corporations, but only with member banks, they are called "bankers' banks."

3. Member Banks. Banks chartered by the federal government must join the Federal Reserve System. Banks chartered by a state may do so if they wish. Today, approximately 5000 federally chartered and 1000 state-chartered banks, holding three-quarters of the nation's total bank deposits, are Federal Reserve members. All Fed members must (and other banks may) join the *Federal Deposit Insurance Corporation.*

4. Board of Governors. The Federal Reserve System is controlled by its Board of Governors. The board consists of a chairperson and six other members, each appointed for a 14-year term by the President with the consent of the Senate. The board, however, is independent of the President and the Senate. Although subject to political pressures, the Fed legally exercises its own best judgment regarding the use of its credit and banking powers.

POWERS OF THE FEDERAL RESERVE

1. Setting the Reserve Ratio. Each business day, a bank pays out and receives money. Because on some days it may pay out more money than it receives, it must keep a money reserve. The Federal Reserve Board of Governors determines the size of this reserve by setting the proportion of reserves to deposits—the *reserve ratio.*

By raising the reserve ratio, the Fed forces its member banks to increase their reserves. They can therefore lend less money. This should lead to fewer loans and a decline in business expansion. Conversely, the board may encourage business expansion by lowering the reserve ratio and thus permitting member banks to lend more money.

2. Setting the Discount Rate. If a member bank needs funds, it may borrow from a Federal Reserve bank. The interest rate charged by the Federal Reserve usually is called the *discount rate.* When the Fed raises the discount rate, the member banks in turn raise their interest rate to their customers, and business expansion may slow down. The board may achieve the opposite effect by lowering its discount rate.

3. Engaging in Open-Market Operations. The Federal Reserve banks buy and sell government securities by dealing with individuals and corporations in the open market. When they sell government securities, the Federal Reserve banks receive payment in checks drawn on their member banks. By cashing these checks, the Federal Reserve banks decrease the cash reserves of their member banks and thereby reduce the ability of the member banks to make loans. Conversely, by buying government securities, the Federal Reserve banks increase the cash reserves of their member banks, thus pumping money into the economy. The Federal Reserve Board directs open-market operations.

4. Setting the Margin Requirement. When investors buy stock on margin, they pay for the securities in part with their own cash and borrow the remainder from their stockbrokers. The Federal Reserve fixes the amount that may be borrowed—*the margin requirement*—as a percentage of the dollar value of the stock purchase.

When the economy is depressed, the Fed may reduce the margin requirement to encourage investment. When the economy is expanding rapidly, the Fed may increase the margin requirement to discourage overspeculation.

TAXATION (FISCAL POLICY)

GOVERNMENT EXPENDITURES

1. Local governments spend money to provide schools, libraries, hospitals, public welfare, police and fire protection, courts of justice, sanitation, local roads, streets, and parks.

2. State governments spend funds to provide state police, courts, highways, hospitals, and parks. States also provide *grants-in-aid,* or *state aid,* to local governments for public welfare and education.

3. The federal government spends large sums for national security, including the maintenance of the armed forces and the development of nuclear and other weapons. It provides money for foreign aid; space exploration; aid to veterans, farmers, workers, and businesses; interstate highways; national parks; and grants-in-aid to state and local governments for road-building, education, conservation, housing, and other social programs. Also, the federal government makes sizable interest payments on the enormous national debt.

INCREASING GOVERNMENT EXPENDITURES: REASONS

1. Increasing Population. As the American population has increased, federal, state, and local governments have provided services for many more people. As the percentage of the population over 65 and under 21 has increased, governments at all levels have increased their spending for aid to the aged and for education.

2. Government Responsibility for Social Welfare. The depression of 1929 led the various levels of government to accept greater responsibility for the people's welfare. The federal government provided aid sometimes directly, as to the farmer, and sometimes indirectly through grants-in-aid to state and local governments. Also, as more persons moved into cities, governments have spent more money on the problems of urbanization.

3. Cold War. Following World War II the United States became the leader of the free nations in their efforts to contain aggressive communism. The federal government sharply increased its expenditures for national defense, foreign aid, and localized conflicts, as in Korea and Vietnam.

4. Improvement in Technology. To improve our national defense, the federal government has borne great costs for the development of new weapons. The federal government also has assumed the major role in space exploration. A number of government agencies were created to regulate areas of technological progress, such as transportation, communication, and drug manufacturing. All levels of government have spent heavily to provide roads and highways for cars and trucks.

GOVERNMENT REVENUES

1. Theories of Taxation. (a) *Ability to Pay.* This theory holds that the government should tax individuals according to their income. The person with the greater income has the greater ability to pay and should bear a greater part of the tax burden. This theory underlies the income tax. (b) *Benefit.* This theory holds that the government should tax the people according to benefits, or gains, they receive. This theory underlies the gasoline tax in those states that use the funds received from the tax for roadbuilding.

2. Tax Rates as Percentages of Income. (a) *Progressive.* The federal income tax is an example of a progressive, or graduated, tax. A person earning a greater income pays taxes at a higher percentage. People earning extremely low incomes pay no income tax at all. For years, the tax laws divided taxpayers into more than a dozen different groups, or brackets. Those in the lowest bracket paid at a relatively low rate (in 1986, 11 percent of their taxable incomes). Those in the highest bracket paid at higher rates (up to 50 percent in 1986). In the *Tax Reform Act of 1986,* Congress made sweeping revisions in the tax laws, reducing the number of brackets to two (15 percent and 28 percent) as of 1988. The act removed an additional 6 million low-income people from the tax rolls altogether. The act also closed numerous "loopholes" in the old tax laws by eliminating many deductible items from individual and business tax returns.

(b) *Proportional.* An example of a proportional tax would be an income tax that taxed everyone at the same rate. (c) *Regressive.* A regressive tax requires a person earning a smaller income to pay a higher percentage of that income for the tax than does a person with a larger income. A cigarette tax is an example of

Berryman in The Washington Star

"Now you must do your duty . . . spend it!"

At what phase of the business cycle might Uncle Sam lower taxes? Would he then want the public to spend or to save its additional income? Explain.

a regressive tax. The laborer who smokes a pack of cigarettes a day pays as much tax as a millionaire who also smokes a pack a day. The laborer is therefore being taxed at a much higher rate in proportion to income than the millionaire. Economists consider the general sales tax as a regressive tax.

3. Major Sources of Revenue

a. Local Sources. Local governments generally secure their largest revenue from the real estate property tax. They may also derive income from the sales tax, minor business taxes, transit fares, water-service fees, and traffic fines. Also, they receive large sums in state and federal aid. Some cities impose an income tax on residents and a payroll tax on commuters working in the city.

b. State Sources. State governments usually secure their largest revenues from the income tax and commodity taxes. The latter include general sales taxes and taxes on specific items such as gasoline, alcohol, and cigarettes. States also receive revenue from licenses, minor business taxes, property taxes, and the inheritance, or estate, tax. In addition, they receive grants of federal aid.

c. Federal Sources. The federal government secures most of its revenue from the individual income tax, the corporate income tax, and the Social Security, or payroll, tax. The federal government also levies excise taxes on gasoline, alcohol, tobacco, telephone service, and new car purchases; tariffs on imports; and an inheritance, or estate, tax.

"Taxes," according to Supreme Court Justice Oliver Wendell Holmes, "are what we pay for civilized society."

4. Government Use of Taxation for Social and Regulatory Purposes. The power of taxation may be used to bring about certain social and economic goals:

a. To further housing construction and attract new industries, local governments sometimes offer limited exemptions from the property tax.

b. To encourage philanthropy, the federal government and the states permit charitable contributions, within limits, to be deducted from taxable income.

c. To aid the elderly, the federal government and some states permit persons over 65 to take a double personal exemption from their income taxes.

d. In part to discourage the consumption of liquor and tobacco, both of which may be harmful to the individual, the federal government and most states levy heavy excise taxes on these products.

e. To battle recession and spur economic growth, Congress in several years—most recently 1986—lowered federal taxes. By reducing individual income taxes, such laws made it possible for individuals to buy more goods and services, and also provide more funds for investment. By reducing corporate income taxes, such laws make it possible for corporations to increase dividends to stockholders and to expand their capital investment programs.

f. Congress may also raise taxes to reduce consumer and corporate spending and thus help check rising inflation. Moderate tax increases passed Congress in 1982 and 1984. Because higher taxes are unpopular, however, political lead-

Courtesy of Times-Picayune and Copley News Service

ers try to avoid tax increases whenever possible. Congressional leaders and the President depicted the Tax Reform Act of 1986 as "revenue neutral"—neither raising taxes nor lowering them.

FEDERAL BUDGET AND THE NATIONAL DEBT

1. Federal Budget. The President, assisted by the Office of Management and Budget, draws up the annual federal budget and submits it for approval to Congress. The budget is an estimate of income, expenditures, and the allocation of funds among the government departments and agencies for the following fiscal year (beginning October 1 and ending the following September 30).

When income exceeds expenditures, the government operates at a surplus and may use the surplus funds for debt reduction. The government is then said to have a *surplus budget.* When income equals expenditures, the government is said to have a *balanced budget.* When expenditures exceed income, the government operates at a deficit and must borrow funds, thereby increasing its debt. The government is then said to have a *deficit budget.*

2. The Federal Budget From 1931 to the Present. Since 1931 the government of the United States has had only seven surplus budgets. The major factors producing deficits since 1931 have been the depression of 1929 and subsequent recessions, World War II, the Cold War, the Korean War, the space race, the Vietnam conflict, and increased spending for human needs. Since 1931 the national debt has risen from $17 billion to over $2 trillion (two thousand billion dollars).

President Reagan, who took office in 1981, had made campaign pledges to increase spending for national defense while balancing the budget through cuts in spending for social services. The Reagan administration carried out the largest peacetime military buildup in United States history. The defense budget rose from $170.7 billion in 1981 to $290 billion in 1987. The government also made sharp cuts in social programs such as welfare, Medicaid, food stamps, student loans, and rental assistance. Nonetheless, domestic spending also continued to grow. As a result, rather than cutting deficits, President Reagan presided over the biggest budget deficits in the nation's history—reaching over $200 billion in 1986 and adding a total of $1 trillion to the national debt over the first six years of the Reagan presidency.

3. Efforts to Reduce Federal Budget Deficits. In the 1980s, as the federal debt mounted above $2 trillion, Americans became concerned that continued federal budget deficits indicated serious problems. Economists warned that federal deficits contributed to inflation and high interest rates—both undermining economic prosperity. Many Americans concluded that federal spending—especially for welfare programs and defense—had ballooned out of control. Demands arose for reevaluation of government programs, tighter eligibility requirements for welfare, elimination of waste and fraud in defense contracts, and possibly transfer of some domestic programs to state and local control. Also

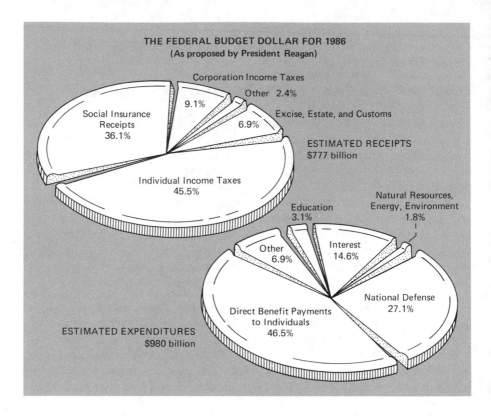

THE FEDERAL BUDGET DOLLAR FOR 1986
(As proposed by President Reagan)

Corporation Income Taxes
Other 2.4%
Social Insurance Receipts 36.1%
9.1%
Excise, Estate, and Customs
6.9%
ESTIMATED RECEIPTS
$777 billion
Individual Income Taxes 45.5%

Natural Resources, Energy, Environment 1.8%
Education 3.1%
Other 6.9%
Interest 14.6%
National Defense 27.1%
Direct Benefit Payments to Individuals 46.5%
ESTIMATED EXPENDITURES
$980 billion

voices were raised urging support for a Constitutional amendment to require the federal government to achieve a balanced budget each year.

The *Gramm-Rudman-Hollings Act* of 1985 tried a different approach. It set a timetable for step-by-step reductions in the budget deficit, beginning with a deficit ceiling of $148 billion in 1987 and reaching zero deficit in 1991. The act provided for automatic across-the-board spending reductions in the event that Congress failed to meet the deficit-reduction targets each year through legislation. However, the Supreme Court ruled in 1986 that the act's mechanism for automatic cuts by the controller general violated the Constitutional separation of powers. The Court's ruling left the main parts of the act in effect, but returned to Congress the politically unpopular task of actually making the "automatic" spending cuts.

4. Dispute Over Deficit Spending and the Mounting National Debt

a. Arguments Against. (1) By borrowing, the present generation is shifting the burden of payment onto future generations. (2) As the national debt has mounted tremendously, it requires heavy interest payments—about $150 billion annually, or about 18 percent of our current budget expenditures. (3) The government is setting the American people a poor example by living beyond its means and constantly borrowing. (4) By its deficit financing, the government pumps additional money into the economy and furthers inflation. If inflation is to be kept under control, the government must move toward a balanced budget. (5) By showing neither the ability nor the desire to restrain the rising national debt, the government is risking the loss of confidence in its financial stability.

b. Arguments For. (1) Future generations will benefit from past expenditures—to win World War II, contain aggressive communism, establish national parks, combat pollution, and construct public roads and buildings. Therefore, future Americans should bear part of the cost. (2) Individuals are accustomed to borrowing money or paying on time for a car, or a house, or appliances. They do not feel it is financially unhealthy to be in debt. (3) The American people have rejected the alternatives to deficit spending: taxation increased to intolerable levels or reduction of essential government services. (4) By selling small-denomination bonds to average citizens, the government encourages thrift and gives many people a personal interest in public finance. (5) By borrowing and incurring budget deficits during periods of depression, the government puts funds into the economy. Government spending stimulates production and creates jobs, thereby helping to improve economic conditions. (6) Although the national debt has increased to more than $2 trillion, as a percent of our gross national product (GNP) the debt has decreased from 145 percent at the end of World War II to the recent figure of 50 percent.

c. Conclusions. Most Americans agree that the government should (1) reduce the cost of government by eliminating waste, duplication, and red tape, (2) maintain essential domestic services and social programs, and (3) use the higher tax collections of prosperous years to achieve some debt reduction.

————————— MULTIPLE-CHOICE QUESTIONS —————————

1. Which is *not* a characteristic of business depressions? (a) decline in employment (b) increase in government spending for relief (c) increase in bank loans (d) decline in imports.

2. Which was an important factor contributing to the Great Depression of 1929? (a) unsound expansion of credit (b) large military expenditures (c) increased importation of foreign goods (d) government restrictions on business activity.

3. The decline in the relative purchasing power of farmers and industrial workers in the 1920s contributed to the depression of 1929 because this decline (a) led to strikes and farm agitation (b) led to a decline in the debtor class (c) kept a close balance between production and consumption (d) limited the domestic market for industry's products.

4. Which was a significant result of the depression of 1929? (a) elimination of the business cycle (b) establishment by the federal government of certain safeguards against depression (c) failure of the Republican party to win the Presidency since then (d) sharp increase in the proportion of Americans engaged in agriculture.

5. Responsibility for maintaining a healthy economic system in the United States is (a) centralized under the director of the budget (b) left to private industry

(c) accepted as a function of the federal government (d) delegated entirely to the Federal Reserve System.

6. The President's Council of Economic Advisers is responsible for (a) preparing the budget (b) analyzing economic conditions (c) reviewing the work of the independent agencies (d) improving the efficiency of government operations.

7. According to many economists, which action by the federal government would contribute the most to the control of inflation? (a) increasing government spending (b) lowering the social security tax (c) cutting federal spending while increasing taxes (d) encouraging foreign investments in the United States.

8. When Congress authorizes a reduction in the federal income tax rate, it is generally trying to (a) stabilize prices (b) balance the federal budget (c) increase consumer spending (d) decrease defense spending.

9. The term "built-in stabilizer" refers to government action designed to (a) reduce the possibility of an economic crisis (b) increase government control over banks (c) maintain a balanced budget (d) equalize the tax burden.

10. Which would be the most valid argument for reducing federal income tax rates despite a deficit budget? (a) Purchasing power will be increased, the economy will be stimulated, and income tax receipts will rise. (b) Those members of Congress supporting the tax cut will benefit politically. (c) Business executives will invest less, and overproduction will be reduced. (d) Deficit financing will lower the price level and therefore increase consumption.

11. The Federal Reserve System helps to stabilize the economy of the United States by (a) preparing the federal budget (b) insuring deposits in savings banks (c) chartering new banks (d) controlling the credit activities of member banks.

12. If the Federal Reserve System wished to cut down on the loans made by member banks, it could (a) lower the margin requirement (b) lower the discount rate (c) raise the reserve ratio (d) order all loans stopped.

13. The term "open-market operations" refers mainly to the (a) speculation in stocks by members of the stock exchange (b) purchase and sale of government securities by the Federal Reserve Banks (c) making of loans by the Federal Reserve to its member banks (d) regulation of the margin requirement by the Federal Reserve Board.

14. When the Federal Reserve Board of Governors raises the margin requirement, it is attempting to (a) decrease the reserves of member banks (b) promote consumer spending (c) discourage excessive speculation in securities (d) stimulate a sluggish stock market.

15. Which theory of taxation is the basis for requiring individuals to pay higher tax rates on higher incomes? (a) stake in society (b) benefits received (c) ability to pay (d) automatic stabilization.

16. A bridge toll is based upon the taxation principle of (a) ability to pay (b) benefits received (c) controlling consumption (d) regulating business.

17. Which is considered a good example of a progressive tax? (a) a sales tax (b) an excise tax (c) a real estate tax (d) an income tax.

18. In the United States, which government action to deal with unemployment and economic depression would most likely be favored by large corporations? (a) establishing a federal public works program (b) reducing the supply of money and credit (c) increasing tax credits for investments (d) raising the minimum wage.

19. Which statement best explains why war may be a major cause of inflation? (a) Foreigners decline to buy products from countries at war and as a result people lose jobs. (b) War goods compete for production with consumer goods, creating a decrease in the amount of products for consumption. (c) Valuable labor is lost as

the military drafts workers for the war effort. (d) People spend less money because they do not have confidence.

20. Which pairs the major source of revenue of the federal government with the major source of revenue of local governments in the United States? (a) excise taxes—sales taxes (b) tariffs—inheritance taxes (c) employment taxes—corporation taxes (d) income taxes—property taxes.

21. The federal government obtains the greatest percentage of its revenue from (a) personal income taxes (b) corporate income taxes (c) import taxes (d) excise taxes.

22. Which is a consequence of regressive taxes such as sales taxes? (a) The poor benefit at the expense of the wealthy. (b) Middle-income people pay the least tax. (c) No one pays taxes on necessities. (d) The wealthy pay a smaller proportion of their income as taxes than do the poor.

23. A federal budget represents a (a) legal limit on spending for the fiscal year (b) program to pay the national debt (c) plan for spending accompanied by an indication of sources of income to meet these expenditures (d) request by Congress for funds from the Treasury.

24. Which item in the federal budget costs the American taxpayer the most money? (a) interest payments on the national debt (b) national defense (c) direct benefit payments to individuals (d) salaries of civil service employees.

———————————————— **ESSAY QUESTIONS** ————————————————

1. The following have been used by the federal government to help prevent or control depression: (a) public works projects (b) minimum wage laws (c) parity payments to farmers (d) the Federal Reserve Board's control over the volume of money and credit (e) unemployment insurance (f) lower income taxes. For each item, (1) state which cause of depression it is designed to prevent or control and (2) explain how it is expected to work.

2. The business cycle has been a characteristic of economic life in the United States. (a) Name one phase of the business cycle and describe the characteristic features of that phase. (b) Explain two controls by which the Federal Reserve Board attempts to stabilize the economy. (c) In what phase of the business cycle is the United States at the present time? Present two evidences to support your opinion.

3. (a) Give one reason for the increase in expenditures by local governments and give one different reason for the increase in expenditures by the federal government. (b) Give one argument for and one argument against a reduction of the corporate income tax at the present time. (c) Give one argument for and one argument against the statement that the size of our present national debt is a danger to our economy.

4. Give one reason to explain why you would agree or disagree with each of the following statements: (a) The budget of a local government generally reflects the economic and social goals of the community. (b) Cuts in personal income taxes will increase the gross national product. (c) The growth of the national debt has been a stimulus to the economy. (d) All state banks should be compelled to join the Federal Reserve System. (e) The automatic stabilizers built into our economic system since 1933 will prevent any severe depression. (f) the increase in government expenditures—federal, state, and local—must come to a halt. (g) Government efforts to halt a recession are much more popular than government efforts to halt runaway inflation.

5. Inflation has become a major economic problem in the United States. (*a*) Explain what is meant by the term *inflation*. (*b*) During which phase of the business cycle is inflation most likely to occur? Defend your answer. (*c*) Select *one* item from each of the three following groups. For each item selected, discuss how it could play a role in the struggle to control inflation: (1) strong labor unions or large corporations (2) defense expenditures or social welfare programs (3) government tax policy or Federal Reserve credit policy.

PART 6. Workers Struggle for an Increased Share of the National Income

THE INDUSTRIAL REVOLUTION CREATES LABOR PROBLEMS

With the factory system, workers became dependent for their livelihood upon factory owners. In the early years of the Industrial Revolution, employers (1) paid workers low wages for long hours, (2) employed women and children, (3) introduced machines that displaced skilled workers and could be run by unskilled ones, (4) compelled workers to conform to the speed of the machines, and (5) maintained unsafe, unsanitary, and badly lighted factories.

WORKERS TURN TO UNIONS—COLLECTIVE BARGAINING

Workers desired to improve labor conditions. They soon found that by individual bargaining, that is, by appealing singly to the employer, they could not very well improve conditions. The individual could be discharged by the employer without seriously affecting production.

Workers came to realize that they would be in a stronger position by *collective bargaining,* that is, by uniting as a group to make demands upon the employer. Under collective bargaining, workers could threaten to strike, thereby halting production and hurting the employer. In order to bargain collectively, workers formed labor unions.

LABOR UNIONS AFTER THE CIVIL WAR

In the post-Civil War era, workers faced large, wealthy, national corporations employing thousands of workers. To win concessions from these powerful employers, workers turned to strikes and formed nationwide labor organizations.

KNIGHTS OF LABOR

1. Structure and Early Successes. Organized by *Uriah S. Stephens* in 1869, the Knights of Labor admitted all workers, both skilled and unskilled. Despite differences in occupation and skill, all workers in an area became members of the same local chapter.

Under *Terence V. Powderly* as "Grand Master Workman," the Knights in the 1880s urged an eight-hour day, the abolition of child labor, and various other political reforms. Although Powderly personally frowned upon strikes, the Knights of Labor won several important industrial battles and by 1886 reached their peak membership of over 700,000. Thereafter, the Knights declined in power and by 1895 had virtually disappeared.

2. Reasons for Decline

a. Unsuccessful Strikes. Beginning in 1886 the Knights lost several important strikes that were called without adequate preparation and finances.

b. Admission of Unskilled Workers. Unskilled members of the Knights of Labor who went on strike could be replaced easily. Also, workers in local chapters lacked common economic interests, and skilled members were unwilling to strike in support of the unskilled.

c. Haymarket Affair (1886). When Chicago strikers, demonstrating for an eight-hour day, were brutally treated by the police, the workers organized a protest meeting in Haymarket Square. Someone, unidentified to this day, threw a bomb at the police, killing seven people and wounding more than sixty. Eight radicals were arrested, tried, and found guilty of murder. Although the Knights of Labor condemned the Haymarket Square bombing, public opinion wrongly identified organized labor with violence.

John P. Altgeld, newly elected governor of Illinois, in 1893 reviewed the case. He pardoned the three convicted men still alive, believing that their trial had been unfair and that the evidence pointed to their innocence.

AMERICAN FEDERATION OF LABOR (A.F. of L.)

1. Aims and Structure. Organized by *Samuel Gompers* in 1881, the American Federation of Labor shunned political crusades. It emphasized "bread and butter" unionism: the furthering of the economic well-being of its members.

Gompers' organizational policies made the A.F. of L. more successful than the Knights of Labor. (a) The A.F. of L. admitted mostly skilled workers. They could strike with greater hope of success than could the unskilled members of the Knights. (b) The A.F. of L. organized workers into separate *craft unions.* A craft, or trade, union is limited to workers of a particular skill; for example, a carpenter and a plumber, although both construction workers, would belong to different unions. By combining workers with the same economic interests, A.F. of L. craft unions could serve their members more effectively than the Knights' local chapters.

2. Significant Early Strikes

a. Homestead Steel Strike (1892). Workers at the Carnegie Steel Company in Homestead, Pennsylvania, belonged to an A.F. of L. union. They went out on strike to protest a reduction in wages. The workers fought a bloody battle with 300 Pinkerton detectives hired by the company to guard the plant and help break the strike. To prevent further violence, the governor of Pennsylvania sent in the state militia. Eventually, the union's resources were exhausted, and the strike collapsed.

b. Anthracite Coal Strike (1902). The United Mine Workers, an A.F. of L. union, went on strike for union recognition, shorter hours, and higher wages. As winter approached, President Theodore Roosevelt summoned both sides to the White House, but the mine owners stubbornly rejected the union's offer to have the dispute arbitrated. The President then threatened to seize the mines, whereupon the owners agreed to accept a Presidential arbitration commission. The commission awarded the workers a wage increase and a nine-hour day, but denied them union recognition.

By using Presidential powers to settle a labor-management dispute, Theodore Roosevelt set a precedent and became known as a friend of labor.

3. Growth. Despite occasional setbacks, the A.F. of L. prospered. Its membership increased from 100,000 in 1890 to 4 million in 1920 and almost 11 million in 1955. The A.F. of L. faced difficult times during the prosperous 1920s and the early years of the 1929 depression. It experienced great growth during World War I, the New Deal Era, and World War II. In the 1950s the A.F. of L. consisted of over 100 member unions. Almost all were craft unions, such as the International Association of Machinists, the United Brotherhood of Carpenters and Joiners, and the American Federation of Musicians.

4. Leaders. Samuel Gompers, an immigrant from England and a member of the Cigar Makers' Union, organized the A.F. of L. and served as its president for some 40 years. A practical man who rejected radicalism, Gompers urged labor to benefit from a capitalist economy by forming strong unions and gaining high wages. His successor, *William Green,* who served from 1924 to 1952, continued Gompers' emphasis on craft unionism. Green was succeeded by *George Meany,* who later merged the A.F. of L. with the Congress of Industrial Organizations.

CONGRESS OF INDUSTRIAL ORGANIZATIONS (C.I.O.)

1. Industrial Unionism. An industrial union consists of all workers— skilled, semiskilled, and unskilled—in a given industry. In 1935 a small group of A.F. of L. leaders, who headed not craft but industrial unions, urged the expansion of industrial unionism. The most notable of these leaders was the United Mine Workers' head, *John L. Lewis.* He condemned the A.F. of L. for its neglect of the many semiskilled and unskilled workers in the expanding mass production industries.

2. Development of a New Nationwide Organization. Industrial union leaders formed the *Committee for Industrial Organization* and unionized the workers at leading mass-production companies. To organize the workers, the C.I.O. utilized a new weapon, the sit-down strike. The employees not only refused to work, but in addition refused to leave the factories, thereby preventing the companies from operating with strikebreakers. By 1939, when the Supreme

Court declared the sit-down strike illegal, C.I.O. unions had won recognition in the automobile, steel, rubber, oil-refining, and textile industries.

The C.I.O., with its large membership, represented a threat to the craft unions' control of the A.F. of L. Consequently, the A.F. of L. suspended the industrial unions and ordered the dissolution of their committee. Instead, in 1938, the industrial unions established their own nationwide organization, the *Congress of Industrial Organizations.*

3. Growth. In the 1950s the C.I.O. had almost 5 million members in over 40 member unions, mostly industrial, such as the United Steel Workers and the United Automobile Workers.

4. Leaders. The first president of the C.I.O. was John L. Lewis. He spurred organizational drives and fought to keep the C.I.O. free of Communist influence. Lewis' policies were continued by both subsequent heads of the C.I.O.: *Philip Murray* (1940–1952) and *Walter Reuther* (1952–1955).

AMERICAN FEDERATION OF LABOR AND CONGRESS OF INDUSTRIAL ORGANIZATIONS (AFL-CIO)

1. Reasons for Unity. In 1955 the A.F. of L. and the C.I.O. merged to form a single organization, thereby ending their 20-year split. This merger was the work chiefly of a new generation of labor leaders, especially George Meany, president of the A.F. of L., and Walter Reuther, president of the C.I.O. These labor leaders expected that a unified labor movement would (*a*) strengthen labor's influence nationally, and (*b*) spur union harmony by preventing membership raids and jurisdictional strikes.

2. Structure. (*a*) The AFL-CIO consists of about 94 affiliated unions with a total membership of some 14.3 million workers. (*b*) It is governed by an executive council composed of the AFL-CIO president, a secretary-treasurer, and 33 vice presidents. (*c*) Its activities are financed by taxing each affiliated union a small monthly amount per member. (*d*) Its national headquarters are in Washington, D.C.

3. Leaders. George Meany was unanimously elected first president of the AFL-CIO. In 1979, after 24 years as "Mr. Labor," Meany retired. *Lane Kirkland,* formerly the secretary-treasurer, was unanimously elected second AFL-CIO president. He immediately called upon all nonmember unions to join the labor federation.

INDEPENDENT UNIONS NOT AFFILIATED WITH THE AFL-CIO

(1) The *United Mine Workers,* originally affiliated with the A.F. of L., helped form the C.I.O., then returned to the A.F. of L., and later became independent. (2) A number of unions were expelled from the C.I.O. in 1949–1950 on the

charge of Communist domination. (3) The 90,000-member *United Transportation Union,* the largest union of railroad employees, withdrew from the AFL-CIO in 1986 in a dispute over recruitment of new members. However, many other railway employees belong to such AFL-CIO affiliates as the *Transport Workers Union* and the *Brotherhood of Railway and Airline Clerks.* (4) The *National Education Association,* representing some 1.6 million teachers and other educators, is another major independent union. Other teachers belong to an AFL-CIO affiliate, the 460,000-member *American Federation of Teachers.*

These and other independent unions have a total membership of 2 million persons.

UNORGANIZED WORKERS: THE GREAT MAJORITY

1. Extent. The American civilian labor force numbers some 116 million workers, 17.3 million of whom are union members. Among employed workers less than 19 percent belong to unions (down from 24.1 percent in 1979). The vast majority of American workers are unorganized.

2. Reasons

a. Occupational Factors. Self-employed workers, such as small storekeepers and many equipment repairers, are both workers and owners. Government employees enjoy civil service status, which provides job security, regular pay increases, sick leave, and retirement benefits. Agricultural laborers and household workers are often transient workers who go from one employer to the next. Professionals, such as doctors, lawyers, accountants, and engineers, are highly trained, well-paid workers who generally consider unions unbecoming to professional dignity. Many professional groups have societies capable of serving functions similar to those of unions. Many workers are entering new, rapidly growing nonunionized service and technical fields. These workers operate high-technology computer and telecommunications equipment and possess sophisticated skills that do not conform to the blue-collar union image.

b. Satisfactory Conditions. Workers feel no need of unions when they have high wages and good working conditions. They may owe such good conditions to general economic prosperity, to the spread of union-won benefits to nonunion workers, and to the deliberate policy followed by certain employers to keep workers from joining unions. An employer may try to discourage unionization by granting workers benefits such as profit-sharing plans, medical and hospital care, pensions, and recreational facilities. This policy is called *welfare capitalism.*

c. Antiunion Sentiment. Some employers vigorously combat union organizational drives. This attitude prevails among large commercial farmers in the West and among industrialists in the Deep South.

d. Restrictive Union Practices. To assure employment and decent wages to their present members, some unions severely restrict the admittance of new members. The "father-and-son" unions, especially in the building and printing trades, limit new admissions to close relatives of present members.

GOALS OF MANAGEMENT AND LABOR

1. Common Goals. To make possible higher dividends for stockholders and higher wages for workers, management and labor both favor (a) a prosperous company with increasing productivity, (b) an expanding economy with rising living standards, and (c) our system of free enterprise under government regulation. Unlike European labor unions, which have frequently supported Socialist and Communist policies, organized American labor has remained true to Gompers' teachings that labor should benefit from capitalism. Most American workers have rejected anticapitalist organizations, such as the American Communist party.

2. Goals of Management. Industrialists have consistently aimed at (a) managing their companies with as little interference from unions as possible, (b) increasing productivity by instituting more efficient methods and utilizing labor-saving machinery, (c) requiring unions and workers to live up to the terms of their labor contract, (d) hiring, promoting, and firing workers as required by company needs, and (e) maintaining an *open shop*. In theory, an open shop permits an employer to hire both union and nonunion workers; in practice, most open-shop companies hire nonunion workers only.

3. Goals of Labor Unions

a. Traditional Goals. Unions have worked for (1) recognition of the union as the sole bargaining agent of the workers, (2) higher wages and shorter hours, (3) good working conditions, including safety devices on machinery and well-lighted, well-ventilated factories, (4) job security, including seniority to enable older workers to gain promotions and avoid layoffs, and also including a union voice regarding the introduction of laborsaving machinery, (5) a *union label* to identify union-made products, thus enabling consumers to support unions by buying only goods with this label, (6) the *checkoff* system, which requires an employer to deduct union dues from the workers' pay and forward the lump sum to the union, and (7) union security, through either the *union shop* or the *closed shop*. In a union shop the employer may hire union or nonunion workers, but all workers must join the union within a specified time or lose their jobs. In a closed shop the employer may hire only workers who are already union members. (The closed shop was outlawed by the Taft-Hartley Act.)

b. More Recent Goals. Unions have also sought (1) the *guaranteed annual wage*, assuring each worker 52 weekly paychecks a year regardless of whether the employer can provide a full year's work, and (2) *fringe benefits,* including paid vacations and holidays, pay for sick leave, hospital and medical care, group life insurance, and pensions.

PEACEFUL METHODS OF SETTLING LABOR-MANAGEMENT DISPUTES

Most labor-management disputes are settled peacefully, and with little publicity, by the following methods: (1) *Collective Bargaining*. Employer and union representatives meet, negotiate directly, settle the issues, and agree to a labor contract. (2) *Mediation*. A disinterested third party, who has the confidence of both the employer and the union, brings about an acceptable agreement by inducing each side to make concessions. A staff of trained mediators is available through the *Federal Mediation and Conciliation Service*. (3) *Arbitration*. The employer and the union together agree on a neutral third party as arbitrator, to hear the dispute and hand down the decision, or *award*. The parties agree in advance to accept the arbitrator's award. (4) *Fact-Finding Board*. In strikes affecting the welfare of the nation, the President may appoint a fact-finding board to hear the dispute and hand down a recommendation. Although the board's recommendation is not binding, the disputing parties usually accept it for fear of adverse public opinion. (The fact-finding method is sometimes used by governors and mayors to settle local labor disputes.)

COSTS OF INDUSTRIAL WARFARE

A small number of labor-management disputes erupt into industrial battles, frequently accompanied by much publicity. Industrial warfare causes hardship. (1) Employers suffer halted production, decreased profits, and unfavorable publicity. (2) Workers are unemployed and lose income while their union suffers unfavorable publicity. (3) Consumers endure a shortage of products or a loss of services. (4) The government experiences a loss of tax revenues and sometimes a scarcity of goods or services essential to the national welfare.

WEAPONS OF UNIONS

(1) *Strike*. Employees refuse to work until the employer agrees to a labor contract acceptable to the union. (2) *Strike Fund*. This money serves to sustain union members and pay for union activities during a strike. (3) *Picketing*. Workers parade outside the strikebound premises. They seek to enlist public support and to deter strikebreakers from taking their jobs. (4) *Boycott*. Workers request consumers not to patronize the strikebound company. (5) *Publicity*. Unions appeal for public support through mass demonstrations, newspapers, radio, and television.

WEAPONS OF EMPLOYERS

(1) *Strikebreakers*. To fill the jobs of strikers, the employer hires other workers, called strikebreakers or, derogatorily, *scabs*. (2) *Financial Resources*. When a strike halts production and curtails business income, most corporations have

Morris for Wide World Photos

Nonprofit enterprise.

How are strikes costly to the worker, the employer, the public, and the government? What are the other methods of settling labor-management disputes?

sufficient financial reserves to meet their continuing costs and to pay dividends to stockholders. (3) *Lockout.* The employer keeps the workers from their jobs until the union agrees to a labor contract acceptable to management. (4) *Injunction.* Upon the request of either a company or the federal government, a court may issue an order, called an *injunction.* It forbids the union to strike, picket, or boycott, on the ground that such union action may damage the employer unfairly or harm the national welfare. Violators of the injunction are liable to fine or imprisonment, or both, for *contempt of court.* (For injunction provisions in federal laws, check the Index for the 1932 Norris–La Guardia Act and the 1947 Taft-Hartley Act.) (5) *Publicity.* Employers present their case to the public through the mass media.

LABOR AND POLITICAL ACTION

1. Early Efforts. In the 1880s Samuel Gompers urged members of the A.F. of L. to work within the two major parties by punishing enemies and rewarding friends. The A.F. of L. did so by endorsing prolabor candidates regardless of party label. However, once elected, these candidates did little to help unions. They owed their election chiefly to financial contributors and political leaders, and felt little obligation to organized labor.

2. Labor Disputes Spur Political Activity

a. Pullman Strike (1894). Workers at the Pullman car plant near Chicago went on strike to protest wage cuts of up to 40 percent, which were not accompanied by rent reductions in the company-owned town. These workers belonged to the American Railway Union, an industrywide union led by *Eugene V. Debs.* To support the strikers, railroad employees refused to handle trains with Pullman cars. Most railroad transportation out of Chicago halted.

Attorney General *Richard Olney,* formerly a railroad lawyer, acted to break the strike. Using the Sherman Antitrust Act, he secured an injunction against the union as a "conspiracy in restraint of trade." When Debs violated the injunction by continuing the strike, he was jailed for contempt of court. President Cleveland meanwhile sent federal troops to Chicago, ostensibly to assure delivery of the United States mail. Cleveland's action was protested as unnecessary by Illinois governor Altgeld. The arrival of federal troops led to mob protests and violence. With troops on the scene and Debs in jail, the Pullman strike collapsed. It marked the first effective use of the injunction against a labor union.

b. Danbury Hatters Strike (1902). Striking workers of the Loewe Hat Company in Danbury, Connecticut, organized a successful boycott of the company's products. The union and its members were sued by the company, which claimed the boycott was a "conspiracy in restraint of trade" violating the Sherman Antitrust Act. In a Supreme Court decision in 1908, the union and its members were found guilty and ordered to pay burdensome cash damages.

c. Results. The Pullman and the Danbury Hatters strikes convinced labor leaders that they had to secure legislation to keep the injunction and the antitrust law from being used against unions. Labor became increasingly active in political campaigns and in 1914 gained some relief when Congress passed the Clayton Antitrust Act (see below).

3. More Recently: Considerable Political Activity. In 1943 the C.I.O. organized the *Political Action Committee (PAC).* It not only endorsed candidates but fought to secure nominations for friends of labor and contributed campaign funds. The PAC also engaged in the hard work of politics: ringing doorbells, printing literature, holding rallies, providing speakers, and getting out the prolabor vote. Following the merger of the A.F. of L. and the C.I.O. in 1955, the AFL-CIO assigned its political efforts to the *Committee on Political Education (COPE).*

FEDERAL LEGISLATION AIDS LABOR: EARLY 20TH CENTURY

1. Department of Labor (1913). Congress created a separate Department of Labor to "foster, promote, and develop the welfare of the wage earners of the United States." The department focuses on labor as it gathers statistics, studies problems, publishes periodicals and pamphlets, and enforces most federal labor laws.

2. Clayton Antitrust Act (1914). In addition to its provisions against monopolistic business practices, the act states that labor is not a commodity and, therefore, legitimate union activities are not subject to antitrust laws. The act also prohibits the use of federal injunctions in labor disputes "unless necessary to prevent irreparable injury" and guarantees a trial by jury to persons accused of contempt of court for violating an injunction.

Samuel Gompers hailed the Clayton Act as the worker's "Magna Carta," for the act designed to protect labor. In practice, the act helped unions very little against injunctions. The courts applied the "irreparable injury" clause to grant injunctions halting many strikes and boycotts.

3. Adamson Act (1916). To head off a threatened railroad strike, this act legislated an eight-hour day for railroad employees.

4. Norris–La Guardia Act (1932). (a) This act prohibited federal courts from granting injunctions against workers who engaged in strikes, boycotts, or peaceful picketing. (b) It made the yellow-dog contract unenforceable. Under such a contract, workers seeking employment had to state that they were not union members and would not join a union during their employment.

FEDERAL LEGISLATION AIDS LABOR: THE NEW DEAL

Labor began an era of great gains under the New Deal. Having strongly supported Franklin D. Roosevelt for President, unions now enjoyed his support. Also, as a result of the depression, public opinion was increasingly sympathetic to workers' needs.

1. National Industrial Recovery Act (1933). This act called for National Recovery Administration (NRA) codes of fair competition whose labor provisions would prohibit child labor and set maximum hours and minimum wages. Section 7a of the NIRA guaranteed workers the right to "organize and bargain collectively through representatives of their own choosing."

To evade Section 7a, however, many employers created and dominated *company unions.* The employer coerced the workers into joining the company union and thus deterred them from joining a union of their own choice. In 1935 the Supreme Court declared the NIRA unconstitutional. (For reasons, check the Index.)

2. Wagner (National Labor Relations) Act (1935). This act replaced the defunct Section 7a of the NIRA. The Wagner Act forbade employers to (a) interfere with labor's right to organize, (b) interfere in the operation of unions, (c) use *blacklists* of active union members to be denied jobs as "trouble-makers," (d) hire labor spies to infiltrate unions and secure confidential information about their members and plans, (e) organize company unions, (f) discriminate against union members, and (g) refuse to bargain collectively with employees. It created the *National Labor Relations Board* (NLRB) to enforce these prohibitions and to hold elections among the workers to determine their choice of a union, if any.

By guaranteeing collective bargaining, the Wagner Act was largely responsible for the subsequent growth in legitimate union membership. From 1935 to 1941 more than 300 company unions were dissolved, and the number of workers in genuine unions grew from under 4 million to over 10 million. Employer groups protested that labor received too much power, without restrictions, by the Wagner Act. (Its provisions were severely modified by the 1947 Taft-Hartley Act. Check the Index.)

3. Social Security Act (1935). This act began as a modest insurance program to combat economic insecurity due to unemployment and old age. Proponents of Social Security argued that it was self-financing and humanitarian, protecting individuals against hazards over which they had little control. Opponents argued that it was "socialistic," substituting government assistance for private initiative, and that it weakened the individuals' will to work.

As Social Security became widely accepted, the law was amended many times to extend coverage, increase benefits, and provide the aged with medical care.

    a. *Old-Age and Survivors Insurance (OASI).* Check the Index.

    b. *Unemployment Insurance.* The 1935 Social Security Act authorized the federal government to levy a payroll tax on employers with four or more workers and to grant each state 90 percent of the money collected within its borders, provided that the state establish a satisfactory unemployment insurance system. Within two years every state had done so.

Systems of unemployment insurance vary from state to state. They cover few workers in agriculture but most workers in industry. In general, the state systems grant an unemployed worker a weekly benefit, calculated according to previous earnings and limited to a certain number of weeks. The worker must report regularly to a State Employment Office, which lists job openings and helps the unemployed person find suitable work.

    c. *Medicare for the Aged.* Check the Index.

4. Fair Labor Standards (Wages and Hours) Act (1938) This act replaced the defunct NRA codes in regard to fair labor standards. For most workers in interstate commerce, it (a) set a minimum wage of 40 cents per hour and a workweek of 40 hours, (b) required payment for overtime (beyond 40 hours) at the rate of time and a half, and (c) prohibited most child labor.

This act has been revised many times to keep up with the rising cost of living.

The latest revision raised the hourly minimum to $3.35. What effect may the minimum wage have on the hiring of unskilled workers? of youthful workers?

STATE LEGISLATION AIDS LABOR

Most industrial states improved the conditions of labor by requiring (1) *worker's compensation* insurance to protect workers in case of occupational disease or job accident, (2) *factory inspection* to ensure proper sanitation, sufficient lighting, and safety devices on dangerous machinery, (3) *protection of women and children* to limit their hours of work and keep them from hazardous occupations, and (4) *compulsory education* to keep children in school and out of the labor market.

LABOR AND THE WORLD WAR II ERA

1. No-Strike Pledge. Realizing that victory depended upon an ever-increasing supply of the implements of war, both the A.F. of L. and the C.I.O. pledged a policy of no strikes. To settle labor disputes peacefully, the government established the *War Labor Board* (WLB). During the war the time lost due to walkouts, mostly not union-called, was less than one percent.

2. Labor Shortages. The demands of the armed forces for personnel and of industry for workers resulted in labor shortages. The government established the *War Manpower Commission* to shift workers from nonessential to essential industries, to "freeze" workers in essential industries, and to train new workers, especially women, for jobs in defense industries.

3. Strikes in the Immediate Postwar Era. Now free of their no-strike pledge, labor unions began walkouts for higher wages. Unions pointed out that (a) take-home pay was sharply reduced by the loss of overtime, (b) the purchasing power of the dollar was cut by inflation, and (c) business profits were at an all-time high.

When long strikes occurred in major industries, unions aroused public resentment. Unions were blamed for delaying the production of long-awaited consumer goods and feeding the forces of inflation.

CRITICISMS OF LABOR UNIONS IN THE POSTWAR ERA

1. Limits Upon Union Membership. Some unions restricted the admission of new members, often accepting only relatives of current members, charging high initiation fees, and discriminating against blacks and other minority applicants. These practices prevented new workers from competing with union members for jobs in closed-shop industries.

2. Opposition to Laborsaving Machinery. Some unions fought the introduction of automated machinery, claiming that such machines would decrease the number of jobs.

3. Featherbedding. Some unions forced employers to retain unneeded help—a practice called *featherbedding.* For example, the railroad brotherhoods compelled the railroads to keep coal-stoking firemen on the trains even though no coal was used in oil-burning diesel locomotives.

4. Lack of Union Responsibility. Some unions failed to keep their members from violating the union's contract with the employer. One such violation was the *wildcat strike*—a spontaneous walkout by workers without the approval of their union.

5. Lack of Financial Statements. Some unions did not publish financial statements. Their members and the general public had no knowledge of the unions' income and expenditures.

6. Lack of Union Democracy. Some unions were controlled by small groups of insiders. Rank-and-file members, sometimes through indifference and sometimes through fear, had little say in union affairs.

7. Racketeer Influence. Some unions were controlled by racketeers. They treated union funds as their own and paid themselves excessive salaries. They employed strong-arm methods to suppress critics within the union and to force the union upon employers. In return for personal favors, they granted employers lenient terms in "sweetheart" labor contracts.

8. Communist Influence. Especially during the depression years of the 1930s, Communists worked hard to gain control of the American labor movement. However, only a few unions fell under Communist leadership.

9. Jurisdictional Strikes. Such a strike came about when two unions competed for control of the same workers. For example, the carpenters' union and the stagehands' union each claimed jurisdiction over workers building movie sets. In the ensuing strike the employer was caught in the middle and suffered from the interruption of production.

TAFT-HARTLEY (LABOR-MANAGEMENT RELATIONS) ACT (1947)

Partly because of the previous criticisms of labor unions, the Republican-controlled Congress in 1947 passed the *Taft-Hartley Act.* President Truman vetoed the bill, but a combination of Republicans and southern Democrats overrode the veto. The Taft-Hartley Act provided as follows:

1. Reaffirmed Collective Bargaining. The law reaffirmed the right of workers to organize and bargain collectively.

2. Outlawed the Closed Shop. The law prohibited the closed shop but permitted the union shop, unless contrary to state regulations. Section 14b of the Taft-Hartley Act authorized states to bar the union shop by passing "right-to-work" laws. (Check the Index.)

3. Prohibited Unfair Union Practices. The law prohibited unions from (a) refusing to bargain collectively with employers, (b) engaging in a jurisdictional strike, (c) engaging in a *secondary boycott,* an action against a business dealing with a firm involved in a labor dispute (for example, when a union requests the public not to buy from a retail store that sells goods of a manufacturer whose workers are on strike), (d) protecting jobs by certain forms of featherbedding, (e) charging excessive initiation fees, (f) contributing funds to candidates for federal office, and (g) denying responsibility for contract violations, especially wildcat strikes.

4. Established Requirements for Unions. The law required unions to file with the government (a) annual financial reports and (b) affidavits that union officials were not members of the Communist party.

5. Established New Regulations for Strikes. (a) Sixty-Day "Cooling-Off" Period. The law required unions to notify employers of intent to strike and then wait 60 days. (b) Eighty-Day Temporary Injunction. In strikes affecting the national welfare, the law empowered the federal government to secure a temporary injunction restraining the union from striking for an additional 80 days. During both the 60-day and 80-day periods, labor and management could seek peaceful settlement of their dispute.

CONTROVERSY REGARDING THE TAFT-HARTLEY ACT

1. Opposition by Unions. Most union leaders condemned the Taft-Hartley Act because they opposed (a) the abolition of the closed shop, since, under the union shop, the union had no power over hiring, (b) the right granted to the states to bar even the union shop, (c) the use of a temporary injunction, and (d) the anti-Communist oath, not required of any other segment of American society.

2. Approval by Major Corporations. Most corporate leaders hailed the Taft-Hartley Act for (a) prohibiting unfair practices by unions, (b) outlawing the closed shop and thus allowing employers to hire anyone they wanted, (c) providing a cooling-off period to encourage peaceful collective bargaining, and (d) insisting that unions and their members honor labor contracts.

3. Observations. (a) Unions continued to gain—growing in membership from 14 million in 1947 to 17 million in 1957 and winning higher wages and many fringe benefits. (b) Some states, mostly in the South, have "right-to-work" laws, outlawing the union shop. These laws, union leaders claimed, hampered unions in organizing workers. (c) Organized labor stepped up its efforts to rid itself of Communist influence. Today, in organized labor, Communist influence is at an all-time low. (d) Employers gained some relief from unfair labor practices. (e) In general, the Taft-Hartley Act brought little change into the power relationship between unions and employers.

LANDRUM-GRIFFIN (LABOR-MANAGEMENT REPORTING AND DISCLOSURE) ACT (1959)

1. Background: McClellan Senate Investigating Committee. Investigating corruption in labor unions, the McClellan Committee concentrated upon the powerful truckers' union, the *International Brotherhood of Teamsters*. Although Teamster officials were reluctant witnesses, the hearings disclosed a shocking picture of racketeering, misuse of union funds, and abuse of union power for personal advantage.

2. AFL-CIO and the Teamsters Union. Following disclosures before the McClellan Committee in 1957, the AFL-CIO acted to enforce its ethical practices code. Its executive council ordered the Teamsters to get rid of its vice president, *James Hoffa,* and other officials considered corrupt. Instead, the Teamsters elected Hoffa as president. Thereupon, the AFL-CIO expelled the Teamsters. The Teamsters increased their membership and for ten years Hoffa retained control. (In 1967 he was imprisoned for jury tampering and mail fraud.) By 1987 the Teamsters had improved their image and were readmitted to the AFL-CIO.

3. Landrum-Griffin Act. To combat corrupt union practices and to assure democracy in union affairs, Congress passed the Landrum-Griffin Act:

a. Union Elections. Union elections, by secret ballot, must be held at least every three years for local offices and every five years for national offices. Each candidate must be permitted to inspect the membership lists and have observers at the polls. Criminals convicted of serious offenses may not serve as union officials until five years after being released from prison. Communist party members may not serve as union officials until five years after leaving the party.

b. Bill of Rights. To protect members against coercion by union officials, this "bill of rights" guarantees freedom of speech and assembly, and the right to participate in union matters. No member may be disciplined by union leaders without a written statement of charges, time to prepare a defense, and a fair hearing. If these rights are violated, a union member may seek a federal court injunction against the officials of the union.

c. Financial Reports. Unions must file with the Secretary of Labor detailed financial reports, including salaries of and loans to union officials, and loans to business concerns. Union officials must report any monetary benefits received from an employer. Employers must report any loan or payment made to a union or to union officials. Persons filing reports must keep their records for five years.

d. Picketing and Secondary Boycotts. The law (1) prohibited picketing by one union for recognition if an employer has already recognized another union, and (2) strengthened prohibitions against secondary boycotts.

Supporters hailed this law as an effort to curb racketeering and safeguard the rights of union members. Many labor leaders, however, condemned this law, arguing that its (a) "bill of rights" would enable disgruntled members to obstruct legitimate union activities, (b) prohibition of picketing for recognition would prevent honest unions from ousting racketeer-controlled unions, and (c) provisions would have no effect on the Teamsters.

4. The United Mine Workers Elections (1969, 1972). Insurgent rank-and-file miners, whose leader Joseph Yablonski had been murdered, challenged the 1969 reelection of W. A. (Tony) Boyle as president of the United Mine Workers. They charged fraud and other election irregularities in violation of the Landrum-Griffin Act. Their charges were upheld by a federal court, which ordered a new union election. Held in 1972 under strict Labor Department supervision, the election enabled the insurgents to oust Boyle and elect their reform candidate. (In subsequent trials, Boyle was found guilty of instigating the murder of Yablonski.)

RECENT LABOR TRENDS AND PROBLEMS

1. Weaknesses of the AFL-CIO

a. Internal Dissension. Despite the merger of the A.F. of L. and the C.I.O. in 1955, labor has not achieved internal harmony. The AFL-CIO remains divided into two camps: the former A.F. of L. leaders are generally conservative and favor craft unionism; the former C.I.O. leaders are generally more progressive and favor industrial unionism.

In 1967 Walter Reuther, president of the United Automobile Workers, condemned the AFL-CIO for failing to extend "equal rights and equal opportunities to every American" and for failing to organize the many industrial, farm, and white-collar workers. In 1968 he led his union out of the AFL-CIO. (In 1981 the UAW, then headed by Douglas Fraser, reaffiliated.)

b. Failure to Expand Membership. In 1955 the combined membership of the AFL-CIO and independent unions totaled 17 million, or 25 percent of the labor force of 68 million. By 1980 unionized workers had increased to 22.4 million, but the total labor force had jumped to 107 million so that union members represented only 20.9 percent.

AFL-CIO membership, at a peak of 16 million in 1955, was down to 14.3 million in 1987. Despite the expectations raised by its creation, the AFL-CIO has proved unable to organize the vast majority of workers.

2. "Right-to-Work" Measures. Section 14b of the Taft-Hartley Act permitted states to adopt "right-to-work" measures prohibiting the union shop. Some 20 states, mostly in the South, have such measures that prohibit compulsory union membership by stating that no worker can be compelled to join a union in order to hold a job.

Supporters argue that "right-to-work" measures (a) protect the democratic right of workers to join or not to join a union and (b) encourage honest unionism, since workers may resign from corrupt unions without losing their jobs.

Opponents argue that "right-to-work" measures (a) weaken unionism by limiting a union's control over its members, (b) deny the democratic principle of majority rule, since a minority of workers may remain outside a union approved by a majority, and (c) enable nonunion workers to benefit from the union's efforts without paying a fair share of union costs. Labor's efforts to secure repeal of Section 14b have so far failed.

3. Problems of Wages

a. Money Wages vs. Real Wages. Unions realize that an increase in *money wages*, that is, wages measured in dollars, is often offset by rising prices, which reduce *real wages*, that is, wages measured in purchasing power. For example, if over a three-year period workers have received a wage increase of 8 percent while the cost of living has risen 15 percent, the workers are worse off than before. Since World War II, the cost of living has been steadily rising. Some unions consequently had their labor contracts include an escalator clause providing for a cost-of-living adjustment (COLA) in wages. This adjustment is made according to changes in the cost of living as indicated in the *Consumer Price Index,* which is compiled by the Department of Labor's Bureau of Labor Statistics.

b. Consumer Price Index (CPI). The CPI measures the change in the prices of goods and services as compared to prices in the base year. The CPI currently measures the prices paid by urban consumers for 400 commonly purchased goods and services—the *market basket.* Each item is weighted to reflect its relative importance in the consumer's budget. Obviously, milk, purchased every day, has a greater weight than a haircut, needed only once in several weeks. The CPI is not foolproof, for over the years: (1) a higher price may reflect an improved quality of goods, and (2) the market basket may neglect significant changes in the consumer's purchasing habits. For example, in 1983, the government revised the CPI's housing component. The Bureau of Labor Statistics stopped calculating housing costs on the basis of house prices and mortgage costs, both of which were soaring at the time. Instead, the bureau switched to a "rental equivalent"—the cost of renting a house of similar size and characteristics. This had the effect of slowing the rise in the CPI. The CPI, nevertheless, remains a highly regarded measure of the cost of living. In 1987 the CPI weights for various goods and services were revised to reflect changes in consumer spending over the previous decade.

The current CPI uses 1967 as the base year, with an index of 100. Since this base year, the CPI has recorded an almost continuous process of inflation. At the start of 1987, the CPI was about 330. This meant that the amount of goods bought for $1.00 in 1967 cost $3.30 in 1987, indicating that the dollar's purchasing power had fallen considerably.

4. Automation. Following World War II, labor became greatly concerned over automation—the use of computers and other automatic devices, chiefly electronic, to control the operation of machines. Unions knew that automation increased productivity, that is, output per worker, enabled workers to receive higher wages, provided better products at lower cost, and created new, higher-skilled jobs in the manufacture, service, and use of automatic equipment. But unions feared that automation would displace large numbers of workers. For example, in New York City alone, automatic elevators in skyscrapers replaced some 40,000 elevator operators.

Unions have responded to automation by seeking a voice, with management, in determining the introduction of automated equipment and also by seeking to provide job security for their current members.

5. Davis-Bacon Act. This 1931 law provided that construction workers on federally financed projects be paid the prevailing wages for similar work in the area. As interpreted by the Labor Department, this provision came to mean union wages. Organized labor approved this act for protecting decent wage standards. Business groups condemned this act for favoring unions, raising construction costs and furthering inflation, and denying work to nonunion help and companies.

Management's efforts to secure repeal or modification of the Davis-Bacon Act have so far failed.

6. Problems of Strikes Affecting the Public Welfare. Following World War II, the government and the public became increasingly concerned over labor-mangement disputes affecting national security and the public welfare. These included strikes by steelworkers, dock workers, airline mechanics, and railroad employees. Several times, the government employed the 80-day Taft-Hartley injunction, but its use proved to be of questionable effectiveness.

Some members of Congress proposed legislation to (a) outlaw industrywide strikes and compel unions to deal with only one employer at a time, (b) require labor and management to accept compulsory arbitration, or (c) permit the government to seize and operate an essential industry involved in a strike pending a labor contract.

Unions opposed all these proposals as restrictions on their economic power. Management suspected that government arbitration would favor unions with their large blocs of votes. Management furthermore considered government seizure of plants as a threat to private ownership. The basic problem remains: How should a democratic society provide for the settlement of strikes affecting the national welfare?

7. Givebacks. In the early 1980s, unions were under pressures for concessions from previously won wages and fringe benefits—concessions generally known as *givebacks*. These pressures, which caused a considerable loss of jobs for union members, included: (a) *An ailing economy.* With two recessions coming back-to-back, unemployment among all American workers stood at 9 percent, or about 9 million persons. (b) *Foreign competition* from low-wage countries such as Brazil in South America, and the Philippines, South Korea, Japan, Taiwan, and Hong Kong in Asia. American auto industry officials claimed that their Japanese competitors—who sold millions of cars in America—paid lower wages of about $8 per hour per worker that became a per-car labor-cost

advantage of $1000 to $1500. American clothing workers' union leaders estimated that more than half of all women's and children's apparel sold in America
was imported from low-wage countries. (c) *Failing American companies.* A number of companies, unable to compete and operate profitably, went out of business, ending the jobs of thousands of workers. In addition to these pressures upon
unions to protect jobs, a number of companies demanded givebacks. The companies threatened to move and build new plants in low-wage southern and western areas of the United States, and to farm out work to and purchase supplies
from low-wage countries.

In numerous cases, unions agreed to cut back wages, forgo cost-of-living increases, and reduce paid vacations and pension benefits. Some unions made no-
strike pledges. In return, the union received the company's assurance that it
would maintain existing production facilities, provide a profit-sharing plan for
workers, and offer the union a voice in setting company policy. Do these developments indicate that unions and mangement are moving from an adversarial
relationship to a cooperative one?

──────────────── **MULTIPLE-CHOICE QUESTIONS** ────────────────

1. An important reason for the decline of the Knights of Labor was the
   (a) organization of the Socialist party (b) high cost of membership (c) conflict between skilled and unskilled workers (d) passage of antilabor laws by the government.
2. During the period 1865 to 1900, labor-management disputes were often marked
   by (a) a willingness by both sides to have the disputes arbitrated (b) violence on
   both sides (c) federal support of the strikers (d) government mediation.
3. At its beginning, the A.F. of L. aimed to (a) unite skilled and unskilled workers into
   one union (b) establish industrial unions (c) form craft unions of skilled workers
   (d) campaign actively for the election of its members to public office.
4. One provision of the Clayton Act concerning labor resulted from the (a) opposition
   of the A.F. of L. to the Taft-Hartley Act (b) failure of the Landrum-Griffin Act to
   end union racketeering (c) Supreme Court decision declaring the National Industrial Recovery Act unconstitutional (d) injunctions issued against labor under the
   Sherman Antitrust Act.
5. In the 1930s which issue caused a split within the A.F. of L. and led to the formation of an independent C.I.O.? (a) the sit-down strike (b) the reelection of Franklin
   D. Roosevelt (c) industrial unionism (d) the National Labor Relations Act.
6. The organizational principles of the Congress of Industrial Organizations reflected
   the (a) increased need for skilled workers (b) rise of mass-production industries
   (c) opposition by many labor leaders to the political involvement of the A.F. of L.
   (d) decline in union membership during the New Deal.
7. Which statement about organized labor today is true? (a) All large unions are affiliated with the AFL-CIO. (b) Unions today favor "givebacks." (c) Less than one-
   quarter of the labor force belongs to unions. (d) Craft-industrial union rivalry
   ceased with the formation of the AFL-CIO.
8. Today, which group is most completely unionized? (a) automobile workers
   (b) office workers (c) lawyers (d) farm employees.

9. The procedure by which representatives of employees deal directly with representatives of employers to determine working conditions is known as (a) arbitration (b) collective bargaining (c) injunction (d) mediation.

10. When labor and management agree in advance to settle a dispute by accepting the decision of a third party, they are relying upon (a) arbitration (b) conciliation (c) the checkoff system (d) a secondary boycott.

11. Which two practices are now forbidden? (a) lockouts and injunctions (b) yellow-dog contracts and secondary boycotts (c) secondary boycotts and strikes (d) blacklists and injunctions.

12. A system under which an employer, by agreement with the union, deducts union dues from employees' wages and turns them over to the union is known as (a) checkoff (b) collective bargaining (c) processing tax (d) transfer payment.

13. "Fringe benefits" include (a) pensions and paid vacations (b) a worker's right to refuse to join a union (c) labor practices limiting the amount of work that a union member may do (d) a guaranteed annual wage.

14. During the 20th century, federal legislation in the area of labor-management relations has most frequently been based on the Constitutional power of Congress to (a) enforce the Fourteenth Amendment (b) levy and collect taxes (c) establish lower courts (d) regulate interstate commerce.

15. The National Labor Relations Act (a) led to a rapid increase in labor union membership (b) led to a marked decline in the use of the closed shop (c) encouraged the use of injunctions by employers (d) made legal the use of strikes and picketing.

16. One purpose of the Social Security Act of 1935 was to (a) protect workers against accidents on the job (b) provide national health insurance (c) encourage states to set up unemployment insurance programs (d) establish a minimum wage for industries engaged in interstate commerce.

17. In most states, funds for unemployment insurance come from (a) appropriations by Congress (b) appropriations by the state legislature (c) contributions by the employees (d) payments by the employers.

18. The author of the quotation, "Confronted with a contracting number of unionized jobs in an expanding labor force, unions have fought one another for control of work opportunities," is probably trying to prove that (a) unemployment has decreased union strength (b) the A.F. of L. and C.I.O. should again split (c) jurisdictional strife is a major labor problem (d) unions are fighting for an expanded labor force.

19. A work stoppage called without official union approval is known as a (a) lockout (b) wildcat strike (c) sit-down strike (d) closed shop.

20. When a strike threatens the national health and safety, the Taft-Hartley Act empowers the President of the United States to (a) forbid the calling of the strike (b) request an injunction to halt the strike temporarily (c) provide for government operation of the plants threatened by the strike (d) provide for compulsory arbitration.

21. An action against an employer who uses or sells products from an establishment where the workers are on strike is called a (a) lockout (b) general strike (c) jurisdictional strike (d) secondary boycott.

22. The author of the statement, "Railroads would have fewer financial difficulties if unions would permit them to eliminate unnecessary jobs," believes that (a) unions are blocking automation (b) the closed shop is a valuable protection for labor (c) many railroads are owned by labor unions (d) featherbedding is expensive.

23. The Senate committee investigating labor racketeering acted within the Constitution by seeking to (a) destroy the principle of collective bargaining (b) provide evi-

dence for criminal action against labor racketeers (c) provide Congress with information on which to base legislation (d) force the AFL-CIO to expel the Teamsters.

24. A major purpose of the Landrum-Griffin Act was to (a) reestablish the closed shop (b) replace the injunction provisions of the Taft-Hartley Act (c) strengthen the position of the AFL-CIO (d) promote democratic operation within labor unions.

25. Organized labor opposes "right-to-work" laws because these laws (a) are contrary to the Taft-Hartley Act (b) prohibit the union shop (c) limit unemployment insurance benefits (d) restrict the right to strike.

26. "The American worker is primarily interested in real wages." This statement is valid because real wages represent the (a) minimum wages that the unions are demanding (b) amount of money the worker receives as a regular weekly wage (c) amount of money the worker takes home after taxes have been deducted (d) amount of goods and services the worker's dollars will buy.

27. The basic purpose of the Consumer Price Index is to measure the (a) amount of goods and services produced annually (b) value of stock traded daily on the New York Stock Exchange (c) relative change in the cost of living (d) productivity rate of the average worker.

28. Which situation will occur if the prices of goods and services increase while income remains constant? (a) The quantity of goods purchased will increase. (b) The amount of money in personal savings accounts will increase. (c) The quality of goods and services will improve. (d) Real purchasing power will decrease.

29. In the United States, which headline describes an event that would be *least* likely to cause an increase in the Consumer Price Index? (a) "Bumper Harvest of Vegetables Expected in California" (b) "Thousands of Texas Cattle Slaughtered When Harmful Pesticides Are Found in Their Feed" (c) "Frost Hits Orange Groves With Worst Florida Weather Ever" (d) "United States Imposes Oil Embargo to Force Middle East Settlement."

30. The purpose of an escalator clause in a labor-management contract is to (a) protect the seniority rights of workers in the event of unemployment (b) provide for a periodic increase in pension benefits (c) keep real wages reasonably stable (d) protect collective bargaining rights not guaranteed by state or federal laws.

31. A generally accepted long-range effect of automation on the labor force is that there will be (a) a decrease in its total size (b) a decrease in the percentage of skilled workers (c) an increase in the percentage of unskilled workers (d) an increase in the percentage of professional and technical workers.

32. The introduction of the newest machinery into a factory could benefit both labor and management by (a) decreasing the number of workers needed (b) increasing borrowing costs to pay for the machinery (c) increasing worker output per hour (d) selling the old machinery at a profit.

33. A graph shows that output per worker-hour has increased from 100 in the base period of 1972 to 130 by 1987. A labor union in 1987 could *best* use these data to support (a) an increase in membership dues (b) a campaign against racial discrimination in employment (c) an expansion of its apprenticeship program (d) a drive for a shorter workweek.

34. "Labor unionism in the United States came into its own in this period. It was also a lean time." This statement best applies to the period (a) 1865 to 1900 (b) 1901 to 1920 (c) 1933 to 1940 (d) 1953 to 1965.

35. Labor union membership in the United States (a) has increased steadily since the 1930s (b) includes over half of the labor force (c) has sharply increased since the AFL-CIO merger (d) has been declining in recent years.

36. Which act would the President probably use as a basis for intervening in a strike that might endanger the national health or the safety of the United States? (a) Clayton Antitrust Act (b) Taft-Hartley Act (c) Norris-La Guardia Anti-Injunction Act (d) National Labor Relations Act.

37. Increases in the minimum wage may result in (a) employers hiring more part-time workers than full-time employees (b) increased number of teenagers earning higher wages (c) reduced job prospects for unskilled workers (d) greater preference among employers for hiring minority-group members.

38. On which issue would a steelworkers' union and a large steel corporation most probably agree? (a) the extent of automation in the production of steel (b) the salaries paid to unskilled steelworkers (c) the necessity for limits on steel imports (d) the length of the workday in the steel plants.

39. The best indicator of a person's social status in the United States is the person's (a) political affiliation (b) occupation (c) religious affiliation (d) national origin.

———————————— **MATCHING QUESTIONS** ————————————

Column A

1. First head of merged AFL-CIO
2. Political leader who helped settle coal strike of 1902
3. Head of United Mine Workers and first president of C.I.O.
4. Founder of A.F. of L.
5. Second leader of merged AFL-CIO
6. Founder of Knights of Labor
7. Labor leader arrested during Pullman strike
8. Senator who sponsored New Deal law guaranteeing collective bargaining
9. President of United Automobile Workers who led his union out of the AFL-CIO
10. Senator who sponsored a law to curtail abuses by labor unions

Column B

a. John P. Altgeld
b. Eugene V. Debs
c. Samuel Gompers
d. Lane Kirkland
e. John L. Lewis
f. George Meany
g. Terence W. Powderly
h. Walter P. Reuther
i. Franklin D. Roosevelt
j. Theodore Roosevelt
k. Uriah S. Stephens
l. Robert A. Taft
m. Robert F. Wagner, Sr.

———————————— **ESSAY QUESTIONS** ————————————

1. To answer this question refer to the information on labor union membership from 1900 to the present, on pages 324–340. Explain *one* reason to account for the increase or decrease in union membership for each of the following periods: (a) 1900 to 1920 (b) 1920 to 1935 (c) 1935 to 1960 (d) 1960 to the present.

2. Both the Knights of Labor and the Congress of Industrial Organization (C.I.O.) consisted of industrial unions. (a) Discuss *two* factors that led to the decline of the Knights of Labor. (b) Discuss *two* factors that led to the growth of the Congress of Industrial Organizations. (c) Explain *one* reason why the C.I.O. succeeded whereas the Knights of Labor failed.

3. In 1955 the American Federation of Labor and the Congress of Industrial Organizations merged. (a) Describe *two* circumstances that led to the formation of the A.F. of L. (b) Discuss *two* circumstances that led to the formation of the C.I.O. (c) Discuss briefly *two* reasons for the merging of the A.F. of L. and the C.I.O. (d) Has the merger of the A.F. of L. and the C.I.O. strengthened the labor movement? Defend your answer by presenting *two* arguments.

4. Show how each of the following has been a problem for organized labor: (a) automation (b) jurisdictional disputes (c) racketeering (d) "right-to-work" laws (e) foreign competition (f) inflation (g) large numbers of unorganized workers.

5. The federal government has, through legislation, court decisions, and intervention by the executive department, frequently exerted a strong influence on the relations between labor and management. (a) Discuss *two* actions by the federal government that exerted a strong influence on the relations between labor and management during the period from 1880 to 1940. (b) Discuss *two* actions by the federal government that exerted a strong influence on the relations between labor and management during the period from 1945 to the present.

6. (a) State *one* specific provision of the Taft-Hartley Act and *one* specific provision of the Landrum-Griffin Act. (b) Show why you consider *each* provision you have chosen to be either beneficial *or* harmful to labor union members.

7. Discuss each of the following, giving *two* specific facts to support *or* refute each statement: (a) The Industrial Revolution spurred the growth of national labor organizations. (b) Changed conditions contributed to the rapid rise in union membership after 1933. (c) The Taft-Hartley Act marked a change in the government's policy toward labor organizations. (d) Union organizations engage in a wide variety of activities in addition to working for improved wages and hours. (e) Good labor-management relations are essential to the welfare of the United States. (f) As automation increases, the result will be mass unemployment. (g) Minimum wage laws are beneficial to workers with low skills.

8. A dockworkers' union objects to the use of automated loading machines on the docks. The shipping companies consider the machines necessary and need workers to run the machines. (a) Identify the *two* groups in conflict and briefly state *one* argument of each to support its position. (b) Describe in detail a process by which the groups involved might settle this conflict. (c) List *two* provisions of such a settlement and explain why you consider each provision to be a fair compromise.

PART 7. Foreign Trade Promotes the Welfare of the Nation

1. Imports. (a) American consumers purchase imports of foodstuffs (coffee, sugar, cocoa, fish, meat, fruits, and nuts) and manufactured goods (Japanese automobiles, TV sets, and cameras, English textiles, German chinaware, French perfumes, Canadian farm equipment, Italian typewriters, and Swiss watches). (b) American manufacturers utilize imports of metals (copper, aluminum, nickel, tin, and iron ore) and other vital products (crude oil, wood pulp, newsprint, and natural rubber). American manufacturers also import large amounts of machinery, especially telecommunications apparatus. From 1966 to 1985 our merchandise imports rose from $25 billion to $339 billion annually.

2. Exports. (*a*) American farmers export much agricultural produce (wheat, corn, soybeans, and tobacco). (*b*) American corporations export large amounts of manufactured goods (electrical equipment, metalworking machinery, computers, agricultural implements, chemicals, medicinals, paper, textile products, trucks, and automobiles). From 1966 to 1985 our merchandise exports rose from $29 billion to $214 billion annually.

Our principal suppliers, and also our chief customers, are Canada, Japan, Mexico, Britain, and West Germany.

3. As an Industry. International trade requires import and export firms, oceangoing freighters, dock and storage facilities, and banking services. These enterprises provide business and employment opportunities.

THE TARIFF: MEANING OF TERMS

(1) A *tariff* is a tax, or duty, placed on goods imported from foreign countries. (2) A *revenue tariff* seeks to provide income for the government. Its rates are low so as not to discourage imports. (3) A *protective tariff* seeks to protect domestic manufacturers from foreign competition. Its rates are high so as to discourage imports. (4) *Free trade* means the international exchange of goods unhampered by any barriers, such as tariffs.

OTHER BARRIERS TO WORLD TRADE

1. Barriers Deliberately Established. In addition to high protective tariffs, nations may employ (*a*) *import quotas,* limiting the amount of goods permitted to enter the country, (*b*) *currency controls,* restricting the amount of foreign money available to domestic importers for the purchase of goods from abroad, (*c*) *embargoes,* halting trade in part or in full with certain countries, and (*d*) *direct control,* as in Communist nations, where the government itself owns and controls the means of producing and distributing goods.

In recent years nations have used trade as an economic weapon. The United States in 1960 embargoed trade with Communist Cuba and in 1980–1981 temporarily embargoed grain exports to the Soviet Union to express American opposition to the Soviet invasion of Afghanistan. The Soviet Union has often directed foreign trade for political purposes, such as bolstering the faltering economy of Communist Cuba.

2. Barriers Due to Economic Conditions. (*a*) *Similar Products.* Nations with similar products have no reason to trade with one another. For example, Argentina sells little to the United States because we produce an abundance of meat and wheat, Argentina's chief exports. (*b*) *Poverty in Underdeveloped Nations.* Many developing nations lack sufficient goods to export and sufficient funds with which to pay for essential agricultural, industrial, and petroleum imports.

PROTECTIVE TARIFFS: EVALUATION

1. Arguments for. (a) By protecting domestic manufacturers from foreign competition, especially from goods produced by cheap labor, tariffs help American business prosper, provide jobs for workers, keep wages high, and raise the nation's standard of living. (b) They help "infant industries" to survive the difficult starting years. (c) They encourage diversified industries. The national economy does not become dependent on a limited number of products. They spur economic self-sufficiency, essential in case of war. (d) To abandon tariffs for industries that have been protected would cause great hardships to these industries and their workers. (e) While following a policy of high protective tariffs, the United States became the world's leading industrial power.

The policy of creating heavy barriers to foreign trade in order to encourage domestic industry is called *economic nationalism.*

2. Arguments Against. (a) By reducing international trade, tariffs discourage *specialization.* By specializing, nations concentrate on those goods that they can produce most efficiently. For example, because of its climate and soil, Brazil grows coffee; because of its mineral deposits, Chile mines copper; because of its technical know-how, the United States produces computers. (b) Tariffs prevent healthy competition from abroad. Competition compels manufacturers to modernize their production methods and improve the quality of their products. (c) Tariffs enable domestic manufacturers to monopolize the home market and raise prices. (d) Tariffs hurt American exports because foreign nations retaliate by raising their tariffs on American goods, and because foreign merchants, unable to sell their goods to the United States, lack the dollars with which to buy our goods. A decrease in exports means smaller profits for American corporations and fewer jobs for American workers. (e) By preventing the free flow of goods, tariffs create ill will among nations.

TARIFF HISTORY OF THE UNITED STATES

1. To the End of the War of 1812 (1789–1815): Revenue Tariffs. Seeking income, the new government levied only revenue tariffs.

2. To the Civil War (1816–1860): Protective Tariffs. To protect the industries that arose with the War of 1812, the government levied high protective tariffs in 1816, 1828, and 1832. These tariffs aroused bitter sectional conflict between the industrial North and the agricultural South. With the Compromise Tariff of 1833, the government reduced tariffs but continued to provide some protection.

3. To the Beginning of the New Deal (1861–1933): High Protective Tariffs. During the Civil War, the Republican party gained control of the government and in 1861 passed the Morrill Tariff Act, inaugurating an era of very high protective tariffs. For almost 75 years, the general trend of American tariffs was upward, with two exceptions during Democratic administrations. President Cleveland urged Congress to lower tariffs, but the resulting *Wilson-Gorman Tariff* in 1894 lowered rates so little that Cleveland let it become law without his signature. President Wilson in 1913 pushed through Congress the much lower *Underwood Tariff.* Since imports into the United States were sharply reduced by the outbreak of World War I in 1914, the Underwood Tariff had little effect. Following the war, the Republicans regained control of the government and restored high protective tariffs. President Harding approved a large increase in tariffs by signing the 1922 *Fordney-McCumber Tariff,* and President Hoover approved the highest tariff ever, the 1930 *Hawley-Smoot Tariff.* Hoover's action came at the beginning of the Great Depression and against the advice of over 1000 American economists.

4. To the Present (1934–): Sharply Lower Tariffs

a. Reciprocal Tariff Acts. In 1934 President Roosevelt, a Democrat, secured passage of the first *Reciprocal Trade Agreements Act,* providing for lower rates through reciprocal action with other nations. This law (1) authorized the President to negotiate agreements with foreign countries and set new tariff rates and (2) permitted reductions up to 50 percent in existing rates. This transfer of rate-making power from Congress to the President displeased the high-tariff lobbyists, who had been able to influence members of Congress by appeals to protect industry in home districts. The President, they feared, would consider tariff problems not from a local, but from a national point of view.

Under the 1934 act, the United States negotiated agreements with many countries for the reciprocal lowering of tariff rates on each other's exports. As American exports increased, subsequent Congresses extended the reciprocal tariff program and authorized further rate cuts. By 1962 our average reciprocal tariff rates were some 80 percent below Hawley-Smoot levels.

b. Trade Expansion Act of 1962. This law was passed to strengthen the bargaining position of American trade negotiators, especially in dealing with the *European Economic Community*—a unified tariff area formed in 1957 and popularly known as the *Common Market.* (Check the Index.)

The law authorized the President to (*a*) reduce existing tariffs up to 50 percent in negotiating reciprocal agreements with foreign countries, (*b*) raise tariffs on goods from any country that places unreasonable restrictions on American goods, and (*c*) help domestic industries and workers injured by increased imports. Industries could be helped by raising tariffs according to an "escape clause" in the law, or by granting technical assistance, loans, and tax benefits. Workers could be helped by programs of retraining and relocation to other job centers.

In 1967 the United States, the Common Market members, and some 40 other free-world nations agreed to the largest tariff reduction ever, a cut averaging one-third of rates then in effect, to be applied over a period of five years.

c. World Trade Accord of 1979. After lengthy negotiations, the leading western trade nations—the United States, Common Market members, Scandinavian countries, Canada, Australia, and Japan—reached agreement on a new trade accord. It called for (1) tariff reductions on industrialized goods by an average of one-third over the next eight years, (2) tariff reductions on agricultural produce, and (3) reductions and removals of nontariff barriers to world trade by forbidding high customs evaluations of imports that had raised duties, by standardizing health and safety codes that had obstructed trade in certain goods, and by eliminating government export subsidies and countervailing (offsetting) import duties. The accord was viewed as a rebuff to the world's rising spirit of protectionism.

The accord was criticized by certain developing, or Third World, nations because it (1) did not provide preferential trade treatment for their products and (2) did nothing to shift wealth from the richer to the poorer nations.

WORLD TRADE: MEANING OF TERMS

1. The *balance of trade* refers to the international flow of goods. If exports exceed imports, a nation is said to have a *favorable* balance of trade; if imports exceed exports, a nation is said to have an *unfavorable* balance of trade.

2. The *balance of payments* refers to the international flow of funds. If funds earned abroad exceed funds spent abroad, a nation is said to have a *favorable*, or *surplus*, balance of payments; it is called a *creditor nation*. If funds spent abroad exceed funds earned abroad, a nation is said to have an *unfavorable*, or *deficit*, balance of payments; it is called a *debtor nation*.

AMERICA'S POSITION IN WORLD TRADE (TO THE 1930s)

1. To World War I: Debtor Nation. In the 19th and early 20th centuries, the United States was a debtor nation. From the 1870s on, we had a favorable balance of trade, as our exports of goods exceeded our imports. However, our net earnings from trade were insufficient to offset the heavy outflow of funds resulting from foreign investments here. British and other Western European investors had helped finance American economic growth by purchasing government bonds, corporate securities, and real estate. Their earnings on these investments resulted in a continuous outflow of funds from the United States. To World War I we had an unfavorable balance of payments and remained a debtor nation.

2. Changes During World War I. Led by Britain and France, the Allies placed large orders for American foodstuffs, war implements, and other items. Impeded by the war, European exports to us fell off considerably. The European nations paid for American goods by (a) selling their holdings of American real estate, stocks, and bonds, (b) shipping gold to the United States, and (c) borrowing large sums from American bankers and investors and from the United States government.

3. Following World War I: Creditor Nation. The United States became a creditor nation. (a) During the war, foreigners sold a large part of their investments here; therefore, their earnings from the United States dropped sharply. (*b*) The Allies began making payments on their war loans, thereby increasing the inflow of funds into the United States. (*c*) The value of our exports greatly exceeded the value of our imports. (*d*) Americans used their favorable financial position to invest in foreign business enterprises, such as plantations, mines, oil wells, and factories. By the end of the 1920s, private investors had placed about $14 billion abroad. The earnings from these investments made for a sizable inflow of funds into the United States, thereby enhancing our position as a creditor nation.

4. Decline of Foreign Trade After 1929. In the 1930s American foreign trade dropped sharply. (*a*) The Hawley-Smoot Tariff established our highest rates ever, and many foreign countries retaliated by raising their tariffs on American goods. (*b*) The depression of 1929 caused a worldwide decline in purchasing power. (*c*) American investors, fearful for the security of their money, refrained from lending money to foreign countries, which therefore lacked funds to buy American goods. (*d*) Many foreign countries defaulted on their existing debts to the United States.

FOREIGN TRADE IN THE 1930s: MEANS OF PAYING INTERNATIONAL DEBTS

1. Goods, or Visible Items. International debts can be paid in goods, called *visible exports* or *visible items.* This is the major method of repaying international debts. In the 1930s the debtor nations were unable to sell many goods to the United States because of the depression, which sharply decreased American demand, and because of the exceedingly high rates of the Hawley-Smoot Tariff.

2. Services and Other Invisible Items. International debts can also be paid in *invisible exports,* or *invisible items.* These include services such as insurance protection, shipping facilities, and tourist accommodations. In the 1930s, because of the depression, debtor nations faced decreased American demand for such services. Other invisible items in international exchange include foreign investments and earnings on such investments. In the 1930s Americans sent little capital abroad for investments, and foreigners had limited investments in the United States.

3. Gold. International debts could be paid in gold. In the early 1930s the debtor nations were unable to pay the United States in gold, since the United States already owned most of the world's gold supply. What little gold the debtor nations did possess, they needed as backing for their currencies.

ATTEMPTS TO REVIVE WORLD TRADE (SINCE THE 1930s)

Most free nations have accepted, to some extent, the following ideas designed to revive world trade: (1) International trade is a two-way transaction, meaning that a nation exporting goods must be willing to accept imports in payment. (2) Creditor nations must assist debtor nations by granting them loans. (3) Prosperous and advanced nations must assist poor and developing nations by loans and technical assistance. These ideas led to new American policies and new international agencies.

1. United States Reciprocity Agreements. Starting in 1934 the United States took the lead in reviving world trade by negotiating agreements for the reciprocal lowering of tariff rates.

2. United States Export-Import Bank. In 1934 the United States established the *Export-Import Bank.* This agency provides low-cost loans to (a) foreign governments and companies for purchases of goods from the United States, and (b) American businesses engaging in international trade. The Export-Import Bank has concentrated its loans most heavily in Latin America.

3. Specialized Agencies

a. *The International Bank for Reconstruction and Development,* established in 1945, is more commonly called the *World Bank.* It provides loans, especially to underdeveloped nations, for economic development. These include projects to facilitate the production of goods for export. To date, the World Bank has loaned many billions of dollars to underdeveloped countries.

b. The *International Monetary Fund* (IMF), established in 1945, encourages nations to maintain stable currencies. To assist a nation that has an excessively unfavorable balance of payments, and that has little gold reserves, the IMF lends that nation the needed foreign currency. Repayment of the loan is expected within a period of several years.

4. United Nations Economic and Social Council. This major UN organ, established in 1945, devotes much work to international economic matters, including world trade. The council maintains regional economic commissions to study problems and make recommendations. It supervises loans and technical assistance to developing nations through the *UN Development Program.*

5. United States Foreign Aid Program. Since 1945 the United States has expended over $300 billion in military and economic aid to about 140 pro-Western and neutral nations. This program stimulated world trade because (a) the receiving nations used most of these funds to buy goods abroad, especially from the United States, (b) through the *Marshall Plan,* the United States helped revive the post-World War II economies of the nations of Western Europe and thus helped restore them to world trade, and (c) through the *Point Four* program, the United States helped raise production and purchasing power in the underdeveloped countries. (For more details on foreign aid, check the Index.)

6. General Agreement on Tariffs and Trade (GATT). In 1947 GATT, originally proposed by the United States, was established by most non-

Communist nations. Together, these nations accounted for over 80 percent of the world's trade. GATT represents a multilateral (many nations) approach to the problem of reducing trade barriers. It has three main features: (a) a list of existing tariff reductions, (b) a code to govern exports and imports, and, most important, (c) meetings to further international trade. GATT members have held numerous bargaining sessions at Geneva, Switzerland.

AMERICAN BALANCE OF PAYMENTS PROBLEM TO THE LATE 1980s

From the 1950s onward, the United States incurred substantial balance of payments deficits—the result of the following:

1. Deficit-Producing Factors. (a) *Military Spending.* The United States expended funds to maintain American forces abroad on bases and in battle. (b) *Foreign Economic Aid.* About 25 percent of our foreign aid was not spent in the United States and represented a drain on American funds. (c) *Tourism.* Many Americans went abroad and spent far more money overseas than did foreigners visiting the United States. (d) *Private Loans and Investment.* Lured by profitable business opportunities, American corporations invested large sums abroad, building factories and buying foreign companies. (e) *Unfavorable Balance of Trade.* In 1971, for the first time in 75 years, the United States imported more goods than it exported. Each year since 1976, the United States has had a substantial deficit in its merchandise trade balance. These deficits can be attributed, among other things, to the high price of imported oil in the 1970s, to a troubled world economy that cut the demand for American goods and services in the 1980s, and to the rise of strong new industries (in countries such as Japan, South Korea, and Brazil) that competed with United States producers on world and domestic markets.

2. Steps to Remedy the Balance of Payments Deficit

a. Reduce Foreign Aid. The government cut our foreign aid program, thereby reducing the flow of American dollars out of the country.

b. Refuse International Settlements in Gold. The government suspended the settlement of international transactions in gold. Since foreign governments could no longer exchange their American-held dollars for gold, this move protected our dwindling gold reserves. (By 1970 gold stocks had fallen to $11.1 billion.)

c. Devalue the American Dollar. In 1971 the leading non-Communist industrial nations reached agreement for the United States to revalue the American dollar downward, and for Japan and Germany to revalue their currencies upward. By this agreement, the overall devaluation of the American dollar was 12 percent. In 1973 the American dollar was devalued an additional 10 percent. Further devaluations against the Japanese and German currencies became necessary in the mid-1980s.

The devaluation of the American dollar in relation to foreign currencies was expected to have the following effects: (1) Increased exports of American goods. Foreigners would find American goods less costly and therefore would buy more of our products. (2) Decreased imports of foreign goods. Americans would find foreign products more expensive and therefore would buy fewer imported goods. (3) Fewer Americans traveling abroad. Since American dollars would buy less of foreign currencies, American tourists would curtail trips abroad because of the increased expense. (Conversely, European tourists would find trips to the United States less expensive.)

d. Keep Tourists in the United States. Americans were encouraged to tour the United States as the government sponsored a "See-America-First" effort.

e. "Buy-American" Campaign. Many Congressional appropriations specified that the government "buy American." Federal contracts were to be given to domestic manufacturers, except where foreign prices were substantially lower.

f. Encourage Foreign Investments in the United States. Congress eased the tax burden on earnings of foreign investors here.

g. Limit Specific Imports. From the late 1970s onward, the government helped bring about limits, or quotas, on imports of shoes from Taiwan and South Korea and on imports of color television sets and automobiles from Japan. The government also acted to stem imports of steel, mainly from the Common Market nations. In addition to reducing imports of such products, these actions were designed to aid domestic manufacturers and workers.

h. Spur Energy Measures to Decrease Oil Imports. Congress enacted various energy laws designed to decrease American consumption of oil and encourage greater use of domestic coal resources. Such laws would enable the United States to reduce its imports of oil.

i. Curtail Inflation. Successive Presidents have taken various steps to reduce inflation. In that way, they have sought to reduce the prices of American exports, making them more attractive to foreign buyers.

j. Expand Markets for United States Exports. The government has negotiated a lowering of tariffs and other barriers to United States exports. It has also sought to persuade exporters such as the European Community and Japan, which compete with the United States for customers abroad, to end subsidies to their own farmers and manufacturers. Such subsidies are unfair, United States officials argue, since they make those nations' exports cheaper and thus more attractive to buyers. (At the same time, other countries have accused the United States of unfairly subsidizing its own exports through such measures as farm subsidies and export credits.)

k. Help Solve Developing Nations' Debt Problems. During the 1960s and early 1970s, in their efforts to build up local industries and improve living standards, the developing nations incurred huge international debts. These nations borrowed heavily from private banks in the United States and other industrial countries and from such international agencies as the World Bank and the International Monetary Fund (IMF).

But high oil prices in the late 1970s and a sharp downturn in demand in the early 1980s made it impossible for many developing nations to meet their debt payments. Among the nations with the highest debts were Mexico, Brazil, and Nigeria.

The debt crisis alarmed both bankers (who wanted their money back) and world leaders (who feared the political impact of a widespread economic collapse). Officials of the United States and other nations sought ways to resolve the debt crisis and restore growth to the world economy. Only when such growth was restored, said United States leaders, would the market for our exports again expand.

As a first step, lenders rescheduled many of the developing nations' debt payments (that is, they stretched the payments out over a longer period). In 1985 United States Secretary of the Treasury *James A. Baker III* proposed a more ambitious program that became known as the *Baker Plan*. In line with the Reagan administration's emphasis on free-market solutions, the Baker Plan stressed a need for debtor nations to begin by abandoning policies that interfered with free enterprise. Subsequently, international lending agencies and private bankers would advance millions of dollars in new loans to help get the debtor nations back on their feet. While the plan attracted interest among both industrial and developing nations, it was not immediately put into effect.

——————— MULTIPLE-CHOICE QUESTIONS ———————

1. Which situation best illustrates the concept of the interdependence among nations? (a) adoption of a policy of economic nationalism (b) establishment by a nation of a system of high protective tariffs (c) sale of goods by one nation to obtain scarce resources from another nation (d) expansion of international sporting events.

2. After 1865, industrialists argued for a high protective tariff because it would (a) increase competition (b) reduce income taxes (c) help the United States gain friends among British manufacturers (d) help the United States become self-sufficient.

3. During the period 1865 to 1890, the general policy of Congress regarding the tariff was to (a) lower rates (b) raise rates (c) give the President more responsibility for adjusting rates (d) encourage reciprocal trade agreements.

4. One effect of high protective tariffs in the United States was (a) fewer industries (b) lower prices paid by consumers for foreign goods (c) higher prices paid by consumers for domestic goods (d) lower prices paid by consumers for domestic goods.

5. The first tariff act with a considerable reduction in rates after the Civil War was enacted during the administration of (a) Woodrow Wilson (b) Warren G. Harding (c) Herbert Hoover (d) William McKinley.

6. The statement that the United States became a creditor nation after World War I means that (a) our national debt was decreasing (b) the debt of foreign governments to the United States was greater than the debt of the United States to foreign governments (c) our budget was balanced (d) Americans earned more money in foreign countries than foreigners earned in the United States.

7. If the United States lowers tariffs on imports from Britain, and Britain does the same for imports from the United States, such an agreement illustrates (a) cooperative marketing (b) tariff reciprocity (c) the protective tariff (d) free trade.

8. One reason why Congress passed reciprocal tariff legislation in the 1930s was to (a) establish free trade (b) increase our foreign markets (c) help make the United States self-sufficient (d) keep out goods produced by cheap foreign labor.

9. Who was empowered to revise tariff rates under the Reciprocal Trade Agreements Act? (a) the President (b) the secretary of commerce (c) the Federal Trade Commission (d) the Interstate Commerce Commission.

10. Brazil exports coffee to the United States, and we export cars to Brazil. Each country concentrates on those goods that it can produce best, thereby illustrating the principle of (a) free trade (b) specialization (c) protectionism (d) mercantilism.

11. The Trade Expansion Act of 1962 indicated (a) an increase in protectionist sentiment (b) our willingness to make further trade concessions (c) the growing opposition to foreign aid (d) our unwillingness to continue reciprocal agreements.

12. Under 1962 tariff legislation, the President was granted increased powers chiefly to meet the competition of the (a) Latin American nations (b) European Common Market (c) Sino-Soviet bloc (d) newly independent nations of Asia and Africa.

13. Which has an immediate effect on the balance of payments of the United States different from the effect of the other three? (a) the export of merchandise from the United States (b) Americans traveling abroad (c) grants under our foreign aid program (d) the purchase of foreign securities by Americans.

14. The flow of gold out of this country from 1957 to 1967 indicated that (a) our foreign expenditures were greater than our foreign income (b) the nations of the world were returning to the gold standard (c) European nations were refusing to buy American products (d) our government was removing idle gold from Fort Knox.

15. A nation seeking to encourage development of its resources and industries would most likely adopt an economic policy that includes (a) an increase in investments abroad (b) invitations to foreigners to invest in the nation (c) reductions in government spending (d) high tax rates on industrial profits.

16. Which action by the federal government would be most beneficial to United States industries that face plant closings and worker layoffs? (a) elimination of investment tax credits (b) stricter enforcement of the present antitrust laws (c) passage of stronger laws to protect the environment (d) agreements with foreign nations voluntarily to limit their exports to the United States.

17. Which would be most likely to result from the devaluation of the United States dollar? (a) French goods would cost less in the United States. (b) More United States citizens would be able to afford to travel abroad. (c) Foreigners would be able to afford more United States products. (d) The value of foreign currencies would decrease.

———————————————— ESSAY QUESTIONS ————————————————

1. (a) Discuss *two* reasons why some people believe that high tariffs promote prosperity. (b) Giving *two* specific facts, explain why international trade is necessary to maintain a high level of prosperity in the United States today.

2. Discuss the relationship of the tariff issue to *each* of the following controversies: (a) North against South—from 1824 to the Civil War (b) industry against agriculture—from the Civil War to 1913.

3. In 1962 Congress passed the Trade Expansion Act to meet "new challenges and opportunities." (a) In *two* ways, explain what was "new" about the "challenges and opportunities" confronting the United States in international trade following World War II. (b) Show how *two* provisions of this trade program met these "challenges and opportunities." (c) Discuss what is meant by the statement that tariff policy demands a balancing of special interests against the national interest.

4. (a) Explain the difference between an unfavorable balance of trade and an unfavorable balance of payments. (b) Discuss *three* reasons why the United States since the 1950s has had an unfavorable balance of payments. (c) Explain any *two* steps that might help remedy our unfavorable balance of payments.

5. The United States balance of trade reflects the effect of certain economic factors upon major United States industries. For example: scarcity affects our domestic oil industry, competition affects our domestic automobile industry, and surplus affects American agriculture. (a) For any *two* of these industries, explain how *each* is affected by the stated economic factor. (b) Show how *each* of these industries affects the United States balance of trade.

UNIT VII Americans Develop a Distinctive Way of Life

PART 1. The American People Come From Many Lands

THE UNITED STATES, A NATION OF IMMIGRANTS

All Americans are immigrants or the descendants of immigrants.

1. Before the European Discovery of the New World. Thousands of years ago, migratory peoples crossed the Bering Strait region from Siberia in Asia into Alaska in North America. Their descendants spread out over the unpeopled Western Hemisphere and became known as Indians and Eskimos. Polynesians from southeast Asia reached the islands of Hawaii, and their descendants became known as Hawaiians.

2. In the Thirteen English Colonies. Settlers came by the thousands. They were mainly from England and other areas of the British Isles, although a sizable number came from western Europe. Blacks from Africa were involuntary immigrants, brought here as slaves. By 1775, the 13 colonies had a population of over 2.5 million people. It was a pluralistic society, diverse as to race, religion, and nationality.

3. Since the American Revolution to Today. Over 52 million people have migrated to our shores. They have come from far-flung areas of the world. From the Western Hemisphere came Canadians, Mexicans, West Indians, and South Americans. From Asia came Chinese, Japanese, and Filipinos. From Africa came blacks, mainly from its northwestern region. The overwhelming majority of immigrants came from Europe.

REASONS FOR EUROPEAN IMMIGRATION: THE PUSH AND THE PULL

1. Economic. (a) The Push. European farmers were discouraged as they tried to reap an adequate crop from small and worn-out lands. Farmers were driven from the soil as the agricultural revolution brought about a change from subsistence to large-scale commercial farming. European city workers were disheartened by low wages, and many workers faced unemployment as the Industrial Revolution hastened the use of machines. (b) The Pull. Immigrants looked to America as a land of opportunity, where fertile lands could be acquired at little or no cost and where the expanding economy provided steady employment at decent wages.

2. Political. (a) The Push. Most European governments were controlled by the upper classes, and the common people had little or no say in po-

356

litical matters. *(b) The Pull.* Immigrants looked to democratic America, where the ordinary citizen had a strong voice in the government.

3. Social. *(a) The Push.* European society was characterized by rigid class distinctions, few educational opportunities for the lower classes, and discrimination against religious minorities. As World War I approached, most governments required young men to serve terms of compulsory military service. *(b) The Pull.* Immigrants looked to America as a land of equality, where they could rise in social status, provide an education for their children, practice their religion without fear, and be free of compulsory military service.

These reasons, which motivated European immigrants, were in large measure true as well for other immigrants throughout our history.

IMMIGRATION FROM THE END OF THE REVOLUTIONARY WAR TO THE CLOSE OF THE FRONTIER (1783–1890)

1. Major Periods of Immigration

a. To the Age of Jackson (1783–1830). At first, immigrants came in a slow but steady stream. Immigration increased as travel became easier with the close in Europe of the Napoleonic Wars in 1815. During the years 1821 to 1830, 143,000 immigrants came to the United States.

b. To the Beginning of the Civil War (1831–1860). In the next three decades, immigrants came in rapidly rising numbers: 1831 to 1840: 600,000; 1841 to 1850: 1.7 million; 1851 to 1860: 2.6 million. Most of these immigrants came from Ireland and Germany. (1) The Irish, long denied self-government by Britain, received their main stimulus to migrate in the 1840s, when Ireland was afflicted by a potato famine. They settled in compact areas in East Coast cities such as Boston and New York. They found work in mills and factories and in construction gangs building canals and railroads. (2) Germans who had migrated for economic reasons were joined, after the failure of the revolution of 1848, by German liberals and intellectuals, who came to escape political persecution. The Germans settled chiefly on farms and in cities of the Midwest. They became prominent in making watches, optical equipment, pianos, beer, and medicinals.

c. To the Close of the Frontier (1861–1890). After being temporarily slowed by the Civil War, immigration again began rising, from 2.8 million in the years 1871 to 1880, to 5.2 million in the years 1881 to 1890. Immigrants continued to come from Ireland and Germany. Farmers came from the Scandinavian countries of Sweden, Norway, and Denmark to look for abundant and fertile soil. The Scandinavians settled mainly in the Upper Mississippi region. The post-Civil War European immigrants were attracted by the claims of labor-recruiting agents and by advertisements of steamship companies and land-grant railroads, and by "America letters" of praise sent by earlier immigrants.

To our Pacific coast came thousands of Chinese immigrants fleeing famine, oppressive government, and civil war. They found work as cooks, laundry workers, miners, and construction laborers.

2. Americans Welcome Immigration. Most Americans considered immigrants an asset to our growing nation. Immigrants represented *(a)* workers for factories, mines, and railroads, *(b)* farmers for western lands, *(c)* consumers for the products of agriculture and industry, *(d)* persons of special abilities, talents, and skills, and *(e)* military strength for the nation.

Americans took pride in their country's tradition as a haven for the oppressed. *Emma Lazarus* expressed the feelings of most Americans in her poem "The New Colossus," inscribed on the base of the Statue of Liberty in New York Harbor: "Give me your tired, your poor, your huddled masses yearning to breathe free."

3. "Old Immigrants" From Europe: Characteristics. Historians have traditionally referred to the Europeans who arrived before 1890 as the "old immigrants." They originated chiefly from northern and western Europe: Great Britain, Ireland, Germany, Holland, France, and the Scandinavian countries. They arrived while the frontier was still open, and many settled on farms in the West. It has been claimed that, since these "old immigrants" possessed customs and traditions similar to those of Americans, they adjusted easily to American ways of life.

IMMIGRATION FROM THE CLOSE OF THE FRONTIER TO THE BEGINNING OF WORLD WAR I (1890–1914)

1. "New Immigrants" From Europe: Characteristics. Historians have traditionally referred to the Europeans who arrived after 1890 as the "new immigrants." They came in greater numbers than immigrants had ever come before. From 1901 to 1910 some 8.8 million persons entered the United States. Unlike the "old immigrants," the "new immigrants" originated chiefly in southern and eastern Europe: Italy, Greece, Austria-Hungary, Serbia, Rumania, Russian Poland, and Russia. They arrived when the frontier was closed and settled chiefly in the cities as factory workers. It has been claimed that, since the "new immigrants" possessed customs and traditions different from those of Americans, they experienced difficulty in adjusting to American ways of life.

2. Typical Migratory Groups. *(a) Italians,* mainly from southern Italy and Sicily, fled poor soil and high land rents. They settled in Atlantic and Gulf coast cities and formed ethnic enclaves. These neighborhoods were often called "Little Italys." They found work in highway and railroad construction, in the building industry, and in the garment trades. *(b) Greeks,* mainly tenant farmers, fled poverty. They settled in northeastern cities, worked in mines and on railroads, and opened small retail businesses. *(c) Poles,* the most numerous of the Slavic-speaking peoples who migrated, fled the Austro-Hungarian and Russian empires to escape tyrannical government, heavy taxes, and, as World War I approached, compulsory military service. They settled in cities in the northeast, forming "Little Polands," and worked in meat-packing plants, steel mines, coal mines, and textile factories. *(d) Jews* in Russia and in Russian-controlled Poland had long been forced to live in special districts or ghettos called the *Pale of Settlement,* and had been subjected to educational restrictions and to legal and economic discrimination. They now fled Czarist-inspired outbreaks of anti-Semitic violence, called pogroms. Jews settled in northeastern cities, worked in the needle trades, and pioneered in the new motion picture and radio industries. *(e) Japanese* workers, permitted after 1885 to migrate by their government, came to our Pacific coast, especially California. Some worked in the fishing and canning industries but most turned to agriculture.

3. Opposition to Immigration. Some Americans disapproved of the "new immigrants," arguing as follows: *(a)* With the frontier closed, there was no more free or cheap land for immigrants. *(b)* American industry had sufficient workers, and "new immigrants" competed with and took jobs away from native Americans. This argument was emphasized by labor unions. *(c)* The "new immigrants" were difficult to Americanize. They had little education. They settled in large cities, creating their own ghettos, and felt no need to learn American ways. Their ghettos were becoming breeding places of disease and crime. *(d)* Some people argued that the "new immigrants" were physically and mentally inferior to the "old immigrants." This was known as the "theory of Nordic supremacy."

4. In Defense of the "New Immigrants." *(a)* The "new immigrants" assimilated as well as had the Irish and German "old immigrants." Critics of the "new immigrants" forgot that the Germans, too, had clung to their native tongue and that the Irish had been impoverished and uneducated. The Irish and the Germans had also been accused of being clannish and of not assimilating quickly into the American Protestant society. *(b)* The "new immigrants" who flocked to the cities were joined by native-born Americans who moved in from the farms. Both groups contributed to the urban problems of slums, disease, and crime. Again, critics of the "new immigrants" forgot that the Irish, too, had settled in the cities. *(c)* The "new immigrants" provided the additional workers needed by our growing industry. Furthermore, they stimulated industrial growth by enlarging the domestic market for goods. *(d)* Reputable scientists rejected the theory of Nordic supremacy as false. *(e)* The "new immigrants" contributed greatly to American life.

IMMIGRATION FROM THE END OF THE WORLD WAR I DECADE TO THE PRESENT (1920–1980s)

1. Declining Number of Immigrants. *(a)* The United States in the 1920s and afterward enacted immigration laws severely curtailing the entry of immigrants. *(b)* European dictators, unwilling to lose workers and soldiers, opposed emigration. *(c)* During the Great Depression, beginning in 1929, the United States was not a land of economic opportunity. *(d)* World War II (1939–1945) made travel difficult.

2. Immigrants From Europe Fleeing Dictatorship

a. Before America's Entrance Into World War II (1941). In three major European nations, dictators seized power—Communist Russia under Lenin and then Stalin, Fascist Italy under Mussolini, and Nazi Germany under Hitler. The dictators persecuted their political opponents, economic or class enemies, subject nationalities, religious minorities—especially Catholics and Jews—and intellectuals. From 1937 to 1941, some 300,000 refugees fled from European dictatorships to the United States. Among them were a large number of talented persons—musicians, writers, aviation pioneers, and scientists—who enriched American life.

b. After World War II Ended (1945). Refugees and displaced persons (DP's), totaling several million in Europe, included (1) the few survivors of the German concentration camps, (2) slave laborers, chiefly East Europeans, who had been forced to work in Germany during the war and who refused to return home to Communist rule, and (3) escapees from Communist rule in Eastern Europe, such as the Hungarians who fled their homeland when their 1956 revolt against Soviet domination was crushed by Russian forces.

Over 500,000 refugees and displaced persons were allowed into the United States above the yearly immigration quotas by the provisions of special Displaced Persons Acts.

3. Other Refugees From Communist Rule

a. Cubans. In 1959 Fidel Castro seized control of Cuba and thereafter established a totalitarian Communist regime. Over 500,000 Cubans fled to the United States, settling chiefly in Florida. Workers found employment in the construction and tourist industries; professionals continued their careers as engineers, technicians, dentists, and doctors; merchants opened retail stores; business executives started cigar-making, shoe-manufacturing, and banking companies.

b. Indochinese. Following the 1975 Communist takeovers in Cambodia, Laos, and South Vietnam, over one million persons fled their homelands. Some feared imprisonment or execution for having opposed the Communists. Others fled renewed warfare in Cambodia between rival Communist factions. Still others fled Communist tyranny and harsh living conditions. By 1981 over 375,000 of these homeless people had been admitted to the United States, and many had settled along the Pacific coast.

"NATIVIST" HOSTILITY TO IMMIGRANT GROUPS

The policy of favoring native-born Americans and opposing immigrant groups uncritically became known as *nativism*.

1. "Know-Nothing" Opposition to Irish and Germans—Before the Civil War. The most influential nativist group in the mid-19th century was the *Know-Nothing party*. It was so called because its members, pledged to secrecy, answered "I know nothing" when asked about the party's activities. The

Know-Nothings condemned the Irish and German immigrants for taking jobs away from native-born Americans, for being clannish and failing to assimilate into American society, and especially for being Roman Catholic. The Know-Nothings purported to defend Protestantism against Catholicism; they sought to limit office-holding to native-born Americans; to require 21 years for naturalization, and to restrict immigration. In the 1850s, the party died out.

2. Pacific Coast Opposition to Orientals—After the Civil War to the 1920s

a. Anti-Chinese Agitation. Pacific coast nativists aroused widespread anti-Chinese feeling. They accused the Chinese of being cheap "coolie" labor, serving as strikebreakers, following strange customs, and of being unassimilable into American society. The nativists secured passage of state and local laws discriminating against Chinese workers and shopkeepers; nativists also used mob violence to terrorize the Chinese communities. In 1882 Congress passed the *Chinese Exclusion Act.* Thereafter, as some Chinese returned to their Asian homeland and others moved eastward, anti-Chinese agitation subsided in the Pacific coast area.

b. Anti-Japanese Agitation. In the early 1900s, nativists aroused fury against Japanese immigrants. Agitators, pointing to Japan's victory in war against Russia (1904–1905), portrayed the Japanese immigrants as a "Yellow Peril" endangering America. San Francisco labor unions accused them of threatening the living standards of American workers; mobs rioted; state and local governments passed discriminatory laws. In 1906 the San Francisco School Board ordered all Orientals to attend a segregated school. When the Japanese government protested to Washington, President Theodore Roosevelt pressured the San Francisco School Board to rescind the segregation order. Roosevelt also negotiated the 1907 *Gentlemen's Agreement* by which Japan agreed to deny passports for America to Japanese laborers. Although Japanese immigration was so curtailed, anti-Japanese agitation continued for many years.

3. Opposition to Minority Religious Groups—From the 1890s to the 1930s

a. Anti-Catholic Agitation. Nativists were perturbed that many of the "new immigrants"—from Italy, Poland, and Hungary—were Catholics. Agitators berated Catholic parents for sending their children to Catholic parochial schools; called attention to growing Catholic political power as Irish politicians gained influence over many East Coast city governments; and warned against "papal conquest" of the United States. Nativists founded several secret anti-Catholic societies, but they were short-lived. After 1915 the theme of anti-Catholicism was circulated by the revived Ku Klux Klan.

b. Anti-Jewish Agitation. Nativists were also anti-Semites—persons who are prejudiced against Jews as a group and therefore support discrimination and persecution of Jewish people. The nativists were perturbed that many of the "new immigrants"—from Eastern Europe—were Jews. Agitators stressed that Jews observed different customs and labeled Jews as ambitious, greedy, and materialistic. In the 1890s, serious anti-Semitic demonstrations took place in several northern towns and in the rural South. In the 1920s, anti-Semitism increased. Employers rejected qualified Jewish job applicants, colleges set quotas restricting the admission of Jewish students, and real estate agents practiced discrimination. In the rural South and Middle West, the Ku Klux Klan stressed anti-Semitism.

4. In Wartime, Hostility to Persons Related to the Enemy

a. World War I (1917–1918)—Hostility to German Americans. After the United States entered the war in 1917, nativists acted to wipe out every aspect of German culture in the United States. In many instances, concert and opera groups ceased performing German music; town officials removed German names from streets and buildings; schools stopped teaching the German language, "sauerkraut" was renamed "liberty cabbage" and "hamburgers" became "Salisbury steaks." Using laws against espionage and sedition, the government arrested some 1500 pacifists, socialists, and pro-Germans. With the end of World War I, anti-German agitation ceased.

b. World War II (1939–1945)—Hostility to Japanese Americans. With the Japanese attack upon Pearl Harbor (1941), Pacific coast residents were gripped by hysteria against Japanese Americans. They were wildly—and falsely—rumored to be a "fifth column" engaged in espionage and sabotage on behalf of the Japanese emperor. In early 1942, on the ground of military necessity, the Japanese Americans were removed from the Pacific coast into the interior. Over 110,000 people, of whom 70,000 were American citizens, were taken from their homes and jobs. Placed in inhospitable relocation centers, they were kept behind barbed wire and under armed guard. Despite the harsh treatment most Japanese Americans were determined to prove their loyalty to America. They gave blood to the American Red Cross, purchased United States war bonds, and taught the Japanese language to army interpreters. Some 12,000 Japanese Americans served in combat units in Europe, suffered heavy casualties, and won numerous decorations. After the war, although a majority of Japanese Americans returned to the Pacific coast, many went to live elsewhere in the United States. They now found greater acceptance by their fellow Americans.

HARDSHIPS OF IMMIGRATION—TO THE EARLY 20TH CENTURY

Most immigrants faced severe hardships: (1) Of leaving. They were uprooted, severing ties with their relatives, friends, and native lands. (2) Of the journey. Being poor, they came in the ship's least desirable section—a crowded and unsanitary area called steerage. (Across the Atlantic the trip by sailing vessel lasted up to three months; after the 1850s, the trip by steamboat took about ten days.) (3) Of adjustment. Immigrants had to find a job and a place to live as well as adjusting to a new language and culture.

FROM IMMIGRANT TO AMERICAN

Most immigrants (1) at first faced discrimination in work, living quarters, and educational opportunities, (2) then proceeded with *acculturation*, learning the language and other aspects of American culture, and (3) finally achieved *assimilation*, becoming part of the American way of life. First-generation immigrants found assimilation more difficult than did their children and grandchildren.

Historical Analysis. *Which is the most satisfactory concept of Americanization?*

Anglo-Conformity. This earliest concept held that our predominantly Anglo-Saxon or British stock had molded a fixed, homogeneous American culture. It was rooted in the English language, English political institutions (as modified by the American experience), and English social patterns. To achieve Americanization, immigrants were expected to divest themselves of their native cultures and to conform to Anglo-American ways. *Anglo-conformity* had strong support among the "old immigrants" coming before 1890 and from 1929 to 1965 in the national origins plan.

Melting Pot. This later concept held that all immigrants to America have contributed to "God's crucible, the great Melting Pot" from which has emerged a homogeneous—but constantly changing—American culture. In the early 20th century, this concept was popularized by Israel Zangwill in his play *The Melting Pot* (1914). The *melting-pot* concept found strong support among the "new immigrants" coming after 1890 as properly recognizing their contributions to the American way of life.

Cultural Pluralism. This recent concept held that all immigrants should absorb those aspects of a uniform culture essential for the functioning of our democratic society, but that they may preserve certain facets of their own heritages. American culture therefore should consist of a homogeneous center—of the English language, political ideals, and economic institutions—surrounded by heterogeneous ethnic patterns, especially in social and intellectual life. American society thusly was described as a mixing bowl, a cultural mosaic, or a symphony of cultures. Since World War II, as minority groups have asserted their own "identities," the concept of *cultural pluralism* has received increasing support.

REGULATIONS AFFECTING THE FLOW OF IMMIGRATION

1. Early Steps Restricting Immigration. (a) The *Chinese Exclusion Act* (1882) began the prohibition of the immigration of Chinese. The law was passed following Pacific coast agitation against cheap "coolie" labor. The prohibition lasted until World War II. (b) The *Gentlemen's Agreement* (1907) contained a promise by the Japanese government to deny passports to Japanese laborers seeking to migrate to the United States. In 1924 Congress prohibited all Japanese immigration to the United States, thereby ending the Gentlemen's Agreement. (Check the Index.) *(c)* The *Literacy Test Act* (1917) required immigrants to be able to read English or their own language before entering the United States. This act was passed over a veto by President Wilson, who insisted that literacy indicated not mental ability, but merely the opportunity to go to school.

2. Further Immigration Restrictions Following World War I—Reasons. *(a)* With the Communist seizure of Russia (1917), many Americans opposed immigration for fear that foreign radicals would infiltrate the United States. *(b)* Disillusioned with the results of World War I, many Americans reverted to our traditional foreign policy of isolation. This came also to mean opposition to immigration. *(c)* With the beginning of the depression of 1920–1921, workers feared unemployment. Labor unions insisted that immigration threatened the jobs of American workers. *(d)* Employers too favored immigration restrictions to keep out foreign radicals who might spur labor unrest. *(e)* The literacy test proved ineffective in limiting immigration. Between 1918 and 1921, of 1.5 million immigrants, those excluded because they failed the literacy test numbered only 6000.

3. Restrictive Immigration Laws Following World War I

a. **Two Emergency Immigration Acts.** These acts, passed in 1921 and in 1924, began the sharp curtailment of immigration from outside the Western Hemisphere. The 1924 act also contained regulations constituting the 1929 National Origins Plan.

b. **National Origins Plan of 1929.** This plan (1) permitted no more than 150,000 immigrants from outside the Western Hemisphere to enter the United States per year, (2) allotted each country a quota in proportion to the number of persons in the United States having that national origin according to the census of 1920, (3) granted each eligible nation at least 100 immigrants per year, (4) placed no restrictions on immigration from the Western Hemisphere, and (5) prohibited all immigration from Asian countries.

4. Immigration Laws Following World War II

a. **Displaced Persons Acts.** (Check the Index for Displaced persons.)

b. **McCarran-Walter Immigration and Nationality Act of 1952**

(1) Internal Security Provisions. To preserve our internal security against Communist infiltration, the law provided for careful screening of immigrants, for revoking the citizenship of recently naturalized persons who joined pro-Communist organizations, and for deporting undesirable aliens.

(2) Immigration Provisions. The law *(a)* kept the national origins system, set a limit of 154,000 immigrants per year from outside the Western Hemisphere and granted each eligible nation a quota based on the 1920 census, *(b)* allowed each Asian nation a quota, usually 100 immigrants per year.

(3) Arguments for the Immigration Provisions. (a) The total of 154,000 admissions per year from outside the Western Hemisphere prevented the flooding of the United States with immigrants. *(b)* The use of the national origins system preserved the "nationality makeup" of our population. *(c)* The law rejected any racial bias by admitting immigrants from Asian nations.

(4) Arguments Against the Immigration Provisions. (a) The United States, with its relatively low population density, could absorb more immigrants. *(b)* The national origins quotas discriminated against people from eastern and southern Europe and from Asia. The law assigned a quota of 109,000 out of a total of 154,000 to three countries: Britain, Germany, and Ireland. Unused quotas could not be given to nations that had already filled their quotas.

President Truman vetoed the McCarran-Walter bill as "repressive and inhumane," but Congress overrode the veto. Subsequently, Presidents Eisenhower, Kennedy, and Johnson all requested a revision of our immigration laws.

c. Immigration Act of 1965 (With 1976 Revisions)

(1) Provisions. For countries outside the Western Hemisphere, the law *(a)* abolished the National Origins Plan, *(b)* established a quota of 170,000 immigrants per year, *(c)* set a limit of 20,000 immigrants per year from any one nation, and *(d)* provided standards for admitting immigrants according to the following preferences: (1) close relatives of United States residents, (2) scientists, artists, professional people, and skilled and unskilled workers needed to fill labor shortages, and (3) refugees from Communist rule and from natural calamity.

For countries within the Western Hemisphere, the law introduced for the first time a quota of 120,000 immigrants per year and, by the 1976 revisions, subjected them to the same provisions as other immigrants—to a limit of 20,000 per year from any one nation and to preferential standards of admission.

(2) Significant Changes. (a) This law replaced the National Origins Plan, stressing race and nationality, by a preference system emphasizing family relationship, value to the United States, and motive for migrating. *(b)* It ended the favored position of north and west European nations, and placed them on an equal footing with other countries. Fewer immigrants have come from Great Britain, Ireland, and Germany. *(c)* It permitted an increase in the number of immigrants from Asia, Africa, and southern and eastern Europe. More immigrants have come from Indochina, Taiwan, the Philippines, Italy, Greece, and Portugal. *(d)* The law reduced the number of Western Hemisphere immigrants from about 150,000 unlimited entrants in 1965 to a quota maximum of 120,000. *(e)* The 1976 revisions reduced Mexican immigration from an annual average of 40,000 to the legal limit of 20,000; spurred illegal Mexican immigration; and increased legal immigration from the Caribbean and Central America.

(3) Criticisms and Further Proposals. (a) Each foreign country, regardless of its population, economy, and government, receives the same immigrant quota limit. *(b)* The legal immigration ceiling of 290,000 per year has been surpassed by the coming of illegal immigrants and by the President's power to exempt refugee groups from the legal ceiling. The United States needs a new realistic maximum immigration ceiling set somewhere between 500,000 and 1 million persons

per year. *(c)* The United States should adopt a flexible quota system, varying the number of immigrants permitted to enter each year according to economic conditions within the United States. *(d)* The preference system for admitting immigrants should be simplified. *(e)* The illegal immigrants now in the United States—between 3 million and 6 million—should be granted amnesty and permanent residency status. *(f)* To discourage further illegal immigration, the United States should require national identity cards as a condition for employment and penalize employers who hire illegal aliens not possessing such cards.

d. Refugee Act of 1980. As countless refugees fled from their native countries—such as Cuba, Haiti, Ethiopia, Somalia, Uganda, Afghanistan, and Vietnam—Congress enacted the 1980 Refugee Act. It (1) defined refugees as people outside their native countries who are unwilling to return because of fear of persecution (this definition did not limit refugees to Communist-led nations only); (2) increased the number of refugees to be admitted annually to 50,000—in addition to the existing special programs for Indochinese and Cuban refugees; (3) empowered the President to admit additional refugees in emergency situations; (4) established the position of *United States Coordinator of Refugee Affairs* to administer the law.

e. Immigration Reform and Control Act of 1986

(1) *Provisions.* (a) The law barred employers from hiring illegal immigrants. The law established civil penalties of $250 to $10,000 for each illegal immigrant hired. It provided for criminal penalties of up to a $3,000 fine and six months' imprisonment for employers who showed a "pattern or practice" of hiring illegal immigrants. (b) The law made it illegal for an employer to discriminate against legal immigrants. (c) The law offered legal status, or amnesty, to immigrants who could prove that they had entered the United States illegally before January 1, 1982, and had resided here continuously since that time. For five years, such people (with certain exceptions based on age, disability, and pregnancy) would not be eligible for welfare, food stamps, and many other government benefits. (d) The law offered amnesty to illegal immigrants who had worked in the United States for at least 90 days between May 1985 and May 1986. (e) The law opened the way for people who benefited from the amnesties to become United States citizens. (f) The law provided for the admission of up to 350,000 immigrants for seasonal farm work in the fiscal years 1990 to 1993, if a shortage of seasonal workers existed. Such immigrants could qualify for permanent residence status after three years. (g) The law set aside $1 billion a year for four years to help state governments provide public assistance, health care, and education to people who benefited from the amnesties.

(2) *Significance.* The 1986 act concluded a six-year effort to satisfy the competing demands of widely varying interest groups—notably employers, Hispanic-rights groups, and financially pressed state officials. The act grew out of a concern among many people that illegal immigration had grown to unacceptable levels. Estimates of the number of illegal immigrants in the country in 1986 ranged upward from the official guess of between 3 and 5 million. By granting amnesty to many of the illegal immigrants already here and tightening controls

© Punch/Rothco

*"Good morning, Ms. Lazarus. Give me your tired,
your poor, your huddled masses yearning to breathe
free, the wretched refuse of your teaming shore. Send
these, the homeless, tempest-tossed, to me."*

against further illegal immigration, officials hoped, in the words of President Reagan, to "regain control of our borders."

(3) Criticisms. (a) The Chamber of Commerce of the United States argued that the bill would be a burden on employers. First, employers might be subject to fines if they hired persons who held forged citizenship documents. Second, employers might face lawsuits from legal immigrants or citizens who charged discrimination in hiring. *(b)* Some critics objected, claiming that illegal immigrants should be punished rather than granted amnesty. *(c)* Other critics argued that the act would encourage job discrimination. They said that employers who were worried about the penalties for hiring illegal immigrants might refuse to hire people who looked "foreign"—including legal immigrants and American citizens of Hispanic ancestry. *(d)* Mexican government officials claimed that the act would harm United States-Mexican relations. They said that the large number of Mexican citizens who crossed illegally into the United States made an important contribution to both nations' economies, and that such immigration served as a "safety valve" at a time when Mexico's economy was under severe stress. Mexican officials said that the United States and Mexico should have negotiated a joint strategy for dealing with the problem of illegal immigration.

CONTRIBUTIONS OF IMMIGRANT GROUPS TO AMERICA

Although specific groups have been identified with particular American developments, all immigrants have had an impact upon the United States.

1. Economic. *(a) In Agriculture.* In the 19th century, blacks raised cotton at first on southern plantations and later as sharecroppers; German, Scandinavian, and British-Canadian farmers settled the Midwest and the Great Plains. In the 20th century, Mexicans in labor gangs harvested the crops of the Southwest;

Japanese and Italians engaged in truck farming. *(b) In Transportation.* The Irish helped build the Erie Canal and other eastern canals. The Irish and Italians constructed many bridges and railroads. In the Far West, the Chinese built the Union Pacific Railroad. *(c) In Mining and Industry.* The Welsh worked in the coal mines, as did the Poles, other Slavic peoples, and Hungarians. These latter three groups also mined iron ore and labored in the steel mills. The English helped establish the New England textile mills, which later utilized Irish and French Canadian workers. The Germans were occupied in the optical, piano construction, beer-brewing, and chemical industries. The Jews, followed by Italians, helped develop the garment industry. Jews also played a major role in beginning the radio and movie industries. *(d) As Consumers and Workers.* Immigrants increased the demand for the products of agriculture and industry, thereby encouraging American economic growth. Also, by coming in great numbers, during times of business expansion, immigrants served to prevent any shortage of labor.

2. Political. That newly naturalized citizens vote as a "bloc" is a myth. Depending upon the issues, immigrant groups may differ one from the other and even within the same group. Further, as newcomers, immigrants probably are swayed less by party loyalty and more by the issues. Nevertheless, reflecting their ties to the "old country" and their economic status in American society, immigrant groups have voted in major part along predictable lines. For example: In the Presidential election of 1920, ratification of the Treaty of Versailles was urged by the Democratic candidate, James Cox. The treaty, however, was opposed by many ethnic groups. It failed to provide independence for Ireland, said Irish Americans; it was too harsh upon Germany, said German Americans; it did not grant Italy its territorial demands, said Italian Americans. Such opposition to the treaty helped build an overwhelming election victory for Republican Warren Harding.

3. Cultural. Immigrants to America brought their native cultural heritages. With time certain features of these heritages died out while other features became part of American life. In foods, we eat hamburgers and frankfurters named after German cities, English muffins, Irish stew, Hungarian goulash, Chinese chop suey, Jewish delicatessen, and Danish pastry. In music, we listen to Italian operas, German symphonies, black spirituals, Spanish tangos, Rumanian dances, and Polish mazurkas. In literature, we read the plays of England's Shakespeare and Norway's Ibsen and the novels of France's Hugo and Russia's Tolstoi. In sports, we follow football developed from England's rugby, jai alai popularized in Latin America, bowling introduced by the Dutch, and ice hockey developed in Canada. Our art, social studies, philosophy, ethics, and science have borrowed from the great people of all ages and all places. Perhaps our most important inheritance, an outgrowth of our population diversity, is the American spirit of toleration and fair play.

——————————— **Multiple-Choice Questions** ———————————

1. The earliest known people in the New World were   (a) natives who originated here   (b) migratory groups who came from northeast Asia   (c) voluntary immigrants from northwestern Europe   (d) seafaring groups from Hawaii.

2. Which was an important cause of immigration to the United States in the 1840s?   (a) the Napoleonic Wars   (b) changes in our immigration policy   (c) revolutions in Europe   (d) completion of the first transcontinental railroad.

3. Which event had the *most* immediate effect upon immigration to the United States?   (a) the defeat of Mexico by the United States in 1848   (b) the potato famine in Ireland in the 1840s   (c) the Communist seizure of power in Russia in 1917   (d) the independence of Belgium, recognized in 1839.

4. In which period did the largest number of immigrants enter the United States?   (a) 1789–1810   (b) 1840–1860   (c) 1870–1890   (d) 1890–1910.

5. The United States had a liberal immigration policy during most of the 19th century because   (a) many members of Congress were foreign-born   (b) the population of the United States remained constant   (c) there was a shortage of labor in the United States   (d) prosperous times in Europe discouraged immigration to the United States.

6. In the latter part of the 19th century, a liberal immigration policy was generally opposed by   (a) eastern manufacturers   (b) land speculators   (c) labor unions   (d) railroad companies.

7. Where can an expression of the philosophy of the United States concerning immigration be found?   (a) in Washington's Farewell Address   (b) on the base of the Statue of Liberty   (c) in the Clayton Act   (d) in the Gettysburg Address.

8. Which statement is true of the immigration policy of the United States in the late 19th century?   (a) Restrictions were placed on Mexican agricultural workers.   (b) Quotas were assigned to European countries.   (c) Chinese immigration was prohibited.   (d) Japanese immigration was limited.

9. Jews in Czarist Russia suffered from government-inspired outbursts of violence known as   (a) pogroms   (b) quotas   (c) Soviets   (d) ghettos.

10. One problem common to most groups that emigrated to the United States was that they were   (a) resented by earlier immigrants   (b) denied the right to own property   (c) persecuted because of their religious views   (d) denied admission to the public schools.

11. Imagine a Polish immigrant family arriving at New York in 1905. The family consisted of four members: husband, age 43; wife, age 37; son, age 19; and daughter, age 8. Which family member probably assimilated most easily into the American way of life?   (a) husband   (b) wife   (c) son   (d) daughter.

12. The immigrant who came to an American city at the turn of this century was *more* likely to have had what advantage over the migrant of today?   (a) familiarity with the English language   (b) eligibility for welfare assistance   (c) availability of jobs for unskilled labor   (d) existence of integrated housing patterns.

13. The melting-pot theory of Americanization holds that American culture   (a) is homogeneous, with contributions of all immigrant groups blended together   (b) is inferior to British culture   (c) is heterogeneous, with each ethnic group preserving its own individuality   (d) contains almost no aspects attributable to Anglo-Saxon immigrants.

14. The analogy of an orchestra to describe contemporary United States attitudes toward immigrants reflects the idea that   (a) the characteristics and customs of im-

migrants are the same as those already existing in society   (b) individuals from different cultures can contribute to society without giving up their cultural characteristics   (c) society will not become harmonious until the old customs of different cultures are forgotten (d) different cultures should be judged by their esthetic qualities.

15. Which was *not* true of immigration to the United States during the 19th century?   (a) Economic opportunity attracted many immigrants.   (b) Political oppression in their homelands caused people to emigrate.   (c) Religious persecution in their homelands was a cause of emigration.   (d) Occupational qualifications were important for admission.

16. The "new immigrants" who came to the United States after 1890 settled mainly in the cities because   (a) the industrial establishments were advertising for skilled artisans   (b) good housing was available in the large urban centers   (c) most had always lived and worked in cities   (d) most were too poor to establish themselves as farmers.

17. An indication that recently arrived immigrants to the United States were involved in the process of assimilation would be their   (a) use of their native language at home   (b) conformity to their traditional ethnic customs   (c) attendance in an English language literacy class   (d) marriage to other members of their same nationality.

18. Which of the following differed in purpose from the other three?   (a) Gentlemen's Agreement   (b) National Origins Plan   (c) Displaced Persons Act   (d) Chinese Exclusion Act.

19. One of the items below is a main topic in an outline, and three are subtopics. Which is the main topic?   (a) negotiation of the Gentlemen's Agreement   (b) establishment of the quota system   (c) passage of the McCarran-Walter Act   (d) influence of nativism on American immigration policy.

20. Which is the *most* valid generalization pertaining to the concept of nativism?   (a) Nativism stems in part from economic fears.   (b) Nativism is essentially sectional in character.   (c) Nativist movements are present only in free democratic societies.   (d) Racial prejudice is the strongest factor in explaining nativism.

21. The charge made by nativist groups in the United States that Italian immigrants sent their children to parochial schools *most* clearly supports the idea that   (a) nativist activity was restricted to the Eastern cities   (b) all immigrants have faced opposition from nativists   (c) immigrants refused low wages in order to avoid criticism   (d) nativism was based, in part, on religious bias.

22. During the 19th century, discrimination against immigrants to the United States was mainly based on the belief that immigrants   (a) lowered urban property values   (b) would have too great an influence on the enactment of legislation favorable to European nations   (c) lowered the scale of wages because they were willing to work for less money   (d) placed an undue burden on available social services.

23. Which phrase has most often been associated with nativist groups?   (a) "free and unlimited immigration for all"   (b) "the right to trial by jury"   (c) "America for the Americans"   (d) "protection of the rights of minorities."

24. From 1920 to 1965, immigration to the United States was influenced by laws based on the "national origins" principle. This principle was widely criticized, however, because it   (a) permitted unlimited entry to Orientals   (b) favored migration from Northern and Western Europe   (c) gave large quotas to immigrants from Latin America   (d) restricted the admission of French Canadians.

25. Which was true of the McCarran-Walter Act?   (a) The quota for Asians was low-

ered. (b) All literate persons could enter the country and become citizens.
(c) Aliens could be deported if they were found to have Communist affiliations.
(d) The quota system for Latin America was revised.

26. The Immigration Act of 1965 provided that the United States (a) retain the national origins system (b) prohibit immigrants from the Western Hemisphere (c) admit more German immigrants (d) give high priority to needed professional people.

27. Immigration to the United States has been beneficial chiefly because immigrants have (a) brought over much-needed investment capital (b) been an important factor in our recent population growth (c) provided willing tenants for our cities' apartment dwellings (d) contributed to our social and economic development .

28. Which was characteristic of the United States immigration laws during the period 1920 to 1960? (a) They led to a decrease in the number of industrial workers in the United States. (b) They reflected discriminatory practices against certain national groups. (c) They permitted large numbers of immigrants to enter the country. (d) They failed to recognize the rising threat of communism to internal security.

29. Which statement best describes the present immigration policy of the United States? (a) It gives preference to immigrants with relatives in the United States (b) It permits unlimited immigration from all Western countries. (c) It encourages unskilled laborers to come to the United States. (d) It excludes immigrants from Communist countries.

30. Which statement concerning immigration to the United States is best supported by historical evidence? (a) Industrial growth led to a decreased demand for cheap labor. (b) Organized labor generally favored unrestricted immigration. (c) The quota laws were designed to prevent discrimination in immigration. (d) The diversity of the immigrant population created a pluralistic society.

31. Which development has promoted the concept of a pluralistic society in the United States since the end of World War II? (a) the decrease in immigration from Western Europe (b) the growth of movements supporting civil rights (c) recent amendments to the Constitution (d) efforts to encourage the preservation of ethnic heritages.

32. In the United States, recent objections to the growing number of illegal aliens in this country have been prompted mainly by (a) traditional prejudices against certain European ethnic groups (b) persistent unemployment in the United States (c) concern over the rapidly increasing birthrate in the United States (d) concern about the financial support given to other nations by illegal aliens.

ESSAY QUESTIONS

1. Describe *one* economic, *one* political, and *one* social condition in Europe that led to immigration to the United States. Illustrate *each* case by specific reference to any European country.

2. Some historians have classified the European peoples coming to America into two groups: "old immigrants" and "new immigrants." For these two groups describe *(a) three* ways in which they were different and *(b) three* ways in which they were similar.

3. When considering immigration into the United States, *most* Americans think of im-

migrants from Europe. *(a)* Explain *one* reason why most Americans usually think of immigrants from Europe. *(b)* Name any *two* non-European immigrants to the United States and describe *from where, when,* and *why* they came. *(c)* Are the reasons for coming of non-European immigrants similar to or different from those of European immigrants? Defend your answer.

4. Explain *one* reason for the attitude of *each* of the following groups toward immigration: *(a)* Know-Nothings, *(b)* railroad builders in the 1860s, *(c)* labor unions of the 1880s, *(d)* the Ku Klux Klan of the 1920s.

5. The McCarran-Walter Act, our basic immigration law from 1952 to 1965, was the subject of much dispute. *(a)* Explain *two* arguments in support of this law. *(b)* Explain *two* arguments in opposition to this law. *(c)* In your opinion which set of arguments seems more valid? Defend your answer.

6. In regard to the Immigration Act of 1965, *(a)* state *three* of its major provisions and *(b)* for *each* provision stated, explain fully why you approve or disapprove of it.

7. *(a)* Which group was treated more harshly: German Americans during World War I or Japanese Americans during World War II? Present *two* arguments to support your opinion. *(b)* Briefly provide a generalization regarding the effect of war upon minority-majority relations. Be careful not to make too sweeping a statement.

8. *Agree* or *disagree*, presenting *two* arguments to support your opinion, with *each* of the following statements: *(a)* The diversity of the American people has strengthened our democracy. *(b)* The melting-pot theory provides a more accurate explanation of American culture today than does cultural pluralism. *(c)* Although the immigrant experience has been both bitter and sweet, in the long run the sweet has far exceeded the bitter.

9. America owes its greatness, in part, to its liberal immigration policy of the 19th and early 20th centuries. *(a)* Discuss *three* ways in which immigrants contributed to America's greatness. *(b)* Explain *two* problems that the liberal immigration policy posed for the United States.

PART 2. Some Disadvantaged Groups in the American Population Strive to Better Their Conditions

INDIANS

MORE HUMANE TREATMENT SINCE THE 1880s

(For earlier treatment, check the Index.)

With the Indian wars over and most Indians confined to reservations, the nation began to reassess its Indian policies. In 1877 President Rutherford B. Hayes informed Congress that "Many, if not most, of our Indian wars have had their origin in broken promises and acts of injustice on our part." In 1881 *Helen Hunt Jackson* further awakened the nation to its shameful treatment of the Indians through her book *A Century of Dishonor*. To make amends, Congress passed the following legislation:

1. Dawes General Allotment Act (1887). This act provided that *(a)* each Indian family head be allotted a 160-acre farm out of reservation lands, *(b)* each allottee who adopted the "habits of civilized life" be granted American citizenship, and *(c)* "surplus" reservation lands remaining after the allotments be available for sale to white settlers.

The Dawes Act, although well intentioned, did not benefit the Indians. Since most Indians were unfamiliar with farming and were assigned poor lands, they were often unable to secure a living. Many Indians did not wish to become "civilized" as reflected in the white culture but sought to retain their own tribal cultures. Finally, chiefly as a result of the "surplus" land provision, the Indians by the 1930s had lost 90 million out of 140 million acres of their reservation lands.

2. Snyder Indian Citizenship Act (1924). In recognition of the many Indians who volunteered for military service during World War I, this act granted American citizenship to all Indians born in the United States. (It applied to about one-third of the Indian population who had not yet acquired citizenship.)

3. Wheeler-Howard Indian Reorganization Act (1934): *(a)* ended land allotments, restored unsold "surplus" lands to tribal ownership, and began the repurchase of lands for Indian use, *(b)* authorized the tribes to form corporations with power to launch tribal business enterprises, and *(c)* provided for elected tribal councils with significant powers over their people. The act reversed previous federal policies by restoring the tribe as the center of Indian life.

THE INDIANS TODAY: A DISADVANTAGED MINORITY

1. Indian Population. In 1492 Indians residing in what is now the United States were estimated to number 850,000. By 1890, after four centuries of contact with white people, the Indian population had dropped to fewer than 300,000. Today the Indian population is sharply up. One Indian author claims that there are 500,000 Indians living in the cities, 100,000 in scattered eastern bands, and 400,000 on the reservations.

2. Problems Facing the Indians. *(a) Poor Health.* In infant mortality, malnutrition, and infectious diseases, Indian rates are much above the national average. The reservation Indian has a shorter life expectancy than the average American. *(b) Poor Education.* Many Indians are illiterate. Many Indian children achieve only grade school educations—their school dropout rate is almost double the national figure. *(c) Poverty.* Many Indians occupy substandard dwellings; they lack training to hold down decent jobs; three-quarters of Indian families earn considerably less than the national average.

3. Indian Moods and Demands. Indians today are no longer willing to accept passively an inferior status. They have become more active in pressing their demands for justice and equality. They speak of "Indian power" and inform whites that "Indians discovered America." They want to *(a)* preserve their Indian identity and culture, *(b)* have the government honor its treaties with their ancestors, *(c)* receive massive government aid for reservations to improve social services—health, housing, and schools—and to attract industries, and *(d)* control their own lives and not have Indian policies set by the "great white father" in Washington. Responding to this demand, the government has named Indians to head its Bureau of Indian Affairs.

AMERICANS OF SPANISH ORIGIN

THE SPANISH HERITAGE OF THE UNITED STATES

Spain financed the 1492 expedition of Columbus that reached the New World. Spanish explorers led the first expeditions into Florida and the American Southwest. The Spanish founded the first American cities: in 1565 St. Augustine, Florida, and in 1605 Santa Fe, New Mexico.

First to reach the New World, the Spanish introduced horses and cattle. Based on these two animals, the Spanish began, in the United States Southwest, the ranch system and the cattle industry. In other ways, the Spanish contributed to American culture in the Southwest: Spanish law regarding land titles, water rights, and mining rights; Spanish architecture in homes and churches, and Spanish foods, music, clothes, and art.

Our Spanish heritage is also reflected in our population makeup. In the mid-1980s, Hispanic Americans numbered more than 17 million, placing them after blacks as the nation's second largest minority. Of these Hispanic Americans *(a)* Mexican Americans comprised 61 percent. They resided overwhelmingly in five Southwestern states: Arizona, California, Colorado, New Mexico, and Texas. *(b)* Puerto Ricans made up 17 percent. They lived mainly in southern New York

State and New Jersey. *(c)* Cubans, most of whom had fled from their island home after Fidel Castro established a Communist state, numbered 6 percent. They lived mainly in Florida, especially in the Miami area. *(d)* Persons from Central and South America and others of Spanish origin totaled 16 percent.

MEXICAN AMERICANS IN OUR POPULATION

1. By Annexation of Territory (mid-19th century). With the admission to the Union of Texas (1845), victory in the Mexican War and the acquisition of the Mexican Cession (1848), and the payment for the Gadsden Purchase (1853), about 100,000 Mexicans came under American rule and became American citizens. At first they were known as Mexican Americans, or "Mexicanos." They later were called Chicanos, a contraction of the word "Mexicanos." With time, large numbers of American settlers of European background entered the Southwest. Called "Anglos" by the Mexican Americans, these newcomers soon became the majority.

As inhabitants of the United States, the Mexican Americans faced many difficulties. Scorned by the Anglos, the Chicanos were stereotyped as lazy, cowardly, and dishonest. The Chicanos further were easily identifiable. Most were *mestizos* of mixed Spanish and Indian ancestry; all spoke Spanish, worshipped as Roman Catholics, and identified with Spanish culture. Some Mexicans claimed ownership of lands based on old Spanish and Mexican grants, which documents were in many cases lost or destroyed. Many Mexican land claims, consequently, were thrown out by the American authorities and the lands assigned to newly arrived Anglo claimants.

2. By Legal Immigration (20th century). Mexicans were driven by poor economic conditions to leave their native land and migrate to the United States, especially to the Southwest. While some helped build railroads or worked in mines, most became migratory farmhands. At harvesttime, they went from one large farm to another, picking crops—citrus fruits, berries, vegetables, sugarcane, and cotton. Unskilled laborers, they received poor housing and low wages. Constantly on the move and working in crews with other Mexicans, they had little contact with Americans. Out of work during the off-season, they lived on the outskirts of such large cities as San Antonio and Los Angeles in ghettos or "shantytowns" called *barrios*.

During the World War II years, Mexican workers were needed to offset labor shortages in American industry, railroad transportation, and agriculture. By special arrangement between the United States and Mexican governments, more than 300,000 Mexicans were admitted on a temporary basis as "contract laborers," or *braceros*. Since World War II, the number of Mexican immigrants has remained high.

3. By Illegal Immigration—The "Wetbacks" (20th century). Many Mexicans—in some years numbering one million—have entered the United States illegally. These illegal immigrants possibly were unaware that they were exempted (until 1976) from quota restrictions, perhaps felt they could not pass the literacy test requirement of reading a language or could not meet the health standards, or wished to avoid the expense and delay of securing American *visas* (entry permits). Since some illegal Mexican immigrants entered the United States by crossing the Rio Grande—some swimming across it—they all became known as "wetbacks."

Many illegal immigrants did not remain permanently in the United States. Some, after working for a while and accumulating money, voluntarily returned to Mexico. Others were eventually caught and deported to Mexico by the Border Patrol of the *United States Immigration and Naturalization Service*. During a five-year period in the 1950s, the number deported back to Mexico reached the staggering total of 3.8 million.

Check the Index for the 1986 Immigration Act.

MEXICAN AMERICAN MOODS—SINCE WORLD WAR II

During the war, some 500,000 Mexican Americans served in the armed forces. Learning skilled trades and seeing that people outside the *barrios* lived better lives, many Mexican Americans returned home determined to improve conditions for themselves and their communities.

WHAT DO THE MEXICAN AMERICANS WANT?

1. In Education. Mexican American children have fared poorly in the public schools. Chicano leaders demand upgrading of facilities for these children, by using bilingual teachers who can provide instruction in Spanish, teaching English as a second language, and introducing courses in Chicano history and culture.

2. In Employment. Mexican Americans, being mainly unskilled and semiskilled workers, earn low wages. (Illegal Mexican immigrants—the wetbacks—often work for less than the minimum wage.) Mexican Americans have a higher than average unemployment rate, which is in part caused by the increasing use of farm machines. In 1965 *Cesar Chavez*, head of the United Farm Workers—an AFL-CIO union—began to organize California's grape pickers. *La Huelga* (the strike) became the rallying cry for the Chicano farm workers. Chavez received support from influential Anglo political, religious, and labor figures. After five years, Chavez won contracts from the grape owners that provided for union recognition, higher wages, and health and welfare benefits. In cities, Mexican American workers seek government programs of vocational training and job placement. In the early 1970s, the Amalgamated Clothing Workers Union (AFL-CIO) organized low-paid Mexican American workers in the Texas garment industry.

3. In Housing. Mexican Americans in the *barrios* reside in run-down, dilapidated buildings. They demand that these structures be torn down and replaced by low-rent public housing units.

4. In Health. As compared to the Anglos, the Mexican Americans have an infant mortality rate that is three times higher and a life expectancy that is some ten years lower. They demand more and improved public health services.

5. Treatment by Law-Enforcement Agencies. Mexican Americans are bitter regarding their treatment by the various city and state police departments and the Border Patrol of the Immigration Service. They claim that the law-enforcement personnel—overwhelmingly Anglos and constantly looking for illegal Mexican wetbacks—are prone to violence against persons of Spanish origin. Leaders demand that these agencies instruct their personnel to respect the civil rights of all suspects and to spur the hiring of qualified Mexican American personnel.

6. Voice in Government. Leaders prod their followers to take an active part in politics—joining political parties, attending meetings, registering, and voting—so as to make government responsive to their needs.

7. Acceptance as Mexican Americans. The Mexican Americans demand that the Anglos accept them as equals and respect their Spanish and Indian culture.

PUERTO RICANS IN OUR POPULATION

1. Background. Victorious in the Spanish-American War, the United States in 1898 annexed the Caribbean island of Puerto Rico. In 1917 the United States granted the islanders American citizenship, thereby permitting them to move freely to the mainland.

2. Emigration From Puerto Rico to the Mainland. Starting in the early 1940s, Puerto Ricans arrived in large numbers, attracted by jobs available during wartime and the postwar boom. By 1960 one million Puerto Ricans resided in and about New York City.

They provided the unskilled and semiskilled labor, previously performed by European immigrants who, curtailed by restrictive laws, were now a mere trickle. The Puerto Ricans secured jobs in the garment trades; the transport industry; hotels, hospitals, and restaurants; and small consumer goods factories.

3. Return to the Island. Starting in the early 1960s, the number of Puerto Ricans returning to the island roughly equaled those coming to the mainland. The returnees were motivated by (a) discrimination and unemployment on the mainland, (b) improved living standards, educational and health facilities, and job opportunities on the island, and (c) a desire to bring up their children within the Latin culture.

PUERTO RICAN MOODS AND DEMANDS

The Puerto Ricans on the mainland want to be considered as equals, treated with dignity, and permitted to enjoy the benefits of American life. They want better educational facilities for their children and more of vocational training programs, low-rental public housing projects, and public health centers.

To further these goals, the Puerto Ricans have various self-help organizations and also benefit from the following government efforts: (1) The New York State Commission on Human Rights combats discrimination in housing and jobs. (2) The federal *Equal Employment Opportunity Commission* acts to prevent discrimination in employment. (3) The *Voting Rights Act of 1965* declared that a sixth grade education in Spanish in Puerto Rico was evidence of literacy for voting purposes. In 1973 a federal district court ordered the New York City Board of Elections to print all election materials in Spanish as well as English so as to assist Puerto Rican voters. (4) In 1970 New York City instituted its college plan of *open admissions*. The plan guaranteed all high school graduates admission to one of the city's two- or four-year colleges, with remedial classes to make up for any educational deficiencies. Within one year, the number of Puerto Rican college students doubled.

WOMEN

TO THE MID-19TH CENTURY—WOMEN'S INFERIOR STATUS

Women (1) were under the legal authority of their husbands or fathers; (2) could own property under certain circumstances, but upon marriage women surrendered control of their property to their husbands; (3) were restricted economically to household and farm activities and denied equal opportunity in business and the professions; (4) received little schooling, limited to household tasks and moral training, or none at all, and were restricted in access to higher and professional education; and (5) were denied the right to vote and otherwise participate in political affairs.

WOMEN'S PROGRESS IN EDUCATION

1. Elementary and Secondary Education for Girls. In the early 19th century, most children—boys and girls—received little or no formal education. By 1860 children in the North had available a free elementary education because of the rise of tax-supported public schools. Later in the 19th century, with the growth of tax-supported public high schools, young girls had available a secondary-level education preparing them for citizenship and homemaking as well as an occupation or admission to institutions of higher learning.

2. Higher Education for Women

a. Pioneers in Higher Education for Women. (1) *Emma Willard* in 1821 founded in New York State the Troy Female Seminary, later renamed the Emma Willard School. Enrolling young women on a tuition basis, the school offered instruction in the "household arts" and in subjects of higher learning—notably mathematics, science, history, and training for teaching careers. (2) *Catherine Beecher* devoted her life to seeking for women equal opportunity with men for higher education. She wrote, lectured, and established "female colleges" in Connecticut and in the Midwestern states of Ohio, Illinois, Iowa, and Wisconsin. (3) *Mary Lyon* in 1837 established in Massachusetts, *Mount Holyoke Seminary,* which later became the first full-fledged women's college. Mary Lyon sought to keep the tuition fees reasonable by having the students undertake various school maintenance chores. Mount Holyoke offered a general college-level program and prepared many women to become teachers. It set the pattern for the establishment of other Northeast women's colleges such as *Barnard, Bryn Mawr, Radcliffe, Smith, Vassar,* and *Wellesley.*

   b. Coeducation. In the 1830s, *Oberlin College* in Ohio became the first coeducational college. Oberlin's example, of admitting women as well as men students, was soon followed by other Midwestern institutions.

   In recent years, the trend toward college coeducation has accelerated. Women's colleges such as Hunter, Vassar, and Skidmore have enrolled men; men's colleges such as Yale and Princeton have opened their facilities to women.

   c. Higher Education Today. The federal government has been a powerful force combating sex discrimination by institutions of higher learning. The 1964 *Civil Rights Act* prohibited discriminatory practices by employers against women. Using this provision, the Department of Health, Education, and Welfare pressured colleges and universities to take "affirmative action" regarding the hiring and promoting of women faculty members. The 1972 *Higher Education Act* prohibited public colleges and universities from discriminating against women in school admission policies. Any higher learning institution violating this prohibition faces the loss of federal aid funds.

   Today, despite minor complaints, women generally have achieved equal access with men to higher educational opportunities.

WOMEN'S PROGRESS IN ECONOMIC MATTERS

   1. The Industrial Revolution Spurs Employment for Women. As women found work outside the home, they were able to be economically independent of male relatives. Such work, requiring minimal physical exertion, resulted from several inventions of the Industrial Revolution—first textile machines and later sewing machines, typewriters, and telephones. As more women joined the labor force, they sought better conditions by joining labor unions. In 1911 about 150 workers, mostly women, died in New York City as a result of a fire and the lack of safety facilities, at the Triangle Shirtwaist Company. This shocking event led to state laws regulating wages, hours, and factory conditions—especially for women and children—and led also to many garment workers joining the *International Ladies Garment Workers Union* (ILGWU).

   During wartime, women have found greater employment opportunities to increase production and to replace men taken for military service.

2. Women Pioneers in the Professions. Women, long accepted as teachers of young children, began to overcome obstacles keeping them from other professions. *(a) Elizabeth Blackwell* was rejected by eight medical schools before being accepted, as a joke, by vote of the student body, at the Geneva, New York, College of Medicine. She graduated in 1849 at the head of her class. *(b)* Her sister-in-law, *Antoinette Louisa Blackwell,* became the first fully ordained female minister in the United States when in 1852 she took the pulpit of the Congregational Church at South Butler, New York. *(c) Ellen H. Richards,* the first woman admitted to the Massachusetts Institute of Technology, graduated with a degree in chemistry. In 1894 in Boston, she began the first school lunch programs, thereby enabling mothers to hold jobs without having to worry about the midday feeding of their school-age children.

3. Women Workers in the Economy Today. Nine out of every 20 workers are women. Women's major occupations are in clerical, sales, and technical jobs (46 percent); as accountants, doctors, lawyers, teachers, and other professionals (23 percent); in service jobs such as in hospitals, restaurants, and beauty parlors (19 percent); and as factory workers, especially in the textile and clothing industries (9 percent). The average income of women workers is 64 percent that of men because women *(a)* perform the lower-paying jobs, *(b)* lose seniority by leaving jobs to bear children and raise families, and *(c)* face discrimination based on sex in hiring, wage, and promotion practices.

4. Government Protection for Working Women. Benefiting from general worker-protection laws, women workers also benefit from special laws. Many states limit women's working hours and prohibit women's employment in "hazardous occupations." New York and some other states require employers to give women and men "equal pay for equal work." The 1964 Civil Rights Act bars employers, employment agencies, and labor unions from discriminating against women in hiring and salary offers, in job referral, and in apprenticeship programs. To investigate complaints of discrimination, the act established a federal *Equal Employment Opportunity Commission.*

5. Remaining Economic Demands of Women. *(a)* They want to overcome bias—by some unions against admitting women members, by some lending institutions against granting mortgages and other forms of credit to women, and by some employers against hiring and promoting women. *(b)* Women want to overcome prejudice by the general public against women in certain occupations such as driving taxicabs, piloting airplanes, or preparing prescriptions. Women protest advertisements that portray them as living only to please men and as belonging in the home attending to domestic chores. *(c)* Women want all states to adopt "equal pay for equal work" laws.

WOMEN'S LEGAL PROGRESS IN FAMILY MATTERS

1. Legal Disabilities of Married Women: In Early America. Upon marriage, a woman became a "chattel" or property of her husband. Married women were classified with minors and mental defectives as not legally responsible; they could not sue or be sued except through their husbands; they surrendered control of any property to their husbands; if they worked, their wages belonged to their husbands; any children resulting from the marriage belonged to the husband.

2. Gains Made by Women in Family Law. Since the laws concerning marriage and divorce are powers reserved to the states under the Constitution, women sought legal reforms through state legislatures. In New York State, *Elizabeth Cady Stanton,* the suffragette, and *Ernestine Rose,* a Jewish immigrant originally from Poland, led the legal reform movement. Their efforts were supported by well-to-do New Yorkers who wanted to safeguard their daughters' dowries and inheritances. In 1848, the state legislature passed the *Married Women's Property Act,* which allowed the property of the wife at the time of marriage to remain under her control. In 1860 New York State enacted further laws giving women the right to sue and be sued, to control their own wages and personal property, and to exercise joint guardianship of minor children.

Today, women in most (but not all) states have achieved legal equality with men and, in cases of divorce, are considered the preferred guardians of minor children.

WOMEN'S PROGRESS IN POLITICAL MATTERS

Those women who militantly sought to gain women the suffrage—the right to vote—were known as suffragettes.

1. Leading Suffragettes. *(a) Susan B. Anthony* was the outstanding 19th-century suffragette leader. She devoted her life—writing, lecturing, organizing, and agitating—in the cause of women's suffrage. She worked especially to secure a women's suffrage amendment to the Constitution. In 1920, some 14 years after her death, the nation ratified such an amendment—the Nineteenth—and in her honor popularly called it the Susan B. Anthony Amendment. *(b) Lucretia Mott* and Elizabeth Cady Stanton issued the call for and directed the first women's rights convention held in 1848 at Seneca Falls (New York). *(c) Lucy Stone,* who graduated from Oberlin College in 1847, later married Henry Blackwell, but insisted upon retaining her maiden name and being known as Mrs. Stone. (Today women, usually in the professional field, who, after marriage, continue to use their original names are known as "Lucy Stoners.") *(d) Amelia Bloomer* for a time edited a newspaper supporting temperance, abolition of slavery, and women's rights. She is best remembered, however, for her wearing of "sensible" clothing—a short dress and loose trousers gathered at the ankle—which trousers became known popularly as "bloomers."

2. Major Events in the Struggle for Women's Suffrage. In 1848 the *Women's Rights Convention,* held at Seneca Falls, New York, drafted a declaration that paraphrased the Declaration of Independence by stating that "all men and women are created equal," listing women's grievances against a man-dominated society, and demanding for women opportunities in education, the business world, and professions as well as rights regarding property, child guardianship, and voting. In 1869 the Territory of Wyoming granted the vote to women. By 1900 four western states permitted women to vote, and by 1914 twelve other states had so acted. By 1920, in recognition of the contribution of women to the American effort in World War I, the states quickly ratified the Nineteenth Amendment prohibiting the states and the federal government from denying the right to vote to citizens "on account of sex." Thereafter, on the federal level, women won election to Congress and secured appointment to Cabinet posts and to judgeships. They also gained important state and local offices.

3. The Women's Liberation Movement Today. The struggle for women's rights languished temporarily following the adoption in 1920 of the Nineteenth Amendment but burst into full public view in the 1960s with an outpouring of college courses, lectures, magazine articles, books, and organizations. The struggle for women's rights now became known as the *Women's Liberation Movement,* or popularly as Women's Lib. Its active participants became known as *feminists* or sometimes as militant feminists.

Gloria Steinem presented the women's viewpoint in a new magazine. *Betty Friedan* founded the major feminist group, the *National Organization for Women* (NOW). By the early 1970s, NOW had about 100 chapters throughout the nation and some 10,000 members, mainly white, middle-class, professional women. NOW seeks to gain "full equality for women in America in a truly equal partnership with men." In political matters, NOW urges ratification to the Constitution of an amendment guaranteeing women equal rights with men.

4. The Proposed Equal Rights Amendment (ERA). In 1972 Congress overwhelmingly proposed an Equal Rights Amendment (ERA) stating that "equality of rights under the law shall not be denied or abridged by the United States or by any state on account of sex."

Feminists were jubilant. They argued that ERA would assure women equal treatment with men in conducting a business, in receiving payment for similar types of work, in setting the age for attaining legal adulthood, and in gaining admission to tax-supported educational institutions.

Opponents of the amendment, including some women, were fearful. They argued that ERA would end the preference usually given mothers in child-custody cases arising out of divorces, would make women eligible for all types of military duty, and would prohibit state laws extending protections to women—forbidding them to work on night shifts or in hazardous occupations.

ERA required ratification within seven years, by three-fourths, or 38, of the states. By early 1979, with the seven-year deadline at hand, ERA had only 35 ratifications. Although Congress extended the deadline until 1982, supporters failed to get the necessary ratifications and the amendment died.

BLACKS

BLACKS IN AMERICA: FROM COLONIAL TIMES TO WORLD WAR II

For background to 1900, check the Index.

DURING AND AFTER WORLD WAR I

1. In the Armed Forces. Some 400,000 blacks served in the armed forces. Barred from the Marines and assigned only to menial tasks in the Navy, most black recruits ended up in the Army. Trained in army camps throughout the nation, many black recruits encountered considerable discrimination from whites and the resulting frictions led to a number of riots.

Some 100,000 blacks were shipped overseas to France, half in service and half in fighting units. Black fighting units achieved commendable records, and many individual blacks won citations for bravery. Blacks were moved by President Wilson's talk of making the world "safe for democracy." They hoped that, in the postwar years, America would expand democracy to its black citizens. Instead, in the 1920s, America moved, in the words of President Harding, to "return to normalcy," that is, the status quo of the late 19th century.

2. Migration to Northern Cities. During World War I, a third of a million blacks, lured by jobs in war industries, moved from the South to northern (and western) cities. After the war, they continued to move northward, as expanding industries hired black workers. In securing jobs, blacks benefited unexpectedly from the restrictive immigration laws of the 1920s which sharply curtailed the admission of white European workers. From 1910 to 1930, the black population in the North more than doubled.

3. Northern Discrimination. Northern blacks freely exercised their right to vote, but they encountered other forms of discrimination. *(a) Socially.* Blacks were crowded into slum areas, or ghettos, where they inhabited rundown, unsanitary housing for which they paid high rents. Their children attended neighborhood schools that were segregated usually not by law, but because of residential patterns. Such segregated black schools were often inferior to schools in white neighborhoods. *(b) Economically.* Blacks got the lowest-paying jobs, had little opportunity to advance, and were barred from most labor unions and professional organizations.

4. Effect of the 1929 Depression. Generally unskilled and poorly paid, northern blacks were particularly hard hit by the depression of 1929. In 1932 they overwhelmingly voted for Franklin D. Roosevelt and his promise of a

"New Deal." Under Roosevelt the status of blacks improved, as New Dealers fought the depression and provided jobs and housing for blacks and whites.

BLACK PROGRESS STARTING WITH WORLD WAR II

1. Gains During the War

a. **Reawakening of Public Concern.** As the United States fought to destroy German nazism with its racist ideas, many Americans realized that *(a)* racial discrimination at home was morally unjust, and *(b)* black soldiers who serve their country deserved equality for themselves and their families. Americans were also influenced by the 1944 publication of a study of the American black written by the Swedish sociologist *Gunnar Myrdal.* Entitling his work *An American Dilemma,* Myrdal pointed out to Americans the contradiction between their belief in democracy and their treatment of blacks.

b. **In the Armed Forces.** About one million blacks were part of the American military force. Although not treated fully as equals, they found conditions had improved as compared to World War I. The black recruits of World War II (1) were admitted to the Marine Corps, (2) were trained for more skilled tasks and received higher ratings in the Navy, (3) experienced less discrimination in the Army, and (4) participated in fewer racial riots.

Half a million blacks served overseas both in service and fighting units. Many black units as well as individuals were cited for distinguished action.

c. **In Employment.** To combat hiring discrimination, President Franklin D. Roosevelt established a temporary *Fair Employment Practices Committee* (FEPC). It sought to prevent discrimination by defense industries against workers because of "race, creed, color, or national origin." From 1941 to 1945 the number of black workers in war plants quadrupled, and many blacks advanced to more skilled and better paying jobs.

2. Gains Since World War II

a. **State and Local Antidiscrimination Efforts.** In 1945 New York State passed the first law against discrimination in employment, the *Ives-Quinn Act.* Subsequently, New York State prohibited discrimination in housing and places of public accommodation and in admission to educational institutions. The *New York State Division of Human Rights* investigates and tries to end discriminatory practices.

Today about 30 states in the North and West have fair employment practices laws. About ten states have laws requiring fair practices in the rental and sale of housing units. Also a number of cities have local antidiscrimination ordinances.

b. **Private Efforts Against Discrimination.** Corporations sought qualified blacks for skilled factory, clerical, and managerial positions. Industrial unions extended membership to blacks. Major league baseball dropped its unwritten color bar in 1947 and admitted the first black ballplayer, *Jackie Robinson.* Movie producers stopped portraying blacks as happy-go-lucky stereotypes and started presenting them as well-rounded human beings with their fair share of human strengths and weaknesses. Advertising agencies began including blacks in their magazine and television displays. Insurance companies invested funds for buildings and businesses in inner-city areas.

   c. Federal Efforts on Civil Rights. President Truman prohibited discrimination in the hiring and promoting of federal employees and began the integration of personnel in the armed forces. Truman also appointed a *Committee on Civil Rights,* that submitted the historic report "To Secure These Rights." The committee asserted that racial and religious discrimination prevents achievement of the American ideal of democracy. It proposed federal laws to bar discrimination in voting and employment.

   President Truman repeatedly requested such legislation, but could not prevail over southern Senators armed with the filibuster. Nevertheless, Truman had elevated civil rights into a major national issue.

   Thereafter, all three branches of the federal government became increasingly involved in civil rights matters—as discussed in the following pages.

PROBLEM OF SEGREGATION IN EDUCATION

   1. Background. Because the Fourteenth Amendment guarantees all citizens "equal protection of the laws," the constitutionality of state and local segregation laws has often been challenged before the Supreme Court. In 1896, in *Plessy vs. Ferguson,* which involved a Louisiana law segregating railroad passengers, the Supreme Court held constitutional state laws giving blacks facilities that are *separate but equal.* Thus fortified, the South pressed forward with segregation. However, facilities for blacks were almost always inferior to those for whites. In education, black schools were poorly constructed and equipped, black teachers poorly trained and paid.

   2. The Supreme Court Holds That "Separate Educational Facilities Are Inherently Unequal" (1954)

   a. Supreme Court Decision. In 1954, in *Brown vs. Board of Education of Topeka* (Kansas), the Supreme Court unanimously decided that segregation of black children in public schools violates the Fourteenth Amendment. Chief Justice *Earl Warren* pointed out that (1) education plays a vital role in training children for citizenship, employment, and use of leisure, (2) separating black children from others solely on the basis of race "generates a feeling of inferiority" that may affect them "in a way unlikely ever to be undone," and (3) therefore, "separate educational facilities are inherently unequal."

   In 1955 the Supreme Court empowered federal district courts to supervise plans of state and local authorities for achieving school desegregation with "all deliberate speed."

   b. Support for the Decision. In the North the Supreme Court decision was praised for upholding American democratic beliefs in human dignity and equality of opportunity. In the South it was (1) accepted by a minority of whites, who urged obedience to the law, (2) praised by many religious leaders, who condemned segregation as morally wrong, and (3) hailed by blacks, who felt that segregation meant second-class citizenship.

    c. **Opposition to the Decision.** (1) *Southern White Groups.* The White Citizens Councils and the Ku Klux Klan defended segregation as part of the southern way of life. These groups used publicity, economic pressure, threats, and sometimes violence against advocates of integration. (2) *Southern State Legislatures.* Several legislatures approved *interposition resolutions,* defying the desegregation decision on the ground that the federal government has no constitutional power over education. Interposition was based on the pre-Civil War doctrine of nullification. (Check the Index.) This and other evasive tactics the Supreme Court declared unconstitutional.

    d. **Crisis in Little Rock, Arkansas.** In 1957 Governor Orval Faubus used the Arkansas National Guard to prevent nine black children from entering an all-white school in Little Rock. After a meeting with President Eisenhower, Faubus obeyed a court order to withdraw the National Guard. When a mob kept the black children from the school, Eisenhower ordered United States army units to Little Rock to restore order. Under federal protection the nine blacks attended the previously all-white high school.

3. Developments on the Educational Front: In the South

    a. **Substantial Acceptance.** Six states with small black populations—Delaware, Kentucky, Maryland, Missouri, Oklahoma, and West Virginia—faced little public opposition to desegregation. The District of Columbia, with its black majority, also achieved desegregation.

"This place isn't big enough for both of us, mac."

Englehardt in The St. Louis Post-Dispatch

b. Token Acceptance. The 11 states of the former Confederacy resisted the Supreme Court decision. In 1963–1964 only 2 percent of their black students attended desegregated schools. In the *Deep South* states, where the black population is largest, white opposition to integration was strongest.

c. Federal Pressure for Integration. The 1964 *Civil Rights Act* allowed the federal government to deny financial aid to state programs practicing discrimination. The 1965 *Elementary and Secondary Education Act* authorized federal funds for distribution to local school districts. Thereupon, the United States *Office of Education* required southern school districts desiring federal aid to submit and implement certain "guidelines"—plans for the desegregation of school faculties and pupils. In 1969 the Supreme Court, under Chief Justice *Warren Burger,* unanimously held that all districts must "terminate dual school systems at once."

d. Further Integration in the South. For the 1971–1972 school year, the federal government claimed that over 90 percent of southern black children were attending desegregated schools. Critics claimed that this figure reflected only the end of dual school systems, whereas many black children were still segregated within school systems, and that the number actually integrated was only 38 percent.

4. Developments on the Educational Front: In the North

a. Toward School Integration. Although some northern cities enforced legal segregation, most contained black residential ghettos that caused school segregation not by law—*de jure,* but in fact—*de facto.* Public schools in black areas tended to be more crowded and less well-equipped than schools in white areas. Northern communities experienced mass demonstrations and boycotts by black groups protesting school segregation. Many school boards thereupon took steps to integrate "fringe area" schools and to permit open enrollment by blacks in underpopulated white schools.

These steps failed to satisfy some civil rights groups. They demanded that all schools achieve racial balance, by mass busing of both black and white pupils if necessary. As some black groups insisted upon total integration, some white parents formed groups to defend the *neighborhood school policy.*

b. Toward "Quality Education." Many school boards made efforts to improve facilities in ghetto schools and provide "quality education." They assigned additional teachers, reduced class sizes, scheduled special classes, and made available more textbooks and other instructional materials.

c. Toward School Decentralization. Some civil rights groups realized that integration of school systems in large cities would take many years or would be impossible because of the large black populations in the inner cities. These civil rights groups have demanded school decentralization. They wished to replace the centralized school administration, which they claimed was bureaucratic and dominated by whites, with local school boards, each controlling its own neighborhood schools. They argued that black community school boards could best provide for the education of black children.

Opponents of decentralization feared that local control would result in a lowering of educational standards and enable extremist groups to dominate ghetto schools, harass the teaching staff, and introduce questionable courses of study.

5. The Busing Issue

a. For Busing. In 1971, in *Swann vs. Board of Education of Charlotte-Mecklenburg* (North Carolina), the Supreme Court unanimously upheld the busing of children as a proper means of overcoming deliberate southern state-imposed school segregation. Thereafter, lower federal courts ordered extensive busing to overcome "de jure" school racial imbalance in the South and also "de facto" imbalance in midwestern and far western cities. These latter busing orders aroused much public resentment.

b. Limits on Busing. In 1974 Congress approved a provision that limited busing. Except where necessary to protect the constitutional rights of minority-group children, the law barred federal courts from ordering busing beyond the school closest or next closest to the child's home.

c. Against Busing. In 1974 the Supreme Court, in *Milliken vs. Bradley*, decided by 5 to 4 that the courts could not order busing when segregation resulted from living patterns rather than discrimination by school boards. The decision put an end to mandatory cross-busing of black children in the urban Detroit school district with the white children in the suburban Detroit school districts. The Court majority held that, unless the districts involved had deliberately practiced discrimination, the Constitution did not require interdistrict busing.

d. Latest Developments. In 1979 in cases involving two northern cities (Columbus and Dayton, Ohio), the Supreme Court found that the school boards had deliberately pursued segregationist policies in the past and ordered the school boards to "eliminate the effects of past discrimination" by undertaking extensive busing programs.

Editorial cartoon by Pat Oliphant. Copyright, The Washington Star.
Reprinted with permission.

"Into the bus, off the bus, into the bus, off the bus— man, what an education!"

During the 1980s, although school segregation remained widespread and busing continued in some places, there was a trend away from mandatory busing. One reason was the tendency of federal courts to conclude that remaining segregation was largely *de facto* (for example, caused by housing patterns) rather than *de jure* (caused by deliberate governmental policies). A second reason was that the Reagan administration went to court on several occasions to support school districts seeking an end to mandatory busing.

6. Affirmative Action in Education: The Bakke Case (1978). The 1964 Civil Rights Act prohibited discrimination based on race by any educational institution receiving federal funds. Citing this provision, the Office of Education urged college and university admissions offices to redress past discrimination by programs to benefit minority groups—programs known as *affirmative action.* At the Davis Medical School of the University of California, the admissions office set aside 16 out of 100 positions in the freshman class for members of minority groups—blacks, Mexicans, and Asians.

Allan Bakke, a white engineer who had served with the Marines in Vietnam, determined to become a doctor. He twice applied to the Davis Medical School and was twice rejected—although his medical aptitude test scores were higher than some minority applicants who gained acceptance. Bakke felt that he was a victim of the Davis admissions program of *minority quotas,* or *reverse discrimination.* He took legal action claiming that he was being denied his Constitutional rights under the "equal protection" clause of the Fourteenth Amendment and was being subjected to racial discrimination for being white, in violation of the 1964 Civil Rights Act.

In 1978, the Supreme Court, by a 5-to-4 vote, handed down a complex decision of two major parts: *(a)* Bakke must be admitted to the Davis Medical School, and the Davis affirmative action program with its set quota for minority students is invalid because it is biased against nonminority applicants. (This part of the decision appealed to persons opposed to quotas and in favor of merit selection of applicants.) *(b)* Race and ethnic origins may be considered as one of many factors in establishing programs of college admissions. (This part of the decision appealed to persons who supported affirmative action to assist the victims of past discrimination.)

Many observers held that the Supreme Court decision was ambiguous and confusing, and that further lawsuits would be brought to challenge affirmative action programs. (For affirmative action in employment, check the Index for the Weber Case.)

CIVIL RIGHTS PROBLEMS IN VOTING AND OTHER AREAS

1. Two Civil Rights Voting Acts. These acts, passed in 1957 and 1960, spurred federal efforts on behalf of citizens denied the right to vote. To protect voting rights, these acts required court procedures, which proved to be cumbersome and time-consuming.

These two laws helped increase the number of black voters, but slowly. Civil rights leaders demanded further laws against discrimination.

2. Continuing Struggle for Civil Rights (1960–1964)

a. Nonviolent Protests by Blacks. Southern black "sit-ins" at "for whites only" lunch counters and "ride-ins" on segregated buses furthered desegregation.

b. March on Washington. In 1963 some 200,000 blacks and whites demanded further civil rights legislation by participating in an orderly and peaceful "March on Washington." They heard the Reverend Martin Luther King, Jr., head of the Southern Christian Leadership Conference, cry out eloquently, "I have a dream" of equality, of brotherhood, and of freedom and justice.

c. Violence Against Blacks and Civil Rights Workers. Although black leaders stressed nonviolence, the surge of demonstrations aroused violence by white segregationists. In the South black demonstrators were subjected to strong-arm tactics by police: clubbings, fire hoses, and mass arrests. Blacks also experienced threats and violence from private individuals. Blacks' houses and churches were damaged by "hate bombings." Black and white civil rights workers were assaulted, and several were murdered. In the North blacks faced heckling and counterdemonstrations. "The fury of bigots and bullies," President Johnson said, "served to strengthen the will of the American people that justice be done." In 1964 he secured passage of an inclusive civil rights act.

3. Comprehensive Civil Rights Act of 1964. *(a) Voting.*

The law prohibited election officials from applying different standards to black and white voting applicants and declared, as evidence of literacy, a sixth grade education. *(b) Public Accommodations.* The law forbade discrimination in most places of public accommodation: hotels, motels, restaurants, lunch counters, retail stores, gas stations, theaters, and sports arenas. *(c) Public Facilities.* The law prohibited discrimination in government-owned or -operated facilities such as parks, swimming pools, and libraries. *(d) Federally Assisted Programs.* The law authorized the federal government to withhold financial aid from state and local programs involving discrimination. *(e) Employment.* The law prohibited discriminatory practices by most employers, employment agencies, and labor unions. To promote compliance, the law created an *Equal Employment Opportunity Commission.*

4. The Twenty-Fourth Amendment (1964).

This amendment prohibited the use of a poll tax as a requirement for voting in elections for federal officials. It affected the five southern states that still had poll taxes.

5. Voting Rights Act of 1965

a. Background. Amidst much publicity, southern officials thwarted a black voter registration drive at Selma, Alabama. There, out of 15,000 eligible blacks, the number registered was only 335. Blacks thereupon marched through Alabama from Selma to Montgomery to focus the nation's attention upon southern racial barriers to voting. The violence with which blacks and civil rights workers were treated shocked the nation. Identifying the Ku Klux Klan as a source of the violence, President Johnson denounced its members as a "hooded band of bigots" and insisted that "every American citizen must have an equal right to vote." Congress quickly enacted the *Voting Rights Act of 1965*.

b. Provisions. (1) In any state or county where less than half of the voting-age population was registered or had voted in 1964, all literacy and other qualification tests were suspended. This provision applied immediately to five southern states and parts of two others. (2) The attorney general was empowered to send federal examiners to any county practicing voting discrimination. These registrars were authorized to register all would-be voters who met the state's age and residency requirements. This provision replaced the time-consuming court processes required by previous laws. (3) The attorney general was empowered to file suits challenging the constitutionality of state poll taxes. This provision affected four southern states.

c. Developments. The Supreme Court almost unanimously held Constitutional the 1965 Voting Rights Act. This law, Chief Justice Warren wrote, was an appropriate means for enforcing the Fifteenth Amendment and wiping out racial discrimination in voting. The Supreme Court also struck down Virginia's state poll tax as a burden irrelevant to voting qualifications and in violation of the Fourteenth Amendment.

6. Overview: Increase of Southern Black Voters. In 1957 the proportion of eligible southern blacks registered to vote was 25 percent. Thereafter, additional black voters enrolled. They were aided by federal voting laws, federal court decisions, drives by civil rights organizations, cooperation of some southern registrars, and the efforts of federal examiners. Recently, the proportion of eligible southern blacks registered was over 65 percent.

Since the late 1960s, blacks have been elected to public offices even in the Deep South, and white candidates have appealed for black votes.

7. Destructive Protests in Black Ghettos (1964–1967). In "long hot summers," blacks in northern and western cities expressed discontent by conducting bloody and destructive riots. The most violent riots came in the Harlem section of New York, in the Watts section of Los Angeles, in Newark, and in Detroit. Mobs wantonly destroyed property and maintained a reign of terror leading to many injuries and deaths. The riots perturbed many Americans who supported the civil rights movement but who expected blacks to behave responsibly. President Johnson, while cautioning blacks against violence, appointed an Advisory Commission on Civil Disorders.

8. Report of the Kerner Commission (1968). With Governor *Otto Kerner* of Illinois as chairperson, the commission's 11 members came from major groups in American life: Democrats and Republicans, labor and industry, North and South, white and black. The commission issued a unanimous report.

    a. **General Conclusions.** "Our nation is moving toward two societies, one black, one white—separate and unequal." This trend threatens our "basic democratic values."

    b. **Riot Findings.** The Commission found that the riots were not the result of an organized conspiracy, although it acknowledged that calls for violence by militant black leaders contributed to a climate conducive to rioting. The commission placed the chief blame for the urban riots on conditions resulting from "white racism." This racism, the commission wrote, leads to discrimination in employment, education, and housing, and it implants in many blacks a sense of degradation, misery, and hopelessness.

    c. **Goals.** The commission opposed racial separatism as leading to a permanently divided country. It favored immediate enrichment of ghetto life and long-range integration of blacks into society outside the ghetto.

    d. **Recommendations.** (1) Creation of additional jobs by governments and private industry. (2) On-the-job training, partly subsidized by the government, for the "hard-core" unemployed. (3) Increased efforts to eliminate *de facto* school segregation and to improve schools serving disadvantaged children. (4) Public welfare improvements such as federally financed income payments to the needy so as to enable black families to remain together. (5) Additional public housing for low- and moderate-income families.

    Civil rights leaders approved the report and hailed its conclusion that the riots ought to be blamed on "white racism." Critics generally did not reject the entire report but condemned it for *(a)* not sufficiently pointing out black progress since World War II, *(b)* excusing black participants of any blame for the riots, and *(c)* raising black expectations by recommendations that could not be implemented because funds were not available.

9. Civil Rights Housing Act of 1968

    a. **Background.** Despite President Johnson's urging, Congress failed to pass a bill outlawing discrimination in the rental and sale of housing. In Congress Southerners opposed to civil rights legislation received support from some Northerners, whose constituents feared that the influx of blacks into a white neighborhood would lower property values and destroy the character of the community. In 1968 the Senate approved an "open housing" bill and sent it to the House, where opponents were able to delay its consideration.

    b. **Passage of the Civil Rights Bill.** While the bill was stalled, Martin Luther King, Jr., in Memphis, Tennessee, was assassinated by a white man. His death, mourned by both whites and blacks, created an emotional atmosphere that spurred quick House approval of the open housing bill. President Johnson hailed the bill as evidence that "America does move forward."

    c. **Provisions.** (1) The law barred discrimination in the rental and sale of 80 percent of the nation's housing. (2) The law provided stiff penalties for persons guilty of intimidating or injuring civil rights workers. (3) It provided penalties for persons who travel from one state to another to incite a riot and for persons who provide firearms for use in a riot.

10. Voting Rights Acts of 1970 and 1975. These laws together extended to 1982 the provisions of the 1965 act protecting southern black voters. The 1970 law also *(a)* suspended all literacy tests as a voting qualification and *(b)* set a 30-day residency requirement for voting in Presidential elections. The 1975 law also required—in voting districts where less than half of the voting-age population had registered or voted in 1972 and where more than 5 percent belong to a single-language minority—that election materials be printed, in addition to English, in the minority language. In 1982 Congress passed a law extending for 25 years a section of the 1965 Voting Rights Act. Under this law, states where low minority voting turnout was common, or where discrimination has been practiced in the past, were required to submit any changes in election procedures for federal government approval.

11. Affirmative Action in Employment

a. The Weber Case (1979). The Kaiser Corporation and the United Steel Workers Union agreed to establish a voluntary affirmative action plan. This voluntary plan called for special programs to train workers for skilled craft jobs, available to blacks and whites on a 50-50 basis. Brian Weber, a white, worked at the Kaiser plant in Louisiana where the training program had 13 openings. Weber lacked sufficient seniority to secure one of the six places reserved for whites, but he had more seniority than two of the blacks accepted for the program. Weber brought suit charging "reverse discrimination" in violation of the 1964 Civil Rights Act, which prohibits racial discrimination by employers and unions.

The Supreme Court, by a 5-to-2 vote, decided against Weber and held that the Kaiser plan—with its numerical quota giving special preference to black workers—was legal. The Court majority claimed that the Kaiser plan was within the spirit of the 1964 Civil Rights Act—"to improve the lot of those who had been excluded from the American dream for so long." The Court minority deplored the decision as a misreading of the 1964 Civil Rights Act.

There's a long, long trail a-winding—

Shanks in The Buffalo Evening News

Civil rights groups hailed the Weber decision as a go-ahead signal for extensive affirmative action programs. The Supreme Court majority, however, had emphasized that its decision was a narrow one—applying only to a voluntary plan adopted by private parties and not involving any government action.

In 1982 a Reagan Justice Department official declared that the Weber case had been "wrongly decided," its racial quota was "unacceptable," and its precedent should be challenged by another lawsuit.

b. Memphis Firefighters vs. Stotts (1984). To settle a discrimination suit brought by black firefighters, the city of Memphis, Tennessee, agreed in 1977 to adopt an affirmative-action hiring program. Later, during a budget crisis, the city, following a seniority policy based on a "last-hired, first-fired" principle, sought to lay off some of the recently hired black firefighters. A federal court ordered the city to change its policy in order to protect the black firefighters' jobs. The city did so and was sued by three white firefighters who had been laid off for a month in 1981. The whites claimed that they were the victims of racial discrimination. In 1984, by a 6-to-3 vote, the Supreme Court decided in favor of the white firefighters. The Court majority ruled that the Civil Rights Act of 1964 permitted "bona fide" (good faith) seniority systems. It said federal courts could not overturn such systems in order to help minority individuals who had not themselves suffered proven instances of discrimination.

c. Wygant vs. Jackson Board of Education (1984). By a 5-to-4 majority, the Supreme Court overturned a Michigan school board's policy of letting minority group teachers keep their jobs while white teachers with more seniority were being laid off.

d. Local 93 of the International Association of Firefighters vs. City of Cleveland (1986). To settle a job-discrimination suit brought by blacks and Hispanics, the city of Cleveland agreed to give temporary preference to minority group members in hiring and promotion within the city's fire department. Whites brought suit, supported by the Reagan administration, which argued that preferences for minorities can be justified only when those who benefit are personally identified as victims of discrimination. The Supreme Court rejected the administration's argument and ruled against the whites. By a 6-to-3 majority, the Justices held that federal courts have broad powers to approve affirmative-action plans in hiring and promotion.

e. Local 28 of the Sheet Metal Workers vs. Equal Employment Opportunity Commission (1986). By 5 to 4, the Supreme Court ruled that a lower court could order a New York City sheet metal workers' union to increase its minority membership to 29 percent by 1987. In the same case, the Court ruled 6 to 3 that judges may order racial preferences in union membership in order to correct serious cases of discrimination.

f. United States vs. Paradise (1987). The Supreme Court by a 5-to-4 vote upheld a federal district court's order that, to redress past discrimination against black officers, the state of Alabama had to observe strict racial quotas and promote one black state trooper for each white person who was promoted.

THE STATUS OF BLACKS TODAY

1. Continued Black Discontent. Despite their betterment, many blacks remain discontented. They complain that not enough is being done to dispel white notions of racial prejudice such as white *ethnocentrism*, or the emotional attitude that whites are superior to black people, and white *xenophobia*, or the fear of black people as strange and different. Blacks protest, also, that in every phase of life they are in an inferior position to whites. *(a) Education.* Proportionately fewer black than white students gain a high school and college education. *(b) Jobs and Wages.* Blacks are concentrated in low-wage occupations. A disproportionately large number of blacks work as unskilled workers and service workers. *(c) Unemployment.* Blacks suffer twice the unemployment rate of white workers. *(d) Housing.* Many blacks are confined to slum areas and have no access to decent housing in better neighborhoods. *(e) Health.* Blacks have an average life expectancy of 71 years as compared to 75 years for whites.

2. Organizations to Improve the Condition of Blacks

a. Civil Rights Organizations: Efforts to Achieve Black Integration

(1) National Association for the Advancement of Colored People. A biracial group founded in 1909, the NAACP is the largest and best known of the civil rights organizations. A major figure in its founding and early thinking was the black historian and educator *William E. B. Du Bois.* He sharply disagreed with Booker T. Washington (check the Index). Du Bois deplored Washington's emphasis on vocational training as a narrow education for blacks, rejected Washington's temporary acceptance of voting discrimination, and derided Washington's policy of "gradualism." Du Bois urged blacks to struggle militantly for full civil rights.

The NAACP has worked to stop lynchings, to end school segregation, and to secure laws for fair practices in employment and housing. The NAACP has employed publicity, lobbying, and legal action, which achieved a major triumph in the 1954 Supreme Court decision against public school segregation. *Roy Wilkins*, as executive secretary, presented the NAACP viewpoint: that blacks want to live as free and equal Americans. (In 1977 Wilkins retired and was succeeded by *Benjamin L. Hooks.*)

(2) National Urban League. A biracial group founded in 1910, the league has helped blacks to adjust to city life as they came from the rural South. It has worked to better conditions for blacks in health, housing, employment, and recreation. In charge of the league's work is its executive director, a position occupied since 1981 by *John E. Jacob.*

(3) Southern Christian Leadership Conference. Founded in 1957 by a group of southern black leaders, the SCLC has opposed discrimination in the use of public facilities, in employment, and in voting. The leading spirit and first pres-

ident of the SCLC was the Reverend *Martin Luther King, Jr.* Inspired by Thoreau's essay "On Civil Disobedience" and by Gandhi's use of passive resistance against British rule in India, King urged blacks to struggle against injustice by nonviolent resistance. King effectively used nonviolent methods many times, starting in 1955–1956 with an economic boycott that compelled Montgomery, Alabama, to desegregate the city buses. In 1964 King was awarded the Nobel Peace Prize. In 1968, when King went to lead a protest march for striking sanitation men, mainly black, in Memphis, Tennessee, he was murdered by a white man. Despite this tragic death, the SCLC reaffirmed its belief in King's philosophy of nonviolence. The current head of the SCLC is the Reverend *Joseph E. Lowery.*

In summary, these three groups have stood for operating within the law, employing nonviolence, and seeking black equality and integration into American society. Their policies stand in contrast with other groups discussed below. These groups urge black nationalism and are considered "militants."

b. The Black Muslims: A Black Nationalist Group to Achieve Black Separation. The Black Muslims are both a religious sect and a nationalist group. Their Muslim religion teaches them to observe clean living and hard work, and to refrain from alcohol, tobacco, and drugs. They have rejected Christianity as the "white people's religion." They hold that white people are evil and therefore seek complete separation from the white world. In some American cities, the Black Muslims maintain their own schools, stores, temples (mosques), and other community facilities. Although the Black Muslims claimed to oppose violence, they were uncompromisingly militant and maintained a trained, armylike corps, the Fruit of Islam. In recent years, the Black Muslims eased their antiwhite stand and turned away from militancy.

Elijah Muhammad, the Black Muslim founder, claimed to have met "Allah on earth" in 1929 and thereafter called himself "Allah's messenger." *Malcolm X,* who became a Black Muslim while serving a jail sentence for burglary, was for many years Muhammad's top aide. His *Autobiography of Malcolm X* provides a fascinating view of his life and ideas. In 1963 Malcolm X and Elijah Muhammad had a falling-out, and in 1965 Malcolm X was assassinated by three Black Muslims. (In 1975 *Wallace Muhammad* succeeded his father as Black Muslim head.)

c. The Black Panthers: A Revolutionary Organization to Overthrow the Existing System and Achieve Black Liberation. Organized in 1966 in Oakland, California, the Black Panther party said that its purpose was to protect ghetto blacks against "police harassment." Its early leaders were *Huey Newton* and *Eldridge Cleaver.* Claiming to be for "self-defense," the Black Panthers affected a military stance, prominently displayed guns, and often came into conflict with the law. They called for a revolutionary struggle of all oppressed peoples, black and white, to overthrow the existing American system, which they labeled as "racist, fascist, and imperialist." By conducting antidrug clinics and children's breakfast programs, the Black Panthers spread their influence among ghetto inhabitants.

In the 1970s the Black Panthers moderated their radicalism and placed greater emphasis upon community programs and political action.

RESULTS OF THE "BLACK REVOLUTION"

1. Meaning. The term "black revolution" encompasses the entire post-World War II civil rights movement and the improvement in the status of blacks.

2. Signs of Progress. The problems of blacks were brought to the attention of the public and became a national issue. Blacks were emboldened to speak up and act in their own behalf. As one result, southern blacks made considerable progress in exercising their right to vote. Progress was also made in desegregating public schools and places of public accommodation, and in gaining labor union membership and better employment opportunities for blacks. Many blacks entered into the middle class. A few entered into the upper class. Most significantly, the civil rights movement convinced most Americans that discrimination is morally wrong.

3. Criticisms and Responses. Some whites have opposed, in part or in whole, the black civil rights movement. In the South, many whites feel that black aspirations threaten the traditional southern way of life. In the North, some whites in cities and suburbs feel that black aspirations threaten their jobs and neighborhoods. This hostile reaction among whites, evidenced by demonstrations against civil rights activities and by votes against candidates favoring civil rights, has been called the "white backlash."

a. Criticism. Blacks are demanding too much too soon. They have made considerable gains since World War II. Now, instead of making additional demands, they should learn to use their gains, extend them to all blacks, and give white communities time to adjust to new conditions.

a. Response. Blacks were guaranteed their freedom and their political and civil rights by the reconstruction amendments. They have waited over 100 years for these guarantees to be honored. Blacks demand no more than equality with whites and will accept no less.

b. Criticism. Blacks are not making sufficient efforts to lift themselves out of poverty and ghetto life. They demand that the government do for them what they should be doing for themselves. After all, white immigrants faced similar handicaps. But white immigrants worked hard and escaped from the ghetto by their own efforts.

b. Response. Blacks are seeking to improve themselves, but they are deliberately kept down by discrimination, especially in employment and housing. Therefore, they need government help to outlaw discrimination. Also, when the white immigrants arrived, industry needed their unskilled labor; but when blacks came to the cities, industry had become more mechanized and had fewer jobs for unskilled workers.

c. Criticism. Blacks have rioted in our cities, looted and destroyed property, battled the police, caused injuries and deaths, and fomented disrespect for authority. They must not be permitted to destroy "law and order."

c. Response. Blacks have rioted out of a sense of misery and frustration. They had appealed peacefully to the "white power structure" for help in overcoming their problems—but to little avail. "Law and order" should mean not repression but equality and opportunity.

─────────────── **MULTIPLE-CHOICE QUESTIONS** ───────────────

1. "Many, if not most, of our Indian wars have had their origin in broken promises and acts of injustice on our part." The author of this statement would most likely agree that the history of United States treatment of American Indians was primarily the result of (a) prejudice toward Indian religions (b) the desire for territorial expansion (c) a refusal of Indians to negotiate treaties (d) opposing economic and political systems.

2. The book *A Century of Dishonor* deals with dishonor caused by (a) Indians against white settlers (b) whites against Indian tribes (c) Americans against Canadians (d) Americans against Mexicans.

3. For American Indians, one effect of life on the reservation has been continued (a) awareness of cultural identity (b) increases in average life span (c) opportunity for assimilation (d) emphasis upon materialism.

4. Some leaders of the Seneca Iroquois taught that the Seneca should stay away from alcohol, observe traditional Iroquois religious festivals, and reject the European lifestyle. Which activity of present-day American Indians would be most consistent with these teachings? (a) establishing tourist trade on the reservations (b) teaching the children the tribal language (c) leaving the reservations and blending into the dominant society (d) setting up industrial companies on the reservations.

5. Which means for redressing grievances is applicable to American Indians but is usually not applicable to other minority groups? (a) nonviolent marches to draw attention to injustices (b) equal employment opportunity laws (c) boycott of all products manufactured in the United States (d) collective lawsuits to recover ancestral lands.

6. The Indians' desire today to retain their heritage reflects the concept of (a) Anglo-conformity (b) melting pot (c) cultural pluralism (d) ethnocentrism.

7. Which best accounts for the large number of Spanish-speaking people in the United States today? (a) The Spanish Civil War resulted in a large influx of refugees. (b) Many supporters of deposed Latin American dictators came to the United States. (c) The United States gained control of areas once controlled by Spain. (d) The United States and Spain entered into an agreement to permit unlimited immigration.

8. Among Americans of Spanish origin, the *largest* group is composed of (a) Cubans (b) Puerto Ricans (c) Mexican Americans (d) South Americans.

9. The Spanish heritage is *most* evident in which American economic activity? (a) growing cotton (b) raising cattle (c) drilling for oil (d) manufacturing shoes.

10. Spanish settlers founded the oldest city in the United States. This city is (a) Miami (b) Santa Fe (c) Los Angeles (d) St. Augustine.

11. Illegal Mexican immigrants coming into the United States frequently are known as (a) barrios (b) visas (c) braceros (d) wetbacks.

12. Cesar Chavez is best known as a (a) labor leader (b) member of the United States Senate (c) professor of history (d) clothing manufacturer.

13. The history of Americans of Spanish origin shows that (a) a democratic government insures equality for all (b) a tribal form of society is best for minority groups

(c) prejudice against minority groups is an obstacle to their development (d) public education insures equal opportunity for minority groups.

14. Most Puerto Ricans coming to the United States mainland faced all the following problems *except* (a) learning the English language (b) gaining American citizenship (c) securing a job (d) adjusting to urban life.

15. Which is a more serious problem for urban minorities today than it was for urban immigrants a generation ago? (a) shortage of jobs for the unskilled (b) income taxes (c) inadequate housing (d) inadequate health care.

16. The activities of various minority groups such as Hispanics and Indians to advance their rights are an indication that (a) minority groups are decreasing in number (b) majority rule is no longer functioning (c) the federal courts have abandoned civil rights (d) laws alone cannot solve all the problems of society.

17. The 19th-century Industrial Revolution had a major influence on the position of women in United States society because it (a) made it possible for women to work in the factories (b) gave women equal employment status with men (c) provided for equal pay for equal work (d) decreased the demand for women as unskilled laborers.

18. Which invention resulted in a large increase in the number of women workers? (a) steam locomotive (b) typewriter (c) electric light bulb (d) automatic elevator.

19. The women's rights movement in the United States has been *least* successful in achieving the right of women to (a) register and vote (b) own property (c) have equal job opportunity (d) dress as they choose.

20. Which has had the *least* effect on increasing the employment of women in the post-World War II era? (a) increase in the number of clerical and office jobs (b) increase in the number of service occupations (c) passage of minimum wage laws requiring higher hourly rates (d) passage of laws forbidding discrimination against women in employment.

21. Women face serious inequities in employment. Evidence to support this statement shows that most women are (a) failing to complete high school (b) unwilling to assume the responsibilities of administrative positions (c) able to accept only part-time employment at low wages (d) employed at jobs that offer few chances for advancement.

22. In its statement that "all men and women are created equal," the Seneca Falls Convention was paraphrasing (a) the Declaration of Independence (b) the Preamble to the Constitution (c) Calhoun's Exposition and Protest (d) Lincoln's Gettysburg Address.

23. Susan B. Anthony is best known for her efforts to gain for women (a) equal employment opportunities (b) admission to colleges (c) the right to vote (d) the right to own property.

24. The Equal Rights Amendment was (a) withdrawn by Congress (b) declared unnecessary by the Supreme Court (c) unable to secure the required number of state ratifications (d) opposed by the National Organization for Women.

25. Some advertisements show women as being concerned mainly with pleasing men. A major objection to such advertisements is that women (a) can be easily misled by false advertising (b) dominate the advertising field (c) will be discouraged from entering the labor market (d) are exploited for the purpose of selling certain products.

26. Which is a valid conclusion based on the history of the feminist movement in the United States? (a) The feminist movement has achieved nearly all its goals. (b) Women have obtained the right to vote but have made very few social or economic gains. (c) Although women have made many gains, the need for further im-

provement still exists. (d) The feminist movement of the 1970s has had little impact upon society.

27. The first major surge of black migration to northern cities took place during the (a) Civil War (b) reconstruction era (c) New Deal (d) World War I.

28. In 1954 the Supreme Court handed down a decision involving segregation in the schools. This decision (a) reversed the "separate but equal" doctrine (b) reaffirmed the "separate but equal" doctrine (c) left questions of segregation up to the states (d) gave the federal government control over all private schools.

29. On which part of the Constitution did the Supreme Court base its 1954 decision in *Brown vs. Board of Education of Topeka?* (a) "general welfare" clause (b) Congressional power to regulate interstate commerce (c) "necessary and proper" clause (d) "equal protection of the laws" clause of the Fourteenth Amendment.

30. The Constitutional argument advocated by some sections of the South against federal action for integration in education is based upon (a) delegated powers (b) division of powers (c) the system of checks and balances (d) the elastic clause.

31. Following 1964, which factor most sped integration in public schools in the Deep South? (a) Southern white opinion shifted in favor of integration. (b) Southern blacks participated in demonstrations. (c) Southern school districts complied with Office of Education "guidelines" in order to qualify for federal funds. (d) Most southern legislators supported school integration to gain black votes.

32. The post-World War II migration of blacks from the rural South to the urban North resulted in (a) decreased employment of blacks in industry (b) a general decline in living standards of northern whites (c) increased pressure for equality (d) black economic control of some northern cities.

33. Which is the main reason for the continued existence of *de facto* segregation in many city schools? (a) Local laws often prohibit integration of schools. (b) Supreme Court rulings on segregation do not apply to city schools. (c) Segregated housing patterns exist in many school districts. (d) Many community groups advocate segregated schools.

34. The surge of the civil rights movement following 1945 *best* illustrates the idea that (a) the most effective leadership comes from state legislators (b) laws are more effective when backed by constructive action of individuals and organizations (c) militancy is the result of Communist conspiracies (d) the courts will not become involved in social issues.

35. Since 1964, a motel owner may legally deny a black's request for a room if (a) there is a local "Jim Crow" ordinance (b) the motel is not directly engaged in interstate commerce (c) the black is not an American citizen (d) there are no vacancies.

36. Which way of protecting black voters was first provided in the Voting Rights Act of 1965? (a) suspension of literacy tests in certain states (b) court injunctions to prevent unfair voting practices (c) reduction of the number of Representatives of a state that limits black voting (d) use of federal troops on election day.

37. Martin Luther King, Jr., was most closely identified with (a) practicing nonviolent direct action (b) undermining the NAACP (c) investigating the "black power" movement (d) demanding creation of a civil rights commission.

38. Which is the most significant reason why so many blacks in the United States have found it difficult to escape from the ghetto and poverty? (a) The urban ghetto provides job opportunities for its inhabitants. (b) In many areas of employment, opportunities for blacks remain limited. (c) Federal courts have ruled unfavorably in most civil rights cases. (d) Black leaders lack interest in significant social changes.

39. The headline: "Elected Black Officials: 2,621 and Rising" most probably reflects the fact that (a) the Twenty-Sixth Amendment to the Constitution has been ratified (b) racial discrimination is rapidly disappearing in the United States (c) the federal government has established a quota for elected black officials (d) recent legal actions and voter registration drives have increased the number of black voters.

40. Which statement is an example of ethnocentrism? (a) "What we need is a return to the good old days." (b) "My party's candidate can make our country strong again and lead it to world leadership." (c) "Change is inevitable. We must attempt to adjust to new conditions." (d) "We are a superior society. All others are barbaric."

41. Which situation best illustrates the idea of affirmative action? (a) An organization actively recruits qualified women and members of minority groups for an on-the-job training program. (b) A corporation hires people on a first-come, first-served basis. (c) A university's sole criterion for admission is performance on an entrance examination. (d) A graduate school accepts all students who apply.

—————————————— **ESSAY QUESTIONS** ——————————————

1. Indians today claim that they are a disadvantaged minority in the American population. *(a)* Discuss *two* arguments to support this claim. *(b)* To better their social and economic conditions most rapidly, should Indians remain on or leave the reservations? Present *one* argument to defend your answer.

2. *(a)* Discuss *two* reasons why the Dawes General Allotment Act (1887) failed to benefit the Indians. *(b)* Show *two* ways in which the Wheeler-Howard Indian Reorganization Act (1934) sought to remedy Indian grievances against the Dawes Act.

3. Similarities and differences often exist between present and past situations. For Mexican Americans in the United States today and any one European immigrant group in 19th-century America, compare their conditions so as to show *(a) two* similarities and *(b) two* differences.

4. *(a)* In the 1940s Puerto Ricans in large numbers began leaving the island and coming to the mainland. Describe *two* conditions that attracted them to the mainland. *(b)* By the 1960s, Puerto Ricans in considerable numbers were returning to the island. Discuss *two* reasons for their return.

5. For over two centuries, women in America have struggled to overcome disadvantages and to secure equal rights. *(a)* Discuss *three* evidences to prove that women, in the early 19th century, were a disadvantaged group. *(b)* Explain *one* way in which the status of women has been altered by *each* of the following: (1) the leadership of determined women in the 19th century (2) The Industrial Revolution as it developed toward the latter part of the 19th century (3) the civil rights ferment of the post-World War II years (4) the need for workers during major wars.

6. Agree or disagree with *each* of the following statements and present *two* arguments to support your opinion: *(a)* Women are basically unwilling to assume positions of leadership in the business world. *(b)* The Equal Rights Amendment failed because it attempted to go too far too fast. *(c)* Since men generally become the family breadwinners, they should receive preference over women in regard to college and professional school admissions. *(d)* American voters would support a woman of ability and proven political experience as a candidate for the Presidency. *(e)* Today the women's rights movement still has a number of items of unfinished business.

7. During the past 100 years the issue of civil rights has frequently played a significant role in the United States. Describe *two* ways in which *each* of the following has af-

fected the cause of civil rights: *(a)* Presidents, *(b)* Congress, *(c)* the Supreme Court, *(d)* state legislatures, *(e)* organizations of private citizens.

8. Congress has passed laws—in 1957, 1960, 1964, 1965, and 1970—to assure black voting rights. *(a)* Explain *two* reasons why more than one law was necessary. *(b)* Evaluate *two* provisions of the Voting Rights Act of 1965. *(c)* Discuss *two* effects upon the South attributable, at least in part, to these federal voting laws.

9. Using *two* facts, agree *or* disagree with *each* of the following statements: *(a)* In the United States, blacks were greatly affected by World War II. *(b)* In their efforts to secure equal rights, blacks have had little help from the United States Constitution. *(c)* Blacks in the North face problems different from the problems of blacks in the South. *(d)* Blacks will find their efforts toward improving their conditions hindered by rioting and violence. *(e)* Today, many blacks can improve conditions for themselves and their families through their own efforts. *(f)* Busing of children is a proper way of achieving school integration. *(g)* Since the end of World War II, blacks in the United States have achieved remarkable gains.

10. "The Declaration of Independence was written over 200 years ago, and the search for equality has been going on ever since." Select *one* group—women, American Indians, blacks—and for that group: *(a)* Cite some of the conditions that prevented that group from attaining equality as expressed in the Declaration of Independence. *(b)* List some of the actions taken by that group to change the conditions given in answer to *a*. *(c)* Evaluate the extent to which the actions cited in answer to *b* alleviated the conditions given in answer to *a*.

11. "Certain groups in society are sometimes stereotyped into specific roles." Select *one* group—Mexican Americans, Puerto Ricans, women—and for that group: *(a)* Describe *two* different roles that society has assigned to that group, thus creating a stereotype. *(b)* Show by specific examples how *two* of the following have or have not reinforced the stereotype: advertisements, literature, television programs, or movies. *(c)* Using at least *two* specific examples, show how a member of *one* of the groups listed above has or has not been affected by the stereotype assigned to that group by society.

12. In the mid-1980s, unemployment statistics showed that the percentage of unemployed blacks was more than double the percentage of unemployed whites. *(a)* Discuss *two* reasons why the percentage of unemployed blacks was double the percentage of unemployed whites. *(b)* Describe *one* way by which the government has already acted or could in the future act to reduce black unemployment. *(c)* Describe *one* way by which blacks, by themselves, could act to reduce black unemployment.

PART 3. The American People Face Problems Arising From Population Trends

OUR GROWING POPULATION

GROWTH OF THE AMERICAN POPULATION TO 1900

Every ten years the government takes a population count, called a *census*. It is required by the Constitution so as to apportion members of the House of Representatives among the states according to population. In 1790, at the first census, the United States contained almost 4 million people. By 1860 our population had risen to over 31 million, an average increase per decade of almost 35 percent. By 1900 Americans totaled almost 76 million, an average increase per decade of almost 25 percent.

Our population growth, from 4 million in 1790 to 76 million by 1900, resulted from (1) a comparatively high birth rate, as Americans proved able to feed and clothe large families, (2) some decrease in the mortality rate, primarily due to medical advances, and (3) a continuous stream of immigrants.

GROWTH OF THE AMERICAN POPULATION IN THE 20TH CENTURY

1. Statistical Data

The 1980 census was criticized for supposedly undercounting aliens and members of minority groups, especially in large cities such as Detroit and New York. These urban centers were concerned because the census population figures determine apportionment of seats in the House of Representatives and amounts of state and federal aid. The Census Bureau denied any significant undercount and insisted that the 1980 figures were "by far the most accurate census ever taken."

2. Analysis

a. From 1910 to 1940. In this period, the population increased, but at a declining rate. Fewer immigrants came because of (1) World War I, (2) restrictive immigration laws (1921–1929), and (3) the depression of the 1930s. Facing

POPULATION GROWTH, 1900–1980

YEAR	POPULATION IN MILLIONS	INCREASE OVER PRECEDING CENSUS	
		IN MILLIONS	IN PERCENT
1900	76	13	21
1910	92	16	21
1920	106	14	15
1930	123	17	16
1940	132	9	7
1950	151	19	15
1960	179	28	19
1970	203	24	13
1980	227	24	12

difficult economic times, young people postponed marriage, and existing families remained small.

b. From 1940 to the Present. In this period, the population has increased at a higher rate than in the 1930s. During World War II, young people had their lives disrupted, but afterward, finding jobs plentiful, they rushed to marry and raise large families, thereby creating a postwar "baby boom." The high birth rate in America continued to about 1970, then dropped sharply.

3. Aspects of the 1980 Census

a. Population Shifts. The region that showed the greatest population growth was the *Sunbelt*—the South and Southwest. The states whose population growth gained them the largest increases in the House of Representatives were Florida—four more; Texas—three more; and California—two more. The states that lost the most Representatives were Northeast: New York—five fewer; and Illinois, Ohio, and Pennsylvania—each two fewer.

b. Population Density. The average number of persons per square mile is called the *population density*. The greatest population density existed in the small industrialized North Atlantic states: 979 persons per square mile for New Jersey, 903 for Rhode Island, 733 for Massachusetts, and 639 for Connecticut. The large Rocky Mountain states (whose land is devoted chiefly to mining and grazing) and Alaska (a frontier state) had the smallest population density: about 5 people per square mile for Montana and Wyoming, 7 for Nevada, and less than one person per square mile for Alaska.

For the entire United States, the population density was 64 persons per square mile. This figure was quite high when compared to 5 for Australia and Libya, 6 for Canada, 9 for Saudi Arabia, and 31 for the Soviet Union. However, the figure for the United States was quite low when compared to 449 for Israel, 593 for Britain, 643 for West Germany, 811 for Japan, and 842 for Belgium.

PROBLEMS CREATED BY OUR GROWING POPULATION

As our nation's population continues to grow, we shall need more of everything: (1) more *goods*—food, clothing, homes, and appliances, (2) more *services*—doctors, dentists, teachers, schools, recreational facilities, and transportation, and (3) more *jobs*—to provide employment.

DIFFERING VIEWS ON AMERICAN POPULATION GROWTH

1. Approval. For most of our history, Americans have viewed our expanding population as an asset: more settlers, more workers, more consumers, more soldiers, more talented individuals.

2. Recent Concern. In messages to Congress, President Nixon declared that Americans took 300 years (to 1917) to number 100 million; they took 50 years (to 1967) to achieve the second 100 million, and if the existing growth rate continued, they would reach the third 100 million by the year 2000. In 1972 a federal Commission on Population Growth and the American Future submitted a report concluding that *(a)* "neither crisis nor complacency is in order," *(b)* "no substantial benefits would result from continued growth of the nation's population," and therefore *(c)* it would be advisable that America slow—and gradually stop—the growth of its population. Recent projections suggest a population of some 265 million people in the year 2000.

OUR YOUTHFUL POPULATION

AFTER THE "BABY BOOM"

1. Statistical Data (1950–1984)

AMERICANS UNDER 30, 1950–1984

YEAR	TOTAL POPULATION (MILLIONS)	PERSONS UNDER 30 (MILLIONS)	PERCENT OF POPULATION
1950	151	74.8	49.7
1970	203	106.9	52.6
1980	227	113.3	50.0
1984	236	113.1	47.9

2. Analysis. From 1950 to 1970, the under-30 population gradually increased to more than half the total population. Because of the post-World War II "baby boom," the 20–29-year age bracket was for a time our fastest-growing group. In recent years the birth rate had declined, and so had the under-30 proportion of the population. By the mid-1980s, the under-30 population was 48 percent of the total population.

3. Impact of Our Under-30 Population

a. Special Wants. (1) For *consumer goods:* convenience foods, highly styled clothing, flashy cars, rock and roll music, youth-oriented movies, television programs, and magazines; and, upon marriage: homes, home furnishings, and appliances. (2) For *educational facilities:* technical, college, and graduate facilities. From 1965 to 1982, the number of college students more than doubled—from 5.9 million to 12.4 million. (3) For *employment:* additional jobs for younger people, who traditionally have a higher unemployment rate than older persons.

b. Political Influence. Beginning in the 1960s, the under-30 group—especially college students—showed great interest in political affairs by supporting Presidential candidates and lobbying among members of Congress. In 1971 youths at age 18 received the right to vote in all elections—federal, state, and local—by the Twenty-Sixth Amendment.

OUR SENIOR POPULATION

INCREASING NUMBER OVER 65

1. Statistical Data

AMERICANS 65 YEARS AND OLDER, 1850–1980

YEAR	TOTAL POPULATION (MILLIONS)	PERSONS OVER 65 (MILLIONS)	PERCENT OF POPULATION
1850	23	.6	2.6
1900	76	3.1	4.1
1950	151	12.2	8.1
1960	179	16.5	9.2
1970	203	20.0	9.9
1980	227	25.5	11.2

2. Reasons. The steady increase in the percentage of persons over 65 is due to (a) *improvements in general welfare:* better food, housing, sanitation facilities, working conditions, and recreational opportunities, and *(b) improvements in medical science:* new drugs, advanced surgical techniques, additional medical facilities, and the development of *geriatrics*—a special branch of medicine concerned with older people. The mortality rate per 1000 persons has fallen from 17.2 in 1900 to 8.7 in 1985. Also, the life expectancy has increased from less than 50 years in 1850 to over 71 years for men and 78 years for women today.

PROBLEMS FACING OUR SENIOR POPULATION

1. Forced Retirement—Previously at Age 65. Many 65-year-old workers, in good health and with a life expectancy of 14 more years, dreaded the change from purposeful activity to idleness. Their complaints led some corporations to try *flexible retirement*—judging each worker's health and outlook, or *gradual retirement*—reducing the work load gradually for workers past 65.

In 1978 Congress passed a *retirement age* measure prohibiting mandatory retirement for most workers in private industry before age 70.

2. Use of Leisure Time. Retired workers may keep occupied by engaging in a part-time business or job, doing charity work, pursuing a hobby, taking courses, and joining *golden age* or *sixty-plus* clubs.

3. Housing. Older people need small, low-cost homes with features to prevent accidents: ramps instead of stairways, handgrips at the bathtubs, and nonskid floors. Since the 1950s Congress has passed housing acts with provisions to benefit older persons.

4. Income. Most retired persons face a problem of "making ends meet." Although retired workers have lower living expenses, they no longer receive a wage or salary. They must now depend upon their pensions, savings and investments, and Social Security.

5. Social Security: Old Age and Survivors Insurance (OASI)

a. Coverage. Social Security at first covered only employees working for business concerns. It has gradually been extended to include almost the entire working population. *Compulsory* coverage is required of self-employed persons (such as farmowners, shopkeepers, accountants, lawyers, and doctors), most domestic help, most farm workers, and all members of the armed forces.

Voluntary coverage is offered to employees of state and local governments, and to clergy and other employees of nonprofit organizations. These workers may be covered if they and their employers are willing to pay the required Social Security taxes.

b. Benefits. Social Security provides old-age insurance. Upon retirement at the age of 65, insured workers are entitled to monthly benefits determined according to earnings, years at work, and number of dependents. Lower benefits are paid to workers who choose to retire at age 62. Full benefits are paid to totally disabled workers regardless of age. Social Security also provides survivors insurance. Upon the death of the insured, benefits are due to the spouse and minor children. Social Security benefits are generally exempt from income taxes.

Benefits have been increased to keep pace with the rising cost of living. Since 1975 benefits have been tied to increases in the Consumer Price Index. In 1985 the average monthly benefit for an aged couple was $776.

c. Financing the Plan. Employee and employer contribute equally. The tax rate, increased many times, now pays for hospital insurance as well as for old-age and survivors insurance. In 1977, aware that the number of Social Security retirees had increased markedly and that Social Security benefit payments were outrunning the system's income, Congress sharply increased Social Security taxes.

d. Social Security Reform Law (1983). Alarmed at calculations showing that the Social Security system was heading for bankruptcy, Congress adopted a reform law in 1983. The 1983 law (1) speeded up planned increases in Social Security taxes on employers and employees, (2) increased taxes even further for the self-employed, (3) for the first time, required employees of the federal government and of nonprofit organizations to join the Social Security system, and (4) delayed scheduled cost-of-living increases in benefits for six months. By 1988, employers and employees were paying 7.51 percent each on the first $45,000 of annual income.

A major reason for worries about the Social Security system was the steady aging of the United States population, with relatively fewer working-age people having to support a system that benefited relatively more retired people. In the mid-1980s there were three workers for every retired person. Some experts predicted that by the year 2020 there would be only two workers for every retired person.

6. Inflation. A major problem facing the aged is *inflation*—a continual increase in the general price level and therefore a corresponding decrease in the purchasing power of the dollar. Since World War II, the United States has been in an inflationary cycle. During the war, consumers had a great amount of money to spend; but the economy, concentrating on war production, did not provide sufficient consumer goods and services. As demand exceeded supply, consumers bid against each other and drove prices upward. After World War II, prices continued to spiral upward, as the government removed price controls, labor unions secured wage increases, business concerns expanded their profit margins, and federal deficit budgets pumped additional money into the economy. Since 1939 our cost of living has increased fivefold, meaning that the purchasing power of the dollar has fallen some 80 percent.

Inflation harms persons receiving fixed incomes, especially retired individuals. With their pension benefits, Social Security checks, and interest on savings providing a fixed income, our senior citizens are most cruelly hurt by the declining value of the dollar. To ease this situation, Congress several times increased Social Security benefits and also tied benefits to rises in the Consumer Price Index.

Earthbound in the space era.

Ivey in The San Francisco Examiner

7. Medical Care

a. Medicare for the Aged Under Social Security

(1) Background. First officially proposed in 1945 by President Harry Truman, Medicare won the support of liberals and labor unions. Advocates argued that Medicare was necessary for Americans over 65 because, as a group, they possessed limited finances, suffered disproportionately more from illness, and were therefore most burdened by high medical costs. Medicare was opposed by conservatives and doctors' groups led by the *American Medical Association.* They argued that Medicare was unnecessary in view of existing private health insurance plans and of state aid programs. Further, the AMA feared that Medicare might lead to government control of all medical care or *socialized medicine.*

(2) Medicare: Provisions. In 1965 President Johnson requested and Congress passed a "Medicare" bill. Revised several times, "Medicare" now offers persons over 65 the following: *(a) Basic Hospital Insurance Plan.* This plan provides (1) hospitalization up to 60 days for each illness, after the first $492 of cost; (2) nursing home care, fully paid up to 20 days; (3) part-time skilled health care at home; (4) 80 percent of the cost, after the first $75, for hospital outpatient services; and (5) hospice care (a hospice is a facility that cares for patients with terminal illnesses). *(b) Voluntary Medical Insurance Plan.* This plan provides for 80 percent of the cost, after the first $75, for services of physicians and surgeons, surgical dressings and appliances, diagnostic tests, home health care, and other medical services. This voluntary plan is financed by a small monthly premium paid by the enrollee and matched by the federal government. Both plans permit the patient free choice of hospitals, nursing homes, and doctors.

(3) Medicare: Costs. Federal spending for Medicare—hospital and medical insurance—has risen dramatically from $4.7 billion in 1967 to $75 billion in 1986.

b. Medicaid: State Health Program.
For needy persons of all ages not eligible for Medicare, the states administer programs of health aid called *Medicaid.* In the 1965 law that established Medicare, the federal government also offered financial support—eventually ranging from 40 to 80 percent of the total cost—for state medical assistance programs. Subject to federal guidelines, each state sets its own eligibility and benefit standards. As with Medicare, federal spending for Medicaid has risen substantially, to $26 billion in 1986.

OUR URBAN POPULATION

INCREASING NUMBER OF URBANIZED AMERICANS

Americans have been steadily leaving the countryside and moving into *metropolitan areas*—defined as consisting of central cities and their surrounding suburbs. We have become overwhelmingly an urban people. (An urban area is defined by the Census Bureau as a place with 2500 or more inhabitants.)

1. Statistical Data

AMERICANS LIVING IN CITIES, 1790–1980

Year	Total Population in Millions	Distribution by Percent		Cities Over 1 Million	Cities of 100,000 to 1 Million
		Urban*	Rural		
1790	4	5.1	94.9	0	0
1850	23	15.3	84.7	0	6
1900	76	39.7	60.3	3	35
1950	151	64.0	36.0	5	101
1960	179	69.9	30.1	5	125
1970	203	73.5	26.5	6	147
1980	227	73.7	26.3	6	163

*An urban area is defined by the Census Bureau as a place with 2500 or more residents.

2. Urbanization by States and Cities: 1980 Census. The most highly urbanized states, with more than 80 percent of their people living in urban areas, were California, New Jersey, Rhode Island, Hawaii, Nevada, New York, Utah, Florida, Arizona, Massachusetts, Illinois, Colorado, and Maryland. The most rural states, with more than 50 percent of their population still living in the rural areas, were Vermont, West Virginia, South Dakota, Mississippi, Maine, North Carolina, and North Dakota.

Our six most populous cities were New York, Chicago, Los Angeles, Philadelphia, Houston, and Detroit.

REASONS FOR THE GROWTH OF CITIES

1. Industrial Revolution. As industries arose, workers congregated about the factories. These workers added to existing city populations or created new cities. Because urban dwellers needed food, clothing, entertainment, and professional services, still more people came to the cities.

2. Social and Cultural Attractions. Many people were attracted to cities by social and cultural facilities: colleges and universities, theaters and movies, symphonies, libraries, and lecture forums.

3. Improved Transportation and Communication. The railroads, telegraph lines, and telephones that served the cities enabled the city dwellers to (a) obtain foodstuffs and other essentials, (b) distribute the products of city factories throughout the land, and (c) conduct business transactions quickly and efficiently from a central office.

4. Decreasing Farm Population. Farmers and farm laborers were driven from the countryside by the *(a)* drabness and hardships of farm life, *(b)* low agricultural prices and difficult times, especially following the Civil War and again following World War I, and *(c)* increased mechanization and growth of commercial farming.

5. Immigration From Europe. During the 19th century, some "old immigrants," especially the Germans and Irish, settled in cities. After the close of the frontier, the "new immigrants" overwhelmingly settled in cities. These urban settlers found jobs in city factories and other businesses. As newcomers unfamiliar with American culture, they preferred to live among fellow immigrants who spoke their native tongue. Ethnic groups congregated in special sections of a city, thereby forming ghettos.

6. Migrations of Blacks and Hispanics. *(a) Blacks.* In the 20th century, blacks left the rural South for urban centers. Some blacks moved to cities in the South, but more moved to cities in the West and North. By 1980 blacks in large numbers inhabited America's most populous cities. *(b) Hispanics.* By 1980 most Puerto Ricans lived in and around New York City, Mexican Americans resided mainly in the cities of the Southwest and West, and most Cubans had settled in the Florida cities of Tampa and Miami.

GOVERNMENTAL PROBLEMS OF CITIES

1. Corruption and Political Machines. In the late 19th and early 20th centuries, city "bosses" ruling political machines dominated and victimized a considerable number of cities. They corrupted city governments by selling justice in local courts, giving city franchises and contracts to business executives in return for presents and favors, and filling city jobs with unqualified political appointees.

Most political machines were eventually ousted from power through the combined efforts of reform leaders, crusading newspapers, and an aroused citizenry. In the early 20th century the muckraker *Lincoln Steffens* did much to make the public aware of corruption in city government by his book *The Shame of the Cities.* Today, although occasional cases of corruption among city officials are still disclosed, bossism does not present nearly the problem that it did at the turn of the century.

2. City-State Relationship. City governments are "creatures of the state." They were created by state-granted charters and exercise powers as enumerated in these charters. Some cities complain that the state does not grant them sufficient *home rule.* Cities generally must obey state directives on local problems and must secure permission from the state legislature to widen their powers over such matters as transportation and taxation. Many cities also complain that the state treats cities unfairly by collecting more money in state taxes from city residents than the state returns to the cities in the form of services and state-aid funds.

3. Demands for More City Services. Cities have faced demands from their inhabitants for more and better services. City aid is especially needed in ghettos occupied by disadvantaged blacks and other minorities. As a result, cities have expanded their facilities in recreation, education, housing, transportation, welfare assistance, and public health; and city expenditures have soared.

4. Decrease in the City Tax Base. Especially since the end of World War II, middle-class and upper middle-class families have left the cities for more spacious homes in the suburbs. They reasoned that they would be escaping the

From The Herblock Gallery *(Simon & Schuster, 1968)*

"Help!"

What problems face our cities? What steps have been taken by the cities to deal with these problems? By the federal government?

city's crowded living, its social problems, and its taxes, and yet would be living near enough to the city to reach it by auto or commuter train. Businesses, too, fled the major cities, in part to be near the labor supply in suburbs and in part to escape what are called "nuisance" city taxes, such as on commercial rents and gross business receipts.

The outflow of businesses and affluent families decreased the tax base of large cities. This decrease came at a time when the cities' need for revenue was greatest. Cities felt compelled to raise the rates of existing taxes, to increase transportation fares, and to impose new taxes, including a city income tax.

PUBLIC HEALTH

Since city dwellers live close together, diseases may spread easily and become epidemics. Consequently, cities maintain public health services such as hospitals, clinics, and visiting nurses. In addition, cities insure a pure water supply and proper sewage disposal, and enforce sanitation laws. In recent years, cities have also taken steps to combat air and water pollution.

PREVENTION OF CRIME

The crime rate in many cities is high. (1) Most cities contain many people. Some have great wealth. Others are poor. (2) Some poor slum inhabitants are tempted into crime. (3) Some poor youths join gangs. They see this as an escape from lack of jobs, guidance, and recreational facilities. (4) Other youths have turned to illegal and habit-forming drugs. Since such drugs are expensive, these youths may become criminals to secure the monies necessary to support a drug habit. To remedy causes of crime, cities provide guidance counselors to assist youths, offer drug prevention programs in schools, and construct low-cost housing to wipe out slums. Cities also maintain police forces to apprehend criminals and municipal courts to try them and impose jail sentences. With the influx of blacks and other minorities, some cities have (1) given the police special training in understanding and dealing with disadvantaged minorities, (2) established boards to hear complaints of police abuse, and (3) hired minority group members as police.

MASS TRANSPORTATION

Cities are being "choked to death" by the ever-increasing number of motor vehicles, private and commercial. Streets are too narrow, parking facilities inadequate. Cities have attempted to meet these problems by improving subway and bus services, building expressways around and through cities, and constructing parking areas at city outskirts, where commuters can leave their autos and take public transportation.

The federal and some state governments have provided funds to help cities expand their mass transit facilities.

EDUCATION

Cities administer their own educational systems, although these are financed in part by state and federal funds and are subject to state supervision. Cities have faced demands for (1) *more education:* pre-kindergarten classes, adult education courses, and two- and four-year community colleges, (2) *better education:* newer buildings, more teachers, and up-to-date teaching materials, such as language laboratories, modern science equipment, and recently published textbooks, and (3) *school integration*—since the 1954 Supreme Court decision in *Brown vs. Board of Education of Topeka.* (Check the Index.)

HOUSING AND URBAN RENEWAL

1. Cost of Slums. Slum areas are typified by *tenement houses*—buildings that are filthy, overcrowded, run-down, poorly ventilated, inadequately heated, and poorly protected against fires. Slum areas usually lack sufficient recreational facilities. Inhabitants generally have few occupational skills and are often unemployed. Compared to the rest of the city, slum dwellers are more susceptible to disease, and more slum youths turn to juvenile gangs and crime. Slum areas therefore require more city services.

2. First Remedial Efforts: Late 19th and Early 20th Centuries. As cities grew, Americans became increasingly concerned over slums. *Jacob Riis,* a journalist, in 1890 publicized the evils of New York City slums in his book *How the Other Half Lives. Jane Addams* established *Hull House* in Chicago, and *Lillian Wald* established the *Henry Street Settlement* in New York City. These settlement houses, located in slum areas, provided playgrounds, meeting rooms, and libraries, and offered classes from nursery school to adult education.

Cities and states passed *tenement laws,* requiring slum landlords to improve their buildings by providing fire escapes, additional sanitary facilities, and better ventilation, heating, and lighting. However, these laws were not strictly enforced.

While the slums remained, the slum population changed. As the Irish, Polish, Italian, and Jewish immigrants learned American ways and improved their economic status, they gradually moved out of the slums. Their dwellings were taken over by incoming blacks and Hispanics.

3. Housing and the New Deal

a. Purposes. From 1929 to 1933 housing construction declined sharply. President Franklin D. Roosevelt moved to stimulate the building industry in order to (1) provide jobs in construction and related industries, and (2) further social reform. Estimating that one-third of the nation was ill-housed, President Roosevelt wanted to strike at the problem of substandard and insufficient housing.

b. New Deal Housing Efforts

(1) Mortgage Insurance. The *Federal Housing Administration* (FHA) insured mortgage loans thus guaranteeing their repayment. This insurance en-

couraged banks and other credit institutions to lend money for new homes and home repairs. The FHA set construction standards for builders who desired FHA-guaranteed loans. Eventually, the FHA insured almost one-half of all mortgages on one- to four-family homes.

(2) *Low-Cost Housing and Slum-Clearance Projects.* The *Public Works Administration* (PWA) and later the *United States Housing Authority* (USHA) administered funds for demolishing slum buildings and construction housing projects. The USHA could provide up to 90 percent of the cost of approved state and local projects by means of long-term, low-interest loans. The USHA could also make outright grants so as to reduce construction costs and assure low rentals.

c. **Significance.** These New Deal housing agencies began federal efforts to solve the housing problem. From 1933 to 1941 they helped bring about a considerable increase in the construction of dwelling units. Construction, however, still remained far below the needs of the people. During World War II, housing construction again declined sharply.

4. Housing and Urban Renewal Since World War II

a. **Need for Housing.** The American people have needed much additional housing to (1) make up for the limited construction during the years of the depression and World War II, (2) fill the requirements of our growing population, and (3) meet the demands of the rising numbers of urban and suburban dwellers.

b. **Private Builders.** The building industry responded by increasing construction to record levels, achieving an average of over one million nonfarm dwelling units annually. These builders constructed apartment houses for middle- and upper-income families and "mass-produced" one- and two-family houses. They avoided slum clearance and low-income housing, as these projects are financially risky.

c. **Federal Efforts.** Since 1965 the Cabinet-level *Department of Housing and Urban Development* has administered the many federal housing laws. The department has (1) offered FHA insurance for mortgage loans on housing construction, (2) assisted communities to build low-rental public housing by approving projects and granting low-cost loans or outright subsidies to assure low rentals, (3) provided loans to colleges and universities for student and faculty housing, (4) provided loans and grants to state and local agencies to further housing for the elderly and to spur urban renewal projects, and (5) enforced nondiscriminatory practices in the rental and sale of most housing.

d. **In Recent Years.** In the early 1980s, economic conditions caused private housing construction to slump drastically. The demand for homes was adversely affected by (1) high unemployment that decreased the number of potential buyers, (2) inflation that sharply raised the initial price of homes (average new-home prices passed the $100,000 mark in 1984 for the first time), and (3) high interest rates that caused mortgage costs to skyrocket. Housing construction perked up during periods of rising economic activity later in the 1980s, and housing became more affordable as interest rates fell.

5. Observations Regarding Housing

a. From 1940 to 1980, according to census reports, America achieved considerable progress in housing. While the population increased 72 percent, from 132 million to 227 million, occupied housing units increased 129 percent, from 35 million to 80 million. Moreover, the number of substandard housing units decreased sharply. Despite the overall progress, however, millions of Americans still lacked decent housing.

b. Federal housing programs designed to aid low-income families have proved disappointing. Although a number of projects have been built, construction has been far below planned goals. Also, government efforts to eliminate some slums have been offset by the influx of people crowding into and expanding other slums.

The problem of slum clearance has been complicated by several factors: (1) Spending for slum clearance, although substantial, has proved insufficient to do the job of urban renewal. (2) Many people have become indifferent, if not opposed, to low-rent housing projects. Taxpayers object to the seemingly endless demands for government housing funds. Low-income families resent the barracks-like appearance and strict management of housing developments. Social reformers have found that better housing by itself has failed to eradicate juvenile delinquency and crime among project tenants. These objections may help explain why voters in notable instances have rejected bond issues to finance state and public housing programs.

FAIR REPRESENTATION FOR CITIES: LEGISLATIVE REAPPORTIONMENT

1. Background: Rural Overrepresentation. From the late 19th century to the early 1960s, rural voters were overrepresented at the expense of urban voters in the federal House of Representatives and in almost all state legislatures. As population shifted from rural to urban and suburban areas, state legislators failed to reapportion because of inertia, disagreement on new election district boundaries, or deliberate intent to maintain rural control of the state legislature. For example, in Tennessee, a rural district of 3500 people and an urban district of 78,000 people each elected one legislator.

For many years the Supreme Court held that reapportionment was not a legal matter to be judged by courts, but rather a political issue to be decided by Congress, state legislatures, and the people.

2. Supreme Court Decisions: More Representation for Urban Areas

a. *Baker vs. Carr (1962).* The Supreme Court decided that federal courts may consider the constitutionality of state election districts. The Court reasoned that some districts may be so "arbitrary and capricious" as to violate the

Fourteenth Amendment clause that requires states to provide all persons with "equal protection of the laws."

b. Wesberry vs. Sanders (1964). The Supreme Court decided that "as nearly as is practicable, one man's vote in a Congressional election is to be worth as much as another's." The Court held that the Constitution established the principle of equal representation in the House for equal numbers of people.

c. Reynolds vs. Sims (1964). The Supreme Court established the "one person, one vote" rule: that election districts for both houses of state legislatures must be approximately equal in population.

3. Effects of the Decisions. Most states reapportioned election districts on a more equitable basis. The result has been increased representation for cities and suburbs in both houses of state legislatures and in the federal House of Representatives. City officials hope that this change will mean greater attention by legislatures to urban problems.

POVERTY AMONG RURAL AND URBAN PEOPLES

PROBLEMS OF POVERTY (1960 TO MID-1980s)

1. Extent of Poverty (1960). Despite our post-World War II affluence, 10 million American families lived in poverty, with yearly incomes of less than $3000. These 10 million impoverished families, about 4 million rural and 6 million urban, totaled 35 million individuals, or about 20 percent of our total population. For poverty data for the mid-1980s, see page 419.

2. Causes of Poverty. *(a) Lack of Training.* Many Americans never had vocational or professional training. Filling only low-skill or no-skill jobs, they received little pay and faced frequent unemployment. *(b) Worn-Out Farms.* Many small farmers, working a few acres of exhausted land, eked out a difficult living. They lacked the capital to acquire sizable fertile lands and to buy expensive machines. A number of rural poor abandoned their farms and moved to the cities, but, lacking education and skills, they remained impoverished. *(c) Old Age.* With medical science prolonging life, the number of aged has steadily increased. Unable to find work, many older persons slipped below the poverty level. *(d) Death or Desertion of the Father.* Many families were plunged into poverty when the father died or deserted the family. The mother, lacking job skills and burdened by young children, frequently was unable to support the family. *(e) Discrimination.* Minority groups faced discrimination in education, housing, and jobs. They suffered poverty because of discrimination and their lack of skills.

Children of impoverished families were often born into an environment of despair and hopelessness, and did not receive the training necessary to rise out of poverty. From generation to generation, they remained locked in a cycle of poverty.

3. Pockets of Poverty. *(a) Appalachia.* In this mountainous area, from Pennsylvania to Alabama, many coal miners lost their jobs when coal mines were worked out and when the coal industry adopted automatic mining equipment. Also, many subsistence farmers were fighting a losing battle with the poor soil. *(b) New England Textile Towns.* Textile workers lost their jobs when many companies moved to the South, where wages were lower, or to Puerto Rico, where tax benefits were available. Other textile mills closed their doors because they were unable to withstand competition from newer domestic and foreign plants. *(c) Indian Reservations.* American Indians living on government reservations generally had poor land and few vocational skills. *(d) Big-City Slums.* Members of minority groups, living in slum areas, suffered chronic poverty.

4. Costs of Poverty. *(a)* Impoverished Americans burden their communities for welfare assistance, public health services, and expanded police and fire protection. Since their earnings are small, they are "taxeaters," not taxpayers. *(b)* They do not contribute proportionately to the nation's production of goods and services. *(c)* They tend to lose faith in the American way of life and may fall prey to extremist teachings.

PRESIDENT JOHNSON AND THE "WAR ON POVERTY" (1964–1969)

As part of his *Great Society,* President Johnson moved to arouse the national conscience by declaring "unconditional war on poverty." Congress created the *Office of Economic Opportunity (OEO).*

1. Some OEO Antipoverty Programs. *(a)* The *Job Corps* enlisted youths who were out of school and unemployed, and gave them remedial education and job training at special camps. *(b)* The *Neighborhood Youth Corps* provided underprivileged youths with summer and part-time community jobs, as in libraries and parks. *(c) Community Action Programs* undertook local projects with federal funds to provide health services, legal services, job training, and work for needy persons. *(d) Project Head Start* provided training to help disadvantaged preschool children so that they could succeed in their schooling.

2. Other Antipoverty Laws. The *Appalachian Redevelopment Act* provided funds for aid to Appalachia: road-building, land improvement, and the construction of health centers. The *Regional Development Act* provided funds for similar aid to other depressed areas.

3. Debate Over the "War on Poverty." Critics condemned the OEO for squandering government funds, encouraging boondoggling (valueless work), permitting graft and corruption, providing political patronage, and tolerating administrative mismanagement. Supporters, while conceding mistakes, insisted that the "war on poverty" awakened the nation to realize the problem and was directly and indirectly helping millions of impoverished Americans.

SUBSEQUENT POVERTY DEVELOPMENTS AND DATA

1. Dismantling the OEO. In 1973 President Nixon began to dismantle the Office of Economic Opportunity. Citing the need to improve efficiency and avoid duplication of services, he transferred most OEO activities to other federal agencies. For example, the Job Corps was moved to the Labor Department and Head Start to Health, Education, and Welfare. President Ford in 1975 established the *Community Services Administration* (CSA). It replaced the OEO and took over OEO's Community Action Program. In 1981 President Reagan abolished the CSA as Congress approved reduced funds in block grants for the states to continue various community services.

2. Comprehensive Employment and Training Act (CETA) of 1973. President Nixon secured this act. It eliminated many federal manpower programs and authorized federal grants to local and state agencies to operate their own manpower programs geared to community needs. CETA's activities were sharply reduced in the 1980s as Congress voted budget cuts requested by the Reagan administration.

3. Recent Poverty Data (Mid-1980s). For 1985 the Census Bureau reported that the poverty threshold for a nonfarm family of four was $10,989. This sharp increase from less than $3000 in 1960 reflected the impact of inflation. For 1985 the Census Bureau also reported that the number of impoverished persons was 33 million, or 14 percent of the population. These figures were a modest increase over 1980 but a decrease from the 1960 figures of 35 million and 20 percent. Some 7 million families were classified as poor in 1985, a drop of over 3 million from 1960. Experts believed that two reasons for the decrease were expansion of the economy and government programs to help poor people.

4. Criticism of Poverty Data. Critics claim that the Census Bureau figures on poverty are misleading because the bureau determines how many persons fall into the poverty category by counting only money income. Many of these persons, however, receive from the government nonmoney income such as food stamps, school lunches, medical benefits (Medicaid and Medicare), and subsidized low-rental housing. If these nonmoney items were counted, critics claim, far fewer people would fall below the poverty level.

——————— **MULTIPLE-CHOICE QUESTIONS** ———————

1. Which development has most aggravated the problem of satisfying unlimited human needs with limited resources? (a) increasing population (b) declining agricultural productivity (c) expanding international trade (d) increasing cost of industrial production.
2. At the present time, the population of the United States is (a) stationary (b) declining (c) increasing at a slower rate than in the 19th century (d) increasing at a faster rate than in the 19th century.

3. In 1980 the population of the United States reached about (a) 60 million (b) 75 million (c) 260 million (d) 227 million.

4. According to the 1980 census, which area showed the most rapid rate of population growth? (a) Sunbelt (b) Middle West (c) Northeast (d) Middle Atlantic.

5. The most densely populated area in the United States is the (a) South (b) Far West (c) Rocky Mountain region (d) Northeast.

6. Which is true of population trends in the United States? (a) The closing of the frontier marked an end of major population shifts. (b) The population of the United States is characterized by immobility. (c) Population shifts have political effects. (d) Economic development has had little effect on population trends.

7. The percentage of people over 65 in the United States has doubled since 1900. This is largely due to (a) an increase in immigration (b) improvements in medical science (c) the adoption of Social Security (d) the increase in homes for the aged.

8. The existence of organizations such as the American Association of Retired Persons indicates that senior citizens are (a) applying increased political pressure to achieve their goals (b) becoming less powerful in United States society (c) no longer interested in working through the political process (d) satisfied that their goals are being achieved.

9. The purpose of Social Security was to (a) provide cheap life insurance (b) curtail employers' profits (c) help relieve workers from the fear of destitution (d) provide more business for the big insurance companies.

10. Until the 1980s a group *not* protected by Social Security was (a) workers in interstate industries (b) white-collar workers (c) workers in the building industries (d) federal employees.

11. Over the years, the Social Security tax has (a) gone up (b) gone down (c) been paid entirely by the employer (d) remained fixed at the present level.

12. In the early 1980s, the Social Security system was a matter of public concern because (a) many employers refused to collect Social Security taxes (b) labor unions complained that benefits were insufficient (c) the cost of benefits was depleting the system's funds (d) doctors were refusing to care for Medicare patients.

13. The expression "Don't trust anyone over 30" was related to the (a) conflict between age groups in American society (b) opposition by civil rights groups to national political leaders (c) basis for conflict between college faculties and students (d) criticism of law-enforcement officers for lenient treatment of law violators.

14. An important effect of the population shifts from East to West and from rural to urban areas has been to (a) decrease the need for governmental services (b) reduce the food supply (c) weaken regional differences (d) increase traffic hazards.

15. The "generation under 30" in the United States has had an impact in many areas of our society. This impact has been *most* directly evident in its effect on (a) patterns of fashion and taste (b) demands made by organized labor (c) advancement of technology in business and industry (d) the federal government's farm policy.

16. The addition of medical insurance provisions to Social Security reflects concern with the (a) hazards of industrial employment (b) rising proportion of young people in our population (c) retirement problems of an increasingly large number of elderly persons (d) decline in job opportunities in economically depressed areas.

17. A period of inflation would probably have the most unfavorable effect on (a) the owner of a small business (b) a person living on a fixed pension (c) an industrial laborer (d) a common stockholder in a corporation.

18. Which of the following statements regarding Medicare is *not* correct? (a) It was first

officially proposed by President Truman. (b) It was supported by the American Medical Association. (c) It is financed through Social Security taxes. (d) It provides plans for paying hospital costs as well as doctor bills.

19. To take advantage of population trends in the United States since 1945, a retail merchant would be *most* likely to establish a new store in (a) a suburban shopping center (b) the central area of a large city (c) a small town in a farming region (d) a community where there is one major employer.

20. The term "home rule" deals with the relationship of (a) cities to suburbs (b) cities to state governments (c) cities to the federal government (d) states to the federal government.

21. Which is an important result of the movement of people from the cities to the suburbs? (a) an increase in the proportion of low-income families in the cities (b) a decline in the urban crime rate (c) a decline in urban renewal and planning (d) a decline in the cost of public transportation in the cities.

22. City governments do *not* deal with the problem of (a) immigration regulations (b) fire protection (c) sanitation (d) education.

23. Which factor is most closely related to the high crime rates in urban areas? (a) the movement of wealthy people into the "inner city" (b) the social and economic problems found in the "inner city" (c) the declining political power of urban areas (d) the failure of the federal government to provide money for local law-enforcement activities.

24. Most criminologists believe that the best way to prevent convicts from repeating criminal acts is to (a) widen use of the death penalty (b) spend a greater per capita amount on police protection (c) improve physical conditions in the prisons (d) change the ex-convict's environment through counseling and rehabilitation.

25. Which has been a result of the movement of the population from urban to suburban areas? (a) a decrease in the value of property in most rural areas (b) an increase in the importance of the city as a commercial center (c) an intensification of financial problems in many cities (d) an increase in the educational cost per pupil in suburban areas.

26. The agency placed in charge of directing President Johnson's "war on poverty" was (a) the Job Corps (b) Project Head Start (c) the Office of Economic Opportunity (d) CETA.

27. The federal government has sponsored programs of public housing because (a) the Constitution prohibits states from enacting housing laws (b) there is a surplus in the Treasury (c) there is a need to provide adequate housing for low-income groups (d) private builders have urged public housing projects.

28. Which best accounts for the fact that many businesses have left large urban areas? (a) increasing rates of taxation (b) increasing shortages of labor (c) lack of adequate housing (d) decrease in the number of available social services.

29. The Federal Housing Authority has encouraged private investors in housing by guaranteeing (a) profit to the builder (b) a buyer for the property (c) the repayment of mortgage loans (d) rent controls.

30. Which principle was involved in the Supreme Court decision on reapportionment in *Baker vs. Carr?* (a) separation of church and state (b) separation of powers (c) "separate but equal" (d) equal protection of the laws.

31. The Supreme Court decision on reapportionment in *Reynolds vs. Sims* spurred (a) a shift in political power from rural to urban areas (b) an increase in Republican strength in state legislatures (c) better representation of farm interests in state legislatures (d) an increased representation in Congress for states with growing populations.

32. Which area probably contains the *smallest* percentage of impoverished families? (a) an Indian reservation in New Mexico (b) a ghetto in Los Angeles (c) a textile town in Rhode Island (d) a suburb of Boston.

——————————— ESSAY QUESTIONS ———————————

1. An important population shift in the United States during the 20th century has been from rural to urban or suburban areas. *(a)* Explain briefly *two* reasons for this shift in population. *(b)* Discuss *three* problems facing cities as a result of this shift.

2. *(a)* Discuss *two* reasons why the percentage of persons over 65 in our population has more than doubled since 1900. *(b)* State *two* problems that face our senior citizens. *(c)* For *each* problem stated, discuss *one* effort that can be made either by the individual or by the government to provide a solution.

3. Discuss how *each* of the following population factors has had a significant effect on life in the United States: *(a)* numerical increase of "youth" *(b)* increase in the number of aged and retired persons *(c)* mobility of the population *(d)* concentration of population in urban areas.

4. The housing problem in American cities has two aspects: insufficient housing and inadequate housing. *(a)* Explain *each* of these aspects of the housing problem. *(b)* Show how *each* of the following either helped or hindered the solution of the housing problem: (1) tenement laws (2) World War II (3) private builders (4) Federal Housing Administration (5) black migration into northern cities.

5. President Johnson proclaimed a "war on poverty." *(a)* Discuss *three* factors that have kept many American families living in poverty. *(b)* Describe *two* programs sponsored by the federal government to break the "cycle of poverty." *(c)* Do you think that poverty can be completely eliminated? Give *two* arguments to defend your answer.

6. Since its inception in 1935, offering old-age pensions to a limited number of workers, Social Security benefits and coverage have been extended to additional groups. *(a)* Identify *three* groups that were included under Social Security in the years after 1935. *(b)* Name *two* forms of expanded benefits provided by Social Security after 1935. *(c)* Why was Congress so willing to expand coverage and increase benefits? Explain. *(d)* In 1950 there were 14 people paying into the system for *every* one receiving benefits. By 1980 the ratio was 3 to 1. Explain the significance of these data. *(e)* To meet the problem facing Social Security, there are three choices: cut benefits, raise taxes, or use funds from the general Treasury. Which course of action do you approve? Defend your answer.

7. Leaders of cities throughout the United States have been confronted with many problems. Among these problems are: costly social services, wage demands of public employees, movement of the wealthy and middle classes from cities to the suburbs, deterioration of housing in cities, outmoded design of the cities, and failure of cities to attract new industries. *(a)* Select *one* of the problems listed above. For the problem selected, (1) discuss *two* conditions which led to the development of that problem, and (2) discuss at least *two* results of that problem. *(b)* For the problem selected in answer to *a*, discuss *one* solution that has been proposed or implemented to deal with that problem. Tell why that solution is or is not likely to be effective.

PART 4. The American People Create a Rich and Varied Culture

EDUCATION

IMPORTANCE OF EDUCATION

Education serves American children by (1) teaching basic skills, especially reading, writing, and arithmetic; (2) training for employment; (3) encouraging constructive use of leisure time; (4) explaining complex world affairs; (5) making possible upward social mobility—that is, improving their status in society; and (6) preparing for the responsibilities of American citizenship.

GOVERNMENT RESPONSIBILITY FOR EDUCATION

1. As a State and Local Function. Although the Framers were well aware of education's importance, they made no mention of education in the Constitution. Most likely they were influenced by the colonial school experience and considered education to be a function of the various religious groups and of local or state governments. The Tenth Amendment to the Constitution declares that all powers not given to the federal government nor prohibited to the states are reserved to the states or to the people. Education consequently became a "reserved" power.

2. As a Federal Function. Although the Tenth Amendment made education a reserved power, the Constitution did not prohibit the federal government from encouraging, financing, and guiding education. By granting Congress the power to dispose of territory belonging to the United States, the Constitution enabled Congress to designate lands for the use of public education. By granting Congress the power to collect taxes for the "general welfare," the Constitution enabled Congress to appropriate money for education as part of "general welfare." By granting Congress the powers to "support armies" and "maintain a navy," the Constitution enabled Congress to provide money for education as essential to national defense.

DEVELOPMENT OF FREE PUBLIC SCHOOLS

1. In the Young Nation (To the 1820s). The states generally left education—as in colonial times—to towns and to religious and other private groups. Children of well-to-do families that could afford the tuition went to private schools. Some children of poorer families attended religious schools or, especially in New England, public primary schools maintained by towns. These children, in the public mind, were considered as "paupers."

2. The Educational Awakening (1800s Through the 1860s)

a. The Free Public School Issue

(1) Opposition. Well-to-do persons claimed that taxing them to provide education for the children of the poor was unjust. Some argued that children of the poor did not need and could not benefit from an education. Religious leaders warned that secular public schools would not provide moral instruction.

(2) Support. The principle of free, tax-supported public schools became firmly established by the 1860s, especially in the North. Its victory was spurred by major developments, notably the granting of the vote to all men and the growing spirit of Jacksonian democracy. The free public school movement had many supporters.

Democratically minded persons insisted that all children receive an equal opportunity for education to develop their own potentials and to preserve our democratic way of life. Nationalists wanted all children educated regarding our nation's history, heroes, and holidays so as to foster patriotism. City workers demanded free public schools so as to educate their children and remove children from the labor market. Humanitarians sought to remove the "pauper" stigma from children attending free schools and to lessen child labor. Educators envisioned the free public schools as the best way to provide children with civic, vocational, and moral training.

b. Two Leaders of the Free Public School Movement

(1) In 1837 *Horace Mann* became the secretary of the newly founded Massachusetts Board of Education. Mann *(a)* aroused the public to the need for free, tax-supported schools, *(b)* raised professional standards by establishing the first state-supported teacher-training school, and *(c)* introduced compulsory attendance, less rigid discipline, and a more varied curriculum. Horace Mann is known as the "father of the American public school."

(2) *Henry Barnard* improved the public schools in Connecticut and Rhode Island. In 1867 he became the first United States Commissioner of Education.

4. To the Present. Educators and political leaders have greatly expanded free public school systems by *(a)* providing elementary schools throughout the nation, *(b)* developing public high schools and gradually raising the age for compulsory education to 16, and, in a few states, to 17 or 18, *(c)* equipping schools with facilities such as libraries, science laboratories, museums, gymnasiums, vocational shops, and homemaking and business-machine rooms, *(d)* enlarging the scope of the high school to include—in addition to the traditional preparation for college—training for citizenship, for the use of leisure time, and for gainful employment, and *(e)* offering students greater attention to their individual needs, a wider selection of courses, and a more democratic school atmosphere.

Today 39 million pupils between the ages of five and 17 (or 88 percent of all children in that age group) are enrolled in public school systems, preparing themselves for life through education.

PRIVATE ELEMENTARY AND SECONDARY SCHOOLS

Supported largely by tuition payments, these schools enroll some 12 percent of the student population. They are of three types: (1) schools for special children—physically handicapped, mentally retarded, or exceptionally bright, (2) "prep" and other exclusive schools for upper-class children—often providing intensive preparation for college, and (3) the largest number—private religious or parochial schools. About 64 percent of the private-school enrollment is in Roman Catholic parochial schools, down from 84 percent in 1964. Protestant, Jewish, and other congregations also operate private schools, with a sharp rise in fundamentalist Protestant schools in recent years. Like the public schools, the private and parochial schools must meet the educational standards set by state boards of education.

Supporters claimed that private schools better provide for children's special needs, more easily introduce educational innovations, allow teachers greater freedom, and preserve America's cultural diversity. Opponents claimed the private schools engender feelings of separation in students and create "class" and religious divisions undercutting efforts to develop an American sense of values.

In recent years, as the costs of education have soared, especially due to inflation, some Catholic schools have closed and Catholic leaders have requested state and federal funds for parochial schools. They point out that (1) Catholic parents whose children attend parochial schools are paying tuition in addition to taxes supporting public education and (2) the parochial schools relieve the public schools of heavy financial and educational burdens. Opponents of public funds for parochial schools include most Protestant and Jewish groups and most public school educators. They insist that the First Amendment, separating church and state, prohibits the granting of public funds for church-controlled schools.

BRIEF SURVEY OF HIGHER EDUCATION

1. To the Civil War. Before 1860 various religious groups founded about 200 colleges. Originally, these schools prepared students for the ministry and taught Latin, Greek, grammar, and philosophy. Later, as they began preparing students for other vocations, they expanded their courses of study. Also, a few states founded state universities, which offered courses in the liberal arts and in various professional subjects.

2. Later Developments. Since 1860 American colleges and universities have grown in number and broadened their scope. *(a)* The *Morrill Act* (1862) granted federal lands to states to support colleges teaching agriculture and the mechanical arts. This act helped increase the number of state colleges and universities. Furthermore, it stimulated the movement toward more practical subjects such as agricultural science, home economics, veterinary medicine, and engineering. Among the well-known land-grant colleges today are the state universities of Wisconsin, Illinois, Texas, and California. *(b)* Technical schools, usually privately endowed, were founded to train chemists, physicists, architects, and engineers. Examples are the Massachusetts Institute of Technology and the California Institute of Technology. *(c)* Graduate schools were established to enable students to pursue advanced studies concentrating on research. Graduate studies were spurred at Yale, Harvard, and Johns Hopkins.

3. Higher Education Today

a. By Types. The United States contains some 2000 colleges and universities, classified as follows: (1) Slightly more than one third are church-controlled institutions, mostly Protestant and Roman Catholic. (2) Slightly less than one-third are privately controlled. (3) One-third are publicly controlled—by states, cities, or school districts. American colleges and universities may also be classified according to their programs: (1) Slightly more than two-thirds offer a four-year course, and many offer graduate work. (2) Slightly less than one-third are community, or junior, colleges that offer a two-year course, enabling students to prepare for a technical career or to transfer to a four-year college.

b. Some Problems. (1) Colleges and universities had 12 million students in 1980 but, due to a drop in school age population, faced declining enrollments. This decline may force the closing of lesser known and poorly financed schools. (2) Colleges and universities also face sharply rising costs due to inflation. In 1976, the City University of New York abandoned its 125-year tradition of free higher education and imposed tuition. (3) Colleges and universities faced decreasing federal aid as the Reagan administration curtailed funds for constructing college facilities and providing loans and grants to college students.

EDUCATIONAL ISSUES AND PROBLEMS TODAY

1. Integration of Public Schools.   (Check the Index.)

2. Need for Adult Education.
Adults have increasingly shown interest in courses to improve their written and spoken English, to learn new vocational skills, and to broaden their cultural horizons. Their interest has resulted in additional night schools, college extension courses, forums, lectures, and study groups.

3. Education for National Defense: Challenge of Soviet Russia.
Americans were startled by the Soviet Union's early leadership in the space race when, in 1957, the Soviets launched the world's first artificial satellite, Sputnik I. Americans began to reexamine our educational system. Many observers made the following conclusions: *(a)* In science, mathematics, and technical subjects, Soviet high school graduates, after ten years of study, were far ahead of American graduates after 12 years. *(b)* The Communist society channeled its ablest students into the fields of science, mathematics, and engineering by offering incentives of higher pay, better living conditions, and community approval. American society did not provide comparable incentives, and many American students preferred nontechnical occupations.

Congress passed the *National Defense Education Act* (1958) providing for *(a)* grants to states for the purchase of textbooks and other materials needed to strengthen the teaching of science, mathematics, and foreign languages, *(b)* grants to states for programs to locate and encourage gifted students, and *(c)* loans and graduate fellowships for college students, especially for those interested in teaching. (The act has been extended several times and expanded to include grants to states for the purchase of instructional materials for English and history.)

4. Finances for Elementary and Secondary Schools

a. State and Local Support. Public education has been financed mainly by state and local taxes. In the mid-1980s the average annual expenditure for public education was more than $3400 per pupil. This average figure, however, had wide variations from state to state. Relatively wealthy states spent considerably more than other states. Alaska spent more than $6800 per pupil, while New York and New Jersey spent about $5200. The poorer rural southern states of Alabama and Mississippi each spent just over $2200, and Utah spent slightly less. The southern states as a group lagged behind the rest of the nation in educational spending.

b. Debate Over Federal Aid

(1) Supporters. Many educators and political leaders urged that federal funds be used for the overall improvement of public education. They argued that federal funds are necessary to raise educational spending in the poorer states up to the national level.

Per Pupil Education Expenditure, by State, 1985

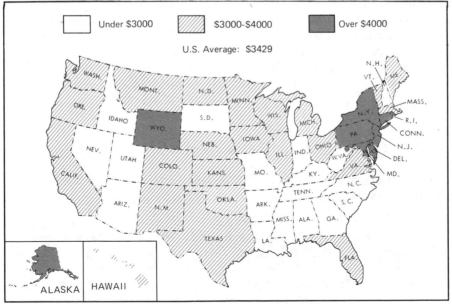

Federal Spending for Education, 1970–1985

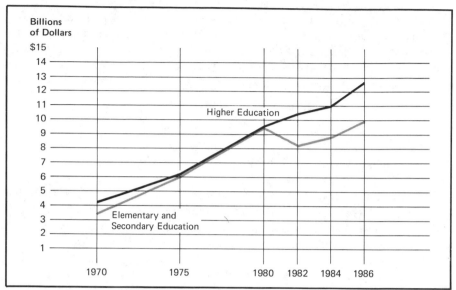

(2) Opponents. States' rights advocates feared that federal aid might erode state control of education. Roman Catholic leaders opposed any federal program that omitted funds for parochial schools. They rejected the argument that the First Amendment, separating church and state, prohibited government grants to church-controlled schools.

c. Elementary and Secondary Education Act (1965). By gearing federal education aid to the "war on poverty" and adopting a new approach to the parochial school issue, President Lyndon Johnson gained quick Congressional passage of this law. It provided (1) funds to the nation's public school districts based on their number of children from impoverished families (the school districts used these funds to hire more teachers, raise teachers' salaries, construct new buildings, and provide special courses), and (2) grants to states for the purchase of textbooks, library books, and audiovisual aids to be shared by public, private, and parochial school students.

This act (1) satisfied Roman Catholic leaders by providing instructional materials for parochial students, (2) satisfied advocates of separation of church and state by giving public officials control of the shared resources and by granting aid to parochial students rather than to parochial schools, and (3) set a precedent of direct federal aid for overall improvement of the public schools.

5. Other Federal Spending for Education. In addition to educational spending for national defense and for public school improvement, the federal government has provided funds on the public school level to *(a)* aid the education of handicapped children and *(b)* subsidize school lunches for needy children. On the college level, the federal government has provided funds to *(a)* enable war veterans—of World War II, Korea, and Vietnam—and military volunteers to secure a college education (under the popularly named G.I. Bill of Rights), *(b)* spur construction of college buildings, *(c)* expand college teaching facilities in medicine and related areas, *(d)* guarantee private low-interest bank loans for the education of qualified college students, and *(e)* give federal scholarships—called "educational opportunity grants"—to needy college students.

The Reagan administration slowed the rapid rise (since 1965) of federal spending for education. President Reagan also had Congress lump together many educational programs into a single block grant with minimal federal regulations for spending the funds. In this way Reagan sought to diminish the federal educational role and return more educational decisions to the states and localities.

6. Court Decisions Affecting Educational Finances. *(a)* In *Robinson vs. Dicenso* (1971) the Supreme Court declared unconstitutional the Rhode Island law that provided state funds to help pay salaries of parochial school teachers of nonreligious subjects. The Court held that such a law violated the First Amendment by requiring the state to keep parochial schools under surveillance, thereby causing "excessive entanglement." *(b)* In 1971 several lower courts held unconstitutional the reliance chiefly upon local property taxes for financing public education. Within a state, poor districts obtained much less money per child for education than did rich districts. In *Rodriguez vs. San Antonio School District* (1973) the Supreme Court upheld the property tax as a method of financing public school systems. The majority opinion held that the "equal protection" clause of the Fourteenth Amendment did not require "absolute equality" and that education is not listed in the Constitution as a fundamental right. The majority opinion further stated that reform in financing public education should come, not from the Supreme Court, but from the states. The minority opinion attacked the decision as a "retreat from an historic commitment to equality of educational opportunity."

7. Recent Educational Issues

a. Should the Cabinet-level Department of Education be abolished and some of its functions transferred to a federal educational foundation?

b. Should the federal government grant tuition vouchers to parents to be used to pay for their children's education in either private or public schools?

c. Should children of illegal aliens in the United States continue to be entitled to a free public school education?

d. Does the Supreme Court decision in *Lau vs. Nichols* (1974)—ordering the public schools to take extra steps to educate students who lack an adequate understanding of English—require that these students be given a bilingual education (in their native tongue and English) or that these students be given an intensive course in English as a second language?

e. Should prayer be encouraged in the public schools? If yes, what steps might be taken to overturn the Supreme Court decision holding unconstitutional the recitation of an official but nondenominational public school prayer in *Engel vs. Vitale* (1962)? (Check the Index.)

f. What can be done to improve students' proficiency in mathematics and the sciences?

g. Should public school teachers have the right to strike?

h. Are public school teachers paid an adequate salary?

i. Should a board of standards be established to certify elementary and high school teachers on a national basis?

j. What can be done to improve parents' confidence in the public schools?

SOCIAL REFORM

HUMANITARIANISM: MEANING AND AMERICAN ORIGINS

Humanitarians feel deep concern for and seek to improve the welfare of unfortunate or disadvantaged human beings. The earliest humanitarian movements in the United States arose amidst the democratic atmosphere and industrial growth of the Jacksonian Era. (1) Since democracy teaches respect for the life of each individual, it encouraged Americans to concern themselves with helping unfortunates. (2) The early Industrial Revolution called attention to unfortunates, as it accentuated certain evils such as slums, poor working conditions, and child labor. (3) By creating wealth, the Industrial Revolution provided humanitarians with money and time to combat social injustices.

MOVEMENTS FOR HUMANITARIANISM AND SOCIAL REFORM

1. Improved Treatment of the Insane and Criminals. *Dorothea Dix,* in the 1840s, worked to secure better treatment of the insane, improve conditions in prisons, and abolish imprisonment for debt. In her day the insane were treated as criminals. Prisons were filthy, and prisoners were often treated cruelly. Today the insane are treated as mentally sick persons. Criminals in prisons are given training to help prepare them to earn an honest livelihood. Imprisonment for debt has ended.

In 1971 inmates in various prisons, notably at *Attica,* New York, staged revolts indicating that they were greatly dissatisfied with conditions and far from society's desired goals of their reform and rehabilitation.

2. Care for Sick and Wounded Soldiers. *Clara Barton* aided Union soldiers during the Civil War by providing medical and nursing care. In 1881 she organized and for many years headed the *American Red Cross.* It serves today not only war casualties but also peacetime disaster victims.

3. Care for the Physically Handicapped. The *Perkins Institute,* founded in Boston in 1832, became famous for aiding deaf and blind persons. It sent *Anne Sullivan* to teach *Helen Keller* to overcome her physical handicaps. In later years, Helen Keller became reknowned as an advocate of humane treatment for the deaf and the blind.

Today, many charitable organizations collect funds to help the physically handicapped: the ill, the deaf, the blind, and the crippled. The federal and state governments also provide funds for programs to help these unfortunate persons.

4. Prohibition of Intoxicating Beverages. Beginning in the early 19th century, many Americans urged prohibition of alcohol to protect the home against drunkenness and to prevent workers from squandering their wages at the corner saloon. In 1851 *Neal Dow* secured prohibition in Maine, and this example was followed by several other states. In 1874 *Frances Willard* helped found the nationwide *Woman's Christian Temperance Union (WCTU)*. Another prohibition group was the *Anti-Saloon League*.

During World War I, when grain used in making liquor was needed for food, Congress proposed the *Eighteenth Amendment* prohibiting the manufacture and sale of intoxicating beverages. Overwhelmingly adopted, this amendment was hailed in 1928 by Herbert Hoover as a "great social and economic experiment, noble in motive." Nevertheless, it was defied by the public, opened a profitable field for bootleggers and gangsters, and led to general disrespect for the law. In 1933 the Eighteenth Amendment was repealed by the *Twenty-First Amendment.* Today, all states have ended prohibition but exercise supervision over the sale of intoxicating beverages.

5. Women's Rights.   (Check the Index.)

6. Philanthropy. Philanthropists are persons of great wealth who donate large sums to promote the welfare of society. Their motives may have been to benefit society, to erase an unfavorable public image, or to perpetuate a name.

a. Peter Cooper, inventor and iron industry leader, promoted the arts and encouraged scientific training by founding in New York City a school and cultural center, *Cooper Union.*

b. Andrew Carnegie, steel magnate, provided free public libraries and established the *Carnegie Endowment for International Peace.* He also built the *Hague* (Holland) *Peace Palace,* which today houses the International Court of Justice.

c. John D. Rockefeller, oil millionaire, endowed the *University of Chicago.* Through the *Rockefeller Foundation,* he provided grants to other colleges and universities and encouraged research programs in the social sciences and humanities. He also founded an institute for medical research, now called *Rockefeller University.*

d. J. Pierpont Morgan, the banker who organized railroad mergers and steel combinations, was a leading art collector. He bequeathed his valuable books, manuscripts, and art works to establish in New York City the Morgan Wing of the Metropolitan Museum and the *Morgan Library.*

e. Daniel Guggenheim, a copper-mining magnate and industrialist, established the *Guggenheim Fund for the Promotion of Aeronautics,* and the *Guggenheim Foundation* to further "the well-being of mankind."

f. Andrew W. Mellon, banker and aluminum manufacturer, gave funds for establishing in Washington, D.C., the *National Gallery of Art.*

g. *Henry Ford*, automobile manufacturer, established the *Ford Foundation*. It grants funds to universities, medical schools, and hospitals and finances studies of such problems as civil liberties and international peace.

7. Other Social Movements. Discussed throughout the book are other humanitarian and social reforms: abolition of slavery, settlement houses in slums, free public schools, low-cost public housing, and Social Security.

SCIENCE

OBSERVATIONS ON SCIENCE IN AMERICA

1. Colonial Times to the 1950s. For the fundamental concepts of *pure* or *basic science*, Americans relied largely on European scientists. Pure or basic scientists seek knowledge for its own sake without direct regard for its use. For pure science, Europeans had the advantages of established universities, research facilities, science associations, and financial resources.

Meanwhile, American scientists excelled in *practical* or *applied science*. Americans were concerned with inventions to solve problems: such as separating the seed from the cotton fiber and cultivating large farms in a labor-scarce society. Americans became known for their resourcefulness and inventiveness—traits encompassed by the term "Yankee ingenuity."

2. In Recent Times. American scientists continued with practical research but also began to delve deeply into basic research. This emphasis reflected the following factors: *(a)* American scientists became increasingly aware that discoveries in basic research are essential for progress in practical areas. *(b)* Because World War II brought so much destruction to Europe, Americans could no longer depend upon European scientists for basic research discoveries. *(c)* America emerged from World War II with an undamaged homeland, tremendous financial resources, and excellent research facilities. *(d)* Because of its high standard of living and atmosphere of freedom, America attracted to its shores many capable foreign scientists—the so-called *brain drain*. *(e)* Because science and industry are interdependent, many American corporations spent large sums on R and D—research and development. These corporations established and staffed their own research facilities and permitted their scientists, within reason, to engage in basic research. Corporate research laboratories originated such familiar products as artificial grass, or astroturf (Monsanto), nylon (Du Pont), and the solid-state transistor (Bell Telephone Laboratories). *(f)* More aware than ever before of the importance of science in coping with national problems, the federal government appropriated tremendous sums for scientific research.

3. Federal Support for Science. The federal government sometimes assigns funds for scientific research and development to "in-house," or government, scientists, but more frequently it gives grants and makes contracts for the

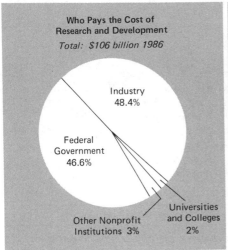

Who Pays the Cost of Research and Development
Total: $106 billion 1986

- Industry 48.4%
- Federal Government 46.6%
- Other Nonprofit Institutions 3%
- Universities and Colleges 2%

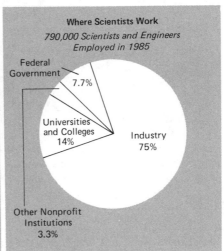

Where Scientists Work
790,000 Scientists and Engineers Employed in 1985

- Federal Government 7.7%
- Universities and Colleges 14%
- Industry 75%
- Other Nonprofit Institutions 3.3%

work to be done by university and industry personnel. The tremendous increase in federal support for scientific research resulted from the high cost of research, the complexity of research (all the "easy" discoveries seemingly have been made) and the importance of science to national defense, and worldwide prestige.

Some scientists welcomed government aid, since it enhanced the status of science and provided funds. Other scientists feared that government aid would lead to political domination of scientists and compel researchers to seek specific practical goals, rather than allow them to investigate freely.

4. From Individual to Team Research. Through the 19th century, creative individuals usually worked by themselves or with a few assistants and some achieved major scientific discoveries. By the mid-20th century, modern research became complex, often involving several scientific areas, so that no one person possessed complete "expertise." Modern research equipment was expensive, such as the big telescope to see deeply into the heavens, and the atomic smasher to peer deeply into the atom. Scientific progress became too important to industry and government to leave to chance discoveries of individuals, no matter how creative.

The creative individual therefore gave way to the creative scientific team. Under centralized supervision, each team member pursued experiments and contributed knowledge to enable the team to solve the overall research problem.

Examples of modern research teamwork include: (1) The Manhattan Project consisted of scientists and technicians who, working together during World War II, produced the first atomic bomb, and (2) the creation of nylon by a group of Dupont researchers, who together synthesized this most useful product.

AMERICAN SCIENTISTS, 19TH AND 20TH CENTURIES

MEDICAL SCIENTISTS	CONTRIBUTIONS
Virginia Apgar	Devised Apgar Test to judge infants' health.
William Morton	Use of ether as an anesthetic during surgery.
Walter Reed	Discovery of mosquito as carrier of yellow fever.
Helen Brooke Taussig	Developed operation to cure "blue-baby" condition.
Selman Waksman (naturalized American)	Antibiotic "wonder drug" streptomycin.
Alice Hamilton	Pioneer in industrial toxicology.
Jonas Salk	First polio vaccine, given by injection.
Albert Sabin	Second polio vaccine, taken by mouth.
Rosalyn S. Yalow	Nobel Prize (1977) for hormone research.

ATOMIC SCIENTISTS	CONTRIBUTIONS
Albert Einstein (naturalized American)	Theory of relativity, including the formula $E = mc^2$ (tremendous energy from small amount of matter); told President Roosevelt in 1939 that Nazi scientists were working to build an atom bomb; advised the President to institute an American atom bomb project.
Harold C. Urey	Discovery of "heavy" hydrogen for nuclear research.
Ernest O. Lawrence	Cyclotron, a machine for studying the atom.
Enrico Fermi (naturalized American)	First nuclear chain reaction (Chicago, 1942).
Leona M. Libby	Work on Manhattan Project to build first nuclear reactor.
J. Robert Oppenheimer	Head of Los Alamos group that built first atom bomb.
Edward Teller (naturalized American)	Research leading to hydrogen bomb.
Glenn T. Seaborg	New chemical elements and radioactive isotopes.
Maria Goeppert-Mayer	Nobel Prize (1963) for analyzing the structure of atomic nuclei.

OTHER SCIENTISTS	CONTRIBUTIONS
John J. Audubon	Detailed paintings printed as *The Birds of America*.
Asa Gray	Study of plants in North America.
Louis Agassiz	Study of glaciers, fossils, and fishes.
Maria Mitchell	Discovery of comet (1847), later named for her.
Luther Burbank	Crossbreeding for new and improved varieties of plants, especially the Idaho potato.
Albert Michelson	Accurate measurement of speed of light.
Robert H. Goddard	First liquid-fuel rocket (1926)—later used for space exploration.
Wallace Carothers	Nylon, developed in Du Pont Company laboratories.

5. All Persons Welcome as Scientists. American science knows no boundaries of race, religion, or nationality. For example, to produce an atomic bomb during World War II, the United States mobilized scientists from all over the world: Albert Einstein, a refugee from Nazi Germany; Edward Teller, from pro-Nazi Hungary; Enrico Fermi, from Fascist Italy; and Niels Bohr, from Nazi-occupied Denmark; as well as native-born Americans, such as J. Robert Oppenheimer and Harold C. Urey.

LITERATURE AND THE ARTS

OBSERVATIONS ON AMERICAN LITERATURE AND ART

1. American culture took root in colonial times. As colonists built cities and acquired wealth, they became interested in the arts. They attended theatrical performances and musical concerts. A few American painters received recognition in England as well as in America. Writers turned out some excellent political and religious discourses.

2. In the 19th century, writers produced the first significant American fiction and poetry. They dealt with our past, with current issues, and with broad moral and philosophical questions. American painters portrayed famous Americans and scenes of everyday life.

3. In the 20th century, American writers sought to explore human motivations and to understand individuals in their complex societies. Painters experimented with new forms, notably abstract art. Composers produced traditional classical works and delved into electronic music. Other composers developed the musical comedy into a major American art form.

4. Since World War II, private and public efforts have brought literature and the arts to more and more Americans, a development called the *cultural explosion.* Television producers presented fine documentaries, dramas, concerts, literary discussions, and educational programs. Publishers expanded the market for books by producing less expensive paperbacks. Municipal leaders, using public and private funds, helped build new museums and cultural centers. In 1965 Congress encouraged culture and scholarship by creating and providing funds for the *National Foundation on the Arts and Humanities.*

SOME AMERICAN WRITERS: COLONIAL PERIOD

Cotton Mather and Jonathan Edwards, both members of the New England clergy, wrote on religious themes. Benjamin Franklin praised hard work, thrift, and sound judgment in his *Poor Richard's Almanac* and in his *Autobiography.* In political affairs, Thomas Paine urged independence in his pamphlet *Common Sense;* Thomas Jefferson wrote the *Declaration of Independence;* Alexander Hamilton, James Madison, and John Jay defended the federal Constitution in essays published together as *The Federalist.*

AMERICAN WRITERS, 19TH CENTURY

Writers	Typical Works
Washington Irving	"The Legend of Sleepy Hollow" and "Rip Van Winkle," stories based on folklore of the Hudson River valley.
James Fenimore Cooper	*The Last of the Mohicans* and *The Deerslayer,* adventure novels of frontier settlers and Indians.
Harriet Beecher Stowe	*Uncle Tom's Cabin,* novel dramatizing the plight of slaves.
George Bancroft	*A History of the United States,* in ten volumes, extolling American democracy and patriotism.
Ralph Waldo Emerson	"Self-Reliance," "Experience," and "Fate," essays on the dignity of the individual; "Concord Hymn," poem about the beginning of the American Revolution.
Henry David Thoreau	*Walden* and *Civil Disobedience,* autobiographical works urging individual freedom and self-reliance.
Nathaniel Hawthorne	*The Scarlet Letter* and *The House of the Seven Gables,* novels set in New England.
Henry Wadsworth Longfellow	"The Song of Hiawatha" and "The Courtship of Miles Standish," poems based on American folklore and history.
Edgar Allan Poe	"The Fall of the House of Usher," short story of horror and mystery; "The Raven" and "Annabel Lee," poems.
Emily Dickinson	"I'm Nobody, Who Are You?", "Because I Could Not Stop for Death," and other poems about the self and destiny.
James Russell Lowell	*Biglow Papers,* poems against the Mexican War and slavery.
Louisa May Alcott	*Little Women* and *Little Men,* popular novels about childhood.
Walt Whitman	*Leaves of Grass,* poems praising democracy and individualism; "O Captain! My Captain!", honoring Abraham Lincoln.
Herman Melville	*Moby Dick,* a novel about whaling, considered an allegory symbolizing the struggle between good and evil.
Emma Lazarus	"The New Colossus," a poem from which come the words on the Statue of Liberty ("Give me your tired . . .").
Samuel L. Clemens (Pen name: Mark Twain)	*The Adventures of Tom Sawyer* and *The Adventures of Huckleberry Finn,* novels of youthful adventure on the Mississippi River.

AMERICAN WRITERS, 20TH CENTURY

Novelists	Typical Works
Edith Wharton	*The House of Mirth* and *The Age of Innocence,* about high society; *Ethan Frome,* a New England tragedy.
Upton Sinclair	*The Jungle,* "Oil," and "Boston," stories of social protest.
Willa Cather	*O Pioneers!* and *A Lost Lady,* about life on the fading frontier; *Death Comes for the Archbishop,* about Roman Catholicism in the Southwest.
Sinclair Lewis	*Babbitt* and *Main Street,* criticisms of middle-class life; *Arrowsmith* about an idealistic doctor; *It Can't Happen Here,* against fascism.
Edna Ferber	*Cimmaron* and *Giant,* novels of western life; also collaborated on such plays as *Dinner at Eight.*
William Faulkner	*The Sound and the Fury* and *Absalom, Absalom!,* about the decay of southern society.

Ernest Hemingway	*For Whom the Bell Tolls*, against fascism; *The Old Man and the Sea*, a fishing tale.
Katherine Anne Porter	*Pale Horse, Pale Rider* and *Ship of Fools*, works of political and social realism.
John Steinbeck	*The Grapes of Wrath*, problems of migratory farm workers in the 1930s.
Mary McCarthy	*The Groves of Academe*, satirizing college life; *The Group*, tracing the experiences of eight Vassar women.
James Baldwin	*Go Tell It on the Mountain*, autobiographical story of a black child growing up in Harlem.
Alice Walker	*The Color Purple*, story of a southern black woman's trials and triumphs.

POETS	TYPICAL WORKS
Marianne Moore	"In Distrust of Merits" mourning war and human failure, and "Poetry," praising its usefulness.
Robert Frost	"Mending Wall," "Birches," and "The Death of the Hired Man," about rural New England.
Carl Sandburg	*Chicago Poems* and *The People, Yes*, praising democracy and the common people. (Also wrote a biography of Abraham Lincoln.)
Edna St. Vincent Millay	"The Harp Weaver," about a mother's love for her son, and "Lament," a meditation on a father's death.
Stephen Vincent Benét	*John Brown's Body*, about the Civil War.
Gwendolyn Brooks	Poet and novelist of black urban life.

PLAYWRIGHTS	TYPICAL WORKS
Eugene O'Neill	*The Emperor Jones, Strange Interlude*, and *Ah, Wilderness!*, psychological analyses of human character.
Lillian Hellman	*The Children's Hour, The Little Foxes*, and *Watch on the Rhine*, all plays made into films.
Maxwell Anderson	*Valley Forge, Elizabeth the Queen, Winterset*, and *Knickerbocker Holiday*, about historical events.
Robert Sherwood	*Abe Lincoln in Illinois*, about his early career; *There Shall Be No Night*, condemning Russia's attack on Finland.
Tennessee Williams	*The Glass Menagerie* and *A Streetcar Named Desire*, studies of human emotions and frustrations.
Lorraine Hansberry	*A Raisin in the Sun*, first Broadway play by a black author (1959).
Arthur Miller	*Death of a Salesman* and *All My Sons*, concerned with moral questions of individuals and society.

HISTORIANS	TYPICAL WORKS
Frederick Jackson Turner	*The Frontier in American History.*
Vernon L. Parrington	*Main Currents in American Thought*, weaving together history and literature.
Charles A. Beard	*An Economic Interpretation of the Constitution*, about the economic interests of the Founders.
Margaret Leech	*Reveille in Washington* (the Civil War), *In the Days of McKinley* (the late 19th century).
Bruce Catton	*The Centennial History of the Civil War*, a multivolume work, including *The Coming Fury* and *Never Call Retreat.*
Barbara W. Tuchman	*The Guns of August*, on the causes of World War I; *A Distant Mirror*, about 14th-century Europe.

Arthur M. Schlesinger, Jr.	*The Age of Jackson; The Age of Roosevelt,* on the New Deal; *A Thousand Days,* about the Kennedy administration.
Frances FitzGerald	*Fire in the Lake,* prize-winning study of the American experience in Vietnam.

AMERICAN COMPOSERS, 19TH AND 20TH CENTURIES

COMPOSERS	TYPICAL WORKS
Stephen C. Foster	"My Old Kentucky Home," "Oh! Susanna," and "Old Black Joe," songs of blacks and the South.
John Philip Sousa	"Semper Fidelis" and "Stars and Stripes Forever," patriotic marches.
Amy Marcy Cheney (known as Mrs. H. H. A. Beach)	*Gaelic Symphony,* first symphonic work by an American woman (1896).
Victor Herbert	*Babes in Toyland* and *Naughty Marietta,* operettas.
Irving Berlin	*Annie Get Your Gun,* musical comedy; "White Christmas" and "God Bless America," popular songs.
George Gershwin	*Porgy and Bess,* folk opera of black life; *An American in Paris* and *Rhapsody in Blue,* symphonic jazz.
Aaron Copeland	*Billy the Kid, Rodeo,* and *Appalachian Spring,* ballets.
Ruth Crawford Seeger	*Sacco-Vanzetti* and *Chinaman, Laundryman,* works for piano and voice on political and social themes; collections of American folk songs.
Richard Rodgers	*Oklahoma!, South Pacific, The King and I,* and *The Sound of Music,* musicals.
Leonard Bernstein	*Wonderful Town* and *West Side Story,* musicals.

AMERICAN PAINTERS, 18TH, 19TH, AND 20TH CENTURIES

PAINTERS	TYPICAL WORKS
John Singleton Copley	Portraits of colonial Americans such as Paul Revere.
Gilbert Stuart	Portraits of early Americans such as George Washington.
Mary Cassatt	"The Boating Party" and "In the Park," scenes of leisure.
Winslow Homer	"The Herring Net" and "The Life Line," seascapes; also Civil War sketches.
Thomas Hart Benton	Historical murals; also scenes of the Midwest.
Grant Wood	Scenes of the Midwest such as "American Gothic."
Anna Mary (Grandma) Moses	Farm scenes and landscapes in "primitive" style; had no formal art training.
John Steuart Curry	Scenes of the Midwest such as "Baptism in Kansas" and "Tornado."
Georgia O'Keeffe	Stark, almost abstract paintings of natural objects such as rocks and clouds.
Jackson Pollock	Abstract paintings with new techniques, such as "Autumn Rhythm."

AMERICAN SCULPTORS, 19TH AND 20TH CENTURIES

SCULPTORS	TYPICAL WORKS
Augustus Saint-Gaudens	The "Standing Lincoln" in Lincoln Park, Chicago.
Malvina Hoffman	The 100 life-size bronze statues in "Races of Mankind" exhibit, Field Museum of Natural History, Chicago.
Daniel Chester French	"The Minuteman" at Concord; the "Seated Lincoln" in Washington, D.C.
Louise Nevelson	"Scavenger art" using such materials as wheels and furniture parts.
Alexander Calder	Abstract sculpture; stabiles and mobiles.

AMERICAN ARCHITECTS, 19TH AND 20TH CENTURIES

ARCHITECTS	TYPICAL WORKS
Louise Bethune	One of the first architects to use steel frames and concrete slabs; store building, Buffalo, New York.
Henry H. Richardson	New York State Capitol at Albany (Romanesque features).
Julia Morgan	San Simeon, the California home of publisher William Randolph Hearst; Fairmont Hotel in San Francisco.
Louis Sullivan	Early modern skyscrapers (believed that the form of a building should express its purpose).
Cloethiel Woodward Smith	Laclede Town, St. Louis; townhouses in Reston, Virginia.
Frank Lloyd Wright	Johnson Wax Building in Racine, Wisconsin; Guggenheim Museum in New York City (believed that a building should harmonize with its surroundings).

———— IDENTIFICATION QUESTIONS: WHO AM I? ————

Susan B. Anthony	Andrew Carnegie	Horace Mann
Henry Barnard	Peter Cooper	John D. Rockefeller
Clara Barton	Dorothea Dix	Elizabeth Cady Stanton

1. I was a pioneer for free public education. I made the school system of Massachusetts a model for other states.
2. I organized and for many years served as president of the American Red Cross.
3. I was an untiring advocate of giving the vote to women. An amendment to the Constitution has been named for me.
4. I donated money to establish free public libraries.
5. I brought about important reforms in the treatment of insane people and criminals.
6. I established a New York City school to serve as a civic center and to train students in the arts and sciences.
7. I endowed the University of Chicago and founded an institute for medical research.

—————————— MULTIPLE-CHOICE QUESTIONS ——————————

1. Historically, free public education in the United States has been urged as necessary (a) for the effective functioning of a democracy (b) for promotion of the arts (c) to instill moral qualities in the citizenry (d) for scientific advancement.

2. Statistics show that, as a group, persons with more education will earn higher incomes than those with less education. This information leads to the conclusion that (a) educators control the job market (b) a poorly educated person has no hope of earning a good living (c) education is a major route for disadvantaged groups to improve their status (d) college-educated persons need not fear unemployment.

3. "Education is a great equalizer of the conditions of people—the balance wheel of the social machinery. It does better than to disarm the poor of their hostility toward the rich; it prevents being poor. . . . " According to this statement, the most important goal of education is to (a) increase social tension (b) encourage social mobility (c) initiate cultural assimilation (d) develop cultural pluralism.

4. The first colleges in New England were organized primarily to (a) teach medicine and law (b) teach the practical arts and sciences (c) prepare persons for the ministry (d) train gentlemen-farmers.

5. During the period 1825 to 1860, which was an important factor in the movement for a tax-supported public school system? (a) unpopularity of religious schools (b) heritage of state-supported schools in Europe (c) leadership of wealthy groups who believed in equal opportunity (d) influence of the wage-earning class in cities.

6. The Morrill Act of 1862 aided education by giving (a) each state the right to control its own schools (b) colleges funds for research (c) each state public land, the income from which was to be used for agricultural colleges (d) the federal government a grant of money to set up an office of education.

7. Today, most policy decisions affecting public schools in the United States are made by (a) federal courts (b) Congress (c) local boards of education (d) the secretary of education.

8. Which best explains why the federal government played a minor role in education until recent years? (a) Historically, education has been regarded as the responsibility of the localities and states. (b) Until recently, parents have been financially responsible for their children's education. (c) The federal government could not afford to provide aid until after World War II. (d) All Presidents, until after World War II, opposed federal aid to education.

9. A basic reason for federal expenditures for education is the (a) attempt to centralize education under a single agency (b) concern for the full development of the nation's human resources (c) desire to eliminate the existing dual system of private and public education (d) need to justify high federal income taxes.

10. Which event spurred Congress to pass the National Defense Education Act of 1958? (a) the Soviet launching of Sputnik I (b) China's explosion of its first atomic bomb (c) the seizure of power in Cuba by Fidel Castro (d) French expulsion from Vietnam.

11. Beginning in the 1950s the federal government aided college education by all of the following except (a) loans for construction of college classrooms (b) grants for purchase of equipment (c) special tax exemptions for parents supporting children at college (d) scholarships for needy students.

12. Which statement regarding the Elementary and Secondary Education Act of 1965 is not true? (a) It was related to the "war on poverty." (b) It granted money to states for the purchase of instructional materials to be used by parochial school stu-

dents. (c) It began federal aid to public education. (d) It provided federal aid directly to school districts.

13. Today, public education in the United States is supported by (a) local governments only (b) state governments only (c) the national government only (d) local, state, and national governments.

14. Which is a valid statement about education in the United States today? (a) The number of high school graduates has fallen since 1900. (b) The federal government is spending a larger amount of money in support of education than all state and local governments combined. (c) A wide range of educational issues are being discussed today. (d) Private schools are gradually replacing public schools.

15. Advocates of a pluralistic society would probably support which activity in the public schools? (a) compulsory recitation of prayers (b) development of ethnic studies courses (c) elimination of bilingual programs (d) censorship of library materials.

16. In which aspect of public education have federal and state courts been *least* involved? (a) religious observances in the schools (b) tax bases for support of public education (c) grading standards and policies (d) racial balance of school populations.

17. An old Chinese proverb states, "Give a man a fish and you feed him for a day. Teach a man to fish and you feed him for a lifetime." The proverb could best be used in support of which United States government program? (a) food stamps (b) agricultural subsidies (c) aid to education (d) Medicare.

18. The main theme of the literature of New England during the early colonial period was (a) economic (b) imperialistic (c) religious (d) scientific.

19. *The Jungle* by Upton Sinclair and *The Grapes of Wrath* by John Steinbeck are both examples of literature that helped to (a) increase the feeling of national pride (b) bolster the economy (c) stimulate interest in free public education (d) create a climate for reform.

20. Which has been a major theme of art and literature in the United States in the 20th century? (a) benefits of modern technology (b) importance of religious values (c) appreciation of nature (d) understanding individuals in their complex society.

21. During the 20th century, American cultural life has been most influenced by (a) business cycles (b) European cultural developments (c) technological advances (d) wealthy patrons of the arts.

22. Which statement best expresses the viewpoint of the quotation, "Art thrives most where commerce has enriched the busy coast"? (a) Great artistic advances are most likely to occur during periods of economic prosperity. (b) Free enterprise is necessary for artistic expression. (c) The creativity of the artist must not be restricted. (d) Most great works of art have been produced for export.

23. The pure scientist would be most concerned with (a) purifying gasoline so as to achieve more miles per gallon (b) producing complex computers (c) writing manuals for operating nuclear generators (d) studying the basic truths of our universe.

24. The practical scientist (a) seeks knowledge for its own sake (b) usually disregards the findings of pure science (c) searches for new and useful products (d) has contributed little to the American standard of living.

25. Which best explains why, in the United States today, individuals are less likely to be credited with inventions, discoveries, and breakthroughs? (a) Individuals are less interested in public recognition. (b) Accomplishments are frequently the result of team effort. (c) Private investment for research has decreased sharply. (d) Governmental grants for research have been eliminated.

26. Which is the most accurate statement concerning scientific development? (a) The future of science is completely predictable. (b) Humanity must find a balance between the risks and the opportunities being created by scientific progress. (c) The interaction of science and society is less important today than in earlier ages. (d) Today's social structure is keeping pace with the invention of new machinery.

——————— MATCHING QUESTIONS: SCIENCE ———————

Column A—Achievements

1. Used ether as an anesthetic
2. Developed antibiotic streptomycin
3. Propounded theory of relativity
4. Hormone research
5. Constructed first nuclear reactor
6. Discovered how yellow fever is spread
7. Developed cyclotron
8. Created first polio vaccine
9. Studied nature through glaciers, fossils, and fishes
10. "Blue-baby" operation
11. Developed hydrogen bomb
12. Launched first liquid-fuel rocket

Column B—Scientists

a. Louis Agassiz
b. John J. Audubon
c. Luther Burbank
d. Albert Einstein
e. Enrico Fermi
f. Robert H. Goddard
g. Ernest O. Lawrence
h. Albert Michelson
i. William Morton
j. J. Robert Oppenheimer
k. Walter Reed
l. Jonas Salk
m. Helen Brooke Tausig
n. Edward Teller
o. Rosalyn S. Yalow
p. Selman Waksman

——————— MATCHING QUESTIONS: LITERATURE ———————

Column A—Themes

1. Pursuit of a white whale
2. Novel about plight of slaves
3. Fascism anywhere as a threat to liberty everywhere
4. Praise of hard work and thrift
5. Experiences of frontier settlers and Indians
6. Poems in praise of democracy and individualism
7. Life on the frontier
8. Conditions of migratory farm workers
9. Account of a boy's life on the Mississippi
10. Poems critical of the Mexican War and slavery
11. Folklore of the Hudson River valley

Column B—Literary Works

a. *Poor Richard's Almanac*
b. *O Pioneers!*
c. *The Adventures of Huckleberry Finn*
d. *Moby Dick*
e. *Walden*
f. *Go Tell It on the Mountain*
g. *Uncle Tom's Cabin*
h. *Leaves of Grass*
i. *For Whom the Bell Tolls*
j. *The Grapes of Wrath*
k. *Rip Van Winkle*
l. *The Last of the Mohicans*
m. *Biglow Papers*

__ MATCHING QUESTIONS: LITERATURE AND THE ARTS __

Column A—Works

1. Biography of Lincoln
2. *The Guns of August*
3. *Porgy and Bess*
4. *Main Street*
5. "American Gothic"
6. *A Raisin in the Sun*
7. Guggenheim Museum, New York City
8. "The Boating Party"
9. *Walden*
10. "God Bless America"
11. "Seated Lincoln," Washington, D.C.
12. San Simeon
13. *The Centennial History of the Civil War*
14. "Mending Wall"
15. "The Harp Weaver"

Column B—Creators

a. Irving Berlin
b. Mary Cassatt
c. Bruce Catton
d. Ralph Waldo Emerson
e. Daniel Chester French
f. Robert Frost
g. George Gershwin
h. Lorraine Hansberry
i. Winslow Homer
j. Sinclair Lewis
k. Edna St. Vincent Millay
l. Julia Morgan
m. Eugene O'Neill
n. Carl Sandburg
o. Henry David Thoreau
p. Barbara Tuchman
q. Grant Wood
r. Frank Lloyd Wright

——————————— ESSAY QUESTIONS ———————————

1. Throughout the history of the United States, our practices and policies in the field of education have been influenced by our national ideals and by historical developments. Give *two* specific examples to prove the truth of this statement for *each* of the following periods: *(a)* 1829–1860 *(b)* 1860–1945 *(c)* 1945–present.

2. The United States today faces the problem of equalizing educational opportunities. *(a)* Show in *two* ways how this problem arose out of conditions in American life. *(b)* Describe in *one* way how this problem affects the welfare of all the American people. *(c)* Illustrate *two* ways by which this problem was tackled by the federal government.

3. Scientific and technological progress in America has been closely related to the needs of society. For each of the following periods in American history, *(a)* name *one* scientific or technological advance and *(b)* show how this advance met the needs of society at that time: (1) 1750–1850 (2) 1850–1900 (3) 1900–1950.

4. Scientific research and development today receive financial support from *(a)* large, science-oriented corporations and *(b)* the federal government. Explain *one* advantage and *one* disadvantage of each of these sources of financial support for science.

5. Among its many functions, literature may help the reader escape from reality or face the problems troubling society. *(a)* Indicate which function of literature you consider more important—escapism or social consciousness. Give *one* argument to support your opinion. *(b)* Name *one* literary work that you consider an example of escapism and provide *one* reason to support your opinion. *(c)* Name *one* literary work that you consider an example of social consciousness and provide *one* reason to support your opinion.

6. "Who reads an American book or goes to an American play or looks at an American picture or statue? What does the world yet owe to American physicians or surgeons? What new substance have their chemists discovered?" This was a criticism by an English writer in 1820. For each of *three* of the areas indicated (literature, theater, medicine, science, sculpture, painting), discuss *two* achievements to prove that the United States, by today, has increased or has influenced the world's knowledge.

7. Agree or disagree with each of the following statements and present *two* reasons to support your opinion: *(a)* The granting of federal funds for public education will eventually lead to federal control of public education. *(b)* The local property tax, as a major source of funds for public schools, has many disadvantages. *(c)* American education and cultural life have been greatly enhanced by the contributions of wealthy business and banking leaders who turned to philanthropy.
(d) Humanitarian movements, many begun in the early 19th century, still continue today. *(e)* The construction of the atom bomb during World War II proves that science knows no boundaries of religion or nationality. *(f)* The development of technology has improved the quality of American life. *(g)* Science has given humanity the power either to create a better world or to destroy civilization. *(h)* The works of painters can be used as a source of historical understanding. *(i)* Financial support for the arts by the federal government is both good and bad. *(j)* There is greater creativity in the arts when a nation is troubled than when it is contented.

8. In your school, you are currently receiving an education. *(a)* Describe *two* ways in which this education has been of benefit to you. *(b)* Discuss *two* ways in which this education could be improved. Support your opinion with facts.

UNIT VIII Political Developments Mirror a Changing and Complex America

PART 1. The Republicans Dominate the Post-Civil War Period (1869–1885)

BRIEF SURVEY OF NATIONAL DEVELOPMENTS

1. Economic. *(a)* Business leaders transformed America from an agricultural to an industrial nation. In business, they achieved wealth and power; they disdained the people who devoted themselves to politics. *(b)* Settlers occupied the last frontier, the Great Plains. *(c)* Employed by large, impersonal corporations and paid low wages, workers turned to nationwide labor organizations, first the Knights of Labor and then the American Federation of Labor. *(d)* Faced with unfair railroad practices and falling agricultural prices, farmers formed the Granger movement and joined the Greenback-Labor party.

2. Social. *(a)* Workers flocked to the cities for jobs. Increasingly, Americans experienced the problems of urbanization. *(b)* After being slowed down by the Civil War, the flow of immigrants picked up rapidly.

3. Political

a. Major Parties and Their Supporters. The Republicans were the party of eastern business and banking interests, of western farmers, and of pro-Union patriots. The Democrats found strong support among southern whites and northern urban dwellers. In times of economic distress, the Democrats also made inroads among the western farmers.

b. Issues. Having preserved the Union, the Republicans sought to keep war hatreds alive by "waving the bloody shirt." The Democrats urged the nation to forget the bitterness of the war. In 1877 this issue disappeared. On economic matters, the two parties differed only in that the Republicans favored higher tariffs than did the Democrats. Both parties favored the laissez-faire doctrine that the government should not interfere with business. Neither party came to grips with the newly emerging economic and social issues: abuses by big business and the needs of workers, farmers, and immigrants. In Presidential elections, the parties largely neglected issues and concentrated on personalities and emotions. From 1868 through 1880 the Republicans won each Presidential election, but they failed to maintain control of both houses of Congress for any length of time.

445

GRANT ADMINISTRATION: 1869–1877 (REPUBLICAN)

MAJOR POLITICAL ASPECTS

1. Election of 1868. General Ulysses S. Grant, who accepted the Radical Republican reconstruction policies, received the Republican nomination. Following a bitter "bloody shirt" campaign, Grant defeated the Democratic candidate, former Governor of New York *Horatio Seymour.*

2. Grant and the Presidency. Inexperienced in politics, inept in choosing assistants, insensitive to public needs, and inclined to defer to Congress, Grant has been judged among the least successful of Presidents. Although personally honest, Grant permitted his administration to be marked by corruption.

3. Election of 1872. The Republicans renominated Grant despite internal party opposition. A Liberal Republican group, seeking honesty in government and a more lenient policy toward the South, chose their own Presidential candidate, *Horace Greeley,* the editor of the New York *Tribune.* The Democrats also nominated Greeley, although he long had been their bitter critic. Grant's wartime record, the "bloody shirt," heavy campaign contributions by business executives, and Democratic distaste for Greeley, all combined to give Grant an easy reelection.

4. Corruption: A Period of "National Disgrace." *(a)* Grant's private secretary was connected with a scandal in which Treasury officials accepted bribes not to collect taxes from a group of St. Louis distillers, the *Whisky Ring.* *(b)* Grant's secretary of war took graft from agents he appointed to posts on Indian reservations. *(c)* Grant's Vice President and several members of Congress received bargain-priced stock to prevent investigation of a fraud by a railroad construction company, the *Crédit Mobilier.*

The Grant Era was also marked by corruption on the state level (by southern carpetbag governments) and on the municipal level (notably by the *Tweed Ring* in New York City).

Grant has not been blamed for causing such corruption. It probably resulted from the lowering of ethical standards during the war and from the postwar em-

GRANT ADMINISTRATION: IMPORTANT DOMESTIC LEGISLATION

Laws	Purposes
Force Acts (1870–1871)	Use federal troops to protect southern blacks.
Amnesty Act (1872)	Restore rights of most Confederate leaders.
Coinage Act (1873)	End coinage of silver.
Specie Resumption Act (1875)	Redeem greenbacks in gold.

phasis by business leaders upon material gains. However, Grant has been blamed for assisting guilty officials to escape punishment and for failing to fight for honesty in public life.

SIGNIFICANT FOREIGN AFFAIRS: THE *ALABAMA* CLAIMS

Grant's Secretary of State, Hamilton Fish, a capable official, negotiated an agreement with Britain for an international court of arbitration to settle the *Alabama* claims. The United States received compensation for damages caused by British-built war vessels turned over to the Confederacy.

HAYES ADMINISTRATION: 1877–1881 (REPUBLICAN)

MAJOR POLITICAL ASPECTS

1. Election of 1876

a. Candidates and Issues. The Republicans nominated the honest and conscientious Governor of Ohio, *Rutherford B. Hayes.* The Democrats chose the reform Governor of New York, *Samuel J. Tilden,* who had smashed the corrupt Tweed Ring. Both candidates represented the business community, supported sound money, urged civil service reform, and favored ending Radical reconstruction in the South. In the campaign, the Republicans "waved the bloody shirt," and the Democrats emphasized the corruption of the Grant Era.

b. The Disputed Electoral Vote. Tilden received 184 electoral votes, Hayes received 165, and both candidates claimed the remaining 20 votes: 1 from Oregon and 19 from the three southern states that still had carpetbag governments. Congress established an electoral commission whose eight Republicans outvoted its seven Democrats and assigned all 20 votes to Hayes. Despite Tilden's 200,000 popular majority, Hayes became President. Hayes was denounced by the Democrats as "His Fraudulency" and "Old Man Eight to Seven."

c. End of Reconstruction. To appease the Democrats, Hayes promised to withdraw federal troops from the South. Once in office, he did so. The remaining carpetbag governments collapsed, and reconstruction was over.

2. Beginnings of Civil Service Reform. Hayes antagonized the regular, or "stalwart," Republicans by trying to curtail political patronage: dismissing unneeded and incompetent employees; forbidding officeholders from being assessed political contributions; and naming as secretary of the interior the Liberal Republican advocate of civil service reform, *Carl Schurz.*

3. Hayes' Antilabor Acts. *(a)* Hayes employed federal troops in 1877 against the railroad strikers. *(b)* Hayes vetoed a Chinese exclusion bill, claiming that it violated our treaty with China. He was condemned as favoring cheap immigrant-Chinese labor.

4. Silver Coinage. Passed over Hayes' veto, the *Bland-Allison Act (1878)* provided that the government purchase and coin a limited quantity of silver.

GARFIELD-ARTHUR ADMINISTRATION: 1881–1885 (REPUBLICAN)

MAJOR POLITICAL ASPECTS

1. Election of 1880. The Republican convention, split between rival factions, turned on the 36th ballot to a compromise candidate, Ohio Representative *James A. Garfield.* The Democrats nominated a former Union general, *Winfield S. Hancock.* The campaign was undistinguished as to issues, but the Republicans were well organized and expended heavy funds. Despite a very slim lead in popular votes, Garfield won easily in the electoral college.

2. Assassination of Garfield (1881). In office less than four months, Garfield was fatally shot by a disappointed office seeker. He was succeeded by Vice President *Chester A. Arthur.*

3. Arthur as President (1881–1885): The Office Makes the Person. Though he had been a machine politician, Arthur rose to the responsibilities of office by maintaining an able and honest administration. He began modernization of the American navy by constructing steel warships; fought corruption; and strongly supported civil service reform.

IMPORTANT DOMESTIC LEGISLATION

(1) The *Chinese Exclusion Act* (1882), passed after revision of our treaty obligations with China, suspended the immigration of Chinese laborers. (2) The *Pendleton Act* (1883) set the basis for the federal civil service system.

PART 2. Seesawing Election Results Reflect a Period of Turmoil (1885–1901)

BRIEF SURVEY OF NATIONAL DEVELOPMENTS

1. Continuation of Post-Civil War Economic and Social Trends. *(a)* Business leaders continued to expand their industrial empires. In 1901 steel magnates and bankers formed America's first billion-dollar corporation, the United States Steel Corporation. *(b)* By the turn of the century, settlers completed the closing of the frontier. *(c)* Immigrants entered in increasing numbers. Many were "new immigrants" from southern and eastern Europe. *(d)* Workers, more discontented than ever before, joined unions and engaged in strikes. They lost the Homestead Steel strike (1892) and the Pullman strike (1894). *(e)* Agricultural prices continued to fall, causing farmers to create the Populist party.

2. Political Developments. *(a) Issues.* In 1884 both parties emphasized personalities and appealed to emotions. In subsequent elections, the parties paid increasing attention to issues, such as the tariff and currency. *(b) First Moves Away From Laissez-Faire.* Congress began government regulation of the economy with the Interstate Commerce Act (1887) and the Sherman Antitrust Act (1890). *(c) Populist Party.* This third party, which advocated many reforms, had a brief existence. Created in 1891, it disappeared after losing the 1896 Presidential election.

FIRST CLEVELAND ADMINISTRATION: 1885–1889 (DEMOCRATIC)

MAJOR POLITICAL ASPECTS

1. Election of 1884. The Republican convention nominated former Representative from Maine and Secretary of State, *James G. Blaine.* Republican reformers, dubbed the "Mugwumps," refused to support Blaine, since he had been linked to political dishonesty. The Democrats nominated a reform candidate, *Grover Cleveland.* As mayor of Buffalo and governor of New York, Cleveland had won a reputation for integrity.

The campaign highlighted bitter personal attacks. Just before the election, a Blaine supporter in New York labeled the Democrats as the party of "Rum, Romanism, and Rebellion." This prejudiced attack, most historians believe, rallied Roman Catholic voters to Cleveland. He carried New York State by slightly more than 1000 out of 1.1 million votes and won the election narrowly by 219 electoral votes to 182 for Blaine.

2. Cleveland and Civil Service Reform. Cleveland doubled the number of federal positions filled by merit examinations. However, as the first post-Civil War Democratic President, he also had to satisfy his party's demand for patronage. Cleveland provided jobs for "deserving Democrats," but he insisted that they be honest and capable. Cleveland proclaimed that "public office is a public trust."

3. Restored Prestige of the Presidential Office. Cleveland reasserted executive independence of the legislature. He fought efforts by the Republican-controlled Senate to limit executive appointive powers. He vetoed many special pension bills for Civil War veterans, claiming that the bills were based on dishonest or farfetched claims. Cleveland guarded the public interest by compelling the return of 80 million acres of public land held illegally by lumber and railroad companies.

Cleveland devoted his annual message to Congress in 1887 to demanding lower tariff rates. When the Senate rejected such a measure, Cleveland had a major issue for the 1888 Presidential election.

Cleveland has been criticized for viewing his Presidential role as chiefly negative (the prevention of dishonesty) and, except for the tariff issue, for not providing constructive leadership. Nevertheless, Cleveland is considered to be outstanding among the 19th-century Presidents following Lincoln.

IMPORTANT DOMESTIC LEGISLATION

(1) The *Hatch Act* (1887) provided for agricultural experiment stations. (2) The *Dawes Act* (1887) offered land and citizenship to Indians. (3) The *Interstate Commerce Act* (1887) began federal regulation of railroads.

HARRISON ADMINISTRATION: 1889–1893 (REPUBLICAN)

MAJOR POLITICAL ASPECTS

1. Election of 1888. The Democrats renominated Grover Cleveland and endorsed tariff reform. Cleveland therefore lost support among protectionist Democrats.

The Republicans nominated Indiana's *Benjamin Harrison*. A grandson of former President William Henry Harrison, he had been a Union general and supported high tariffs. His campaign benefited from lavish funds contributed by industrialists favoring protection. Part of these funds was used for bribes and other dishonorable election tactics. Although Cleveland outdrew Harrison by 100,000 popular votes, Harrison narrowly carried many large states and won the election by an electoral vote of 233 to 168.

2. Harrison and the Presidency. Harrison did not assert Presidential authority but deferred to the wishes of the Republican party leaders. In making appointments to major posts, Harrison carried out his campaign managers' election deals. He allowed party leaders to distribute the many post office jobs to loyal party workers. In legislation, Harrison permitted the Republicans in Congress to set their own goals.

3. First Billion-Dollar Congress (1889–1891). With Republicans controlling both houses, Congress *(a)* reduced federal revenues by raising tariff rates to a level that decreased imports, and *(b)* increased federal expenditures by voting "pork barrel" public works and by authorizing veterans' pensions previously vetoed by Cleveland. These measures wiped out the surplus of federal funds. This Congress authorized expenditures of almost $1 billion.

4. Congressional Elections of 1890. The Republicans overwhelmingly lost control of the House of Representatives. Consumers blamed the high Republican tariff for a sharp rise in the cost of living. Farmers blamed the Republicans for failing to raise agricultural prices. Especially in the Midwest, farmers deserted the Republican party to vote for candidates of the Farmers' Alliances, the forerunners of the Populist party.

IMPORTANT DOMESTIC LEGISLATION

(1) The *McKinley Tariff Act* (1890), providing high rates, was passed by logrolling between eastern protectionist Republicans and western farm and silver interests. (2) The *Sherman Silver Purchase Act* (1890) increased government purchases and coinage of silver. (3) The *Sherman Antitrust Act* (1890) declared business efforts in "restraint of trade" illegal.

SIGNIFICANT FOREIGN AFFAIRS: THE PAN-AMERICAN CONFERENCE

Secretary of State James G. Blaine organized and in 1889 presided over a Pan-American Conference, held at Washington, D.C.

SECOND CLEVELAND ADMINISTRATION: 1893–1897 (DEMOCRATIC)

MAJOR POLITICAL AND ECONOMIC ASPECTS

1. Election of 1892. The Republicans renominated Harrison, although he lacked public appeal. The Democrats selected Cleveland. Both major party platforms straddled the currency issue. The Populists presented their first Presidential candidate, General *James B. Weaver*. The Populists' *Omaha Platform* demanded unlimited coinage of silver and other reforms.

In polling over one million popular votes and 22 electoral votes, the Populists cut considerably into Republican strength in the Midwest. Thus aided, Cleveland defeated Harrison by an electoral vote of 277 to 145. He became the only President to serve two nonconsecutive terms.

2. Cleveland Faces Economic Problems. A conservative, sound-money, business-oriented Easterner, Cleveland had little contact with the discontented groups: western silverites, midwestern farmers, and urban workers. Cleveland possessed only a limited knowledge of complex economic problems.

a. Panic of 1893. Cleveland took the oath of office as the nation experienced the *Panic of 1893,* which began a severe depression. Railroads, banks, and industrial enterprises went into bankruptcy. Farmers suffered further declines in agricultural prices. Workers suffered sizable wage cuts, and some 20 percent were unemployed.

b. Cleveland Antagonizes Silverites and Farmers. Cleveland blamed this depression on a single cause: the government's purchase of silver. Therefore, he pressured Congress to repeal the Sherman Silver Purchase Act and authorized the Treasury to obtain gold by selling bonds. Cleveland's actions preserved the gold standard but did not noticeably improve economic conditions.

c. Cleveland Antagonizes Workers. Cleveland ignored the demands of Populist *Jacob Coxey* that the government provide the unemployed with work on a national road-building program. When *Coxey's Army* of 500 demonstrators arrived in Washington, Coxey was arrested for walking on the Capitol grass, and his "army" melted away. Cleveland further antagonized labor by using troops and an injunction in the Pullman strike (1894).

3. Congressional Elections of 1894. The Democrats suffered heavy losses, as the Republicans regained control of the House of Representatives and as the Populists increased their vote substantially.

IMPORTANT DOMESTIC LEGISLATION

(1) The repeal of the *Sherman Silver Purchase Act* (1893) ended the government's buying of silver for coinage. (2) The *Wilson-Gorman Tariff Act* (1894) lowered tariff rates so little that Cleveland, disgusted, permitted it to become a law without his signature. It also provided for a small income tax, which the Supreme Court in 1895 declared unconstitutional.

SIGNIFICANT FOREIGN AFFAIRS: THE OLNEY INTERPRETATION

In 1895 Cleveland's Secretary of State, Richard Olney, intervened in a boundary dispute between British Guiana and Venezuela. The dispute led to an expansion of the Monroe Doctrine by the *Olney Interpretation*.

McKINLEY ADMINISTRATION: 1897–1901 (REPUBLICAN)

MAJOR POLITICAL AND ECONOMIC ASPECTS

1. Election of 1896. Dominated by *Marcus A. Hanna,* a wealthy business executive turned politician, the Republican convention nominated the former Governor of Ohio, *William McKinley.* He supported the gold standard and opposed free silver. Meanwhile, silver and farm leaders had wrested control of the Democratic party from Cleveland and the conservative business interests. The Democratic convention chose former Representative *William Jennings Bryan.* The Populists, in a supreme effort to achieve free silver, also nominated Bryan. With huge campaign funds and with Hanna's skillful management, McKinley won the election by an electoral vote of 271 to 176.

2. Return of Economic Prosperity. *(a)* Farmers experienced rising agricultural prices. Foreign markets grew, as crop failures struck Europe. Currency expanded, as the supply of gold increased with new discoveries in Alaska, Australia, and South Africa, and with improved gold-mining methods. *(b)* Business leaders, recovering from the depression, increased production and made higher profits. *(c)* More workers found jobs and earned higher wages.

3. Disappearance of the Populist Party. Following the 1896 election and the revival of farm prosperity, the Populist party fell apart. Some Populist leaders and policies reappeared later in the progressive movement.

4. Election of 1900. The Republicans renominated William McKinley, claimed credit for economic prosperity, and pledged to maintain the "full dinner pail." The Democrats renominated William Jennings Bryan, who renewed his call for cheap money and condemned as imperialism the territorial acquisitions following the Spanish-American War. By an even greater margin than previously, McKinley defeated Bryan.

IMPORTANT DOMESTIC LEGISLATION

(1) The *Dingley Tariff Act* (1897) raised tariff rates to new highs. (2) The *Gold Standard Act* (1900) made all paper money redeemable in gold.

SIGNIFICANT FOREIGN AFFAIRS

1. Turn to Imperialism. Responding to public pressure over events in Cuba, McKinley led the United States into war with Spain (1898). The Spanish-American War marked the emergence of the victorious United States as a world power with colonial possessions in the Caribbean and the Pacific. McKinley also secured a joint resolution in Congress for the annexation of Hawaii (1898).

2. Concern Over Trade With China. Secretary of State *John Hay,* announced the *Open Door Policy* (1900) to assure all nations equal trading rights in China. Shortly afterward, Hay persuaded the nations that suppressed the Boxer Rebellion in China not to annex Chinese territory.

——————— MULTIPLE-CHOICE QUESTIONS ———————

1. "In an age characterized by few diplomats and by Presidents and lawmakers now half-forgotten, history was made by economic giants." The author of this quotation is probably (a) opposed to the Republican party (b) questioning a democratic form of government (c) supporting socialism (d) attempting to interpret an era.
2. During the period 1865 to 1900, big business (a) was strictly regulated by federal laws (b) lost many important strikes (c) experienced substantial growth (d) developed friendly relations with labor unions.
3. The industrial growth of the United States between 1865 and 1890 was aided by the (a) government policy of protective tariffs (b) financial policies of the Federal Reserve Banks (c) dominance of the Populist party in national politics (d) passage of laws to restrict immigration from Europe.

4. During the period 1865 to 1900, the federal government did *not* take any action to (a) curb big business (b) relieve human distress during a depression (c) curb the activities of labor unions (d) regulate railroads.

5. Which was a significant characteristic of politics during the quarter century following the Civil War? (a) beginning of the abolition of the spoils system (b) greater concern by Presidents for foreign affairs than for domestic affairs (c) disappearance of third-party movements (d) domination of national politics by the Democratic party.

6. The policies of the Republican party in the period following the Civil War were most favorable to the interests of (a) southern farmers (b) northern industrialists (c) wage earners (d) debtors.

7. Between the Civil War and the Spanish-American War, the most controversial domestic issue in the United States was (a) internal improvements (b) labor unions (c) cheap money (d) treatment of the Indians.

8. If you had been a member of the Republican party in the 1880s and had advocated reform, you would have been called a (a) Mugwump (b) muckraker (c) carpetbagger (d) scalawag.

9. Which was the major issue in the Presidential campaign of 1896? (a) government ownership of railroads (b) monetary policy (c) imperialism in the Far East (d) removal of troops from the South.

10. "The change came in the nineties, and it was more than mere coincidence that it accompanied the coming of age of our industrial system." This statement refers to the period in which the United States (a) began a policy of westward expansion (b) adopted a policy of isolation (c) became involved in imperialism (d) first enforced the Monroe Doctrine.

11. Which factor best explains the disappearance of the Populist party? (a) adoption of unlimited silver coinage (b) ratification of the income tax amendment (c) return of farm prosperity (d) government ownership of railroads.

12. Which of the following terms has the *least* relationship to Presidential campaigns from 1868 through 1900? (a) "the bloody shirt" (b) "Alabama Claims" (c) "Old Man Eight to Seven" (d) "Rum, Romanism, and Rebellion."

———— IDENTIFICATION QUESTIONS: WHO AM I? ————

Chester A. Arthur	James A. Garfield	Rutherford B. Hayes
James G. Blaine	Ulysses S. Grant	William McKinley
William Jennings Bryan	Horace Greeley	Horatio Seymour
Grover Cleveland	Benjamin Harrison	Samuel J. Tilden

1. I was victorious in a disputed Presidential election. I alienated many members of my party by withdrawing the last remaining federal troops from the South.

2. During my administration, the United States won a short war and acquired an overseas empire. The slogan "the full dinner pail" was used in one of my campaigns.

3. I was the first Democrat elected to the Presidency after the Civil War. I supported the principle that "public office is a public trust."

4. I was the editor of the New York *Tribune*. I received both the Liberal Republican and Democratic nominations for the Presidency in 1872, but I lost the election to the regular Republican candidate.

5. President for less than four months, I was assassinated by a disappointed office seeker. My death hastened passage of a civil service reform law.

6. I won an electoral college majority although my opponent received more popular votes than I did. The first Congress of my administration voted expenditures of close to $1 billion.
7. A Democrat and reform Governor of New York, I lost the disputed Presidential election of 1876.
8. Despite my oratorical ability and my claim to speak for the farmers and workers, I lost two successive Presidential elections to the same Republican candidate.

—————————————— **ESSAY QUESTIONS** ——————————————

1. Allan Nevins subtitled his biography of Grover Cleveland "A Study in Courage." *(a)* Discuss *three* of Cleveland's actions as President to prove he was a man of courage. *(b)* For each of the actions discussed above, give *one* argument supporting *or one* argument opposing Cleveland.
2. In the era from the end of the Civil War to 1901, three major economic developments were (1) the growth of big business, (2) discontent among workers, and (3) discontent among farmers. *(a)* Describe *one* specific event illustrating each development. *(b)* Show how a federal action or law attempted to deal with a problem created by each development.
3. Two issues that faced the United States after the Civil War were civil service reform and the tariff. *(a)* Compare the attitude of Hayes with the attitude of Arthur toward civil service reform. *(b)* Compare the attitude of Cleveland with the attitude of McKinley toward the tariff.
4. The following statements all refer to the era from the end of the Civil War to 1901. Agree or disagree with each statement, giving *two* reasons to support your point of view: *(a)* Presidential elections emphasized personalities rather than issues. *(b)* President Grant must be blamed for the corruption that marked his administration. *(c)* The McKinley administration reflected the interests of the business community. *(d)* The United States had little interest in foreign affairs. *(e)* The power and prestige of the Presidency were not high.

PART 3. The Progressive Era Marks an Upsurge of Reform (1901–1921)

THE PROGRESSIVE MOVEMENT

PROGRESSIVISM: MEANING AND OBJECTIVES

Influencing politics in the early 20th century, progressivism was a movement to improve American life by expanding democracy and achieving economic and social justice. Progressives were optimistic and forward-looking. They generally did not seek to restore the rural America of the past, but rather they accepted urbanization and industrialization. They hailed the benefits of the machine age but sought to correct its evils.

1. Political Reforms. Shocked by the sorry state of everyday politics, progressives planned *(a)* to wipe out such practices as graft, machine politics, and business domination of government, and *(b)* to set up political procedures to assure the people closer control over the government. The remedy for the evils of democracy, progressives believed, is more democracy.

2. Social and Economic Reforms. Appalled by the poverty afflicting many Americans, progressives planned *(a)* to eliminate practices harming farmers, workers, tenement dwellers, and consumers, and *(b)* to expand government regulation over our economy so as to further the public interest.

SOURCES OF PROGRESSIVE STRENGTH

1. Farmers. Although they had abandoned the Populist party, farmers retained the Populist heritage. They wanted tighter regulation of railroads, lower tariffs, and easier credit.

2. Urban Middle Classes. Many professional people, storekeepers, and small business owners were alarmed by the power of giant trusts and political machines. They favored lower tariffs, more government regulation of industry, and the extension of democracy.

3. Workers. Laborers looked to the government for laws regulating work by women and children, protecting workers from dangerous machinery, and easing the financial hardships caused by industrial accidents.

4. Writers. Critics analyzed American society and wrote of the need for reform. These writers included Frank Norris, Gustavus Myers, Ida Tarbell, Ray Stannard Baker, Upton Sinclair, and Lincoln Steffens; they are generally known as *muckrakers.*

5. Political Leaders. Progressives were found not only in the short-lived Progressive party of 1912, but more significantly in both major parties. Progressive leaders achieved office and furthered reform at all levels of government.

MAJOR PROGRESSIVE LEADERS

Reformer	Party	Major Office
Tom Johnson	Democrat	Mayor of Cleveland
Samuel "Golden Rule" Jones	Republican; Independent	Mayor of Toledo
Robert La Follette	Republican	Governor of Wisconsin
Charles Evans Hughes	Republican	Governor of New York
Hiram Johnson	Republican	Governor of California
Theodore Roosevelt	Republican	President of the United States
Woodrow Wilson	Democrat	President of the United States

ACCOMPLISHMENTS OF THE PROGRESSIVE MOVEMENT

1. Political Reform

a. City and State Action. (1) *Direct primaries* enabled voters rather than party bosses to nominate candidates. (2) *Corrupt practices laws* regulated political contributions and campaign spending. (3) The *Australian ballot* allowed citizens to vote in secrecy. (4) The *initiative* and *referendum* provided voters with a greater voice in making laws. (5) The *recall* enabled voters to oust unsatisfactory elected public officials. (6) The *commission* and *city manager* forms of municipal government reduced the power of political machines. (7) Municipal and state *civil service examinations* reduced the number of positions available to political machines for patronage. (8) *Woman suffrage* in the states extended democracy.

b. Federal Action. (1) *Direct election of Senators* was achieved by the Seventeenth Amendment (1913). (2) *Nationwide woman suffrage* was guaranteed by the Nineteenth Amendment (1920).

2. Social and Economic Reform

a. City and State Action. (1) *State regulation of intrastate railroads and public utilities* improved service and reduced rates. (2) *Consumer protection laws* assured honest weights and unadulterated foods. (3) *Fair tax laws*, by taxing incomes, relieved the burden on owners of real estate. (4) *Child labor laws* set a minimum age for employment and prohibited children from working in dangerous occupations. (5) *Labor laws affecting women* set minimum wages and maximum hours for female workers. (6) *Welfare benefits* were enacted for dependent children, widows, and the aged. (7) *Factory inspection laws* improved sanitation, lighting, and safety. (8) *Workers' compensation laws* protected workers and their families in case of on-the-job accidents.

b. Federal Action. (1) Expanded federal *regulation of railroads, industrial combinations, and banks* protected the public interest. (2) *Conservation measures* preserved America's natural resources. (3) *Consumer protection laws* required pure foods and drugs. (4) An *income tax* was authorized by the Sixteenth Amendment (1913). (5) *Legitimate union activities* were exempted from antitrust prosecution, and the use of injunctions in labor disputes was limited. (6) Federal funds were used for long-term, low-interest *loans to help farmers.*

WEAKNESSES OF THE PROGRESSIVE MOVEMENT

1. Uneven Pattern of Reform. In some states, the progressives achieved very little; in other states, with vigorous leaders, the progressives achieved much. The leading progressive states included New York, New Jersey, California, Oregon, Michigan, Ohio, and Wisconsin.

2. Court Roadblocks. The courts at first held illegal considerable progressive legislation affecting economic matters such as minimum wages for women. The states claimed that such laws were a valid exercise of the states' "police powers." The courts, however, frequently ruled that such laws violated the "due process" clause of the Fourteenth Amendment.

3. Survival of Political Machines. The progressives failed to end the power of political machines. Party bosses learned to evade the reform laws. The progressives were unable permanently to overcome public apathy, which continued to be the greatest enemy of successful democratic government.

DISAPPEARANCE OF THE PROGRESSIVE MOVEMENT

By the early 1920s, progressivism had died out because many progressive reforms had become law and the public had lost its enthusiasm for further reforms. Also, the American people had turned their attention from domestic matters to foreign affairs with the coming of World War I. After the war, Americans were tired of public affairs and looked on reform with apathy.

HERITAGE OF THE PROGRESSIVE MOVEMENT

(1) The progressives promoted the belief that government has the responsibility to act for the people's welfare. The Progressive Era marked the transition from laissez-faire to government regulation of the economy. (2) The progressives demonstrated the ability of our democratic institutions to meet problems arising out of urbanization and industrialization. Further, they showed the need for tackling such problems on the city and state levels as well as on the federal level. (3) The progressives believed that a President should provide strong and effective national leadership. This concept was illustrated, for the first time since the days of Abraham Lincoln, by both progressive Presidents: Theodore Roosevelt and Woodrow Wilson.

THEODORE ROOSEVELT ADMINISTRATION: 1901–1909 (REPUBLICAN)—THE "SQUARE DEAL"

MAJOR POLITICAL AND ECONOMIC ASPECTS

1. Roosevelt Becomes President. President McKinley was assassinated six months after his second inauguration. He was succeeded in office by his Vice President, Theodore Roosevelt.

2. Roosevelt's Background and Personality. A member of a prominent family and a graduate of Harvard, Roosevelt early decided upon a career in politics. He acquired considerable experience, serving as a New York State Assembly member, a federal civil service commissioner, a New York City police commissioner, and assistant secretary of the Navy. During the Spanish-American War, Roosevelt organized and led a volunteer cavalry regiment, the *Rough Riders*. Elected governor of New York in 1898, Roosevelt achieved civil service and tax reforms, and demonstrated his independence from state Republican leaders, who became eager to be rid of him. He was "kicked upstairs" in 1900, receiving the nomination for the Vice Presidency, a position without power or influence. With McKinley's assassination, Roosevelt at the age of 42 became our youngest President ever.

Roosevelt was a man of tremendous energy and varied activities: rancher and sportsman, historian of the West, and politician. A dramatic and popular figure, Roosevelt was affectionately acclaimed by millions as "Teddy."

3. Roosevelt's Views

a. **Strong Leadership.** Roosevelt considered himself morally bound as President to further the interests of the people. During his tenure he focused public attention upon national problems and won public support for progressive solutions. Roosevelt effectively utilized the power and prestige inherent in the office of President and referred to the White House as a "bully pulpit." He proposed the *stewardship theory*—that the President was a "steward of the people" on whose behalf the President must provide strong leadership.

b. **"Square Deal."** Roosevelt believed that the government should (1) assure honesty and fairness in both government and business, and (2) give greater economic opportunity to the individual. He proclaimed that the theme of his administration was to afford all groups—business leaders, laborers, farmers, and consumers—a *square deal.*

4. Election of 1904.
Roosevelt's Square Deal and his strong leadership evoked great public enthusiasm. In the election of 1904, he overwhelmingly defeated the colorless and little-known Democratic candidate, Judge Alton B. Parker. Now President by election, Roosevelt proceeded even more vigorously, and although Congress was controlled by conservative Republicans, he secured significant progressive legislation.

5. Roosevelt's Relationship to Progressivism.
Roosevelt did not create the progressive movement, but he supported many progressive reforms as essential to save our democratic, capitalist system from both the extreme left and the extreme right. He opposed Socialists and other radicals who urged an end to private enterprise. At the same time, Roosevelt condemned those persons of wealth who resisted change and who abused their power. He accused them of "arrogant stupidity" and called them "malefactors of great wealth." Roosevelt represented the middle-class progressives, whose method was moderate reform.

6. Roosevelt Provides Vigorous Government

a. **Curbing "Bad" Trusts.** Roosevelt insisted that big business adjust to the public welfare. Roosevelt approved "good" trusts but condemned "bad" trusts. In 1902 Roosevelt instituted an antitrust suit against a railroad holding company, the *Northern Securities Company.* Roosevelt won dissolution of this monopoly by a 5-to-4 decision of the Supreme Court. Roosevelt hailed the decision as indicating the power of the federal government to regulate business

THEODORE ROOSEVELT ADMINISTRATION: IMPORTANT DOMESTIC LEGISLATION

LAWS	PURPOSES
Pure Food and Drug Act (1906)	Protect the consumer.
Meat Inspection Act (1906)	Protect the consumer.
Hepburn Act (1906)	Expand the powers of the Interstate Commerce Commission.

combinations. In all, Roosevelt began over 40 antitrust suits. He thus gained his reputation as a "trust buster."

b. Settling the Anthracite Coal Strike (1902). The United Mine Workers went out on strike in 1902 for union recognition, shorter hours, and higher wages. With coal scarce and winter approaching, Roosevelt summoned mine-owners and union leaders to the White House. Union chief John Mitchell offered to submit the issues to arbitration, but the mine-owners refused. When Roosevelt threatened to seize the mines, the owners agreed to accept a Presidential arbitration commission. Its decision, reflecting moderate progressivism, awarded the workers a wage increase and shorter hours but denied them union recognition.

In contrast with Cleveland during the Pullman strike, Roosevelt emerged as a friend of labor. Also, by settling the strike, Roosevelt established a precedent for expanded Presidential powers.

c. Conserving Natural Resources. Roosevelt had lived in the West and personally witnessed the depletion of natural resources. As President, Roosevelt (1) increased substantially the national reserves of forests, coal lands, and waterpower sites, (2) secured passage of the *Newlands Act* (1902) to finance irrigation projects, (3) encouraged the conservation efforts of the *Forest Service,* directed by *Gifford Pinchot,* and (4) in 1908 summoned a *Governors' Conference* at the White House to spur conservation. By his leadership, Roosevelt propelled conservation into national significance.

d. Protecting the Consumer and the Railroad User. To achieve these ends, Roosevelt urged and secured legislation from Congress.

SIGNIFICANT FOREIGN AFFAIRS

Roosevelt envisioned the United States as a major power playing a leading role in an interdependent world. Advocating that the United States "speak softly and carry a big stick," Roosevelt modernized the army, built a strong navy, and pursued an active foreign policy.

1. Revolt in Panama (1903). Roosevelt aided the successful revolt of the province of Panama against Colombia. By a treaty, the United States then gained control over the Panama Canal Zone.

2. Roosevelt Corollary to the Monroe Doctrine (1904). This statement declared the United States the international policeman of the Western Hemisphere. It arose out of the Venezuela debt dispute and the Dominican Republic debt default.

3. Settlement of the Russo-Japanese War (1905). Roosevelt arranged for Russia and Japan to end their war by a peace conference at *Portsmouth,* New Hampshire. For this effort, Roosevelt received the 1906 Nobel Peace Prize.

4. Gentlemen's Agreement (1907). Roosevelt halted immigration of laborers from Japan by negotiating the *Gentlemen's Agreement* with that nation.

TAFT ADMINISTRATION: 1909–1913 (REPUBLICAN)

MAJOR POLITICAL ASPECTS

1. Election of 1908. The Republican convention, at the recommendation of Roosevelt, nominated his secretary of war and then good friend, *William Howard Taft.* Promising to continue Roosevelt's policies and benefiting from Roosevelt's popularity, Taft defeated William Jennings Bryan, whom the Democrats selected as their candidate for the third and last time.

2. Taft: Background and Personality. Taft had served as federal judge, governor of the Philippines, and secretary of war—all appointive positions that afforded him little experience in dealing with legislators and voters. Jovial and easygoing, Taft lacked the personality to dramatize issues, to arouse public support, and to battle with Congress for his program. Furthermore, he held a limited view of the President's role and was unwilling to utilize fully his powers as chief executive. Taft recognized the need for further progressive measures but was basically conservative.

Taft displayed personal integrity and a keen legal mind. Although these qualities later enabled Taft to serve effectively as Chief Justice of the Supreme Court (1921–1930), they did not suffice to let him master the problems facing him as President.

3. Taft Antagonizes the Progressives

a. Tariff Issue. Taft called Congress into special session to lower tariff rates. However, by fighting only halfheartedly to keep Senate protectionists from enacting high rates, Taft dismayed the progressives. When Taft signed the resulting Payne-Aldrich Tariff and acclaimed it the best ever, he further alienated the progressive Republicans, now known as "insurgents."

b. Conservation Issue. Taft supported the secretary of the interior, Richard Ballinger, in a conservation controversy with Roosevelt's friend, Gifford Pinchot, head of the Forest Service. Although Taft favored conservation, his role in this controversy widened the breach between Taft and the progressives, who favored Pinchot.

c. Issue of Reform in the House of Representatives. Taft failed to support the Republican progressives in their effort in 1910 to limit the power of the Speaker of the House of Representatives, the conservative *Joseph G. ("Uncle*

Joe") *Cannon.* Nevertheless, the Republican insurgents joined with the Democrats and ended Cannon's dictatorial rule. They stripped the Speaker of his power to appoint members of House committees and excluded him from membership on the powerful Rules Committee.

By Taft's handling of these issues, he heightened the division in the Republican party between the "Old Guard" conservatives and the insurgents.

4. Split Between Taft and Roosevelt. While Taft moved closer to the Old Guard, Roosevelt voiced support for the insurgents. Differences in personality accentuated the political issues between the two men, and they became bitter enemies. In 1912 Roosevelt challenged Taft for the Republican Presidential nomination, announcing: "My hat is in the ring."

5. Accomplishments of the Taft Administration. *(a)* Although in office only half as long as "trust buster" Roosevelt, Taft instituted twice as many antitrust suits. *(b)* Taft increased the number of federal employees under civil service. *(c)* Congress proposed the Sixteenth Amendment for a national income tax, and the Seventeenth Amendment for the direct election of Senators. (In 1913 both amendments became part of the Constitution.) *(d)* Congress increased the powers of the Interstate Commerce Commission.

IMPORTANT DOMESTIC LEGISLATION

(1) The *Payne-Aldrich Tariff Act* (1909) maintained high import duties. (2) The *Mann-Elkins Act* (1910) authorized the Interstate Commerce Commission to regulate telephone and telegraph companies. (3) The *Physical Valuation Act* (1913) empowered the Interstate Commerce Commission to determine the value of each railroad's property as a basis for setting fair rates.

SIGNIFICANT FOREIGN AFFAIRS

Taft encouraged Americans to look for investment and trade opportunities in Latin America, especially in Honduras, Haiti, and Nicaragua. In 1911 Taft sent marines to Nicaragua to protect American investments. By giving strong diplomatic and military support to American business interests abroad, the Taft administration became identified with the practice of *dollar diplomacy.*

WILSON ADMINISTRATION: 1913–1921 (DEMOCRATIC)— THE "NEW FREEDOM"

MAJOR POLITICAL ASPECTS

1. Election of 1912. President Taft dominated the Republican convention and won renomination on the first ballot. Roosevelt's supporters claimed fraud, hastily created the *Progressive party,* and with great fervor nominated Theodore Roosevelt. Because Roosevelt often said that he was as "strong as a bull moose," the new party became known as the *Bull Moose party*. After a bitter struggle between conservatives and progressives, the Democratic convention nominated the choice of the progressives, *Woodrow Wilson*.

In many ways, the programs of Wilson and Roosevelt were similar: greater political democracy and more social and economic reforms. Roosevelt and Wilson differed, however, in that Roosevelt supported high tariffs, considered business consolidation inevitable, and urged that giant corporations be permitted to exist, but under government regulation. Wilson favored lower tariffs, opposed business consolidation, and urged the government to break up giant corporations.

Wilson won the election. The combined popular votes for Roosevelt and Taft showed that the Republican split made Wilson's election possible. However, the combined popular votes for Wilson and Roosevelt indicated a victory for progressivism.

2. Wilson: Background and Personality. The son of a southern minister, Woodrow Wilson received a fine education and excelled in politics and public speaking. When he became a professor of history, he compared the American and British political systems in his famed study *Congressional Government*. In 1902 he was appointed president of Princeton University. By his efforts to improve education and to end snobbish eating clubs at Princeton, Wilson attracted public attention. Elected Governor of New Jersey in 1910, he pushed a progressive program through the legislature.

A "scholar in politics," Wilson personified intellect, reason, and logic. He was a man of high moral principles and an idealist who found it difficult to compromise on basic issues. Although he lacked warmth in his personal relationships, Wilson could sway crowds by his eloquent prose and effective oratory.

3. Wilson's Views

a. Strong Leadership. Believing that the President of the United States should give the country strong leadership, Wilson utilized his Presidential powers to the fullest. In 1913 he called Congress into special session and appeared personally before Congress—a practice unused since Jefferson's day—to request legislation. He employed the power of patronage to swing necessary Senate votes, and he appealed to the people and won public support to influence wavering Congress members. For his strong leadership in securing legislation, Wilson is rated a highly successful President.

b. "New Freedom": A Progressive Program. Wilson distrusted the extremes of great wealth and radical agitation. For his goals, he used the term the "New Freedom" to preserve and strengthen our democratic, capitalistic society by progressive reforms: lower tariffs, an improved banking system, stronger regulation of business, and protection for unions and workers.

4. Election of 1916. Wilson narrowly defeated the Republican candidate, Charles Evans Hughes. Both candidates represented the progressive viewpoint, but Wilson won reelection with the slogan "He kept us out of the war."

WILSON ADMINISTRATION:
IMPORTANT DOMESTIC LEGISLATION

Laws	Purposes
Underwood Tariff Act (1913)	Reduce tariff rates; institute an income tax.
Federal Reserve Act (1913)	Create an effective national banking system.
Clayton Act (1914)	Strengthen antitrust regulations; exempt unions from antitrust suits; limit injunctions in labor disputes.
Federal Trade Commission Act (1914)	Prevent unfair business practices.
La Follette Seamen's Act (1915)	Improve working conditions on American merchant vessels.
Adamson Act (1916)	Establish an eight-hour day for railroad workers.
Federal Farm Loan Act (1916)	Provide low-interest loans for farmers.

Nevertheless, in 1917 the United States entered World War I. As Americans turned their energies from reforms to war, the Progressive Era came to an end.

SIGNIFICANT FOREIGN AFFAIRS

1. Difficulties With Mexico. When Wilson took office in 1913, Mexico was in the midst of revolution. Wilson refused to recognize the military regime of General Huerta and instead adopted a policy of *watchful waiting*. After a dispute with Huerta involving American sailors, Wilson ordered the navy to occupy the port of Vera Cruz. Soon afterwards, the reformer Carranza became President of Mexico.

In 1916 Wilson ordered American troops under General John J. Pershing to cross into Mexico to hunt Pancho Villa, who had conducted guerrilla raids into the United States. In 1917 Wilson withdrew our troops from Mexico and recognized the Carranza regime as the *de jure* (rightful) government.

2. Interest in the Caribbean. Wilson claimed to oppose "dollar diplomacy," but he continued Taft's policies in Nicaragua and also sent troops to Haiti and the Dominican Republic. In 1917, to provide protection for the Panama Canal, the United States paid Denmark $25 million for the Virgin Islands.

3. World War I. In 1914, when World War I began, Wilson urged Americans to remain neutral. He protested violations of our "freedom of the seas" both by British warships and by German submarines. In 1917, as a result of Germany's unrestricted submarine warfare, Wilson asked Congress for a declaration of war against Germany. Wilson inspired Americans to a victorious war effort.

In 1918 Wilson proposed his idealistic *Fourteen Points* for a postwar settlement. Wilson helped draw up the *Treaty of Versailles*, the peace treaty with Germany, and incorporated in it his plan for a *League of Nations*. In 1919, to arouse public support for the treaty, Wilson undertook a speaking tour, which ended when he suffered a paralytic stroke. Thereafter, the Senate rejected the treaty.

WILSON ADMINISTRATION AFTER WORLD WAR I (1918–1921)

1. End of the Progressive Movement. The progressive spirit disappeared as *(a)* popular attention centered upon the battle over the Treaty of Versailles, and *(b)* Wilson fell seriously ill and could not provide effective leadership, although he remained President till March 1921. Among the last measures reflecting progressive influence were the Eighteenth Amendment (prohibition) and the Nineteenth Amendment (woman suffrage).

2. Transition to a Peacetime Economy and Labor Strife. As the government quickly ended all wartime economic controls, the cost of living rose sharply, and the United States experienced postwar inflation.

Labor unions, seeking to maintain their members' living standards, called a series of strikes. The steelworkers and the Boston police lost their strikes. The coal miners won a partial victory. Equating strikes with radicalism, public opinion turned against labor unions.

3. Public Hysteria: The "Red Scare." Alarmed by the Communist seizure of Russia in 1917, the American people feared "Red" threats within the United States. Attorney General *A. Mitchell Palmer* conducted raids seeking subversive aliens and Communists. He arrested and held innocent persons, often in violation of their Constitutional rights. By the end of 1920, however, public hysteria subsided.

———————————— **MULTIPLE-CHOICE QUESTIONS** ————————————

1. The progressive movement of the early 20th century sought to (a) free the individual from dependence on the government (b) solve the political and social problems created by industrialism (c) preserve an agrarian America (d) provide government ownership of the major industries.
2. A major objective of the progressive movement was to (a) end overseas expansion (b) increase the supply of money (c) assure more democracy in government (d) end government ownership and operation of the post office.
3. The progressive movement urged (a) the use of the initiative and referendum (b) consolidation in industry (c) more financial aid to the railroads (d) close ties between government and business.
4. Which correctly pairs a progressive governor and his state? (a) Charles Evans Hughes—California (b) Robert La Follette—Wisconsin (c) William Jennings Bryan—Nebraska (d) Hiram Johnson—Texas.
5. The progressive movement (a) urged a policy of laissez-faire (b) had the support of a group of influential writers (c) had no success at the city government level (d) eliminated political machines as an influence in American government.

6. Which statement best represents Theodore Roosevelt's attitude toward trusts?
   (a) "Good" trusts should be allowed to exist but under government supervision.
   (b) There should be no interference with the organization of trusts. (c) The federal government should encourage the formation of trusts. (d) All trusts should be abolished.

7. Which statement best expresses an opinion of Theodore Roosevelt?
   (a) Combinations in industry are a result of economic law and must be protected.
   (b) Latin American nations can conduct their own affairs without interference from the United States. (c) Natural resources must be used for the benefit of all the people. (d) The states and not the federal government must protect public welfare.

8. In which area did Theodore Roosevelt exert *least* influence? (a) conservation (b) tariff reform (c) railroad regulation (d) antitrust actions.

9. In the Spanish-American War, Theodore Roosevelt (a) commanded the American army (b) led a volunteer regiment, the Rough Riders (c) served as secretary of the Navy (d) negotiated the treaty of peace with Spain.

10. Which term is *not* associated with Theodore Roosevelt? (a) square deal (b) big stick (c) Red scare (d) trust buster.

11. In 1908 Taft secured the Republican Presidential nomination (a) with Theodore Roosevelt's aid (b) by battling against Theodore Roosevelt (c) as a dark horse following a convention deadlock (d) as the candidate of the "Old Guard."

12. Which is the most valid statement concerning the terms "progressive" and "conservative" as used in politics? (a) They refer to things that do not really exist. (b) Their meanings are dependent on the time period. (c) The ideas indicated by the terms are usually not understood. (d) They can apply only to people, not to ideas.

13. The Progressives were most antagonized by President Taft when he (a) signed the Payne-Aldrich Tariff Act (b) instituted antitrust suits (c) urged adoption of the Sixteenth Amendment (d) placed additional federal employees under civil service.

14. President Taft's foreign policy was most closely associated with the term (a) watchful waiting (b) strenuous life (c) dollar diplomacy (d) hands off Cuba.

15. Which was a third party that played a prominent part in the election of 1912? (a) Greenback-Labor (b) Populist (c) Democratic (d) Progressive.

16. Woodrow Wilson entered politics following a successful career as (a) historian and educator (b) minister and religious reformer (c) lawyer for large corporations (d) banker engaged in foreign investments.

17. As part of his New Freedom, Wilson advocated (a) repeal of restrictions on immigration (b) broader responsibility of government in social and economic areas (c) passage of antidiscrimination laws (d) open diplomacy instead of secret treaties.

18. President Wilson did *not* request Congress to enact a law to (a) lower tariff rates (b) establish the Federal Reserve System (c) inaugurate Social Security (d) create the Federal Trade Commission.

19. Which Constitutional amendment *least* reflected an objective of the progressive movement? (a) the income tax (b) direct election of Senators (c) two-term limitation upon any one person as President (d) nationwide woman suffrage.

20. Which of the following had most to do with the decline of the progressive movement? (a) Wilson's belief in weak Presidential leadership (b) American participation in World War I (c) disappearance of the Progressive party (d) the Senate's rejection of the Treaty of Versailles.

——————————————— **ESSAY QUESTIONS** ———————————————

1. In the early 20th century the United States experienced an era of reform resulting from the progressive movement. *(a)* Show *one* way in which the progressive movement was similar to *and one* way in which it was different from the earlier Populist movement. *(b)* Describe *two* political and *two* social or economic reforms achieved by the progressive movement. *(c)* Explain *two* weaknesses of the progressive movement. *(d)* Describe *one* way in which the progressive movement has had an influence upon American life today.

2. State whether you agree or disagree with each of the following statements and give *two* facts to support your point of view: *(a)* Theodore Roosevelt deserved the title of "trust buster." *(b)* Theodore Roosevelt awakened the United States to the need for conservation. *(c)* Theodore Roosevelt was a pioneer in the efforts of the United States to promote world peace. *(d)* Theodore Roosevelt followed the same philosophy in regard to the power of the President as did James Buchanan.

3. In connection with the life of Woodrow Wilson, discuss *each* of the following: *(a) two* outstanding aspects of his career before 1912, *(b) one* reason why he was able to secure the Democratic Presidential nomination in 1912, *(c) one* reason why he won the election of 1912, *(d) two* important domestic reforms achieved during his administration, *(e) one* reason why his administration marked the decline of the progressive movement.

4. For *each* of the following comparisons, state which President, you think, handled the matter better and defend your answer: *(a)* Theodore Roosevelt and Cleveland in regard to a labor dispute, *(b)* Taft and Cleveland in regard to the tariff issue, *(c)* Theodore Roosevelt and Taft in regard to enforcing the antitrust law, *(d)* Theodore Roosevelt and Wilson in regard to securing progressive legislation.

PART 4. The Republicans Dominate the Post-World War I Era (1921–1933)

BRIEF SURVEY OF NATIONAL DEVELOPMENTS

ECONOMIC

1. "Golden Twenties": Booming Business. Following a brief depression in 1920–1921, the American people entered upon an era of prosperity. Corporations grew bigger as executives constructed new plants and concluded mergers. Enterprising business leaders ventured into new fields: automobiles, chemicals, radio, and movies. Output and profits increased, as did employment opportunities and wages. The American economy enjoyed widespread public confidence.

2. Flaws in the Business Boom. Not sharing in the general prosperity were certain "sick" industries, namely coal mining and textiles. Also, agriculture experienced overproduction, and railroads faced competition from newer means of transportation. Furthermore, consumers found their purchasing power not rising sufficiently to absorb the increasing output of goods. Finally, many Americans, seeking to "get rich quick," speculated excessively in real estate and in the stock market.

3. Great Depression (Beginning in 1929). In late 1929 the values of stocks fell abruptly. This stock market crash signaled the onset of the Great Depression. Production, prices, and profits declined sharply, as did wages and employment. The mood of most Americans veered swiftly from confidence to despair.

SOCIAL

1. New Nativism. As an outgrowth of the "Red Scare" of 1918 to 1920, a new nativist, antiforeign movement arose. The most notorious group, the Ku Klux Klan, which had been revived in 1915, grew in membership and spread bigotry against minority groups: foreigners, blacks, Catholics, and Jews. However, by the late 1920s, the influence of the Klan declined, as the American people recoiled against the Klan's lawlessness, corruption, and intolerance.

2. Prohibition Era. With the ratification of the Eighteenth Amendment in 1919, the United States inaugurated nationwide prohibition. Instead of improving American life, prohibition provided profitable opportunities for criminal syndicates, encouraged bootleggers and speakeasies, fostered alliances between gangsters and corrupt politicians, and bred public disrespect for the law. In 1933 the Twenty-First Amendment repealed prohibition.

3. Loss of Idealism. Americans of the "Golden Twenties" lost the social concern characteristic of the Progressive Era. In foreign affairs, they wished to withdraw into isolation. In domestic affairs, they saw little need for reform.

4. Undercurrent of Protest. Many intellectuals and youths rejected conformity and complacency. *Sinclair Lewis,* typical of the protesting writers, criticized American culture and values. Young people rebelled against uniformity by acclaiming a new musical form, jazz. Many young women, called "flappers," defied social standards by unconventional dress and behavior. These young people, who felt out of place in postwar America, constituted the "lost generation."

POLITICAL

(1) The Democratic party was enfeebled by factional quarrels. Progressives battled conservatives, and eastern big-city political bosses contended against southern and western rural leaders. The Democrats lost three successive Presidential elections: 1920, 1924, and 1928. (2) The Republican party was dominated by conservative business types (who supplied the campaign funds) and by

"Old Guard" professionals (who provided political leadership). The Republicans won the three successive Presidential elections.

HARDING ADMINISTRATION: 1921–1923 (REPUBLICAN)

MAJOR POLITICAL ASPECTS

1. Election of 1920. The Democratic convention, after a bitter struggle, gave a 44th ballot nomination to Ohio Governor *James M. Cox*. Heeding Wilson's plea that the election be a "great and solemn referendum" on the League of Nations, Cox campaigned vigorously for American membership.

When the Republican convention failed to select a nominee on the first six ballots, a small group of political bosses met privately in a "smoke-filled room" and threw their support to a "dark horse" candidate, Ohio Senator *Warren G. Harding*. He was nominated on the tenth ballot. Campaigning from his front porch, Harding dealt with the League issue evasively. He failed also to spell out his domestic policies. He did, however, capture the public mood with his promise of a "return to normalcy." Harding won the election overwhelmingly.

2. Harding and the "Return to Normalcy." An easygoing person, Harding possessed a limited understanding of national problems. He ignored the developments of the Progressive Era and returned to the domestic policies of the Republican party of McKinley's time. He favored *(a)* less government: reduced federal spending and the restricted use of Presidential powers, *(b)* pro-business policies: higher tariffs, lower taxes, and inactivity by government regulatory agencies, and *(c)* a foreign policy tending toward isolation.

3. Scandal at the National Level. Harding was an honest but pliable man who, like Grant, was unable to protect his postwar administration from scandal. *(a) Charles R. Forbes,* head of the Veterans Bureau, pocketed millions through various shady deals. (In 1925 Forbes was sentenced to prison.) *(b) Harry M. Daugherty,* Harding's political patron and attorney general, was involved, together with others, in substantial kickbacks following the rigged sale of government property. (Eventually, one man committed suicide and another went to jail, but Daugherty was saved twice by a hung jury.) *(c) Albert Fall,* Secretary of the Interior, secretly gave private business executives liberal leases to government oil reserves at *Elk Hills,* California, and *Teapot Dome,* Wyoming. In return, Fall received considerable "loans" and gifts. (Subsequently, the leases were cancelled, and Fall was sentenced to jail, the first Cabinet officer so dishonored.)

In 1923, soon after the public became aware of this corruption, Harding suffered a severe illness and died. He was succeeded by his Vice President, *Calvin Coolidge*.

IMPORTANT DOMESTIC LEGISLATION

(1) The *Emergency Quota Act* (1921) severely restricted immigration. (2) The *Veterans Bureau Act* (1921) created a single agency to administer veterans' benefits. (3) The *Fordney-McCumber Tariff Act* (1922) provided high tariffs.

SIGNIFICANT FOREIGN AFFAIRS

1. Return to Isolation. Harding interpreted his election to mean rejection of the League of Nations. To replace the Treaty of Versailles, Harding arranged a separate peace treaty with Germany that did not provide for American membership in the League.

2. Washington Conference (1921–1922). Charles Evans Hughes, Secretary of State, summoned and presided over this international conference. It concluded the *Five-Power Agreement,* providing for partial naval disarmament, and the *Nine-Power Agreement,* pledging respect for the territorial integrity and independence of China.

COOLIDGE ADMINISTRATION: 1923–1929 (REPUBLICAN)

MAJOR POLITICAL AND ECONOMIC ASPECTS

1. Calvin Coolidge: Background and Personality. Calvin Coolidge, a descendant of New England colonists, rose slowly in Massachusetts politics and in 1918 became governor. Coolidge won national attention when he called up the state National Guard to maintain order during a Boston police strike and proclaimed, "There is no right to strike against the public safety." Coolidge received the Republican Vice Presidential nomination in 1920, and, upon Harding's death, he became President. He "cleaned house" by prosecuting the Harding appointees involved in scandals. For many Americans, Coolidge came to represent "normalcy" combined with honesty.

2. Election of 1924. The Republican convention gave a first-ballot nomination to the President and urged the nation to "keep cool with Coolidge." The Democratic convention, deadlocked for more than 100 ballots, finally named a "dark horse" candidate, the conservative corporation lawyer *John W. Davis.* Both the Republican and the Democratic nominees disappointed reform groups, who established a Progressive party and nominated Wisconsin Senator *Robert La Follette.*

While Coolidge claimed credit for prosperity and Davis attacked the Harding scandals, La Follette concentrated upon vital issues and proposed reforms: more aid for farmers, further curbs on the use of injunctions in labor disputes, government ownership of railroads and waterpower resources, and higher income taxes. La Follette polled almost 5 million votes, more than polled by any previous third-party candidate; Davis received almost 8.5 million; Coolidge, however, won easily with more than 15 million.

3. Business Administration. Insisting that "the business of America is business," Coolidge believed that the government should encourage business but regulate it as little as possible. Coolidge favored reduced government spending and low taxes, and vetoed government aid for farmers and government operation of the water power plant at *Muscle Shoals,* Alabama. He made no effort to restrain stock market speculation. Although the Coolidge years were prosperous, Coolidge's failure to act in economic matters helped bring on the Great Depression.

IMPORTANT DOMESTIC LEGISLATION

(1) The *Immigration Act* (1924) tightened immigration restrictions. (2) The *Soldiers' Bonus Act* (1924), passed over Coolidge's veto, provided World War I veterans with paid-up life insurance policies.

SIGNIFICANT FOREIGN AFFAIRS

Secretary of State Frank B. Kellogg and Foreign Minister Aristide Briand of France arranged for over 60 nations to sign a pact "outlawing" war. The *Kellogg-Briand Pact (Pact of Paris)* of 1928, although lacking provision for enforcement, was welcomed by Americans.

HOOVER ADMINISTRATION: 1929–1933 (REPUBLICAN)

MAJOR POLITICAL AND ECONOMIC ASPECTS

1. Election of 1928. After Coolidge announced "I do not choose to run," the Republican convention gave a first-ballot nomination to Secretary of Commerce *Herbert Hoover.* A "dry" (supporter of prohibition) and a successful business executive, Hoover told the American people that they were nearer than ever before to "the final triumph over poverty."

The Democratic convention nominated New York Governor *Alfred E. Smith.* A grandson of Irish immigrants, Smith had risen from the "sidewalks of New York" to the governor's mansion and had provided efficient and humane state government.

As a Presidential candidate, however, Smith labored under several handicaps. As a Roman Catholic—the first nominated by a major party—Smith lost votes because of religious bigotry, especially in Ku Klux Klan strongholds in the South. As a "wet" (antiprohibitionist), and as a big-city resident, Smith was mistrusted by the predominantly "dry" southern and midwestern rural voters. Most important, Smith could not overcome the Republicans' claim that they had engendered prosperity. Smith pulled almost double the vote of the 1924 Democratic candidate and carried many large cities. However, Hoover handily won the election and was the first Republican since reconstruction to carry five states of the "Solid South."

2. Hoover: Background and Views. Educated at Stanford University as a mining engineer, Hoover became a self-made millionaire. During and after World War I, he directed food relief programs for the Belgians and other European peoples, gaining renown as an administrator and humanitarian. His work as secretary of commerce (1921–1928) further enhanced his reputation.

Hoover credited America's greatness and prosperity to free enterprise and "rugged individualism." He argued that government interference in business endangered economic progress and personal liberty. The government, he held, should serve business by levying high tariffs and low taxes, practicing economy, and maintaining a balanced budget.

3. Hoover's Efforts to Combat the Depression. (a) When the depression of 1929 began, Hoover at first believed that the economy was basically sound and would recover, as in the past, through the workings of natural economic factors. Nevertheless, to halt the depression, Hoover requested business leaders voluntarily to maintain employment, wage scales, and capital investment. However, faced by falling prices, production, and profits, they were unable to do so. As conditions worsened, the Democrats made substantial gains in the 1930 Congressional elections. (b) Thereafter, Hoover secured increased appropriations for a limited federal public works program. Although modest, this program was greater than any attempted previously. Also, he secured establishment of the *Reconstruction Finance Corporation* (RFC), to provide federal loans to hard-pressed banks, life insurance companies, railroads, and other businesses. Hoover's efforts proved inadequate to stop the depression, which reached its lowest depth in the years 1932 and 1933.

4. Hoover's Rejection of Additional Measures to Combat the Depression

(a) Hoover opposed proposals for direct federal relief to unemployed workers. (b) Hoover refused to expand the federal public works program. (c) He opposed the request of unemployed veterans for immediate payment of their World War I bonuses (not due until 1945).

In these times of despair, surprisingly few Americans turned to violence or to radical political parties. Americans overwhelmingly remained faithful to their traditions and patiently awaited the Presidential election of 1932.

IMPORTANT DOMESTIC LEGISLATION

(1) The *Agricultural Marketing Act* (1929) tried to raise farm prices by establishing a Federal Farm Board with funds to purchase surplus produce. (2) The *Hawley-Smoot Tariff Act* (1930) raised tariffs to the highest levels ever.

SIGNIFICANT FOREIGN AFFAIRS

1. Improving Relations With Latin America. Hoover refused to intervene in Latin America to protect American economic interests, thus rejecting dollar diplomacy. In 1933 he withdrew American marines from Nicaragua.

2. Furthering Naval Disarmament. At the *London Naval Conference* (1930), the United States, England, and Japan extended for five years the limits on their navies.

3. Voicing Opposition to Japanese Aggression. When Japan invaded China's northern province of Manchuria in 1931, Secretary of State *Henry L. Stimson* informed Japan that the United States would not recognize any seizure of territory by force.

————————— MULTIPLE-CHOICE QUESTIONS —————————

1. "The public mood zigzagged from one extreme to the other: first hysteria over radicalism, then complacency over good times, and finally gloom when the depression began." Which period is being described? (a) 1860s (b) 1890s (c) 1920s (d) 1930s.
2. In the "return to normalcy" following World War I, a policy of the government was to (a) keep federal expenditures at a minimum (b) prosecute monopolies (c) encourage the growth of labor unions (d) follow a low-tariff policy.
3. In the 1920s the domestic policies of the federal government were primarily concerned with (a) protecting business interests (b) furthering social reform (c) negotiating reciprocal trade agreements (d) improving the national banking system.
4. During the 1920s Congress and the President approved legislation providing for (a) conservation of natural resources (b) increases in tariff rates (c) regulation of the sale of stocks and bonds (d) guaranteed prices for farm products.
5. The enactment of prohibition in the United States during the 1920s involved an attempt to legislate (a) public morality (b) political responsibility (c) civil rights (d) cultural assimilation.
6. A study of the 1920s reveals that (a) the people preferred Presidents who exerted the full power of the office (b) the people favored a continuous buildup of armaments (c) law enforcement was difficult in the face of opposition to prohibition (d) social reform movements tended to increase because of prosperity.
7. In the 1920s which policy was most inconsistent with the fact that we were a creditor nation? (a) our tariff policy (b) our neutrality policy (c) our disarmament policy (d) our policy toward Latin America.
8. In which national election was the "Solid South" first broken? (a) 1920 (b) 1924 (c) 1928 (d) 1932.
9. The Teapot Dome Scandal involved (a) import duties on tea (b) excise taxes on the sale of beverages (c) overcutting in government forest lands (d) liberal leases of government oil reserves.
10. Before becoming President in 1929, Herbert Hoover had been all of the following *except* (a) mining engineer (b) administrator of Belgian food relief (c) Governor of California (d) secretary of commerce.

11. The most dramatic event that occurred during Hoover's first year as President was the (a) stock market crash (b) beginning of our Social Security system (c) Japanese invasion of Manchuria (d) repeal of prohibition.

——————— MODIFIED TRUE-FALSE QUESTIONS ———————

1. In 1920 a group of Republican political bosses meeting in a "smoke-filled room" arranged for the Presidential nomination of *James M. Cox.*
2. The Presidential candidate of the Progressive party who in 1924 polled almost 5 million votes was *Theodore Roosevelt.*
3. A position held by both Charles Evans Hughes and Frank B. Kellogg was *secretary of state.*
4. The author of the statement, "I do not choose to run," issued in 1927, was *Calvin Coolidge.*
5. The first Roman Catholic to be nominated by a major party for the Presidency was *Alfred E. Smith.*
6. In the elections of 1930, the *Progressive* party substantially increased its representation in Congress.
7. In spite of a protesting petition of over 1000 economists, President Hoover signed the *Fordney-McCumber* Tariff Act.
8. To provide loans to distressed railroads, banks, and life insurance companies, President Hoover approved the establishment of the *Federal Trade Commission.*

——————————— ESSAY QUESTIONS ———————————

1. The years from 1921 to 1929 have been characterized as an era of *political conservatism, economic prosperity,* and *social conformity.* For *each* of the italicized terms in the preceding sentence, discuss *one* fact to support *and one* fact to refute the accuracy of the statement.
2. Warren G. Harding has been associated with the term "return to normalcy." *(a)* Discuss *two* reasons why the voters in the election of 1920 welcomed Harding's promise of a "return to normalcy." *(b)* Discuss *one* domestic and *one* foreign policy of the Harding administration, showing how each reflected the search for "normalcy." *(c)* Were the scandals of the Harding administration part of or alien to "normalcy"? Give *one* argument to support your point of view. *(d)* The Coolidge administration has been considered as representing "normalcy" combined with honesty. Agree or disagree with this statement, giving *two* arguments to support your point of view.
3. Agree or disagree with *each* of the following statements, giving *two* reasons to support your point of view: *(a)* In his career until 1928, Herbert Hoover received excellent training for the Presidency. *(b)* Hoover had great difficulty in winning the Presidential election of 1928. *(c)* President Hoover provided effective leadership to combat the depression of 1929. *(d)* In foreign affairs, the Hoover administration compiled a successful record.

PART 5. The Democrats Introduce the "New Deal" and Then the "Fair Deal" (1933–1953)

BRIEF SURVEY OF NATIONAL DEVELOPMENTS

ECONOMIC

1. Partial Recovery With the "New Deal." The Democrats led by Franklin D. Roosevelt began the *New Deal,* a program of strong government intervention in the economy to combat the depression. By 1939, 5 million persons previously unemployed were back at work, industrial and farm prices were up significantly, as were workers' wages, and the total national income had almost doubled. The recovery, nevertheless, was only partial, and relief needs remained heavy, since over 8 million workers were still unemployed.

2. Full Recovery With World War II. After war started in Europe in 1939, the United States hurried its own military preparedness and offered "all aid short of war" to Britain. In 1941 the United States was forced into active battle by the Japanese attack upon Pearl Harbor, Hawaii. War needs stimulated industry to produce to capacity and to absorb the remaining unemployed. Wartime prosperity carried over into the postwar years.

SOCIAL DEVELOPMENTS

1. Restoration of Confidence. Abandoning the despair of the depression, the American people reasserted their natural optimism. When faced by Fascist and Communist ideologies, the American people reaffirmed their faith in their own institutions: regulated capitalism and democratic government.

2. Cultural Developments. Through its *Works Progress Administration,* the New Deal provided work for destitute artists, musicians, writers, and actors. Apart from the WPA, novelists and playwrights tackled current problems, thereby heightening social consciousness. Their messages, as well as purely escapist stories, reached wide audiences by means of the newly developed "talking" motion picture. Also, Americans depended increasingly on the radio for entertainment, newscasts, and political addresses. In the years after World War II, the radio was to an extent replaced by television.

3. Post-World War II "Red Scare." With the beginning of the cold war between the United States and the Soviet Union, the American people once more became concerned with the danger of domestic Communists. Their fears were heightened by the disclosure of several spy cases, the most notable involving a former State Department employee, Alger Hiss.

a. Laws Against Subversion. The 1940 *Smith Act* made illegal teaching the violent overthrow of any government in the United States. In the *Dennis* case (1948–1949), the Smith Act was used by the Justice Department to successfully prosecute 11 top domestic Communists, and the law was held Constitutional by the Supreme Court. The 1950 *Internal Security (McCarran) Act* placed further restrictions upon domestic Communists and their organizations. The major provision of the law required Communist and Communist-front organizations to register with the Department of Justice. (This provision was negated in 1965 when the Supreme Court held that Communists could not be compelled to register because of the Fifth Amendment protection against self-incrimination.)

b. Congressional Investigations. House and Senate committees conducted hearings to uncover Communist agents in strategic positions. Senator *Joseph McCarthy* of Wisconsin made newspaper headlines by charging that the State Department contained a large number of Communists. McCarthy's charges, investigated by a special Senate committee, were found to be half-truths and untruths. Undaunted, McCarthy continued his attack, accusing Secretary of State George C. Marshall of disloyalty and charging the Democratic administrations with "twenty years of treason." McCarthy's supporters praised his efforts to alert the nation to the danger of Communist subversion. McCarthy's detractors labeled him a demagogue whose wild and reckless charges divided the nation and fanned public hysteria. (Later, McCarthy directed his charges against members of the Republican administration of President Eisenhower. In 1954 McCarthy was officially condemned by the Senate for "unbecoming" conduct, and his influence rapidly declined.)

POLITICAL

1. Democrats: A Victorious Coalition. Starting in 1932, the Democratic party forged a successful coalition: factory workers, liberal business leaders, ethnic minorities, and intellectuals—mostly from the big cities; traditional Democrats in the South; and small farmers. The Democratic party won five consecutive Presidential elections.

2. Republicans: Defeated and Divided. The Republicans labored under severe handicaps. At first, they were blamed for the so-called "Hoover depression" and were identified with upper-class interests. Later, they were split on New Deal reforms. Some Republicans urged total rejection of the New Deal; others favored retention of certain New Deal measures. Then, as the nation approached World War II, the Republicans were split on foreign policy between midwestern isolationists and eastern internationalists. After the war, the Republicans gained strength, but not sufficiently to win the 1948 Presidential election.

FRANKLIN D. ROOSEVELT ADMINISTRATION: 1933–1945 (DEMOCRATIC)—THE "NEW DEAL"

MAJOR POLITICAL AND ECONOMIC ASPECTS

1. Election of 1932. Although aware that the public blamed President Hoover for the depression, the Republican convention renominated him. The Democratic convention gave a fourth-ballot nomination to New York Governor *Franklin D. Roosevelt*. The two candidates disagreed basically regarding the economy. Roosevelt insisted that the government should take firm steps to insure the well-being of the people. Hoover argued for the continuation of only limited interference in the economy. Roosevelt won overwhelmingly, and the Democrats also secured substantial majorities in both houses of Congress.

2. Franklin D. Roosevelt: Background and Personality. A member of a wealthy New York landowning family, Franklin D. Roosevelt was educated at Harvard and at Columbia Law School. He served a term in the New York State legislature and in 1912 supported Woodrow Wilson, who appointed him assistant secretary of the Navy. Roosevelt demonstrated resourcefulness and also absorbed Wilsonian progressivism and idealism. Nominated for Vice President in 1920, Roosevelt, together with Presidential nominee James M. Cox, battled unsuccessfully for the League of Nations. In 1921 Roosevelt was paralyzed by an attack of polio. He fought back and, although never again able to walk unaided, he recovered sufficiently to resume political activity. In 1928, while Presidential candidate Alfred E. Smith lost the election and failed to carry New York State, Roosevelt narrowly won the New York governorship. His progressive administration provided care for the aged and aid for the unemployed.

Roosevelt possessed personal warmth, self-confidence, tremendous energy, and a zest for life. A master politician and a skilled orator, Roosevelt commanded widespread public loyalty.

3. Roosevelt Provides Strong Leadership. Like his distant cousin "Teddy" Roosevelt, Franklin Roosevelt used the Presidency as an office of moral and political leadership.

a. Bank Holiday. For a month before his inauguration, Roosevelt observed that depositors, fearful of bank failures, were making "runs" on their banks to withdraw cash, thereby compelling many banks to shut their doors. Immediately upon taking office, Roosevelt closed all banks by declaring a *bank holiday*. He called Congress into special session and quickly obtained legislation empowering Treasury officials to examine the banks and reopen those that were solvent. Roosevelt's vigorous action restored public confidence not only in the banks but also in the federal government.

b. The "Hundred Days." The banking act was the first of many laws enacted by Congress during the three months of its special session. Roosevelt proposed many new laws and, using his position as party leader and public orator, secured passage of every major proposal. This period of the New Deal has become known as the "Hundred Days."

c. Press Conferences. Roosevelt held frequent press conferences and utilized them to present his ideas to the public and to dominate newspaper headlines.

d. "Fireside Chats." Roosevelt used the radio to reach into the American home with his "fireside chats." In an informal manner, he addressed his listeners as "my friends" and gained public support for his programs.

Roosevelt reestablished the Presidency as a position of leadership. In doing so, he stirred vigorous controversy, and no President since Lincoln has evoked so much public love or hate. Most historians agree that Roosevelt ranks among our greatest Presidents.

4. Roosevelt Constructs the New Deal

a. Concern With the "Forgotten Man." Roosevelt pledged himself to "a new deal for the American people." He offered help for the average citizen, the "forgotten man at the bottom of the economic pyramid."

b. Use of the "Brain Trust." Respecting academic scholarship, Roosevelt sought the help of a group of college professors, who were soon dubbed by the newspapers as the "brain trust." From the clash of ideas among these and other advisers, Roosevelt was able to evaluate alternative proposals and to determine the government's course of action.

c. Disregard of Laissez-Faire. To combat the depression, Roosevelt committed the government to an ever-increasing role in the economy. His New Deal completed the transition from laissez-faire to regulated capitalism.

d. Pragmatic, or Practical, Approach. In his 1933 Inaugural Address, Roosevelt said, "This great nation will endure, revive, and prosper. . . . The only thing we have to fear is fear itself. . . . This nation asks for action and action now." Roosevelt favored bold experimentation: "Above all, try something." He adopted the pragmatic approach of trial and error.

e. New Deal Goals: Relief, Recovery, Reform. The New Dealers sought (1) *relief*—to assist distressed persons through direct money payments, jobs, and mortgage loans, (2) *recovery*—to lift the nation out of the depression through aid to farmers, business owners, and workers, and (3) *reform*—to eliminate abuses in the economy and to prevent future depressions through protection of bank depositors, investors, consumers, the aged, and the unemployed.

f. Growth of Federal Power. The federal government greatly expanded its role in our society. The full extent of federal activity is revealed best by the listing of New Deal laws and agencies (see page 481).

5. Election of 1936. The American people overwhelmingly reelected Roosevelt over the Republican candidate, Kansas Governor Alfred M. Landon. Roosevelt won all but two states and almost 61 percent of the popular vote.

6. New Deal and the Supreme Court

a. The Supreme Court Temporarily Checks the New Deal. Dominated by a conservative majority, the Supreme Court threw out several early New Deal laws, notably, in 1935, the National Industrial Recovery Act and, in 1936, the Agricultural Adjustment Act. Roosevelt complained that the Supreme Court was living in the "horse and buggy" age, and he feared for the fate of other New Deal laws.

b. Roosevelt's Court Plan Is Rejected by Congress. Encouraged by his overwhelming reelection in 1936, Roosevelt proposed a Court reorganization plan that would have permitted him to appoint up to six additional Supreme Court Justices. Roosevelt's enemies labeled his plan "Court-packing" and accused the President of trying to upset our traditional separation of powers. The bill was defeated in Congress, by the votes of Republicans and many Democrats.

c. The Supreme Court Reverses Itself. Meanwhile, the Supreme Court adopted a more liberal position. In 1937, by a vote of 5 to 4, the Court held constitutional two major New Deal laws: the National Labor Relations Act and the Social Security Act. Thereafter, a conservative Justice resigned, enabling Roosevelt to appoint a New Dealer to the Court—the first of several such appointments. Roosevelt later claimed that he had lost the battle but won the war.

7. End of the New Deal (By 1939).

Although Roosevelt remained in office until 1945, by 1939 he had ceased to expand the New Deal. *(a)* Southern Democrats, mainly conservative, had split from the liberal wing of the party in the 1937 Supreme Court fight. They were further alienated in 1938 by the Wages and Hours Act, which they viewed as a threat to the use of cheap labor by southern industry. Thereafter, southern Democrats in Congress joined with Republicans to create a formidable opposition to any further New Deal proposals. *(b)* Because the economy had achieved some recovery, the public lost its enthusiasm for further reforms. *(c)* Americans shifted their attention from domestic to foreign affairs, as international crises pointed toward a second World War.

8. Evaluation of the New Deal

a. Arguments For. Supporters praised the New Deal for (1) restoring courage and optimism to the people and improving the economic status of most Americans, (2) providing work relief, which enabled the unemployed to retain their self-respect and which enriched the nation with roads, public buildings, dams, and parks, (3) increasing government spending, thereby offsetting declines in private spending and helping the economy to recover from the depression, (4) reducing unemployment by 5 million and treating the remaining unemployed humanely, (5) successfully regulating capitalism and introducing laws of permanent value, and (6) expanding federal power over our economic system and yet maintaining democratic methods and personal freedoms.

b. Arguments Against. Critics condemned the New Deal for (1) failing to gain the confidence of the business community, (2) wasting money on valueless make-work, or "boondoggling," through its work-relief projects, (3) unbalancing the budget and increasing the national debt through a program of deficit spending, (4) failing to eliminate unemployment, which stood at 8 million in 1939, (5) interfering excessively with free enterprise, engaging in "socialistic" experiments, and passing unconstitutional and highly controversial laws, and (6) increasing the number of federal employees and creating a bureaucracy of agencies with vast powers over the economy.

c. Revolution or Evolution? (1) Critics, pointing to deficit spending and the growth of federal power, especially over the economy, claimed that the New Deal was a revolution—a break with American tradition. (2) Supporters, pointing to our Populist and Progressive heritage, and to the preservation of our capitalist democracy, claimed that the New Deal represented evolution—in harmony with American tradition.

9. Breaking the Two-Term Tradition

a. Election of 1940. The Democratic convention focused its attention upon the world crisis. Nazi German armies had overrun France and were threatening Britain; and Japan had overrun most of coastal China. To retain experienced leadership, the Democrats nominated Roosevelt for an unprecedented third term. Meanwhile, the Republicans nominated *Wendell Willkie,* the president of a large utility company, and a liberal and internationalist. Willkie supported most of Roosevelt's foreign policies and also many New Deal reforms. However, he opposed federal ownership of power plants, as in the TVA, and the breaking of the two-term tradition.

Roosevelt won the election by a substantial margin. His third term was chiefly concerned with foreign affairs and with America's participation in World War II.

b. Election of 1944. The Democrats nominated Roosevelt for a fourth term. The Republicans selected the young and energetic Governor of New York, *Thomas E. Dewey.* Being mildly liberal and internationalist, Dewey raised few issues. He charged the fourth-term candidate with being "tired" and insisted that it was "time for a change." Roosevelt demonstrated his popularity by easily winning the election.

Within three months after his fourth inauguration, President Roosevelt suffered a massive stroke and died. He was succeeded by Vice President *Harry S Truman.*

SIGNIFICANT FOREIGN AFFAIRS

1. Good Neighbor Policy Toward Latin America. By pursuing the *Good Neighbor Policy,* Roosevelt *(a)* expanded our Latin American trade so as to combat the depression, and *(b)* won Latin American friendship so as to unite the Western Hemisphere against Fascist aggression.

2. Recognition of the Soviet Union (1933). Roosevelt recognized the 16-year-old Soviet regime, but relations remained unfriendly. The United

NEW DEAL: IMPORTANT DOMESTIC LEGISLATION

Laws	Purposes
Federal Emergency Relief Act (1933)	Provide grants to states for relief of destitute persons.
Agricultural Adjustment Act (1933)	Raise farm prices by curtailing production.
National Industrial Recovery Act (1933)	Speed business recovery by codes of fair competition.
Reciprocal Trade Agreements Act (1934)	Increase foreign trade by reciprocal lowering of tariffs.
National Labor Relations Act (1935)	Guarantee workers the right to organize and bargain collectively.
Social Security Act (1935)	Protect workers by insurance for unemployment and old age.
Agricultural Adjustment Act (1938)	Raise farm prices by curtailing production through soil conservation programs.
Fair Labor Standards Act (1938)	Establish minimum wages and maximum hours; prohibit most child labor.
Food, Drug, and Cosmetic Act (1938)	Protect consumers by proper labeling and advertising.

NEW DEAL AGENCIES

Agencies	Purposes
Civilian Conservation Corps (CCC)	Provide work for the unemployed.
Public Works Administration (PWA)	Same as above.
Works Progress Administration (WPA)	Same as above.
Home Owners Loan Corporation (HOLC)	Provide mortgage loans for homeowners facing foreclosure.
Federal Deposit Insurance Corporation (FDIC)	Protect depositors in case of bank failure.
Tennessee Valley Authority (TVA)	Improve economic conditions in the Tennessee Valley through development of hydroelectric power.
Securities and Exchange Commission (SEC)	Protect investors by supervising issuance of securities and regulating stock exchanges.
Rural Electrification Administration (REA)	Bring low-cost electricity to farm families.

States and the Soviet Union did not increase trade with each other nor, until 1941, did they cooperate against the Axis menace.

3. From Isolation to Leadership of the Free World. Roosevelt alerted the American people to the danger of aggression by the Rome-Berlin-Tokyo Axis. After World War II began in Europe (1939), Roosevelt extended all aid short of war to Great Britain and other nations fighting the Axis. Following the Japanese attack upon Pearl Harbor (1941), Roosevelt led the United States to military victory and helped plan the *United Nations*.

TRUMAN ADMINISTRATION: 1945–1953 (DEMOCRATIC)— THE "FAIR DEAL"

MAJOR POLITICAL AND ECONOMIC ASPECTS

1. Harry Truman: Background and Personality. A Missouri farm-boy by birth, Truman held various jobs and, during World War I, served as an army officer. After an unsuccessful haberdashery store venture, Truman turned to politics and was elected county commissioner. He administered county affairs efficiently, and in 1934 was elected to the United States Senate. As chairman of the Senate committee investigating military contracts, Truman saved government funds, sped war production, and gained a national reputation. At the 1944 Democratic convention, Truman won the Vice Presidential nomination.

Well-read in American history, Truman viewed the Presidency as an office of power and leadership. He acted with authority and demonstrated intelligence, imagination, and courage. Truman was above all a "fighter" and a champion of the average citizen. According to historians, Truman "grew on the job" and fulfilled his responsibilities competently. His record contrasted sharply with those of Grant and Harding, who were also postwar Presidents.

2. Transition to Peacetime. *(a)* Bowing to strong public pressure, Truman permitted the hasty demobilization of the armed services. To adjust to civilian life, veterans availed themselves of the *Servicemen's Readjustment Act* (1944), popularly called the *G. I. Bill of Rights*. Under this law, veterans were entitled to unemployment pay; medical care; loans for buying a home, farm, or business; and payments for continuing their education. *(b)* Heeding the business community, Congress denied Truman's request for continuation of strong price controls. Meanwhile, labor unions gained considerable wage boosts. With prices and wages rapidly rising, the nation experienced serious inflation.

3. Election of 1948. The Republicans, confident of victory, again nominated New York Governor Thomas E. Dewey. Republican confidence was based upon their success in 1946, when they had gained control of both houses of Congress, upon predictions of public-opinion polls, overwhelming newspaper support, and dissension in the Democratic party.

The Democratic convention nominated President Truman. Thereupon, Southern Democrats, who opposed Truman's strong stand on civil rights, organized the *States' Rights* or *Dixiecrat party* and nominated South Carolina Governor *J. Strom Thurmond*. Left-wing Democrats, who opposed Truman's efforts to halt the spread of Russian influence, founded a *Progressive party* and nominated a former Vice President, *Henry A. Wallace*. His candidacy fell increasingly under Communist domination.

While Dewey waged a colorless campaign to avoid offending voters, Truman fought vigorously. He undertook "whistle-stop" railroad tours, berated the "do-nothing" Republican Congress, and projected an image as an unassuming but concerned human being. Truman won an upset victory, with 24 million popular votes and 303 electoral votes to Dewey's 22 million popular votes and 189 electoral votes. (Thurmond and Wallace each polled slightly over a million popular votes, and Thurmond also won 39 southern electoral votes.)

4. "Fair Deal"

a. Relationship to the New Deal. Truman knew that Wilson's New Freedom had ended with World War I. He was determined that Roosevelt's New Deal should survive World War II and continue, improved and expanded, as the *Fair Deal.*

b. Opposition in Congress: The Conservative Coalition. During Truman's two terms in office, the conservative coalition of Republicans and Southern Democrats mustered sufficient votes to defeat Fair Deal proposals for (1) civil rights legislation: an anti-lynching law, an anti-poll-tax law, and a Fair Employment Practices Committee (FEPC), (2) compulsory health insurance, and (3) federal aid to education.

Congress also rebuffed President Truman by overriding his strongly worded vetoes of measures designed to (1) curb labor unions, (2) protect internal security, and (3) continue restrictions on immigration.

c. Accomplishments

(1) Continuation of Existing Laws. Truman secured passage of Fair Deal proposals to expand Social Security coverage and benefits, raise the minimum wage, provide funds for slum clearance and low-income housing projects, and maintain farm price supports.

(2) New Laws. Truman secured laws establishing the Atomic Energy Commission, unifying the armed services, and committing the government to a policy of full employment.

(3) Civil Rights. Truman appointed a *Committee on Civil Rights,* which in 1947 issued the historic report "To Secure These Rights." It called the nation's attention to the unfinished business of ending racial and religious discrimination. Truman incorporated the recommendations of the committee into his legislative program but they were defeated in Congress. (Through an executive order, Truman began desegregating the armed services.) Truman's efforts awakened the nation's conscience to the problem of discrimination.

5. Other Developments. *(a) Loyalty Program.* Truman established loyalty boards to investigate federal employees and remove disloyal persons and other security risks. Of almost 3 million government employees investigated, some 2000 resigned and 200 were dismissed. *(b) Steel Strike of 1952.* After union and management failed to agree upon a new labor contract, Truman ordered Secretary of Commerce Charles Sawyer to seize the steel mills. Before the Supreme Court, (1) the steel companies challenged the seizure as a violation of the Fifth Amendment, which prohibits the federal government from taking private property without "due process of law," and (2) government attorneys defended the seizure as a war measure necessary to assure steel production for the Korean fighting front. The Supreme Court declared the seizure illegal, thus checking the power of the executive branch. The steel mills were returned to their owners, and the workers went out on strike and after two months secured a new contract.

IMPORTANT DOMESTIC LEGISLATION PASSED WITH TRUMAN'S APPROVAL

(1) The *Employment Act* (1946) affirmed the responsibility of the federal government to "promote maximum employment" and established the *Council of Economic Advisers.* (2) The *Atomic Energy Act* (1946) ordered government control over atomic research and production, and established a civilian *Atomic Energy Commission (AEC).* (3) The *National Security Act* (1947) unified the armed forces—Army, Navy, and Air Force—by creating a single *Department of Defense.*

IMPORTANT DOMESTIC LEGISLATION PASSED OVER TRUMAN'S VETO

1. The *Taft-Hartley (Labor-Management Relations) Act* (1947) placed restrictions upon labor unions. (Congress did not agree with Truman's veto message that the law showed prejudice against unions.)

2. The *McCarran (Internal Security) Act* (1950) called for strict regulation of pro-Communist activities within the United States and created the *Subversive Activities Control Board.* (In his veto message, Truman claimed that this law punished men not for committing crimes, but for holding unpopular opinions.)

3. The *McCarran-Walter (Immigration and Nationality) Act* (1952) restated the national origins quota system. (Truman argued that this law unfairly restricted immigration from much of the world.)

SIGNIFICANT FOREIGN AFFAIRS

1. Japanese Phase of World War II and the Atomic Bomb. To speed the end of the war and save countless American battle casualties, Truman authorized the use of the newly developed atomic bomb. Eight days after the bombing of the Japanese city of Hiroshima, Japan surrendered.

2. United Nations. Truman obtained overwhelming Senate ratification of American membership in the world organization.

3. Cold War. As Russia expanded its power in Europe and Asia, Truman countered with the American policy of *containment.* The Truman administration originated the *Truman Doctrine,* the *Marshall Plan,* and the *Point Four Program.* It helped establish the NATO military alliance. In the Far East, Truman began the nonrecognition policy toward Communist China and sent American forces to help repel the North Korean Communist invasion of South Korea.

——————— MULTIPLE-CHOICE QUESTIONS ———————

1. The major reason why Franklin D. Roosevelt won the Presidential election of 1932 was (a) his oratorical ability (b) the split in the Republican party (c) the support of his distant cousin, Theodore Roosevelt (d) the fact that the public associated the depression with Hoover.

2. Which statement about Franklin D. Roosevelt before 1932 is *not* true? (a) He was born into a wealthy family. (b) He was the Democratic Vice Presidential candidate in 1920. (c) He supported Theodore Roosevelt in the election of 1912. (d) He served as governor of New York.

3. Which term is *not* associated with the New Deal? (a) rugged individualism (b) the forgotten man (c) the brain trust (d) fireside chats.

4. The careers of Theodore Roosevelt and Franklin D. Roosevelt were similar in that each (a) led the cause for peace but involved the United States in a major war (b) led the fight for progressive ideas (c) succeeded to the Presidency upon the death of the previous President (d) mediated a dispute between major world powers.

5. The policies of Theodore Roosevelt and Franklin D. Roosevelt that differed most dealt with the (a) conservation of natural resources (b) protection of the consumer (c) power of the Presidency (d) countries of Latin America.

6. The statement, "Like Franklin D. Roosevelt, this President concerned himself primarily with domestic reform during his first years in office, and with foreign affairs in subsequent years," applies most accurately to (a) Woodrow Wilson (b) Herbert Hoover (c) Harry S Truman (d) William McKinley.

7. Woodrow Wilson and Franklin D. Roosevelt were alike in that both (a) were Republicans (b) favored creating an organization for world peace (c) requested Congress to establish the Tennessee Valley Authority (d) died in office.

8. Why did President Franklin D. Roosevelt ask Congress to increase the number of Supreme Court Justices? (a) The Court had declared several New Deal laws unconstitutional. (b) There was too much work for nine persons. (c) More experienced Justices were needed on the Court. (d) Until 1932 there had usually been more than nine judges on the Supreme Court.

9. An important reason for the opposition to Franklin D. Roosevelt's proposal to "reform" the Supreme Court was that this change would have (a) encouraged the appointment of inexperienced justices (b) been contrary to a tradition established by President Washington (c) lengthened the terms of the Justices of the Supreme Court (d) weakened the system of checks and balances.

10. Which group most consistently opposed New Deal legislation? (a) industrialists (b) labor union members (c) farmers (d) blacks.

11. New Deal legislation helped protect investors by (a) nationalizing all banks (b) preventing the practice of buying on margin (c) regulating the issuance of securities (d) determining dividend rates.

12. A feature of our economic life during the period 1933 to 1945 was that (a) the United States shifted from a creditor to a debtor nation (b) our farm population increased (c) the output of goods decreased (d) the number of persons at work increased.

13. An important criticism of the New Deal was that it (a) greatly increased the national debt (b) weakened the power of the chief executive (c) did not deal with important issues (d) promoted the idea of laissez-faire.

14. The New Deal of President Franklin D. Roosevelt could best be described as a policy which tended toward the (a) introduction of an economic policy of laissez-faire

(b) growth of federal power (c) enforcement of a strict interpretation of the Constitution (d) placement of strong emphasis upon states' rights.

15. The New Deal advanced the principle that (a) corporations should operate without government interference (b) government officials should inform the public of major political decisions (c) the President should determine foreign policy (d) the government should become more involved in the social and economic life of the people.

16. A reason for Roosevelt's election to a fourth term in 1944 was the (a) strength of his running mate, Henry A. Wallace (b) support given him by powerful third parties (c) ratification of the Twentieth Amendment (d) reluctance of voters to change leaders in the midst of a great crisis.

17. The administrations of Grant, Harding, and Truman were similar in that all three (a) were Republican (b) were marked by a return to isolationism (c) were followed by the election of a President from a different party (d) faced problems resulting from a recent war.

18. Which is the chief reason why the leaders of the Communist party in the United States were convicted of violating the Smith Act? (a) They had pledged allegiance to a foreign nation. (b) They had given government secrets to Soviet Russia. (c) They had conspired to overthrow the government of the United States by force. (d) They had ridiculed the courts and government of the United States.

19. An aim of the federal internal security program was to (a) remove subversives from government positions (b) provide for worker's compensation in industry (c) train able-bodied citizens for military duty (d) restrict the use of wiretapping.

20. In winning the Presidential election of 1948, Truman was most helped by (a) the endorsement of Henry A. Wallace (b) the strong support of southern Democrats (c) editorial support of most newspapers (d) his own determination to carry his campaign to the voters.

21. Truman's views regarding Presidential powers were most similar to those of (a) Harding (b) Wilson (c) Coolidge (d) McKinley.

22. Which term is *not* associated with the career of Truman? (a) whistle-stop campaign (b) policy of containment (c) the hundred days (d) "To Secure These Rights."

23. One Fair Deal proposal *not* passed by Congress during the Truman administration was to (a) provide federal aid for education (b) expand Social Security benefits (c) raise the minimum wage (d) provide funds for low-income housing projects.

24. One measure passed by Congress during the Truman administration that became law with the President's signature was the (a) Taft-Hartley Labor-Management Relations Act (b) McCarran Internal Security Act (c) McCarran-Walter Immigration Act (d) Employment Act.

25. President Truman (a) initiated important foreign policies (b) gave little support to the United Nations (c) requested Senator Joseph McCarthy to investigate federal employees for security risks (d) advocated a return to isolation.

26. Which was an outstanding achievement of the Truman administration? (a) passage of civil rights legislation (b) revision of the Taft-Hartley Act (c) formation of the NATO alliance (d) termination of the Korean War.

ESSAY QUESTIONS

1. Designed to meet the domestic problems of the United States in the 1930s, the New Deal continues to influence our way of life today. *(a)* Explain *two* conditions that helped to produce the Great Depression in the United States. *(b)* Show how *three* New Deal laws passed in the 1930s still affect us today.

2. The administration of Franklin D. Roosevelt was marked by various reform measures. *(a)* Discuss briefly an important law that was passed in relation to *each* of the following: (1) conservation, (2) housing, (3) labor, (4) agriculture. *(b)* In regard to a dispute that arose between the executive department and the Supreme Court during this period, describe the main issue and the outcome of the dispute.

3. Agree or disagree with *each* of the following statements, presenting *two* arguments to support your point of view: *(a)* Franklin D. Roosevelt was well-qualified for the Presidency. *(b)* Franklin D. Roosevelt made excessive use of Presidential powers. *(c)* The New Deal had much in common with the Progressive movement of the early 20th century. *(d)* The New Deal was more successful in achieving reform than in promoting recovery.

4. *(a)* In connection with the life of Harry S Truman, discuss *each* of the following: (1) *two* domestic problems that faced him as President and the steps that he took to solve each problem, (2) *one* reason why he won the Presidential election of 1948, (3) *one* reason why he was unable to secure Congressional passage of much Fair Deal legislation, (4) *two* foreign policies initiated during his administration. *(b)* How would you rate Truman in comparison with Warren G. Harding, the President following World War I? Present *two* facts to support your answer.

PART 6. Americans Choose as Leaders Both Republicans and Democrats (1953 to the Present)

BRIEF SURVEY OF NATIONAL DEVELOPMENTS

ECONOMIC AND SOCIAL

1. Prosperous America. Despite moderate-to-serious inflation, heavy taxation, and several recessions, most Americans continued to enjoy unprecedented prosperity. Their affluence was reflected in the growth of suburbs; the sales of automobiles, home appliances, and television sets; the expansion of airplane transportation; and the increase in leisure time. Nevertheless, considerable numbers of our people still lived in poverty.

2. Problem of Improving American Life. Critics of our "affluent society" urged Americans to be less concerned with seeking consumer goods and more concerned with improving their communities. This criticism stirred public discussion and eventually led to government action. Cities and states raised their taxes to improve public services. In the 1960s the federal government began new programs to fight poverty, expand medical care, combat the pollution of our air and water, and improve education.

3. Emphasis Upon Education. As Americans entered upon the "age of automation," the "atomic age," and the "space age," they became increasingly concerned with education. Citizens viewed education as essential for individual advancement and national survival. In the 1960s local governments increased their educational expenditures, and the federal government greatly expanded its aid to education.

4. Civil Rights Movement. Blacks and other minorities made progress toward overcoming discrimination, exercising their right to vote, and improving their economic status. These gains resulted from a favorable climate of public opinion, from the work of civil rights organizations, and from the activities of business and labor leaders, various state governments, and the federal government.

POLITICAL

1. Major Parties and Their Supporters. The Republican and Democratic parties each consisted of diverse groups functioning in a loose coalition. Each party reflected the same wide spectrum of political and economic opinion, although with different emphasis. The Republicans tended to outdraw the Democrats in attracting conservatives, business leaders, and well-to-do farmers. In contrast, the Democrats tended to lead the Republicans in attracting liberals, laborers, and small farmers.

2. Issues. In Presidential elections, each party generally sought to occupy the middle-of-the-road position in order to appeal to the greatest number of voters. Both parties supported American leadership in world affairs. They differed as to degree and method rather than as to goals. The Republicans generally accepted basic New Deal-Fair Deal reforms. (An exception took place in 1964, when the Republican Presidential candidate, Senator *Barry Goldwater,* taking a more conservative position, was soundly defeated.) Presidential campaigns tended to blur issues and to emphasize each candidate's personality and experience.

EISENHOWER ADMINISTRATION: 1953–1961 (REPUBLICAN)

MAJOR POLITICAL AND ECONOMIC ASPECTS

1. Election of 1952. The Republican convention witnessed a bitter struggle between "Mr. Republican," Ohio Senator *Robert A. Taft,* and the popular General *Dwight D. Eisenhower.* The Senator was the candidate of the more conservative and isolationist "Old Guard" Republicans; the General was supported by the party's liberal and internationalist wing. The convention gave a first-ballot nomination to Eisenhower and then selected, as his running mate, California Senator *Richard M. Nixon.* Eisenhower promised to lower taxes and to reduce government regulation of the economy. He criticized the Truman administration for excessive spending, incompetence, and its conduct of the Korean War. Republicans argued that, after 20 years of Democratic control of the Presidency, it was "time for a change."

The Democratic convention, wide open because President Truman refused to run again, nominated Illinois Governor *Adlai E. Stevenson.* He pointed to the nation's prosperity, defended the Democratic conduct of foreign affairs, and warned the people that no easy solutions existed for our many complex problems.

Eisenhower, who presented a fresh face in politics and a promise of new leadership, especially to end the Korean War, easily won the election.

2. Election of 1956. Again, Eisenhower and Stevenson contested for the Presidency. This time, Eisenhower campaigned on his record of "peace and prosperity." Stevenson attacked Eisenhower for favoring big business and mishandling foreign affairs. The Democrats also warned the nation that Eisenhower, having suffered a heart attack in 1955 and undergone an intestinal operation in 1956, could be only a "part-time President." Stevenson, however, was fighting a losing battle. By a somewhat greater margin than in 1952, Eisenhower repeated his election triumph.

3. Observations Upon the Election Results

a. Eisenhower twice carried several states of the traditionally Democratic "Solid South." Many white southern voters deserted the Democratic party because they opposed its strong civil rights program. Also, they favored Eisenhower's opposition to the further growth of federal power.

b. In 1956 Eisenhower received a heavy black vote in northern cities. These blacks supported Eisenhower because they (1) acclaimed the Supreme Court decision against segregation, handed down during his first term, and (2) felt that the Democratic party was dominated by Southerners, who opposed civil rights legislation.

c. Eisenhower's impressive victories testified to his popularity among the American people, who affectionately called him "Ike." However, other Republican candidates ran far behind Eisenhower, and the Republicans controlled Congress for only two of Eisenhower's eight years in office.

4. Eisenhower: Background and Personality. "Ike" was brought up in Kansas and held a night job while at high school. He secured an appointment to West Point, graduated in 1915, and subsequently served in varied army positions. During World War II, Eisenhower was advanced by President Roosevelt, over numerous senior officers, to the command of American forces in Europe. Eisenhower led the invasion of North Africa (1942) and the assault across the English Channel into France (1944). After the war Eisenhower served briefly as President of Columbia University and in 1950 was appointed by President Truman to be the first commander of the military forces of NATO.

Eisenhower had a warm personality with the ability to get diverse people to work together. Honest, sincere, and unpretentious, Eisenhower was one of our most popular Presidents.

5. Eisenhower Favors Bounds Upon Presidential Power. Eisenhower disapproved the practice, identified with his predecessors Roosevelt and

Truman, of strong Presidential leadership. Eisenhower urged restoration of the traditional separation of powers between the executive and Congress. He proposed legislative programs, but he held that Congress members should vote according to their own views and remain free from executive pressures. Eisenhower was willing to exercise leadership by "influencing people," but he refrained from "desk-pounding."

6. Eisenhower Advocates "Modern Republicanism." Eisenhower defined "modern Republicanism" as a middle-of-the-road approach which was "conservative when it comes to money and liberal when it comes to human beings." The chief principles of "modern Republicanism" were the following:

a. Accepting Basic New Deal-Fair Deal Reforms. Eisenhower secured measures to expand Social Security benefits and coverage, to raise the minimum wage, to further slum clearance and low-cost public housing, and to extend the reciprocal tariff program.

b. Limiting Federal Power. Eisenhower opposed the expansion of federal activity as leading to "statism" and threatening personal liberties. He favored making the federal government "smaller" by transferring some of its activities to the states and to private enterprise.

(1) To Expand the Power of States. Eisenhower approved a law shifting from the federal government to individual states the title to offshore lands. California, Texas, and Louisiana thus received lands rich in oil. He also authorized New York State, instead of the federal government, to cooperate with the Canadian Province of Ontario in building hydroelectric power plants on the St. Lawrence River.

(2) To Encourage Private Enterprise. Eisenhower ended the price and wage controls of the Korean War period. He secured flexible instead of rigid price supports for agriculture as a step toward withdrawing all government controls. He condemned the Tennessee Valley Authority as "creeping socialism" and urged that, in the future, waterpower sites be developed by private enterprise. Further, to assure a "smaller" federal government, Eisenhower urged reducing expenditures and balancing the national budget. (Despite rising welfare, defense, and space needs, Eisenhower was able to balance the budget in three of his eight years as President.)

7. Other Developments

a. Eisenhower's Illnesses. During his Presidency, Eisenhower suffered three serious illnesses: a heart attack, an intestinal obstruction, and a mild stroke. These illnesses made the public realize that, if the President were disabled, there was no Constitutional way to replace him. (This situation was remedied, in 1967, by the adoption of the Twenty-Fifth Amendment.)

EISENHOWER ADMINISTRATION:
IMPORTANT DOMESTIC LEGISLATION

Laws	Purposes
Civil Rights Acts (1957, 1960)	Protect voting rights of all Americans.
National Defense Education Act (1958)	Improve teaching of science, mathematics, and foreign languages.
Landrum-Griffin Labor-Management Act (1958)	Further democracy in labor unions and prevent union corruption.

b. Civil Rights. The Eisenhower years witnessed considerable activity in civil rights. In 1954 the Supreme Court outlawed segregation in public schools. In 1957 Eisenhower ordered army units to Little Rock, Arkansas, to prevent mob rule and enforce federal court orders for school integration. In 1957 and in 1960, Congress enacted civil rights laws.

c. Space Program. In 1957 Russia seized initial leadership in space by orbiting the world's first human-made satellite, *Sputnik I.* To speed up American efforts in space, Eisenhower secured from Congress (1) increased funds for space programs, (2) establishment of the *National Aeronautics and Space Administration* (NASA), and (3) the National Defense Education Act.

SIGNIFICANT FOREIGN AFFAIRS

1. Far East. *(a) Korea.* The Eisenhower administration concluded truce talks in 1953 ending the war in Korea and thereafter signed a mutual defense treaty with South Korea. *(b) Indochina.* The United States attended the 1954 Geneva Conference on Indochina, but did not sign the final agreements, which partitioned Vietnam. Thereafter, Eisenhower gave aid to the non-Communist regime of South Vietnam, and Secretary of State John Foster Dulles helped create the *Southeast Asia Treaty Organization* (SEATO).

2. Atoms for Peace. Eisenhower's plan for peaceful uses of atomic energy led to the creation of the *International Atomic Energy Agency.*

3. Middle East. *(a) Egypt.* Eisenhower opposed the 1956 invasion of Egypt by Israel, Britain, and France. Eisenhower's stand caused a sharp but temporary split with our traditional allies. *(b) Eisenhower Doctrine.* In 1957 Eisenhower offered any Middle Eastern nation economic aid, and, if threatened by Communist aggression, military aid. In 1958 Eisenhower sent American troops to help sustain the government of Lebanon.

4. Summit Conferences. Eisenhower met twice with the leaders of Britain, France, and Russia to seek to ease international tensions. The *Geneva Conference* of 1955 radiated cordiality but brought no concrete results. The *Paris*

Conference of 1960 collapsed when Soviet Premier Khrushchev made an issue of an unarmed American U-2 spy plane downed over the Soviet Union.

5. Cuba. In 1959 Eisenhower recognized the new Cuban regime of Fidel Castro. In January 1961, after Castro seized American property and harassed American officials, Eisenhower broke diplomatic relations.

KENNEDY ADMINISTRATION: 1961–1963 (DEMOCRATIC)— THE "NEW FRONTIER"

MAJOR POLITICAL AND ECONOMIC ASPECTS

1. Election of 1960. The Democratic convention gave a first-ballot nomination to Massachusetts Senator John F. Kennedy. He had actively sought the nomination and had proved his vote-getting ability by winning seven Presidential primaries. To strengthen the ticket in the South, Kennedy selected as his running mate Texas Senator *Lyndon B. Johnson*.

The Republican convention gave a first-ballot Presidential nomination to Vice President Richard M. Nixon. He had the overwhelming support of party workers and the endorsement of President Eisenhower. For the Vice Presidential nomination, Nixon decided upon the American Ambassador to the United Nations, *Henry Cabot Lodge*.

The election of 1960 introduced a new campaign technique. Kennedy and Nixon met in a series of four television encounters, popularly called "debates." Both candidates answered questions posed by panels of news correspondents, but the candidates did not cross-examine each other directly. The debates were viewed by an audience of over 80 million Americans.

Kennedy charged that, under the Eisenhower administration, the United States had suffered a decline in world power and prestige. Nixon answered that "American prestige is at an all-time high." The candidates also differed regarding ways to spur the nation's economic growth. Kennedy urged increased government action to "get the country moving again." Nixon called for economic growth through private enterprise and individual initiative.

John F. Kennedy won the election: Kennedy—34,227,000 popular votes and 303 electoral votes; Nixon—34,109,000 popular votes and 219 electoral votes. (Virginia Senator Harry Byrd received 15 electoral votes from unpledged southern electors.) Despite the narrow popular margin of Kennedy's victory, the Democrats retained substantial control over Congress.

2. Observations Upon the Election Results

(a) Kennedy became the first Roman Catholic and, at age 43, the youngest person ever to be elected President. *(b)* Kennedy's Roman Catholicism played a part in the election, although both candidates deplored religion as a campaign issue. Kennedy's religion probably helped him in the large industrial states, es-

pecially in the Northeast, where the Catholic population is large. His religion probably lost him votes in the small rural states, especially in the South and Midwest, where the Catholic population is small and anti-Catholic prejudice strong. *(c)* Kennedy won overwhelming support from minority groups and labor unions. These people believed that Kennedy's election would bring strong civil rights laws and government action to improve economic conditions. *(d)* Like Truman and Stevenson before him, Kennedy failed to hold the "Solid South" intact. The Democratic ticket lost Virginia, Tennessee, and Florida to the Republicans and also lost unpledged electors from Alabama and Mississippi. White Southerners who deserted the Democratic party did so chiefly because of Kennedy's stand on civil rights and his religion.

3. Kennedy: Background and Personality. John F. Kennedy was the great-grandson of an immigrant who had left Ireland during the potato famine of the 1840s. He was the son of Joseph Kennedy, a self-made millionaire who was active in Democratic politics and served under President Franklin Roosevelt as chairman of the Securities and Exchange Commission and as Ambassador to Britain. The elder Kennedy instilled in his children a strong sense of family loyalty, a competitive spirit, and an interest in public service. Young "Jack" Kennedy majored in political science at Harvard University and graduated with honors. During World War II he served in the navy. Returning to Massachusetts, Kennedy won election in 1946 to the House of Representatives, and in 1952 to the Senate.

Attractive and youthful-looking, Kennedy displayed dignity and self-assurance. Possessing a sense of history, Kennedy had written two books: *Why England Slept,* discussing Britain's appeasement of Nazi Germany, and *Profiles in Courage,* describing valiant deeds of American Senators. Kennedy adhered to the Roosevelt-Truman view that the President should exercise strong leadership.

4. Kennedy's Inaugural Address (1961). Kennedy reaffirmed America's determination to "pay any price, bear any burden, meet any hardship, support any friend, oppose any foe to assure the survival and the success of liberty." Speaking to "those nations who would make themselves our adversary," Kennedy asked "that both sides begin anew the quest for peace." Kennedy concluded with an appeal to his fellow Americans: "Ask not what your country can do for you—ask what you can do for your country."

5. "New Frontier"

a. Meaning. As the frontier of the 19th century had provided Americans with opportunity in the West, so the "new frontier" of the 1960s meant opportunity in the areas of technology, science, and social relations. To describe the program of his administration, Kennedy used the term *New Frontier.*

b. Accomplishments. Kennedy secured Congressional approval for the modernization of existing programs: expanding Social Security coverage and benefits, raising the minimum wage, furthering slum clearance and public housing, and lowering tariff barriers. Kennedy also won approval for some less con-

KENNEDY ADMINISTRATION: IMPORTANT DOMESTIC LEGISLATION

Laws	Purposes
Area Redevelopment Act (1961)	Help economically depressed areas.
Manpower Development and Training Act (1962)	Retrain destitute farmers and chronically unemployed workers.
Trade Expansion Act (1962)	Permit tariff reductions, in forthcoming trade negotiations.
Medical Education Act (1963)	Provide student loans; improve teaching facilities in medicine and related fields.
Mental Retardation and Health Centers Act (1963)	Provide funds for research and treatment of mental retardation.

troversial new measures: combating mental retardation, improving medical education, and assisting economically distressed areas and persons.

c. **Opposition in Congress.** On more controversial measures, Kennedy faced strong opposition from the conservative coalition of Republicans and southern Democrats. He did not secure legislation for (1) tax reduction, (2) federal aid to elementary and secondary education, (3) medical care for the aged under Social Security, and (4) voting rights and equal treatment for blacks in places of public accommodation. (During Johnson's administration, Congress enacted all these Kennedy proposals.)

6. Assassination of President Kennedy (November 1963)

a. **Tragic Events.** In Dallas, Texas, President Kennedy met death from a sniper's bullet. His suspected assassin, Lee Harvey Oswald, was quickly arrested by the police. Oswald, who had lived in the Soviet Union and who claimed membership in a pro-Castro group, denied the charge. Two days later, as Oswald was being moved to the county jail, he was shot and killed by a Dallas resident who had greatly admired the late President.

b. **The New President.** Within two hours after the assassination, Vice President Johnson was sworn in as President. Johnson moved quickly to express the nation's grief and to restore public determination to move "toward a new American greatness."

c. **Investigating Commission.** At President Johnson's request, Supreme Court Chief Justice Earl Warren headed a special commission to investigate the Kennedy assassination. After conducting a ten-month inquiry and evaluating the testimony of over 500 persons, the Warren Commission concluded that Oswald was the assassin and that he had acted alone.

SIGNIFICANT FOREIGN AFFAIRS

1. Peace Corps. President Kennedy created this agency to send skilled and idealistic Americans to assist underdeveloped nations.

2. Cuba. In 1961 Kennedy permitted American-trained Cuban exiles to invade Castro's Cuba at the *Bay of Pigs*. The invaders were crushed. In 1962 Kennedy ordered a naval quarantine of Cuba and secured from Soviet Premier Khrushchev the removal of offensive missiles from Cuba.

3. Alliance for Progress. Kennedy initiated this program of aid and reform to improve the living conditions of the masses of Latin America.

4. Limited Nuclear Test Ban Treaty. In 1963, after many years of negotiations, the United States, Great Britain, and Russia agreed to ban all but underground nuclear tests.

5. Vietnam. Kennedy stepped up military aid to the government of South Vietnam, which was battling Communist guerrillas, the *Vietcong*.

JOHNSON ADMINISTRATION: 1963–1969 (DEMOCRATIC)— THE "GREAT SOCIETY"

MAJOR POLITICAL AND ECONOMIC ASPECTS

1. Johnson: Background and Personality. The son of a Texas farmer, Lyndon B. Johnson attended Southwest Texas State Teachers College and worked to help pay his way through school. After teaching for a year, Johnson turned to politics. In 1937 Johnson won election to the House of Representatives. Johnson was the first member of Congress to enlist in World War II and served in the navy.

In 1948 Johnson won election to the Senate, and in 1953 he was chosen Senate Democratic Leader. As Senate majority leader during the last six years of the Eisenhower administration, Johnson cooperated with the executive branch in furthering legislation. In particular, he helped overcome southern opposition to the Civil Rights Acts of 1957 and 1960.

In 1960 Johnson made a bid for the Democratic Presidential nomination but lost to John F. Kennedy. Thereafter, Johnson accepted Kennedy's invitation to take second place on the ticket. As Vice President, Johnson assisted Kennedy in major governmental matters.

A determined yet sensitive man, Johnson desired public approval, but not at the price of abandoning his principles. Johnson excelled in working with people of divergent views and achieving satisfactory compromises. He often quoted the Biblical prophet Isaiah, "Come now, and let us reason together."

2. Johnson's Views

a. Strong President. Johnson believed in strong Presidential leadership, having admired Franklin D. Roosevelt as "one of the giants of all times." Johnson welcomed power and used it to further his goals for the public welfare. In dealing with Congress from 1964 to 1966, Johnson, in the words of one historian, "rang up a remarkable record" by a "furious display of coaxing, cajoling, compromising, and plain arm-twisting."

b. Desire for Consensus. A goal of political leadership, Johnson held, is to make the people aware of their "fundamental unity of interest, purpose, and belief." He asked his supporters and his opponents to remember that "there are so many more things in America that unite us than can divide us." Johnson sought broad national agreement, or *consensus*.

3. Election of 1964. The Democrats nominated Lyndon B. Johnson for President and Minnesota Senator *Hubert H. Humphrey* for Vice President. The Republicans nominated Arizona Senator Barry M. Goldwater for President. The Goldwater nomination was a victory for Republican conservatives over the party's previously dominant liberal wing. Goldwater received only lukewarm support, if any, from many liberal Republicans.

Goldwater claimed that he offered voters "a choice not an echo." He urged a tougher foreign policy toward the Communist world. He opposed the growth of federal power as threatening personal freedom and claimed that civil rights matters belonged to the states.

Johnson argued that his foreign policy, being tough but flexible, furthered world peace. He insisted that the expansion of federal power was essential to protect civil rights and to further the nation's liberty and progress.

The American people gave Johnson a landslide victory: Johnson—43 million popular votes, 44 states, and 486 electoral votes; Goldwater—27 million popular votes, 6 states, and 52 electoral votes.

4. Observations Upon the Election Results

(a) Johnson's popular vote—43 million, or 61 percent of the total—was greater than that polled by any previous Presidential candidate. *(b)* Johnson swept many other Democrats into House and Senate seats. The Democratic gains in the House were considered sufficient to break the power of the conservative Republican-southern Democrat coalition. *(c)* Goldwater polled some 7 million votes fewer than Nixon in 1960, indicating that many Republicans had deserted him.

5. "Great Society"

a. Meaning. Johnson asserted that humanity now possessed the capacity to end war, eradicate poverty and racial injustice, dispel ignorance, share abundance, overcome disease, revitalize cities, and, in general, permit people to enjoy a life of freedom and prosperity. To describe the goals of his administration, Johnson employed the term *Great Society*.

b. "Great Society" Congress (1965–1966). Controlled by huge Democratic majorities, the 89th Congress responded favorably to Johnson's requests for far-reaching legislation. According to some historians, this first Great Society Congress could be compared with great productive Congresses of the past: the first New Freedom Congress of the Woodrow Wilson administration and the first New Deal Congress under Franklin D. Roosevelt.

JOHNSON ADMINISTRATION:
IMPORTANT DOMESTIC LEGISLATION

LAWS	PURPOSES
Civil Rights Act (1964)	Prohibit discrimination in voting, employment, and places of public accommodation.
Economic Opportunity Act (1964)	Inaugurate programs for the "war on poverty."
Voting Rights Act (1965)	Strengthen previous voting rights laws.
"Medicare" Act (1965)	Provide medical care for the aged under Social Security.
Elementary and Secondary Education Act (1965)	Grant funds directly to public schools; provide instructional materials for public, parochial, and private school students.
Higher Education Act (1965)	Continue grants for college construction and student loans.
Appalachian Development Act (1965)	Aid the distressed Appalachian region.
Immigration Act (1965)	Admit immigrants on the basis of family relationships and national needs.
Clean Rivers Restoration Act (1966)	Provide funds for sewage treatment plants.
Truth in Packaging Act (1966)	Require accurate labeling of foods, drugs, and cosmetics.
Meat Inspection Act (1967)	Improve inspection of intrastate meat-processing plants.
Civil Rights Act (1968)	Ban racial discrimination in the sale and rental of most housing.
Truth in Lending Act (1968)	Require lenders to state the true cost of consumer credit.
Omnibus Crime Control Act (1968) and Gun Control Act (1968)	Grant funds to improve local law enforcement; ban interstate mail-order sales of handguns, shotguns, and rifles; prohibit their sale to minors.

c. Ninetieth Congress (1967–1968). As a result of the Congressional elections of 1966, the Democrats retained control of both houses of Congress but with significantly reduced majorities. The Democratic setback was attributed to a "white backlash" against strong civil rights legislation, protests against inflation, and uneasiness regarding the war in Vietnam.

SIGNIFICANT FOREIGN AFFAIRS

1. Dominican Republic (1965). Fearing that a Dominican civil war might lead to a Communist takeover, President Johnson intervened with American troops. Although Johnson's action was resented by many Latin Americans, it helped restore peace on the island and enabled the Dominican people to elect a pro-Western regime.

2. Vietnam. Johnson began air strikes against North Vietnam and sharply increased American forces in the South. He also launched "peace offensives" seeking negotiations. These were spurned by Hanoi.

Johnson's Vietnam policies faced criticism at home from "hawks," who demanded stepped-up military effort, and from "doves," who urged a reduction in military activity. Also, the cost of the Vietnam War retarded the programs of Johnson's Great Society. In 1968 Johnson again halted the bombing of North Vietnam, whereupon Hanoi agreed to peace negotiations.

NIXON ADMINISTRATION: 1969–1974 (REPUBLICAN)

MAJOR POLITICAL AND ECONOMIC ASPECTS

1. Election of 1968

a. The Candidates. The Republican convention gave a first-ballot nomination to *Richard M. Nixon.* A middle-of-the-roader, Nixon was acceptable to both liberal and conservative wings of the Republican party. To strengthen the ticket in the South, Nixon selected as his Vice Presidential running mate Maryland Governor *Spiro T. Agnew.*

The Democratic convention gave a first-ballot nomination to *Hubert H. Humphrey.* When President Johnson announced that he would not run again, Vice President Humphrey fell heir to the President's political support: labor unions, and city and state party organizations. For the nomination, Humphrey was opposed by Senators Eugene McCarthy of Minnesota and Robert F. Kennedy of New York, both outspoken critics of the Vietnam war, who clashed in five successive primaries. (Humphrey entered the race too late to run in any Presidential primaries.) Kennedy won all but one of these primaries, but, immediately after his victory in California, he was assassinated by an Arab immigrant from Jordan, presumably incensed by Kennedy's pro-Israel statements.

Humphrey's delegates controlled the convention. They nominated Humphrey and his Vice Presidential choice, Maine Senator *Edmund S. Muskie.*

George C. Wallace, former Governor of Alabama and advocate of segregation and states' rights, ran as a third-party candidate. In most states, his name was listed under the banner of the American Independent party.

b. The Campaign. Nixon blamed the Johnson-Humphrey administration for the Vietnam war, the high crime rate, and the urban riots. He urged the voters to elect "new men" with "new ideas." Humphrey asserted that the voters could "trust" him to lead the nation to peace and prosperity. Wallace urged a return to "law and order" by strengthening the power of the police to deal with crime and with student and black riots. Wallace also called for the repeal of federal laws on "open housing" and voting rights, and for the end of federal efforts to desegregate the public schools.

ELECTION RESULTS IN 1968

CANDIDATE	POPULAR VOTE		STATES WON	ELECTORAL VOTE
	IN NUMBER	IN PERCENT		
Nixon	31,770,000	43.4	32	301**
Humphrey	31,271,000	42.7	13*	191
Wallace	9,897,000	13.4	5	46

*Plus the District of Columbia.
**Although Nixon won the popular vote in North Carolina, one elector from that state voted for Wallace.

2. Observations Upon the 1968 Election Results

(a) Nixon won a close victory. Of 73 million popular votes cast, his lead over Humphrey was about 500,000. Nixon's percentage of the popular vote (43.4) was the smallest of any successful Presidential candidate since 1912, when Woodrow Wilson was elected, also in a three-way contest. *(b)* By winning an electoral majority, Nixon prevented the election from going into the House of Representatives, where the naming of the next President might have been subjected to political pressures and to delay. *(c)* Despite Nixon's victory, both branches of Congress remained strongly Democratic. *(d)* In what had once been the traditionally Democratic Solid South, Humphrey carried only Texas; Nixon and Wallace each won five states. *(e)* Wallace polled 9.9 million popular votes, the most ever received by a third-party candidate. However, Wallace's percentage of the popular vote (13.4) was smaller than that for Bull Moose candidate Theodore Roosevelt in 1912 (27.4) or Progressive candidate Robert La Follette in 1924 (16.6). Wallace polled half of his popular vote in the South. *(f)* Nixon inherited the problems that plagued the Johnson administration: the Vietnam war, the arms race, urban rehabilitation, and racial tensions. After his election, Nixon declared that the great objective of his administration would be national unity: "to bring America together."

3. Election of 1972. The Republican convention nominated President Richard M. Nixon and Vice President Spiro T. Agnew for a second term.

The Democratic convention gave a first-ballot nomination to South Dakota Senator *George McGovern.* He had headed the Democratic reform commission which had required convention delegations to give greater representation to women, blacks, young people, and ethnic minorities—groups whose active leaders favored McGovern. He went on to win delegates in ten primary contests and in many state conventions. A right-wing challenge to McGovern ended when a would-be assassin shot and paralyzed Alabama Governor George Wallace, thereby ending Wallace's campaign for the Democratic nomination. McGovern selected as his running mate *Sargent Shriver.* He had been first head of the *Peace Corps* and was related through his wife to the Kennedy family.

In gaining the nomination McGovern had alienated many labor leaders and state political bosses. In his campaign, McGovern's promises—of immediate peace in Vietnam, sharp cuts in military funds, and drastic social reforms—failed to gain him sufficient public support. Meanwhile, the Nixon team campaigned on the administration's record: in foreign affairs—withdrawal of 500,000 troops from Vietnam, the journeys to Peking and Moscow, and the SALT pacts limiting missile arsenals; in domestic matters—efforts to curtail inflation and opposition to busing pupils to achieve racial integration. Nixon's reelection chances seemingly were not hurt when Republican partisans were caught attempting to "bug" the Democratic headquarters in Washington at the Watergate apartments. (After the election, the *Watergate Affair* became a major issue of political corruption and morality involving leading Republican figures.)

Nixon won an overwhelming victory: Nixon—46 million popular votes, 49 states, with 521 electoral votes; McGovern—29 million popular votes, one state (Massachusetts) and the District of Columbia with 17 electoral votes. Nixon's victory, however, did not carry over into the Congressional elections and the Democrats retained substantial control of both houses of Congress.

4. Nixon: Background and Views

A native Californian, Nixon worked in the family gasoline station and grocery store while attending Whittier College. He majored in history and showed a talent for politics. At Duke University Law School he compiled an excellent record. During World War II, Nixon secured a naval commission, requested combat-zone duty, and was promoted to lieutenant commander. In 1946 Nixon was elected to the House of Representatives, where he became known as a member of the Un-American Activities Committee investigating Communist influence in the United States. In 1950 he won election to the Senate. In 1952 and again in 1956, he was running mate of Dwight D. Eisenhower. As Vice President, Nixon gained valuable executive experience. He represented the United States on trips to South America, and to Poland and the Soviet Union. During Eisenhower's illnesses, Nixon presided at meetings of the Cabinet and other executive agencies.

In 1960 Nixon was the Republican Presidential nominee but narrowly lost the election to Democrat John F. Kennedy. In 1964 he campaigned for the Republican Presidential candidate Barry M. Goldwater. Later Nixon worked to repair the liberal-conservative split that threatened Republican party unity, and in 1966 he campaigned for Republican candidates.

On the nature of the Presidency, Nixon quoted with approval the views of two strong Presidents: Theodore Roosevelt and Franklin D. Roosevelt. Nixon said that "the days of a passive Presidency belong to a simpler past." He affirmed that today the President "must take an activist view of his office. He must articulate the nation's values, define its goals, and marshal its will."

5. Major Domestic Events

a. Supreme Court Appointments. In his first term, Nixon appointed four members to the Supreme Court: as Chief Justice, Warren Burger; and as Associate Justices, Harry Blackmun, Lewis Powell, and William Rehnquist. In contrast with the previous Warren Court majority, which had been liberal and had interpreted the Constitution broadly, the four Nixon appointees were considered conservatives who favored a stricter interpretation of the Constitution and judicial self-restraint.

b. Revenue Sharing. In 1971 Nixon urged increased federal revenue sharing with the states, especially replacing many grants-in-aid earmarked for specific programs with funds not restricted as to use or limited only within broad categories. In this way, Nixon argued, the states would assume more responsibility in dealing with local problems. In 1972 Congress passed a *Revenue-Sharing Act* providing federal monies to be distributed over a five-year period, one-third to the states and two-thirds to the local governments.

c. Fight Against Inflation. The Nixon administration battled inflation by such traditional methods as reduced federal spending to decrease demand and higher interest rates to discourage borrowing and also by temporary wage and price controls—but all without success. The cost of living as measured by the Consumer Price Index (with the 1967 base year having an index of 100) rose from 108 in 1969 to 148 in 1973. Inflation remained serious and showed little sign of easing.

d. Energy Problems

(1) Background. The American people for years benefited from cheap and plentiful supplies of energy—coal, natural gas, and oil. Americans used energy for heating and cooking, generating electricity, producing agricultural and industrial goods, and powering transportation. With 6 percent of the world's population, we have consumed 30 percent of the energy used by the people of the world. By the early 1970s, experts warned Americans that the nation was consuming far more energy than it was producing and was heading into an energy crisis. Specifically regarding oil, the United States then daily imported 6 million barrels—of which over a million barrels came from Arab sources.

(2) Arab Oil Embargo. In late 1973 with the outbreak of the fourth Arab-Israeli war, the oil-rich Arab states, working through OPEC, raised oil prices substantially and totally embargoed oil shipments to the United States. In early 1974 the Arabs ended their oil embargo against the United States. The Arab states thusly made the American people realize that the United States was dependent upon foreign energy sources and faced a serious energy crisis.

(3) Nixon's Energy Plans. In response to the energy crisis, President Nixon recommended both immediate and long-range programs. Immediately, to overcome the oil shortage caused by the Arab embargo, the President urged the American people to lower house heating thermostats, to limit automobile speeds to 50 miles per hour, and to form more car pools. For the long range, the President urged a variety of actions: construct more electric power plants using coal and nuclear fuel; build the Alaska pipeline to make available oil from Alaska's North Slope; explore for more American natural gas and oil supplies, especially by drilling in *offshore* areas; encourage the surface or *strip-mining* of the tremendous coal reserves in our western states; and pursue methods of tapping solar energy, extracting shale oil, and converting coal into natural gas and oil.

e. *The Resignation of Agnew as Vice President.* Under investigation for alleged kickbacks, fraud, and income tax evasion while Baltimore County Executive and Maryland Governor, Spiro Agnew in late 1973 pleaded "no contest" to the tax evasion charge and resigned as Vice President of the United States. Sentenced to three years' probation and a fine, Agnew was the first Vice President in American history to be forced from office because of criminal charges.

Acting under the Twenty-Fifth Amendment, President Nixon nominated his choice for Vice President—the Republican minority leader in the House of Representatives, Gerald R. Ford. Overwhelmingly approved by Congress, Ford in December 1973 took the oath of office as Vice President.

f. *Watergate and the Nixon Resignation*

(1) Background. Overshadowing President Nixon's second term was *Watergate*—a word that carried two meanings. *(a)* In general, Watergate meant the series of political scandals affecting the Nixon administration. The *Committee to Reelect the President* had accepted secret and illegal contributions from corporations and dairy cooperatives that could benefit from administration favors. White House officials had sought to use the Internal Revenue Service to harass administration "enemies." President Nixon had donated his Vice Presidential papers to the National Archives, but the donation was illegally backdated so as to provide a substantial tax deduction—later disallowed. *(b)* Specifically, Watergate meant the 1972 break-in at Democratic national headquarters in Washington at the Watergate Apartments to steal documents and "bug" the offices, and the subsequent efforts to hide involvement of top administration officials by a cover-up. Caught in the break-in, the Republican partisans were arrested and brought to trial.

(2) Highlights. For almost two years Watergate dominated the news and revealed a complicated, often confusing sequence of political intrigue.

a. Investigations. Two newspapers, the *Washington Post* and *The New York Times,* pursued investigations of Watergate. They publicized their findings, voiced their suspicions—especially regarding the President's role—and sustained public concern. The Senate established a bipartisan *Committee on Presidential Campaign Activities.* The committee held hearings, called witnesses, and uncovered further evidence damaging to the administration. A *special prosecutor* named by the attorney general investigated the Watergate affair and brought criminal charges against a number of administration officials, most of whom had already resigned from office.

b. Court Actions. Defendants charged with Watergate offenses or Watergate-related offenses were tried in various federal courts in Washington and New York. Some defendants pleaded guilty and offered to provide evidence for the prosecution in the hope of receiving lighter sentences. Other defendants received jury trials. Some 30 persons, charged with various Watergate offenses—including burglary, obstructing justice, fraud, and lying to a grand jury—were found guilty and given jail sentences. Those defendants involved specifically with the Watergate break-in and cover-up were tried in the Federal District Court for Washington, D.C., under Judge *John Sirica.*

c. The Tapes. The existence of tapes, ordered by President Nixon of all White House conversations, was revealed by a witness before the Senate Investigating Committee. Thereafter the Senate committee and the special Watergate prosecutor both requested the President to provide them with specific tapes relevant to their investigations. With great reluctance, the President yielded some tapes and provided edited transcripts of 42 others. The evidence so made available, although not conclusive, was damaging to the President, who had claimed no knowledge of the Watergate break-in before it occurred and no knowledge of the cover-up until nine months later. The tapes, according to leading Republicans in Congress, portrayed "shabby, immoral performances" by the administration.

Soon afterward special prosecutor *Leon Jaworski* requested additional Watergate-related tapes, but President Nixon refused the request. The President based his refusal on the doctrine of *executive privilege.* Under this doctrine, which is not stated in the Constitution but is implied by the system of separation of powers, Nixon claimed the right to maintain the confidentiality of Presidential records and to defend executive power against encroachment. Opposing Nixon's claim to executive privilege, Jaworski secured from District Court Judge Sirica a subpoena, or court order, directing Nixon to yield the tapes. The President appealed this subpoena, eventually to the Supreme Court.

In July 1974 the Supreme Court in an 8-to-0 decision ordered the President to surrender the tapes. In his decision, Chief Justice Warren Burger stated that the doctrine of executive privilege exists not as an absolute but as a relative right, and therefore that in this case executive privilege must yield to the need for evidence in Watergate trials. Although expressing disappointment, President Nixon agreed to obey the Supreme Court decision.

d. The Impeachment Proceedings. Meanwhile, the bipartisan *House Judiciary Committee* had been holding hearings to consider possible impeachment charges against the President. With a considerable number of Republicans joining the Democrats, the committee approved two Articles of Impeachment: the first dealt with Nixon's role in the Watergate cover-up, the second with Nixon's abuse of Presidential powers for personal purposes. While the committee was so acting, Nixon complied with the Supreme Court order by turning over the subpoenaed tapes, one of which revealed that he had halted an FBI investigation of the Watergate break-in immediately after it had occurred. Since Nixon had previously denied knowledge of the Watergate cover-up for nine months, this revelation destroyed Nixon's credibility with most Americans and eroded his support in the Congress. The President was advised, by Republican leaders, that the House of Representatives would overwhelmingly approve the impeachment charges and that the Senate would sustain them by far more than the necessary two-thirds vote.

e. The Resignation. On August 9, 1974, Richard M. Nixon resigned—the first President in American history to do so. In a televised speech to the American people, Nixon admitted that some of his judgments had been wrong, insisted that at all times he had been concerned with the best interests of the nation, explained that he was resigning because he no longer had a "strong enough political base in Congress," and expressed the hope that his resignation would begin the desperately needed process of "healing the wounds of this nation." Nixon's successor, Gerald Ford, upon being sworn in as President, called upon the nation to "bind up the internal wounds of Watergate" and asserted that "our long national nightmare is over."

(3) Significances. Watergate undoubtedly had both bad and good effects. The bad effects included public cynicism toward politicians individually and the political system generally (only 38 percent of the voting-age population went to the polls in the 1974 elections, the lowest voter turn-out in almost 30 years); endangering the ability of the Republican party to function effectively; and a blot on the American political record comparable to the Teapot Dome scandal of the Harding administration and to the various corruptions that marred the Grant administration.

Most observers, however, preferred to stress that Watergate, although a shameful episode, had good effects, especially in proving the strength and competence of our democratic institutions:

a. *Freedom of the press worked.* Protected by the First Amendment, newspapers opposed to the administration were able to focus and sustain public attention upon Watergate scandals.

b. *The two-party system worked.* The Democrats in control of Congress functioned effectively and reasonably in opposition to the Republican administration.

c. *Checks and balances worked.* The Congress was able to check the executive by investigating the actions of top administrative officials. The House was able to check the President by instituting impeachment proceedings. The Supreme Court was able to check the President by deciding that the Presidential claim of executive privilege to withhold tapes was in this case not valid.

d. *Government by law worked.* Ours is a government of laws, not of persons. The laws must be enforced, fairly and impartially, regardless of the individuals involved. No one, not even the President of the United States, is above the law.

e. *The powers of the Presidency were weakened and the powers of Congress were strengthened.* During this century the trend has been for the President to exercise greatly increased powers. This trend has been deplored, by some observers, as leading the nation to an all-powerful or "imperial Presidency." The trend was reversed, at least temporarily, by Watergate. The powers of the President were sharply curbed as Congress reasserted its authority, not only by investigations and impeachment proceedings but also by the following legislative actions: The *Budget Reform Act* gave Congress a larger voice in the budget-making process. The *War-Powers Resolution,* passed over Nixon's veto, required the President to secure Congressional approval for any extended combat service by American troops abroad. An appropriations bill provision cut off funds so as to compel Nixon to halt American bombing raids in Cambodia.

f. *Public esteem of Congress rose.* Americans by the millions viewed the televised hearings of the Senate Committee on Presidential campaign activities and the House Judiciary Committee. They were impressed by their members of Congress—serious, concerned, and working hard to resolve complicated issues. Americans gained a greater understanding of the operation of Congress and the complexities of government.

g. A reform era began. Almost all states passed campaign reform laws, as did Congress for federal elections. In general these laws set limits on campaign contributions so as to reduce the influence of wealthy donors on candidates for office. Some candidates themselves revealed their net worth and accepted only small campaign donations.

h. Our democratic system worked. Faced by the Watergate crisis, the Constitutional procedures inscribed almost 200 years earlier proved resilient. They provided the methods and agencies to investigate the scandals, to punish the

NIXON ADMINISTRATION: IMPORTANT DOMESTIC LEGISLATION

LAWS	PURPOSES
Coal Mine Health and Safety Act (1969)	Reduce coal mine hazards; provide benefits for disabled miners.
Air Quality Standards Act (1970)	Produce a 90 percent pollution-free auto engine.
Organized Crime Control Act (1970)	Increase federal powers over interstate gambling and organized crime; make bombings a federal offense.
Voting Rights Act (1970)	Set voting age at 18 for all elections. (Supreme Court disallowed this provision for state and local elections, making necessary the Twenty-Sixth Amendment.)
National Cancer Act (1971)	Allot funds to expand cancer research.
Social Security Act (1972)	Raise Social Security taxes; increase benefits; provide for future cost of living benefits tied to Consumer Price Index.
Product Safety Act (1972)	Create a commission to enforce safety standards for many household items.
Revenue-Sharing Act (1972)	Distribute federal funds to state and local governments for use as they see fit.
Water Pollution Act (1972)	Clean up rivers and lakes by providing federal funds to state and local governments mainly for sewage plants.
Agricultural Act (1973)	Provide direct cash subsidies to farmers if "target prices" of basic crops fall below market prices.
Alaska Pipeline Act (1973)	Construct Alaska oil pipeline; bar environmental suits opposing the pipeline.
War-Powers Resolution (1973)	Require the President to secure Congressional approval for any extended combat use of American forces abroad.
Budget Reform Act (1974)	Enlarge role of Congress in determining the federal budget.

wrongdoers, to compel a President to resign, and to effect a smooth transition of executive power to a new President. Upon taking the Presidential oath, Gerald Ford noted the strength of our political democracy by saying, "Our Constitution works. Here the people rule."

SIGNIFICANT FOREIGN AFFAIRS

1. Vietnam. President Nixon sought a negotiated peace that would preserve American honor and vital interests. Nixon had his national security adviser, *Henry Kissinger,* undertake secret talks with the North Vietnamese. In 1973 Kissinger and the Hanoi negotiator reached a detailed truce agreement. Nixon thus brought to an end a long and costly war that had deeply divided the American people.

2. Congress and Foreign Affairs. With Nixon under attack because of Watergate, Congress reasserted its authority over foreign affairs:

   a. Cambodian (Khmer) Bombing Cutoff. Not included in the Vietnam agreement, Cambodia remained a battleground between anti-Communist government forces and Communist troops. To support the Cambodian government, Nixon maintained American bombing raids against Communist forces, and many Congress members feared further American military involvement. Using its power to withhold funds, Congress compelled Nixon to accept an August 1973 cutoff of all bombing in Cambodia.

   b. War-Powers Resolution of 1973. In ordering American forces into combat in Vietnam, three successive Presidents—Kennedy, Johnson, and Nixon—had used the Presidential power of commander in chief but had not secured a Congressional declaration of war. In 1973 Congress limited Presidential war-making powers by enacting, over President Nixon's veto, the *War-Powers Resolution.*

3. Asian Policy. Speaking at Guam in 1969, the President told our Asian friends that the United States would keep its treaty commitments and would provide economic and military assistance, but that we would look to the nation directly threatened, except for a nuclear threat, to provide the personnel for its own defense—a statement called the *Nixon Doctrine.*

4. Middle East. President Nixon pledged continued American support for Israel and its right to exist. In the 1973 Arab-Israeli War, Nixon resupplied the Israelis with essential military equipment. Nixon also bettered American relations with moderate Arabs as he urged a just Mideast peace and Secretary of State Henry Kissinger negotiated troop disengagement agreements for the Israeli-Egyptian and Israeli-Syrian fronts.

5. Détente With Russia. In 1969 President Nixon declared that Soviet-American relations were ready to move from the confrontation of the cold war era to negotiation in a new era of *détente* (check the Index). Nixon's declaration was viewed favorably by the Soviet Communist party head Brezhnev.

6. Arms Limitations. The Nixon administration began negotiations with the Soviets in the *Strategic Arms Limitation Talks (SALT).* In 1972 in Moscow, President Nixon signed two SALT I pacts limiting missile arsenals.

7. Improved Relations With Communist China. President Nixon ended over two decades of isolation between the United States and China. In 1972 Nixon visited China, a trip he called a "journey for peace."

FORD ADMINISTRATION: 1974–1977 (REPUBLICAN)

MAJOR POLITICAL AND ECONOMIC ASPECTS

1. Ford Takes Office (August 9, 1974). Immediately upon Nixon's resignation, Vice President Gerald R. Ford was sworn in as President. Ford delivered a brief and simple Inaugural Address. Since he had become Vice President by provisions of the Twenty-Fifth Amendment and President by resignation of his predecessor, Ford remarked, "I am acutely aware that you have not elected me as your President by your ballots. So I ask you to confirm me as your President with your prayers."

2. Ford: Background and Views. In 1935 Gerald R. Ford graduated from the University of Michigan, where he had starred as a football player. In 1941, after alternately working as a sports coach and attending school, he secured his law degree from Yale. During World War II he enlisted in the Navy, rising to the rank of lieutenant commander. In 1948 he won election from Michigan to the House of Representatives, the first of 13 successive victories. In Congress Ford earned a reputation as fair, trustworthy, sensible, and hard-working. Although Ford took partisan stands on issues, his manner was such that he enjoyed great popularity. In 1965 his fellow Republicans elected Ford as House minority leader.

Ford described his political outlook in these words: "I would say I am a moderate on domestic issues, a conservative in fiscal affairs and a dyed-in-the-wool internationalist in foreign affairs."

3. Ford's Initial Moves

a. Rockefeller for Vice President. With the Vice Presidential office again vacant, Ford acted quickly, under the Twenty-Fifth Amendment, to nominate his choice—oil millionaire and former New York State Governor Nelson Rockefeller. Congress overwhelmingly approved the nomination.

b. Unconditional Pardon for Nixon. President Ford granted Richard Nixon an unconditional pardon for all federal offenses which he "committed or may have committed or taken part in" while President. In accepting the pardon, Nixon expressed regret for "my mistakes over Watergate" and the anguish caused the nation but made no admission of any illegal acts. The Ford pardon of

Nixon aroused much criticism and led to a House of Representatives inquiry. Ford agreed to testify before the House panel—the first time on record that an American President submitted to questioning before a Congressional body. Ford stressed the following: "there was no deal"; Nixon had been sufficiently punished; Nixon's acceptance of the pardon was in effect an admission of guilt; and Ford's motive in granting the pardon was "to shift our attentions from the pursuit of a fallen President to the pursuit of the urgent needs of a rising nation."

4. Economic Matters

a. The 1973–1975 "Inflationary Recession." President Ford faced the problem of dealing with this recession—until then the longest and most severe of the post-World War II years. Whereas recessions generally bring falling prices, this recession was complicated by sharply rising prices and strong inflation. It presented unusual problems of an "inflationary recession."

b. Disagreement Over Remedies. President Ford, a Republican, held that the best way to improve the economy was to curtail inflation. To this end he sought to limit government services and hold down federal spending. Congress, heavily Democratic, wanted to stimulate the economy and reduce unemployment by increased government spending. Congress voted increased funds for government services and public-sector jobs. Ford consistently vetoed such bills. In his two years in office, Ford used the veto—on economic and other bills—a total of 66 times and was overridden 12 times.

In 1975 the United States emerged from its sixth postwar recession.

IMPORTANT DOMESTIC LEGISLATION

1. Public Education Act (1974). This act continued federal funding for public elementary and secondary schools; restricted busing for integration to no farther than the school next closest to the child's home.

2. Campaign Reform Act (1974). This act provided substantial federal funding of Presidential campaigns; established a federal Elections Commission; limited contributions by wealthy individuals.

3. "Government in Sunshine" Act (1976). This act required some 50 government agencies to operate "in sunshine" by conducting their activities in full view of the press and the public.

4. Other Legislation. (a) Provided federal funds to states and cities to meet urban mass-transit needs, (b) provided federal loans to New York City to help stave off municipal bankruptcy, (c) extended to 1982 the voting rights protection of the 1965 law, (d) continued federal revenue sharing, and (e) extended American jurisdiction over fishing in waters up to 200 miles offshore.

OTHER DEVELOPMENTS

1. No Comprehensive Energy Program. President Ford proposed removing all price controls on oil and natural gas, thereby raising prices, curtailing consumption, and spurring the search for new domestic oil and gas fields. Opposed to the President's plans, Congress favored maintaining price controls to protect consumers. The President and Congress did not provide any comprehensive program to deal with our energy crisis.

2. Investigations of Intelligence Agencies. Select committees of the House and the Senate conducted thorough investigations of America's two major intelligence agencies, the CIA and the FBI. While reporting that the agencies in the main performed responsibly, the investigations focused attention upon agency abuses and errors in judgment. The CIA kept American citizens under surveillance (although specifically prohibited by law) and engaged in assassination plots abroad. Both the CIA and the FBI illegally opened mail, monitored telegrams, maintained wiretaps, conducted break-ins, and investigated dissidents and civil rights groups.

As a result of these investigations, both the CIA and the FBI undertook major reorganizations to eliminate illegal activities. Also, President Ford issued an executive order to curb abuses by restricting the surveillance of American citizens and otherwise limiting the intelligence agencies' domestic activities, by clarifying the responsibility of each agency, and by establishing a Civilian Oversight Board to check on these agencies.

Most Americans felt that strong but legally acting intelligence agencies were essential for the national security.

SIGNIFICANT FOREIGN AFFAIRS

1. Vietnam. In 1975 Hanoi, in violation of the Paris truce agreement, mounted a massive offensive and gained control of South Vietnam. President Ford made no move to return American forces to Vietnam, secured funds from Congress to assist some Vietnamese refugees to come to the United States, and proclaimed that America would remain strong.

2. Angola. Becoming aware that the Ford administration was sending covert aid to pro-Western forces in the Angolan civil war, Congress prohibited such aid by enacting the *Clark Amendment*.

CARTER ADMINISTRATION: 1977–1981 (DEMOCRATIC)

MAJOR POLITICAL AND ECONOMIC ASPECTS

1. Election of 1976. The Democratic convention gave a first-ballot nomination for the Presidency to former Georgia Governor James Earl (Jimmy) Carter. For over a year Carter had entered many Presidential primaries and amassed sufficient delegates to assure his nomination. Carter selected as his running mate for the Vice Presidency liberal Minnesota Senator *Walter Frederick (Fritz) Mondale.*

ELECTION RESULTS IN 1976

CANDIDATE	POPULAR VOTE		STATES WON	ELECTORAL VOTE
	IN NUMBER	IN PERCENT		
Carter	40,300,000	51	23*	297
Ford	38,600,000	49	27	241

*Plus the District of Columbia.

The Republican convention gave a first-ballot nomination to President Gerald Ford. The President had narrowly withstood a powerful challenge by former California Governor *Ronald Reagan*—the idol of conservative Republicans. To restore party harmony, Ford named as his running mate for the Vice Presidency conservative Kansas Senator *Robert Dole*.

In the election campaign, Ford stressed his Presidential record: restoring public confidence in the integrity of the government, keeping America at peace, curtailing inflation, and leading the nation out of a recession. Carter stressed that "it was time for a change" and that he represented a "fresh face"—not part of the Washington establishment—who would curtail bureaucracy and improve government operations. Ford and Carter met in three television debates, viewed by 90 million people, in which the candidates responded to questions posed by a panel of experts.

2. Observations on the 1976 Election Results

(a) Carter won a very narrow victory, carrying the South and most industrial states of the Northeast and Midwest. In several large industrial states, the vote was so close that a small shift in the popular tally would have changed those states' electoral results. *(b)* Despite Carter's narrow victory, the Democrats retained overwhelming control of both branches of Congress. *(c)* Carter was the first candidate from the Deep South to be elected President since the 1848 election of Zachary Taylor. Observers interpreted Carter's victory to mean that the American people had overcome prejudices arising out of the Civil War and reconstruction. *(d)* Carter's victory was significantly helped by the 1974 Federal Campaign Reform Act. It provided Carter—being relatively unknown nationally and having limited financial support—with federal funds to contest the Presidential primaries. In the general election, the law kept the campaign spending by the two major parties more or less equal; in previous elections, the Republicans usually had a financial advantage. *(e)* Out of 150 million eligible American voters, about 80 million voted in the 1976 election. Although this was a record number, in percent it was the lowest turnout since the 1948 election. Why, political observers asked, did so many people fail to vote? Some possible answers were mistrust of government arising out of the Watergate scandals, cynicism regarding candidates and their preelection promises, general apathy, and doubts about the ability of government to significantly improve our society.

3. Carter: Background and Views. A sixth-generation Georgian, Carter studied at the Georgia Institute of Technology and then at the United States Naval Academy. Carter graduated in 1946 and pursued a career in the Navy's nuclear submarine service. Upon the death of his father in 1953, Carter left the Navy and returned to Georgia to manage the family agribusiness. He became interested in Georgia politics, winning election to the state senate and in 1970 becoming governor. Limited to one term as governor by the Georgia constitution, Carter then turned his energies toward achieving the Presidency.

Carter saw himself as an "activist" President, seeking excellence in behalf of the nation. In his Inaugural Address, Carter set a moral tone, saying "our commitment to human rights must be absolute, our laws fair, our natural beauty preserved; the powerful must not persecute the weak, and human dignity must be enhanced."

4. The Nation's Economic Difficulties. The Carter administration faced complex economic problems, most of long standing: unemployment at the 7 percent level, mounting inflation, high interest rates, an unfavorable balance of trade, declining value of the dollar in relationship to Japanese and most West European currencies, decrease in labor productivity, and fear of a new recession. The administration's ability to deal with these problems was complicated by the prevailing national mood. Many citizens were skeptical regarding the ability of the federal government to remedy economic problems. Many citizens also resented their heavy tax load and demanded lower and fewer taxes. (This taxpayer revolt was highlighted in California. There voters easily approved *Proposition 13,* which sharply reduced property taxes even though it might mean a decrease in local and state government services.) By 1980, the nation's economic problems had worsened.

5. Relations Between the Administration and Congress. President Carter had difficulty getting his legislative programs through Congress even though he and the majority in Congress were Democrats. Carter took office while Congress was still asserting its own authority against the executive—a process that began as an aftermath of the Watergate scandals. Carter also was an "outsider" to Washington and inexperienced in dealing with Congress. Carter requested Congress to act quickly on many complex and controversial issues. Congress, however, preferred to move slowly and to tailor its lawmaking to what it perceived as the national consensus.

IMPORTANT DOMESTIC LEGISLATION

1. Social Security Act (1977). This act raised the tax rate and maximum salary base so as to insure the solvency of the Social Security system by increasing its income.

2. Minimum Wage Act (1977). This act raised the minimum wage, in four steps, to $3.35 by 1981.

3. Strip Mining of Coal Act (1977). This act permitted most strip mining of coal, provided the land was restored to good environmental condition.

4. Civil Service Reform Act (1978). This act improved efficiency of civil service workers and eased regulations for discharge of incompetent ones.

5. Comprehensive Energy Act (1978). This act permitted the price of newly discovered natural gas to rise slowly until controls were removed in 1985; encouraged homeowners to save energy by insulating their homes; taxed gas-guzzling cars beginning with 1980 models; encouraged industry to expand its use of coal.

6. Further Energy Measures (1980). Congress sought to spur production of synthetic fuels by establishing a government agency—the *Synthetic Fuels Corporation;* it placed a windfall-profits tax on domestic oil companies.

7. Refugee Act (1980). This act broadened the definition of refugees; it permitted additional refugees to enter the United States.

8. Waste Cleanup Act (1980). This act provided for the cleanup of chemical waste sites.

9. Other Legislation. *(a)* Prohibited American companies from participating in the Arab trade boycott against Israel, *(b)* raised the mandatory retirement age for most workers in private industry from 65 to 70, *(c)* allowed the proposed Equal Rights Amendment an additional 39 months to secure the necessary 38 state ratifications, *(d)* provided loan guarantees to aid the Chrysler Corporation to avoid bankruptcy, *(e)* created two Cabinet-level departments—of energy and of education, *(f)* provided partial deregulation for the banking, trucking, and railroad industries, *(g)* strengthened safety standards for nuclear power plants, *(h)* with few exceptions, denied federal funds for abortions, and *(i)* endorsed President Carter's call for a worldwide boycott of the 1980 summer Olympic Games at Moscow to protest the Soviet invasion of Afghanistan.

SIGNIFICANT FOREIGN AFFAIRS

1. Human Rights. President Carter launched a human rights campaign, explaining that since all UN members were pledged to respect human rights, their treatment of political prisoners and dissidents was a matter of international concern. Carter's emphasis on human rights was resented by the Soviet Union, by several East European Communist nations, and by a number of Third World dictatorships. Thereafter, President Carter toned down his human rights campaign, although he claimed that it had improved conditions in several nations.

2. Repeal of Arms Embargo Against Turkey. President Carter secured Congressional approval to lift the arms embargo against Turkey. The President hoped that this move would strengthen the NATO alliance.

3. Panama Canal Treaties. President Carter secured narrow Senate ratification of these treaties providing for the transfer of ownership and management of the canal to Panama by the year 2000.

4. Camp David Summit Meeting. President Carter acted as host and mediator at this 1978 meeting of President Sadat of Egypt and Prime Minister Begin of Israel. The meeting resulted in two agreements that President Carter hailed as a major step toward peace in the Mideast.

5. Diplomatic Recognition to China. President Carter in 1979 extended full diplomatic recognition to Communist China and ended diplomatic and military (but not economic) ties with Nationalist China on Taiwan.

6. Soviet Invasion of Afghanistan. President Carter condemned the Soviet invasion of Afghanistan in 1979 and took various economic and political steps to make the Soviets "pay a concrete price for their aggression." One step was a request to the Senate to delay consideration of the SALT II Treaty.

7. Carter Doctrine. President Carter warned the Soviet Union in 1980 that any attempt to gain control of the Persian Gulf region, with its important oil resources, "will be regarded as an assault on the vital interest of the United States" and "will be repelled by any means necessary, including military force." This statement regarding the Persian Gulf region became known as the *Carter Doctrine.*

8. American Hostages in Iran. President Carter condemned Iran for holding some 50 American diplomatic personnel as hostages and, to secure their release, exerted various political and economic pressures against Iran. In 1981 the hostages were released just as Carter left office as President.

REAGAN ADMINISTRATION: 1981– (REPUBLICAN)

MAJOR POLITICAL AND ECONOMIC ASPECTS

1. Election of 1980. President Carter withstood a belated challenge to his renomination by Massachusetts Senator Edward (Teddy) Kennedy. The President secured an easy first-ballot renomination at the Democratic convention; also renominated was his running mate, Walter Mondale.

Former California Governor Ronald Reagan won numerous Republican primaries and gained an easy first-ballot nomination at the Republican convention. As his running mate, Reagan named the former CIA director and UN Ambassador *George Bush.*

John Anderson, a Republican member of Congress from Illinois, who had sought the Republican nomination but realized that he would not secure it, announced that he would run for the Presidency as an independent.

ELECTION RESULTS IN 1980

CANDIDATE	POPULAR VOTE		STATES WON	ELECTORAL VOTE
	IN NUMBER	IN PERCENT		
Reagan	43,900,000	51+	44	489
Carter	35,500,000	41+	6*	49
Anderson	5,700,000	7	0	0

*Plus the District of Columbia.

In the election campaign, Carter emphasized that he had maintained peace, was experienced, and represented the liberal traditions of the Democratic party; also he portrayed Reagan as a "dangerous" leader. Reagan blamed Carter for the nation's economic woes—double-digit inflation, heavy unemployment, high interest rates—and for America's "humiliation" over the hostages held in Iran. Portraying Carter as a "weak" leader, naive about Soviet intentions, Reagan called upon the voters to choose strong, conservative leadership.

2. Observations on the 1980 Election Results

(a) Although pollsters had predicted a close election, Reagan won an easy victory in the popular vote and a landslide electoral vote. Reagan's victory indicated that he benefited from a crossover by many traditional Democratic voters— union members, ethnic and religious minorities, Southerners, and urban dwellers. (b) Reagan's victory helped the Republicans gain control of the Senate for the first time in 26 years. A number of conservative Republicans defeated liberal Democratic Senators. In the House of Representatives, the Republicans gained 35 seats so that—although the Democrats remained in control—a possible coalition of Republicans and conservative Democrats could dominate the House. (c) John Anderson, as an independent, polled 7 percent of the popular vote, but his candidacy did not affect the outcome of the election. (d) Carter's defeat marked the first time since the defeat of Herbert Hoover in 1932 that an elected incumbent President had lost the bid for reelection.

3. Election of 1984.
The Republicans confidently nominated Reagan and Bush for a second term.

The Democrats selected as their Presidential candidate Walter Mondale, the Vice President of the Carter administration. To dramatize his candidacy and to attract voters, Mondale chose as his running mate a woman, a Representative from Queens, New York, *Geraldine Ferraro*. She was the first woman ever to be named on the national ticket of a major party.

Reagan and Mondale met in two television debates, responding to questions posed by a group of panelists. In the election, Reagan had many advantages— especially a prosperous economy. While Mondale carried only the District of Co-

ELECTION RESULTS IN 1984

| CANDIDATE | POPULAR VOTE | | STATES WON | ELECTORAL VOTE |
	IN NUMBER	IN PERCENT		
Reagan	52,610,000	59	49	525
Mondale	36,451,000	41	1	13

lumbia and his home state of Minnesota for 13 electoral votes, Reagan won a landslide victory with 49 states and 525 electoral votes.

4. Reagan: Background and Personality. Born into a poor family, Ronald Reagan grew up in Illinois in a small-town environment. He attended Eureka College in Illinois, supported by a partial scholarship and by money he earned from working. He majored in economics, won letters in three major sports, acted in school plays, and served as president of the student body. After graduation in 1932, Reagan worked as a radio sportscaster, then as a Hollywood film star—making some 50 pictures over 30 years—and also as a host for television programs. While in Hollywood, Reagan several times headed the film actors union—the Screen Actors Guild.

Reagan's increasingly conservative views led him in the 1960s to an active role in the Republican party. He soon displayed great skill as a campaign orator. In 1966 Reagan was elected to his first public office—governor of California—and four years later won reelection. As governor, Reagan was viewed as an efficient executive who chose capable assistants and delegated authority, and who achieved compromises with Democratic state legislators.

In 1980 Reagan secured the Republican nomination and was elected President, becoming at age 69 the oldest person ever elected to that office. In his Inaugural Address, Reagan called upon Americans to "begin an era of national renewal," for, he said, "we are too great a nation to limit ourselves to small dreams."

According to observers, Reagan is a decent, sincere, and honorable person, with a friendly manner and easy charm, who is pragmatic and flexible. When in the third month of his term, Reagan was wounded in the left lung by a bullet fired by a would-be assassin, Reagan demonstrated courage—walking into the hospital despite his pain and loss of blood—and a sense of humor—quipping to his wife, Nancy, "Honey, I forgot to duck." Reagan recovered rapidly and soon resumed his full Presidential duties.

In July 1985 President Reagan underwent surgery for the removal of a cancerous growth. His doctors assured the public that his chances of recovery were excellent. What effect would Reagan's surgery and recovery have upon the remainder of his term in office?

5. Reagan's Views. In domestic matters, Reagan's views marked a 180-degree turn away from governmental policies begun by F. D. Roosevelt's New

Deal and embodied in Harry Truman's Fair Deal and Lyndon Johnson's Great Society. Reagan held that the federal government had become too large and too involved in business matters and in the daily lives of individuals. It was time, Reagan said, to get the government "off our backs," and to release the productive initiatives of American business leaders and citizens. He therefore favored sharply curtailing federal regulations and transferring power to state and local units of government. Reagan believed in *supply-side economics*—the theory that our economy could be improved by increasing the supply of goods and services. He therefore supported tax cuts that would give incentives to businesses to produce more and to individuals to provide more funds for investment. Also, he advocated a balanced budget.

In foreign affairs, Reagan held the Soviet Union to be the major threat to American security and world peace. He therefore urged increased military spending to improve our national defenses and enable the United States to negotiate with the Soviets from a position of strength.

As for his task as President, Reagan believed, according to observers, that he should set policy, make the big decisions, and act vigorously to secure public and Congressional support—but that the follow-up details and problems should be handled by his assistants starting at the Cabinet level.

6. Reagan Administration—To Date

a. Domestic Matters

(1) Farm Exports. Responding to farmers' pleas, President Reagan ended the embargo on grain exports to the Soviet Union imposed by President Carter after the Soviet Union sent troops into Afghanistan in 1979.

(2) Business Deregulation. Under a policy of *deregulation,* President Reagan delayed or lifted various economic regulations affecting business. He abolished the remaining price controls on United States-produced oil.

(3) Domestic Spending. President Reagan got Congress to step up defense spending and sharply cut such social programs as welfare grants, Medicaid, food stamps, rental assistance, and student loans. He said that a "safety net" of welfare programs would protect the very poor. Critics said that too much money was going for defense, and cuts in social programs were causing widespread suffering among the poor.

(4) Tax Cuts. President Reagan secured Congressional approval in 1981 for a three-year tax cut in line with the theory of supply-side economics. The goal was to make more money available to individuals and to the businesses that supply goods and services to the economy, thereby spurring investment, production, and consumption, and promoting economic growth.

(5) Social Security. To restore the Social Security system to financial health, President Reagan approved bipartisan measures to cut Social Security benefits and increase the system's income.

(6) Budget Deficits. President Reagan and Congress clashed over ways to deal with huge—and growing—budget deficits. The President wanted to make further cuts in domestic spending; opponents said many social programs had al-

. sic 'em . . . !"

© Pletcher/Rothco

ready been cut too deeply. The President repeatedly argued against broad-based tax increases; opponents said raising taxes might be the only way to balance the budget. The President favored a Constitutional amendment to require a balanced budget; instead, Congress approved the Gramm-Rudman-Hollings Act of 1985 establishing a procedure for making automatic, across-the-board spending cuts in several steps if necessary to balance the budget by 1991. (See page 318.)

(7) Tax Reform. The President and Congress worked out a bipartisan tax reform bill that made sweeping changes in the federal income tax system. Under the *Tax Reform Act of 1986,* basic tax rates were simplified and reduced, and many deductions and tax breaks were gradually phased out or eliminated. (See page 314.)

(8) Pollution Control. President Reagan and Congress compromised on a measure to expand the pollution-control program dealing with toxic wastes and on an act to protect the nation's underground water supply. However, the President vetoed as "too expensive" a 1986 bill that would have extended and renewed the Clean Water Act of 1972. In early 1987, Congress overrode the President's veto and authorized spending $20 billion to clean up and protect the nation's water.

(9) Drugs. President Reagan and Congress created a major new program to fight the battle against illegal drugs.

(10) Immigration. The *Immigration Reform and Control Act of 1986* offered amnesty to illegal immigrants who had lived in the United States for more than four years and barred employers from hiring illegal immigrants. (See page 366.)

(11) Farm Subsidies. The Reagan administration tried to trim government farm programs. Nonetheless, government spending on farm programs reached record levels as farmers suffered a prolonged crisis. Under the bipartisan *Food Security Act of 1985*, the government paid higher subsidies to farmers while hold-

ing grain prices down in an effort to boost grain exports and win new markets for United States crops. (See p. 271.)

(12) *Supreme Court Appointments*. President Reagan appointed new members to the Supreme Court—*Sandra Day O'Connor*, the first woman Justice, in 1981, and *Antonin Scalia* in 1986. The President elevated Justice *William H. Rehnquist* to the position of Chief Justice upon the retirement of Warren Burger in 1986.

(13) *Economic Recovery*. The economy plunged into recession in 1981–1982, but economic growth had resumed by 1984.

b. Foreign Affairs

(1) *Soviet Union*. President Reagan at first took a hard line against the Soviet Union, calling it an "evil empire." He sharply stepped up defense spending, and called for a massive new space-based defense system—the *Strategic Defense Initiative*, or "Star Wars." He condemned the Soviets for shooting down a South Korean passenger jet. In 1985 and 1986, as the Soviets appeared willing to reduce international tensions, President Reagan held face-to-face talks with Soviet leader *Mikhail Gorbachev*. Both made far-reaching arms-control proposals. In 1987 they signed a treaty to scrap intermediate-range missiles. (See page 713.)

(2) *Poland*. When Poland's Communist leaders imposed military rule in 1981, President Reagan criticized both Poland and the Soviet Union. He imposed limited economic sanctions on both countries.

(3) *El Salvador and Nicaragua*. The Reagan administration took extensive measures to oppose Communist expansionism in Central America. It stepped up aid to the government of El Salvador, which was battling leftist rebels. Accusing Nicaragua's Sandinista government of supporting the Salvadoran guerrillas, the United States organized and armed a force of Nicaraguan guerrillas (known as *contras*) to oppose the Sandinistas. Meanwhile, United States leaders formed closer military and economic ties with other Central American nations that shared concerns about the Sandinistas. Critics in Congress argued that United States policies were too confrontational and might lead to another Vietnam-style war.

(4) *Anti-Communist Moves*. Under the *Reagan Doctrine*, the administration announced that it would support "freedom fighters" opposing hard-line leftists and Communist regimes. Besides the contras, fighters receiving United States aid included guerrillas in Afghanistan and Angola.

(5) *Caribbean Aid*. President Reagan proposed a *Caribbean Basin Initiative* of trade and economic aid to friendly Caribbean and Central American nations.

(6) *Grenada*. United States troops led an invasion of the Caribbean island nation of Grenada in 1983, ousting the Marxist government.

(7) *Lebanon*. The President sent Marines to Lebanon to join a multinational force to help deal with chaotic conditions that followed Israel's 1982 invasion. After a suicide truck-bombing killed 241 Marines in October 1983, the President withdrew the troops.

(8) *Bombing of Libya*. Accusing Libya of major responsibility for international terrorism and of attacks on United States military planes over the Mediterranean, the United States bombed Libyan cities and air bases in 1986. The death toll included two American pilots and a reported 58 Libyans.

(9) Trade Problems. Arguing in favor of free trade, the Reagan administration opposed protectionist measures that some members of Congress proposed for dealing with the nation's unprecedented trade deficits. Through talks and various pressures on Japan, the European Community, Canada, and others, the administration sought to increase United States exports while holding down imports.

(10) Falklands. The Reagan administration sided with Britain in that nation's 1982 war with Argentina over the South Atlantic Falkland Islands (or Malvinas).

(11) Philippines. When President *Ferdinand Marcos* of the Philippines was accused of election fraud in 1986, United States officials disavowed Marcos, formerly considered an ally. President Reagan extended a warm welcome to Marcos's popular successor, *Corazon Aquino.*

(12) Latin America. The Reagan administration applauded the return of civilian rule to several Latin American nations, including Argentina and Brazil, as well as the fall of Haitian dictator "Baby Doc" Duvalier.

(13) South Africa. While denouncing South Africa's *apartheid* system of racial separation under white-minority rule, President Reagan did not shy away from cooperation with the South African government. He described his policy as one of *constructive engagement,* or quiet persuasion. Under pressure from Congress, the President agreed to limited economic sanctions against South Africa in 1986.

(14) Fighting Drugs. The Reagan administration sent United States military planes and troops to help the government of Bolivia fight the illegal cocaine trade.

"You mean our arms sales to Iran didn't help?"

copyright 1987 by Herblock in The Washington Post

(15) Iran and Iraq. While affirming a position of neutrality in the Iran-Iraq war, the United States secretly provided help to both sides.

(16) Iran Arms Sales. A major controversy erupted late in 1986 when the public learned of secret United States arms sales to Iran (a nation that President Reagan had condemned as a supporter of terrorism) and of the diversion to Nicaraguan contras of profits from the Iran arms sales. The diversion occurred at a time when Congress had barred United States military aid to the contras (a bar that had later been lifted). The President himself denied having known of the diversion. Congressional committees and other official bodies in 1987 launched investigations. (See pages 646–647.)

——————————— MULTIPLE-CHOICE QUESTIONS ———————————

1. Which statement regarding the Presidential election of 1952 is *least* valid?
   (a) Eisenhower enjoyed great popularity. (b) Stevenson defended Truman's record. (c) Settlement of the Korean War was a major issue. (d) The Republican candidates for Congress helped assure Eisenhower's victory.

2. Which term is *not* associated with the career of Dwight D. Eisenhower? (a) modern Republicanism (b) Atoms for Peace (c) time for a change (d) a choice not an echo.

3. During the Eisenhower administration, Congress passed laws affecting all of the following *except* (a) civil rights (b) education (c) protection of the consumer (d) labor unions.

4. Which was a major aim of the Eisenhower administration? (a) balancing the budget (b) compulsory health insurance (c) repealing Social Security (d) raising tariffs.

5. In foreign affairs, the Eisenhower administration (a) ended American aid to South Vietnam (b) sent American troops to Egypt (c) achieved a truce in Korea (d) refused to take part in summit conferences.

6. Which of the following was *not* a factor in the Presidential election of 1960? (a) the religion of the Democratic candidate (b) television "debates" (c) a split in the Republican party (d) black demands for additional civil rights legislation.

7. John F. Kennedy was *not* (a) a mining engineer and self-made millionaire (b) author of *Profiles in Courage* (c) in the navy during World War II (d) United States Senator from Massachusetts.

8. Presidents Eisenhower and Kennedy were *least* in agreement regarding (a) raising the minimum wage (b) support for the UN (c) lowering tariff barriers (d) the use of Presidential powers.

9. Which foreign policy did President Kennedy inherit from his predecessors and carry to a successful conclusion? (a) establishment of the Peace Corps (b) limited nuclear test ban (c) war in Vietnam (d) reunifying Germany.

10. Which statement regarding Lyndon B. Johnson is *not* true? (a) He was born in Texas. (b) He was educated at the Naval Academy at Annapolis. (c) He greatly admired Franklin D. Roosevelt. (d) He served as Senate majority leader.

11. Lyndon B. Johnson and Andrew Johnson, on succession to the Presidency, each faced the problem of (a) limiting the power of the Supreme Court (b) providing foreign aid to Europe (c) insuring civil rights for minority groups (d) appointing a Vice President.

12. President Johnson's desire for a consensus refers to his (a) disregard of public opinion (b) distrust of public opinion polls (c) seeking of strong public support for his policies (d) advocacy of extreme measures to achieve his goals.

13. Which man served as secretary of state under both President Nixon and President Ford? (a) Nelson Rockefeller (b) John Foster Dulles (c) Walter Mondale (d) Henry Kissinger.

14. Which measure, first proposed by President Truman, was achieved during the Johnson administration? (a) St. Lawrence Seaway (b) medical care for the aged under Social Security (c) aid to Appalachia (d) reciprocal tariff program.

15. Some Presidents of the United States have based their refusal to permit members of the White House staff to answer certain questions before Congressional investigating committees on the basis of (a) executive privilege (b) due process (c) the Fifth Amendment (d) executive clemency.

IDENTIFICATION QUESTIONS: WHICH PRESIDENT AM I?

Dwight D. Eisenhower   Richard M. Nixon   James E. (Jimmy) Carter
John F. Kennedy   Gerald R. Ford   Ronald W. Reagan
Lyndon B. Johnson

1. I called for a national "war on poverty."
2. I was forced to resign because of the Watergate affair.
3. I secured removal of Soviet offensive missiles from Cuba.
4. I was in office when the Supreme Court decided the case of *Brown vs. Board of Education of Topeka.*
5. I hosted the Camp David Summit meeting to spur Middle East peace.
6. I became Vice President through the Twenty-Fifth Amendment and President upon the resignation of my predecessor.
7. Facing tremendous budget deficits, I secured Congressional approval for cuts in social services previously considered untouchable.
8. I signed the immigration bill that ended the national origins system.
9. I secured establishment of the National Aeronautics and Space Administration (NASA) to direct space research.
10. I was the first Roman Catholic to be elected President.
11. I appointed the first woman member to the Supreme Court.
12. I began the policy of *détente* with the Soviet Union.
13. I extended full diplomatic recognition to the People's Republic of China.
14. I opposed America's traditional allies upon their invasion of Egypt.

———————— ESSAY QUESTIONS ————————

1. *(a)* In *each* of the following areas, describe briefly a problem faced by President Eisenhower: (1) segregation (2) labor-management relations (3) the cold war. *(b)* Show *one* way in which the Eisenhower administration attempted to deal with *each* of these problems.

2. The frontier of the 1800s was a vast, unexplored region of adventure and opportunity. The New Frontier of the Kennedy administration referred to another avenue of opportunity, that of technological, social, and scientific development. *(a)* Show *two* ways in which the federal government played an important part in the development of the frontier from 1783 to 1890. *(b)* Show *two* ways in which the Kennedy administration attempted to solve the problems of the 1960s.

3. Choose *three* of the following aspects of the Great Society program: *(a)* aid to education *(b)* civil rights *(c)* Social Security *(d)* urban development *(e)* antipoverty projects. For *each* aspect chosen, explain (1) how it represented a continuation of a policy adopted by a previous administration, and (2) how it marked an advance in the intellectual or economic well-being of the United States.

4. The Constitution of the United States provides for a system of checks and balances among three equal branches of government—legislative, executive, and judicial. However, at different times in history, one branch has been viewed as being more powerful than the other two. *(a)* For either the Nixon Era (1968–1974) or the Carter Era (1976–1980), explain why *one* specific branch of government was viewed as being more powerful at any time during that period. Use specific examples to support your answer. *(b)* Discuss *two* possible effects upon our system of checks and balances if an amendment was adopted limiting any one person to a single Presidential term of six years.

5. Since President Richard M. Nixon resigned from office in August 1974, some observations, both general and specific, such as those listed below, have been made: *(a)* No person is above the law. *(b)* The balance of power feature of our Federal Government has been strengthened. *(c)* The United States constitutional system insures orderly succession to the Presidency. *(d)* This resignation by President Nixon will not solve our number-one economic problem—inflation. *(e)* The events leading to President Nixon's resignation were similar to those that led to the impeachment of President Andrew Johnson in 1867. Select *three* of the preceding statements, and using specific information related to the Presidency, either support *or* refute *each* of the statements selected.

6. The period during which executive power is being transferred is difficult under any form of government. *(a)* Describe and evaluate the effectiveness of the Twenty-Fifth Amendment to the Constitution in providing for Presidential succession. *(b)* Show how the Ford administration was (1) in *one* way different from and (2) in *one* way similar to the policies of the preceding administration.

7. The process by which President Reagan was elected in 1980 was more democratic than the way in which Abraham Lincoln was elected in 1860. *(a)* Select *three* areas from the list. For *each* area chosen, discuss how a development in that area since Lincoln's election has made Presidential elections more democratic. Use specific historical information to support your position.

Constitutional amendments
Court decisions
Legislation
Nominating procedures
Technology

(b) Identify and explain *one* criticism that has been made of the current process of selecting a President. Discuss a change that has been proposed to deal with this criticism.

UNIT IX   American Foreign Policy Moves From Isolation to World Leadership

PART 1. Introduction

MAKING OF FOREIGN POLICY TODAY

1. Preeminent Position of the President. The President determines and carries out American foreign policy. This authority derives from the Constitutional powers to receive ambassadors (and therefore to recognize or refuse to recognize foreign governments), to command the armed forces, to negotiate treaties, and to appoint major foreign affairs officials.

The President also has *extra-Constitutional powers:* to rally public opinion, to visit foreign countries, and to sign executive agreements. (Such agreements, between the President and the head of a foreign nation, do not have the status of treaties and therefore do not require Senate ratification. An example was the 1940 exchange of 50 "over-age" American destroyers for naval bases on British territory in the Western Hemisphere—an exchange known as the *Destroyer-Naval Base Deal.*)

2. The President's Assistants. The President receives assistance, information, and advice from many appointed government officials. Two major assistants are *(a)* the assistant for national security affairs—a member of the White House office, and *(b)* the secretary of state—a member of the Cabinet. The national security assistant, an expert on foreign affairs, is the President's loyal supporter, confidant, and *personal adviser.* This adviser directs a small staff to help in analyzing and making recommendations regarding the national interest and foreign policy. The secretary of state, usually a political appointment, is the President's *official adviser.* The secretary has the responsibility of administering the State Department with its myriad divisions, its many ambassadors and ministers stationed abroad, and its over 30,000 staff members. Both the national security assistant and the secretary of state help implement the President's foreign policy decisions by undertaking foreign trips, negotiating with foreign leaders, and testifying before Congressional committees.

The President also receives information and advice from other top State Department personnel such as American ambassadors to foreign countries, American representatives to international organizations, and the head of the *Agency for International Development* (AID), which directs our foreign aid program; from the secretary of defense and the *Joint Chiefs of Staff* of the armed forces; from other Cabinet members whose departments affect or are affected by foreign developments; and from the director of the *Central Intelligence Agency* (CIA), which coordinates American intelligence activities related to national security. The President and the key advisers on foreign policy and national defense together constitute the *National Security Council.* The President, however, makes the final decisions on foreign policy and bears the final responsibility.

3. Role of Congress. The Senate's "advice and consent" are necessary to approve major Presidential appointments, including foreign service personnel, and to ratify treaties. Appointments require a majority vote; treaties, a two-thirds vote. Approval of both houses of Congress is necessary for expenditures in the area of foreign affairs. Both the Senate Foreign Relations Committee and the House International Relations Committee hold hearings, question witnesses, and make recommendations. Congress also has the power to regulate commerce with foreign nations, to voice its opinion upon foreign policy by means of a joint resolution, and, finally, to declare war.

Congress may respond to a President's foreign policy initiative in either *(a)* a *partisan* way, such as in 1919–1920, when generally Senate Republicans clashed with Senate Democrats and defeated President Wilson's treaty for American membership in the League of Nations, or *(b)* a *bipartisan* way, such as in 1945, when both major parties overwhelmingly approved President Truman's request for American membership in the United Nations.

4. Other Influences. The President may be influenced by *(a)* predecessor's policies, the views of our allies, the efforts of the United Nations; *(b)* the pressures of lobbyists representing domestic groups—such as business, labor, veterans, and ethnic minorities, and also of lobbyists representing foreign governments; and *(c)* the attitudes of the mass media, educational associations, and poll-taking organizations—which help shape and record public opinion. No matter how great the President's powers, no President has long maintained a foreign policy at sharp variance with public opinion.

GOALS OF AMERICAN FOREIGN POLICY

1. General Statement. The purpose of American foreign policy is to protect and preserve the *national interest*. What specifically constitutes the national interest?

2. Specific Goals

*a. **Political.*** To assure the survival of the United States as a free and independent nation; defend its territories and people; protect American citizens in foreign countries; further democratic ideals throughout the world and view favorably any nation sharing our democratic outlook; disapprove of and, depending upon the circumstances, oppose any nation maligning democracy and advocating a conflicting governmental system such as military dictatorship, fascism, and communism.

*b. **Military.*** To maintain a strong military establishment; secure strategic military bases outside the United States; join in agreements and alliances for mutual protection, preferably with nations sharing our democratic philosophy; prevent any potentially hostile power from gaining military bases that could menace the United States; and, with the danger of nuclear war today between the United States and the Soviet Union threatening near-total destruction of both nations, prevent misunderstandings and resolve issues peacefully so as to avoid an all-out nuclear war.

   c. Economic. To assist American farmers and manufacturers who *export* products to foreign markets; assist American corporations that *import* raw materials, farm produce, and some manufactured goods from foreign nations; protect American workers and businesses against competition of underpriced foreign-made goods produced by cheap labor; protect *foreign investments* of American individuals and corporations against harassment and *nationalization* (seizure) of their properties without payment of fair compensation by foreign governments; secure repayment of governmental and private loans made to foreign nations.

   3. Priorities in Foreign Policy Goals. The United States has pursued foreign policies that apparently are in conflict—but not really so. In each case, American leaders have had to decide among several foreign policy goals by setting *priorities*—that is, which goal is first and which goals are of lesser importance.

   Although one American goal has been to further foreign trade, since 1960 the United States has maintained an embargo on trade with Communist Cuba—an apparent conflict. Not so, for American leaders have given priority to another goal: to stop the spread of Communist influence in the Western Hemisphere. By denying Cuba access to American markets to sell its raw materials and access to American industry to purchase machinery and replacement parts, American leaders have expected to weaken Cuba economically, thereby lessening its ability to influence other Latin American nations toward communism. The United States thus sacrificed the less important goal, trade, and opted for the more important one, stopping the spread of Communist influence.

   Although another American foreign policy goal has been to further democracy, the United States has given substantial economic aid to Latin American military dictatorships—an apparent conflict. Not so, for American leaders have given priority to another foreign policy goal: to further hemispheric unity for mutual protection. American leaders further realize that we could not overthrow the military dictatorships and reshape the political life of these Latin American countries without intervening in their internal affairs—a course of action incompatible with American democracy.

AMERICAN FOREIGN POLICY: HIGHLIGHTS TO THE POST-CIVIL WAR ERA

   1. Policy of Isolation. George Washington, in his *Farewell Address* (1796), urged the young republic to further foreign trade but avoid permanent alliances with foreign nations. Evolving into a policy of isolation and endorsed by subsequent American leaders, Washington's advice guided American foreign policy for over 100 years. It did not prevent the War of 1812, which involved the United States in the Napoleonic Wars. But, thereafter, it enabled the American people to concentrate upon domestic issues and upon foreign affairs affecting the

Western Hemisphere—especially the independence of Latin America and our expansion westward to the Pacific.

2. Monroe Doctrine. James Monroe, in his message to Congress in 1823, stated that *(a)* the Western Hemisphere was no longer open to European colonization, *(b)* the United States would not interfere in the internal affairs of European nations, and *(c)* any attempt by a European power to intervene in the Americas would be regarded as "dangerous to our peace and safety."

The American people approved the Monroe Doctrine as a logical extension of our policy of isolation, since it attempted to isolate the entire Western Hemisphere from European affairs. Latin Americans, who had just won their independence, welcomed the Monroe Doctrine as an offer of assistance against would-be European aggressors. The first real application of the Monroe Doctrine took place just after the Civil War when the United States persuaded France to withdraw its troops from Mexico—an event called the Maximilian Affair.

3. "Manifest Destiny." Many Americans in the early 19th century believed that the United States had a *manifest destiny* to expand to the Pacific coast. James Polk, in his Presidential campaign in 1844, demanded the "reannexation of Texas" and the "reoccupation of Oregon." Just before Polk took office, Congress approved the annexation of Texas. Thereafter, Polk led the United States in a war against Mexico and secured the Mexican Cession territory, including California. He compromised with Britain and agreed to divide the Oregon Country at the 49th parallel. Polk's expansionism enabled the United States to reach the Pacific coast.

PART 2. The United States Undertakes a Policy of Imperialism

REASONS FOR AMERICA'S TURN TO IMPERIALISM

Following the Civil War, and definitely by the 1890s, the United States began to extend its control over "backward" or weaker areas, especially in Latin America. Mexico, the Caribbean region, Central America, and parts of South America and the Pacific came under our influence. The major reasons are as follows:

1. Industrial Revolution. Spurred by Civil War needs, American industry had grown tremendously. Industrialists began to look abroad for *(a)* new sources of raw materials, *(b)* additional markets for manufactured goods, and *(c)* places to invest surplus capital.

American merchants and sugar planters as well as missionaries had already pioneered the way overseas.

2. Close of the Frontier. By 1890 the American West was sufficiently populated for the frontier to be considered closed. This development motivated

American manufacturers and investors to look beyond our borders for economic opportunities.

3. Example of European Nations. The major as well as many lesser European powers were engaged in imperialist ventures. Britain purchased control of the Suez Canal, established domination over Egypt, and planned a "Cape-to-Cairo" empire in Africa. France annexed Indochina. Russia secured border territories from China. Belgians took over the Congo. Such developments stimulated American interest in empire-building.

4. American Nationalism. Expansionists in the United States urged that America assume its rightful place as a great power by embarking upon a policy of imperialism. Most influential were the lectures and writings of Captain *Alfred Mahan.* In his book *The Influence of Sea Power Upon History,* Mahan urged the United States to "look outward": to expand foreign markets, construct a powerful navy, and acquire overseas bases. (Mahan had a notable admirer in Theodore Roosevelt.)

Some historians maintain that overseas imperialism was a logical continuation of America's earlier pursuit of manifest destiny.

FIRST COLONIAL ACQUISITIONS

1. Alaska

a. Purchase From Russia (1867). Russia proposed to sell Alaska to the United States, and Secretary of State William Seward agreed to the purchase. Seward's reasons were (1) gratitude to Russia for its support of the Union during the Civil War, (2) a desire to reduce foreign possessions in North America, and (3) the belief that Alaska contained vast natural resources. Because many people thought the territory a "barren icebox," Alaska, costing $7.2 million, was called "Seward's Folly."

b. Statehood (1959). Our forty-ninth state, Alaska ranks first in area (being more than twice the size of Texas) but next-to-last in population (having about 520,000 inhabitants). About 80,000 of Alaska's people are native Inuits (Eskimos) and Indians.

c. Importance. Alaska (1) has natural resources of timber, fur, fish, coal, oil, and gold, (2) is located along the polar air routes to northern Europe and Asia, and (3) is adjacent to Soviet Siberia. Alaska contains major air bases, as well as missile-warning systems.

2. Samoan Islands and Midway. The Samoan Islands in the South Pacific served American merchant ships as supply harbors and coaling stations. In 1899 several of the islands were formally annexed by the United States. Also annexed was the Central Pacific island of Midway. Today, American Samoa and Midway are American colonies that provide the United States with naval and air bases.

3. Hawaii

a. Acquisition (1898). Hawaii, a group of islands in the Central Pacific, 2400 miles off the California coast, (1) served American merchant ships as a supply and refueling station, (2) drew American missionaries, who converted the natives to Christianity, and (3) attracted American investors into Hawaiian sugar plantations. Most Hawaiian sugar was sold in the United States.

In 1893 revolutionists, mainly American settlers, overthrew the anti-American native Queen Liliuokalani. The revolutionists established a temporary republic and asked for annexation by the United States. Annexation was delayed by the opposition of President Cleveland, who believed that most native Hawaiians preferred independence. In 1898, however, with McKinley in the White House, the United States annexed Hawaii.

b. Statehood (1959). Our fiftieth state, Hawaii ranks forty-seventh in area but thirty-ninth in population, with about one million inhabitants. One-fourth of these are white, one-fourth are of Japanese ancestry, and the rest are of Hawaiian, Filipino, and other extractions.

c. Importance. Hawaii (1) produces sugar and pineapples, (2) attracts many tourists, and (3) contains the major American military installations in the Central Pacific, including the naval base at Pearl Harbor.

SPANISH-AMERICAN WAR (1898)

1. Cuban Background of the War

a. Early American Interest. Americans had long been interested in the Spanish colony of Cuba. They recognized Cuba's strategic location in the Caribbean Sea. Located at the entrance to the Gulf of Mexico, the island is within 90 miles of the Florida coast. Americans feared for our security if Cuba passed from Spanish into stronger European hands.

Before the Civil War, Southerners wanted to annex Cuba as another pro-slave state. In 1854 three American diplomats declared that, if the United States could not purchase Cuba, it would be justified in seizing Cuba by force—a declaration known as the *Ostend Manifesto*. Although repudiated by the United States government, the Ostend Manifesto reflected considerable American sentiment. After the Civil War, American interest in Cuba temporarily subsided.

b. Despotic Spanish Rule. Spain denied the Cubans civil liberties and political rights, levied heavy taxes, restricted foreign trade, and ruthlessly suppressed several rebellions. In 1895, as a depression hit the island, Spain faced another Cuban revolt for independence.

2. Causes of the Spanish-American War

a. Humanitarianism. Americans sympathized with the desire of the Cuban people for independence. Americans were outraged when Spain's General Valeriano Weyler placed Cuban civilians in concentration camps to prevent them from aiding the revolution. Some 200,000 concentration camp inmates, mainly women and children, died of hunger and disease.

b. Economic Interests. American merchants traded with Cuba to the amount of $100 million per year. American investors had placed $50 million in Cuban sugar and tobacco plantations. Our trade and investments suffered from unsettled conditions.

c. "Yellow" Journalism. The "yellow" press—especially William Randolph Hearst's New York *Journal* and Joseph Pulitzer's New York *World*— sought to increase newspaper circulation by sensational treatment of news from Cuba. Journalists exaggerated stories of Spanish atrocities and falsified news pictures while playing down atrocities by the Cuban revolutionaries. The yellow press also gave sensational treatment to the *De Lome Letter.* Written by the Spanish minister in Washington to a friend in Cuba and stolen from the Havana post office, this private letter belittled President McKinley as a weak, incompetent politician. By its treatment of such news stories, the yellow press enraged the American people against Spain.

d. Sinking of the Maine. In 1898, the American battleship *Maine,* visiting in Havana, Cuba, was blown up with a loss of 260 American lives. The cause of the explosion remains unknown, but the American people blamed Spain. They were goaded to do so by the yellow press; by jingoists who boasted of the nation's strength; and by imperialists, who wanted an overseas empire.

3. Outbreak of the War. President McKinley had sought to avert war and urged Americans to remain calm regarding Cuba. Now, with the sinking of the *Maine,* McKinley demanded that Spain proclaim an armistice, end the concentration camps, and negotiate with the rebels. Although Spain's reply was conciliatory, McKinley finally yielded to American public sentiment for war. At his request, Congress approved the use of American armed forces in Cuba. Congress also recognized the independence of Cuba and declared that the United States would not annex Cuba but would leave "control of the island to its people"—a self-denying declaration known as the *Teller Resolution.*

Historical Analysis. *Did American business interests favor war with Spain over Cuba?* Historians have long debated this issue.

Yes. War would advance the political fortunes of the Republican party, considered probusiness, by finally solving the Cuban problem. It would spur business growth in the United States. War would end Spanish control in Cuba so that American merchant interests could greatly expand their Cuban trade. By delaying American intervention, the fighting between revolutionists and Spanish forces dragged on, causing additional damage and destruction to Cuban properties owned by American investors. Without American intervention, "radical" revolutionaries might seize control of Cuba and institute policies harmful to American business interests.

No. Peace was strongly desired by American business interests. Peace news sent Wall Street stock prices up whereas war news depressed stock prices. War would threaten and probably end the business recovery in progress in the United States. War would be fought in Cuba and cause great damage and destruction of Cuban property owned by American investors. An independent Cuba might adopt policies harmful to American business interests.

4. Conduct of the War. With "Remember the *Maine!*" as their battle cry, American forces swept quickly and easily to victory. In the Pacific, Commodore *George Dewey* led an American naval force to destroy the Spanish fleet at Manila, the capital of the Philippines, and an American army took possession of the city. In the Caribbean, American naval units destroyed the Spanish fleet at Santiago, Cuba. Meanwhile, American forces captured this city after a battle famed for the dash up San Juan Hill by Theodore Roosevelt and his Rough Riders.

In this "splendid little war," so called by the American diplomat John Hay, more American soldiers died from tropical diseases, especially yellow fever, than from Spanish guns. Some years after the war, *Walter Reed,* an army surgeon, discovered that the disease is transmitted by a certain kind of mosquito. This discovery led to the wiping out of yellow fever.

5. Treaty of Paris (1898). Thoroughly beaten, Spain agreed to the following: *(a)* Cuba was freed of Spanish control, *(b)* Puerto Rico, in the Caribbean, and Guam, in the Pacific, were ceded to the United States, and *(c)* the Philippine Islands, in the Pacific, were sold to the United States for $20 million.

6. Significance. The United States emerged from the Spanish-American War as a world power with colonies in the Caribbean and the Pacific. Anti-imperialists were alarmed. In the Presidential election of 1900, Democrat William Jennings Bryan warned that imperialism abroad would lead to despotism at home. Disregarding this warning, the people reelected William McKinley, who had campaigned on the issue of the "full dinner pail," but who represented imperialism.

AMERICAN RELATIONS WITH CUBA

1. Temporary American Occupation. After the Spanish-American War, the United States temporarily took charge of Cuba, establishing schools, building roads, providing sanitation, and wiping out yellow fever. Americans also assisted the Cubans in drawing up a democratic constitution. In 1902, in keeping with the Teller Resolution, American forces withdrew from the island.

2. American Protectorate Over Cuba: The Platt Amendment. Under strong American pressure, the Cubans included in their constitution the *Platt Amendment.* It provided that Cuba would *(a)* not sign any foreign treaty that threatened its independence, *(b)* allow the United States to intervene in Cuba to preserve Cuban independence and to protect life, liberty, and property, and *(c)* grant the United States naval bases. Under the last provision, Cuba leased to the United States the naval base at *Guantanamo Bay.*

The Cubans lacked political experience. For years their governments alternated between weak, inefficient regimes and tyrannical military dictatorships. The island abounded with corruption, fraud, violence, and revolt.

Using the Platt Amendment, the United States intervened four times in Cuba to restore order and safeguard American lives and investments. Our interventions aroused resentment among Cuban nationalists. In 1933, however, although Cuba was in the midst of another revolt, President Franklin D. Roosevelt did not intervene. Instead, in 1934, as part of his Good Neighbor Policy, he abrogated (abolished) the Platt Amendment. With Cuban consent, the United States retained the naval base at Guantanamo Bay.

3. Economic Ties. Although the Platt Amendment was ended, the United States continued to dominate the Cuban economy. Americans had over $1 billion invested in Cuban public utilities, railroads, iron and nickel mines, and sugar and tobacco plantations. The United States provided the chief market for Cuban agricultural and mineral exports, and was the chief source of Cuban imports of manufactured goods. American tourists flocked to Cuban vacation resorts.

The Cuban economy provided the people with no more than a very low living standard. Few farmers owned their own land, and farm workers received low wages. Because Cuba was largely dependent upon the sugar crop, the entire economy frequently suffered from world competition and low prices.

4. Hostility (Since 1959). *Fidel Castro,* leading Cuban rebels, overthrew the dictatorship of Fulgencio Batista and seized power. As Castro aligned himself with the Communist world, relations between Cuba and the United States deteriorated. (Check the Index for "Cuba, under Castro.")

PUERTO RICO: AN AMERICAN SHOWCASE

1. Political Evolution: From Colony to Commonwealth

a. Foraker Act (1900). Congress provided that the President of the United States appoint the island's governor and the upper house of its legislature but that the Puerto Ricans elect the lower house.

b. Jones Act (1917). Congress granted the Puerto Ricans American citizenship and the right to elect both houses of the Puerto Rican legislature.

c. Elected Governor (1948). Congress passed a law to permit the Puerto Ricans to elect their own governor. They chose, as their first elected governor, *Luis Muñoz Marín.* Elected for four consecutive terms until he retired in 1965, Muñoz Marín helped shape modern Puerto Rico. He furthered economic progress through Operation Bootstrap and achieved commonwealth status.

d. Commonwealth Status (Since 1952). Congress empowered the Puerto Ricans to draw up their own constitution. Under Muñoz Marín's leader-

Caribbean Area

ship, the islanders overwhelmingly chose to become freely associated with the United States as a self-governing *commonwealth*. (1) Puerto Ricans elect their own legislators and governor, who deal with local matters. (2) Puerto Ricans are American citizens. However, as long as they reside in Puerto Rico, they do not vote in Presidential elections and do not elect members of Congress. They do, however, send a resident commissioner to Washington with power to speak, but not to vote, in the House of Representatives. (3) Puerto Ricans are subject to most federal laws. They serve in the American armed forces, and their products enter the mainland free of tariff duties. However, individuals and corporations on the island are exempt from federal income taxes.

    e. Political Developments. Until recently, a majority of Puerto Rican voters approved the commonwealth status; very few desired independence. But a large minority favored statehood, which would mean voting in federal elections—and also paying federal income taxes. In the 1976 elections, the Puerto Ricans narrowly elected as governor *Carlos Romero Barcelo,* an advocate of statehood. This surprising result, although probably reflecting economic discontent, spurred interest in statehood.

    In 1979 President Carter, citing "humane considerations," freed from American prisons four Puerto Rican independence nationalists—one who in 1950 had attempted to assassinate President Truman and three who in 1954 had sprayed gunfire into the House of Representatives and wounded five members of Congress. Their unconditional release was opposed by Puerto Rico's governor as menacing public safety and encouraging terrorism. The best-known terrorist group demanding Puerto Rican independence calls itself the *Armed Forces of National Liberation* (FALN).

Forces favoring statehood lost Puerto Rico's governorship in 1984 to *Rafael Hernández Colón,* who favors a continuation of commonwealth status. The parties favoring statehood and commonwealth are relatively equal in strength. A much smaller third party favors Puerto Rican independence.

2. Economic Developments

a. Problem of Poverty. Despite fertile soil, favorable climate, and good crops of sugar and tobacco, the Puerto Ricans subsisted for a long time at minimal living standards. (1) The island lacks sufficient area to support its rapidly growing population in agriculture. In contrast to a population density of 67 inhabitants per square mile for the United States, Puerto Rico now has a population density of 955. (2) Most Puerto Rican land was held by American corporations. Eighty percent of the islanders were landless. (3) The island's economy depended upon sugar. A drop in world sugar prices meant depression.

b. Operation Bootstrap: Efforts to Improve Conditions. In the early 1940s, Puerto Rico initiated a program to improve its economy. Since Puerto Rico was trying "to lift itself by its own bootstraps," the project became known as *Operation Bootstrap.* (1) *Limits on Landholdings.* Puerto Rico began enforcing a law, passed in 1900, limiting corporate land ownership to 500 acres. The government bought up the excess holdings and distributed the land to agricultural cooperatives and individual farmers. (2) *Tourism.* The Puerto Rican government encouraged the building of hotels and developed the island as a resort area. Beaches, gambling casinos, the *Pablo Casals Music Festival,* and touches of Spanish culture all attracted American vacationers. (3) *Social Welfare Projects.* The Puerto Rican government paved roads, built hydroelectric plants, provided public health facilities, constructed low-income housing projects, and substantially increased educational expenditures. Instruction is in Spanish; the chief second language studied is English. Literacy has risen to about 95 percent. (4) *Industrialization.* "Operation Bootstrap" especially emphasized attracting American capital and industry. The Puerto Rican government offered new factories, easy credit, and vocational training of workers. Most important, corporations in Puerto Rico are exempt from federal income taxes. Over 1000 new enterprises, manufacturing textiles, electrical equipment, plastics, chemicals, and many other products, were set up on the island and provided many jobs.

c. Results. Today, Puerto Rico's income from manufacturing exceeds that from agriculture. The people's standard of living has risen substantially; it is among the highest in Latin America. On the other hand, the unemployment rate in Puerto Rico has been above 20 percent, the per capita income remains considerably lower than on the United States mainland, and many Puerto Ricans are dependent upon federal food stamps and other welfare programs.

3. Emigration to the Mainland and Back. (Check the Index.)

PANAMA CANAL

1. American Interest. Americans long desired a canal across the Isthmus of Panama to connect the Atlantic and Pacific oceans. By eliminating the long voyage around South America, a canal would shorten the boat trip between our east and west coasts and would lower the cost of transporting goods. The Spanish-American War pointed up the need for a canal to *(a)* provide greater mobility for our naval fleets, *(b)* protect our new colonial empire, and *(c)* further commerce from the Atlantic Coast with the Far East.

2. American Diplomatic Moves

a. With Great Britain. In the *Clayton-Bulwer Treaty* (1850), the United States and Great Britain agreed to share control of any canal across Central America. In 1901 Secretary of State John Hay negotiated the *Hay-Pauncefote Treaty,* by which Britain agreed that the United States alone would build and operate the canal. In return, the United States pledged to open the canal to ships of all nations.

b. With the French Canal Company. A private French company, under *Ferdinand de Lesseps,* builder of the Suez Canal, had attempted to construct a canal in Panama but had failed. The United States agreed to pay $40 million to this French company for its property and its franchise rights.

c. With Colombia. In 1903 Secretary Hay negotiated a treaty with Colombia to pay that nation $10 million and an annual rental of $250,000 for the right to build a canal across its northern province of Panama. The treaty was rejected by the Colombian senate, which hoped for better terms the following year when the French company's franchise would expire. Rejection of the treaty worried the French canal company, inflamed the people of Panama, and enraged President Theodore Roosevelt.

d. Roosevelt and the Panama Revolution. Roosevelt privately expressed the wish to see Panama independent of Colombia. Shortly afterward, a revolt broke out. The United States openly aided the revolt by sending naval vessels to prevent Colombian troops from entering Panama. Later, Roosevelt boasted, "I took the Canal Zone." Roosevelt's actions earned us ill-will throughout Latin America. (In 1921 the United States attempted to placate Colombia by a payment of $25 million.)

e. Treaty With Panama. Hay now negotiated a treaty with the new Republic of Panama, whose minister was the former official of the French canal company, *Philippe Bunau-Varilla.* The Hay–Bunau-Varilla Treaty (1903) provided for (1) American control, "in perpetuity," of the Canal Zone, a strip of land ten miles wide across the isthmus, (2) American intervention in Panama when necessary to preserve order, and (3) payment to Panama of $10 million and an annual rental of $250,000 for the Canal Zone. (The annual rental was increased several times up to $2.3 million.)

3. Building the Canal

    a. George W. Goethals, an army engineer, had charge of building the canal. To solve the problem of the uneven terrain, Goethals built huge locks to raise and lower ships. In 1914 the 50-mile canal was opened to traffic.

    b. William C. Gorgas, an army medical officer, wiped out malaria and yellow fever in the Canal Zone. By maintaining proper sanitation, Gorgas enabled the workers to complete the canal.

    4. Protecting the Canal. The United States *(a)* fortified the Canal Zone, *(b)* converted the Caribbean into an "American lake," by extending American influence and military bases throughout the area, and *(c)* in 1917 purchased from Denmark an additional Caribbean base, the Virgin Islands.

    5. Panamanian Nationalism and the Canal Zone. By the 1960s Panamanians strongly resented American control over the Canal Zone "in perpetuity" as well as the comfortable life of American personnel, in contrast with the poverty of most Panamanians. In 1964 a Canal Zone incident involving the unauthorized flying of the American flag by American high school students sparked a series of anti-American riots. Thereafter the United States and Panama began negotiations to revise the status of the Canal Zone.

    6. The 1977 Canal Treaties. After 13 years of intermittent talks spanning four American Presidential administrations, United States and Panama negotiators agreed to replace the 1903 Hay–Bunau-Varilla pact with two new treaties. The *"Transfer of Ownership"* treaty provided that *(a)* the United States transfer ownership and control of the canal to Panama by the year 2000, *(b)* until then the United States operate the canal but assign an increasing role to Panamanians, *(c)* Panama assume control of most of the Canal Zone—those areas not essential for defense or operation of the canal, and *(d)* Panama receive $50 to $70 million annually out of canal tolls and also extensive American economic aid. The *"Neutrality"* treaty *(a)* guarantees the neutrality of the canal from the year 2000 onward and *(b)* gives the United States (as later spelled out) the right to intervene militarily to defend the canal's neutrality.

    In Panama, the voters by better than 2 to 1 approved the treaties.

    In the United States, President Carter exerted much political pressure to secure Senate ratification. A considerable number of Americans had strong doubts regarding the advisability of the treaties. The antitreaty arguments included the following: *(a)* The United States had acquired its rights to the Panama Canal legitimately, had built the canal despite considerable hardship, and should not now surrender these rights. *(b)* Panama is not entitled to the huge sums to be paid out of canal tolls and extended as American economic aid. *(c)* Americans working on the canal eventually will lose their jobs. *(d)* Panamanians lack the skill and ability to operate the canal. *(e)* The canal is vital to American national security.

    The Senate ratified the two treaties by identical votes of 68 to 32—one vote above the two-thirds required by the Constitution. President Carter hailed ratification stating that these treaties "symbolize our determination to deal with the developing nations of the world . . . on the basis of mutual respect."

EXPANSION OF THE MONROE DOCTRINE IN THE CARIBBEAN

In 1823 the United States issued the Monroe Doctrine to keep European powers from extending their control in the Western Hemisphere. Beginning in 1895, the United States interpreted the Monroe Doctrine so as to justify its own political and economic domination of the Caribbean area.

1. Venezuela Boundary Dispute (1895). Great Britain and Venezuela had long disputed the boundary between Venezuela and British Guiana. The disputed area, where gold was discovered, extended north to the mouth of the Orinoco River. Britain had rejected several proposals for arbitration.

In 1895 *Richard Olney,* secretary of state under President Cleveland, demanded that Britain submit to arbitration. Olney *(a)* claimed that British pressure on Venezuela violated the Monroe Doctrine, and *(b)* asserted that the United States may intervene in all Western Hemisphere affairs because "the United States is practically sovereign on this continent"—the *Olney Interpretation* of the Monroe Doctrine. Britain dismissed Olney's arguments, but, after Cleveland indicated that the United States was ready to use force, Britain agreed to arbitration. British Guiana was awarded most of the disputed territory, but Venezuela retained the mouth of the Orinoco River.

The Olney Interpretation greatly perturbed the Latin American nations, which foresaw intervention by the United States in their internal affairs.

2. Venezuela Debt Dispute (1902). Venezuela defaulted on debts owed to citizens of Italy, Great Britain, and Germany. The European powers sent warships to compel repayment of the debt by blockading Venezuelan ports. President Theodore Roosevelt feared that the naval display might lead to permanent occupation of Venezuela, in violation of the Monroe Doctrine. Roosevelt secured arbitration of the dispute and withdrawal of the warships.

3. Dominican Debt Default (1904–1905). The Dominican Republic (sometimes called Santo Domingo) failed to repay loans to European creditors. President Roosevelt opposed European intervention as a violation of the Monroe Doctrine, but he authorized intervention by the United States to protect the European creditors. In 1905 the United States took control of Dominican finances and initiated the repayment of Dominican debts.

Roosevelt justified his interference in Dominican affairs by asserting that, in case of "chronic wrongdoing" by any Western Hemisphere nation, the United States would exercise "international police power." This *Roosevelt Corollary* to the Monroe Doctrine was part of Roosevelt's "big stick" policy, a term derived from his expression, "Speak softly and carry a big stick."

The Roosevelt Corollary pleased European and American investors, for it indicated that we would intervene, if necessary, to protect their investments. It enraged Latin Americans by implying that they needed help from the United

States to manage their affairs. (In opposition to the Roosevelt Corollary, the Latin American nations denied the right of any country, European or American, to use force to collect foreign debts.)

4. "Dollar Diplomacy." President Taft endorsed the Roosevelt Corollary and expanded our role as "policeman" of the Western Hemisphere. Taft offered American business interests in the Caribbean the full military and diplomatic support of the government, a policy called *dollar diplomacy*. Taft encouraged American bankers to expand their loans to Honduras, Haiti, and Nicaragua. After disturbances in Nicaragua, Taft in 1912 sent marines to that country to protect American lives and property and to restore order.

President Wilson continued American intervention in the Caribbean. In 1915 Wilson sent marines to occupy Haiti, and the United States took control of Haiti's finances. In 1916 he ordered marines to restore peace in the Dominican Republic. Wilson's greatest Latin American problem, however, was Mexico.

AMERICAN RELATIONS WITH MEXICO: AN UNEVEN RECORD

1. Relations in the 19th Century. Because of the annexation of Texas and the Mexican War of 1846–1848, Mexicans had considerable ill will toward the United States. Mexican sentiments changed when the United States, from 1862 to 1867, invoked the Monroe Doctrine and helped overthrow a French protectorate in Mexico under the Emperor Maximilian.

2. American Investments in Mexico. *Porfirio Diaz*, Mexican dictator from 1884 to 1911, favored the landowning aristocracy and welcomed foreign, especially American, investors. Diaz issued a code granting landowners the right to subsoil minerals. Americans invested over $1 billion in Mexican cattle ranches, railroads, mines, and oil wells.

3. Mexican Revolution of 1911. Many Mexicans were dissatisfied with Diaz. Peons—peasants who worked on large estates—wanted their own land, nationalists resented foreign investors, and supporters of democracy demanded representative government. In 1911 revolutionists ousted Diaz, and Mexico entered upon an era of turmoil. In 1913 General *Victoriano Huerta* seized control. His dictatorial regime was opposed by reform-minded Mexicans under *Venustiano Carranza*. Mexico experienced civil war.

4. Wilson's Policies Toward Mexico

a. "Watchful Waiting" (1913–1914). Wilson refused to recognize the Huerta regime, claiming that it lacked the consent of the Mexican people. Wilson also resisted demands to send troops into Mexico to protect American lives and property. Instead, he applied various pressures against Huerta: ordering American forces to occupy the Mexican seaport of Vera Cruz so timed as to keep European arms from Huerta and permitting American arms to go to Carranza. Huerta finally fled from Mexico. Wilson's policy toward Mexico under Huerta became known as "watchful waiting."

b. Pursuit of Pancho Villa (1916–1917). After Wilson recognized the Carranza government, a rival Mexican leader, Pancho Villa, led several raids into the United States and murdered a number of Americans. Wilson ordered American forces under General John Pershing into northern Mexico to seize Villa, but he eluded capture.

5. Troubled Relations (Following 1917). The Mexicans resented Wilson's occupation of Vera Cruz and the pursuit of Villa into Mexican territory. They further feared "Yankee imperialism" and American economic power. During World War I and afterward, Mexico was unfriendly toward the United States.

In turn, many Americans disliked the actions of the Mexican government. American Catholics protested Mexico's seizure of Church lands and the supplanting of parochial schools by state-controlled schools. American oil interests objected to Mexico's nationalization in 1938 of all foreign-owned oil properties.

6. The Good Neighbor Policy (Since 1933). President Franklin D. Roosevelt acknowledged Mexico's right to seize the oil properties but requested fair compensation for the foreign investors. Mexico complied with this request. The friendly conclusion to this dispute improved Mexican-American relations. In World War II, Mexico was a firm ally of the United States.

7. Mexican-American Relations Today

a. Energy Supplies. In the 1970s, Mexico discovered huge new deposits of natural gas and oil. Mexico became the leading supplier of United States oil imports.

b. Economic Troubles. Mexico's economic prosperity, fed by the oil boom, lasted until the early 1980s, when its economy plunged into recession. Declining oil prices in the mid-1980s made the recession worse. Mexico struggled to keep up payments on its massive foreign debt, which passed the $100 billion mark in 1986. Officials voiced concern that the economic troubles would lead to an increase in illegal immigration into the United States.

c. Illegal Immigrants. In the mid-1980s, United States immigration officials were taking more than one million Mexicans a year into custody at the border with Mexico and deporting them as illegal immigrants. Many other Mexicans crossed the border illegally without being detected. Mexicans made up by far the largest portion of the officially estimated 3 million to 5 million illegal immigrants living in the United States. (Other estimates put the figure much higher.) Illegal immigration had become a major source of friction between the two nations. Many in the United States argued that Mexican "illegals" were taking jobs away from American citizens, depressing wages, and adding to welfare costs. Mexicans, on the other hand, argued that the immigrants benefited the United States economy by taking jobs no one else wanted and provided a "safety valve" for Mexico's political and economic woes. Mexican officials argued that the United States should have negotiated with Mexico on the issue of illegal immigration rather than dealing with it through the Immigration Reform and Control Act of 1986. (See page 366.)

d. Illegal Drug Traffic. United States officials claimed that Mexico was a major source of the illegal drugs entering this country. On occasion, Mexico and the United States have cooperated on campaigns to destroy marijuana and opium-poppy fields in Mexico. Nonetheless, the United States charged that some high-level Mexican officials took part in the flourishing drug trade.

e. Assembly Plants in Border Towns. Taking advantage of Mexican wage rates that are much lower than United States rates, many American businesses have set up assembly plants just across the border in northern Mexico. These so-called *maquiladora* plants provide desperately needed jobs for Mexican workers and help United States firms to hold down costs. However, labor unions argue that the *maquiladora* plants take jobs away from American workers. The plants perform such tasks as sewing clothing and assembling television sets, which are then sent back to the United States. During the mid-1980s, the *maquiladora* plants were multiplying rapidly as the declining value of the Mexican peso made such arrangements more and more attractive to United States firms.

PART 3. The Good Neighbor Policy Replaces Imperialism in Inter-American Affairs

MOVEMENT FOR PAN-AMERICANISM

1. Aims. *Pan-Americanism* seeks cooperation among the nations of the Western Hemisphere to achieve common goals such as improved trade relations, greater political stability, military defense, and cultural interchange.

2. Beginnings (In the 1820s). *Simon Bolivar,* the Latin American liberator, issued the call for the first Pan-American conference. This first meeting was a failure, and interest in Pan-Americanism declined afterward.

3. Revival (In the 1880s). *James G. Blaine,* American secretary of state, revived the idea of inter-American cooperation by calling for another Pan-American conference. Convened in 1889, this meeting agreed to establish an information center, which later developed into the *Pan-American Union.* This organization was housed in Washington, D.C., in a building donated by Andrew Carnegie.

4. Limited Accomplishment. Subsequent Pan-American conferences to 1928 achieved little of practical value. The Latin American nations mistrusted the United States. They feared that our support of Pan-Americanism was designed to further American domination of the Western Hemisphere.

REASONS FOR LATIN AMERICAN MISTRUST OF THE UNITED STATES

The Latin American nations mistrusted the United States because of (1) our annexation of Texas, (2) the Mexican War and our annexation of the Mexican Cession, (3) the Olney Interpretation of the Monroe Doctrine, (4) the Spanish-American War and our annexation of Puerto Rico, (5) the Platt Amendment, making Cuba a protectorate, (6) our role in the revolt of Panama against Colombia, (7) the Roosevelt Corollary to the Monroe Doctrine, and (8) our interventions in the Dominican Republic, Nicaragua, Haiti, and Mexico.

AMERICAN EFFORTS TO DISPEL MISTRUST

Herbert Hoover moved the United States to improve Latin American relations. As President-elect, Hoover made a successful goodwill tour of Latin America. His State Department disowned the Roosevelt Corollary. Despite several Latin American revolutions and debt defaults, Hoover refused to intervene. In 1933 he withdrew American marines from Nicaragua.

GOOD NEIGHBOR POLICY (STARTING IN 1933): OBJECTIVES

President Franklin D. Roosevelt and Secretary of State Cordell Hull labored to win Latin American goodwill by the "policy of the good neighbor." Their objectives were as follows: (1) *Friendship.* By respecting the rights of others, Americans hoped to overcome the hostility that many Latin Americans felt toward the United States. (2) *Trade.* With the United States in the midst of the Great Depression, Americans hoped to increase trade with Latin America and spur our economic recovery. (3) *Defense.* As the Nazis rose to power in Germany and as war clouds gathered over Europe and Asia, Americans wanted to strengthen hemispheric defenses. They sought to forestall Nazi influence in Latin America and to assure inter-American military cooperation.

GOOD NEIGHBOR POLICY IN PRACTICE

1. Retreat From Imperialism. *(a)* In 1934 American marines were withdrawn from Haiti, and the United States gave up its protectorate over Cuba by abrogating the Platt Amendment. *(b)* In 1936 the United States surrendered its right to intervene in the internal affairs of Panama. *(c)* In 1938 Secretary of State Hull acknowledged Mexico's right to expropriate American oil properties.

2. Pan-Americanization of the Monroe Doctrine at Various Conferences. *(a)* In 1933 the United States agreed that "no state has the right to intervene in the internal or external affairs of another," thereby formally abandoning the Roosevelt Corollary. *(b)* In 1936 the American republics pledged to consult together in case of a threat to the peace of the Americas. *(c)* In 1938 they further agreed that a threat to the peace of any one of them would be considered a threat to all. Thus the *unilateral* (one-nation) interpretation of the Monroe Doctrine was replaced by a *multilateral* (many-nation) interpretation. The Monroe Doctrine, henceforth to be interpreted and enforced not by the United States alone but by all American republics, became a Pan-American doctrine.

3. Strengthening Economic Ties. *(a)* In 1934 the United States created the Export-Import Bank. This agency granted low-cost, long-term loans to Latin American nations for building roads and for developing their natural resources. It also provided credit facilities to encourage inter-American trade. *(b)* In 1934 Congress passed the Reciprocal Trade Agreements Act. Hull negotiated trade agreements, providing for the mutual lowering of tariff barriers, with a number of Latin American nations.

4. Strengthening Social and Cultural Ties. The United States and Latin America used literature, art, music, science, education, radio, the press, movies, and goodwill tours to promote better understanding. In 1941, to strengthen hemispheric bonds, the United States established the Office of Inter-American Affairs.

GOOD NEIGHBOR POLICY: EFFECTIVE DURING WORLD WAR II

With the chief exception of Argentina, the nations of Latin America cooperated with the United States during World War II.

1. Upon the Outbreak of War (1939). The American republics declared their neutrality and forbade belligerents from entering a safety zone that ranged from 300 to 1200 miles off the coast of the Americas.

2. Following the Nazi Conquest of Western Europe (1940). When Nazi Germany overran France and Holland, the American republics feared that the Nazis would try to occupy the colonies of these two nations in the Western Hemisphere. These consisted of *(a)* Dutch Guiana and French Guiana in South America, and *(b)* Dutch Aruba and Curaçao; and French Guadeloupe and Martinique in the Caribbean. The American republics agreed that they would jointly take control of these colonies if necessary to prevent their seizure by Nazi Germany.

3. Following the Japanese Attack on Pearl Harbor (1941). The American republics declared the Axis powers a threat to the liberty and independence of the Americas, and recommended the severing of diplomatic relations.

Thereafter, most Latin American nations assisted the United States. They *(a)* severed diplomatic relations with Italy, Germany, and Japan, and declared war against them, *(b)* arrested Axis agents, seized Axis airplanes and ships, and prohibited Axis propaganda, *(c)* granted the United States military bases, and *(d)* increased the production of strategic raw materials. In addition, Mexico and Brazil sent troops to the fighting fronts. (For later developments, check the Index for Latin America.)

REASONS FOR ARGENTINE OPPOSITION TO THE UNITED STATES

1. Hemispheric Leadership. Intensely nationalistic, Argentina considered itself the logical leader of the nations of Latin America. Consequently, Argentina resented American leadership in the Pan-American movement.

2. Economic Competition. Both Argentina and the United States exported much wheat and beef, and competed for world markets. Argentina found the chief market for its exports in Europe, particularly Britain and Germany. In turn, Britain invested large funds in Argentina. Consequently, Argentina was economically more closely tied to Europe than to the United States and looked on the United States as an economic competitor.

3. Nazi Influence. Argentina was the target of German efforts during the Hitler regime to spread Nazi propaganda and implant Nazi influence. This campaign was furthered by the German and Italian immigrants in Argentina, by the economic ties between Germany and Argentina, and by Argentine army officers, many trained by Germans. During World War II, Argentina served as a center of Axis activity in the Western Hemisphere. Not until 1944, when Germany's defeat appeared inevitable, did Argentina break relations with Germany.

—————————— MULTIPLE-CHOICE QUESTIONS ——————————

1. The foreign policy of a nation is based *primarily* on that nation's interpretation of its (a) moral commitments to others (b) imperialist desires (c) people's demands (d) national interests.

2. Which power of the President is related *least* to the control of foreign policy? (a) commanding the armed forces (b) calling Congress into special session (c) negotiating treaties (d) receiving ambassadors.

3. Because of the treaty-making procedure provided in the Constitution, some Presidents have (a) negotiated executive agreements instead of treaties (b) vetoed proposed Constitutional amendments curbing the treaty power (c) obtained advisory opinions from the Supreme Court before submitting treaties to the Senate (d) referred treaties to the House of Representatives instead of to the Senate.

4. Which is a check on the President's control of foreign policy? (a) Congress must approve appropriations. (b) The House of Representatives must approve Presidential appointments. (c) The Senate can remove ambassadors. (d) The Central Intelligence Agency must approve the admission of foreign diplomats to the United States.

5. Which sequence best shows the historical development of a 19th-century colonial power? (a) nationalism, imperialism, industrialization (b) imperialism, nationalism, industrialization (c) nationalism, industrialization, imperialism (d) industrialization, imperialism, nationalism.

6. "In our infancy we bordered upon the Atlantic only; our youth carried our boundary to the Gulf of Mexico; today, maturity sees us upon the Pacific. Whether they will it or not, Americans must now begin to look outward." This late 19th-century quotation best reflects a United States foreign policy of (a) imperialism (b) isolationism (c) collective security (d) peaceful coexistence.

7. Which is the *most* valid conclusion that can be drawn concerning the territorial acquisitions of the United States? (a) There was little interest in adding territory before the Civil War. (b) Expansion frequently brought involvement with foreign nations. (c) Peaceful means were always used to obtain additional territory. (d) Desires for land were limited to the North American continent.

8. Which best explains why the United States made few foreign investments prior to 1890? (a) There was no excess capital to invest overseas. (b) Investments in foreign countries were prohibited by Congress. (c) The development of the western United States offered better investment opportunities. (d) Foreign nations generally would not accept United States investments.

9. A *major* reason for United States empire-building at the turn of this century was the belief that colonies (a) could serve as an outlet for eventual surplus population (b) would help the United States to increase its trade and industrial development (c) would provide the skilled labor needed in our industrial society (d) would enable the United States to replace France as the major world power.

10. United States foreign policy toward nations in the Caribbean has been motivated most by (a) social and humanitarian concerns (b) a desire to establish democratic governments in the area (c) economic and military concerns (d) a desire for noninvolvement.

11. In the United States, which group benefited most from the establishment of overseas colonies during the late 19th century? (a) factory workers (b) members of the armed forces (c) investors and manufacturers (d) farmers.

12. The earliest colonial acquisition of the United States was (a) Alaska (b) Hawaii (c) Puerto Rico (d) the Virgin Islands.

13. Since World War II, Alaska's strategic importance has increased because of the (a) discovery of new gold mines (b) large-scale mining of uranium deposits (c) air routes across the Arctic (d) achievement of statehood.

14. The admission of Hawaii as our fiftieth state (a) granted equality with the older states to an area with an Asian majority (b) extended our defenses against China to the mid-Pacific (c) caused widespread economic problems on the mainland (d) permitted unlimited Hawaiian immigration to the mainland.

15. The United States declaration of war on Spain is an example of (a) Presidential leadership in the face of Congressional disapproval (b) army maneuvers making war inevitable (c) the influence of the press on popular opinion (d) the unanimous opinion of business leaders in favor of war.

16. The peace treaties ending the Mexican War of 1846 and the Spanish-American War of 1898 were similar in that both (a) ceded land to the United States (b) created a mutual defense pact (c) addressed the question of neutrality rights on the high seas (d) established a strong union of friendship between the countries involved in the treaty.

17. An important result of the Spanish-American War was that it (a) strengthened American control in the Caribbean (b) increased the rivalry between the United States and Russia (c) forced Spain to recognize the Monroe Doctrine (d) assured the election of Theodore Roosevelt as President in 1900.

18. Conclusions about the relations between the United States and Spain before the Spanish-American War would probably be most valid if based on (a) editorials published in newspapers during that time (b) biographies of Presidents William McKinley and Theodore Roosevelt (c) the diary of a member of the crew of the battleship *Maine* (d) government documents, as interpreted by historians with different viewpoints.

19. The Platt Amendment provided that the United States (a) annex Cuba (b) maintain a protectorate over Cuba (c) withdraw American investments from Cuba (d) send an American to serve as President of Cuba.

20. Puerto Rico is represented in the United States House of Representatives by (a) its governor (b) an elected commission of three (c) a delegate who may speak but not vote (d) one elected Representative.

21. Which term is used to describe Puerto Rico's relationship to the United States today? (a) colony (b) state (c) trust territory (d) commonwealth.

22. The Hay-Pauncefote Treaty between the United States and Great Britain was concerned with the (a) boundary between Maine and Canada (b) building a canal across Panama (c) disposition of the Samoan Islands (d) Bering Sea seal fisheries.

23. The United States built the Panama Canal to (a) improve its national defenses (b) increase the prosperity of Central America (c) force the reduction of railroad rates (d) fulfill our treaty obligations to Britain.

24. In 1917 the United States purchased the Virgin Islands to (a) secure tropical products (b) secure a naval base on the Caribbean Sea (c) secure an air base for trans-Atlantic aviation (d) protect American settlers.

25. Which occurred during the last quarter of the 19th century? (a) Maximilian Affair (b) Venezuela boundary dispute (c) occupation of Vera Cruz (d) opening of the Panama Canal.

26. Which combines a period in United States history with a phase of foreign policy dominant at that time? (a) 1865–1890—active leadership in world affairs (b) 1890–1903—rejection of opportunities for imperialism (c) 1904–1910—active role in Caribbean area (d) 1910–1918—isolation from world struggles.

27. Which idea was a corollary to the original Monroe Doctrine? (a) The Western Hemisphere is closed to further colonization. (b) The United States has the right to intervene in Latin America. (c) The United States will not intervene in the affairs of Europe. (d) The United States will respect European colonies already established in the New World.

28. The United States used the Roosevelt Corollary to justify (a) intervention in Cuba's rebellion against Spain (b) requests to Latin American countries to join in enforcing the Monroe Doctrine (c) reversal of the policy followed in the Maximilian Affair (d) intervention in the financial affairs of certain Caribbean republics.

29. Dollar diplomacy was used by Presidents Taft and Wilson to (a) aid nations in Asia (b) protect United States investments abroad (c) promote an economic union of European nations (d) encourage adoption of reciprocal tariff agreements.

30. During the late 1920s and early 1930s, United States foreign policy changed most significantly in respect to (a) Canada (b) Great Britain (c) Latin America (d) Germany.

31. Pan-Americanism is chiefly a movement to (a) unite the countries of North America under one government (b) strengthen our military bases in Canada (c) bring about cooperation among the republics of the Western Hemisphere (d) protect the Panama Canal.

32. A sharp contrast in our relations with Latin America is evident between (a) dollar diplomacy and our 1912 intervention in Nicaragua (b) the Roosevelt Corollary and our intervention in Haiti (c) the Olney Interpretation and the Good Neighbor Policy (d) "watchful waiting" and nonrecognition of the Huerta government.

33. When the United States grants specific import privileges to a foreign nation in return for similar privileges for the United States, the agreement is a (a) balance of payments (b) common market (c) protective tariff (d) reciprocal trade pact.

34. The Good Neighbor Policy was promoted by the (a) Platt Amendment (b) "big stick" policy (c) Roosevelt Corollary (d) multilateral interpretation of the Monroe Doctrine.

35. The United States does not trade extensively with Argentina because Argentina (a) exports goods that we also export (b) does not want more foreign trade (c) has nothing to export (d) is tied to the Russian trade bloc.

36. Which of the following countries gave us the *least* cooperation during World War II? (a) Venezuela (b) Brazil (c) Mexico (d) Argentina.

———————————— **MAP QUESTIONS** ————————————

For each area described below, write *both* its name and the letter indicating its location on the map.

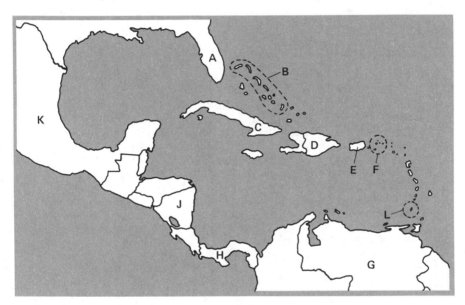

1. Acquired by the United States as a result of the Spanish-American War, this area now has the status of a commonwealth.
2. This area, a protectorate of the United States from 1901 to 1934, later experienced a revolution led by Fidel Castro.
3. Conditions in this area, once ruled by Maximilian, caused President Woodrow Wilson to adopt a policy of "watchful waiting."
4. This area, once considered as an alternate canal route, was occupied by United States troops for most of the years from 1912 to 1933.
5. In 1917 the United States strengthened its naval control of the Caribbean region by purchasing this area from Denmark.
6. This area gained its independence with the aid of President Theodore Roosevelt, who was interested in acquiring the right to build a canal.
7. A boundary dispute in this area led to the issuance of the Olney Interpretation.

——————— MODIFIED TRUE-FALSE QUESTIONS ———————

1. The American battle cry in the Spanish-American War was *"Remember the Alamo!"*
2. The effort by the government of Puerto Rico to improve economic conditions on the island was called *Operation Bootstrap.*
3. The President who first proclaimed the "big-stick" policy was *William McKinley.*
4. The author who urged imperialism in his book *The Influence of Sea Power Upon History* was *Richard Olney.*
5. That the United States would not annex Cuba was stated by the American Congress in the *Foraker Act.*
6. The army surgeon who discovered that yellow fever is transmitted by a certain kind of mosquito was *William Seward.*
7. The naval base that Cuba leased to the United States is located at *Santiago.*
8. The army engineer who had charge of building the Panama Canal was *George W. Goethals.*

——————————— ESSAY QUESTIONS ———————————

1. Foreign-policy makers seek to protect and preserve the *national interest.* In so doing, they establish policies and often must set *priorities.* (a) Explain the meaning, in regard to foreign policy, of the italicized terms. (b) For the United States today, what would you consider to be *two* major aspects of the national interest? Defend your answer. (c) Suggest *three* foreign policies to further the national interests you have identified. (d) To which *one* of these foreign policies would you give top priority? Why?
2. Many individuals and groups have important roles in the making of American foreign policy. For *each* of the following pairs, (a) explain which *one* is more important in making American foreign policy and (b) give *two* reasons to support your opinion: (1) President *or* Congress (2) Senate *or* House of Representatives (3) White House assistant for national security affairs *or* secretary of state (4) Central Intelligence Agency *or* National Security Council (5) newspapers *or* television.
3. Many historians believe that the war with Spain signaled America's turn to imperialism. (a) Explain *two* reasons why, in the latter 19th century, the United States turned toward imperialism. (b) Present *two* arguments to support the claim that, in the war with Spain, America's motives were imperialistic. (c) Present *two* arguments to disprove this claim. (d) Explain *two* effects of the war upon American foreign policy.
4. Giving *one* specific reason in each case, explain why *each* of the following either improved or worsened relations between Latin America and the United States: (a) Wilson's policy toward Mexico (b) Pan-Americanization of the Monroe Doctrine (c) reciprocal trade agreements (d) Venezuela boundary dispute (e) Theodore Roosevelt's policy toward Panama (f) economic and political developments in Puerto Rico since 1898.
5. The relations between the United States and Latin America are vital to the future welfare of the Western Hemisphere. (a) State specifically *two* policies of the United States toward Latin America as expressed in the Monroe Doctrine of 1823.

(b) Discuss *two* actions of the United States in the period 1890–1930 that aroused ill feeling in Latin America. *(c)* Describe *two* activities of the United States in the period 1930–1945 that fostered goodwill in Latin America. *(d)* Describe *two* reasons for the shift in our policies toward Latin America during the period 1930–1945.

6. World War II provided a test for the effectiveness of the Pan-American movement. *(a)* What is meant by Pan-Americanism? *(b)* Discuss *two* ways in which Latin America aided the United States during World War II. *(c)* Explain *one* reason why Argentina was unwilling to support a policy of hemispheric solidarity.

7. "In the Venezuela boundary dispute, the United States helped protect the territory of Venezuela. In the Dominican debt dispute, the United States prevented European occupation of the Dominican Republic. The nations of Latin America should be grateful for American intervention in these disputes." *(a)* What conclusions could you draw from this statement regarding the nationality and foreign policy views of the speaker? Explain your reasoning. *(b)* What might you expect to be the nationality and foreign policy views of a speaker holding an opposing opinion? *(c)* For *each* of the *two* cases cited in the statement, present *one* argument to support an opposing opinion. *(d)* Do you approve or disapprove the statement that the "nations of Latin America should be grateful"? Give *one* reason to support your viewpoint.

PART 4. The United States Pursues Its National Interests in the Far East

AMERICAN INTERESTS IN THE FAR EAST

1. Economic Interests. In 1783, as the American Revolution ended, an American sailing ship began the first successful voyage to China. Thereafter, American merchants created a small but thriving trade with the Far East, delivering furs and textiles, and bringing back tea, silk, and spices. Following the Civil War, as the United States became more industrialized, American manufacturers and investors looked to the Pacific area for markets, raw materials, and investment opportunities.

2. Religious Interests. American missionaries supplied western medical and agricultural knowledge to the Asians and sought to convert them to Christianity.

3. Colonial Acquisitions. Between 1867 and 1899, the United States gathered a colonial empire in the Pacific: purchasing Alaska, annexing Hawaii, securing Guam and the Philippines as a result of the Spanish-American War, and acquiring Midway, Wake, and some Samoan Islands.

4. Defense. American military leaders used our possessions in the Pacific to establish army, navy, and air bases.

PHILIPPINES

PEOPLE AND ECONOMY

Located in the western Pacific, 7000 miles from California, the Philippines has a population of about 58 million. As a result of Spanish rule, the Filipinos are chiefly Roman Catholic, but a small, cohesive minority are Muslim. The Filipinos have a standard of living low compared to Americans, but good compared to most Asians.

The Filipinos are engaged chiefly in agriculture, raising rice, manila hemp, tobacco, coconut oil, and sugar. The islands contain relatively undeveloped mineral deposits of gold, silver, copper, chromium, and iron. Their industrial plants are concerned chiefly with processing agricultural and forest products. The Philippines trades extensively with the United States.

AMERICAN ANNEXATION

1. Reasons. As a result of the Spanish-American War, the United States annexed the Philippines for *(a)* geographic reasons—to gain an opening to eastern Asia, *(b)* economic reasons—for trade, raw materials, and investments, *(c)* military reasons—to establish a strategic base in the Far East, and *(d)* humanitarian reasons—in the words of President McKinley, "to educate the Filipinos, and uplift and civilize and Christianize them."

2. Filipino Opposition. Many Filipinos had expected the United States to withdraw after 1898 and grant them independence. *Emilio Aguinaldo* led the embittered islanders in revolt against American rule. After three years of fighting and at great cost, American forces suppressed the Filipino rebels.

AMERICAN ACHIEVEMENT IN THE PHILIPPINES

1. Economic Development. American investors furthered the development of Filipino resources and processing industries. American authorities promoted extensive public works and helped peasants purchase small farms.

2. Conquest of Disease. American health officials started sanitation programs, wiped out cholera and smallpox, and built hospitals and health centers.

3. Education. By establishing free public schools, the United States substantially reduced illiteracy. Most Filipinos are able to read and write.

4. Gradual Self-Government. The United States trained the islanders for self-government. Beginning in 1907, the Filipinos elected the lower house of their legislature. By the *Jones Act* of 1916, they received the right to elect both houses of the legislature and were promised eventual independence.

AMERICAN SUPPORT FOR PHILIPPINE INDEPENDENCE

1. Reasons. Americans came to realize that most Filipinos desired independence. American producers of sugar and edible oil wanted tariff protection against incoming Philippine sugar and coconut oil. American workers on the Pacific coast wanted to halt the influx of Filipino immigrants who competed for jobs. American taxpayers wanted to end federal spending in the Philippines. American military leaders, concerned by the distant location of the islands, wanted to end American responsibility for Philippine defense.

2. Tydings-McDuffie (Philippine Independence) Act (1934). This act offered the Filipinos independence after a transition period. The act permitted the gradual imposition of American tariffs and provided for sharp restrictions in Filipino immigration. It also empowered the Filipinos to write a constitution and establish a democratic government. The islanders agreed.

PHILIPPINES IN WORLD WAR II

In December 1941, immediately after bombing Pearl Harbor, Japan invaded the Philippines and quickly overran the islands. General *Douglas MacArthur*, American commander in the Far East, fled to Australia but pledged, "I shall return." In 1944 MacArthur came back with a powerful military force and liberated the islands. Throughout the war, the Filipino people resisted the Japanese occupation and demonstrated their loyalty to the United States.

PHILIPPINES AS AN INDEPENDENT NATION

1. Independence. In 1946, at Manila, the Philippines formally received independence from the United States. It also received extensive postwar economic aid, as well as favorable tariff treatment for its exports.

2. Friendship for the United States. In 1947 the Philippines granted the United States military bases, and in 1951 the two nations signed a treaty of mutual defense. In 1954 the Philippines joined the Southeast Asia Treaty Organization (SEATO). To support the American effort in South Vietnam, the Philippine government sent a token force of troops, chiefly engineers.

3. Presidency of Ferdinand E. Marcos (1965–1986). After being elected president of the Philippines in 1965, Marcos acted as follows:

a. Foreign Policy Shifts. Marcos moved somewhat away from a pro-American and toward an independent foreign policy. He withdrew the Filipino troops from Vietnam. In 1975 and 1976, following American setbacks in Indochina, Marcos entered into diplomatic and trade agreements with the Soviet Union and Communist China. In 1979 and 1983, Marcos secured revisions in the agreement regarding American military bases in the Philippines. While allowing the United States "unhampered" military use, the revisions acknowledged

Filipino sovereignty over the bases and stepped up United States economic and military assistance to the Philippines.

b. Moves Against Muslim Guerrillas. Marcos tried to crush a guerrilla movement that demanded a separate state for the Philippines' Muslim minority. After four years of fighting, in which an estimated 50,000 to 100,000 people died, the Libyan government in 1976 helped to arrange a cease-fire. The cease-fire eventually broke down, as the government and the rebels failed to agree on ways of creating a separate Muslim region within the Philippines. Low-level fighting had resumed by the mid-1980s.

c. Communist Insurgency. After the defeat of a Communist insurgency movement called the *Hukbalahap* (or "Huk"), in the 1950s, Philippine Communists reorganized. A group called the New People's Army launched a second rebellion in 1969. By 1986 the movement had an estimated 20,000 to 30,000 guerrilla fighters.

d. Martial Law. In 1972 Marcos imposed martial law, claiming to have uncovered an assassination plot against Defense Minister *Juan Ponce Enrile.* Marcos arrested many leaders of the political opposition. He initiated censorship, seizing newspapers and television stations owned by his critics. In 1973 Marcos proclaimed a new constitution, enabling him to suspend meetings of the legislature and increase his own power. Under martial law, Marcos cracked down on gang violence and private armies. He built many new roads and public buildings and continued a policy of land redistribution. But the nation's economy limped from bad to worse, and widespread corruption in high places fed public unrest. In 1981 Marcos officially ended martial law while holding firmly to power.

e. Assassination of Benigno Aquino. The leading opposition figure, *Benigno Aquino,* moved to the United States after being freed from jail in 1980. He returned from self-exile in 1983, only to be killed by an assassin as he stepped from his airplane at Manila airport. Marcos' opponents charged that high military officials had plotted and carried out the assassination, but late in 1985 a court found the military defendants not guilty. The court said a lone gunman had shot Aquino. The verdict touched off widespread street demonstrations and protests.

f. Marcos's Fall. To demonstrate what he believed to be his continued popularity, Marcos called an early presidential election for February 1986. Most of Marcos's opponents—except the Communists—rallied behind the candidacy of *Corazon Aquino,* widow of the slain opposition leader. She won enthusiastic support and drew large crowds wherever she went. Although many observers believed Aquino won the election, the Marcos-dominated legislature declared the president reelected. Outraged citizens poured into the streets to protest. United States leaders, who up to that point had firmly backed Marcos, now joined in widespread accusations of election fraud. When several high Philippine military leaders switched their support to Aquino, Marcos, his wife, Imelda, and other high officials fled into exile.

4. Presidency of Corazon Aquino (1986–   ). As president, Aquino faced many problems, among the most serious of which were: *(a)* a potential power struggle between civilian and military officials, *(b)* the Communist and Muslim insurgencies, and *(c)* the Philippines' large foreign debt and shaky economy. One of her first jobs was to oversee the adoption of a new constitution in an attempt to stabilize the country's uncertain democracy. Also on the agenda was negotiating with the United States about its military bases in the Philippines— the largest outside American borders. The existing agreement on the bases is scheduled to expire in 1991.

CHINA

APPEAL TO MODERN IMPERIALISTS (FROM THE MID-19th CENTURY)

China, a land occupying much of eastern Asia, attracted imperialist nations for several reasons: (1) China's huge population offered a tremendous market for manufactured goods and cheap labor for foreign-owned enterprises. (2) China's untapped mineral resources—coal, iron, and tin—attracted investors. (3) China's tea and silk found ready Western markets. (4) China's Manchu government was inefficient and lacked military power to withstand the imperialists.

VICTIM OF MODERN IMPERIALISM

Britain, by the *Opium War* (1839–1842), compelled China to (1) allow imports of opium, a habit-forming narcotic, (2) open additional ports to British trade, (3) cede Hong Kong to Britain, and (4) grant British citizens the privilege of *extraterritoriality.* (This entitled Britons accused of crimes in China to be tried in British courts. Extraterritoriality, soon conceded to other foreign nations, offended Chinese justice and pride.) Britain later established a *sphere of influence* over the Yangtze River valley. (A sphere of influence was a region over which an imperialist nation maintained an *economic monopoly:* licensing businesses, controlling tariff rates, and determining railroad and harbor fees.)

Other foreign nations secured trading and extraterritorial rights in China, annexed Chinese territory, and acquired spheres of influence. France gained a sphere of influence in southeastern China, as did Germany in the Shantung Peninsula. Russia annexed territory in northern China and established a sphere of influence over Manchuria. Japan annexed Taiwan (Formosa).

The imperialist nations seemed poised to annex their respective spheres of influence, thereby threatening further to dismember China.

AMERICAN RELATIONS WITH CHINA

The United States had long conducted a small but profitable trade with China. *Caleb Cushing,* American diplomat, negotiated an 1844 treaty with China securing for Americans the trading and extraterritorial privileges extended to other foreigners. However, unlike most foreign nations in China, the United

States annexed no territory and claimed no sphere of influence. American relations with China therefore remained friendly.

OPEN DOOR POLICY (1899)

With the acquisition of the Philippines in 1898, Americans anticipated an increase in our China trade. Such trade was threatened, however, by the existence of spheres of influence and by the prospect of China's dismemberment. *John Hay,* the American secretary of state, therefore proposed equal trading rights in China for all nations—*the Open Door Policy.* Later, it also came to mean the preservation of China's independence and territory. The "open door" was accepted by the imperialist nations in principle, but not in practice. For many years, it served as the cornerstone of American policy toward the Far East.

Historical Analysis. *Was the Open Door Policy an American blunder?*

No. The Open Door Policy helped protect American trade with China. It underscored American "morality" and decency toward weaker nations in contrast with the "wickedness" of the imperialist powers. It earned for America China's goodwill.

Yes. The Open Door Policy was not fully honored by the imperialist nations, thereby making the United States appear naive and helpless. It entangled the United States in Far Eastern affairs, an entanglement not warranted by our limited trade with China. If a single imperialist nation became dominant in the Far East, as Japan did, the Open Door Policy would present the United States with a dilemma: Either abandon it and risk humiliation or uphold it and risk war.

BOXER REBELLION (1900)

The *Boxers,* a Chinese society encouraged by Manchu leaders, staged an uprising to drive out all foreigners and restore China to isolation. They wrecked foreign property and killed foreign citizens, chiefly missionaries, business managers, and diplomatic officials. The Boxers were suppressed by an international military force of European, Japanese, and American troops.

When the foreign nations demanded compensation from China, Secretary of State Hay urged that China pay not by surrendering territory, but by giving a monetary indemnity. The other nations agreed. (When the foreign powers imposed excessive indemnities, the United States returned half of its indemnity to advance education in China and to enable Chinese students to attend American colleges.)

BRIEF SURVEY OF DEVELOPMENTS IN CHINA TO WORLD WAR II

In 1911–1912 the *Kuomintang,* or *Nationalist party,* under *Sun Yat-sen,* overthrew the feeble Manchu Dynasty and proclaimed a republic. Thereafter, the Nationalists struggled to subdue the local warlords. By 1928 General *Chiang Kai-*

shek had led the Nationalist armies to victory over the warlords, but he now faced a greater threat, the Chinese Communists. Following a period of civil war, the Nationalists and Communists arranged a temporary truce to meet the challenge of Japanese imperialism.

JAPAN

OPENING OF JAPAN (1853–1854)

By the mid-17th century, feudal Japan had withdrawn into isolation, and for 200 years remained unaffected by Western civilization.

In 1853–1854 Commodore *Matthew C. Perry,* heading an American naval squadron, convinced Japan to open certain ports to American trade. Soon afterward, the leading European powers demanded and received similar trade rights. In 1857–1858 *Townsend Harris,* America's first consul to Japan, skillfully negotiated treaties expanding diplomatic and commercial relations between the two countries.

WESTERNIZATION OF JAPAN (STARTING IN 1867)

In 1864 European and American warships bombarded a Japanese seaport in retaliation against antiforeign outbreaks. Impressed by Western military might and fearful of foreign domination, the Japanese rapidly transformed their country from medieval feudalism to modern nationhood. In so doing, the Japanese demonstrated a talent for learning from the West and for adapting Western institutions to their needs.

The Japanese (1) established a strong central government with a constitution that concentrated power in the hands of the Emperor and the military leaders, (2) created a powerful army and navy, (3) ended serfdom and enabled many peasants to become landowners, and (4) encouraged a sweeping program of industrialization. Japan soon produced textiles, steel, machinery, and ships, and became a major trading and manufacturing nation.

JAPAN TURNS TO IMPERIALISM

1. Reasons. *(a)* Japanese industrialists needed raw materials—especially cotton, iron ore, and oil—and markets for their manufactured goods. *(b)* Japanese nationalists sought honor for the emperor and glory for the military forces. They thought that colonies would raise Japan to the rank of a world power. *(c)* Densely populated and lacking arable land, Japan wanted colonial outlets for its surplus population. *(d)* Japan was located within easy reach of the underdeveloped nations of eastern Asia, especially China.

2. Sino-Japanese War (1894—1895). In a short war Japan overwhelmed China and acquired Taiwan and a sphere of influence in Korea. (In 1910 Japan annexed Korea.)

3. Russo-Japanese War (1904–1905). Caused by imperialist rivalries over Manchuria and Korea, this war was fought on Chinese territory and in the nearby Pacific waters. Japan, to the world's surprise, defeated Russia.

 a. Treaty of Portsmouth (New Hampshire). President Theodore Roosevelt brought the warring nations together to negotiate the *Treaty of Portsmouth.* Japan gained from Russia the southern half of Sakhalin Island, the lease of Port Arthur (in China), and Russia's sphere of influence in southern Manchuria. Roosevelt was pleased that the Treaty of Portsmouth did not violate the Open Door Policy. (For his efforts, Roosevelt received the 1906 Nobel Peace Prize.)

 b. Significance. (1) Japanese militarists were cheered by their victory, the first in modern times of an Asian nation over a European power. They became determined to place eastern Asia under Japanese domination. (Later, they promised to bring a *New Order* to this so-called *Co-Prosperity Sphere.*) (2) Japanese officials were satisfied with the treaty, but many Japanese resented the lack of any war indemnity and were dissatisfied with their territorial gains. They blamed President Roosevelt and staged anti-American riots. (3) American government officials realized that Japan had become the major power in the Far East. They feared for the safety of the Philippines and the maintenance of the Open Door Policy. To demonstrate American power, President Theodore Roosevelt sent the American navy on an around-the-world tour with a significant stop at Tokyo, where the navy received a friendly welcome. (4) American people became aroused over what was loosely termed the "yellow peril."

JAPAN AND THE UNITED STATES COME INTO CONFLICT

 1. Japanese-American Conflict of Interests. The Japanese resented the discriminatory immigration policies of the United States, and state and local restrictions against Japanese Americans. (Check the Index for Japanese Americans.) These, however, were minor irritations when compared to the basic conflict of interests—American support of the Open Door Policy versus Japan's ambition to dominate China.

 2. Japan's Twenty-one Demands Upon China (1915). During World War I, with the Western powers preoccupied in Europe, Japan tried to turn China into a protectorate by making the *Twenty-one Demands.* Despite American protests, Japan compelled acceptance of most of these demands by weak, defenseless China.

 After the war the United States called the *Washington Conference* (1921–1922) to discuss naval and Far Eastern problems. Under Western persuasion, Japan joined in the *Nine-Power Treaty,* pledging to respect the principles of the Open Door: *(a)* equal trade rights in China, and *(b)* China's territorial integrity and independence.

 3. Japanese Invasion of Manchuria (1931). In violation of the Nine-Power Treaty, Japan invaded the northern Chinese territory of Manchuria, rich in coal, iron, and fertile soil. The *Lytton Commission,* investigating for the

League of Nations, condemned Japan and recommended that it withdraw its troops. Instead, Japan withdrew from the League.

Henry L. Stimson, the United States secretary of state, informed Japan that America disapproved of the aggression in Manchuria. He declared that the United States would not recognize seizure of territory by force—the *Stimson Doctrine.* Neither the League nor the United States took further action.

By 1932 Japan exercised full control over Manchuria. In violation of the Open Door Policy, the Japanese expelled foreign business interests and monopolized the region's economic development. They built railroads, developed hydroelectric power, and created a sizable iron and steel industry, thereby increasing Japan's economic and military power.

4. Japanese Invasion of China (1937). Japan invaded China proper, seeking to control the entire country. Initially, Japanese armies met with success and occupied most of coastal China. By 1939, however, their advance into the interior was slowed, often to a standstill, by Chinese guerrilla resistance. Meanwhile, the United States, in support of China, *(a)* extended loans for the purchase of war materials, *(b)* permitted American volunteer pilots to fight for China as the *Flying Tigers,* and *(c)* in 1940 embargoed the sale to Japan of scrap metal and aviation gasoline. Also, many American consumers boycotted Japanese goods.

5. Japanese Attack on Pearl Harbor (December 7, 1941). Japanese leaders believed that they had to drive out Great Britain and the United States in order to dominate the Far East. In 1937 Japan joined the Axis alliance of Fascist Italy and Nazi Germany. When World War II began in 1939, Japanese leaders believed that their opportunity was at hand. Britain was at war against Germany; the United States was busy supplying military equipment to the Allied nations in Europe. Consequently, on December 7, 1941, Japan staged a surprise attack against the American naval base at Pearl Harbor, Hawaii. Japanese armies invaded British-held Malaya and the American-held Philippines. (Check the Index for "Japan, and World War II.")

——————— **MULTIPLE-CHOICE QUESTIONS** ———————

1. American merchants began trading with the Far East (a) after the Open Door Policy was announced (b) just prior to the Civil War (c) just after the Revolutionary War (d) during the administration of Theodore Roosevelt.

2. The American record in the Philippines includes all of the following *except* (a) training the Filipinos for self-government (b) developing a highly industrialized economy (c) reducing illiteracy (d) improving health conditions.

3. During the 1920s some Americans urged independence for the Philippines because (a) the Filipinos are brown-skinned (b) the Communists were very powerful in the islands (c) Filipino products were entering the United States without payment of any tariff (d) the islands had no need of American military protection.

4. Since independence, the Philippines has followed a foreign policy that (a) favors Communist China (b) opposes entangling alliances (c) supports the United States (d) seeks strict neutrality in the cold war.

5. A sphere of influence, in the history of China, was a region (a) annexed by a foreign power (b) ruled by foreign missionaries (c) nominally Chinese but controlled economically by a foreign power (d) lacking in Chinese courts.

6. The United States decided on its Open Door Policy at a time when China (a) was in danger of being partitioned by foreign nations (b) refused to trade with non-Asian powers (c) was engaged in a civil war between Communists and Nationalists (d) was undergoing rapid industrialization.

7. The major goal of the Open Door Policy was to (a) aid the Chinese Nationalists against the warlords (b) prevent Japan from invading China (c) weaken the Communist movement in China (d) protect United States trading rights in China.

8. The United States won the friendship of China immediately after the Boxer Rebellion by (a) encouraging Japanese expansion into Manchuria (b) returning a portion of the indemnity payments (c) allowing the admission of Chinese immigrants on a quota basis (d) refusing to recognize Chiang Kai-shek.

9. During the 19th century, which Asian nation reacted to Western imperialism by strengthening itself militarily and economically? (a) Philippines (b) Indochina (c) India (d) Japan.

10. Commodore Perry's visit to Japan sought to (a) open Japanese ports to American merchant ships (b) prevent Japanese domination of China (c) break the British monopoly of Japanese trade (d) settle the controversy over the seal fisheries.

11. Which statement best applies to developments in Japan in the 19th and 20th centuries? (a) Industrialization of Japan has been prevented by its lack of natural resources. (b) Japan has rejected cultural and religious influences of other Asian nations. (c) Historically, Japan has experienced a struggle between centralization and decentralization of authority. (d) Japan has adopted and assimilated Western political and economic institutions.

12. American policies toward the Far East during the period 1900 to 1914 (a) aroused Japanese resentment (b) encouraged German ambitions (c) produced a united China (d) weakened British influence.

13. Which event marked the emergence of Japan as a major power? (a) Sino-Japanese War (b) Russo-Japanese War (c) Twenty-one Demands (d) World War I.

14. The Gentlemen's Agreement between the United States and Japan dealt primarily with (a) racial discrimination (b) trade (c) immigration (d) naval disarmament.

15. The major cause of tension between the United States and Japan during the 1930s was Japan's (a) violation of the Open Door Policy (b) expulsion of American missionaries from Japan (c) refusal to trade with the United States (d) military pact with Russia.

16. The Stimson Doctrine (a) had little effect on Japanese aggression in the 1930s (b) was issued when Japan annexed Formosa (c) placed an embargo on the sale of scrap metal to Japan (d) opposed efforts by the League of Nations regarding Manchuria.

17. Japanese imperialism in the 20th century (a) resulted from the desire for new trade routes (b) sought territory as indispensable for national power and prestige (c) was motivated by strong religious desires to convert peoples (d) planned to give Japan's surplus products to less developed areas.

———————————— **MATCHING QUESTIONS** ————————————

Column A

1. Formulated Open Door Policy
2. Overthrew Manchu regime
3. Led Filipino revolt against United States
4. Stated that the United States would recognize no seizure of territory by force
5. Sponsored bill to offer independence to Philippines
6. Commanded American army forces in the Far East
7. Led Chinese Nationalists against warlords and then against Communists
8. Received Nobel Peace Prize for efforts in ending Russo-Japanese War

Column B

a. Emilio Aguinaldo
b. Chiang Kai-shek
c. Townsend Harris
d. John Hay
e. Douglas MacArthur
f. Ferdinand Marcos
g. Theodore Roosevelt
h. Henry L. Stimson
i. Sun Yat-sen
j. Millard Tydings

DISCUSSION ANALYSIS QUESTIONS:
———————————— **PHILIPPINE ISLANDS** ————————————

Speakers *A, B, C, D,* and *E* are discussing the Philippine Islands. Base your answers to the following questions on their statements and on your knowledge of American studies.

Speaker A: "These poor, uncivilized, unchristianized people need our assistance if they are to be uplifted from their ignorance to a point at least approaching our level of civilization and accomplishment. The Philippines must be ours."

Speaker B: "These islands would certainly make excellent coaling stations for our great naval fleet, which is growing each year as Congress approves additional funds for the construction of new ships."

Speaker C: "The shipping interests really find the Philippines to be excellent trading centers. Furthermore, they can be used to develop our commerce with China and Japan. We can use the islands as stopover and storage points for our merchant fleets."

Speaker D: "We have no alternative but to accept the Philippines as our own. God would not forgive us if we rejected his obvious faith and trust in our nation. Democracy must be carried to the four corners of the globe."

Speaker E: "Were our economic rivals to obtain the Philippines, it would be a commercial disaster for us. We entered the race late, but we must not fall behind now."

1. Each statement made by the speakers could be used to justify (1) imperialism (2) containment (3) coexistence (4) genocide.
2. Speaker A would be willing to accept what the British called the (1) defense of democracy (2) appeasement policy (3) lost cause (4) white man's burden.
3. Which speaker's views are most in accord with an economic interpretation of history? (1) A (2) B (3) C (4) D.

4. Speaker *A*'s views are most similar to those of Speaker (1) *E* (2) *B* (3) *C* (4) *D*.
5. Which speaker *most* shows the influence of the writings of Captain Alfred Mahan? (1) *A* (2) *B* (3) *D* (4) *E*.
6. Which speaker believes that the United States has been chosen to carry out a "divine mission"? (1) *B* (2) *C* (3) *D* (4) *E*.
7. A Spanish cultural contribution to the Philippines disproves part of the statement made by Speaker (1) *A* (2) *B* (3) *C* (4) *D*.
8. When referring "our economic rivals," Speaker *E* is *most* concerned about (1) Canada (2) Russia (3) Britain (4) Italy.

———————————————— **ESSAY QUESTIONS** ————————————————

1. As a result of the Spanish-American War, the United States acquired the Philippines. Discuss *(a) two* reasons why the United States annexed the Philippines *(b) two* problems that the Philippines posed for the United States after annexation *(c) two* reasons why the United States later offered the Philippines independence and *(d) one* way the Philippines was affected by World War II.
2. The United States championed the Open Door Policy with regard to China. *(a)* Briefly state the terms of the Open Door Policy. *(b)* Describe *one* circumstance that led to the issuance of the Open Door Policy. *(c)* Describe *one* incident in which Japan threatened the Open Door Policy during the period 1905 to 1945, and explain *one* action taken by the United States government to resist this threat.
3. Describe *one* action taken by the United States as a result of *each* of the following developments in the Far East: *(a)* emigration from the Far East to the United States between 1875 and 1929 *(b)* Boxer Rebellion *(c)* Russo-Japanese War *(d)* Twenty-one Demands *(e)* Japan's seizure of Manchuria *(f)* Japan's invasion of China proper.

PART 5. The United States Becomes Involved in World War I

EUROPE GOES TO WAR (1914)

Divided into two hostile alliances, the major European nations had provoked each other in a series of international crises. They had turned Europe into a "powder keg" ready to explode into war. When in 1914 a Serbian (Yugoslav) nationalist assassinated the heir to the Austro-Hungarian throne, World War I began. In the initial stage of the war, the conflicting nations were (1) the *Central Powers*—Germany and Austria-Hungary—against (2) the *Allies*—Great Britain, France, Russia, Serbia, and Belgium.

FUNDAMENTAL CAUSES OF WORLD WAR I

1. Nationalism. *(a)* France was determined to retake the French-inhabited provinces of Alsace and Lorraine that were seized in 1871 by Germany after

France's defeat in the Franco-Prussian War. *(b)* Subject nationalities sought in-dependence. Yugoslavs, Czechs, and Slovaks sought freedom from Austria-Hun-gary. Poles, divided among Russia, Austria-Hungary, and Germany, longed to re-create a self-governing Polish state. *(c)* Intense patriotism assured popular sup-port for warlike measures.

2. Imperialism. *(a)* France and Germany clashed over Morocco. *(b)* Rus-sia and Austria-Hungary were rivals in the Balkans. *(c)* Britain and Germany com-peted for imperialist control in Africa and the Middle East, and for world markets.

3. Militarism. *(a)* By peacetime conscription of soldiers, the Continental European nations each sought military superiority. *(b)* Germany had a military tradition and extolled armed might. *(c)* Britain, relying heavily upon its navy for protection, felt threatened by Germany's huge naval building program.

4. International Anarchy. *(a)* No international organization existed with authority to compel nations to obey its decisions. *(b)* The *Hague Court of Arbitration*, a tribunal to settle international disputes, depended on voluntary ac-ceptance of its authority and was ineffective.

OTHER NATIONS ENTER THE WAR

1. The Central Powers were joined by Turkey and Bulgaria.
2. The Allied Powers were joined by more than 25 nations. Most notable

Europe: The Opposing Sides in World War I

were *(a)* in 1914, Japan, which acted primarily to seize German territories in the Pacific, *(b)* in 1915, Italy, which had refused to honor its alliance with the Central Powers and was won over to the Allies by a secret treaty promising territorial gains, and *(c)* in 1917, the United States.

AMERICAN ENTRANCE INTO WORLD WAR I: REASONS

When war started in 1914, President Woodrow Wilson urged the American people to be "neutral in fact as well as in name" and issued a *Proclamation of Neutrality*. However, Americans could not help but take sides. Except for some Irish Americans, traditionally anti-English, and some German Americans, most people strongly sympathized with the Allies. In the administration, Wilson and his advisers mostly favored the Allies.

Despite his pro-Allied leanings, Wilson hoped to keep the United States neutral. In November, 1916, Wilson narrowly won reelection with the slogan, "He kept us out of war." In April 1917, only five months later, Wilson asked Congress to declare war on Germany. The main reasons, according to historians, were the following:

1. Unrestricted Submarine Warfare by Germany. To blockade Britain and counteract British superiority in surface vessels, the Germans resorted to *unrestricted submarine warfare.* The United States contended that German submarines, or *U-boats,* violated international law by interfering with *freedom of the seas: (a)* the right of American merchant ships to trade with belligerents in goods not intended for war use, and *(b)* the right of American citizens to sail on the merchant ships of belligerents. The American people were outraged as German U-boats violated our neutral rights and took an increasing toll of American lives. Before the United States entered the war, over 200 Americans, most traveling on Allied merchant ships, perished as a result of Germany's submarine warfare.

a. Sinking of the **Lusitania** *(1915).* A German U-boat sank the *Lusitania,* a British passenger liner, without first searching for contraband war goods and without providing for the safety of the crew and passengers. More than 1000 persons lost their lives, including over 100 Americans. The United States vigorously protested this "illegal and inhuman act." The Germans replied that the *Lusitania* had carried contraband and that Americans had been warned, by a newspaper advertisement, to stay off the ship.

b. Sussex Pledge (1916). A U-boat torpedoed an unarmed French vessel, the *Sussex,* injuring several American passengers. When President Wilson threatened to sever diplomatic relations, the German government gave the *Sussex Pledge,* not to sink merchant vessels without first attempting to save lives.

c. Unrestricted Submarine Warfare Again (1917). Believing that they now had enough U-boats to starve Britain, the German leaders took the risk of war with the United States and renewed their unrestricted submarine warfare. U-boats soon sank several unarmed American merchant ships. President Wilson ordered guns placed on our merchant ships and shortly afterward asked Congress to declare war.

(In spite of our protests, Britain blockaded our trade with the Central Powers, forced American ships into British ports to be searched, and intercepted American mail. However, Americans were less angered by British than by German acts, since British interference with our neutral rights did not endanger American lives.)

2. Allied Propaganda. Americans were receptive to Allied propaganda. *(a)* We felt a kinship for Britain, based upon a common language, culture, and belief in the democratic way of life. *(b)* Our friendship for France went back to French support of the colonial cause in the American Revolution.

3. Hostility Toward Germany. The American people became increasingly hostile toward Germany because the Germans *(a)* supported a thinly veiled dictatorship controlled by the military and the Kaiser, *(b)* invaded Belgium in violation of a treaty guaranteeing Belgian neutrality, *(c)* waged unrestricted submarine warfare, *(d)* attempted to sabotage American industries, and *(e)* plotted to draw Mexico into war against the United States, as evidenced by the *Zimmermann Note.*

(German Foreign Minister Zimmermann in early 1917 sent instructions to the German minister in Mexico. In the event of German-American hostilities, he was to induce Mexico to declare war against the United States. Mexico might then regain Texas, New Mexico, and Arizona. Intercepted by the British, this secret German message inflamed American war sentiment.)

4. American Economic Interests. Because Britain effectively blockaded the Central Powers, Americans sold foodstuffs and manufactured goods almost entirely to the Allies. Our manufacturers, workers, farmers, and exporters all shared in a period of prosperity. When the Allies exhausted their funds, American investors extended them substantial loans. Americans feared that, if Germany won the war, American loans to the Allies might never be repaid.

5. American Idealism. Americans felt that a better world would emerge if the Allied nations triumphed over the autocratic Central Powers. President Wilson called World War I the "war to end all wars" and proclaimed that "the world must be made safe for democracy."

6. American Security. Germany, if victorious, would have replaced democratic Britain as the dominant European power on the Atlantic. From this location, aggressive, militaristic Germany could have threatened the security of the United States.

AMERICA AT WAR: THE HOME FRONT

1. Increasing Presidential Powers. Wilson provided strong wartime leadership. He received from Congress broad powers to direct the economy and spur the war effort. Wilson commanded an array of government agencies representing a tremendous expansion of federal and executive power.

2. Mobilizing the Economy. The *War Industries Board* allocated raw materials and expanded war production. The *War Labor Board* mediated labor disputes to prevent work stoppages. The *Railroad Administration* took control of the railroads, unifying and improving their operations. The *Shipping Board* built a "bridge of ships" to transport armies and equipment to the European fighting fronts. The *Fuel Administration* stepped up the production of coal, gas, and oil. The *Food Administration* increased farm output and encouraged the public to observe "wheatless" and "meatless" days.

3. Punishing Espionage and Sedition. *(a)* The *Espionage Act* (1917) provided penalties for spying, sabotage, and obstructing the war effort, and banned antiwar materials from the mail. *(b)* The *Sedition Act* (1918) provided penalties for speaking or writing against the American form of government or the war effort. These laws, leading to the arrest of some 1500 pacifists and pro-Germans, reflected wartime unwillingness to tolerate dissent.

4. Financing the War. The government *(a)* raised income taxes and levied new and heavier excise taxes, securing $11 billion, or one-third of the cost of the war, and *(b)* borrowed from the American people by selling them *Liberty* and *Victory Bonds,* securing $21 billion, or two-thirds of the war's cost. The United States lent the Allies $10 billion to purchase war supplies.

5. Providing Military Forces. Congress passed several *Selective Service Acts.* Our armed forces consisted of almost 3 million draftees together with 2 million volunteers. The dispatch of army units to Europe was hastened by desperate Allied appeals for American troops to turn the tide of battle.

MILITARY ASPECTS OF THE WAR

1. Worldwide Involvement. For the first time in history, all major nations throughout the world were involved in the same war.

2. New Weapons. The following were introduced into warfare: dirigibles, submarines, giant artillery guns, tanks, poison gas, and, very significant, the airplane. It was employed at first mainly for observation purposes but later for small-scale bombings and for attacks on ground forces.

3. Naval Warfare. The British navy, aided by the French, maintained control of the Atlantic shipping lanes, combatted the German submarine menace, and effectively blockaded the Central Powers. In 1917 the American navy bolstered the Allied fleets. Together they convoyed merchant and troop ships to Europe.

4. American Military Contribution in Europe. By early 1918, the military situation in Europe was as follows: *(a)* The *western front,* in France, was deadlocked. The opposing armies were dug into the ground for *trench warfare.* *(b)* The *eastern front* was no more. In 1917 Russia had experienced two revolutions and had come under Communist rule. In 1918 Russia withdrew from the war, freeing German forces for transfer to the western front.

The *American Expeditionary Force* (AEF), totaling 2 million soldiers and led by General *John J. Pershing,* turned the tide of battle in France. In 1918 American forces helped halt a German offensive at *Château-Thierry* and *Belleau Wood.* Later they led the Allied end-the-war counteroffensive at *St. Mihiel* and in the *Argonne Forest.*

5. German Surrender. By late 1918 the German High Command under Generals *von Hindenburg* and *Ludendorff* realized that the German armies, although still fighting on foreign soil, had lost the war. Germany sued for peace and on November 11, 1918, ended hostilities by accepting an *armistice.*

PRESIDENT WILSON'S FOURTEEN POINTS

In 1918, before the end of the war, President Wilson addressed Congress on American war aims. His program, which evoked enthusiasm throughout the world, called for a lasting peace based upon *Fourteen Points:* (1) open covenants (treaties) of peace openly arrived at, (2) freedom of the seas, (3) removal of international trade barriers, (4) reduction of armaments, (5) impartial adjustment of colonial claims with due regard for the interests of the native peoples, (6–13) adjustment of European boundaries in accordance with the principle of *nationality,* that is, the right of any national group to self-determination regarding its own government and independent state, and (14) establishment of a League of Nations.

Allied leaders approved Wilson's Fourteen Points only with significant reservations—notably claims to territorial gains and to protection of vital national interests.

TREATY OF VERSAILLES WITH GERMANY (1919)

1. Different Allied Objectives. The "Big Four," the Allied leaders who dominated the peace conference, each sought different objectives. *(a) David Lloyd George,* Prime Minister of Great Britain, sought to expand Britain's colonial empire, preserve its naval and industrial supremacy, and "make Germany pay for the war." *(b) Georges Clemenceau,* Premier of France, sought to make France safe against future German invasion and weaken Germany by imposing military limitations, financial payments, and territorial losses. *(c) Vittorio Orlando,* Premier of Italy, sought to enlarge Italy's territory in Europe and expand its empire overseas. *(d) Woodrow Wilson,* President of the United States, sought to provide a just peace and create a better world by implementing his Fourteen Points.

Out of these different and often conflicting objectives emerged the *Treaty of Versailles,* the result of months of struggle and compromise.

Europe Following World War I

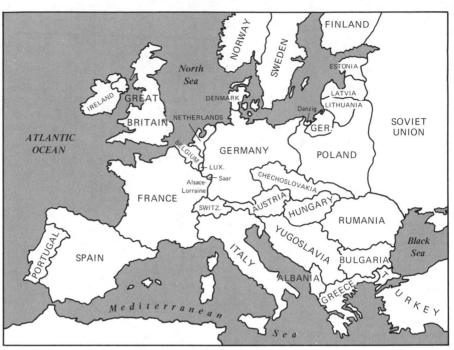

2. Major Treaty Provisions

*a. **Territorial Changes.*** Germany surrendered (1) Alsace-Lorraine to France, (2) minor border regions to Denmark and Belgium, (3) parts of Posen and west Prussia, including a corridor to the Baltic Sea, to the new nation of Poland (this "Polish Corridor" cut off east Prussia from the rest of Germany), (4) Danzig, a Baltic city, which was placed under League of Nations authority to provide Poland with its only seaport.

Except for mainly German-inhabited Danzig, these territorial changes were in accord with the principle of nationality. The territory granted to Poland, however, contained a considerable German minority.

*b. **Colonial Losses.*** Germany ceded all its colonies to the Allies, to be held as League of Nations mandates.

*c. **Disarmament.*** The German army was limited to 100,000 volunteers. Conscription was forbidden. The Rhineland, in western Germany, was demilitarized. The German navy was reduced to a few small ships. Submarines, military aircraft, and war industries were prohibited. These military restrictions were intended to prevent Germany from again waging war.

*d. **War Guilt and Reparations.*** Germany accepted sole responsibility for causing the war and agreed to pay reparations for war damages. After a few payments, Germany repudiated most of the debt.

e. League of Nations. The first article of the treaty provided for the establishment of the League of Nations. (Check the Index.)

Historical Analysis. *Was the Treaty of Versailles harsh or fair?*

A Harsh Treaty That Planted the Seeds of World War II. The treaty took German-inhabited territory away from Germany, forced Germany to give up all its colonies, and compelled it to accept sole "war guilt." It forced Germany to be unarmed while other nations remained armed, and it wounded German pride. Later, by attacking the treaty, the Nazi party gained the support of the German people, achieved power, and brought on World War II.

A Fair Treaty That Was Not Enforced. The treaty transferred German territory chiefly on the basis of nationality, assigned German colonies as League of Nations mandates with the objective of eventual independence, disarmed Germany as a start toward world disarmament, and provided for a League of Nations. The treaty alone cannot be blamed for the German people's later support of Nazism. Furthermore, if the military provisions of the treaty had been enforced, Nazi Germany would not have been able to wage war.

TREATIES WITH THE OTHER DEFEATED NATIONS

The Allies signed separate treaties with each of the other Central Powers. The treaties with Austria and Hungary breaking up the Austro-Hungarian Empire. (1) Austria and Hungary became independent national states. (2) Czechoslovakia, a new republic, was created entirely out of Austro-Hungarian territories. (3) Italy, Rumania, Poland, and Yugoslavia secured areas inhabited by their own nationals. (4) Austria was forbidden *Anschluss,* or union, with Germany.

RESULTS OF WORLD WAR I

1. Social. *(a)* Almost 10 million soldiers were killed and over 20 million wounded. *(b)* Millions of civilians died as a result of the hostilities, famine, and disease. *(c)* The world was left with a legacy of hatred, intolerance, and extreme nationalism.

2. Economic. *(a)* The total cost of the war was over $350 billion. Paying for the war brought heavy taxation and lower living standards to European peoples. *(b)* After the war, international trade suffered because nations raised tariffs and sought economic self-sufficiency. *(c)* In Russia, the Communists seized power and introduced a new economic system. *(d)* Economic dislocations caused by the war helped bring on the Great Depression.

3. Political. *(a)* Three major European dynasties were dethroned: the Hohenzollerns of Germany, the Hapsburgs of Austria-Hungary, and the Romanovs of Russia. *(b)* New nations arose in central Europe. Several contained minority groups (subject nationalities), such as the German-speaking populations of Poland and Czechoslovakia. *(c)* Beset by economic and political discontent, many European nations—notably Russia, Italy, and Germany—turned to dictatorship. *(d)* The League of Nations was established to solve international problems and advance world peace. *(e)* The United States emerged as a leading world power, though reluctant to assume international responsibilities.

——————— MULTIPLE-CHOICE QUESTIONS ———————

1. Which most directly resulted from late 19th-century European nationalism? (a) the economic unification of Europe (b) the creation of strong international peace organizations (c) the development of new European colonies in the Western Hemisphere (d) intensified rivalry and conflict among European nations.

2. The division of the major European powers into two rival alliances in the years preceding 1914 resulted in a (a) reduction of world tensions (b) decline of imperialism (c) decrease in military expenditures (d) series of international crises.

3. The suppression of subject nationalities contributed to the outbreak of World War I. This statement can be illustrated by (a) Austro-Hungarian domination of part of present-day Yugoslavia (b) German domination of Danzig (c) French domination of Alsace and Lorraine (d) German and French domination of Morocco.

4. Which was a characteristic of the period 1900 to 1914? (a) a series of armament races involving European nations (b) a series of Communist revolutions in central Europe (c) an international organization that fostered discussion of common problems (d) the rise of dictatorships in Italy and Germany.

5. President Wilson's policy at the beginning of World War I was to (a) send lend-lease aid to nations attacked by Germany (b) declare war against the Central Powers (c) prohibit trade with warring nations (d) issue a Proclamation of Neutrality.

6. Immediately following the sinking of the *Lusitania,* President Wilson (a) signed a secret treaty to give aid to Britain (b) presented his Fourteen Points as a basis for promoting world peace (c) refused to be stampeded into any hasty act leading to war (d) prohibited Americans from traveling on ships of belligerents.

7. The immediate cause for the entry of the United States into World War I was Germany's (a) attempt to arrange an alliance with Mexico (b) invasion of Belgium (c) resumption of unrestricted submarine warfare (d) campaign of sabotage in the United States.

8. Which is *not* considered a factor that influenced the United States to enter World War I? (a) financial commitments to the Allies (b) desire to gain overseas possessions (c) desire to repay France for its assistance during our Revolutionary War (d) concern over the survival of democracy.

9. The United States raised money to carry on World War I primarily by (a) high protective tariffs (b) the sale of government-owned property (c) loans obtained from the American people (d) loans obtained from the Allied nations.

10. One of the aims of the United States during World War I was (a) the defeat of Japan (b) the collection of indemnities from Germany (c) freedom of the seas (d) the division of Germany into two countries.

11. Which would be consistent with one of the Fourteen Points? (a) the formation of new national states in Europe (b) the permanent separation of East Germany and West Germany (c) a secret military alliance between the United States and Japan (d) an increase in the United States tariff rates to keep out German goods.

12. Which principle of Wilson's Fourteen Points was incorporated in the Treaty of Versailles? (a) open diplomacy (b) removal of economic barriers (c) limitation of armaments for all signers of the treaty (d) a League of Nations.

13. An important result of World War I was that in many European nations (a) living standards rose (b) foreign trade increased (c) nationalism became less intense (d) dictators seized control.

14. Another result of World War I was that the United States (a) became a creditor nation and world power (b) abandoned its interests in the Caribbean area (c) initiated a policy of imperialism in the Far East (d) feared Germany's emergence as an Atlantic power.

15. To find out if the United States fulfilled its war aims in World War I, a historian should (a) study accounts of the war found in United States magazines published during that time (b) compare the conditions leading to United States involvement in the war with the conditions after the war (c) compare maps of Europe in 1914 and in 1920 (d) compare the Republican and Democratic platforms in the election of 1920.

—————— MODIFIED TRUE-FALSE QUESTIONS ——————

1. The *Lusitania,* sunk by a German submarine during World War I, was *an American ship.*

2. In winning the Presidential election of 1916, Woodrow Wilson was aided by the slogan, *"The world must be made safe for democracy."*

3. The Zimmermann Note called for a German offer of American territory to *Japan.*

4. The head of the American Expeditionary Force during World War I was General *John J. Pershing.*

5. In 1918 pacifists in the United States who spoke against American participation in World War I were subject to prosecution under the provisions of the *Sussex Pledge.*

6. Allied territorial claims, often in conflict with the principles of the Fourteen Points, were based upon *secret treaties.*

7. In returning Alsace and Lorraine to France, the Treaty of Versailles was *in accord with* the Fourteen Points.

8. The Treaty of Versailles limited Germany to an army of *one million soldiers.*

—————————— ESSAY QUESTIONS ——————————

1. *(a)* Briefly discuss *three* reasons why the United States entered World War I. *(b)* Evaluate these three reasons, explaining which one you consider most important, which one second in importance, and which one least important.

2. Describe *one* way in which the United States dealt with *each* of the following problems during World War I: *(a)* expanding industrial and agricultural production *(b)* providing personnel for the armed forces *(c)* influencing public opinion.

3. *(a)* List *four* important provisions of the Treaty of Versailles. *(b)* Discuss *two* reasons why Germany criticized this treaty. *(c)* Would you agree or disagree with each of the German criticisms? Explain your answer. *(d)* Did the Treaty of Versailles plant the seeds of World War II? Present *one* argument to support your answer.

4. Describe *two* important results of World War I in *each* of the following areas:
   (a) social *(b)* economic *(c)* political.

PART 6. The United States Is Torn Between Isolation and International Cooperation (1919–1939)

OPPOSING VIEWPOINTS ON AMERICAN FOREIGN POLICY

1. Isolation: The Predominant Sentiment

a. Disillusionment With World War I. Many Americans were disappointed with the results of the war. It had proved costly in American lives and money. Instead of making "the world safe for democracy," it had led to major European dictatorships. Instead of being a "war to end all wars," it had apparently planted the seeds for another world conflict.

b. American Tradition of Isolation. Isolationists claimed that, except for World War I, the United States had consistently and successfully pursued a policy of isolation. Now they demanded that the United States return to and strictly adhere to its traditional policy.

c. Peace Through Isolation. Isolationists argued that America could have peace only by shutting itself off from the rest of the world. Let Uncle Sam "stay on his side of the street" while Europe "stews in its own juice."

Isolationist sentiment was powerful during the 1920s as well as during the depression years, when Americans concentrated upon domestic problems. It found expression in books, plays, and newspapers, and it received strong support from a powerful group of Senators.

2. International Cooperation: The Minority View

a. Defense of World War I. Internationalists defended American entrance into World War I by emphasizing Wilsonian idealism and national security. They claimed that, by rejecting world leadership, the United States endangered its own security and lost the opportunity to assure world peace.

b. Failure of Isolation. Opponents of isolation insisted that isolation had not worked in the past, pointing to American involvement in the Napoleonic Wars (by the War of 1812) and World War I. Now that economic factors and scientific progress had brought nations even closer together, internationalists argued, isolation was unrealistic.

c. Peace Through International Cooperation. Internationalists argued that America could have peace only by cooperating with peace-loving nations against aggression. We cannot "stop the world and get off."

Sentiment for cooperation grew in the late 1930s, as Americans observed

Fascist militarism and aggression. President Franklin D. Roosevelt, who had served under and admired Wilson, worked cautiously but deliberately to swing public opinion away from isolation. However, not until Britain stood alone in World War II did international cooperation achieve acceptance by a majority of Americans.

UNITED STATES REFUSAL TO JOIN THE LEAGUE OF NATIONS

1. Brief Survey of the League of Nations

a. Establishment. Woodrow Wilson believed that the single most important step toward world peace was the League of Nations. Wilson succeeded in placing the League Covenant (Charter) into the Treaty of Versailles.

b. Purposes. By international cooperation, the League proposed to (1) deal with economic and social problems, (2) encourage disarmament, and (3) settle disputes among nations peacefully. If an aggressor nation refused to submit to peaceful settlement, the League could advise, but not force, its member nations to employ coercive measures, called *sanctions.* These might be withdrawing ambassadors; halting trade; and, finally, using military force.

2. Senate Defeat of the Treaty of Versailles and the League

a. Republican Opposition. In control of the Senate, the Republicans consisted of (1) a small group of extreme isolationists, notably *William Borah, Hiram Johnson,* and *Robert La Follette,* and (2) a large group of more moderate Senators, most of whom supported the chairman of the Foreign Relations Committee, *Henry Cabot Lodge, Sr.* Bitterly hostile to Wilson, Senator Lodge determined to humiliate the President, to "republicanize" the Treaty of Versailles, and to protect American sovereignty by adding to the League Charter interpretations, called *reservations.* Lodge held lengthy committee hearings to delay action and win support from the public and the Senate.

b. Arguments Against the League. Lodge and his supporters offered the following arguments: (1) The League might involve the United States in a war, thereby violating the American Constitution, which gives Congress the exclusive power to declare war. (2) The League might interfere in domestic matters, such as tariff and immigration policies. (3) The League would be under the disproportionate influence of Great Britain, since Britain and each of its dominions had a vote in the League Assembly. (4) League membership would involve us in world problems and violate America's traditional policy of isolation.

c. Wilson's Countermoves. Wilson denounced the Lodge reservations. To arouse the people and to bring pressure on the Senate, Wilson undertook an extensive speaking tour. His efforts ended abruptly when, overworked and exhausted, he suffered a paralytic stroke. From his sickbed, Wilson instructed the Democrats in the Senate to reject the Lodge reservations.

d. The Senate Votes. The Senate overwhelmingly defeated the Treaty of Versailles with the Lodge reservations and then also rejected the unamended treaty. In a third and final vote, some Democrats disregarded Wilson's instructions and supported the treaty with the Lodge reservations. The amended treaty, however, fell seven votes short of the required two-thirds majority. (Later, the United States negotiated a peace treaty that ended the war with Germany but that did not provide for a League.)

   e. Who Defeated the Treaty and the League? The Treaty of Versailles was defeated by (1) Lodge, by his insistence on reservations, (2) Wilson, by his refusal to compromise, and (3) the American people. At first, most people probably favored League membership, but they did not speak out with sufficient strength. As the League debate raged, Americans became confused, disillusioned, and unwilling to assume the burdens of world leadership.

   3. Election of 1920 and the League. Appealing to the voters again, Wilson asked that the Presidential election of 1920 be a "great and solemn referendum" on the League. James M. Cox, the Democratic candidate, campaigned vigorously for the League. Warren G. Harding, the Republican candidate, urged a "return to normalcy" but took no definite stand on the League.

   The voters were influenced by other factors, all working against the Democrats: falling farm prices; growing unemployment; disillusionment with the war; and the resentment of various national groups who blamed Wilson for treating Germany harshly, denying territory to Italy, and failing to secure independence for Ireland. Harding won an overwhelming triumph. He interpreted the result to mean that the American people opposed League membership.

HISTORY OF THE LEAGUE: A FAILURE

1. Reasons for Failure

   a. Membership. The League did not include all major nations. The United States never joined. The Soviet Union entered the League in 1934 but was expelled in 1939. Germany and Japan withdrew in 1933, as did Italy four years later.

   b. Voting. League decisions required *unanimous* votes.

   c. Powers. The League lacked the power to tax and to draft an army. Although the League could request money and troops from its members, each state was free to respond according to its own national interests. The League was not a world government, but a weak *confederation*.

   2. Record of Failure. Although the League settled minor disputes between small nations, it failed in major crises to stop *(a)* the Japanese invasion of Manchuria, *(b)* the Italian conquest of Ethiopia, and *(c)* German rearmament, in violation of the Versailles Treaty, and German territorial seizures.

   In 1946 the League disbanded and transferred its properties to the new world organization, the United Nations.

LIMITED INTERNATIONAL COOPERATION BY THE UNITED STATES

1. The United States Cooperates With the League. The United States cooperated with the League by *(a)* joining the *International Labor Organization* (ILO), a League agency to improve world labor conditions, *(b)* working with other League agencies to wipe out disease, suppress slavery, and establish standards in communication and transportation, and *(c)* supporting the League during the crisis over Manchuria. (Check the Index for "Stimson Doctrine.")

2. The United States Joins in Naval Disarmament

a. Early Agreements. To reduce the tax burden and to avoid a naval armaments race, which had helped cause World War I, the United States cooperated with other naval powers in seeking a reduction of naval forces.

(1) *Washington Conference (1921–1922).* The United States, Great Britain, Japan, France, and Italy agreed to stop building capital ships (large warships) for ten years and to maintain capital ships for each nation in a ratio of 5:5:3:1.67:1.67, respectively.

(2) *London Naval Conference (1930).* The United States, Great Britain, and Japan agreed to a ratio of approximately 10:10:7, for five years, for cruisers and destroyers as well as capital ships.

b. Eventual Failure. At the *London Conference* (1935), the United States and Britain faced a Japanese demand for a 10:10:10 ratio, or *parity*. The democracies refused on the ground that Japan had no need of such naval power unless for aggression. No agreement was reached; soon afterward Japan started a new naval race.

3. The United States Joins in International Pacts

a. Nine-Power Treaty at the Washington Conference (1921–1922). The United States, Japan, Britain, France, and five smaller nations agreed to support equal trading rights in China and to respect China's independence, thus reaffirming the Open Door Policy.

b. Kellogg-Briand Pact (1928). Frank Kellogg, United States secretary of state, and *Aristide Briand,* French foreign minister, proposed a pact to settle all disputes peacefully and to outlaw war "as an instrument of national policy." Most nations, including Germany, Japan, and Italy, signed this idealistic statement, also called the *Pact of Paris.*

c. Failure of International Pacts. In the 1930s militarist Japan, Fascist Italy, and Nazi Germany all violated the Kellogg-Briand Pact. Japan also violated the Nine-Power Treaty. Without provision for enforcement, these agreements proved worthless.

FURTHER EVIDENCES OF ISOLATION BY THE UNITED STATES

1. Refusal to Join the World Court. The World Court was established by the League to settle disputes between nations according to international law. Despite the requests of four successive Presidents—Harding, Coolidge, Hoover, and Roosevelt—Senate isolationists managed to keep the United States from membership in the World Court. They insisted that the World Court was a "back door" into the League.

2. Immigration Restrictions. By a series of immigration laws in the 1920s, drastically limiting admissions, Congress expressed American sentiment for fewer world contacts—an aspect of isolationism.

3. High Tariff Policy. Congress restored high import duties and in 1930 passed the highest rates ever, the *Smoot-Hawley Tariff Act.* By such protectionism, Congress reflected the isolationist view in economic matters.

4. Insistence Upon Repayment of War Debts. During World War I the European Allies—mainly Britain, France, and Italy—borrowed $10 billion from the United States, primarily to buy American war materials. Thereafter, the Allies claimed that they could not repay these loans, especially since America's high tariffs made it difficult for them to sell goods here and secure dollars.

The United States refused to cancel the war debts. By 1934, as all debtor nations except Finland had ceased repayments, Congress passed the *Johnson Debt Default Act.* It prohibited public or private loans to any foreign government that had defaulted on debts in the United States.

5. American Neutrality Acts (1935, 1937). As Germany and Italy became more and more aggressive, Americans sensed that Europe was again headed toward war. Congress passed two *Neutrality Acts* which *(a)* prohibited the sale of war implements to belligerents, *(b)* prohibited loans to belligerents, *(c)* prohibited Americans from sailing on ships of belligerents, and *(d)* restricted the entry of American merchant ships into war zones.

These acts surrendered traditional American claims to freedom of the seas. Congress hoped that neutrality would prevent the economic and emotional entanglements that, many believed, had involved the United States in World War I.

6. Unfavorable Response to President Roosevelt's "Quarantine" Speech (1937). After Japan's invasion of China proper, President Franklin D. Roosevelt braved isolationist sentiment by delivering his "quarantine" speech. Citing "the present reign of terror and international lawlessness," Roosevelt warned, "let no one imagine that America will escape . . . that this Western Hemisphere will not be attacked." He compared world lawlessness to an "epidemic of physical disease" and proposed that the aggressor nations be subjected to "quarantine." Deliberately vague, Roosevelt wanted to test the readiness of Americans to support efforts against the aggressors.

Public and press reaction to the speech was generally unfavorable. Americans still believed that they could avoid war by maintaining isolation. Extreme isolationists called Roosevelt a "warmonger."

PART 7. The Allies Defeat the Axis and Win World War II

AXIS NATIONS: JAPAN, ITALY, AND GERMANY

Imperial Japan was controlled by the military, Fascist Italy was led by the dictator *Benito Mussolini,* and Nazi Germany was headed by the dictator *Adolf Hitler.* These nations (1) engaged in one act of aggression after another, thereby violating, without any effective opposition, the major international peace agreements: the Treaty of Versailles, the Covenant of the League of Nations, the Nine-Power Treaty, and the Kellogg-Briand Pact, (2) withdrew from membership in the League, and (3) joined together to form a military alliance, the *Rome-Berlin-Tokyo Axis.*

RECORD OF AXIS AGGRESSION

1. Manchuria. In 1931–1932 Japan invaded and conquered China's northern province of Manchuria. (Check the Index for Manchuria.)

2. Ethiopia. In 1935 Italy invaded the African nation of Ethiopia. The League of Nations branded Italy an aggressor and voted minor economic sanctions but not an embargo on Italy's most essential import, oil. Undeterred by such feeble opposition, Mussolini conquered and annexed Ethiopia.

3. German Remilitarization. Nazi Germany violated the Treaty of Versailles in 1935 by reintroducing conscription and in 1936 by remilitarizing the Rhineland. Hitler encountered no serious Allied opposition although Germany's military strength was then still slight.

4. Spain. In 1936 General *Francisco Franco* began a revolt against the legally elected left-of-center government of Spain. The Loyalists, who supported the elected government, received limited aid from the Soviet Union; Franco received extensive support of troops and equipment from Italy and Germany. After three years of civil war, Franco won complete control and established a military dictatorship. The Spanish civil war served Nazi Germany as a testing ground for new weapons and military tactics, such as dive-bombings and tank assaults, later used in World War II.

5. China. In 1937 Japanese forces from Manchuria invaded China proper. (Check the Index for China.)

Axis Aggressions in Europe   1933–1942

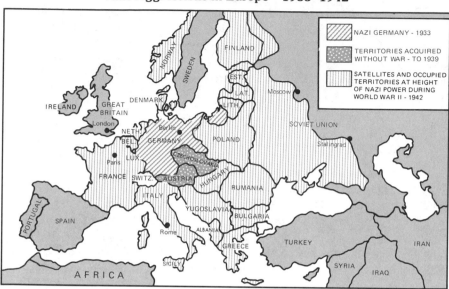

6. Austria. In 1938 Hitler invaded and annexed Austria, claiming that all German-speaking people belonged within one German nation. *Anschluss* (union) of Germany and Austria violated the World War I peace treaties and was never approved by the Austrian people in an honest plebiscite.

7. Czechoslovakia

a. Hitler Demands the Sudetenland. Later in 1938 Hitler claimed the *Sudetenland,* a region in Czechoslovakia bordering on Germany and inhabited by German-speaking people. Although the Sudeten people had not been oppressed, Nazi propagandists manufactured stories of Czech "atrocities." The Czech government refused to yield. It counted on its alliances with the Soviet Union and France, and expected British support. However, Britain and France decided not to risk war but to appease Hitler.

b. Munich Conference. British Prime Minister *Neville Chamberlain* and French Premier *Edouard Daladier,* meeting at Munich with Mussolini and Hitler, agreed to let Hitler annex the Sudetenland. Deserted by its friends, Czechoslovakia yielded. Chamberlain returned to London and proclaimed that he had preserved "peace in our time." Hitler promised that he would demand no more territory.

c. Hitler Seizes the Rest of Czechoslovakia. Six months later, Hitler seized the Slavic-inhabited remainder of Czechoslovakia. In Britain, the Chamberlain government at last realized that Hitler could not be trusted. Britain and France joined in a military alliance and guaranteed protection to Germany's next probable victim, Poland.

8. Albania. In 1939 Mussolini invaded and annexed the Balkan country of Albania, giving Italy control of the Adriatic Sea.

9. Poland

a. Hitler's Demands. In 1939 Hitler demanded the return of Danzig and the Polish Corridor since they were inhabited by German-speaking people.

b. Soviet-German Nonaggression Pact. Before Poland responded, Germany and the Soviet Union announced a ten-year *Nonaggression Pact*. The world was surprised because Hitler had always preached hatred of communism, and Joseph Stalin, the Soviet dictator, had always condemned fascism. (1) The pact enabled the Soviet Union to avoid (for the time being) involvement in a major war and, by its secret clauses, gave Stalin a free hand over eastern Poland and the Baltic states of Estonia, Latvia, and Lithuania. (2) The pact protected Germany against a two-front war and promised Hitler foodstuffs and war supplies from the Soviets.

c. Start of World War II. On September 1, 1939, German troops invaded Poland. Two days later, Britain and France honored their guarantee to Poland and declared war on Germany. World War II had started.

BASIC CAUSES OF WORLD WAR II: AXIS PHILOSOPHY AND AGGRESSION

1. Totalitarianism. The Axis nations were totalitarian dictatorships. They scorned the democratic ideals of civil liberties, dignity of the individual, and world peace; and they openly declared their intent to destroy democracy.

2. Militarism. The Axis nations spent vast sums on armaments, devised new weapons, and prepared their peoples for war. They proclaimed war a glorious adventure and death for the Fatherland the highest honor.

3. Nationalism. Japanese Shinto religious beliefs, Italian dreams of a revival of the Roman Empire, and German "master race" doctrines all fostered a narrow and bigoted nationalism. The Axis nations considered themselves superior and destined to rule over "lesser peoples."

4. Imperialism. The Axis powers embarked upon imperialism with the excuse that they lacked land and resources and were *have-not* nations. Japan expanded into Manchuria and China proper to establish a Japanese-dominated "New Order" in Asia. Italy enlarged its African empire and planned to make the Mediterranean an "Italian lake." Germany annexed Austria and Czechoslovakia as first steps toward domination of Europe and eventually, perhaps, of the world.

SUBSIDIARY CAUSES OF WORLD WAR II

1. Failure of Appeasement. Britain and France followed a policy of *appeasement*—that is, making concessions to the dictators in the hope that they would eventually be satisfied and stop their aggression. Anxious for peace, democratic peoples failed to understand that each concession strengthened the aggressors and emboldened them to make further demands. The chief advocate of appeasement was Neville Chamberlain, and its final application was the transfer of the Sudetenland to Germany by the Munich Conference.

2. Lack of Collective Security. Peace-loving nations, by coordinating their military strength and acting collectively, might have protected each other from aggression. However, the democratic peoples shrank from any kind of military action. The United States was determined to remain neutral. Britain and France delayed the formation of a firm alliance until 1939.

The Communist Soviet Union urged collective security because it feared attack by Nazi Germany. Democratic nations, however, were reluctant to enter into collective security pacts with the Soviet Union because they *(a)* doubted Soviet sincerity, *(b)* feared Communist plans for world revolution, and *(c)* were not eager to protect the Soviet Union. In 1939, the Soviet Union saw an opportunity to turn the Nazi war machine against Britain and France. Thereupon, the Soviets terminated their support of collective security and concluded the Stalin-Hitler Nonaggression Pact.

3. American Neutrality Legislation. By prohibiting loans and the sale of war implements to all belligerents, the Neutrality Acts actually favored the well-armed aggressor nations over their ill-equipped victims. These laws also implied that America would not intervene to check Axis aggression.

WORLD WAR II (1939–1945)

1. Initial German Successes (1939–1940)

a. Conquest of Poland. German armies employing massive air bombings and tank assaults unleashed a "lightning war," or *blitzkrieg,* and destroyed all Polish resistance. Germany annexed western Poland. (As agreed in the Hitler-Stalin Pact, the Soviet Union seized eastern Poland and the Baltic countries.)

b. Conquest of Denmark and Norway. Nazi armies next overran neutral Denmark and Norway. Germany thus gained valuable submarine bases on the Atlantic Ocean.

c. Conquest of France. Nazi armies invaded northern France in 1940 by going through the plains of neutral Holland and Belgium. By this route, the Germans bypassed the Franco-German border with its mountainous terrain and French defensive fortifications, the *Maginot Line.* Nazi armies easily defeated the Allied defenders. The British were able to evacuate most of their troops to England while the French forces fled southward. With Mussolini confident that victory was already won, Italy entered the war. As the Nazi armies continued their advance southward, France surrendered.

In Britain, General *Charles de Gaulle,* determined to liberate France, established the *Free French* movement.

2. Britain Stands Alone (1940–1941)

a. Leadership of Churchill. Winston Churchill, who had repeatedly opposed appeasement of the Nazis, succeeded Chamberlain as Prime Minister. Churchill inspired the English people, as he called upon them to save the world from the "abyss of a new dark age." "I have nothing to offer," he said, "but blood, toil, tears, and sweat."

b. Battle of Britain. For three months (August to October 1940) Britain was subjected to devastating air attacks by the German air force, the *Luftwaffe.* The Royal Air Force, the RAF, however, drove off the Luftwaffe and maintained control of the air lanes. The RAF thus compelled the Nazis to abandon their plans for an invasion of Britain.

3. American Preparedness and Aid to the Allies (1939–1941)

a. Neutrality Act of 1939. As World War II started, President Franklin D. Roosevelt requested Congress to pass the Neutrality Act of 1939. This law permitted belligerents to purchase war materials on condition that they paid cash and carried the goods away in their own vessels. *Cash and carry* was designed to give limited assistance to the Atlantic sea powers (France and Britain) and, at the same time, maintain American neutrality.

b. Changes in Public Opinion. President Roosevelt awakened the American people to the threat to their national security. When France fell in 1940, Americans finally realized that Britain alone stood between them and a hostile Fascist world. For America's self-defense, Congress supported aid to Britain by *all measures short of war.*

c. Military Preparedness. Congress also supported a vast military buildup, approving a two-ocean navy, a huge air force, and the 1940 *Selective Service Act.* It provided for America's first peacetime conscription.

d. Destroyer-Naval Base Deal (1940). President Roosevelt traded 50 "over-age" destroyers to Britain in exchange for military bases on British territory in the Western Hemisphere. Britain needed the destroyers to combat German submarines; the United States used the bases as defensive outposts. (Fearful of delay in the Senate, Roosevelt negotiated this exchange by an executive agreement rather than by a treaty, which would have required Senate approval.)

e. Lend-Lease Act (1941). Realizing that Britain's cash was almost exhausted, President Roosevelt requested legislation to maintain the United States as the *arsenal of democracy.* Congress passed the *Lend-Lease Act* authorizing the President to lend or lease goods to any nation whose defense he deemed necessary for the defense of the United States. Immediately, Roosevelt extended substantial aid to Britain; he later gave aid to other Allies, including the Soviet Union. (Total lend-lease aid amounted to $50 billion.) Roosevelt also ordered that merchant ships carrying lend-lease materials be convoyed by the Navy partway across the Atlantic. When convoys were attacked by German submarines, American warships returned fire, thus beginning a limited naval war.

f. Embargo on Strategic Materials to Japan. The United States opposed Japan's aggression in eastern Asia. In 1940–1941 the United States protested Japanese occupation of French Indochina. Since protests proved ineffective, President Roosevelt embargoed the sale of aviation gasoline and scrap iron to Japan and "froze" Japanese assets in the United States.

4. The Axis Makes Two Mistakes (1941)

a. German Attack Upon the Soviet Union (June 22, 1941). Despite the Soviet-German Nonaggression Pact, Hitler ordered a blitzkrieg against the Soviet Union. Hitler expected a quick victory, but the Soviet Union was a formidable foe. The Nazis occupied much territory but were unable to crush the Soviet armies.

b. Japanese Attack Upon the United States (December 7, 1941). Japan staged a surprise attack upon the American naval base at *Pearl Harbor,* Hawaii, forcing the United States actively into the war. Under General *Hideki Tojo,* the Japanese government planned to humble the United States and assure Japanese domination of eastern Asia. Japan's Axis partners, Germany and Italy, immediately declared war on the United States.

5. The United States Organizes for Victory

a. Presidential Leadership. Franklin D. Roosevelt showed confidence and determination in directing the national war effort. As commander in chief he planned the overall war strategy: first beat Hitler, then Japan. He met with top Allied leaders in several wartime conferences. On the home front, Roosevelt established an array of wartime economic agencies.

b. Economic Mobilization. (1) The *War Production Board* ordered military equipment, shifted peacetime plants to war production, set priorities for raw materials, and built new plants, notably to produce aluminum and synthetic rubber. (2) The *War Labor Board* settled labor-management disputes and tried to prevent strikes. (3) The *War Manpower Commission* trained workers for essential industries, supervised the Selective Service system, and recruited new workers, including several million women. (4) The *Fair Employment Practices Committee* encouraged maximum use of labor by combating racial and religious discrimination in employment. (5) The *Office of Price Administration* combated inflation by imposing price and rent ceilings and by rationing scarce consumer goods, such as sugar, meat, shoes, and gasoline.

c. Civil Liberties. Except for the forced removal of Japanese-Americans from the West Coast to interior relocation centers, civil liberties survived the war strains. The nation experienced little war hysteria. The press and the people remained free to criticize the government, and vigorous debate marked the Presidential election of 1944, in which Roosevelt won a fourth term.

d. Wartime Finances. The federal government greatly increased corporate and individual income taxes and for the first time taxed low-income persons. The number of taxpayers rose from 8 million to almost 55 million. The government introduced a withholding system by which employers deducted in advance the estimated tax from each worker's paycheck to be forwarded to the government. Of the total war cost of $330 billion, taxes provided one-third. The government borrowed the rest through the sale of *war bonds*. From 1940 to 1945 the federal debt rose from under $50 billion to over $250 billion.

e. Military Personnel. With Selective Service draft boards providing most of the recruits, the armed forces enrolled 15 million Americans. At peak strength the army totalled 8.5 million recruits, the navy 3.5 million, and the marines half a million. To release men for frontline duty, women's branches—Army Wacs, Navy Waves, and Women Marines—took over necessary noncombat duties.

6. Victory in Europe

a. From North Africa to Italy. In 1942, a British army under General *Bernard Montgomery* defeated the Germans and Italians at *El Alamein,* Egypt, and pursued them westward. Meanwhile, an Anglo-Canadian-American army under General *Dwight D. Eisenhower* invaded French North Africa and moved eastward. The Allies destroyed the Axis African armies. In 1943 the Allies crossed the Mediterranean and invaded Sicily and southern Italy. Mussolini's Fascist government collapsed, and Italy surrendered unconditionally. To resist the Allied advance northward, Germany rushed troops into Italy.

b. Soviet Counteroffensive. In early 1943, following a six-month battle, the Soviets annihilated a large Nazi army deep inside the Soviet Union at *Stalingrad.* Following this great victory, Soviet armies drove out the Nazis and pursued them through eastern and central Europe. In 1945 the Soviets reached Germany and entered Berlin.

c. Anglo-American Invasion of France. On June 6, 1944 (D Day), American and British forces, led by General Eisenhower, crossed the English Channel and landed in northern France at *Normandy.* This, the greatest waterborne invasion in history, established a major second front. The invading forces met a strong German army, kept from the Soviet front in anticipation of the invasion. Allied forces pushed back the Germans and drove them from France.

d. Surrender of Germany. In 1945 Anglo-American armies crossed the Rhine River in Germany and continued eastward to the Elbe River. Here they met the Soviets driving westward. After Hitler committed suicide, on May 8 (V-E Day), Germany surrendered unconditionally.

7. Victory in the Pacific

a. Initial Japanese Offensive. In 1941–1942 Japanese forces overran the Philippines, the Dutch East Indies, and part of New Guinea. Poised just north of Australia, they were halted by American naval victories in the *Coral Sea* and afterward in the central Pacific at *Midway.*

b. Allied Counteroffensive. In 1942, General Douglas MacArthur started the Allied forces (chiefly American) on an "island-hopping" offensive toward Japan. In 1944, the American navy won a decisive victory at *Leyte Gulf* and American forces returned to the Philippines. In early 1945 they also captured

World War II: Victory in Europe

Arrows show Allied victory routes from the south, the west, and the east. See text, page 579.

World War II: Victory in the Pacific

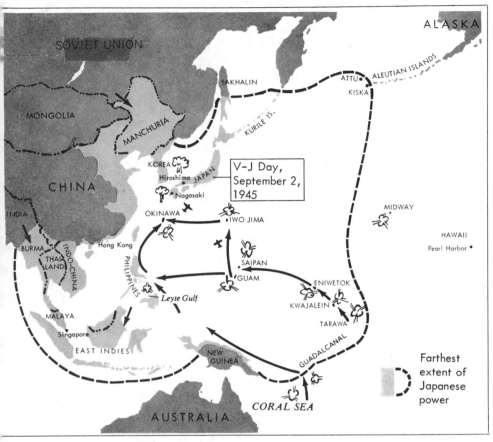

V-J Day,
September 2,
1945

Farthest
extent of
Japanese
power

Arrows show Allied progress in Southeast Asia and in the Pacific. See text, pages 579–582.

Iwo Jima and *Okinawa*. From these islands, American planes launched destructive raids upon Japan.

    c. Atom Bomb and the Surrender of Japan. After Japan belittled the Allied demand to surrender or face "utter destruction," President Truman ordered the air force to use the newly developed atom bomb. Its use, Truman believed, would save countless American (and Japanese) casualties that would result from a seaborne invasion of Japan, and would hasten the end of the war.

    In August 1945 the United States dropped a single atom bomb—the first used in war—on the Japanese city that contained Japanese army headquarters and munitions factories—the city of *Hiroshima*. The bomb killed or injured 130,000 people. Two days later the Soviet Union declared war against Japan and invaded Japanese-held Manchuria. The following day the United States dropped a second atom bomb, this time on the industrial and shipbuilding city of *Nagasaki*. Defenseless against atomic bombings and without allies, Japan surrendered.

SIGNIFICANT FACTS DESCRIBING WORLD WAR II

1. Total War. The war was fought not only by armed forces in battle but also by civilians in factories and homes. Schoolchildren also took part. They collected scrap metal, rubber, and paper, helped air-raid wardens, and assisted in war bond drives.

2. Global War. The war was fought on all major seas and in Africa, Asia, and Europe. It involved almost 60 nations, seven on the side of the Axis. To plan global military strategy, top Allied leaders held several conferences, notably at Teheran, Yalta, and Potsdam.

3. Scientific Progress. Scientists and engineers devised or adapted for war purposes such inventions as radar, guided missiles, jet-propelled planes, magnetic mines, and atom bombs. World War II witnessed the use of blood plasma, penicillin, and sulfa drugs to save lives.

4. Major Role of the Airplane. Fleets of airplanes attacked troop and naval units, destroyed railroads and industrial centers, and prepared the way for invasion. Control of the air was essential to offensive military action.

RESULTS OF WORLD WAR II

1. Economic. *(a)* This most costly war exacted military expenditures of over $1100 billion and caused property damage of over $230 billion. *(b)* European and Asian nations, ravaged by military action, faced difficult problems of economic recovery. *(c)* The Communist economic system spread from the Soviet Union to Eastern and Central Europe, and to several Asian nations.

2. Social. *(a)* This most destructive war left over 22 million military personnel and civilians dead, and over 34 million wounded. For the United States alone, the dead and wounded totaled over one million. *(b)* Several million *refugees* and *displaced persons,* uprooted by the war, needed assistance to rebuild their shattered lives.

3. Political. *(a)* Germany, Italy, and Japan met complete military defeat, and their totalitarian systems were overthrown. *(b)* The United States and the Soviet Union emerged as the major world powers and soon came into a conflict called the *cold war.* *(c)* The Soviet Union acquired an empire of Communist satellite nations. *(d)* The Asian and African colonial peoples became intensely nationalistic and hastened the downfall of Western imperialism. *(e)* Great Britain and France declined as world powers and gradually relinquished major portions of their empires. *(f)* The atomic age brought the problem of achieving international control of atomic energy. *(g)* To preserve peace, the Allies formed a new international organization, the *United Nations.* *(h)* The United States joined the United Nations and otherwise actively assumed the responsibility of world leadership.

———————— **MULTIPLE-CHOICE QUESTIONS** ————————

1. The United States has at times pursued a policy of isolation and at other times a policy of international cooperation. The policy pursued at any given time depends *generally* upon the (a) need to serve what appears to be the national interest (b) desire to secure the support of developing nations (c) demands of the voters as expressed at the polls (d) willingness of Communist nations to remain peaceful.

2. Which factor encouraged an American policy of neutrality during the 1930s? (a) disillusionment with World War I and its results (b) a decline in the military preparedness of other nations (c) the belief that United States participation in World War I had little effect on the outcome (d) the economic prosperity of the period.

3. The United States Senate rejected the Treaty of Versailles mainly because the treaty (a) contained the Covenant of the League of Nations (b) made Germany assume sole guilt for the war (c) required Germany to pay reparations (d) provided for the return of Alsace-Lorraine to France.

4. A principal reason why isolationists in the United States Senate objected to the League of Nations was their opposition to (a) lower tariffs (b) freedom of the seas (c) potential military commitments (d) Soviet and German membership in the League.

5. In which area was the League of Nations most successful? (a) improvement of health conditions (b) achievement of European disarmament (c) arbitration of the Italian-Ethiopian dispute (d) withdrawal of Japanese forces from Manchuria.

6. In 1934 the United States became a member of the (a) World Court (b) Pan-American Union (c) Munich Conference (d) International Labor Organization.

7. "The high contracting parties . . . condemn recourse to war for the solution of international controversies, and renounce it as an instrument of national policy." This quotation is taken from the (a) Treaty of Versailles (b) Kellogg-Briand Pact (c) Nine-Power Treaty (d) Munich Pact.

8. The Kellogg-Briand Pact failed to accomplish its purpose because it (a) was not signed by Germany (b) was signed by too few nations (c) had no provisions for enforcement (d) was rejected by the League of Nations.

9. European nations claimed that they were unable to pay their war debts because the United States did not (a) join the League of Nations (b) sell them enough goods (c) lower its tariff rates (d) join the World Court.

10. A nation that does not give aid to either side in a controversy is said to be (a) a belligerent (b) a buffer state (c) an aggressor (d) a neutral.

11. One similarity between the Embargo Act of 1807 and the Neutrality Act of 1937 is that both (a) distinguished clearly between aggressor and victim (b) showed United States determination to fight (c) abandoned substantially the principle of freedom of the seas (d) discouraged aggression in Europe.

12. United States neutrality legislation of the 1930s was based on the assumption that (a) the rights of neutrals had been established by the War of 1812 (b) isolation interfered with United States expansion in the Pacific (c) a show of force would prevent aggression against the United States (d) the United States could avoid being

drawn into another world war by eliminating some of the causes for our involvement in World War I.

13. The United States contributed to world peace during the period between World War I and World War II by (a) opposing the League of Nations (b) supporting naval disarmament (c) joining the World Court (d) adopting free trade.

14. *Not* a concern of the Washington Conference of 1921–1922 was (a) the burden of naval armaments (b) the Far Eastern imperialistic ambitions of the great powers (c) Japan's economic penetration into China (d) the payment of war debts due the United States.

15. Which resulted from the political confusion and instability in Europe between World War I and World War II? (a) adoption of a policy of isolation by most European countries (b) creation of a united Western Europe (c) stationing of United States troops in European countries (d) emergence of totalitarian regimes in some European countries.

16. During the 1930s the leaders of Germany, Italy, and Japan promoted a warlike attitude among their peoples by (a) stressing the huge indemnities required of them by the Treaty of Versailles (b) playing upon nationalist feelings (c) condemning the League of Nations for refusing them membership (d) pointing to their loss of territory as a result of World War I.

17. Germany's rearmament, starting in 1935, was (a) essential to the policy of collective security (b) encouraged by France (c) in violation of the Treaty of Versailles (d) approved by the London Naval Conference.

18. Hitler argued that Germany should annex the Sudetenland to (a) protect the German-speaking population (b) reduce French influence in central Europe (c) gain control of additional munitions factories (d) prevent Communist seizure of the area.

19. During the Spanish Civil War, General Franco received military aid from (a) Germany and the Soviet Union (b) Germany and Italy (c) Italy and France (d) the United States and Great Britain.

20. The term "appeasement" is often used to describe the (a) Munich Pact (b) Destroyer-Naval Base Deal (c) Stimson Doctrine (d) Rome-Berlin-Tokyo Axis.

21. An international policy whereby nations agree to take joint measures against an aggressor nation is called (a) unilateral action (b) an offensive alliance (c) benevolent neutrality (d) collective security.

22. Which characterized world politics just prior to the outbreak of World Wars I and II? (a) existence of opposing alliances (b) growth of Communist influence in Western nations (c) increased acts of aggression by Western democracies (d) a decline in imperialism.

23. The Nonaggression Pact of 1939, preceding the outbreak of World War II, was between (a) Germany and Poland (b) Germany and the United States (c) Germany and the Soviet Union (d) Great Britain and the United States.

24. World War II started in 1939 when Germany invaded (a) Britain (b) France (c) Poland (d) the Soviet Union.

25. Which was an underlying cause of both World War I and World War II? (a) Japanese imperialism in Asia (b) Italy's demand for control of the Rhineland (c) German ambitions to dominate Europe (d) absence of alliances among nations.

26. During the period 1939 to 1941, United States foreign policy can *best* be described as (a) consistently internationalist (b) aimed at avoiding war at all costs (c) moving steadily toward isolation (d) moving from isolation to active aid for the Allies.

27. In 1940 the United States leased naval bases from Great Britain to (a) cancel Britain's debts from World War I (b) build adequate defenses in the Western Hemisphere (c) gain markets for exports (d) secure sources of uranium.

28. President Roosevelt urged that the United States remain the "arsenal of democracy" when he called for the (a) Neutrality Act of 1939 (b) Selective Service Act of 1940 (c) Destroyer-Naval Base Deal of 1940 (d) Lend-Lease Act of 1941.

29. The Lend-Lease Act of 1941 authorized the President to (a) declare war against Germany (b) trade destroyers for British naval bases in the Western Hemisphere (c) supply equipment to the countries fighting the Axis nations (d) send an expeditionary force to Europe.

30. Which would be classified as a primary source of information on the reasons for the Japanese attack on Pearl Harbor? (a) materials written by Japanese officials prior to the attack (b) accounts of the event found in Japanese newspapers and magazines during that period (c) interviews with American survivors of the attack (d) compilation of the works of several historians who investigated the attack.

31. The internment of Japanese-American citizens during World War II was closely related to the problem of (a) the immigrant quota system (b) the abuse of the welfare system by the United States Congress (c) racial prejudice (d) illegal aliens.

32. A widely adopted means of solving the manpower problem in industry during World War II was to (a) use forced labor (b) raise the immigration quotas (c) employ women (d) abolish relief payments.

33. The United States financed World War II by (a) borrowing from Britain (b) confiscating factories engaged in defense production (c) increasing tax rates and selling war bonds (d) increasing tariff rates.

34. During World War II, the United States (a) gave substantial lend-lease aid to the Soviet Union (b) requested the Soviet Union to send an army to the North African front (c) sent troops to the Soviet front (d) granted recognition to the Communist government in the Soviet Union.

35. Which is the most objective answer to the question of whether the United States should have dropped atomic bombs on Hiroshima and Nagasaki? (a) The answer depends on the facts and interpretations one chooses to accept about the war. (b) The action taken by the United States was unquestionably correct. (c) Since Japan had started the war with a sneak attack on Pearl Harbor, a drastic act of retaliation was necessary. (d) The President's decision to drop the bombs was unconstitutional.

36. Which two countries were on our side in World War I and were our enemies in World War II? (a) Italy and Japan (b) Germany and Japan (c) the Soviet Union and Japan (d) Austria and France.

37. The two nations that emerged as major world powers following World War II were (a) the United States and Great Britain (b) the United States and the Soviet Union (c) the Soviet Union and Germany (d) the Soviet Union and China.

———— **IDENTIFICATION QUESTIONS: WHO AM I?** ————

Neville Chamberlain	Dwight D. Eisenhower	Henri Pétain
Winston Churchill	Warren G. Harding	Franklin D. Roosevelt
James M. Cox	Henry Cabot Lodge, Sr.	Harry Truman
Charles de Gaulle	Douglas MacArthur	Woodrow Wilson

1. As chairman of the Senate Foreign Relations Committee, I led the fight for reservations to the Treaty of Versailles.

2. I delivered my "quarantine" speech to alert the American people to the danger of aggression.

3. I became prime minister of Britain in 1940. I offered my people "blood, toil, tears, and sweat."

4. As Presidential candidate in 1920, I took no clear-cut stand regarding the League of Nations.

5. As commander of the Anglo-American forces in Europe, I led the invasion of France at Normandy.

6. After the fall of France in 1940, I fled to Britain and established the "Free French" movement.

7. As prime minister of Britain I made concessions to Hitler at the Munich Conference. I believed that my policy was preserving "peace in our time."

8. I commanded the Allied forces in the Southwest Pacific. In 1944 I kept my pledge to return to the Philippines.

9. To shorten the war and save American lives, I ordered the use of the atom bomb against Japan.

— DISCUSSION ANALYSIS QUESTIONS: WORLD WAR II —

Speaker A: Actually, from 1939 to 1941, before the German attack on the Soviet Union, the cause of the British and French could really be called the cause of freedom and democracy, for very little else was involved on the Western side.

Speaker B: The Soviet "Red" menace was daily becoming more formidable and Japanese fears rapidly increased. The only way to insure Japanese security was through adequate measures of defense in Manchuria.

Speaker C: The continued militaristic expansion of Japan, with its challenge to law, order, peaceful processes, and territorial integrity, posed an intolerable threat to the future security of the United States.

Speaker D: The Axis forces which had rolled over Austria, Czechoslovakia, Poland, Denmark, Norway, the Netherlands, Luxembourg, Belgium, and France by the middle of 1940 were an extremely serious threat to American security and interests.

1. Which speaker believes that the United States may have misunderstood Japanese movements in East Asia between 1933 and 1941? (a) A (b) B (c) C (d) D.

2. Which two speakers most clearly believe that United States participation in World War II was both necessary and desirable? (a) A and D (b) B and D (c) B and C (d) C and D.

3. Which speaker believes that the issue of fighting for democracy was more valid when World War II began than it was when the Soviet Union joined the Allies? (a) A (b) B (c) C (d) D.

4. Which speaker is most concerned with violations of the Open Door Policy? (a) A (b) B (c) C (d) D.

5. When Speaker D says the Axis forces "rolled over Austria," the event referred to (a) took place some 18 months before the outbreak of World War II (b) was the immediate cause of World War II (c) happened during the first year of World War II (d) was accomplished by Italian troops.

————————————— **ESSAY QUESTIONS** ——————————————

1. *(a)* Describe *two* events or circumstances in the period 1919 to 1920 that kept the United States from membership in the League of Nations. *(b)* Give *two* arguments for and *two* arguments against the entrance of the United States into the League. *(c)* Explain *two* reasons why the League was unable to prevent war.

2. *(a)* Explain *one* reason why the United States adopted the policy of isolation early in its history. *(b)* Give *two* reasons for the change in sentiment between 1919 and 1941 regarding the policy of isolation. *(c)* Referring to these years, describe (1) *one* American action illustrating isolation and (2) *one* American action illustrating international cooperation.

3. In the 1930s some Americans proposed that, in case of a foreign war, the United States maintain neutrality by cutting off all trade relations with the warring powers. *(a)* Show how this proposal developed out of our experience during the years 1914 to 1917. *(b)* State *two* provisions of the Neutrality Acts of 1935 and 1937. *(c)* Explain *one* reason why such neutrality legislation failed to keep the United States out of World War II.

4. In the period between World War I and World War II, democracies and dictatorships were rivals. *(a)* Describe *three* instances of aggression by totalitarian states before World War II. *(b)* Discuss *one* reason why the democracies declared war on Germany when that country attacked Poland. *(c)* Discuss *two* basic causes of World War II.

5. The United States has played a major role in the worldwide struggle against totalitarianism. *(a)* Discuss *two* reasons why the American people are opposed to totalitarianism. *(b)* Describe *three* factors that made it possible for the United States to be the "arsenal of democracy" during World War II.

6. Similar foreign problems arose during the administrations of Woodrow Wilson and Franklin D. Roosevelt. Describe *two* foreign policies of Franklin D. Roosevelt and show how *each* either resembled or contrasted with a foreign policy of Woodrow Wilson.

7. State whether you agree or disagree with *each* of the following statements and give *two* facts to support your point of view: *(a)* Preparedness for war is the best guarantee of peace. *(b)* The United States was right in not joining the League of Nations. *(c)* Appeasement of dictators can preserve the peace. *(d)* The failure of the League proves that wars cannot be prevented by an international organization. *(e)* The causes of World War II were very different from those of World War I.

8. Various factors within the United States have influenced United States foreign-policy decisions. Choose *three* of the factors from the list below. For *each* one selected, show *one* way in which that factor influenced the formulation of a particular foreign-policy decision of the United States. *[Use a different foreign-policy decision for each factor selected.]*

Geographic position	Public opinion
Ideologies	Pluralistic society
Need for trade	

UNIT X
The United States Accepts the Responsibilities of Free World Leadership

PART 1. The United States Is Concerned About the United Nations

STEPS TOWARD THE UNITED NATIONS

1. Atlantic Charter (1941). Roosevelt and Churchill, meeting on board ship in the Atlantic, issued a statement of principles, the *Atlantic Charter*. Remindful of Wilson's Fourteen Points, this document stated that Britain and the United States *(a)* desired no territorial gain, *(b)* respected the right of all peoples to choose their own form of government, *(c)* hoped that all peoples would live in freedom from fear and want, *(d)* believed that nations must abandon the use of force, and *(e)* would seek to establish a "system of general security," implying an international organization.

In 1942 the Allied nations meeting in Washington pledged support for the Atlantic Charter and adopted the name *United Nations* (UN).

2. Yalta Conference (February 1945). The Big Three—President Roosevelt, Prime Minister Churchill, and Premier Stalin—decided upon procedures for voting in the UN Security Council.

3. San Francisco Conference (April–June 1945). Despite the death of President Roosevelt just before the conference, delegates of 50 nations met and completed the UN Charter.

The United States became the first nation to ratify the Charter, as the Senate overwhelmingly approved American membership. Also, the United States provided the UN with headquarters in New York City.

PURPOSES OF THE UNITED NATIONS

The United Nations has as its goals to (1) maintain international peace and security, (2) by collective action, remove threats to the peace and suppress acts of aggression, (3) develop friendly relations among nations, (4) promote respect for human rights without distinction as to race, sex, language, or religion, and (5) encourage international cooperation in solving economic, social, cultural, and humanitarian problems.

ORGANIZATION OF THE UNITED NATIONS

1. General Assembly: The International Forum

a. Membership and Voting. The General Assembly consists of all UN member nations, now totaling 159, each having one vote. General Assembly decisions on "important questions" require a two-thirds majority.

Organization of the United Nations

b. **Powers.** The General Assembly has the power to (1) discuss international problems fully and freely, (2) make recommendations to member nations,
to the Economic and Social Council, and to the Security Council, (3) elect members of other UN organs, (4) with the prior recommendation of the Security
Council, suspend or expel any member nation persistently violating UN principles
and admit any "peace-loving" nation to membership, and (5) approve the UN
budget and apportion expenses among the member nations.

c. **Sessions.** The General Assembly meets in *regular* sessions annually,
for about three months. If necessary, however, the Assembly may be summoned
into *special* session.

2. Security Council: The Executive Agency

a. **Membership.** The Security Council consists of 15 members: (1) Five
are *permanent:* the United States, Great Britain, France, the Soviet Union, and
the People's Republic of China. (2) Ten are *nonpermanent,* each elected for a
two-year term by the General Assembly.

b. **Voting.** Decisions by the Security Council on important matters require the affirmative vote of nine members, including the five permanent members. Thus, by a negative vote, any one of the Big Five can defeat a Security
Council decision, that is, exercise *veto power*. Abstention from voting by a permanent member is not considered a veto.

c. **Powers.** The Security Council bears primary responsibility for maintaining international peace and security. It has the power to (1) investigate dis-

putes endangering world peace, (2) make recommendations for peaceful settlement, and (3) if necessary, call upon UN member nations to take economic or military action against an aggressor nation.

d. Sessions. To be able to deal instantly with any international crisis, the Security Council functions continuously.

3. Secretariat: The Civil Service

a. Personnel and Duties. The Secretariat consists of the *Secretary General* and staff. They are charged with primary loyalty to the United Nations. The Secretary General is appointed (usually for a five-year term) by the General Assembly upon the recommendation of the Security Council. The Secretary General directs the staff, numbering several thousand employees, to perform UN clerical and administrative work. In addition, the Secretary General is authorized to (1) bring to the attention of the Security Council any matter threatening world peace, and (2) perform tasks assigned by major UN organs. Such tasks have included undertaking special diplomatic missions and directing UN emergency military forces.

b. Persons Serving as Secretary General. (1) *Trygve Lie* of Norway (1946–1953), (2) *Dag Hammarskjold* of Sweden (1953–1961), (3) *U Thant* of Burma (1961–1971), (4) *Kurt Waldheim* of Austria (1972–1981), (5) *Javier Pérez de Cuéllar* of Peru (1981–   ).

4. International Court of Justice: The Court for Nations

This Court consists of 15 judges, each elected for a nine-year term by the General Assembly and Security Council. Deciding cases by majority vote, the Court has the power to *(a)* settle legal disputes between nations, and *(b)* grant UN organs advisory opinions on legal questions. Nations submitting disputes to the Court agree in advance to accept its decisions.

5. Trusteeship Council: For Protection of Colonial Peoples

a. Membership and Voting. The Trusteeship Council consists now of the five permanent Security Council members. In 1986 the United States held the last remaining trust territory—certain Pacific islands. (A trust territory was an area placed by the UN under the administration of a member nation.) This council's decisions require a simple majority.

b. Powers. The Trusteeship Council supervised trusteeships so as to safeguard colonial peoples. As trust territories gained independence, the work of the Trusteeship Council diminished.

6. Economic and Social Council (ECOSOC): For Humanity's Welfare

a. Membership and Voting. The Economic and Social Council consists of 27 members, each elected for a three-year term by the General Assembly. Decisions require a simple majority, each member nation having one vote.

***b.* Powers.** The Economic and Social Council is concerned with improving economic, social, cultural, educational, and health conditions throughout the world. ECOSOC may conduct studies and make recommendations to UN member nations and to the General Assembly.

***c.* ECOSOC Commissions and Committees.** (1) The *Commission on Human Rights* seeks to encourage fundamental freedoms for all persons, regardless of race, sex, language, or religion, and (2) other commissions and committees are concerned with such issues as the control of narcotics, prevention of crime, and the status of women.

SPECIALIZED AGENCIES

1. Introduction. The specialized agencies are independent organizations, some predating the United Nations, that came into existence by intergovernmental agreement. They include most (but not all) nations as members; they secure their funds chiefly by voluntary contributions from member nations; they directly serve only those nations that request assistance; and they coordinate their efforts with the UN through the Economic and Social Council.

The United States joined all the specialized agencies, actively participated in their work, and provided them with substantial financial contributions.

2. Major Specialized Agencies

a. The *United Nations Educational, Scientific, and Cultural Organization* (UNESCO) seeks to promote the worldwide exchange of information on education, science, and culture. UNESCO undertakes projects to raise educational standards and to combat ignorance and prejudice. UNESCO bases its work on the statement in its Charter: "Since wars begin in the minds of men, it is in the minds of men that the defenses of peace must be constructed."

b. The *International Labor Organization* (ILO) endeavors to improve world labor conditions. ILO defines minimum labor standards and assists countries in formulating labor laws.

c. The *Food and Agriculture Organization* (FAO) attempts to raise world food and nutrition levels. FAO provides information to improve methods of growing and distributing food.

d. The *World Health Organization* (WHO) seeks to improve world health standards. WHO surveys health conditions, combats mass diseases and epidemics, and helps nations improve public health services.

e. The *International Bank for Reconstruction and Development* (World Bank) encourages world economic progress by providing loans for large-scale projects, such as electric power plants, railroads, and highways.

MAJOR ACTIONS TAKEN BY THE UNITED NATIONS

UN ACTIONS ON SOCIAL AND ECONOMIC MATTERS

1. Children's Fund. In 1946 the General Assembly created the *United Nations International Children's Emergency Fund* (UNICEF). It provides food, vitamins, and medicines to millions of needy children; and it trains nurses to help mothers in proper child care. UNICEF's activities, now permanent, are financed by voluntary contributions of governments and individuals.

2. Declaration of Human Rights. In 1948 the General Assembly approved the *Declaration of Human Rights,* drawn up by the Commission on Human Rights. The declaration states that all human beings are born free and equal and are entitled to *(a) civil rights:* life; liberty; freedom of religion, speech, and assembly; and a voice in their government; *(b) legal rights:* freedom from arbitrary arrest and the right to a fair trial; *(c) economic rights:* employment, participation in labor unions, an adequate living standard, private property, and leisure time; and *(d) social rights:* education and a cultural life. Although these ideals will not soon be realized throughout the world, they provide a "standard of achievement for all peoples and all nations."

3. Genocide Convention. In 1948 the General Assembly adopted the *Genocide Convention.* It declared illegal the deliberate extermination of any human group (as the Nazis had attempted with Jews and gypsies) and provided that violators be tried before an international court. The convention, ratified by over 90 nations, seeks to rally world opinion toward granting all people freedom from fear. After years of controversy, the United States Senate ratified the convention in 1986.

4. Technical Assistance. In 1949 the United Nations and several specialized agencies began the *Expanded Program of Technical Assistance.* This program coordinates efforts to improve social and economic conditions in underdeveloped areas, chiefly in Africa, Asia, and Latin America. Technical experts have helped underdeveloped peoples increase food production, develop natural resources and industries, fight disease, and reduce illiteracy.

UN ACTIONS ON INTERNATIONAL DISPUTES (1946–1949)

With the destruction of World War II fresh in mind, people hoped for a better world, to be achieved in part through the United Nations. The UN recorded some major achievements.

1. Iran (1946). Security Council discussions spurred the Soviet Union to withdraw its troops stationed in Iran during World War II.

2. Greece (1946–1948). The General Assembly requested the Communist nations to cease aiding guerrilla rebels in northern Greece. After Yugo-

International Disputes Considered at the United Nations

slavia broke with the Soviet Union and ceased aiding the guerrillas, the rebellion collapsed.

3. Palestine (1948–1949). The General Assembly approved the partition of Palestine into an Arab state and a Jewish state. When Israel—the new Jewish state—was attacked by the Arab nations, UN mediator *Ralph Bunche* arranged temporary armistices.

4. Indonesia (1947–1949). The Security Council assisted in negotiations that led to Indonesian independence from the Netherlands.

5. Kashmir (Since 1948). The UN helped end hostilities between India and Pakistan over Kashmir.

DISPUTES INVOLVING STRONG SOVIET CONCERNS (1948–PRESENT)

The Soviet Union was not moved to modify its foreign policies by following UN actions and resolutions.

1. Korea (1948–1953). In 1948 a UN commission to unify Korea by elections was denied admission to Soviet-occupied North Korea. In 1950, when North Korea invaded the South, the Security Council was able to approve a resolution for a UN army to help South Korea—only because the Soviet Union was absent from the session.

2. Hungary (1956). The General Assembly resolution—condemning Russia for suppressing a revolt by the Hungarian people—was rejected by the Soviets.

3. Afghanistan (1980). As Soviet troops invaded Afghanistan, a Security Council resolution calling for their withdrawal was vetoed by the Soviet representative, and a similar General Assembly resolution was belittled by the Soviet government.

DISPUTES AFFECTING FORMER BRITISH EMPIRE AREAS (1963–PRESENT)

In dealing with these disputes, the UN had at best questionable success—or none at all.

1. Cyprus (1963, 1974). An east Mediterranean island that received independence from Britain in 1960, Cyprus contains two antagonistic ethnic groups: 80 percent Greek Cypriot and 20 percent Turkish Cypriot. Twice Cyprus was torn by civil war between its Greek and Turkish peoples. Both times the Security Council authorized UN peacekeeping forces that helped restore order but did not resolve the basic Cyprus problem.

2. Rhodesia (Zimbabwe). Britain insisted that the white-minority regime in its African colony of Rhodesia move toward rule by the black majority. Instead, in 1965, Rhodesia declared its independence. Britain secured a Security Council resolution for economic sanctions against the "breakaway" colony but in 1970 vetoed a resolution condemning Britain for not using force to topple the white-minority regime.

For years Rhodesia suffered attacks by black *Patriotic Front* guerrilla groups. In 1979 the white-minority regime agreed to a Rhodesian government chosen in free elections by all citizens. *Robert Mugabe,* a Patriotic Front leader, became prime minister of the country, renamed Zimbabwe. Meanwhile, the UN lifted its economic sanctions.

3. South-West Africa (Namibia). South Africa received this former German colony as a League of Nations mandate. At the UN, South Africa's *apartheid* policies angered the Afro-Asian nations, which secured many General Assembly resolutions condemning South Africa and calling for an end of the South-West Africa mandate. In the 1970s both the Security Council and the World Court declared that South Africa was occupying the territory illegally. In recent years a guerrilla group, the South-West Africa People's Organization (SWAPO), has been fighting for Namibian independence. Although SWAPO and South Africa tentatively agreed in the early 1980s to hold UN-supervised elections on the territory's future, no such elections have taken place. South Africa has insisted that there can be no independence for South-West Africa until Cuban troops leave neighboring Angola. (The Cubans are supporting Angola's leftist government, which is fighting a guerrilla movement supported by South Africa and the United States.)

4. India-Pakistan War (1971). India and Pakistan both received independence in 1947 from Britain. Pakistan consisted of two nonadjacent regions separated by 1000 miles of Indian territory. Aside from their Islamic religion, the West Pakistanis and East Pakistanis had little in common. The West Pakistanis controlled the government and in 1971 sent the army into East Pakistan to suppress demands there for autonomy. The East Pakistanis declared their region independent as the nation of *Bangladesh.* In support of Bangladesh, India sent its army into the East and easily defeated the West Pakistani forces.

Three Security Council resolutions for a cease-fire and withdrawal of forces were vetoed by the Soviet Union. A similar General Assembly resolution was ignored by India as "not very realistic." Meanwhile, the West Pakistan representative denounced the UN as "a fraud and a farce."

ARAB-ISRAELI DISPUTES (1967 TO THE PRESENT)

With the increase in UN membership from the original 50 nations to 159 nations today, the General Assembly contained a sizable bloc—of Communist, Arab, Muslim, and other Third World nations—that was strongly anti-Israel. In the Security Council, the United States usually—but not always—supported Israeli policies.

"**Mirror, Mirror, on the wall! Who's the most influential . . . ?**"

Renault in The Sacramento Bee, Ca.

1. Arab-Israeli War of 1967. Security Council resolutions helped end the fighting. Later, the council adopted *Resolution 242* calling for the *(a)* withdrawal of Israeli forces from the occupied territories, *(b)* right of every Middle Eastern state to live in peace, *(c)* free navigation of international waterways, and *(d)* just settlement of the refugee problem.

2. Arab-Israeli War of 1973. After the Israelis turned the tide of battle against the Arab attackers, the Soviet Union agreed to a Security Council resolution (1) calling for a cease-fire that was accepted by the warring nations and (2) reaffirming the 1967 Resolution 242. The Security Council also approved a UNEF force to separate the opposing armies.

Thereafter, the General Assembly, with its large anti-Israeli bloc, approved an Arab resolution condemning Zionism as "a form of racism and racial discrimination." *Daniel Moynihan,* the American representative, warned that the United States "will never acquiesce in this infamous act."

3. Israeli Raid on the Iraqi Nuclear Reactor (1981). The Security Council passed a resolution to "strongly condemn" Israel for this raid. Israel rejected the resolution as "evidence" of the UN's "biased and one-sided" attitude toward Israel.

4. Israeli Annexation of the Golan Heights (1981). The Security Council approved a resolution calling the annexation illegal. Israel rejected the resolution as "tainted" for ignoring Syria's refusal to seek a peaceful settlement.

5. Israel's Invasion of Southern Lebanon (1982). Security Council resolutions for a cease-fire and withdrawal of Israeli forces were not heeded. A later Security Council resolution threatening sanctions against Israel was vetoed by the United States as "not sufficiently balanced."

OTHER RECENT DISPUTES

The UN's inability to have nations accept its judgments was again illustrated in these disputes.

1. Iran (1979). The Security Council and the World Court called upon Iran to release the Americans held as hostages. Iran disregarded these calls.

2. Falkland Islands (1982). The Security Council passed a resolution calling for Argentina to withdraw its forces invading the British-held Falkland Islands in the south Atlantic. Argentina ignored the resolution.

EVALUATION OF THE UNITED NATIONS

1. Optimistic View: Effectiveness of the UN

a. Almost Universal Membership. The UN is the world's most representative body of nations. It mirrors the hopes and fears of humanity.

b. Availability of Forum. The UN provides a forum where any member nation may present its point of view on world problems.

c. Uniting-for-Peace Resolution. This resolution enables the General Assembly to deal with a threat to world peace if the Security Council fails to act because of a veto.

d. Resolving International Problems. Through the UN, many international problems have been solved, brought closer to a solution, or at least kept from erupting into a major war. Examples of UN achievements include (1) independence for Indonesia and (2) the partition of Palestine.

e. UN Military Forces. The UN has secured the military cooperation of a number of member nations. Examples are (1) the formation of a UN army to repel aggression against South Korea, and (2) the creation of UNEF units to preserve peace in the Middle East, the Congo, and Cyprus.

f. Economic and Social Progress. The Economic and Social Council, the specialized agencies, and the technical assistance programs have worked to improve economic and social conditions in underdeveloped countries.

g. Colonial Independence. The Trusteeship Council has helped colonial peoples form independent nations, including Cameroon, Togo, Somalia, Tanganyika (now part of Tanzania), Rwanda, and Burundi—all in Africa.

h. Preventing International Anarchy. The UN keeps the world from reverting to international anarchy. It enables conflicting nations to speak to each other and enables neutral nations to influence world problems.

2. Pessimistic View: Problems Besetting the UN

a. Blocs Within the UN. The UN contains three blocs: (1) The *Western bloc* (about 50 nations) includes the United States, Western Europe, most of Latin America, and some British Commonwealth members. This bloc generally supports American leadership. (2) The *Soviet Communist bloc* (about ten nations) consistently follows Soviet policy. (3) The *Afro-Asian, or Third World, bloc* (about 90 nations) has grown tremendously with the admission of new UN members. The Afro-Asian nations are opposed to colonialism but hold diverse views on most other international issues.

The existence of blocs is a divisive force within the UN that tends to aggravate international friction.

b. Self-Serving Use of UN Organs and Specialized Agencies. UN members often consider international problems on the basis of individual or bloc interests, rather than on the basis of UN principles. Most Afro-Asian nations approved India's military seizure of Goa—a tiny Portuguese colony on the Indian coast—although the UN Charter prohibits the use of force.

In the 1970s Communist, Arab, and other Third World nations "politicized" the work of specialized UN agencies. At the ILO, the Communist nations secured condemnation of the military regime in Chile for "denying trade union rights." Using a double standard, the ILO did not say a word about the denial of such rights in Communist and many Third World nations. At WHO, the Arab nations secured rejection of a report by WHO experts that Israel had improved the health conditions of Arab peoples under Israeli control. At UNESCO the Arab nations secured condemnation of Israel for archeological excavations in Jerusalem.

In a 1974 speech, the chief American representative to the United Nations deplored bloc voting and self-serving use of the UN by Communist, Arab, and Third World nations. He warned that, by adopting unrealistic, one-sided resolutions, the General Assembly was eroding support for the UN among the American people. He further declared that "when the rule of the majority becomes the tyranny of the majority, the minority will cease to respect or obey it."

In 1977 the United States withdrew from the ILO in protest of the ILO's failure to apply its labor standards equally to all nations, including Communist and Third World countries. In 1980, as the ILO seemed to be abandoning its "politicizing" activities, the United States rejoined the organization.

c. Veto Power. The Soviet Union has used the veto over 100 times, thereby limiting the effectiveness of the Security Council. The United States, Britain, and France have each used the veto far fewer times.

d. Defiance of UN Resolutions. Some nations have defied UN resolutions, claiming that the issue involved was a domestic matter not subject to UN authority or insisting that they were protecting their national interests. Examples of defiance of the UN include (1) the 1948 Arab attack upon Israel, (2) Soviet suppression of the Hungarian rebellion, and (3) South Africa's refusal to recognize UN control of South-West Africa (Namibia).

Bear market.

Crawford. Reprinted by permission of Newspaper Enterprise Association

Bear market *denotes values that are sharply falling. What is the cartoonist saying about UN prestige? about what has caused this trend? What other factors might be considered? How could the UN reverse this trend?*

   e. Lack of Military Power. The UN has no permanent military force. It depends upon member nations to honor resolutions requesting armed personnel. Only 16 nations—then about one-fourth of the UN—heeded the call for troops to aid South Korea.

   f. Financial Difficulties. The UN secures funds for its regular budget by assessing member nations according to their ability to pay. The United States has been assessed 25 percent of the UN regular budget, the Soviet Union 13 percent. Also, the United States has voluntarily contributed up to 45 percent of funds for UN special activities, the Soviet Union 1.5 percent.

   The UN has been in financial straits because some nations have been unable or unwilling to pay their regular assessments and to pay special assessments for UNEF forces. For example, the Soviet bloc and most Arab states refused to pay their share of UNEF Middle East expenses.

   g. Limited Action Against International Terrorism. Extremist groups have employed terrorism—deliberate violence against innocent civilians—so as to further the extremists' political goals. Active terrorist groups have included Turkish and Armenian extremists, Islamic fundamentalists, Croatian separatists (opposed to Yugoslavia), the Irish Republican Army, and West German and Italian revolutionaries. Some terrorist attacks were carried out by governments.

   In recent years, people supporting one side or the other in the Arab-Israeli conflict have been responsible for numerous cases of terrorism. Palestinian extremists have attacked Israelis in isolated villages and crowded cities. Israeli extremists have attacked Palestinians in the occupied West Bank.

   Perhaps most shocking to Americans and Western Europeans have been acts of mass terrorism that have taken the lives of athletes, airline passengers, and other innocent victims. Many such attacks have been carried out by Palestinians and their sympathizers. Among the most dramatic incidents have been the slaying of 11 Israeli athletes at the 1972 Olympic Games in Munich, West Germany; the murder of more than 20 schoolchildren at the Israeli town of Ma'alot in 1974; the killing of 30 civilians in a Palestinian raid on the Israeli coast in 1978; the hijacking of the cruise ship *Achille Lauro* and the killing of an American passenger in October 1985; an attack at the Vienna and Rome airports in December 1985 that killed 20 people; the killing of 20 people on a hijacked Pan American jet at Karachi, Pakistan, in September 1986; and the killing of 22 Jews at a synagogue in Istanbul, Turkey, in September 1986.

   Other major incidents of terrorism not directly attributed to the Palestinian cause included the kidnaping and murder of Italian Premier *Aldo Moro* by leftists in 1978; a boat explosion by Irish extremists that killed Britain's *Earl Mountbatten* in 1979; the assassination of Egyptian President *Anwar Sadat* by Islamic extremists in 1981; a bomb blast that killed Lebanese President-elect *Bashir Gemayel* in 1982; a bomb explosion that killed three South Korean officials on a visit to Burma in 1983; a bombing by Armenian extremists that killed six people at a Paris airport in 1983; the assassination of India's Prime Minister *Indira Gandhi* by Sikh guards in 1984; the bombing in a New Zealand harbor in 1985 by French government agents of a ship owned by the environmentalist organization Greenpeace, killing one person; and the assassination of Sweden's Premier *Olof Palme* by an unknown assailant in 1986.

While most governments condemn terrorism, at least in public, some people have argued that terrorism is a legitimate weapon of the powerless against the powerful. In 1985 the UN General Assembly unanimously voted to condemn all international terrorism as criminal.

3. Realistic View. The United Nations is not meant to be a world government; it is a loose confederation whose member states retain their sovereignty. The United Nations is only an instrument available for their use. Although the UN embodies humanity's highest hopes, its strength and influence will reflect the wishes of the world's peoples and governments.

—————————— MULTIPLE-CHOICE QUESTIONS ——————————

1. "They hope to see established a peace . . . which will afford assurance that all the men in all the lands may live out their lives in freedom from fear and want" is quoted from the (a) Atlantic Charter (b) Genocide Convention (c) United Nations Charter (d) UNESCO Charter.
2. The Atlantic Charter was most similar in its provisions to the (a) Platt Amendment (b) Fourteen Points (c) Stimson Doctrine (d) Kellogg-Briand Pact.
3. Which UN body provides a forum for expression by all UN members? (a) Security Council (b) Trusteeship Council (c) General Assembly (d) World Court.
4. The General Assembly meets (a) in continuous session (b) at least once a year (c) only when called by the Secretary General (d) only in time of emergency.
5. Each nation's voting strength in the General Assembly is according to (a) area (b) population (c) military strength (d) the principle of one vote per nation.
6. Which organ of the UN was given primary responsibility for investigating situations that threaten world peace? (a) the Economic and Social Council (b) the Secretariat (c) the Security Council (d) the Trusteeship Council.
7. The nonpermanent members of the Security Council are selected by the (a) General Assembly (b) Economic and Social Council (c) five permanent members of the Council (d) Secretary General.
8. The Security Council has the power to (a) veto decisions of the General Assembly (b) cancel treaties made by member nations (c) recommend the use of force to stop aggression (d) elect the Secretary General.
9. The veto power in the UN is held by (a) each member of the Security Council (b) each member of the General Assembly (c) only the Soviet Union and the United States (d) the five permanent members of the Security Council.
10. The distribution of power within the Security Council is based on the principle that (a) neutral nations are an effective power bloc (b) important questions are settled by the International Court of Justice (c) agreement among the major nations is necessary if the organization is to succeed (d) large and small nations have equal influence in decisions about world problems.
11. To fill the office of Secretary General of the United Nations, a person must be (a) recommended by the Security Council and appointed by the General Assembly

(b) recommended by the General Assembly and appointed by the Security Council (c) nominated by the Soviet Union and the United States, and elected by the Security Council (d) recommended by the Security Council and elected by the International Court.

12. One function of the Economic and Social Council is to (a) settle boundary disputes (b) promote respect for human rights (c) direct the economies of underdeveloped nations (d) regulate the use of atomic energy.

13. The specialized agency that seeks to promote cultural cooperation and understanding among nations is (a) UNICEF (b) Trusteeship Council (c) WHO (d) UNESCO.

14. A weakness of UNESCO in its efforts to foster world understanding is that it (a) must report to ECOSOC (b) is subject to vetoes by any of the Big Five (c) cannot work within a country unless invited (d) uses Communist personnel chiefly.

15. "Since wars begin in the minds of men" is a phrase used in the UNESCO Charter to emphasize the need for (a) encouraging regional agreements on trade (b) expanding educational opportunities (c) controlling newspapers that stir up controversies (d) stopping research on atomic weapons.

16. The concept of national sovereignty is best defined as a nation's (a) obligation to support the United Nations (b) need to maintain democratic institutions (c) freedom to act independently (d) willingness to make compromises.

17. Which is true of the United Nations but was *not* true of the League of Nations? (a) It includes all the major powers in its membership. (b) It has the power to collect taxes from each member nation. (c) It conducts an international court. (d) It controls a standing army that can be used wherever needed.

18. A significant accomplishment of the UN has been the (a) promotion of health and sanitation programs in underdeveloped nations (b) resolution of international conflicts in Southeast Asia (c) prevention of the collapse of Europe's colonial empires (d) abandonment of imperialism by the larger nations.

19. The United Nations has (a) admitted many new member nations (b) adopted a plan by which nations may withdraw from the UN (c) outlawed atomic weapons (d) established a permanent UN military force.

20. Which is a reason why the UN General Assembly has become more involved in trying to meet international crises than its founders intended? (a) The total membership of the Security Council changes annually. (b) The Security Council has often been unable to take effective action. (c) The Secretary General has lost all influence with the major powers. (d) The major powers have more influence in the General Assembly than in the Security Council.

21. The UN finances its regular budget *chiefly* by (a) charging admission to visitors (b) assessing member nations (c) placing a tax upon citizens of UN member nations (d) selling UN stamps and souvenirs.

22. Which generalization is *best* supported by the record of UN actions? (a) The big powers are abandoning their nationalistic policies. (b) The spirit of nationalism is being replaced by a spirit of internationalism. (c) All nations are ready to abandon their imperialistic policies. (d) Crises in world trouble spots more often end in deadlocks than in permanent solutions.

23. In 1950 the Security Council was able to pass a resolution calling for a UN army to aid South Korea because the Soviet Union (a) approved the resolution (b) was absent from the meeting (c) was prohibited from voting since it was directly concerned with the issue (d) declined to use its veto power.

24. The General Assembly resolution urging the Soviet Union to cease its interference against the Hungarian revolt of 1956 was (a) defeated by its failure to secure a

majority (b) defeated by the use of the veto (c) heeded by the Soviet Union (d) rejected by the Soviet Union.

25. During the 1971 India-Pakistan war over Bangladesh (a) India refused to heed a Security Council cease-fire resolution (b) the United States vetoed a Security Council cease-fire resolution (c) the General Assembly, with the Third World nations divided, was unable to approve any resolution (d) India refused to heed a General Assembly cease-fire resolution.

26. In regard to international crises involving Israel, the Arab-Communist-Third World bloc at the UN has (a) consistently condemned Israel (b) been unable to word resolutions satisfactory to all its members (c) lacked a two-thirds majority needed to pass a General Assembly resolution (d) approved Zionism as an expression of Jewish nationalism.

27. A major criticism of the voting procedure in the Security Council is that (a) the Soviet Union has as much voting power as the United States (b) a veto by any permanent member can prevent or delay action (c) the permanent members have more votes than the nonpermanent members (d) most member nations have no voting power in the Security Council.

28. In getting member states to heed its requests, the United Nations closely resembles (a) the United States under the federal Constitution (b) the United States under the Articles of Confederation (c) Britain in relation to the first British settlements in the New World (d) a holding company in relation to its subsidiaries.

29. Which problem has consistently troubled the United Nations? (a) member nations giving consideration only to their national interests (b) a steady decrease in membership of small nations (c) lack of a public forum where any nation may discuss world problems (d) fair distribution of its budgetary surpluses.

30. The establishment of the United Nations, and the exchange of information among scientists of many nations indicate increasing (a) disillusionment with communism in most countries (b) prosperity and rising standards of living in most developing countries (c) isolationism in United States foreign policy (d) interdependence among nations.

31. Which is a major obstacle to United Nations efforts to deal with international political issues? (a) The small nations dominate the Security Council. (b) Sessions of the UN have been cut short due to lack of funds. (c) UN peacekeeping forces are primarily made up of United States armed forces. (d) The superpowers often do not provide the cooperation necessary for effective UN action.

32. "War is the natural relationship between sovereign nations interrupted occasionally by brief intervals of peace." The writer of this statement probably meant that (a) international organizations should be formed to solve world problems (b) wars are necessary for human progress (c) lasting peace is a realistic goal of nations (d) the present system of nation-states has inherent weaknesses that lead to war.

33. "International crises are not unlike the migration of birds. They leave during one time of year only to return to their original place of departure at another." The author of this statement is probably referring to the fact that most international crises (a) occur most often during the warm seasons of the year (b) spread quickly to many parts of the world (c) are created by those who pursue the elusive dove of peace (d) tend to reappear rather than be resolved.

34. Which group of conditions is most characteristic of Third World, or emerging nations? (a) industrialization, political instability, poor health conditions (b) former colonial areas, high technology, low standard of living (c) stable government, declining population, advanced educational systems (d) poverty, illiteracy, growing population.

35. The aspect of the United Nations that has undergone the most significant change is the (a) method of financing its operation (b) use of the veto power in the Security Council (c) work of the Economic and Social Council in aiding the emerging nations (d) influence of Third World nations in the General Assembly.

————————————— **ESSAY QUESTIONS** —————————————

1. Giving *one* specific example for *each,* show how the United Nations has sought to achieve the following objectives stated in its Charter: *(a)* "to maintain international peace and security," *(b)* "to promote social progress and better standards of life," *(c)* "to reaffirm faith in fundamental human rights."

2. The UN represents an effort to solve the problems of international tension in an age of extreme danger. *(a)* Describe *two* ways in which the UN represents an improvement over the League of Nations. *(b)* Discuss *two* different ways in which the UN attempts to maintain world peace. *(c)* Show how the United States has cooperated with the UN in meeting *two* international crises. *(d)* Explain *two* limitations on the ability of the UN to meet world problems.

3. *(a)* State *two* functions of each of the following specialized agencies associated with the United Nations: (1) WHO (2) FAO (3) ILO (4) UNESCO. *(b)* Discuss *two* weaknesses that hinder the work of the specialized agencies.

4. In 1948 the United Nations issued a Declaration of Human Rights that stressed the right (1) to be protected from mental and physical abuse (2) to such vital needs as food, shelter, health care, and education (3) to enjoy civil and political liberties.

   (a) Using *two* examples from European, Asian, or African experience during any period of history prior to 1948, indicate why the United Nations considered it necessary to issue the Declaration of Human Rights.

   (b) The mere acceptance of the Declaration of Human Rights did not eliminate the violation of human rights. By reference to *two* specific examples outside the United States since 1948, show how the violation of human rights continues to be a major problem in the world. Include in your response the methods by which world reaction has sought to deal with these violations.

5. At a discussion on the United Nations, the following arguments were given:

For the United Nations	*Against the United Nations*
a. The United Nations Charter has avoided the weaknesses of the Covenant of the League of Nations.	*a.* Since the United States pays about 25 percent of the cost of running the United Nations, our country might just as well "go it alone."
b. The war in Korea has tested the strength of the United Nations and proved that it can stop aggression.	*b.* The frequent use of the veto has made the United Nations helpless.
c. The UN serves as a safety valve where nations may talk out problems rather than resort to war.	*c.* By passing partisan and unrealistic resolutions which nations defy, the General Assembly has destroyed the prestige of the UN.

Agree or disagree with any *two* of the arguments above, giving *two* specific facts for each to support your point of view.

6. The United Nations has been the subject of considerable controversy. Giving *two* specific arguments to support your answer, discuss the extent to which you agree *or* disagree with each of the following statements. *(a)* The United Nations has successfully achieved its major aims. *(b)* The United States should withdraw from the United Nations. *(c)* The present "one-nation, one-vote" practice in the General Assembly should be replaced by a weighted system under which extra votes would be given to certain members on the basis of population and economic strength. *(d)* The specialized agencies of the United Nations have made significant contributions toward helping resolve economic and social problems. *(e)* In the future, historians will look back at the UN and judge it to have been as much a failure as was the League of Nations.

PART 2. The United States Faces the Communist Challenge

AMERICAN LEADERSHIP IN WORLD AFFAIRS

With the Japanese attack on Pearl Harbor in 1941, the American people finally realized that the United States had become a major world power and could not protect its national interests by a policy of isolation. American public opinion encouraged the government to pursue a new foreign policy: active American participation and leadership in world affairs.

RECENT OBJECTIVES OF AMERICAN FOREIGN POLICY

(1) Safeguard United States national interests. (2) Avoid the outbreak of a nuclear war. (3) Help other nations improve their social and economic conditions. (4) Promote democracy throughout the world. (5) Protect our friends and allies against Communist expansion.

COLD WAR

1. Origins. The "cold war" originated immediately after World War II as a struggle between the free-world nations, led by the United States, and the Communist nations, led by the Soviet Union. The American people were alarmed by *(a)* the expressed Soviet aim of communizing the world, and *(b)* the expansion of Soviet power into Central Europe and Asia. President Truman began the American policy of keeping Russia from gaining control of any additional territories—a policy called *containment.*

2. Weapons. The cold war has been fought by *(a) propaganda*—in newspapers, on radio and television, in street demonstrations, and at the UN, *(b) diplomatic moves,* at international conferences and in military alliances, *(c) scientific competition,* in developing nuclear weapons and missiles, and undertaking space flights, *(d) economic competition,* in aid to underdeveloped countries, *(e) espionage,* by spy rings, intelligence ships, and data-gathering vehicles orbiting the earth, and *(f) subversion,* chiefly by local Communist groups that have sought to overthrow pro-Western governments by demonstrations, strikes, and guerrilla warfare.

The cold war also has been marked by localized military action but not by all-out war. The world has been living under an uneasy armed truce—an absence of total war but also an absence of genuine peace.

3. Today: A More Complex Situation. Although the cold war originated in a world generally divided into an American bloc and a Soviet bloc, this simple division no longer exists. Each bloc has experienced strains.

In the American bloc, the United States has faced dissent from its major allies—especially Britain and France—over aspects of foreign policy, military matters, and economic programs. In the Soviet bloc, the Soviet Union was defied by Yugoslavia over national communism and challenged by China over Communist leadership and foreign policy.

THE TWO SUPERPOWERS

The Soviet Union and the United States emerged from World War II as the two superpowers. There were no others, for the war had destroyed the might of the two major Axis powers, Germany and Japan; the war had reduced to second-rate status two major Allied powers, France and Britain.

The Soviet Union and the United States are superpowers on the basis of their large populations, their strong and stable governments, their industrial and technological leadership, and their military power, including nuclear weapons and missiles.

A COMPARISON OF THE TWO SUPERPOWERS

1. Government: Dictatorial vs. Democratic

a. Political Parties

(1) Soviet Union. The Communist party is the only party permitted to exist. It selects all candidates for election to office and dominates the government.

(2) United States. Many political parties exist, the two major parties being the Democrats and the Republicans. The major and minor parties check upon each other, present candidates and issues to the people, and compete for support. No one party monopolizes the government.

b. Power Over the Country

(1) Soviet Union. Communist party leaders decide upon Soviet policies, which are then presented to the nation as the not-to-be-challenged Communist position, or *party line.* The party dominates every aspect of Soviet life.

(2) United States. Diverse persons—including elected and appointed government officials; captains of industry, agriculture, and labor; and leaders in education and the information media—all help shape American policies. These policies are subject to public criticism and revision. Because power is diffused, no one group dominates the country.

c. Civil Liberties

(1) Soviet Union. Russian citizens lack basic civil liberties and fear the *secret police* (KGB). Those who speak against the government are regarded as criminals or insane persons.

(2) United States. American citizens are guaranteed their civil liberties by the federal and state constitutions. They can turn to the courts to protect their rights.

2. Economy: Communist vs. Capitalist

a. Industry

(1) Soviet Union. The government owns and operates all industry. The Communists transformed the Soviet Union from an agricultural nation into the world's second-leading industrial nation through a series of *Five-Year Plans.* These emphasized the needs of the state for heavy industry and military equipment. The plans slighted consumer goods, which remain scarce and of poor quality.

(2) United States. Private entrepreneurs—individuals and corporations—own and operate most industry. Competition and the *profit motive* provide personal economic incentives. The government acts chiefly to prevent abuses. America, the world's leading industrial nation, exceeds the Soviet Union in output of capital goods and consumer products.

b. Labor

(1) Soviet Union. Almost all Soviet workers belong to unions dominated by the Communist party. These unions spur the workers to greater productivity. However, they have no say in determining wages and no right to strike. Although the standard of living of Soviet workers is higher than in Czarist times, it remains low by Western standards.

(2) United States. One-sixth of American workers belong to unions, which are free of government domination although subject to regulation. Unions bargain collectively with employers regarding wages and working conditions; they retain the right to strike. American workers enjoy a considerably higher living standard than Soviet workers.

c. Agriculture

(1) Soviet Union. Some 19 percent of the labor force is employed in agriculture. Farmers work on vast state-owned farms or in farm communities called collectives. Agriculture is handicapped by shortages of farm equipment, inefficient production methods, and insufficient fertilizer. The Soviet Union has been importing feed grains in recent years to increase the production of meat.

(2) United States. Less than 3 percent of the labor force is employed in agriculture. Farmers own their own lands or work on giant commercial farms. American farmers utilize much machinery and fertilizer, and employ the latest production methods. They receive government aid to maintain soil fertility, achieve fair prices, and secure agricultural knowledge. American farmers produce crops large enough for domestic consumption and huge exports. In fact, crop surpluses have contributed to serious economic difficulties for farmers in recent years.

3. Culture: Regimentation vs. Freedom

a. Education

(1) Soviet Union. The central government controls education. All children receive compulsory schooling for ten years. Capable students are encouraged to study further, especially in mathematics and the sciences. The Soviet Union produces more engineers and scientists than does the United States. In the humanities, students are not trained to think for themselves but must accept the Communist party line.

(2) United States. The states and localities control education, although the federal government grants funds to expand school facilities, improve instruction, and aid capable students. Most children receive compulsory education to at least the age of 16. The United States turns out far more college graduates than does the Soviet Union. In the humanities, students are encouraged to pursue independent, nonregimented thinking.

b. Literature and Art

(1) Soviet Union. The Soviet regime encourages writers and artists, but it demands that they propagandize for communism. They must seek wide popular appeal, avoid experimentation, and praise the Soviet state. Many Soviet writers resent regimentation and represent a constant pressure upon the Communist party for greater freedom of expression.

(2) United States. The American government is prohibited constitutionally from interfering with free expression. American writers and artists produce works that represent their own taste and outlook on life. Their works may praise or criticize aspects of American culture and governmental policy.

AN OVERVIEW OF SOVIET-AMERICAN RELATIONS

1. 1917–1941: Unfriendly. The Communists resented *(a)* American aid to anti-Communist forces following the Russian Revolution, and *(b)* America's refusal until 1933 to recognize the Soviet Union.

The United States resented *(a)* the Soviet withdrawal from World War I, enabling the Germans to concentrate their military forces on the western front, *(b)* Soviet efforts to spread unrest and revolution in non-Communist countries by means of an organization called the *Comintern,* and *(c)* the Soviet Union's Nonaggression Pact of 1939 with Nazi Germany—an agreement that encouraged Germany to start World War II.

2. 1941–1945: Cooperative. During World War II, the Soviet Union and the United States found themselves fighting against a common enemy, Germany. To create amity with its democratic allies, the Soviet Union dissolved the Comintern. To assist the Soviet Union, the United States *(a)* provided $11 billion of lend-lease equipment, and *(b)* led the Western allies in opening other fronts in Europe by invading southern Italy and northern France. Also, the Soviet Union, the United States, and Britain coordinated military strategy and planned postwar arrangements at top-level conferences at *Teheran, Yalta,* and *Potsdam.*

3. 1945–1963: Generally Unfriendly. As World War II ended, the Soviet Union reverted to its prewar attitude of hostility toward non-Communist countries, especially the United States. Soviet leaders justified their actions by declaring that *(a)* the spread of communism was necessary for the security of the Soviet Union, and *(b)* communism inevitably must triumph over capitalism throughout the world. Until his death in 1953, Stalin pursued a "hard line" toward the West, but his successors have urged *peaceful coexistence.* They have not, however, abandoned the Soviet goal of communizing the world.

American leaders *(a)* held the expansion of Soviet power a threat to the safety of the free world, and *(b)* predicted victory for the American way of life in peaceful competition with communism. In the post-World War II era, American leadership has concentrated upon the defense of the free world against Communist expansion.

4. 1963–1979: A Search for Détente. The first breaks in the Cold War came with agreements on a United States-Soviet "hot line" and a Limited Nuclear Test Ban Treaty in 1963. During the early 1970s, President Nixon sought a wide-ranging relaxation, or *détente,* in United States-Soviet relations. Soviet leader Leonid Brezhnev responded positively. The United States and the Soviet Union expanded their trade and concluded two strategic arms limitation treaties—SALT I, in 1972, and SALT II, in 1979. Détente recognized the basic differences between the two superpowers but also their mutual interest in avoiding a nuclear war.

5. Recently: Renewed Tensions. The Soviet invasion of Afghanistan in 1979 and the United States response marked an end to détente, at least for the time being. In the early 1980s, President Reagan denounced the Soviet Union as an "evil empire" and greatly expanded a United States military buildup begun by President Carter. In 1986 the United States ceased compliance with the unratified SALT II treaty. Although the two superpowers continued negotiations over new arms-control measures, differences over events in Nicaragua, Afghanistan, Angola, Poland, and other countries contributed to the renewal of tensions. (Check the Index for Carter, Reagan, and Détente.)

THE SOVIET UNION DOMINATES ITS EUROPEAN SATELLITES

1. Meaning of Satellites. The *satellites* are the Communist-dominated nations of Eastern and Central Europe that, in most important matters, accept Soviet authority. Communist satellites are Bulgaria, Czechoslovakia, East Germany, Hungary, Poland, and Rumania.

Self-proclaimed *people's republics,* the satellite nations have governments that essentially imitate Soviet domestic practices. *(a)* They are dictatorships, each controlled by its own Communist party. *(b)* They have nationalized industry, tried to collectivize agriculture, and proclaimed master economic plans. *(c)* They have denied many civil liberties and restricted free cultural expression. *(d)* In Poland and Hungary, both predominantly Roman Catholic, the governments have harassed the Catholic Church.

COMMUNIST EXPANSION SINCE 1939

Outright Annexations	Local Communist Parties Seize Control
By the USSR 1. *Countries:* Estonia, Latvia, and Lithuania. 2. *Territories:* from Czechoslovakia, Finland, Germany, Japan, Poland, and Rumania. **By China** *Country:* Tibet.	1. *In Europe:* Albania, Bulgaria, Czechoslovakia, East Germany, Hungary, Poland, Rumania, Yugoslavia. 2. *In Asia:* Cambodia, China, Laos, North Korea, South Yemen, Vietnam. 3. *In America:* Cuba 4. *In Africa:* Angola, Ethiopia, Mozambique.

2. Establishment of Satellites. To help local Communist parties seize and maintain control, the Soviet Union *(a)* fostered Communist regimes in Eastern and Central Europe as its armies pursued the retreating Germans during the closing year of World War II, *(b)* trained local Communists in revolutionary tactics and leadership, *(c)* provided military equipment and advisers for local Communist forces, *(d)* maintained troops in Eastern and Central Europe, and *(e)* violated a Yalta Conference agreement by thwarting free elections in Soviet-occupied nations.

3. Methods of Soviet Control. *(a)* Soviet specialists in political, economic, and military matters "advise" the satellite governments. *(b)* The Soviet Union tries to keep the satellite economies tied to its own by trade treaties. *(c)* Soviet military forces are stationed in some satellite countries; they have also intervened to compel satellite conformity with Soviet policy. *(d)* Soviet generals head a unified military command coordinating Soviet and satellite armed forces within an alliance, the *Warsaw Pact.* (See map, page 617.)

IRON CURTAIN

As part of the cold war, the Communist regimes have kept their people from free contact with Western ideas. They have established restrictions on visitors, newspapers, magazines, books, and movies; they have jammed Western radio broadcasts, especially the *Voice of America* and *Radio Free Europe.* Speaking about this barrier between the Communist nations and the West, Winston Churchill used the term "iron curtain."

TROUBLE BEHIND THE IRON CURTAIN

1. Yugoslavia Since 1945. *Marshal Tito,* Communist ruler of Yugoslavia, defied the Soviet Union and pursued nationalist policies. Tito was emboldened to act independently because Yugoslavia was not occupied by Soviet troops and does not border the Soviet Union.

The Soviet Union and the satellites sought to overthrow Tito by economic pressure, propaganda, and subversion within Yugoslavia. These efforts proved unsuccessful. Since Stalin's death, the Soviet Union and the satellites have somewhat repaired relations with Yugoslavia.

The Western democracies were cheered by Tito's independence of Soviet control and his advocacy of *national communism*. The democracies hoped that other satellites would follow Tito's example. The democracies aided Yugoslavia with loans, food, trade treaties, diplomatic support, and military equipment. The West realizes that Yugoslavia is a Communist nation, but not a Soviet satellite.

Following Tito's death in 1980, most Western nations reaffirmed their support for Yugoslavia's unity, nonalignment, and independence.

2. Power Struggle Following Stalin's Death in 1953. The death of Joseph Stalin signaled a bitter struggle for power among the top Soviet Communists. *Nikita Khrushchev* became first secretary of the Communist party and used that position to eliminate his chief rivals. One was executed; others were demoted to minor jobs. In 1958 Khrushchev, feeling secure, assumed the premiership.

The struggle for power after Stalin's death gave the world an unusual glimpse of the conflict that can exist within the Soviet dictatorship—a conflict that is usually kept well hidden from the public.

3. Downgrading of Stalin (1956). Stalin had used every means of propaganda to encourage hero worship of himself as a great teacher, leader, and military genius. In 1956 Khrushchev began an all-out attack to downgrade Stalin in the eyes of the Soviet people. Khrushchev condemned Stalin for *(a)* purges of military and political leaders on false charges, *(b)* blunders in foreign affairs, *(c)* terror against innocent Soviet citizens, and *(d)* personal cowardice during World War II. After Khrushchev's denunciation of Stalin, the Communist party spread this anti-Stalin line.

In the satellite nations, the anti-Stalin campaign strengthened the Titoist doctrine of national communism and helped set off upheavals, especially in Poland and Hungary.

4. Uprising in Poland (1956). The Polish people engaged in strikes and demonstrations *(a)* to achieve better living conditions, and *(b)* to end Soviet domination. *Wladyslaw Gomulka,* who had been imprisoned as a Titoist, regained the leadership of the Polish Communist party and announced that Poland would seek its own road to socialism. Khrushchev was alarmed by Poland's trend toward independence, but Gomulka reassured him that Poland would remain Communist and allied with the Soviet Union. Khrushchev thereupon pledged not to interfere in Poland's internal affairs.

By this bloodless uprising, Poland under Gomulka achieved *(a)* a measure of independence in domestic matters, enabling Gomulka to end the forced collectivization of agriculture, and *(b)* expulsion of Soviet agents from positions of authority over the Polish army, economy, and government.

5. Revolution in Hungary (1956). The Hungarian people revolted for *(a)* better living conditions, *(b)* the withdrawal of Soviet troops, and *(c)* full national independence. *Imre Nagy,* a Titoist, became head of the government, appointed some non-Communists to his cabinet, and demanded the removal of

Soviet forces. Nagy announced Hungary's neutrality in the cold war and withdrawal from the Warsaw Pact.

Such anti-Soviet moves were more than Khrushchev would permit. In spite of Nagy's appeal to the United Nations and a resolution by the General Assembly, Soviet troops intervened and suppressed the Hungarian freedom fighters. Thousands of Hungarians were killed or deported to Siberia; others fled their native land. The Soviets smashed the Nagy government and replaced it with a puppet Hungarian regime under *Janos Kadar.*

6. Soviet Split With Communist China. (Check the Index.)

7. Removal of Khrushchev (1964). In a surprise development, Khrushchev was removed from power by collective action of the other top Communists. He was denounced for "hare-brained scheming, immature conclusions, and hasty decisions." Khrushchev's removal, according to Western observers, was caused by his worsening of the dispute with China and his failure to improve the Soviet economy. Khrushchev was succeeded in the powerful position of First Secretary by *Leonid Brezhnev.*

8. Invasion of Czechoslovakia (1968). Alexander Dubcek became head of the Czechoslovak Communist party and pledged a program of "liberalization." Dubcek lifted censorship of press, radio, and television, permitted non-Communists to form political groups, and planned to seek trade and loans from the West. To reassure the Soviet Union, Dubcek asserted that Czechoslovakia remained Communist and loyal to the Warsaw Pact.

Soviet leaders, however, feared that the Czechoslovak reforms might spur similar movements in the other satellite nations. Soviet forces, supported by troops of four Warsaw Pact nations—East Germany, Poland, Hungary, and Bulgaria—occupied Czechoslovakia. The Soviets compelled Czechoslovakia to reestablish censorship, ban non-Communist political groups, accept Soviet advisers, consent to the stationing of Soviet troops, and replace Dubcek as head of the Czechoslovak Communist party by the Soviet choice, *Gustav Husak.*

This invasion, condemned by many Western and neutral nations, was also condemned by three Communist states—Yugoslavia, Rumania, and China—and by West European Communist parties. These Communist groups rejected the Soviet claim to have saved Czechoslovakia from "counterrevolutionary forces." They also rejected the Soviet assertion that if a Communist nation endangers socialism at home or in other Communist countries, the Soviet Union has the duty to intervene with military force—the *Brezhnev Doctrine.*

9. Recurrent Unrest in Poland

a. 1970–1971. Polish workers felt their earnings threatened by a new wage incentive system. When the government increased prices of food, fuel, and clothing, workers in coastal cities began riots and demonstrations. As the rioting spread, Gomulka resigned as head of Poland's Communist party and, in a change approved by the Soviet Union, was replaced by Edward Gierek. The

Gierek regime quieted discontent by shelving the wage incentive system and re-voking the price increases, but called for "law, order, and discipline."

b. 1976. Polish workers again rioted to protest government increases in food prices—designed to offset internal inflationary costs and higher priced West-ern food imports. The government rescinded the higher prices, but it also sen-tenced some riot leaders to prison terms.

c. 1979. Karol Cardinal Wojtyla of Poland was elected as Pope in 1978 and took the name *John Paul II.* He is the first Polish pontiff in the history of the Roman Catholic Church. In 1979, as Pope, he visited his homeland, whose peo-ple are overwhelmingly Roman Catholic. Warmly and even emotionally received by huge crowds, the Pope spoke out for human rights, religious liberty, and Cath-olic Church interests; he condemned atheism and questioned Soviet domination of its East European satellites. The visit of this "Slavic Pope" heightened Polish nationalism—to the discomfort of the Soviet Union; it also intensified religious fervor and raised expectations of more personal freedom—to the discomfort of Poland's Communist rulers.

d. 1980–1983. When the government sharply raised meat prices, work-ers throughout Poland walked off their jobs. In Gdansk, a Baltic seaport, shipyard workers selected a strike committee headed by *Lech Walesa.* The strikers de-manded major reforms—relaxation of censorship; free access for religious and labor groups to the mass media; release from jail of the 1976 riot leaders; wage increases; a reduction in the workweek; and, most important, the right to strike through a free labor union, independent of Communist party and government control. After two months of turmoil, the Gierek regime accepted most of the strikers' demands; in return the labor leaders acknowledged the leading role of Poland's Communist party. Then Gierek, supposedly ill, was removed as head of Poland's Communist party.

Solidarity—the 10-million-member independent Polish labor union headed by Lech Walesa—represented an unprecedented development in the Commu-nist bloc. It signified a measure of power and authority separate from the Com-munist party; its existence contradicted Communist ideology requiring complete party supremacy. This situation in Poland was of great concern to Communist leaders in other Soviet-bloc nations and in the Soviet Union.

In 1981 Poland's Communist government was under increasing domestic pressure for further reforms. The government felt compelled to grant (1) private farmers the right to form an independent Rural Solidarity union, (2) university students the right to form an independent union with influence to change from compulsory to optional courses in the Russian language and in Marxism-Lenin-ism, and (3) Solidarity the right to use the mass media and a pledge gradually to reduce the workweek from six to five days. Despite these concessions, bitterness between the government and Solidarity mounted, the economy worsened, and food shortages continued.

In late 1981, General *Wojcieck Jaruzelski* became head of the Polish gov-ernment and Communist party. He faced deteriorating economic conditions, wildcat strikes by Solidarity members, and calls by Solidarity groups for a national referendum on the Communist regime. Jaruzelski acted, possibly with Soviet prodding and approval, to impose martial law; crush Solidarity; arrest Lech Walesa, other Solidarity leaders, and liberal activists; and govern by military force.

The Polish people resented martial law with deep-felt anger; some workers went on strike but they were soon suppressed. For Poland's Catholic Church, Archbishop *Jozef Glemp* assailed martial law and the denial of human rights, and demanded the release of political prisoners, naming Lech Walesa. For the United States, President Reagan blamed Moscow, as well as Warsaw, for the repression in Poland. The United States imposed various economic sanctions against both Poland and the Soviet Union.

By 1983 the Polish Communist regime felt strong enough to free Lech Walesa and other political prisoners, to officially ban the Solidarity union, and to suspend martial law—while retaining sufficient powers to rule dictatorially. Critics of the Polish regime were cheered by the awarding of the 1983 Nobel Peace Prize to Walesa and by the visit to Poland that same year of the Polish-born Pope John Paul II.

e. *Since 1984.* General Jaruzelski has sought a "normalization" of Polish affairs by (1) freeing Solidarity leaders who remained in jail, (2) liberalizing the Communist party leadership, and (3) creating a national consultative council to promote dialogue between the regime and its opponents. Meanwhile, Jaruzelski has attempted to increase foreign trade to help Poland pay back its staggering foreign debt and resolve its severe domestic economic crisis. Critics charged that these moves were merely window dressing. They continued to demand a free trade union movement and genuine political freedom.

TROUBLE WITH WEST EUROPEAN COMMUNIST PARTIES: EUROCOMMUNISM

During the 1970s, the Soviet Union faced an apparent revolt by Communist parties in Western Europe. A number of Communist figures, led by *Enrico Berlinguer,* then head of the Italian Communist party, rejected Soviet dominance of the Communist movement and voiced support for multiparty democracy and nationalism. A French leader stated that his party would pursue "a socialism in the colors of France."

The ideological changes demanded by such Communists were (1) toward democracy—to abide by the results of free, multiparty elections, guarantee civil liberties, and renounce dictatorship—and (2) toward nationalism—to remain independent of Soviet domination and uphold the national interests of their respective countries. This ideology, which became known as *Eurocommunism,* was seen as an attempt to build alliances between Communists, Socialists, and other European leftists.

By the mid-1980s, some Western European Communist parties had returned to the Soviet fold, and Eurocommunism had weakened. The Italian Communist party—Italy's second largest political party—remained the chief supporter of Eurocommunist theories. The decline of Eurocommunism resulted from a strengthening of Social Democratic and other non-Communist leftist parties and from splits within European Communist parties.

PART 3. The United States Promotes the Economic and Military Strength of the Non-Communist World

FOREIGN AID

THE TRUMAN ADMINISTRATION (1945–1953) SHAPES AMERICAN FOREIGN AID POLICIES

First to deal with Communist expansionism in the post-World War II era, the Truman administration countered with three major foreign aid initiatives—the *Truman Doctrine* for Greece and Turkey, the *Marshall Plan* for Western Europe, and the *Point Four Program* for underdeveloped nations. In these areas the Truman initiatives were designed to oppose Communist expansion by improving economic conditions.

1. The Truman Doctrine (1947) for Greece and Turkey. Announcing American policy to "support free peoples" against direct and indirect Communist aggression, President Truman extended economic and military aid to Greece and Turkey. American aid enabled Greece to revive its economy and to suppress Communist guerrilla bands—especially after Tito split with the Soviet Union and ceased helping the Greek guerrillas. American aid strengthened Turkey to withstand Soviet demands regarding the Dardanelles—the waterway connecting the Black and Mediterranean seas.

2. The Marshall Plan (1948–1951). *George C. Marshall,* secretary of state under Truman, offered economic aid to all European nations to help them recover from the destruction of World War II. The plan, accepted by most non-Communist nations of Europe, helped achieve "recovery, not relief." It cost the United States $12.5 billion, spent mostly for American foodstuffs, raw materials, and machinery.

The Marshall Plan was opposed by the Soviet Union and its satellites as an American scheme to dominate Europe. They formed a Communist economic aid plan, the *Council of Mutual Economic Assistance* (COMECON).

3. Point Four Program (1949). As Point Four in America's program to contain communism, Truman offered technical assistance to developing nations in Latin America, the Middle East, Africa, and Asia. American technical specialists helped increase agricultural and industrial output, improve government administration, promote public health, and advance education.

SUBSEQUENT AMERICAN FOREIGN AID INITIATIVES

Administrations following the Truman era continued the foreign aid programs and also, to deal with additional situations, introduced their own initiatives.

1. Food-for-Peace Program (1954). President Eisenhower began making outright gifts or low-cost sales of our surplus food products to help developing nations.

2. Eisenhower Doctrine (1957). Eisenhower offered economic and military aid to the Middle East nations, but most denounced the offer as an American plot to dominate the Arab world. (In 1958 American troops were sent into Lebanon to protect that nation's government against leftist rebels.)

3. Alliance for Progress (1961). President Kennedy substantially increased aid to the nations of Latin America. (Check the Index.)

4. Peace Corps (1961). President Kennedy created this agency. It sends volunteers to developing nations that request aid in implementing programs of technical assistance.

AMERICAN FOREIGN AID: AN OVERVIEW

The United States spends large sums for foreign aid—annually several billion dollars. Currently, American military aid is administered by the Defense Department and economic aid by the State Department's *Agency for International Development* (AID).

From 1945 to the present, the United States has extended over $300 billion in aid to some 140 countries. Of this total, 38 percent has been for military supplies and services and 62 percent for economic and technical aid. One-third of American aid has been in the form of loans that are repayable; two-thirds has been in the form of grants that are outright gifts.

CRITICISMS OF OUR FOREIGN AID PROGRAM

Although most Americans support foreign aid as in the national interest, a minority is opposed, claiming that foreign aid (1) is a burden on the American taxpayer, (2) diverts funds that could be used for domestic purposes, (3) is characterized by inefficient administration, waste, and corruption, (4) creates competition for American manufacturers and farmers by building up foreign industry and agriculture, and (5) has failed to lessen the danger of communism.

FOREIGN AID PROGRAMS OF WEST EUROPEAN NATIONS

The United States has urged the more prosperous free-world nations—notably Great Britain, France, and West Germany—to extend aid to underdeveloped lands. These nations have initiated modest foreign aid programs.

COMMUNIST ECONOMIC OFFENSIVE SINCE 1954

The Communist bloc has offered aid to most underdeveloped nations, both neutral and pro-Western. Communist aid, chiefly loans and skilled personnel, has been accepted by more than 20 countries—notably Argentina, India, Indonesia, Iraq, Syria and Egypt.

To date American foreign aid remains far greater than that extended by the Communist nations.

WEST EUROPEAN ECONOMIC UNITY

THE INNER SIX

The *Inner Six* West European nations—Belgium, France, Italy, Luxembourg, the Netherlands, and West Germany—having cooperated under the Marshall Plan, moved toward further economic unity.

1. First Steps. The Inner Six established an authority to manage their coal and steel resources in the interests of the entire community. They formed a European Atomic Energy Commission to spur atomic research and use for generating electric power.

2. European Economic Community (EEC; Common Market). In 1957 the Inner Six agreed to join in a tariff union. They set up a *European Economic Commission* to *(a)* eliminate internal tariff barriers, and *(b)* establish a unified tariff system on imports from outside the tariff union area. European leaders envisioned a free-trade area—a *Common Market* without human-made barriers to the movement of goods, capital, and labor.

AN ENLARGED COMMON MARKET (SINCE 1973)

Britain twice applied for Common Market membership, but each application was vetoed by France under President de Gaulle. He viewed Britain's membership as a threat to his hopes for French leadership in Western Europe. After de Gaulle retired, Britain again applied for membership and was accepted together with Ireland and Denmark.

In 1973 these three nations officially joined, creating a nine-member Common Market. In 1981 Greece, a developing eastern Mediterranean European nation, was admitted to the Common Market. In 1986, two relatively poor West European nations, Spain and Portugal, were admitted.

The 12 nations have a combined gross national product (GNP) second only to that of the United States.

MILITARY ALLIANCES

NORTH ATLANTIC TREATY ORGANIZATION (NATO)

1. Free-World Fears. In 1948 the free-world nations were shocked by three Soviet-inspired aggressions: (1) the Communist seizure of Czechoslovakia, (2) Soviet pressure upon Finland to accept a mutual assistance pact, and (3) a Soviet attempt to drive the Western powers out of Berlin by a surface route blockade. Made fearful by these Soviet moves, the free-world nations formed the *North Atlantic Treaty Organization.*

2. Defensive Military Alliance. In 1949, 12 nations—Britain, France, Belgium, the Netherlands, Luxembourg, Denmark, Iceland, Italy, Norway, Portugal, Canada, and the United States—signed the *North Atlantic Pact.* They declared that *(a)* they would consider an attack on any one of them as an attack on all, and *(b)* they would come to the defense of the attacked member nation with armed force if necessary.

NATO admitted the eastern Mediterranean countries of Greece and Turkey in 1952, West Germany in 1955, and Spain in 1982, bringing its membership to 16 nations.

Europe: Opposing Western and Soviet Alliances

3. NATO Army. In 1950 the North Atlantic Pact nations authorized a NATO army. Its headquarters are located in Belgium. Its supreme commander has always been an American general.

The United States and other member nations have assigned personnel and equipment to the NATO military establishment. Within Europe, NATO's conventional (nonnuclear) military strength has been far less than that of the Soviet Union and its European allies.

In the 1970s, the Soviet Union built up its supply of medium-range nuclear missiles aimed at Western Europe. Worried European leaders called on the United States to match the buildup. In response, the United States began installing medium-range Pershing 2 and cruise missiles at European bases in 1983. Large protest marches in several European countries greeted the United States move, highlighting divisions within Western Europe over NATO policies. The major opposition parties in both Britain and West Germany have since called for at least partial withdrawal of the missiles. Other European leaders have insisted that the United States missiles are vital to Western Europe's defense.

4. Problems Facing NATO

a. Nuclear Fears. Many NATO members are fearful that, in the event of a Soviet-American conflict, Western Europe would suffer nuclear devastation.

b. French Nationalism. President Charles de Gaulle of France resented what he called United States domination of NATO. In 1967 he ended French participation in NATO military activities, although France remained a member of the alliance. De Gaulle and succeeding French leaders strengthened France's own nuclear forces, which include atomic submarines armed with nuclear missiles.

c. Hostility Between Greece and Turkey. Although Greece and Turkey both joined NATO, the two countries have traditionally been enemies and have clashed bitterly over the island of Cyprus. In 1974 a Greek-backed coup, aimed at uniting Cyprus with Greece, failed and resulted in Turkish armies occupying 40 percent of the island. The Greek government, resenting the lack of NATO support, kept its membership in NATO but withdrew its military forces from the NATO command.

Turkey condemned the action of the United States Congress—cutting off military aid to Turkey—and ordered American forces out of military installations and intelligence posts in Turkey.

In 1978 President Carter requested Congress to lift the three-year-old embargo. He feared that Turkey might further weaken its ties to NATO. Congress narrowly approved an end to the ban. Thereafter, the United States reached agreement with Turkey to provide military and economic aid in return for American use of Turkish military and intelligence posts "within the NATO framework."

d. American Disillusionment With NATO. For years American officials had been unhappy that the NATO powers, economically recovered from World War II, were questioning American leadership and obstructing unified foreign policies.

(1) In the 1973 Arab-Israeli War. The major NATO members, yielding to Arab oil embargo threats, refused permission to the United States to use facilities on their soil for transporting military equipment to Israel. Their refusal compelled the United States to transport the equipment by a more difficult route.

(2) In the 1980–1983 Polish Crisis. When Poland's Communist regime instituted martial law and crushed the independent Solidarity union, President Reagan blamed the repression upon Moscow as well as Warsaw. The United States imposed various economic sanctions against both Poland and the Soviet Union, but America's NATO allies proved reluctant to take similar action. West Germany and France, in particular, were concerned over their considerable trade with the Soviet Union.

(3) In the Natural Gas Pipeline From Siberia to Western Europe. The Soviets gave highest priority to constructing this 2800-mile pipeline—to be built by imports of Western equipment financed by Western loans that would be repaid by the future sale of natural gas in Western Europe. The United States opposed this project because it would provide considerable foreign exchange for the Soviets and would make Western Europe vulnerable to Soviet threats to curtail energy deliveries. The United States urged Western Europe to consider alternate energy sources such as gas from North Sea fields and coal. The United States further prohibited American companies from selling the Soviets equipment for the pipeline project. Despite American objections, West Germany, France, and Italy signed contracts for the future purchase of Siberian gas; also, West German and French manufacturers agreed to sell the Soviets necessary pipeline equipment, and a group of French banks agreed to provide a large Soviet loan to finance such purchases. With our major NATO allies rejecting American pipeline policy and with American companies unhappy over the possible loss of Soviet contracts, the United States in late 1982 lifted its sanctions against the pipeline.

e. Possibility of Communists in NATO Member Governments. NATO since the mid-1970s has faced the possibility of Western Communists in the governments of NATO nations. This problem surfaced as follows:

(1) Portugal. In 1974 an army coup ended over 40 years of conservative dictatorial rule but plunged Portugal into political chaos. For a time, the small Portuguese Communist party seemed likely to seize complete control but was unable to do so. The much larger Socialist party formed a government committed to democracy, economic reform, and active NATO membership—policies supported by subsequent Portuguese governments.

(2) Italy. Following the 1976 parliamentary elections, the Christian Democrats formed a minority government; however, their ability to secure a parliamentary majority depended on tacit Communist cooperation. The Communists indicated that they would accept this arrangement for the time being but that their goal was full membership in an Italian coalition government.

In 1979 the Communists, having received no cabinet positions, caused the fall of the minority government. After the 1979 elections, Italy was governed by coalition regimes that continued to exclude the Communists.

(3) France. In 1981 elections, Socialist François Mitterrand was elected

president and the Socialist party gained a strong majority in the National Assembly. Mitterrand, who took a hard line toward the Soviet Union, nevertheless appointed four Communists to his cabinet. He explained that Communist votes had helped the Socialists attain power, that the four Communists were given technical posts—not militarily sensitive—and that the French Communist party had agreed to support the Socialists' anti-Soviet stands.

The United States voiced grave concern over this development in France as setting an undesirable precedent for other West European countries and threatening the security of NATO.

SOUTHEAST ASIA TREATY ORGANIZATION (SEATO)

1. Defensive Military Alliance (1954). Eight nations—the United States, Great Britain, France, Australia, New Zealand, Thailand, Pakistan, and the Philippines—established SEATO. Each member nation *(a)* agreed that armed aggression against any other member would "endanger its own peace and safety"; *(b)* recognized that civil wars might involve foreign aggression; and *(c)* offered to aid, upon request, the Southeast Asian states of Cambodia, Laos, and South Vietnam.

2. Weaknesses of SEATO. *(a)* SEATO lacked a unified armed force and military command. *(b)* Four important Southeast Asian nations—India, Burma, Ceylon (Sri Lanka), and Indonesia—refused to join SEATO. *(c)* France refrained from active participation in SEATO. *(d)* Displeased by lack of SEATO support in its quarrels with India, Pakistan in 1972 withdrew from SEATO.

3. End of SEATO (1976). Following the Communist triumphs in Indochina, the remaining SEATO members agreed that SEATO should be "phased out."

ADDITIONAL AMERICAN MILITARY ALLIANCES

Today, the United States has military alliances with over 40 nations of the free world. In addition to NATO, the United States has entered into the following military commitments:

1. The Rio Inter-American Defense Treaty (1947) between the United States and the Latin American nations of the Organization of American States (OAS) provides for the common defense of the Western Hemisphere. In 1982 Argentina appealed to the OAS for support in its dispute with Britain over the Falkland Islands. The OAS approved a resolution—with the United States and three Latin American nations abstaining—that affirmed Argentine sovereignty over the Falklands but also declared that Argentina must obey the UN Security Council resolution and withdraw its occupation forces from the Falkland Islands.

2. The Anzus Pact (1951) between Australia, New Zealand, and the United States provided that each nation *(a)* consider an attack upon one of the others as dangerous to its own safety, and *(b)* act to meet the common danger. In 1984 New Zealand banned from its waters nuclear-powered and nuclear-carrying American warships. United States leaders protested, saying that if such a policy spread to other nations, the ability of the United States to defend its allies would be crippled. In 1986 Secretary of State George Shultz announced that the United States no longer felt bound to defend New Zealand under the ANZUS Pact.

Also, the United States maintains military bases in Spain.

COMMUNIST MILITARY ALLIANCES

1. Chinese-Soviet Treaty (1950). The Soviet Union and Communist China signed a 30-year treaty of friendship and alliance, providing for *(a)* mutual military aid if attacked by Japan or an ally of Japan (meaning the United States) and *(b)* consultation on all international matters of mutual concern.

Because Soviet-Chinese relations have been openly strained since 1963 and the two nations have engaged in verbal polemics and border clashes, observers doubted that this alliance had meaning. In 1980 this treaty expired.

2. Warsaw Pact (1955). The Soviet Union and its European satellites formed an alliance providing for a unified Communist military command under a Soviet general. This was designed as a counterweight to NATO.

——————— MULTIPLE-CHOICE QUESTIONS ———————

1. President Franklin D. Roosevelt stated: "We have learned that we must live as men, and not as ostriches, nor as dogs in the manger. We have learned to be citizens of the world, members of the human community." Which attitude does this statement reflect? (a) acceptance of an active role in world affairs (b) acceptance of responsibility for the failure of the United Nations (c) approval of a policy of appeasement toward aggressors (d) approval of our traditional foreign policy in world affairs.

2. Which helps to explain why United States foreign policy today is very *different* from our foreign policy in the early 1800s? (a) Constitutional amendments have restricted the role of the President. (b) Presidents are reluctant to act without direction from the Senate. (c) The United States has evolved from a newly independent nation into a world power. (d) The role of public opinion in determining foreign policy has decreased.

3. In the period following World War II, an important factor influencing the change in United States foreign policy toward internationalism was the (a) emergence of a powerful Soviet Union (b) establishment of a unified Western Europe (c) increased self-sufficiency of the United States (d) heightened hostility of Japan.

4. Which is the *least* valid argument for isolation today? (a) the opportunity for investment at home (b) the protection afforded by the oceans (c) the domestic problems challenging the country (d) the danger of war in Europe.

5. A bipartisan foreign policy is one upon which there is agreement between the (a) House of Representatives and Senate (b) United States and Great Britain (c) President and Secretary of State (d) two major parties.

6. All of the following are characteristics of a democracy *except* (a) majority rule and respect for minority rights (b) existence of the people for the state (c) responsible citizenship (d) government of, by, and for the people.

7. The Soviet leaders claim that the government of the Soviet Union is democratic because (a) elections are held and citizens have the right to vote (b) party patronage is unknown (c) all workers are members of the Communist party (d) each citizen shares equally in goods produced.

8. Which of the following is true of the Soviet Union? (a) Workers have the right to strike. (b) Writers are free to criticize the government. (c) Agricultural shortages have been eliminated. (d) Schools are provided for all children.

9. Which is a characteristic of both capitalism and communism? (a) use of capital (b) a predominantly free-enterprise system (c) government ownership of the major industries (d) government planning of production.

10. Which is a characteristic of all totalitarian societies? (a) Religious worship is forbidden. (b) Voting is not allowed. (c) The government controls the mass media. (d) The government yields to the demands of the people.

11. Which aspect of the United States economic system would be found in any capitalist system? (a) antitrust laws (b) the profit motive (c) minimum-wage scales (d) tariffs on imported goods.

12. Government in the Soviet Union *differs* most from government in the United States with respect to the role the Soviet government plays in (a) maintaining an army (b) determining what goods and services shall be produced (c) allocating funds for advanced scientific research (d) establishing a monetary system.

13. The policy of the Soviet government toward ballet and other forms of the arts is to (a) take no official notice of them (b) denounce them as a waste of time (c) use them to promote the state ideology (d) require all citizens to participate in them.

14. Which was an aim of the United States policy of containment? (a) encouraging the Soviet people to revolt against communism (b) overthrowing the governments of the satellite nations in Eastern Europe (c) encircling the Soviet Union with a belt of neutral nations (d) preventing the further spread of communism.

15. Which of these was created to counteract Soviet propaganda? (a) Comintern (b) Voice of America (c) American Legion (d) Veterans of Foreign Wars.

16. From 1917 to 1941 relations between the United States and the Soviet Union were (a) generally friendly (b) friendly until 1933, then unfriendly (c) generally unfriendly (d) unfriendly until 1939, then friendly.

17. Which traditional foreign policy objective was achieved by the Soviet Union in World War II? (a) control of access routes from the Black Sea to the Mediterranean Sea (b) suppression of Mongol invaders through control of the borders with China (c) creation of a buffer zone in Eastern Europe (d) acquisition of a warm-water port on the Baltic Sea.

18. Which group consists entirely of Soviet satellites? (a) Denmark, Poland, Turkey (b) Czechoslovakia, Greece, Austria (c) Bulgaria, East Germany, Poland (d) Hungary, Israel, Rumania.

19. Estonia, Latvia, and Lithuania are (a) islands taken by the Soviet Union from Japan (b) Soviet satellite nations in the Balkans (c) neutralist nations (d) former independent nations now part of the Soviet Union.

20. From events since 1945, which conclusion about communism may *best* be drawn? (a) It has made no headway in Asia. (b) In different nations, communism is shaped by national needs and goals. (c) Communist nations have moved closer to the Soviet Union. (d) It has been weakened because of the Soviet Union's involvement in Vietnam.

21. Under both Czarist and Communist rule, the Soviet policy toward Turkey has been influenced by the desire to gain control of (a) the Red Sea (b) Gibraltar (c) the Suez Canal (d) the Dardanelles.

22. The Truman Doctrine was a (a) proposal for the peaceful use of atomic energy (b) program for general disarmament (c) policy of extending aid to nations threatened by communism (d) policy of giving technical aid to underdeveloped nations.

23. "A nation on the march can not afford internal unrest." A political leader following this philosophy would most likely favor (a) government ownership of all business (b) provisions for dictatorial powers (c) a policy encouraging political dissent (d) elections at all levels of government freely contested by many political parties.

24. One purpose of the Marshall Plan was to (a) promote political reforms in France (b) convert Germany into an agricultural nation (c) encourage the economic recovery of Western Europe (d) compel the Soviet Union to withdraw its troops from Eastern Europe.

25. Originally, the Marshall Plan was an offer made to (a) all European nations (b) all UN members (c) only English-speaking nations (d) only anti-Communist nations.

26. The most significant result of the Marshall Plan was that it (a) increased American control over the European economy (b) helped to restore the economy of Western Europe (c) aided refugees from the Soviet Union (d) discouraged Western European efforts toward economic integration.

27. Since the 1950s, the actions of most Western European nations toward the United States have (a) consistently supported our trade policy with Communist nations (b) shown increasing independence of our policies (c) required increasing amounts of United States economic aid (d) supported our participation in the conflicts of Asia.

28. The primary purpose of the Point Four Program was to help underdeveloped areas by (a) furnishing technical aid (b) providing food for starving people (c) spreading information concerning the American way of life (d) providing military aid to resist Communist aggression.

29. A basic purpose of the Peace Corps is to provide (a) jobs for unemployed American youths (b) scholarships for Americans to study in foreign countries (c) aid to people in underdeveloped areas (d) relief to Arab refugees in the Middle East.

30. The term "Inner Six" referred to (a) a trade and economic association in Western Europe (b) the Communist parties in Western Europe that have expressed independence of Moscow domination (c) a major power bloc in the United Nations (d) the original members of NATO.

31. Which has been a problem for the members of the European Common Market? (a) conflict between national sovereignty and united action (b) active opposition from the United States (c) decline in living standards of Western Europeans (d) failure to remove tariff barriers within the union.

32. In a sense, the United States has had a "common market" of its own because the original federal Constitution *prohibited* taxes on goods (a) exported from the United States (b) imported into the United States (c) manufactured in the United States (d) shipped from one state to another.

33. Nations have formed international organizations such as the Common Market to (a) provide for military defense (b) insure a sufficient supply of natural resources (c) further their national interests (d) carry out United Nations resolutions.

34. The Common Market has been most successful in (a) reducing tariff rates among member nations (b) encouraging democracy in Eastern Europe (c) bringing political stability to the member nations (d) speeding up the industrialization of Western Europe.

35. Which action was a marked departure from traditional United States foreign policy of the 19th and early 20th centuries? (a) intervening in the Dominican Republic in the 1960s (b) blockading Cuba during the missile crisis (c) refusing to recognize Communist China (d) joining the North Atlantic Treaty Organization.

36. "The parties agree that an armed attack against one or more of them in Europe or North America shall be considered an attack against them all. . . . " This quotation is most closely associated with which concept? (a) collective security (b) intervention (c) ultimatum (d) appeasement.

37. A major reason for creating the North Atlantic Treaty Organization (NATO) was to (a) supervise the West German government (b) protect member nations against Communist aggression (c) distribute Point Four funds (d) regulate world trade.

38. In which respect is our participation in NATO significant? (a) It is our first peacetime military alliance with any European nation. (b) It marks a return to the foreign policy of George Washington. (c) It nullifies the power of Congress to appropriate money for the armed forces. (d) It violates the UN Charter.

39. Which country was *not* a member of the Southeast Asia Treaty Organization? (a) Australia (b) Thailand (c) India (d) the Philippines.

——————————————— ESSAY QUESTIONS ———————————————

1. During the past 50 years, the United States has moved from a policy of isolation to a policy of active leadership in world affairs. Discuss *three* historical events or developments that have led to this change of policy.

2. It is customary for totalitarian countries to attempt to disguise themselves as democracies. *(a)* Describe *three* democratic features of life in the United States that do *not* exist in the Soviet Union. *(b)* Discuss *two* devices used by the Soviet Union to give the impression that it is democratic. *(c)* Discuss *two* differences in economic life between the United States and the Soviet Union.

3. *(a)* How would you characterize our relations with the Soviet Union (1) during World War II and (2) after World War II? Give *two* facts to support your characterization of *each* period. *(b)* Discuss *two* reasons to account for the drastic change in relations that took place following 1945.

4. To win the cold war, the Western democracies must estimate as correctly as possible their own strengths and weaknesses as well as those of the Soviet Union and its satellites. *(a)* Describe *one* strength *and one* weakness of the Western democracies. *(b)* Describe *one* strength *and one* weakness of the Soviet Union and its satellites. *(c)* Discuss *two* different ways by which the United States has attempted to win the cold war.

5. *(a)* Give *two* reasons why the United States has extended military and economic aid to foreign nations since the end of World War II. *(b)* Name *two* American foreign aid programs. *(c)* Explain *one* criticism of American foreign aid. *(d)* Discuss *one* reason why the Communist bloc has undertaken its own foreign aid program.

6. Since World War II, membership in NATO has been a cornerstone of American foreign policy. *(a)* Explain *one* reason why NATO was formed. *(b)* Discuss *two* disputes among NATO members, showing how *each* has weakened the organization. *(c)* In view of these disputes, does NATO retain any value as a military alliance today? Give *one* argument to support your opinion.

7. There are a number of methods that a nation can use to achieve the goals of its foreign policy. Select *two* of the following methods: *(a)* military alliances *(b)* foreign aid *(c)* economic sanctions. For *each* method chosen, explain how a nation used that method to achieve a specific goal of its foreign policy. Discuss the extent to which the method was effective. Use a different nation and a different situation for each method chosen.

——————— **MODIFIED TRUE-FALSE QUESTIONS** ———————

1. Soviet armed might in 1968 suppressed a Communist "liberalization" program in *Bulgaria.*
2. The Point Four Program of the United States closely parallels the United Nations program of *technical assistance.*
3. British membership in the Common Market was approved on a third application. Previously, British membership had twice been vetoed by *Belgium.*
4. The European Communist country that first successfully resisted Soviet domination was *Hungary.*
5. The Truman Doctrine was intended to keep Soviet influence out of Turkey and *Egypt.*
6. The Communists seek to keep democratic ideas from their people by means of a barrier known as the *Warsaw Pact.*
7. The nation that remained a member of the North Atlantic Pact but set the precedent of withdrawing its military forces from the NATO army was *West Germany.*
8. Two NATO members, traditional enemies, that have clashed over Cyprus, are *Britain and Italy.*
9. During the 1973 Arab-Israeli war, American efforts to resupply Israel with military equipment *were not supported* by the major NATO nations.
10. A NATO member having a common frontier with the Soviet Union is *Turkey.*
11. This nation, the homeland of Pope John Paul II and of the Solidarity trade union, is *East Germany.*

PART 4. The United States Deals With Problems Throughout the World

GERMANY

ALLIED DECISIONS REGARDING GERMANY (1945)

At the Yalta and Potsdam Conferences and in other agreements, the United States, Britain, and the Soviet Union made several decisions concerning Germany.

1. Territory. The eastern provinces were detached from Germany, with part occupied by the Soviet Union but most under Polish control. These territorial

Germany Following World War II

The map shows the railroad, highway, and air routes guaranteed to the Western Allies for access across the Soviet zone to Berlin.

changes were meant to be temporary, pending a German peace treaty. The Soviet Union and Poland, however, considered the changes as permanent. (In 1975 the Western powers assented to these boundaries by signing the Helsinki Pact. Check the Index.)

2. Occupation Zones. The rest of Germany was divided into four zones, with the Soviet Union, Britain, the United States, and France each governing one zone. Berlin, lying 110 miles inside the Soviet zone, was likewise divided into four sections, with each of the Allies controlling one section. The three Western Allies were guaranteed access to Berlin by surface and air routes across the Soviet zone. These divisions also were meant to be temporary.

3. Economy. The German economy was to be directed toward agriculture and peaceful industries. War industries were barred.

4. Disarmament. Germany was to be disarmed so as to render it unable to wage aggressive warfare again.

5. Education. German schools were to develop democratic ideas.

6. Denazification. Nazism was to be wiped out completely. All Nazi organizations, including the Nazi party, storm troopers, and the Gestapo (secret police), were dissolved. Active Nazis were not to be allowed to hold public office or other positions of influence. War criminals were to be brought to trial.

Will we learn
the lessons?

Partymiller, The Gazette and Daily, York, Pa.

NAZI WAR CRIMES TRIALS AT NUREMBERG (1945–1946)

An *International Military Tribunal* tried Air Force Minister Hermann Goering and other top Nazi leaders. They were charged with crimes against humanity, violations of international law, and waging aggressive warfare. These trials, it was hoped, would serve to democratize Germany by exposing the evils of Nazism. The tribunal found 19 of the 22 defendants guilty.

THE WEST AND THE SOVIET UNION DISAGREE ON GERMANY

After World War II, the West and the Soviet Union came into conflict over Germany. Each side sought German support for itself. Western plans for German reunification that would swing Germany toward the West were rejected by the Soviet Union. Soviet plans for reunification that would bring Germany into the Communist camp were rejected by the West.

BERLIN BLOCKADE (1948–1949)

Under Stalin, the Soviet Union tried to drive the Western Allies out of Berlin by blockading the surface routes—roads, rails, and canals—between Berlin and the three Western zones of Germany. To thwart this *Berlin Blockade,* the Allies resorted to an *airlift.* This airlift supplied over 2 million West Berliners with the necessities of life. Since the Soviets could not halt the airlift except by shooting down Allied planes, a course that might have started an all-out war, they lifted the blockade after a year.

DEVELOPMENTS IN WEST GERMANY

1. Establishment of the German Federal Republic. Unable to reach an agreement with the Soviet Union for German reunification, the three Western Allies in 1949 combined their zones to form the *Federal Republic of Germany* with its capital at *Bonn.* In 1955 West Germany was granted full sovereignty over domestic and foreign affairs (except for negotiations regarding German reunification and West Berlin) and was admitted to NATO.

2. Government of West Germany. The West German constitution provides for a democratic government with *(a)* a guarantee of civil liberties and free elections, *(b)* a two-house parliament, and *(c)* a chancellor responsible to the *Bundestag,* the popularly elected lower house of parliament.

Germany's two major parties are the *Christian Democrats* and the *Social Democrats.* Although they differ on details, both parties support welfare state measures, NATO membership, and a pro-Western foreign policy. The Christian Democrats for many years controlled the Bundestag.

From 1969 to 1982, the Social Democrats in coalition with the minor Free Democratic party controlled the government, first under Chancellor *Willy Brandt* and then under Chancellor *Helmut Schmidt.* In foreign policy, the Social Democrats favored West European unity in partnership with the United States.

In 1982 the Christian Democrats attracted enough Free Democratic support to gain control of the Bundestag. *Helmut Kohl* became chancellor. In the 1983 elections, the Kohl government won a comfortable Bundestag majority. Kohl pursues a policy of strong West German cooperation with the United States.

DEVELOPMENTS IN EAST GERMANY

1. Establishment of the German Democratic Republic. The Soviet Union in 1949 transformed its zone into the *German Democratic Republic* with its capital at *East Berlin.* This state is a Soviet satellite occupied by Soviet troops. In addition, East Germany maintains its own army of over 170,000 troops and is a member of the Warsaw Pact.

2. Government of East Germany. A self-proclaimed "democratic republic," East Germany is in fact a typical Communist dictatorship with restrictions on civil liberties, a secret police, and only one political party. In 1953 East German riots against the satellite government were repressed by Soviet tanks and troops. Until the 1970s, the Western powers refused to recognize the East German regime.

Since 1971, the head of the East German Communist party has been *Erich Honecker.*

COMPARISON OF THE TWO GERMANYS

1. Area. West Germany comprises 70 percent of the total area of postwar Germany as compared to 30 percent for East Germany.

2. Population. West Germany contains over 75 percent of the German people as compared to less than 25 percent for East Germany.

3. Industrialization. West Germany, the more industrial of the two Germanys, contains the industrial heart of Europe, the Ruhr Valley. East Germany also has industry but is more agricultural than West Germany.

4. Economic System. West Germany has a capitalist economy, typified by private enterprise, free labor unions, and limited government regulation of the economy. East Germany has a Communist economy, typified by government ownership of industry and collectivization of agriculture.

5. Economic Developments Since World War II. Aided by Marshall Plan funds, West Germany made a remarkable recovery from the devastation of World War II. Its cities, transportation systems, and industries were all rebuilt. West Germany became the leading industrial nation of Western Europe with a high standard of living.

In contrast, East Germany made a far slower recovery. For years its cities were not rebuilt, and its people suffered shortages of food and consumer goods. Seeking a better life, many East Germans fled to West Germany, chiefly through Berlin. To stop this flow, the Communists in 1961 built a barbed-wire and concrete barrier, the *Berlin Wall*. In the 1960s East Germany experienced considerable economic growth, but its living standard still remains below that of West Germany.

THE SOVIET UNION PROVOKES ANOTHER CRISIS OVER BERLIN (1958–1961)

In 1958 Soviet Premier Khrushchev announced his determination to drive the Western powers out of West Berlin. If successful, Khrushchev probably expected that West Berlin would be absorbed by East Germany, thereby closing down a "showcase" of democracy and capitalism behind the Iron Curtain.

The Western nations stated their determination to remain in Berlin but indicated willingness to negotiate. Although negotiations failed, the Soviets did not act to drive out the Western powers.

STEPS TO REDUCE TENSIONS OVER BERLIN AND GERMANY (SINCE 1970)

1. West Germany Improves Relations With Communist East Europe (1970–1972). While affirming West Germany's strong adherence to the Western world, Chancellor Willy Brandt moved to "normalize" his country's relations with the Communist nations of Eastern Europe. Brandt signed two treaties—with the Soviet Union and with Poland—by which (1) West Germany accepted the existing Soviet and Polish borders, thereby conceding sizable areas taken from prewar Germany (see map, page 626), and (2) the signatories renounced the use of force and agreed to strive for economic, scientific, and cultural cooperation. These treaties were opposed by many Germans for accepting the territorial losses to Poland and the Soviet Union. In 1972 the treaties secured a minimal approval in the Bundestag.

2. The Four Allied Powers Reach Another Berlin Agreement (1971). The Allied powers reached a new Berlin agreement *(a)* providing for unimpeded road and rail traffic between West Berlin and West Germany, *(b)* permitting personal and business visits by West Berliners to East Germany, *(c)* accepting West German responsibility for West Berlin, and *(d)* allowing the Soviet Union to open a consular office in West Berlin.

3. West Germany and East Germany "Normalize" Their Relations (1972). West Germany and East Germany signed a treaty that *(a)* established formal relations between them, *(b)* called for the two Germanys to cooperate in such areas as sports, environmental control, airlines, and technical knowledge, *(c)* proposed that both Germanys be admitted to the UN (which was done in 1973), and *(d)* left unanswered the question of German reunification.

4. Germany Remains Divided. After East Germany acceded to the 1971 agreement on Berlin, Britain and France opened diplomatic relations with the Communist regime. In 1974 the United States became the last major Western power to establish formal diplomatic relations with East Germany.

MIDDLE EAST

LOCATION AND IMPORTANCE

The Middle East consists of northeastern Africa and southwestern Asia. The region's importance lies in its (1) *vital waterways*—the Suez Canal and the Dardanelles, (2) *valuable oil resources*—in Saudi Arabia, Kuwait, the United Arab Emirates, Libya, Iraq, and Iran, and (3) *strategic location*—at the crossroads of Europe, Asia, and Africa, and on the southern flank of the Soviet Union.

ISRAEL AND THE ARAB STATES

EMERGENCE OF ISRAEL

1. Jewish Claims to Palestine. *Theodor Herzl*, a journalist and Jewish intellectual, founded modern *Zionism*, the movement for a Jewish homeland in Palestine. Zionists pointed out that the Jewish people *(a)* had lived in Palestine during ancient times, and *(b)* needed a refuge from anti-Semitic persecution. In 1917 Britain gave support to the Zionist movement by the *Balfour Declaration*, which viewed "with favor the establishment in Palestine of a national home for the Jewish people." To fulfill the Balfour Declaration, Britain in 1923 received the League of Nations mandate over Palestine.

East Africa and the Middle East

By 1938 over 500,000 Jews had migrated to Palestine. They built modern cities, founded agricultural settlements, started industries, restored desert lands to fertility, improved health standards, and established schools.

2. Arab Opposition and a New British Policy. Opposition to Jewish immigration came from *(a)* Arab nationalists, who desired an Arab Palestine, *(b)* Arab ruling classes, who feared Western ideas of democracy, and *(c)* Arab peasants and nomads, who feared the loss of their traditional ways.

In 1939, just before the outbreak of World War II, Britain severely limited Jewish immigration to Palestine. By so appeasing the Arabs, the Zionists claimed, Britain was violating the Balfour Declaration.

During World War II, 6 million European Jews—men, women, and children—were savagely murdered by the Nazis. Of those who survived, many sought admission to Palestine. Britain, however, still kept the gates closed. Britain's policy was *(a)* defied by Palestinian Jews, who smuggled immigrants into the Holy Land, and *(b)* condemned by the United States.

3. Palestine and the UN. In 1947 Britain turned the Palestine problem over to the UN General Assembly. It voted to *(a)* end the British mandate, *(b)* place Jerusalem under international control, and *(c)* partition Palestine into separate Arab and Jewish states.

Thereupon, in 1948, Israel proclaimed its independence. The Israeli republic is the Middle East's only modern democratic state.

4. Israel Maintains Its Existence

a. Israeli War for Independence (1948–1949). The Arab nations defied the UN decision for a Jewish state and attacked Israel. Despite their numerical superiority, the Arabs were driven back and lost some territory to the Israelis. In 1949 the Arab states accepted, as temporary, the armistice agreements arranged by UN mediator Ralph Bunche.

(The Arab nations also defied the UN decision for a Palestinian Arab state. The areas proposed for such a state were seized—the Gaza Strip by Egypt and the land on the West Bank of the Jordan River by Jordan.)

b. Continued Arab Hostility (1949–1956). (1) The Arab League enforced an economic boycott against Israel and against Western companies doing business with Israel. (2) Under President Nasser, an Arab nationalist, Egypt barred Israeli ships from the Suez Canal. Egyptian artillery on the Sinai Peninsula blockaded ships bound for Israel's southern port of Elath on the Gulf of Aqaba. Egypt allowed guerrilla raids against Israeli border communities.

c. Sinai Campaign (1956). Israel invaded Egypt to wipe out guerrilla bases and end the Aqaba blockade. Israeli forces quickly scattered Nasser's armies and overran the Sinai Peninsula. (Britain and France also invaded Egypt to regain control of the Suez Canal.) The UN secured withdrawal of the invading forces and stationed a *United Nations Emergency Force* (UNEF) in Egypt on the border with Israel and at the tip of the Sinai Peninsula. For ten years Israel was free from Egyptian guerrilla raids and free to use the Gulf of Aqaba.

SURVEY OF ARAB NATIONALISM (SINCE 1945)

1. Roots. Arab peoples became aware of their common cultural background: Arabic language, Islamic religion, and the great Arab civilization of the Middle Ages.

2. Evidences of Arab Unity

a. Arab League. Founded in 1945, the Arab League seeks to unify Arab policy on world issues, especially Arab efforts against Israel.

b. Organization of Petroleum Exporting Countries (OPEC). Founded in 1960, OPEC consists of six non-Arab and seven Arab states—the major oil producer being Saudi Arabia. Dominated by its Arab members, OPEC's economic purpose is to increase its members' oil revenues. (For OPEC and the 1973 Arab-Israeli war, check the Index.)

c. Military Cooperation. In the 1973 Arab-Israeli war, the Arab states rushed troops and planes to the aid of Syria and Egypt.

d. Palestine Liberation Organization (PLO). Because the PLO has been both a unifying and divisive force, it is discussed at greater length below.

PALESTINE LIBERATION ORGANIZATION (PLO)

1. Background. The Palestine Arab refugee problem arose out of the 1948–1949 war, when the Arab nations tried to destroy Israel. Mainly fearing for their safety, some 540,000 Arabs, out of 700,000 in Israeli territory, fled to neighboring Arab nations. After the war, Israel proposed that the refugee problem be part of an overall settlement involving boundaries and diplomatic recognition, but the Arab nations rejected the Israeli proposal.

The Arab nations generally refused to assimilate the refugees into their societies. Many refugees were compelled to live in squalid camps dependent upon international charity for the necessities of life. This environment gave rise to various guerrilla groups committed to destroying Israel. In the mid-1960s, these groups formed an umbrella organization, the *Palestine Liberation Organization* (PLO). Eventually, *Yasir Arafat*—leader of the largest guerrilla group, *Al Fatah*—became head of the PLO.

2. Arab Support for the PLO. In 1974 the Arab nations, meeting in Morocco, declared the PLO the "sole legitimate representative of the Palestinian people" and called for the creation of a Palestinian state. Also in 1974, the Arab nations secured a UN General Assembly invitation for the PLO to take part in its debate on the "Palestine question."

3. PLO as a Divisive Force in the Arab World. In 1970–1971 Palestinian guerrillas threatened the rule of King Hussein of Jordan, but his army drove them from Jordan. In the Lebanese civil war in 1975–1976, leftist Palestinian guerrillas joined with leftist Lebanese Muslims to battle against rightist Lebanese Christian Arabs. Fearful of a hostile leftist regime in Lebanon, Syria sent its army into Lebanon, suppressed the Palestinians and Lebanese Muslims, and enforced a cease-fire. (Check the Index for Lebanon.)

SURVEY OF ARAB DISUNITY

1. Differences Among the Arab Nations. *(a)* Libya, Syria, and Iraq are leftist, radical, and generally pro-Soviet, whereas Saudi Arabia, Jordan, and Tunisia are rightist, conservative, and generally pro-Western. *(b)* Saudi Arabia, Jordan, Morocco, and Kuwait are monarchies headed by hereditary rulers; most others are nominally republics—in reality, military dictatorships and one-party states.

2. Disputes in the Arab World. *(a) Jordan vs. Palestinian Guerrillas (1970–1971).* King Hussein of Jordan thwarted the efforts of the Palestinian guerrillas to overthrow his regime and drove them out of Jordan. They fled northward into Syria and Lebanon. *(b) Algeria vs. Morocco (Since 1975).* These two nations both claim control of phosphate-rich Western (Spanish) Sahara. *(c) Leb-*

anon Civil War (Since 1975). (Check the Index.) (d) Iran-Iraq War (Beginning in 1980). (Check the Index.) Libya and Syria expressed support for Iran, which is not an Arab nation, as a revolutionary Islamic state, while Jordan backed Iraq as defending Arab interests. (e) Syria vs. Jordan (1980). Supporting opposing sides in the Iran-Iraq war, Syria and Jordan became bitter enemies. As Syria and Jordan massed troops, a Saudi Arabian envoy helped defuse the situation, but tension remained. (f) Egypt vs. Libya (Since 1977). These countries became bitter enemies as Egypt, under President Sadat, adopted a pro-American stance, while Libya, under Colonel Muammar al-Qaddafi, moved into the Soviet orbit. In 1977 the two nations clashed in air and land border battles. In 1980, Libya sent troops across its border into Chad. This Libyan invasion, Egypt feared, endangered its security and the security of Egypt's ally, the Sudan. Sadat and Qaddafi called for the overthrow of each other's governments, and Sadat considered Qaddafi a fanatic and terrorist supporter. In 1981, when Sadat's assassination became known, Libya was officially jubilant.

ARAB-ISRAELI WAR (1967)

1. Background. Egypt, Syria, and Jordan, in military alliance, moved their armies toward their borders with Israel. Nasser secured removal of the UNEF and closed the Gulf of Aqaba to Israeli shipping. Meanwhile, Israel called up its military reserves. Eventually war started.

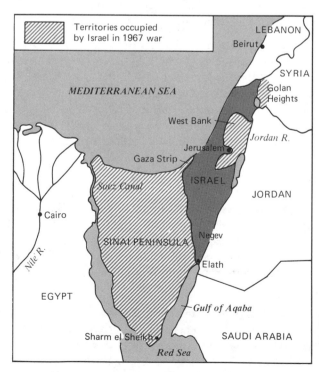

Israel and the
Bordering Arab
States

2. The War. In a six-day war, the Israelis routed the Arab forces and seized (1) from Egypt—the Gaza Strip and the entire Sinai Peninsula westward to the Suez Canal and southward to Sharm el Sheikh, thus opening the Gulf of Aqaba to Israeli shipping, (2) from Jordan—all territory on the West Bank of the Jordan River, including the Old City of Jerusalem; and (3) from Syria—the Golan Heights.

UN Security Council resolutions helped end the fighting.

ARAB HOSTILITY AND DIPLOMACY (1967–1973)

1. No War but No Peace. Arab guerrilla groups raided Israeli settlements and gunned Israeli commercial airplanes at airports in Europe. In 1972 Arab extremists employed Japanese terrorists to massacre innocent civilians at the Tel Aviv airport; Arab terrorists murdered 11 Israeli Olympic athletes and coaches at Munich. In response, Israel raided guerrilla bases in Syria and Lebanon. The main threat to Israel in the late 1960s and early 1970s, however, was Egypt. As Israel bested Egypt in artillery and airplane duels along the Suez Canal, Egypt became dependent upon the Soviet Union for military equipment and 20,000 military personnel.

2. Egypt Under Sadat. In 1970 Nasser died and his position was assumed by *Anwar al-Sadat*. This Egyptian president directed his nation's foreign policy away from dependence on the Soviet Union. In 1972 Sadat ordered the 20,000 Soviet military personnel to leave Egypt. Although they left, the Soviet military equipment remained, and the Soviets continued to supply Egypt with military spare parts.

Sadat was determined to regain Egyptian territory lost to Israel in the 1967 war—if necessary by a new war.

ARAB-ISRAELI WAR (1973)

1. Military Front. By attacking on Yom Kippur, the most holy day of the Jewish religion and one devoted to prayer, the Syrians and Egyptians gained the initial advantage of surprise. Hastily mobilized, Israeli forces slowly reversed the tide of battle. The Israelis advanced against the Syrians on the Golan Heights and crossed the Suez Canal westward into Egypt proper, trapping a large Egyptian force in the Sinai desert. Against this military background, the three warring nations accepted the UN call for a cease-fire.

2. Arab Oil Embargo. The Arab states—especially Saudi Arabia, Kuwait, the United Arab Emirates, Iraq, Libya, and Algeria—possess the world's major known oilfields and have supplied significant amounts of the oil needs of industrialized nations: the United States, West European countries, and Japan. Since 1960, Arab and other oil-producing countries have been joined in the *Organization of Petroleum Exporting Countries* (OPEC), coordinating efforts to increase their oil revenues. With the 1973 Arab-Israeli war, the Arab states acted to further their economic goal and to use oil as a political weapon. They raised oil prices fourfold, reduced shipments to most West European nations and Japan, and totally embargoed oil shipments to the United States. As the diplomatic price for easing their cutoffs, the Arab states demanded that the industrialized nations voice support for the Arab position in the Mideast. Japan and most West European nations did so.

After the UN achieved a cease-fire, American Secretary of State Henry Kissinger negotiated an Israeli-Egyptian troop-separation agreement that restored Egyptian control of both sides of the Suez Canal. Thereafter, most oil-producing Arab states lifted the embargo against the United States.

3. Superpower Involvement. After the outbreak of the 1973 war, the United States acted unsuccessfully to halt the hostilities. The Soviet Union, in contrast, acted to spur hostilities, urging the other Arab states to join in the struggle. As the war took a heavy toll of military equipment, the Soviets airlifted additional supplies to Egypt and Syria. The United States thereupon acted to resupply Israel.

After the Israelis gained the military advantage, the Soviet Union and the United States jointly sponsored a UN resolution that achieved a Mideast cease-fire.

4. Observations: *(a)* Israel "won" the war militarily but "lost" in other ways. With its small population, Israel suffered heavy casualties, although they were only one-tenth those inflicted on the Arabs. With its limited resources, Israel incurred heavy war costs. Finally, Israel was more isolated diplomatically than before. *(b)* Egypt experienced an upsurge of confidence as its armies demonstrated ability to master modern military equipment. *(c)* The United States increased its *leverage*—that is, its ability to influence Mideast affairs. While reaffirming its support for Israel's right to exist, the United States avoided an extreme partisan stand and gained increased respect among moderate Arab nations, especially Egypt. *(d)* The Soviet Union demonstrated its ability to influence Mideast affairs.

RECENT MIDDLE EAST DEVELOPMENTS

1. Rift in Egyptian-Soviet Relations (1976). Sadat, bitter that the Soviet Union had refused to replenish Egypt's weapons and to ease Egypt's debt repayment, ended the Soviet-Egyptian friendship treaty.

2. The Sadat Visit to Israel (1977). President Sadat stated that, to further Mideast peace, he was ready to journey to Israel. Sadat thereupon received an official invitation from Israeli Prime Minister *Menachem Begin*. Sadat became the first Arab leader ever to visit Israel. He received a warm welcome from the Israeli people and addressed the *Knesset*, the Israeli parliament.

Sadat acknowledged that Israel's existence is a fact and stated that "we Arabs welcome you to live among us in peace and security." However, he reiterated

Arab demands for the return of all lands occupied by Israel in the 1967 war and for the recognition of Palestinian rights to a homeland, but he did *not* mention the PLO. In response, Begin praised Sadat for his courage but reiterated Israeli demands for secure borders. In final statements the two leaders pledged "no more war."

The Sadat visit to Israel sharply divided the Arab world. Sadat's initiative was hailed overwhelmingly by the Egyptian people and was approved by the governments of Sudan, Tunisia, and Morocco. Sadat was denounced as a traitor to the Arab cause by the PLO and by the radical Arab states of Libya, Algeria, and Iraq. These states were known as "rejectionists" because they rejected any compromise that provided for the existence of Israel.

For the United States, the Sadat initiative was hailed as a major step toward Mideast peace.

3. The Camp David (Maryland) Conference (1978). Following the Sadat visit to Israel, President Carter invited President Sadat and Prime Minister Begin to meet with him at Camp David. For 13 days, the leaders conferred and reached agreement upon two documents.

a. Framework for Peace in the Middle East. This document dealt with the West Bank of the Jordan River and the Gaza Strip. It provided the following: (1) Palestinians living in these areas will receive self-rule through an elected council. Thereafter, the Israeli military government will end and Israeli troops will be partially withdrawn. (2) Israel, Egypt, Jordan, and the elected Palestinian representatives will begin discussions on the "final status" of the areas. The negotiators will consider the "legitimate rights" of the Palestinians and also the security of Israel.

b. Framework for a Peace Treaty Between Egypt and Israel. This document dealt with the Sinai Peninsula. It provided the following: (1) Israel agreed to return the Sinai Peninsula to Egypt and, within three years, to withdraw all of its troops from the area. (2) Egypt agreed to demilitarize much of Sinai and to permit the stationing of peacekeeping forces in the Sinai along the Israeli border, along the Gulf of Aqaba, and in the Sharm el Sheikh area. (3) Israeli ships were guaranteed free passage through the Suez Canal and the Gulf of Aqaba. (4) Egypt and Israel agreed to negotiate a peace treaty.

The agreements evoked widely different responses. President Carter hailed the agreements, as did the Egyptian and Israeli peoples. The PLO was bitter that its existence had been completely ignored. Syria, the "rejectionist" Arab states, and the Soviet Union denounced the agreements.

4. The Israeli-Egyptian Peace Treaty (1979). This treaty *(a)* reaffirmed the Camp David provisions regarding Israeli withdrawal from the Sinai, the stationing of a peacekeeping force, free passage through the Suez Canal and the Gulf of Aqaba for Israeli ships, and the establishment of normal relations between Israel and Egypt, and *(b)* contained provisions for Israel and Egypt to hold negotiations regarding Palestinian self-rule in the West Bank and the Gaza Strip.

Also, the United States agreed to *(a)* extend economic and military aid to both Israel and Egypt, *(b)* assist Israel in case of Egyptian violations of the peace treaty, and *(c)* take part in negotiations on Palestinian self-rule.

Although the peace treaty was welcomed by the Egyptian people, it received a hostile reception elsewhere in the Arab world. Most Arab nations broke diplomatic relations with Egypt. Saudi Arabia ended economic aid to Egypt, and the Arab League moved its headquarters out of Cairo.

5. Negotiations on Palestinian Autonomy (Beginning in 1979).

These negotiations were attended by Egypt, Israel, and the United States but were boycotted by Palestinians of the West Bank and Gaza and by Jordan. The negotiations soon revealed sharp disagreement. Egypt insisted that the Palestinians be granted full autonomy with the right to establish an independent Palestinian state. Israel asserted its right to establish additional settlements in "Judea and Samaria"—the Biblical names for the West Bank region. Israel rejected any Palestinian state as a threat to its security and as a potential Soviet satellite nation. Israel offered the Palestinians local autonomy with the right to choose between Israeli and Jordanian citizenship. The United States urged compromise and asked the Palestinians to join the talks but condemned new Jewish settlements in the West Bank as "harmful to the peace process."

6. The Syrian-Soviet Treaty (1980).

Increasingly isolated in the Arab world and concerned over the loss of Egyptian support in a future war against Israel, Syria signed a 20-year treaty of friendship with the Soviet Union. The treaty called for the two nations to consult in case of a security threat and to cooperate in military, economic, scientific, and cultural areas. The treaty was viewed as enhancing Soviet influence in the Middle East.

7. Israeli Raid on the Iraqi Nuclear Facility (1981).

Israeli warplanes bombed and destroyed the Iraqi nuclear facility—named *Osirak*—that had been purchased from and was being built by France. Although France intended the Iraqi facility to be used for peaceful purposes, expert opinion was divided as to whether it could have been used to produce nuclear bombs.

Israel justified the raid as an "act of national self-defense," claiming that the Iraqi facility was meant to produce nuclear weapons. The Israelis further pointed out that Iraq considered itself in a "state of war" with Israel; that Iraq had often stated its goal of destroying the "Zionist entity"; and that Iraqi President *Saddam Hussein* was an "evil" and "crazy" person who would not hesitate to use nuclear bombs against Israeli cities.

Iraq insisted that its nuclear facility was designed for peaceful purposes. Iraq further claimed that Israel was seeking to deter Arab technological progress and that Iraq would rebuild the nuclear facility. France warned that before it would help rebuild the destroyed reactor, Iraq had to accept strict safeguards against possible military use.

The UN Security Council voted unanimously to "strongly condemn" Israel for the raid.

8. Assassination of Egypt's President Sadat (1981). While observing a military parade, Anwar al-Sadat was assassinated by four men who were later identified as Egyptian Islamic fundamentalists holding similar beliefs to the religious party in control of Iran. Sadat's death was mourned in Egypt, the Sudan, Israel, the United States, and most pro-Western nations, where he was viewed as a man of courage and peace. His death was greeted with joy by the PLO, Libya, and other "rejectionist" Arab states, where he was viewed as a "traitor" to the Arab cause.

Hosni Mubarak, a former air force commander, had been handpicked by Sadat as his vice president and successor. Mubarak now became Egypt's president. He pledged to continue the peace process.

9. United States Sale of AWACS to Saudi Arabia (1981). The Reagan administration proposed to sell to Saudi Arabia $8.5 billion of military equipment including five Airborne Warning And Control Systems (AWACS) planes. These are complex high-technology radar planes capable of detecting approaching aircraft at a distance of several hundred miles. The administration defended the proposed sale as *(a)* enhancing the military security of the Persian Gulf area against any Soviet threat and *(b)* encouraging the Saudis to be more supportive of American Middle East peace efforts.

Opponents argued that the sale did not serve the "best interest of the United States" because Saudi Arabia *(a)* is an unstable country, creating the danger that the AWACS might fall into unfriendly hands, and *(b)* had been a "negative" influence on the Middle East peace process by financing the PLO, opposing the

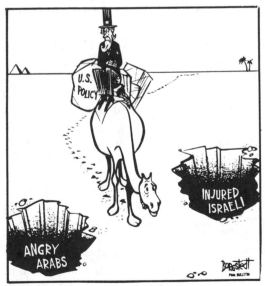

Pitfalls in the Middle East.

Reprinted by special permission of Doug Borgstedt and of The Evening and Sunday Bulletin, Philadelphia, Pa.

Camp David accords, and condemning Egypt. In denouncing the sale, Israeli leaders expressed the fear that Saudi Arabia could use the AWACS to undermine Israeli military security.

The Senate narrowly upheld the AWACS sale. The first of the five planes reached Saudi Arabia in 1986. Meanwhile, Congress had approved further arms sales to the Saudis, although in lesser quantities than President Reagan requested.

10. Israeli Annexation of the Golan Heights (1981).

In the 1967 Arab-Israeli war, Israeli troops captured the Golan Heights from Syria. Previously, Israeli communities lying below the Golan Heights had been subjected, even in peacetime, to sporadic Syrian artillery attacks, compelling the Israeli civilians to seek shelter in underground facilities. For almost 15 years, the Israelis kept the Golan Heights under military rule while Syria pursued a hardline policy against Israel—opposing the Camp David accords and vowing not to recognize Israel. In 1981 Israel formally annexed the Golan heights.

Syria labeled the Israeli annexation a "declaration of war" and secured UN condemnation of Israel. The United States criticized the Israeli action as detrimental to the Middle East peace process.

11. Developments in Lebanon (Since 1975)

a. Civil War. Lebanon's deeply fragmented society has been in turmoil since civil war broke out in 1975. Unlike the usual civil war, in which a single rebel movement fights an existing government, Lebanon's war has been a free-for-all, pitting several rival militias against one another. The weak Lebanese army has been only one faction among many.

Lebanese society is divided mainly along religious lines, with one or more militias representing each religious group—Maronite Christians, Sunni Muslims, Shiite Muslims, and Druses. Further complicating the picture have been armed groups such as the PLO that were formed by Palestinian refugees who fled to Lebanon during the Arab-Israeli wars. In addition, outside powers such as Syria and Israel have intervened.

Syria sent 15,000 troops into Lebanon in 1976 under an Arab League mandate to enforce a cease-fire. For a few years, the fighting died down. But the Lebanese failed to resolve their differences, in particular a dispute about how political power should be shared between Christians and Muslims. Syria's troops remained and took sides, first with right-wing Christian forces, then with left-wing Muslims. Lebanon's civil war rekindled in 1981 and caused massive destruction in the years that followed.

b. PLO Attacks and Israel's 1978 Invasion of Southern Lebanon. PLO commandos used southern Lebanon as a base for attacks inside Israel. In 1978 a PLO squad landed on the Israeli coast and killed 30 civilians. In retaliation, Israeli troops drove into southern Lebanon and occupied it for three months. They withdrew after the UN Security Council had created a 6000-strong peacekeeping force called *Unifil* (United Nations International Force in Lebanon). The Israelis left behind a Lebanese Christian militia that they had organized to prevent the Palestinians from reoccupying southern Lebanon.

 c. Israel's 1982 Invasion. After the Lebanese civil war resumed in 1981, Lebanon's neighbors quickly became involved. Syrian troops battled on the side of Lebanese Muslims and Palestinians. Israeli armed forces bombed the Lebanese capital, Beirut, in 1981 and launched a full-scale invasion of Lebanon in 1982. The Israelis trapped several thousand PLO troops in Beirut and forced their evacuation to Tunisia and other Arab countries far from Israel's borders.

 d. Assassination and Massacres. Lebanon's President-elect *Bashir Gemayel* was assassinated in a bomb explosion in 1982, during the Israeli invasion. Gemayel, the head of the Christian Phalange, was regarded favorably by the Israelis. In retaliation for the assassination, Lebanese Christian militia massacred some 600 Palestinians at two camps in Beirut. Israeli leaders were widely criticized for allowing the Christian troops into the camps.

 e. Suicide Bombings. The United States joined France, Italy, and Britain in creating a multinational force to support the weak Lebanese government and serve as a buffer between rivals in Lebanon. Regarded by leftists and Muslims as serving the interests of rightist Lebanese Christians, the multinational force came under attack. Suicide bombers drove trucks into United States and French military compounds in October 1983, and the ensuing explosions killed 241 Marines and 58 French soldiers. President Reagan withdrew the Marines the following year.

 f. Israeli Withdrawal: 1985. Israel completed the withdrawal of most of its forces from Lebanon in 1985, keeping control of a small "security zone" in southern Lebanon. In addition, the Israelis continued to arm a southern Lebanese Christian militia that served as a buffer against Israel's enemies.

 g. Israeli-Syrian Confrontations. The fighting inside Lebanon has at times pitted Israelis against Syrians on a limited scale. Syria has installed surface-to-air missiles (SAMs) on Lebanese as well as Syrian territory. Syrian missiles have shot at Israeli planes, and Israeli planes have bombed Syrian missile sites.

 12. The Middle East Peace Process. Efforts to put an end to the years of Arab-Israeli hostility have stumbled over two key problems: (1) the refusal of Palestinian leaders to recognize publicly Israel's right to exist as an independent nation, and (2) the refusal of Israeli leaders to recognize publicly the Palestinians' right to self-determination within a homeland of their own. The United States and Israel insist that the Palestinians must formally accept *UN Security Council Resolution 242,* adopted in 1967, which calls for Arab recognition of Israel's existence and borders in exchange for Israeli withdrawal from land occupied in the 1967 war. Palestinians have agreed to accept Resolution 242 only in return for United States and Israeli recognition of a Palestinian right of self-determination.

 a. Israeli-Egyptian Relations. Israel completed the turnover of occupied territory to Egypt in 1982, under the two nations' 1979 peace treaty. Israeli-

There are several
alternatives.

Reprinted with permission from The Minneapolis Tribune

In dealing with the bordering Arab states and with the Palestinians, what alternatives (different policies) are available to Israel?

Egyptian relations, which cooled after the 1982 Israeli invasion of Lebanon, began to warm up again in 1985.

b. President Reagan's Middle East Peace Proposals (1982). President Reagan moved to expand beyond the Camp David framework by calling for direct negotiations between Israel and a joint Palestinian-Jordanian delegation. Reagan proposed: (1) autonomy for the Palestinian inhabitants of the West Bank and Gaza in association with Jordan, (2) no independent Palestinian state, (3) a freeze on Israeli settlements in the West Bank and no Israeli annexation of the region, and (4) negotiations to reach agreement for an undivided Jerusalem. The President reiterated America's commitment to Israel's security and urged the Arab states to "accept the reality of Israel."

President Reagan's proposals met with negative responses. The Israeli government rejected the proposals, claiming that Palestinian self-rule would lead to a Palestinian state endangering Israel's security. The PLO rejected the proposals because they did not provide for an independent Palestinian state. For Jordan, King Hussein claimed that he could not speak for the Palestinians since the Arab League in 1974 had assigned that responsibility solely to the PLO.

c. The Arab Nations' Fez Plan (1982). In a meeting at Fez, Morocco, in 1982, Arab leaders called for (1) total Israeli withdrawal from all lands occupied in the 1967 war, (2) the withdrawal of all Jewish settlements on the West Bank and Gaza Strip, (3) the creation of a Palestinian state with Jerusalem as its capital, and (4) a Security Council guarantee for Middle East peace. Israel rejected the plan.

d. Hussein-Arafat Peace Proposals (1985). After years of estrangement, Jordan's King Hussein and PLO leader Yasir Arafat renewed relations. In 1985 Arafat accepted a peace plan put forth by King Hussein. Under its terms: (1) Israel would withdraw from the Gaza Strip, the West Bank, and East Jerusalem, (2) Jordan and the PLO would agree to peace with Israel, (3) Israel would recognize the Palestinians' right of self-determination, and (4) Palestinians and Jordanians would join in a new confederation. Hussein and Arafat proposed an international peace conference that would include the United States, the Soviet Union, and other permanent members of the UN Security Council. Israel and the United States spurned the Hussein-Arafat plan. In 1986 new tensions arose between the Palestinian and Jordanian leaders.

e. The Superpowers and the Middle East Peace Process. The United States has continued its support for Israel and its friendly relations with Jordan and Egypt. United States leaders seek a Middle East peace conference limited to Israeli, Arab, and United States representatives. The Soviet Union has continued to supply arms to Syria and to maintain friendly relations with Israel's most bitter enemies. However, unlike Syria, which supports anti-PLO factions of Palestinians, the Soviet Union has worked to bridge differences among rival Palestinian factions. Soviet leaders seek a wider Middle East peace conference that would include a Soviet delegation.

IRAN: ANOTHER MIDDLE EAST TROUBLE SPOT

1. Background. Iran is an Islamic state whose people are not Arabs but are mainly Persians. Iran is a major oil producer and a member of OPEC.

Iran was a monarchy ruled by a shah. The last Shah, who ruled from 1941 to 1979, was *Mohammad Reza Pahlavi.* He ruled autocratically, employed secret police, and did not permit political opposition. The Shah did, however, spur economic and social modernization, including land reform, literacy, and women's rights. He followed a pro-Western foreign policy and maintained a "special relationship" with the United States.

2. Upheaval and Unrest

a. Khomeini Seizes Control. By 1979 the Shah faced uncontrollable opposition by workers protesting low wages and inflation, by democratic and radical groups protesting autocratic rule, and by conservative religious groups protesting efforts to modernize the country. As the Shah fled Iran, the country came under the control of *Ayatollah Ruhollah Khomeini.* This Islamic religious leader exercised dictatorial rule. He converted Iran into an Islamic republic based on the principles stated in the Koran, the holy book of Islam.

b. Problems Facing Iran. Iran faced many problems: resentment of Marxist groups at being excluded from the government; resentment of moderate democratic groups at strict observance of the Koran and against Khomeini's dictatorial rule, which included a ban on broadcasts of music, a call for women to cover their heads and dress conservatively in accordance with Islamic tradition, and a shutdown of opposition newspapers; revolts by ethnic minorities—Arabs in the south and Kurds and Turks in the north; assassinations; unemployment; inflation; and a cut in oil production. Nevertheless, Iranian voters approved an Islamic constitution that granted Ayatollah Khomeini dictatorial powers for life.

As the Iranian government increasingly came under the control of the clergy-dominated *Islamic Republican party,* Iran experienced still more violence. The government mounted a crackdown against "counterrevolutionaries," and some 2000 persons were executed. Guerrilla groups opposed to the regime fought street battles against revolutionary guards and planted bombs that took the lives of major figures in the Islamic Republican party and government. The authorities blamed especially a leftist Islamic organization, the *People's Mujahedeen.* The Mujahedeen, who had fought against the Shah, wanted not a clergy-dominated Iran but a modern nation.

3. Problems for the United States

a. Khomeini's Anti-American Attitude. Khomeini spurred anti-American feeling and blamed the United States for Iran's problems. Iran canceled contracts for the purchase of American arms and other goods, curtailed the shipment of oil to the United States, and closed American intelligence posts in northern Iran that had monitored Soviet missile tests.

b. Americans Taken Hostage in Iran. In late 1979, President Carter allowed the Shah to enter the United States for surgery and treatment for cancer. Thereupon, in Teheran, capital of Iran, militants—supposedly students—occupied the American embassy and seized more than 50 Americans as hostages. For release of the hostages, the militants demanded that the United States deliver the Shah to Iran to be punished. The militants, urged on by Khomeini, charged the Shah with massacring antigovernment demonstrators, torturing political prisoners, plundering the nation's wealth, eroding Iran's traditional Islamic values, and placing Iran under the control of the United States.

The Carter administration refused to hand over the Shah and condemned the seizure of the American embassy and its staff as violations of international law and as "blackmail." The United States demanded that the hostages be released unconditionally—a position supported unanimously by the UN Security Council and the World Court. As Iran still refused, President Carter prohibited American purchases of Iranian oil and froze Iranian assets in the United States.

In early 1980, after the Shah had left the country, United States leaders broke diplomatic relations with Iran. They also embargoed American exports to Iran. Later, in April 1980, President Carter ordered a military mission to rescue the hostages. The attempt failed when three helicopters malfunctioned and two aircraft collided over the Iranian desert, killing eight crew members.

c. Release of the American Hostages. In late 1980, the Iranian Parliament proposed to free the fifty-two remaining hostages upon American acceptance of certain conditions. With Algeria serving as intermediary, the United

States and Iran negotiated the following agreement: (1) The United States would not interfere in Iran's internal affairs and would end its embargo against Iran. (2) The United States would return, through Algeria, some $9 to $10 billion of frozen Iranian assets—part to be used to repay American banks for previously made loans to Iran and part to be held to satisfy private American claims against Iran. (3) The two nations would establish an arbitration commission to decide claims of American individuals and corporations against Iran (the hostages were excluded from claiming damages from Iran). (4) Iran could sue in American courts for any of the late Shah's assets discovered in the United States.

On January 20, 1981, as President Reagan was being inaugurated, the hostages, after 444 days of captivity, departed from Iran in an Algerian plane. Several days later, they returned to the United States, where they received heroes' welcomes. As the hostages told of the physical and mental brutality practiced by their Iranian captors, President Reagan expressed America's outrage and cautioned Americans against attempting business with Iran.

4. The Iran-Iraq War (Beginning in 1980). Under the Shah, Iran had been considered militarily strong and had secured Iraq's agreement to a 1975 treaty. This treaty established a boundary between the two nations providing for shared control of the *Shatt al-Arab* waterway at the northern tip of the Persian Gulf. In return, Iran pledged to end its aid to the rebellious Iraqi Kurds.

Under Khomeini, Iran by 1980 was considered militarily weak—its military leaders had been purged, military supplies from the United States were frozen, and Iranian society was chaotic. Thereupon, President Saddam Hussein of Iraq abrogated the "humiliating" 1975 treaty and attacked Iran. Hussein's motives were to gain full control of the Shatt al-Arab waterway, to overthrow Khomeini, who had called upon Iraqis to rebel against the Hussein regime, and to emerge as the Arab "strongman." Iraqi forces penetrated some 30 miles into Iran's oil-rich province of Khuzistan but were contained by fervent Iranian resistance. In 1982 the Iranians mounted a counteroffensive and drove the Iraqi forces out of almost all Iranian territory.

Then began a long but deadly stalemate. Iraq, which seemed to have superior air power, bombed Iranian cities and attacked Iranian oil terminals on islands in the Persian Gulf. Iran, which seemed to have greater ground strength, battered against Iraq armies defending the frontier. Early in 1986, Iranian armies broke across the border and occupied Fao, a short distance inside southern Iraq.

Still the war dragged on. After six years of fighting, analysts estimated the death toll at 250,000 Iranians and 100,000 Iraqis, with an additional 650,000 wounded. Although Iraq called for a settlement, Iranian leaders insisted on the ouster of Iraqi President Saddam Hussein as a condition for ending the war.

The Iran-Iraq war had serious effects. It *(a)* curtailed oil shipments to the West from both Iran and Iraq, *(b)* sharply divided the Arab world as Libya and Syria supported Iran whereas Jordan, Saudi Arabia, and others backed Iraq, and *(c)* raised fears that Iran's revolutionary ideas might spread in the Arab world and endanger "moderate" Arab regimes, such as Jordan and Saudi Arabia.

5. Terrorism and Arms Deals: United States-Iranian Relations. After the Iran hostage crisis of 1979 to 1981, relations between the United States and Iran remained hostile. The United States continued its arms embargo, and its leaders accused Iran of supporting terrorist actions, including incidents in which pro-Iranian militants in Lebanon seized Americans as hostages. President Reagan urged United States allies to join in cutting off arms sales to nations supporting terrorism. He declared he would never negotiate with terrorists.

a. Controversy Over Secret Arms Sales. A storm of controversy arose following the revelation in November 1986 that President Reagan had secretly approved United States arms sales to Iran via Israel. Critics charged that the arms had been a "ransom" for hostages and that the President had violated his own policy against negotiating with terrorists. President Reagan went on television to defend his actions, arguing that the arms deals had been part of a diplomatic initiative to win influence with moderates in the Iranian government and were not "ransom" at all.

The sales of United States arms to Iran took place in 1985 and 1986. At least one hostage was released soon after arms reached Iran. Once the sales became public, President Reagan ordered them stopped.

The arms sale issue stirred vigorous debate in Congress and within the administration. The sales had been handled by the Central Intelligence Agency (CIA) and the National Security Council (NSC), the latter a White House body that normally advises the President on security matters without actively carrying out policy.

b. Controversy Over Secret Funds. A few weeks after the first revelations about arms sales, Attorney General *Edwin Meese III* announced the discovery that between $12 million and $30 million in Iranian payments for the arms had been secretly diverted to the Nicaraguan *contras* (United States-supported rebels fighting Nicaragua's leftist government). This news stirred an even bigger controversy. At the time of the alleged diversions, which took place earlier in 1986, the *Boland Amendment* barred either direct or indirect United States aid to the *contras*.

President Reagan said the NSC staff members responsible for the diversion of funds had resigned or been dismissed. The President added that he himself had neither known about nor approved the diversion of funds.

c. The Iran-Contra Investigations. The new revelations led to a flurry of investigations: (1) President Reagan appointed a three-member committee headed by former Senator John Tower. The report of the *Tower Commission* criticized the President for his detached "management style." (2) Senate and House committees held joint public hearings before a nationwide television audience. Key witnesses included *Rear Admiral John M. Poindexter,* head of the NSC in 1985–1986, and *Lieutenant Colonel Oliver L. North,* an assistant to Poindexter and his predecessors. The two men acknowledged their role in the fund diversions and asserted that they were carrying out policies they believed the President wanted. But Poindexter said he had not told the President. (3) At Meese's request, a federal court appointed an independent prosecutor to determine whether federal laws had been broken.

Courtesy of San Diego Union and Copley News

President Reagan said he was "mad as a hornet" at not being told what his administration was doing. He pledged to cooperate fully with investigators.

Critics of the Reagan administration argued that (1) the arms deals with Iran had indeed begun as an exchange for hostages, (2) administration officials had repeatedly lied to Congress, and (3) decisions about foreign policy had been made in great confusion and in "arrogant disregard of the rule of law." Supporters of the Reagan administration argued that (1) although mistakes had been made, the administration had acted quickly to correct its mistakes, (2) members of Congress had exaggerated problems for partisan political purposes, and (3) secret help for the contras would not have been necessary if Congress had not wavered in its support for the contras' cause.

Congressional investigators finally concluded that the President had not known of the diversion of funds but faulted him for failure to exercise proper authority over the activities of his subordinates.

FAR EAST

CHINA

NATIONALISTS LOSE CHINA TO THE COMMUNISTS (1949)

1. Nationalist Weaknesses. Following World War II the Chiang Kai-shek regime lost support in China because it *(a)* was corrupt and inefficient, *(b)* wasted a considerable portion of the American loans and military supplies, *(c)* failed to earn the soldiers' loyalty and prevent army desertions, and *(d)* ignored the peasants' desire for land and the workers' demand for better living conditions.

The Far East

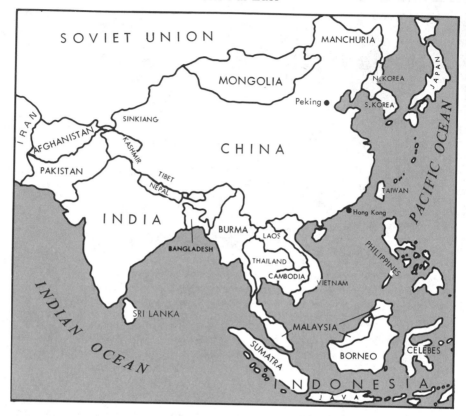

2. Communists Gain China. Chinese Communist armies, strengthened by equipment captured from the Japanese and supplies provided by the Soviet Union, defeated the Nationalists. In 1949 Communist armies drove Chiang Kai-shek to his remaining stronghold, the island of Taiwan (Formosa). The Communists took control of mainland China and rule its current population of over one billion people.

At Peking (Beijing) the Communists proclaimed the *People's Republic of China* under Premier *Chou En-lai* (Zhou Enlai) and Communist party head *Mao Tse-tung* (Mao Zedong). (The spellings in parentheses conform to the Pinyin phonetic transcription system adopted officially by China to replace the Wade-Giles transcription system.)

UNFRIENDLY RELATIONS BETWEEN COMMUNIST CHINA AND THE UNITED STATES (TO 1971)

1. Communist China's Policies. In opposition to the United States, the Communists *(a)* harshly treated American officials, missionaries, and business-people caught in China during the civil war, *(b)* intervened in the Korean War and fought American troops, and *(c)* sent military aid to the Communist forces in Vietnam.

2. America's Policies. In opposition to China, the United States *(a)* recognized the Nationalists on Taiwan as the legal government of China, *(b)* refused to recognize the Peking regime, *(c)* successfully opposed China's bid for admission to the UN, *(d)* embargoed trade with Communist China, *(e)* fought to prevent a Communist takeover in South Vietnam, and *(f)* signed mutual defense treaties to defend South Korea and Taiwan.

3. Dispute Over Taiwan (Formosa). The United States viewed Taiwan as a vital Pacific military base and the Nationalist government as an ally. Consequently, the United States extended economic and military aid to Taiwan and vowed to defend Nationalist-held territory.

Communist China was determined to annex the island and destroy the Nationalist government. The Chinese Communists warned the United States that nothing would deter them from "liberating" Taiwan.

CHINESE-SOVIET SPLIT: IN THE OPEN BY 1963

Despite their 1950 treaty of alliance, China and the Soviet Union gradually became hostile and, by 1963, openly and bitterly disagreed in the following areas.

1. Ideology. *(a) The Soviet Union.* Soviet leaders asserted that world communism can be achieved through peaceful coexistence. They claimed that people, impressed by Soviet achievements, will turn to communism. However, Communists must make every effort to avoid nuclear war. A Communist paradise cannot be built upon millions of corpses. *(b) China.* Mao Tse-tung derided peaceful coexistence as a myth and held the view that war against capitalism is inevitable. If war does come, it will prove America to be a "paper tiger," will end capitalism, and will usher in a glorious Communist future.

2. Soviet Atomic Aid to China. *(a) The Soviet Union.* The Soviets trained Chinese atomic scientists and provided China with a nuclear reactor. When the ideological conflict became acute, the Soviets terminated their aid. *(b) China.* Peking at first complained that Soviet aid was not enough and then deplored its termination.

3. Chinese-Soviet Borders. *(a) The Soviet Union.* Soviet leaders defended the 19th-century treaties that had established the borders between Russia and China. These treaties provided for Russian annexation of sizable territories, including the Amur River valley and the port of Vladivostok. *(b) China.* Chinese leaders argued that the treaties were imperialist-imposed and were no longer valid. In 1969 Chinese and Soviet forces clashed at several border points.

4. World Communist Leadership. *(a) The Soviet Union.* As the oldest and most advanced Communist nation, the Soviet Union claimed the leadership of the Communist bloc. It retained the support of most Communist nations. *(b) China.* The most populous Communist nation, China claimed to be the true interpreter of Marxist-Leninist doctrine and the leader of the Communist world.

CHINA DEVELOPS NUCLEAR WEAPONS: SINCE 1964

In 1964 China set off its first atomic bomb, in 1967 exploded a hydrogen bomb, and in 1970 sent up its first earth satellite, indicating sufficient thrust power to launch ICBMs. China's progress in developing nuclear weapons and missiles caused concern in four nations—India and Japan, whose relations with China had been unfriendly; the Soviet Union, whose long border with China had been the scene of several armed clashes; and the United States, whose leaders considered the possibility of a Chinese missile attack.

RECENT DEVELOPMENTS (SINCE 1966)

1. "Cultural Revolution" (1966–1969). *(a) Reasons.* Aged and ill, Mao Tse-tung wanted to assure the continuation of his policies after his death: (1) *Within the country,* he increased collectivization even over the opposition of the peasants, and (2) *in foreign affairs,* promoted world revolution even at the risk of war. Mao did not want China to use profit as an economic incentive and to lose revolutionary zeal in foreign affairs. Mao's opponents, holding important positions in the Communist party and the government, supported pay raises for workers and private garden plots for peasants, and considered Mao's views inappropriate for building the nation. *(b) Three Years of Turmoil.* Mao moved to crush his opponents by a "great proletarian cultural revolution." He mobilized millions of youths into *Red Guard* groups that denounced and terrorized the opposition. The *Cultural Revolution* shattered Chinese society, fragmented China's Communist party, and undermined production, education, and transportation.

2. Stability and a New Foreign Policy. By 1970 China returned to stability. The Red Guards were disbanded and order was restored by powerful army leaders; production recovered; and the government reflected the control of moderate political leaders under Premier *Chou En-lai.* Then China turned from preoccupation with internal matters to a more active foreign role, especially in improving Chinese-American relations. Soon Chou En-lai invited President Nixon to visit China. Nixon accepted, expressing the hope that this "will become a journey for peace."

3. The Nixon Visit to China (1972). In China, President Nixon spent a hectic week that included sightseeing, entertainment, banquets, a meeting with

Mao Tse-tung, and numerous sessions with Chou En-lai. The visit concluded with the issuance of the *Shanghai communiqué* in which *(a)* the United States agreed that Taiwan is part of China, urged peaceful settlement of the Taiwan issue by the Chinese themselves, and agreed ultimately to withdraw all American forces from Taiwan, and *(b)* the United States and China agreed to peaceful coexistence and to improve and expand their contacts.

This visit, analysts believed, signified the following: *(a) for China*—realization that the major threat to its national interests comes from the Soviet Union rather than the United States and *(b) for the United States*—less fear that China threatens American interests in eastern Asia.

Following the Nixon visit, China and the United States encouraged reciprocal visits by scholars, doctors, musicians, and sports figures and also expanded trade. China placed large orders for American farm produce and bought some American jet airplanes.

4. Power Struggle Following the Deaths of China's Leaders (1976). With the deaths of Premier Chou En-lai and Chairman Mao Tse-tung, China experienced an open struggle for power between radical and moderate Communist party factions. The radicals favored strict adherence to Maoist theories of class warfare, no profit incentives, and "permanent revolution." The moderates stressed pragmatic goals of economic growth and political stability. The moderates attracted support of the industrial managers, government officials, and army leaders.

With the moderates in control, the government acted against four top radical leaders, placing them under arrest on charges of plotting to "usurp party and state power." The government's action against the "gang of four" was cheered by huge demonstrations.

In foreign affairs, the moderate Chinese regime continued Chou En-lai's recent policies: *(a)* rebuffing Soviet efforts to improve relations and *(b)* indicating a strong desire to strengthen friendship with the United States.

5. Full Diplomatic Relations (1979). The United States and China agreed to establish full diplomatic relations. For the United States, this agreement meant breaking diplomatic ties with Taiwan, withdrawing the American forces on that island, and ending its mutual defense treaty with Taiwan. The United States pledged, however, to maintain cultural and economic ties with Taiwan, to sell Taiwan limited supplies of defensive arms, and to remain interested in the peaceful settlement of the Taiwan issue. For China, the agreement meant an implied promise—but no public statement—not to use force to gain control over Taiwan.

Teng Hsiao-ping (Deng Xiaoping), the senior Deputy Communist party chairman, spurred the restoration of full diplomatic relations. A pragmatist and moderate, Teng wanted China to increase trade with and learn from the West so as to hasten China's modernization. Although twice purged during the Mao era, Teng bounced back and became most influential in post-Maoist China.

President Carter hailed the new Sino-American relationship—economically, as furthering trade and, politically, as a "simple reality" that "contributes to the cause of peace." Although the President stated that the normalization of Sino-American relations was not directed against any third nation, the Soviet Union indicated its concern over this development as potentially dangerous to its interests. (In 1981, when the Reagan administration agreed to sell modern American weapons to China, the Soviets deplored the agreement as "highly dangerous for the cause of peace.")

6. Mao Downgraded: New Chinese Leaders. In 1981, the Chinese Communist party gave its official assessment of Mao Tse-tung. Stating that his contributions "far outweigh" his mistakes, the party called Mao a brilliant revolutionary but a blundering national leader. Mao was condemned for the Cultural Revolution, which the party said "was responsible for the most severe setbacks and the heaviest losses suffered by the party, the state, and the people." Mao was also blamed for being arrogant and arbitrary in his later years, for suppressing discussions, and for fostering his own personality cult. The party contrasted Mao's "seeking quick results in economic work" with the efforts for orderly economic development by Chou En-lai and Teng Hsiao-ping.

After this assessment, the party appointed two Teng supporters to major posts: Zhao Ziyang became premier, and Hu Yaobang became party chairperson. Observers pointed out that Teng—now the most powerful leader in China—had arranged an orderly transfer of power to younger persons committed to his views.

In 1987 Hu lost his post in a party upheaval. Observers said Hu was blamed for policies that in 1986 set off serious antigovernment demonstrations by Chinese college students, who demanded more freedom of expression and democracy.

7. China vs. Vietnam: Hostility Between Communist Nations. (Check the Index for Vietnam.)

8. Recent Chinese Foreign Policies. *(a) Toward the Soviet Union.* After years of ignoring each other, China and the Soviet Union began talks in 1982 on normalizing relations. China asked the Soviet Union to cease supporting Vietnam's efforts to control Cambodia, to withdraw its forces from Afghanistan, and to reduce its troops along the Chinese-Soviet border. While the talks made only slow progress, they did lead to a resumption of Soviet technical aid to China. *(b) Toward the United States.* China asked the United States to halt arms sales to Taiwan. The United States promised to reduce such sales. *(c) Toward Great Britain.* China and Britain negotiated a pact on the future status of Hong Kong, which has been ruled by Britain under a 99-year lease from China that expires in 1997. China agreed that for 50 years it would permit Hong Kong to have local self-government under British-style laws and to continue with its capitalist institutions.

JAPAN

TERRITORIAL LOSSES FOLLOWING WORLD WAR II

Japan lost Taiwan and Manchuria to China, and the Kuriles and the southern half of Sakhalin Island to the Soviet Union. The Ryukyu Islands, which contain Okinawa, were occupied by the United States. The Japanese-mandated Mariana, Marshall, and Caroline Islands in the Pacific were transferred to the United States as a UN trusteeship. Korea was divided at the 38th parallel into Soviet and American zones, pending independence.

JAPAN UNDER AMERICAN OCCUPATION (1945–1952)

General Douglas MacArthur, as Supreme Allied Commander in Japan, promoted the following:

1. New Constitution (1947). Japan adopted a democratic constitution that *(a)* renounced the waging of war and the maintainance of offensive armed forces, *(b)* denied the emperor's divine origin but retained him as a symbol of national unity, *(c)* contained a bill of rights guaranteeing civil liberties, including freedom of speech and press, separation of church and state (ending government support for Shintoism), and equality under the law (including equal rights for women), and *(d)* provided for a cabinet responsible to an elected two-house legislature, called the *Diet*.

2. Economic and Social Reforms. Japan *(a)* dissolved the huge business monopolies that had controlled much of its economic life, *(b)* encouraged free labor unions with the right to strike, *(c)* provided farms for landless peasants, and *(d)* reformed education by removing ultranationalist teachers and textbooks and encouraging democratic learning.

3. War Trials. Japanese war leaders were tried before Allied courts on war crime charges: aggressive warfare and atrocities against prisoners. Some Japanese leaders were sentenced to prison; others were executed.

TREATY OF PEACE WITH JAPAN (1952)

Drawn up by the United States, the Japanese peace treaty was accepted by the major Allied nations except the Soviet Union. The Soviet Union refused to sign the treaty chiefly because it confirmed Japan's position as an ally of the United States. (In 1956 the Soviets signed a declaration of peace with Japan.) The 1952 treaty provided as follows:

1. Territory. Japan lost all its conquered territory but retained its four large home islands. (Japan consented to American administration of the Ryukyu Islands, including Okinawa, but retained the right to claim their return.)

2. Reparations. Japan was not required to pay reparations for war damages. However, Japan agreed to contribute goods and services to countries damaged by Japanese aggression in World War II.

3. Defense. Japan was recognized as an independent, sovereign nation possessing the right of military self-defense. In a separate pact, the United States and Japan agreed that American troops remain in Japan.

AMERICAN FRIENDSHIP FOR JAPAN

1. Reasons. *(a)* Because of the reforms introduced in Japan during the American occupation, the United States considers Japan an Asian bulwark of democracy. *(b)* Japan's postwar government, democratically elected and controlled by the Liberal Democratic party, has been stable, capitalist, pro-American, and anti-Communist. Among Japanese voters, Communist influence has been negligible. *(c)* Japan represents a counterbalance to the growth of Communist power in Asia. *(d)* Japan is a valuable ally because of its industrial capacity, productive workers (drawn from a population of 121 million), and strategic location off the Asian continent.

2. Evidences. The United States *(a)* treated Japan generously in the peace treaty, *(b)* extended economic and military aid to Japan, *(c)* kept American forces in Japan for the defense of Japan and other free-world nations in eastern Asia, *(d)* developed close commercial and cultural ties, and *(e)* in 1972 returned the Ryukyu Islands, including Okinawa, to Japan. (In contrast, the Soviet Union has refused to return four small northern islands seized at the end of World War II and repeatedly claimed by Japan.)

RECENT DEVELOPMENTS AND PROBLEMS

1. Limited Rearmament. In accordance with its constitution, Japan maintains only a small military force for "self-defense." But these troops are insufficient to defend the nation. Japanese public opinion, strongly pacifist, remains unwilling to amend the constitution to permit more extensive rearmament. Meanwhile, the people are free of heavy military expenditures and depend on the United States to protect their homeland.

2. Economic Recovery. Under its free-enterprise economic system, postwar Japan achieved a remarkable rate of economic growth. Japan ranks among the world's leading manufacturers of automobiles, steel, computer chips, synthetic fibers, electrical products, and cotton yarns. Its banks and corporations are major investors in other countries. Japan is the world's third-greatest economic power and enjoys a higher standard of living than many European nations. But because of its limited farmland and natural resources, Japan must "export or die."

3. Trade With the United States. Japan provides the second-largest market for American exports and, in turn, finds the United States its best customer. Japanese buy United States beef, citrus fruit, timber, and machinery. Americans purchase Japanese autos, cameras, television sets, and computer chips. American manufacturers of competing products have asked Congress for increased tariff protection, complaining that Japanese wages are lower than those paid American workers and that Japanese business practices are unfair to foreigners trying to do business in Japan. To quiet these protests, Japan has, on several occasions, voluntarily limited its exports to the United States. Japan has also agreed to lower some tariffs and end other restrictive trade practices. United States leaders continue to press Japan for further steps to open its markets to more United States goods and services.

INDIA

BRIEF SURVEY

1. Independence and Government. In 1947 India received independence from Britain. *Jawaharlal Nehru,* India's independence leader, became prime minister and promoted a democratic government. In 1975 Prime Minister *Indira Gandhi*—Nehru's daughter—moved India away from democracy by declaring a "state of emergency," arresting political opponents, and instituting press censorship. In 1977 elections, Mrs. Gandhi and her Congress party were decisively defeated and for three years Mrs. Gandhi was out of office. In the 1980 elections, Mrs. Gandhi achieved a remarkable triumph as her faction of the Congress party won over two-thirds of the seats in the legislature and she again became India's prime minister.

In 1985, as religious unrest swept India, Mrs. Gandhi was assassinated by a member of the Sikh minority which opposed government actions to suppress dissent. Mrs. Gandhi was succeeded in parliamentary elections by her son, Rajiv, who pledged to set India off on a path of increased economic growth.

2. Mixed Economy. To raise the low living standards of its 730 million people, India utilizes a "mixed economy" of private and public enterprise. To supplement private business efforts, the government began five-year plans: constructing irrigation projects, electric power plants, railroads, and steel mills; distributing land to the peasants; and fostering modern farming methods. Nevertheless, India's economy has made slow progress.

3. Foreign Policy of Neutrality. Nehru hoped to devote India's energies to domestic problems. Therefore, in the cold war, Nehru set a policy of nonalignment, or neutrality. Nehru's successors reaffirmed this policy.

COMMUNIST CHINESE AGGRESSION AFFECTS INDIA (1959–1962)

Prime Minister Nehru's friendship for Communist China was shattered by the following Chinese actions:

1. Tibet. In 1959, after eight years of Chinese Communist occupation, the Tibetan people revolted. The Chinese *(a)* suppressed this revolt, taking many Tibetan lives, and *(b)* accused India of having aided the revolt, a charge that Nehru indignantly denied. Nehru condemned China's brutality in Tibet and granted asylum to thousands of Tibetan refugees.

2. Indian Border. For many years China had disputed its boundary with India. In 1959, following the Tibetan revolt, Communist Chinese troops crossed India's northern frontier, attacked Indian border patrols, and occupied large areas of territory claimed by India. In 1962 the Chinese occupied additional territory. Declaring that his country would resist Chinese aggression, Nehru secured military aid from Britain and the United States.

AMERICAN EFFORTS IN INDIA

The United States hopes that India will align itself with the free world because India (1) in Nehru's words, is "firmly wedded to the democratic way of life," (2) has been menaced by China, and (3) has received considerable American economic and military aid. In 1962, during the India-China border dispute, President Kennedy airlifted weapons to India. In 1966, President Johnson authorized wheat shipments to prevent starvation in India.

In 1971, however, President Nixon condemned India for sending its troops into East Pakistan and forcibly gaining independence for Bangladesh.

(For the United States-India dispute over nuclear proliferation, check the Index.)

SOVIET EFFORTS IN INDIA

The Soviet Union seeks to win India to its side or, at least, to keep it neutral in the cold war. (1) The Soviet Union has granted loans for the development of India's heavy industry. (Soviet economic aid to India is far less, however, than that extended by the United States.) (2) In 1963, Soviet leaders voiced support for India in its border dispute with China. (3) In 1971, the Soviet Union signed a 20-year treaty of friendship with India; thereafter, as the India-Pakistan war started, the Soviets supported India by vetoing three Security Council resolutions for a cease-fire and withdrawal of Indian forces. (Check the Index for the Indian-Pakistani war.)

KOREA

KOREA AFTER WORLD WAR II

In 1945, Korea (a colony of Japan since 1910) was divided at the 38th parallel: the north was occupied by Soviet troops, the south by American troops. The USSR defied UN attempts to unify Korea by free elections. In North Korea, the Soviets established a Communist government led by the Korean Workers Communist party head, *Kim Il-Sung,* and equipped a powerful Korean army. In South Korea, UN-supervised elections established an anti-Communist government headed by President *Syngman Rhee.*

COMMUNIST AGGRESSION AGAINST SOUTH KOREA (1950–1953)

In June 1950, without warning, North Korean Communist forces crossed the 38th parallel and invaded South Korea. The UN Security Council, with the Soviet

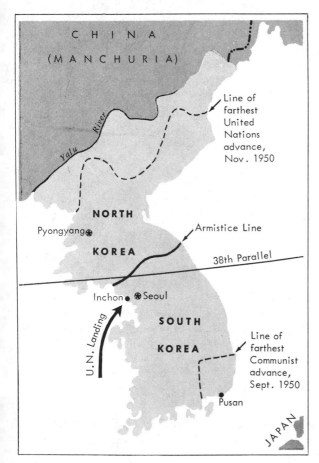

The Korean War

Union absent, promptly recommended that UN members furnish military assistance to South Korea. The UN army consisted chiefly of American and South Korean units, with contingents from 15 other anti-Communist nations. It was headed originally by General Douglas MacArthur.

At first, the UN forces retreated before the Communist assault. After reinforcements arrived, General MacArthur launched a counterattack that carried his forces deep into North Korea close to the Manchurian border. Then, powerful Communist Chinese armies crossed into North Korea, attacked the UN forces, and compelled MacArthur to retreat. By mid-1951 the battle line had stabilized near the 38th parallel.

Meanwhile, the UN General Assembly voted (with opposition only from the Soviet bloc) to declare China guilty of aggression in Korea.

MacARTHUR-TRUMAN CONTROVERSY (1951)

President Truman, as commander in chief of the American armed forces, dismissed General MacArthur for insubordination. Truman charged that the general had repeatedly disregarded instructions to refrain from making foreign policy statements that criticized government policies.

The two men had disagreed sharply. MacArthur advocated carrying the war in Korea to China, especially Manchuria, and urged an all-out war to win victory over communism in Asia. Truman feared that an invasion of Manchuria would lead to war with the Soviet Union. He held that the United States must fight a limited war in Asia so as not to leave Western Europe, the key to American security, defenseless.

TRUCE IN KOREA (1953)

UN and Communist negotiators took two years to agree upon truce terms. The conference was long deadlocked regarding the *repatriation* (return), of prisoners. The UN claimed that many of its prisoners did not want to return to Communist rule; the Communists insisted upon compulsory repatriation. Finally, the conference agreed that all prisoners be given freedom of choice. (Eventually, two of every five prisoners held by the UN refused to return to Communist rule.)

The truce was (1) hailed by the UN as a victory against aggression, (2) criticized by the South Korean government for failing to unify the country under anti-Communist leadership, and (3) greeted by most Americans with relief. The Korean struggle cost the United States $18 billion; 103,000 people were wounded, and 33,000 were killed.

KOREAN DEVELOPMENTS SINCE THE TRUCE

1. Continued American Interest. In support of South Korea, the United States extended considerable economic and military aid, kept many troops there, and signed a bilateral Mutual Defense Pact.

2. Continued Communist Interest. In 1961 the Soviet Union signed a defense treaty pledging to assist North Korea "with all forces and by every means." Communist China also made a similar defense pledge to North Korea.

3. The *Pueblo* Incident (1968–1969). North Korean patrol boats seized the American intelligence ship *Pueblo*. The Communists claimed that the *Pueblo* had intruded into North Korean waters on a hostile mission. The United States answered that the *Pueblo* had been in international waters. To secure the release of the ship's crew, the American negotiator eventually signed a document confessing intrusion into North Korean waters, while publicly repudiating the confession. North Korea freed the *Pueblo* crew.

4. Governmental Changes in South Korea

a. Rhee Regime (1948–1960). In 1960 South Korea was swept by antigovernment riots protesting rigged elections, police terror, corruption, and autocratic rule. Syngman Rhee ended his 12-year presidency by resigning.

b. Park Regime (1961–1979). In 1961 General *Park Chung Hee* seized power. He improved economic conditions and maintained a pro-American foreign policy. In 1972 Park imposed martial law, prohibited political activities, and imposed press censorship. Under these conditions, Park won a public referendum for a constitution enabling him to remain president for life and to rule dictatorially. Park became highly intolerant of dissent.

c. American Criticism of the Park Regime. The United States disapproved of Park's 1972 constitutional changes. Thereafter, the United States criticized the Park regime for its harsh treatment of dissidents and for its use of campaign contributions and bribes to influence American officials.

d. Assassination of Park (1979). Kim Jae Kyu, head of Korea's Central Intelligence Agency, assassinated President Park. Kim's motives were not clearly known—possibly personal quarrels or possibly a policy rift, as Kim felt that Park's repression of opposition threatened the nation's stability.

e. Chun Regime (1980–   ). General *Chun Doo Hwan* seized control of the Seoul government. Pledging to wipe out corruption and to foster a "democracy suited to our political climate," Chun secured public approval of a new constitution containing many democratic features—guarantees of press freedom and habeas corpus, a ban on forced confessions, and a single seven-year presidential term. Meanwhile, Chun enforced martial law, strong press censorship, and repression of dissidents.

In 1981, prior to visiting Washington, Chun ended martial law in South Korea, but his government continued in firm control. In Washington, Chun was reassured by President Reagan that America remained committed to the security of South Korea and would retain there its 39,000 American troops. A State Department official further explained that although "we are for human rights"—which the Carter administration had emphasized—the Reagan administration's preeminent concern was for military security.

As South Korea's scheduled 1988 presidential election approached, United States leaders urged Chun to move as quickly as possible toward full democracy. Riots and unrest accompanied debate over how to choose a new president. Chun's ruling party favored an election by parliament, while opposition leaders called for direct election by popular vote.

NATIONS OF INDOCHINA

CAMBODIA, LAOS, AND VIETNAM

INDOCHINA UNDER FRENCH RULE

In the 19th century, France annexed Indochina—an agricultural region in Southeast Asia. During World War II, while France was overrun by the Nazis, Indochina was occupied by Japanese armies. Indochinese nationalists, opposed to both Japan and France, joined an independence movement called the *Vietminh*. Although this movement contained some non-Communist nationalists, the Vietminh was controlled by Communists and led by Moscow-trained *Ho Chi Minh*.

COMMUNISTS SEEK CONTROL (1946–1954)

After the war, France promised partial independence to the three states of Indochina. The Vietminh rejected the French offer and gained popular support by promising to (1) drive out the French completely and (2) distribute land to the peasants. For eight years, civil war raged in Indochina. In 1954 the Vietminh won the decisive *Battle of Dien Bien Phu*.

GENEVA CONFERENCE: TRUCE FOR INDOCHINA (1954)

The major powers and the states of Indochina sent representatives to Geneva, Switzerland, to negotiate a settlement. The Geneva Agreements, not signed by the United States or South Vietnam, provided as follows: (1) *Laos* and *Cambodia* were recognized as independent. (2) *Vietnam* was divided at the 17th parallel: the North under a Communist government in *Hanoi*, the South under an anti-Communist government in *Saigon*. The people in both the North and the South were to vote by mid-1956 for a single, all-Vietnam government.

DEVELOPMENTS IN VIETNAM

1. Communist North Vietnam. Ho Chi Minh established a Communist dictatorship, strengthened the army, and received considerable Soviet and Chinese aid. The Communists sought control of South Vietnam.

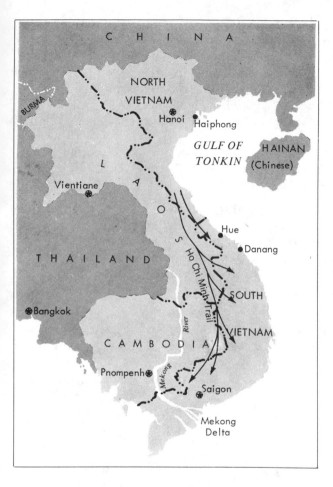

The Vietnam War

2. Anti-Communist South Vietnam. The Saigon government was strongly anti-Communist and rejected plans for all-Vietnam elections. It argued that honest elections were impossible in the Communist north. To undermine the Saigon government, the Communist Vietcong waged guerrilla warfare throughout the south—terrorizing villagers and killing government supporters—and established Vietcong control over large rural areas. Saigon requested and received American aid. American leaders feared that a Communist takeover in South Vietnam might cause the bordering nations in Southeast Asia to fall to the Communists like a row of "falling dominoes."

3. Escalation of the War. In 1964 American naval units patrolled the international waters of the Gulf of Tonkin. When North Vietnamese torpedo boats attacked American destroyers in the gulf, President Johnson ordered an air strike against North Vietnam's naval bases. The President's action received almost unanimous support from Congress in its *Gulf of Tonkin Resolution.* (In 1970 Congress repealed this resolution.)

In 1965, after American bases in South Vietnam had been attacked by Communist forces, President Johnson ordered air strikes against North Vietnamese military targets. The United States increased its forces in South Vietnam, eventually to over 500,000 personnel. Four SEATO members—Australia, New Zealand, the Philippines, and Thailand—augmented the South Vietnamese and American forces.

The Communist nations increased their support for the Vietcong and Hanoi. Moscow provided additional military equipment. Peking assigned service troops to maintain transportation in the North.

4. Debate in America Regarding Vietnam. American public opinion divided sharply regarding Vietnam. *(a)* The "hawks" argued for increased military action to halt aggression and contain Communist expansion in Asia. *(b)* The "doves" urged the United States to seek peace by reducing its military activities in Vietnam. They argued that America (1) had no vital interests in Vietnam and (2) was supporting a Saigon government that commanded no loyalty among the people.

5. The Move to Peace Talks (1965–1968). President Johnson's efforts to arrange peace talks were all unsuccessful until 1968, when Hanoi agreed

**"Tell us again, old one,
what peace was like."**

Mansbridge, © Punch/Rothco

to negotiations. The two nations began talks in Paris. Later the peace talks were expanded to include the Saigon government and the Vietcong. The Paris talks, however, remained deadlocked.

6. Nixon Administration and Vietnam (1969–1974)

a. Vietnamization. Nixon spurred *Vietnamization,* that is, shifting the burden of fighting the war to South Vietnamese forces. By late 1972 he had withdrawn over 500,000 personnel from Vietnam, leaving only 27,000 American troops. American casualty lists grew much shorter.

b. The War Spills Over Into Bordering Nations

(1) Cambodia. In 1970 the Cambodian regime, while reaffirming the country's neutrality, demanded the withdrawal of North Vietnamese and Vietcong forces from bases in Cambodia. Instead, the Communist forces attacked Cambodian towns. Thereupon, President Nixon ordered American forces to join with South Vietnamese troops in a limited "incursion" into Cambodia to destroy the Communist bases.

(2) Laos. In 1970 North Vietnamese and local Communist Pathet Lao forces overran much of southern Laos. In 1971, South Vietnamese forces, with American air support, began a limited "incursion" into southern Laos to disrupt enemy supply routes.

Both incursions aroused much controversy in the United States, again between the "hawks" and the "doves."

c. Secret Peace Talks. Beginning in 1969, Washington and Hanoi had held, near Paris, a series of secret peace talks. The American negotiator was President Nixon's national security adviser, *Henry Kissinger;* the Hanoi negotiator was *Le Duc Tho.* In 1973 they reached an agreement.

7. The Paris Peace Agreement for Vietnam (1973)

a. Major Provisions

(1) Military. (a) The United States, North Vietnam, South Vietnam, and the Vietcong agree to a cease-fire. *(b)* The United States shall withdraw its remaining forces from South Vietnam. *(c)* Hanoi and the Vietcong shall return all American prisoners of war and account for persons "missing in action" (MIA). *(d)* All foreign troops shall be withdrawn from Laos and Cambodia. *(e)* No more troops and military supplies shall be introduced into South Vietnam.

(2) Reunification. The reunification of Vietnam shall be achieved only by peaceful means.

(3) Political Arrangements for South Vietnam. (a) Saigon and the Vietcong each shall retain the areas under its control at the time of the cease-fire. *(b)* The people of South Vietnam have a sacred right to decide their own political future through free elections.

b. Observations. (1) The agreement was a compromise, with neither side gaining all its objectives. The United States did *not* secure the withdrawal of Hanoi's troops out of the South. Hanoi did *not* secure the establishment of a Communist-dominated government in the South. (2) The Vietnamese War cost the United States over an 11-year period $140 billion, more than 300,000 wounded, and 46,000 killed. It was one of the costliest and most divisive wars in American history.

COMMUNIST FORCES TRIUMPH IN INDOCHINA (1975)

1. Cambodia (Kampuchea). The rightist-leaning government faced increasing military pressure from Communist forces: some North Vietnamese units and the local *Khmer Rouge*. The government forces, despite a Congress-imposed cutoff of American air support, withstood the Communist insurgents for more than a year. In early 1975, however, the government forces collapsed, and Communist troops took control of the entire country.

The Khmer Rouge executed Cambodian leaders who had opposed them, forcibly drove urban residents out of the major cities into rural areas, which caused many deaths, and, on charges of spying, seized an American merchant vessel, the *Mayaguez*. When diplomatic efforts failed, President Ford ordered American forces to rescue the crew and vessel, which was done at a cost of almost 70 Americans killed and wounded.

2. Laos. In 1975, following the Communist victories in Cambodia and South Vietnam, the Communist Pathet Lao took full control of the government and country.

In 1976 reports out of Laos indicated that the Pathet Lao held 50,000 rightists and neutralists in harsh prison camps for punishment and "reeducation." Many inmates died from lack of food and medicine.

3. Vietnam. *(a)* The United States withdrew its remaining military forces but continued to give limited economic and military aid to the Saigon regime. *(b)* North Vietnam, in violation of the Paris agreement, increased its forces in the South to an estimated 400,000 troops. In 1975 the North Vietnamese and Vietcong mounted a major offensive and gained full control of the South.

During this final phase of the Vietnam War, the United States proceeded as follows: (1) President Ford pledged that American forces would not return to Vietnam. (2) The United States helped evacuate thousands of South Vietnamese— many of whom had worked with the Americans and feared for their lives under Communist rule. Congress voted funds to assist some 120,000 Vietnamese refugees to come to the United States. (3) President Ford spoke out to reassure our allies by affirming that no "time-tested friends of the United States should worry or fear that our commitments to them will not be honored."

In 1976 reports out of South Vietnam indicated that the Communists held between 100,000 and 300,000 persons in labor camps, where brutal conditions caused many deaths. Also in 1976, the Communists proclaimed the official reunification of the country as the *Socialist Republic of Vietnam*.

REFUGEES FROM INDOCHINA (SINCE 1975)

Following the Communist takeovers in Southeast Asia more than one million people fled from Vietnam, Cambodia, and Laos and became refugees. (1) The earliest refugees were those closely identified with the overthrown anti-Communist regimes, who feared for their lives under Communist rule. (2) The ethnic Chinese, many of families who had lived in Vietnam for generations, were pressured to leave by the Hanoi regime. The Chinese were considered of doubtful loyalty by Hanoi; and they were disliked by the Vietnamese. Many Chinese were compelled to pay large sums to the Hanoi regime before being permitted to depart. (3) Cambodians fled political instability and renewed warfare as Vietnamese troops invaded Cambodia to oust a pro-Chinese regime and install a government subservient to Hanoi. (4) Other refugees fled harsh Communist rule, forced evacuation from cities, and the lack of food, clothing, and other essentials.

Some refugees fled overland to Thailand and China; others fled by sea and became known as the *boat people.* Fewer than half the boat people were estimated to have survived the unsafe vessels, the hazards of the sea, and pirate attacks and to have reached land in the Philippines, Malaysia, Indonesia, and southern Thailand. The refugees were not welcomed—and in many cases were forcibly driven out—by the Southeast Asian nations. These nations insisted they lacked the facilities and resources to care for the refugees and were unwilling to absorb the refugees into their societies.

Many refugees were accepted by the United States and some by other Western nations—notably Canada, Australia, and France. About 250,000 ethnic Chinese found safety in Hong Kong and southern China.

Vietnam meanwhile was viewed with grave mistrust by many Western powers, the Southeast Asian nations, and China.

VIETNAM VS. CHINA: HOSTILITY BETWEEN COMMUNIST NATIONS (BY 1979)

1. Reasons. By 1979 Vietnam had aroused the hostility of Communist China. *(a)* Vietnam indicated its preference for the Soviet Union, which China viewed as its major enemy. In 1978 Vietnam signed a 25-year friendship treaty with the Soviet Union, receiving pledges of economic aid and of "effective measures" in case of attack. *(b)* Vietnam moved to control all Indochina. Whereas Laos yielded to Vietnamese dominance, Cambodia did not. Under *Pol Pot,* this Cambodian regime ruled with great brutality, but it was pro-Chinese. In 1978 Vietnam launched a full-scale invasion of Cambodia, overthrew the Pol Pot regime, and installed a puppet government under *Heng Samrin.* China resented the ousting of its ally and held that Moscow was using the Vietnamese in Asia as it had used the Cubans in Africa. *(c)* Vietnam harassed, exacted funds from, and expelled over 250,000 of its ethnic Chinese residents.

Valtman/Rothco

2. The Limited War (1979). After several border incidents, China announced that it would no longer tolerate "being pushed around" and would act to "teach Vietnam a lesson." Embarking upon a limited invasion, Chinese armies crossed the border into northern Vietnam and met strong resistance. The Soviet Union warned China to withdraw "before it is too late" and speeded military equipment to Vietnam but itself undertook no military moves. After four weeks of fighting, with heavy casualties on both sides, the Chinese withdrew their forces. Thereafter, China and Vietnam engaged in peace talks but arrived at no meaningful understandings.

EFFECTS OF THE VIETNAM WAR ON AMERICAN FOREIGN POLICY

1. The Nixon Doctrine (1969). President Nixon asserted that the United States would continue to play a major role in the Pacific but would seek to avoid involvement in another war like Vietnam. Consequently, Nixon told our Asian friends that the United States would honor its treaty commitments, including military and economic aid, but would look to any Asian nation threatened by internal subversion or nonnuclear aggression to provide the troops for its own defense.

2. War-Powers Resolution (1973). In ordering American forces into combat in Vietnam, three successive Presidents—Kennedy, Johnson, and Nixon—had used the Presidential power of commander in chief but had not secured a Congressional declaration of war. In 1973 Congress moved to limit Presidential war-making powers by enacting, over President Nixon's veto, the *War-Powers Resolution.* It provided that *(a)* a President who commits American troops to combat abroad must present the reasons for doing so to Congress within 48 hours, *(b)* if the President expects to keep American troops in combat abroad for more than 90 days, Congressional approval must be secured, *(c)* if the President does not secure Congressional approval, the military action must be terminated, and *(d)* Congress can order withdrawal of American forces from abroad, before 90 days, by adopting a concurrent resolution not subject to a Presidential veto.

President Nixon condemned the resolution as "clearly unconstitutional" and as undermining "this nation's ability to act decisively" in international crises.

3. Other Effects. *(a) Thailand.* Now bordered by Communist Laos and Cambodia, and fearful that these countries might aid local guerrilla bands, Thailand in 1975 requested the United States to close American bases and withdraw American forces from its soil. The United States agreed. *(b) Angola.* After Portugal withdrew in 1975, Angola experienced civil war between pro-Western and pro-Communist groups. When the United States Congress became aware that the Ford administration was sending covert (secret) aid to the pro-Western forces, Congress voted to prohibit such aid, fearing American involvement in another Vietnam-type situation. *(c) El Salvador.* A number of members of Congress opposed the Reagan policy of economic and military aid to El Salvador to battle leftist guerrillas for fear of another Vietnam-type involvement.

AFGHANISTAN

1. Land and People. Located in west central Asia, Afghanistan is a landlocked country, bordered on the north by the Soviet Union, on the west by Iran, on the south by Pakistan, and at its eastern tip by China (see map, page 648). Afghanistan contains some small, fertile valleys interspersed among large deserts and extensive mountains. The Khyber Pass, 35 miles long, provides a major route through the Hindu Kush Mountains from Afghanistan into Pakistan. Afghanistan's natural resources remain largely untouched except for natural gasfields and coal deposits. Afghanistan is essentially a primitive, underdeveloped country.

The Afghan people, totaling 15 million, are mostly devout Muslims. They belong to a number of different tribes and retain a strong sense of tribal identity and loyalty. They speak Persian or Persian-related languages. Most Afghans live in rural areas and are engaged chiefly in farming. Their per capita income is less than $200 per year, some 80 percent are illiterate, and the average life span is less than 40 years.

2. Pro-Soviet Government (1978). By a 1978 revolution, a pro-Soviet regime seized control. It signed a treaty of "friendship and cooperation" with the Soviet Union and accepted Soviet military and economic advisers. This pro-Soviet regime aroused strong opposition among the people for being "godless" and anti-Islamic, subservient to the Soviet Union, brutal in its treatment of political prisoners, and a threat to the traditional Afghan way of life. The Communist regime proved unable to suppress the rebellious Islamic tribal guerrilla bands, and by late 1979 government leaders were quarreling among themselves.

3. Soviet Invasion (1979–   ). The Soviet Union sided with one faction in Afghanistan's government, helping to install a new president—*Babrak Karmal*—in the capital city of Kabul and sending some 50,000 Soviet troops into the country to crush the rebellious tribal guerrillas. The Soviet Union claimed that its intervention had been requested by the Afghan authorities. Soviet troops met strong and continued resistance.

This invasion—reminiscent of Soviet actions in 1956 in Hungary and in 1968 in Czechoslovakia—was protested by Western and many Third World nations. The United States condemned Russia for "blatant military interference." China termed the invasion a threat to its security. Pakistan, which has housed many Afghan refugees, asked the UN Security Council to consider the situation. The Security Council resolution, calling for the "unconditional withdrawal of all foreign troops from Afghanistan," was defeated by a Soviet veto. Thereupon, the veto-free General Assembly, by a vote of 104 to 18 (with 30 not voting), adopted a resolution strongly deploring the armed intervention in Afghanistan and calling for a withdrawal of all foreign troops. Year after year in the 1980s, the Assembly passed new resolutions calling for an immediate Soviet withdrawal, but to no avail.

The war in Afghanistan was bitterly fought. Charges of torture and other atrocities were leveled against Soviet and Afghan government forces by private groups such as Amnesty International, by human rights reports at the United Nations, and by the United States. On the other hand, the Afghan government accused the guerrillas of atrocities.

THE CARTER DOCTRINE

In his 1980 State of the Union address, President Carter said that the Soviet invasion of Afghanistan threatened the Persian Gulf region (see the map on page 631), with its oil supplies essential to the Western democracies. Soviet forces now were close to the major waterway for transporting Persian Gulf oil, the *Strait of Hormuz*. The President therefore issued a warning that any attempt by outside forces "to gain control of the Persian Gulf region will be regarded as an assault" against the United States and "will be repelled by any means necessary, including military force." This warning became known as the *Carter Doctrine*.

The Soviet Union meanwhile denied any designs on Middle East oil or warm-water ports on the Persian Gulf.

To implement the Carter Doctrine, the United States established a small Rapid Deployment Force, promised economic and military aid to Oman in exchange for air and naval bases near the Persian Gulf and to Kenya for bases on the East African coast, and agreed to grant Somalia credits to purchase military equipment in exchange for the use of a Somali naval and air base at Berbera just south of the Red Sea.

The United States later expanded the Rapid Deployment Force and renamed it the *Central Command,* or *Centcom.* Under Centcom, the United States moved stockpiles of military equipment to bases near the Persian Gulf, ready for use in an emergency. When fully ready (in about 1990), Centcom is to be able to land an estimated 450,000 soldiers in the Gulf area on short notice and under wartime conditions.

Presidents Carter and Reagan sent weapons and other aid to the Muslim resistance fighters in Afghanistan. The Afghan fighters also received aid from Pakistan, Iran, and other nations. The rebels' effectiveness was undermined, however, by quarrels among rival leaders. In 1985 the seven main guerrilla groups joined in an alliance.

THE REAGAN DOCTRINE

In a speech announcing what became known as the *Reagan Doctrine,* President Reagan declared in 1986 that the United States would support what he called "freedom fighters" in their efforts to overthrow oppressive left-wing, especially Communist, regimes. The doctrine applied not only to the rebels in Afghanistan but also to guerrilla movements fighting against the governments of Nicaragua, Angola, and Cambodia. After meeting with several Afghan rebel leaders, President Reagan ordered stepped-up aid to the guerrilla resistance.

NEGOTIATIONS ON THE WAR IN AFGHANISTAN

Pakistan and Afghanistan began UN-sponsored talks in 1982 to try to agree on ways of ending the war. Pakistan is deeply involved because more than 2 million Afghans have fled across the border into Pakistan, and much of the military aid to the resistance is funneled through Pakistan. The talks involved such

© *1986, Washington Post Writers Group; reprinted with permission*

questions as *(a)* a schedule for Soviet troop withdrawal, *(b)* a cutoff of military aid to the rebels, and *(c)* means of monitoring compliance with any agreement.

In 1986 the Soviet Union announced that it was withdrawing 6000 to 8000 of its troops, but more than 110,000 Soviet troops remained in Afghanistan, and fighting continued. A change in leadership of the Afghan government that same year brought no immediate changes in government policies. *Najibullah,* the new Afghan leader, was regarded as strongly pro-Soviet.

LATIN AMERICA

INTER-AMERICAN PACTS AFTER WORLD WAR II

1. Rio Inter-American Defense Treaty. In 1947 the American nations signed the *Rio Treaty* providing that *(a)* an armed attack against any American state shall be considered an attack against all, and *(b)* the other American states shall assist the victim of attack.

2. Organization of American States (OAS). In 1948 the American nations established the *Organization of American States.*

   a. Purposes. The OAS Charter obligates the signatory nations to pursue the following: (1) cooperation in economic and social matters, (2) peaceful settlement of disputes, (3) nonintervention in the internal affairs of any state except to preserve hemispheric security, and (4) collective action against armed attack and against any threat to hemispheric peace.

   b. Major Organs. (1) The *Inter-American Conference* meets once every five years and determines general policy. (2) The *Council,* consisting of representatives of each member nation, is in permanent session. (3) *Meetings of Consultation of Ministers of Foreign Affairs* are held as needed to consider urgent problems. (4) The *Inter-American Defense Board* coordinates hemispheric military defense. (5) The *Pan-American Union* serves as the OAS secretariat.

   c. Strengths. The OAS advances inter-American economic cooperation. It provides a forum for the American nations and makes possible hemispheric solidarity on international problems. Finally, by a two-thirds vote, the OAS may recommend action to protect its member nations.

   d. Weaknesses. The OAS cannot be sure that its members will heed OAS recommendations. Further, the OAS operates on a limited budget and lacks a military force. Finally, many Latin American members resent the United States because of its economic wealth and military power, and complain that the United States dominates the OAS.

BASIC FACTORS UNDERLYING LATIN AMERICAN UNREST

1. Social Factors

   a. Population Explosion. Now totaling over 400 million, the population of Latin America is growing rapidly. By outpacing the growth of Latin America's economy, its population explosion hinders efforts to raise living standards.

b. Population Divisions. The whites, a large minority, are chiefly descendants of Spanish colonists. (In Brazil, most whites are of Portuguese descent.) The whites also include recent immigrants, such as Italians and Germans. Generally, the whites constitute the upper and middle classes. Usually, they own the large estates and occupy high positions in the dominant Roman Catholic Church, in the armed forces, and in the government. The rest of the population consists of a large minority of *mestizos* (people of mixed white and Indian ancestry) and smaller groups of Indians and blacks. These peoples make up the lower classes of city workers and peasants.

c. Illiteracy. While some Latin American countries have literacy rates of 90 percent and above, others have rates as low as 51 percent (Guatemala). The 20th-century trend has been away from church control of education and toward free public schools. However, many children receive no education at all because they begin work at an early age, and because there are not enough schools. In more industrialized countries such as Argentina, Uruguay, Chile, and Costa Rica, illiteracy is low; in less developed lands such as Bolivia, Guatemala, and Haiti, illiteracy is high.

2. Economic Factors

a. Poverty. Latin America is enmeshed in widespread poverty. The average income per person is very low. Great extremes exist between the rich and the poor. Two percent of the people possess 70 percent of the area's wealth. The Latin American masses seek to escape poverty and want more material goods.

b. Agricultural Problems. Most Latin Americans earn their livelihood from agriculture. Yet only 10 percent of the population owns 90 percent of the arable land, much of which is organized into large estates. The *peons*—peasants who work the estates—are practically serfs, many being heavily indebted to the landowners. Reformers have demanded that the large estates be broken up and distributed to the peasants as small family-size farms. In addition to the need for land reform, other problems are primitive equipment, inadequate farming methods, and lack of fertilizer, irrigation, and electrification.

c. One-Product Economies. The wealth of Latin America lies in its mineral resources and agricultural produce: tin in Bolivia; copper in Chile; oil in Mexico and Venezuela; coffee in Brazil, Colombia, Costa Rica, and Guatemala; bananas in Ecuador, Honduras, and Panama. Latin America exports these minerals and foodstuffs, and imports manufactured goods. Its major trading partner is the United States. Most Latin American countries are plagued by economic instability. Any change in the world price of their major export affects their entire economy.

d. Dependence on Foreign Investment. To develop its natural resources and industries, Latin America needs capital. Much of the area lacks a stable, prosperous middle class with funds to invest, however, and many wealthy Latin Americans, fearing revolution, have placed their capital in safe foreign banks. Consequently, Latin America looks for capital and technical know-how to institutions such as the World Bank and to foreign, especially American, investors. Private United States investments in Latin America totaled $29.5 billion in 1985.

Latin America—Annual Per Capita Income

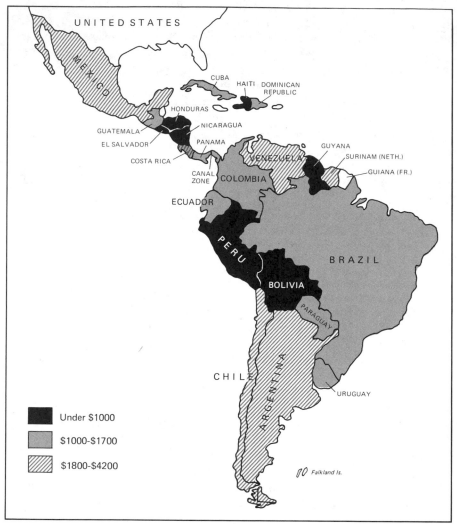

UNITED STATES

MEXICO

CUBA
HAITI DOMINICAN
REPUBLIC
HONDURAS
GUATEMALA
NICARAGUA
EL SALVADOR
PANAMA
COSTA RICA
CANAL
ZONE
COLOMBIA
VENEZUELA
GUYANA
SURINAM (NETH.)
GUIANA (FR.)
ECUADOR

P E R U

B R A Z I L

BOLIVIA

PARAGUAY

CHILE

ARGENTINA

URUGUAY

Falkland Is.

- ■ Under $1000
- $1000-$1700
- $1800-$4200

3. Political Factors

a. Governmental Instability and Military Dictatorships. Latin American nations have democratic constitutions providing for elected executives and legislators. Nevertheless, many Latin American governments are dictatorships. The people lack a democratic tradition, since (1) Spanish colonial rule was autocratic, (2) the masses are poorly educated, (3) the democratically minded middle class is weak, and (4) military leaders have frequently seized the government. Many Latin American nations have been subject to frequent revolutions, but these governmental changes have usually produced few economic and social improvements.

Rocky soil.

Hesse in The St. Louis Globe-Democrat

b. Doubts About Democracy. Latin Americans have had little experience with successful democratic government. Many consider the democratic system weak, easily corrupted, incapable of achieving basic reforms, and subject to manipulation by the wealthy.

COMMUNIST INFLUENCE IN LATIN AMERICA

To expand their influence among the discontented masses of Latin America, local Communist groups have demanded that the workers receive better wages and that the peasants be given their own land. They have stirred up nationalism against "Yankee imperialism" and have urged seizure of foreign-owned properties. The Communists have achieved some following among farm workers, labor unions, college students, and intellectuals.

The Communists have been encouraged by their (1) success under Castro in gaining control of Cuba, (2) use of Cuba to spread Communist influence into other Latin American countries and to stir up an independence movement in Puerto Rico, (3) temporary ascendancy under Marxist-Leninist President Allende in Chile, and (4) influence upon the Sandinista government of Nicaragua.

FACTORS OPPOSING COMMUNIST INFLUENCE

(1) Latin American upper classes—landowners, businesspeople, military leaders, and government officials—have feared the loss of their wealth and power. (2) Many Latin American governments have outlawed the Communist party and have no diplomatic relations with Communist Cuba. (3) The Roman

Catholic Church has condemned communism as antireligious. (4) Many Latin Americans have strong cultural ties to Western nations, especially the United States, France, and Spain. (5) Left-of-center non-Communist groups, determined to achieve reform without totalitarianism, have shown strength. (6) The United States has moved to improve relations and encourage reforms.

CUBA: FROM MILITARY DICTATORSHIP TO COMMUNISM

1. Batista Dictatorship (1952–1959). General *Fulgencio Batista* seized the Cuban government and set up a dictatorship. His regime was marked by corruption and terrorism. Beginning in 1956, Batista faced a rebellion led by *Fidel Castro*. Not yet known as a Communist, Castro promised to restore democracy to Cuba. He gained support among students, peasants, business people, and professional people. Castro waged guerrilla warfare until Batista fled the country. Castro entered Havana and took control.

2. Castro Regime (Since 1959)

a. Denial of Democratic Rights. The Castro government adopted police state practices: suspending the writ of habeas corpus and other civil liberties, stifling press and radio criticism of Castro's policies, refusing to hold free elections, and trying Castro's opponents before military courts without legal safeguards. Over 500,000 Cubans, including former Castro supporters, fled to the United States and other Western Hemisphere nations.

b. Economic Changes. Castro expropriated land from large plantations (chiefly American-owned) for use by the landless peasants under a system of state-controlled cooperatives. Subsequently, Castro expropriated other properties owned by American corporations. In 1960 President Eisenhower responded by halting American imports of Cuban sugar and banning most American exports to Cuba. As its economy deteriorated, Cuba rationed gasoline, clothes, and food and required substantial Soviet aid.

c. Anti-American Attitude. Castro inflamed anti-American sentiment among the Cuban people. He claimed that the United States was imperialist, a supporter of counterrevolutionary forces, and the cause of Cuba's economic woes. Castro denounced the Rio Inter-American Defense Treaty. He challenged America's right to retain its Cuban naval base at Guantanamo Bay. Finally, President Eisenhower in 1961 broke diplomatic relations with Cuba.

d. Communist State. Cuba negotiated an economic pact with the Soviet Union, exchanging Cuban sugar for Soviet manufactured goods, and securing Communist military equipment and technicians. In 1961, for the first time, Castro publicly admitted being a "Marxist-Leninist." He announced plans to transform Cuba into a Communist state.

3. Bay of Pigs Invasion (1961). American-trained Cuban exiles launched a small-scale invasion of Cuba at the *Bay of Pigs.* Although easily crushed by Castro's military forces, the invasion sparked a bitter argument between the Soviet Union and the United States. Premier Nikita Khrushchev demanded that the United States halt its "aggression" against Cuba and warned that the Soviet Union would assist Castro. In reply, President John Kennedy proclaimed American admiration for the Cuban invaders and warned the Soviet Union that the United States would "protect this hemisphere against external aggression."

4. Organization of American States and Cuba (1962). The 21 OAS nations conferred on the problem of Communist Cuba. The conference approved resolutions *(a)* declaring communism incompatible with the principles of the inter-American system, *(b)* warning the peoples of the Western Hemisphere against Communist subversion, and *(c)* removing Castro's Cuba from the Inter-American Defense Board and all other OAS organs.

5. Soviet Missile Bases in Cuba (1962)

a. Crisis. President Kennedy disclosed that the Soviet Union secretly was bringing offensive bombers and missiles into Cuba and building Cuban missile bases—a threat to the security of the Western Hemisphere. The President ordered a quarantine by American naval and air forces on shipments of offensive arms bound for Cuba. He demanded that the Soviets dismantle the Cuban missile bases and withdraw the bombers and missiles. Furthermore, the President warned that if any nuclear missiles were launched from Cuba against the United States, America would reply with a full retaliatory blow against the Soviet Union.

At first, the Soviet Union called the American charges false and labeled the American quarantine "piracy." Then, after several suspenseful days, Khrushchev agreed to dismantle the missile bases and withdraw the offensive weapons. Kennedy agreed to lift the quarantine and pledged not to invade Cuba.

b. Reactions to the Settlement. (1) President Kennedy considered the settlement an honorable accord, not a victory. The President felt relieved that the Soviet offensive weapons were withdrawn in peace. However, the United States is aware that Cuba remains Communist, heavily armed with defensive weapons, and bolstered by Soviet military and technical personnel. (2) Premier Khrushchev called the settlement an example of his policy of peaceful coexistence. He claimed that the American pledge not to invade Cuba ended the need for the missile bases.

6. Communist Cuban Troops in Africa (Since 1975)

a. Angola. In 1975 Cuba sent 15,000 troops to Angola, helping the pro-Soviet faction to gain control of the country. Resenting this intervention, the United States warned Cuba that "we cannot tolerate again a Cuban military adventure anywhere."

b. Ethiopia. In 1977, despite this warning, the Cuban troops in Africa moved to Ethiopia. They assisted the pro-Soviet Ethiopian military regime in battling a Somali rebellion.

7. Soviet Combat Force in Cuba (1979). Check the Index for "Cuba, Soviet force in."

PANAMA: SINCE 1964

(Check the Index.)

DOMINICAN REPUBLIC: FROM DICTATORSHIP TO FREE ELECTIONS

1. Trujillo Dictatorship (1930–1961). General *Rafael Trujillo* seized control of the Dominican Republic, assumed dictatorial rule, suppressed civil liberties, employed terrorism against his enemies, and amassed a tremendous personal fortune. To improve the country, Trujillo built houses, hospitals, schools, and highways, and encouraged industry. In 1961 Trujillo was assassinated by military leaders, supposedly to avenge personal slights.

2. Political Unrest (1961–1965). After Trujillo, the Dominican Republic saw conservative military leaders contend with leftist groups for control. In 1965 the two sides resorted to open civil war.

3. United States and OAS Intervention. President Lyndon Johnson sent American forces into the Dominican Republic—the first direct military intervention by the United States in Latin America in 30 years. Johnson's purposes were to protect American lives and to prevent a Communist takeover. Johnson asserted that "the American nations cannot, must not, and will not permit the establishment of another Communist government in the Western Hemisphere."

In response to a United States request, the OAS established an Inter-American Peace Force. Combining Latin American and United States troops, the OAS army halted the violence in the Dominican Republic.

Many Latin American nations and many domestic critics argued that the Johnson administration had *(a)* exaggerated the danger of a Communist takeover, *(b)* allied the United States with reactionary military forces against forward-looking reformers, and *(c)* earned hemispheric ill will by reviving American intervention in internal Latin American affairs. Administration officials denied these charges, pointing out that the United States *(a)* could more easily prevent than cure a Communist takeover, *(b)* had acted in accordance with the OAS Charter, which permitted intervention to preserve hemispheric security, and *(c)* had welcomed the acceptance of responsibility by the OAS.

4. Subsequent Developments. The Dominican Republic has held a number of presidential elections—all considered relatively honest. The several presidents have sought to improve the economy by attracting tourists and encouraging investments of foreign corporations. Nevertheless, the country faces economic problems, especially high unemployment, considerable inflation, the low world price of sugar—its major export—and the high world price of its imported oil.

LATIN AMERICAN GRIEVANCES AGAINST THE UNITED STATES: A SUMMARY

1. Latin Americans have complained that the United States *(a)* gave them too little foreign aid, *(b)* paid low prices for their exports of raw materials and foodstuffs while charging high prices for their imports of American manufactured goods, *(c)* dominated their economies through its investments, *(d)* supported notorious Latin American dictators such as Batista in Cuba and Trujillo in the Dominican Republic, and *(e)* intervened in internal matters, especially in 1965 in the Dominican Republic.

2. Americans have replied that the United States *(a)* does not have limitless resources and must distribute foreign aid according to need throughout the world, *(b)* determines price according to the economic laws of supply and demand, *(c)* through its investments, has developed the resources of Latin America, at the same time providing employment and paying taxes, *(d)* has had to deal with Latin American dictators, however repugnant, only because they represented official governments, and *(e)* intervened in the Dominican Republic to protect the Western Hemisphere from communism and subsequently received OAS approval for this action.

THE ALLIANCE FOR PROGRESS (1961–1971): A MAJOR UNITED STATES EFFORT TO AID LATIN AMERICA

President Kennedy held that "those who make peaceful revolution impossible will make violent revolution inevitable." Accordingly, he proposed the *Alliance for Progress* to benefit the Latin American masses—not just the privileged few—and thereby eliminate conditions that breed Castro-type revolutions.

1. Plans. In 1961 the United States and the Latin American nations (Cuba excepted) adopted the following program: *(a) Aid.* The Alliance nations agreed to a ten-year, $20 billion aid program for Latin America. Of this sum, the United States was to provide more than half, chiefly as long-term, low-interest loans; the rest was to come from international agencies, Western Europe, Japan, and private capital. *(b) Trade.* The Alliance nations agreed to expand trade and to stabilize prices of Latin America's products, especially coffee and tin. *(c) Reform.* The Alliance nations agreed to improve conditions for the Latin American masses by social and economic reforms: providing free schools for all children, reducing adult illiteracy, eradicating malaria, building public housing, breaking up large estates and giving land to the peasants, and distributing the tax burden fairly.

The Alliance aroused opposition in Latin America from both extremes: left and right. The Communists feared that, if the Alliance improved conditions, they would be less likely to win the support of the masses. The privileged classes feared that if the Alliance achieved its reforms, they would lose their estates and face heavy income taxes.

2. Mixed Record. The United States sharply increased its aid to Latin America. American funds were used for distribution of food and for construction of schools, waterworks, power plants, housing, and highways. These efforts, however, proved to be only a small step toward solving Latin America's massive problems.

On the other hand, *(a)* Latin America did not significantly attract more private American capital, *(b)* most Latin American nations postponed land reforms, *(c)* the prices of most Latin American exports remained low, and *(d)* the per capita GNP (the value of the output of goods and services per person) in Latin America increased only slightly.

In the United States and Latin America, the record of the Alliance for Progress caused considerable disillusionment. Nevertheless, the Alliance received renewed pledges of Latin American support and of United States aid past 1971, the original termination date.

CHILE: FROM MARXIST TO MILITARY RULE

1. The Marxist-Leninist President (1970–1973). *Salvador Allende Gossens,* supported by the Popular Unity coalition of Socialists, Communists, and other leftists, led in a three-person presidential race, winning a popular plurality of 36 percent. He was named president by the Chilean congress even though his supporters were a minority. The congress upheld the Chilean tradition of selecting the first-place finisher.

With socialism as his goal, Allende moved to seize the large estates and distribute the land to peasant cooperatives, to nationalize banks and other businesses, to raise workers' wages while freezing prices, and to expropriate copper mines and other properties, chiefly owned by American companies. Allende affirmed his belief in democracy and permitted non-Marxist parties and news media to exist, but acted to weaken his opponents through legal means. (In 1974, the United States Central Intelligence Agency revealed that, as authorized by the National Security Council, it had conducted undercover activities in Chile, providing funds to keep alive political parties and news media threatened by the Allende government.)

In foreign affairs, Chile resumed diplomatic relations with Castro's Cuba but also proclaimed a policy of cold war neutrality. Allende kept Chile in the OAS and promised to bar any foreign military bases in Chile that might threaten the United States.

By 1973 Allende was unable to govern Chile effectively and to end the economic chaos. He faced political problems: opposition from the parties controlling congress and dissension among the parties in his Popular Unity coalition. Allende also faced economic problems. Chile suffered from food shortages and from severe inflation. The middle and upper classes, constituting half of Chile's population, opposed Allende's expropriation of large estates and nationalization of small businesses. The Allende government was challenged by a series of strikes and demonstrations—all protesting shortages, inflation, and government economic policies.

2. Military Rule (Since 1973). In a swift military coup, marked by bloodshed and the death of Allende, army leaders overthrew the Allende regime and replaced it with a conservative military junta headed by General *Augusto Pinochet Ugarte* as president. The military thus broke a 46-year Chilean tradition of nonintervention in political affairs, believing it necessary to liberate Chile "from the Marxist yoke."

On the economic front, the junta acted to abolish food and price controls, to freeze workers' wages temporarily, and to return most small businesses to their former owners. The junta promised to restore illegally expropriated lands to their former owners and, while retaining Chilean ownership of the copper mines, to negotiate fairly with the American companies regarding compensation for their former holdings. The junta's policies temporarily improved economic conditions and spurred economic growth. However, in the early 1980s, during a worldwide recession, Chile's economy deteriorated and President Pinochet's military government faced serious protest demonstrations.

On the political front, the junta proceeded to outlaw the Marxist political parties that had supported Allende, to abolish the Workers Confederation, which was chiefly Communist-controlled, to recess congress, to prohibit political activity, to end diplomatic relations with Castro's Cuba, to control the press, and to imprison suspected leftists.

In 1977 Chile was condemned for violating human rights by the UN Human Rights Commission and was criticized by President Carter. The junta moved somewhat to improve its human rights record by releasing many political prisoners, abolishing its secret police, and granting labor unions, under certain conditions, the right to strike.

NICARAGUA: FROM DICTATORSHIP TO POLITICAL UNREST

1. The Somoza Regime (To 1979). The Somoza family for almost 50 years ruled Nicaragua as a military dictatorship. The Somozas manipulated elections, crushed political opposition, and employed terror against their enemies. The Somozas furthered Nicaragua's economic growth by building roads, improving port facilities, and developing hydroelectric power. They invested in various business enterprises and amassed a vast family fortune. In foreign policy, the Somoza regime was strongly pro-United States and anti-Communist.

General *Anastasio Somoza Debayle,* who became president in 1967, felt the full force of opposition to dictatorial rule from workers, business leaders, students, professionals, Catholic clergy, and radical Marxists. The opposition was centered in the *Sandinista National Liberation Front*—named after reform leader *Augusto Sandino* who was reputedly killed in 1934 by Somoza orders. Although the Sandinista movement contained many moderates, it was dominated by leftist Marxist leaders. In the 1970s, Sandinista guerrillas, some trained in Cuba and armed with Cuban weapons, mounted attacks to topple the Somoza regime. Nicaragua experienced civil war.

2. Revolution and Unrest. In 1979 the United States, realizing that Somoza's power was fading and fearing "another Cuba" in the Western Hemisphere, moved to shape Nicaraguan developments toward moderate, democratic policies. The United States sought to have the Sandinista movement give greater recognition to its moderate elements. After Somoza had fled Nicaragua, the Sandinistas named a five-member junta to govern the country. The new regime dissolved Congress, seized the Somoza estates and businesses, and pledged to rebuild the country. It requested and received humanitarian and economic aid from the United States.

3. The Reagan Administration and the Sandinistas. By 1982, American officials believed that the Sandinista junta was moving to create a leftist, Marxist regime. The junta had postponed elections, suspended publication of an opposition newspaper, and built up the Nicaraguan military. The Reagan administration ended financial aid to the Nicaraguan regime. Instead, it provided aid to Nicaraguan opponents of the Sandinista regime in the hope of countering the junta's tilt to the left.

The United States also provided covert aid, through the CIA, to anti-Sandinista guerrillas based in Honduras and Costa Rica. These guerrillas were generally called *contras,* for "counterrevolutionaries." President Reagan called them "freedom fighters" for opposing a Marxist government that ruled by military might.

In 1983, Congress approved $24 million in aid to the contras. It refused further aid the next year after hearing charges that the CIA had been involved in mining Nicaraguan harbors. Under the *Boland Amendment* of 1984, Congress forbade both direct and indirect aid to the rebels. Money and supplies continued to reach the contras from the United States and other countries, however, often coming through private sources that were encouraged and monitored by the Reagan administration.

In 1984, Nicaraguans elected a Sandinista, *Daniel Ortega Saavedra,* as president. Nicaraguan opposition leaders and the Reagan administration charged that the elections had been rigged in favor of the Sandinistas.

4. The Reagan Administration and the Contras. In 1985, President Reagan imposed a trade embargo on Nicaragua. He also secured from Congress $27 million in nonmilitary aid for the contras. But Congress turned down the President's request for military support and continued its ban on such aid.

Nicaragua brought charges of aggression against the United States in the World Court, a UN agency. The United States refused to recognize the court's jurisdiction. In 1986 the court ruled that the United States had committed acts of aggression against Nicaragua and had an obligation to pay for damages. The United States vetoed two UN Security Council resolutions urging it to obey the court, and officials said they would ignore the court's ruling.

The United States stepped up aid to countries bordering Nicaragua. It built new airfields and other military facilities in the region and carried out joint maneuvers with Honduran forces. In 1986, after President Reagan warned that the United States faced "the reality of a Soviet military beachhead in Nicaragua," Congress approved both military and nonmilitary aid for the contras. The administration assigned the CIA to oversee contra activity.

In the months after the Congressional decision to aid the contras, major controversies erupted. Congress began investigations to determine (1) whether the CIA or other parts of the United States government had aided the contras in violation of the Boland Amendment between 1984 and 1986, (2) how profits from the secret sale of United States arms to Iran had been diverted to the contras (see page 646), and (3) whether individuals or groups among the contras had engaged in drug smuggling and other illegal activities.

The contras themselves are an alliance of rival factions, ranging politically from moderate to ultraconservative. Under United States pressure, the contras united in 1986 to form the United Nicaraguan Opposition, or UNO.

EL SALVADOR: POVERTY, CIVIL WAR, AND INTERNATIONAL INVOLVEMENT

1. Background—The Christian Democratic Regime. El Salvador is a small, densely populated nation in Central America with a wide disparity in living standards. The large landowners and military leaders are at the top, and the impoverished masses of peasants, farm workers, and urban workers are at the bottom. Until 1979, El Salvador was governed for many years by a succession of military regimes that had little concern for the welfare of the people. Moderate army officers overthrew a right-wing military regime in 1979. After a year of unrest, the moderate officers named a civilian, *José Napoleón Duarte*, as the head of government. The government pursued a program of basic reforms: nationalizing banks and foreign trade, distributing land to the peasants, strengthening control over the army to prevent excessive violence and human rights violations, and scheduling elections in March 1982 for an assembly to draw up a constitution and name an interim president. Duarte, a Christian Democrat, occupied the political center in El Salvador and was supported by economic and military aid from the United States.

2. Rightists, Leftists, and Centrists. The centrist Christian Democrats were opposed by both sides of the political spectrum. The extreme right maintained its own paramilitary forces and used "death squads" to assassinate political opponents. *Roberto D'Aubuisson*, leader of the extreme right-wing Nationalist Republican Alliance, pledged to exterminate the leftist guerrillas and to scrap the banking and land reforms. The extreme left consisted of several guerrilla groups united in the *National Liberation Front* and dominated by Marxists. The guerrillas employed terror against government supporters and attacks against government forces—launching a civil war that in its first two years took more than 30,000 lives. Arms for the guerrillas, American officials charged, were coming from Communist bloc nations and were being funneled into El Salvador through

Cuba and Nicaragua—a charge denied by those countries. The guerrillas boycotted and sought unsuccessfully to sabotage the March 1982 elections.

3. Duarte's Ups and Downs. In the 1982 election, although Duarte's Christian Democrats won 40 percent of the vote and emerged as the largest political party, rightist parties won a majority of seats in the constituent assembly. The assembly replaced Duarte as head of the government and repealed parts of the land-reform laws. Duarte continued to have strong United States backing, and in 1984 he was elected president of El Salvador. The following year his Christian Democrats won a majority of seats in a new national assembly.

Duarte faced three main problems: *(a)* fighting the leftist insurgency, *(b)* establishing civilian control over El Salvador's military forces, and *(c)* restoring a badly damaged economy. After seven years of civil war, the death toll had risen to more than 60,000 people. Tentative peace talks between the rebels and the government failed to produce any settlement. United States aid of more than $600 million strengthened the Salvadorean military, which retained a large degree of independence from civilian control. United States leaders repeatedly urged the military not to interfere in politics. Meanwhile, economic problems grew more serious. Trade unions staged mass demonstrations to protest the government's economic policies, while supporters of the government marched in counterdemonstrations.

PRESIDENT REAGAN'S CARIBBEAN BASIN INITIATIVE

Prompted by developments in El Salvador, President Reagan in 1982 proposed a broad plan to improve the economic well-being of 28 nations in or bordering the Caribbean Sea. He warned that if the United States did not act "decisively in the defense of freedom, new Cubas will arise." Reagan's *Caribbean Basin Initiative* plan consisted of (1) substantially increasing economic aid, (2) except for textiles and apparel, eliminating for 12 years all United States import duties on Caribbean products—a "free trade" policy, (3) encouraging American investment in the Caribbean nations by granting tax incentives, and (4) offering technical assistance to the private sector in the Caribbean nations.

President Reagan's program was favorably received by leaders of most Caribbean nations. It faced criticism in the United States from (1) members of Congress who questioned additional funds for the Caribbean while social programs were being cut at home, and (2) labor and business leaders who feared that increased Caribbean imports would mean fewer jobs for Americans and more competition for American manufacturers.

Congress passed legislation implementing the Caribbean Basin Initiative in 1983. In its first two years of operation, according to administration officials, the plan helped to create some 35,000 new jobs in the Caribbean Basin. However, economic troubles caused United States firms to close down some major operations (banana plantations, bauxite plants, and refineries) in the Caribbean, causing other jobs to be lost.

THE NATIONAL BIPARTISAN COMMISSION ON CENTRAL AMERICA

In 1983 President Reagan established a 12-member bipartisan commission, headed by former Secretary of State Henry Kissinger, to suggest long-term policies to protect United States interests in Central America. The commission's report, delivered in 1984, warned that United States security was endangered by "Soviet and Cuban efforts to penetrate" Central America. The commission's recommendations (some qualified by reservations) were: (1) a five-year economic aid program for the region—to cost $8 billion, (2) a "substantial" increase in military aid to El Salvador—to be linked to progress in protecting human rights, and (3) a series of economic and social initiatives—to increase food aid, further literacy, improve health care, and build housing.

The commission's report was viewed generally as supporting Reagan administration policies, including aid to Nicaraguan rebels battling the Sandinista regime. The report faced considerable criticism in Congress—mainly from Democrats.

THE AMERICAN-LED INVASION OF GRENADA (1983)

Grenada, an island nation in the eastern Caribbean, is the smallest country in the Western Hemisphere. Formerly a British possession, Grenada attained independence in 1974 as part of the Commonwealth. By a nonviolent coup in 1979, a leftist, friendly to Cuba, became prime minister. His regime enlisted the aid of Cuban workers, technicians, and soldiers to build a major airport. United States leaders criticized the project, arguing that the airport might be used by large Communist military jets. Grenadian leaders said the airport's purpose was to open Grenada to large-scale tourism.

In October 1983, the Grenadian regime was overthrown by hard-line Marxists who killed the prime minister and other leaders. A few days later, before dawn on October 25, 1983, about 7000 United States troops, together with a small Caribbean force, invaded Grenada. The United States asserted that the invasion (1) had been requested by a five-nation group called the Organization of Eastern Caribbean States, which considered the hard-line Marxists as aggressive and a threat to the region's stability, and (2) conformed to the OAS Charter permitting "collective action" against threats to "peace and security." The Reagan administration called the invading force a "rescue mission" and said its goals were to (1) protect some 1000 Americans on Grenada—mainly students at a medical school—and keep them from being seized as hostages, (2) restore order and democracy on Grenada, and (3) forestall Soviet-Cuban plans to use Grenada to "export terrorism and undermine democracy."

The invasion quickly succeeded, and most Grenadians seemed pleased. Elsewhere in the world, there was widespread criticism. Major NATO allies deplored the intervention. The UN General Assembly condemned it. A Security Council resolution "deeply deploring" the invasion was vetoed by the United States. Within the United States, many Americans hailed the invasion as a demonstration of United States resolve against communism. Others criticized it as unnecessary and morally wrong.

Moderates backed by the United States took control of Grenada and organized elections. As a result of those elections, held in 1984, *Herbert Blaize* became prime minister at the head of a centrist coalition. Blaize invited President Reagan to visit the island and welcomed him warmly in 1986, after the last United States troops had withdrawn. Fourteen people, described as hard-line Marxists, were convicted of murder in connection with the 1983 coup.

——————————— **MULTIPLE-CHOICE QUESTIONS** ———————————

1. A major problem in the establishment of peace immediately following World War II was the (a) extreme difficulty in reconciling the goals of the victors (b) refusal of the defeated powers to sign the terms of surrender (c) policies of nonalignment adopted by the emerging nations (d) international agreements that have weakened the role of the nation state.

2. Which came first in postwar Germany? (a) admission of West Germany to NATO (b) Berlin blockade (c) building of the Berlin Wall (d) Potsdam Conference.

3. Which was a result of both World War I and World War II? (a) All of Germany was placed under occupation by Allied armies. (b) The United States joined its allies in collecting reparations from Germany. (c) Germany was forced to give up all its African colonies. (d) Germany was forced to transfer territory to Poland.

4. The city of Berlin is located (a) within East Germany (b) within West Germany (c) on the border between East Germany and West Germany (d) on the border between East Germany and Poland.

5. Khrushchev wanted to drive the Western powers from West Berlin because that city was (a) traditionally Communist (b) a valuable seaport (c) NATO military headquarters (d) a showcase of democracy and capitalism behind the Iron Curtain.

6. Western determination to remain in West Berlin was based upon (a) the failure of the 1948–1949 airlift (b) the friendship given to the Western powers by Berliners throughout the 20th century (c) an effort to prevent the return of nazism in West Berlin (d) the recognition that weakness there would encourage Soviet aggression.

7. America gave economic aid to West Germany after World War II to help (a) stop the spread of communism (b) strengthen Germany against France (c) socialize German industry (d) raise the German standard of living above prewar levels.

8. Nazi leaders were charged at Nuremberg with (a) losing the war (b) destroying the German Republic (c) inventing missiles (d) committing crimes against humanity.

9. The Ruhr Valley, considered the industrial heart of Europe, is located in (a) East Germany (b) West Germany (c) France (d) Poland.

10. The Arab attack upon the newly proclaimed state of Israel in 1948 (a) was approved by the UN General Assembly (b) was halted by a UN emergency force (c) sought to destroy the new state (d) sought to create a unified Arab nation.

11. Which represents the *major* goal of Israeli foreign policy? (a) ending Communist influence in the Middle East (b) destroying the Organization of Petroleum Exporting Countries (OPEC) (c) gaining control of both sides of the Suez Canal (d) assuring the physical and economic security of Israel.

12. The waterway that has been a trouble spot in the relations between Egypt and Israel is the (a) Mediterranean Sea (b) Dead Sea (c) Jordan River (d) Gulf of Aqaba.

13. American foreign policy in the Middle East has sought (a) a confrontation with the Soviet Union (b) a compromise settlement of Arab-Israeli issues so as to end the recurrent crises (c) peace in the area enforced by American marines (d) an end to American investments in Arab countries.

14. Which best accounts for the lack of unity among the Arab nations of the Middle East? (a) language differences (b) the interference of major world powers (c) nomadic tribal allegiances (d) conflicting economic and political interests.

15. Several Arab nations in the Middle East have a position of power in world politics primarily because they (a) have developed a sophisticated nuclear weapons technology (b) have developed a highly trained labor force (c) control access to major world transportation routes (d) possess abundant supplies of an essential natural resource.

16. Which is a basic cause of unrest throughout Asia? (a) complete control by European powers (b) lack of important natural resources (c) labor shortage (d) low standard of living.

17. Where does the government of Nationalist China maintain its headquarters? (a) Peking (b) Taiwan (c) Hong Kong (d) Singapore.

18. Since the end of the Cultural Revolution, what has characterized China's foreign policy? (a) supporting the Soviet Union in the UN (b) improving relations with the United States (c) offering aid to SEATO (d) joining in an alliance with India.

19. What was a major point that created disunity between Maoist China and the Soviet Union? (a) Mao Tse-tung's rejection of Marxism (b) Soviet criticism of India (c) the downgrading of Lenin (d) China's claim to territory seized from it by Czarist Russia.

20. On which issue have the Soviet Union and Communist China agreed? (a) the ultimate triumph of communism (b) the pooling of nuclear armaments (c) the validity of 19th-century treaties between Russia and China (d) the leadership of the Communist world.

21. One of the items below is a main topic and three are subtopics. Which item is the main topic? (a) military uses of nuclear energy (b) expansion of communism in Southeast Asia (c) friction between the Soviet Union and China (d) problems of international peace and security.

22. Our efforts to cultivate friendship with Japan were based chiefly upon (a) our desire to import Japanese products (b) our regret for having atom-bombed Hiroshima and Nagasaki (c) the influence of Japanese-American war veterans (d) our fear of further Communist expansion in the Far East.

23. Relations between India and Communist China were strained by (a) Communist China's refusal to provide nuclear weapons to India (b) India's efforts to spread Hinduism (c) Communist China's suppression of the Tibetan revolt (d) Communist China's alliance with Sri Lanka.

24. In recent years, India (a) agreed to divide Kashmir with Pakistan (b) refused to recognize Communist China (c) joined SEATO (d) secured Soviet support before waging war for the independence of Bangladesh.

25. Which statement is most clearly supported by the position of Jews in the Soviet Union, and relations between India and Pakistan? (a) Society has come to accept differing points of view. (b) The effects of World War II have remained fresh in the minds of society. (c) Religion continues to influence people's actions and behavior. (d) Decisions of political leaders are determined by actions of the United Nations.

26. Which statement best explains India's decision to develop nuclear weapons? (a) India's economy could easily afford the cost of developing nuclear capability. (b) India felt other nations which possess nuclear capability were a threat to its security. (c) The dominant religions in India stress military and national pride. (d) The United Nations encouraged India to develop nuclear weapons.

27. After World War II, United States troops occupied part of Korea that had formerly been controlled by (a) Germany (b) China (c) Japan (d) the Soviet Union.

28. Which event in Korea occurred *first?* (a) North Korea's invasion of South Korea (b) the creation of the Republic of Korea (c) intervention of Chinese Communist troops in Korea (d) division of Korea at the 38th parallel.

29. In 1950, although Congress did not declare war, President Truman sent American troops into battle in Korea. The President's authority was based upon his position as (a) head of his political party (b) leader of the free-world nations (c) commander in chief of the armed forces (d) interpreter of the Monroe Doctrine.

30. Which issue was the chief cause of delay in negotiating a truce in Korea? (a) the UN resolution calling Communist China an aggressor (b) the boundary line between North and South Korea (c) the exchange of war prisoners (d) the status of Taiwan.

31. Following the Korean truce (a) Korea was unified (b) Nationalist China obtained Korea (c) Communist influence in Korea was ended (d) Korea remained divided.

32. Which European country was directly involved in the civil war in Indochina from 1946 to 1954? (a) Great Britain (b) France (c) Italy (d) the Netherlands.

33. Which is the most accurate statement concerning United States involvement in the Vietnam conflict? (a) Our involvement resulted from a declaration of war by Congress. (b) Our European allies strongly urged large-scale involvement. (c) Military preparedness of the United States encouraged involvement. (d) Public opinion in the United States became divided over involvement.

34. The 1973 Paris Peace Agreement for Vietnam did *not* include which provision? (a) withdrawal of all American troops from South Vietnam (b) withdrawal of all Hanoi troops from South Vietnam (c) return of all Americans held as prisoners of war (d) Vietnam reunification by peaceful means only.

35. As a result of United States military involvement in Southeast Asia, many members of Congress have attempted to (a) delegate additional powers to the President (b) place greater responsibility for foreign policy on the secretary of state (c) reassert the role of Congress in the formulation of foreign policy (d) eliminate the requirement of a vote of Congress for a declaration of war.

36. The Korean and Vietnam conflicts were similar in that both (a) represented United States efforts to contain communism (b) involved unilateral military action on the part of the United States (c) brought the United States into direct military conflict with China (d) were military defeats for the United States.

37. Which factor had the greatest influence upon the decisions of the United States government to enter the Spanish-American War and to withdraw from the Vietnam conflict? (a) campus demonstrations (b) pressure from large corporations (c) power of the press (d) desire to gain complete victory.

38. Which was the primary effect of the Vietnam conflict on later United States foreign policy decisions? (a) return to a policy of isolationism (b) increased emphasis on the United States military as the world's police force (c) reassessment of commitments to other nations (d) acceptance of the expansion of Chinese influence.

39. "The United States will participate in the defense and development of allies and friends, but we will not and cannot undertake all the defense of the free nations. . . . We will help where it makes a real difference and is considered in our interests." This statement most nearly meant that the United States would no longer (a) become involved in international conflicts (b) police the world single-handedly (c) act as the political leader of the free world (d) finance the economic development of emerging nations.

40. Which nation in the Far East has achieved the greatest degree of industrial development? (a) Burma (b) India (c) China (d) Japan.

41. The author of the statement, "The Japanese are creating their own version of the 20th century," suggests that the Japanese are (a) replacing Japanese values with values from the Western world (b) preserving the cultural patterns of their ancestors (c) integrating Western technology with Japanese culture (d) exporting Japanese-made goods.

42. Which statement would be most *difficult* to prove? (a) Japan's emperors have reigned but have seldom ruled. (b) The workers of the United States are better workers than those of Japan. (c) In the post-World War II period, the United States was the source of much cultural borrowing by the Japanese. (d) Japanese technology today is more advanced than it was in the 1940s.

43. Which has been a *major* obstacle to economic development in Latin America? (a) shortages of unskilled labor (b) shortage of investment capital (c) lack of markets (d) insufficient natural resources.

44. By joining the Organization of American States, the United States (a) achieved cooperation with Canada (b) abandoned the Good Neighbor Policy (c) achieved economic control over the Western Hemisphere (d) reaffirmed its rejection of the Roosevelt Corollary to the Monroe Doctrine.

45. The term "revolution of rising expectations" refers to the (a) desire of Communists to take over more of the world (b) desire of people in developing nations to raise their standards of living (c) demand of workers around the world for collective bargaining (d) hope of the United States to improve relations with China.

46. An important reason for the quarantine ordered by President Kennedy in the Cuban missile crisis of 1962 was to (a) protect refugees escaping from Cuba (b) protect the security of the United States (c) prevent a Cuban invasion of the Dominican Republic (d) prevent Communist China from shipping weapons to Cuba.

47. A unique feature of the Alliance for Progress was the degree to which it required Latin American countries to (a) accept United States military bases (b) make trade concessions for products from the United States (c) institute basic reform programs (d) repress local Communist movements.

48. Since World War II, United States foreign policy toward Latin America has been characterized by (a) approval of Communist states (b) programs to increase economic and technical aid (c) frequent military intervention in political revolutions (d) attempts to secure guarantees of religious freedom.

49. Which situation in developing nations most often hinders efforts to raise their standards of living? (a) continuation of high population growth (b) existence of widespread disease and starvation (c) inability of scientists to significantly increase crop yields (d) reluctance of developing nations to adopt Western technology.

50. Many governments in developing countries are controlled by the military because the military is (a) usually in favor of rapid change (b) supported by democratic political parties (c) usually the most organized and efficient institution (d) dominated by officers who are members of the wealthy class.

51. The European Common Market, the North Atlantic Treaty Organization, and the Organization of American States were formed to (a) provide a way for smaller nations to protect themselves from domination by larger nations (b) serve the self-interest of member nations through regional associations (c) bring about political unity within each grouping (d) decrease cultural and political differences among nations.

52. Which information about country X would be most useful to the head of a government establishing a foreign policy toward country X? (a) an analysis of the national resources and goals of country X (b) a file containing the major public statements made by the leaders of country X concerning their nation's foreign policies (c) an analysis by religious leaders of the major religious groups and beliefs of the people of country X (d) a newspaper report summarizing the treaties and international agreements of country X.

53. Many nations have considered Castro's Cuba a threat because the Castro regime (a) overthrew a democratic Cuban government when taking control (b) has seriously hindered trade among countries of the Western Hemisphere (c) has supported revolutions in various parts of the world (d) has refused to sell sugar or tobacco to industrialized nations.

54. "The lesson of imperial Britain is a lesson for contemporary America. Like the United States today, Britain stood at the center of a great empire." Which is the most valid conclusion that can be drawn from this statement? (a) The influence of domestic politics on United States foreign policy will decrease. (b) The United States will probably embark on a foreign policy of imperialism. (c) The United States will probably expand its naval power. (d) The United States may become less influential in world affairs.

55. Two Communist nations that engaged in a limited war against each other were (a) Iran and Iraq (b) Lebanon and Syria (c) China and Vietnam (d) Laos and Burma.

56. The Soviet invasion of Afghanistan was intended to (a) halt Afghan border raids into the Soviet Union (b) prevent Afghan guerrillas from overthrowing a pro-Soviet Afghan regime (c) scare Pakistan from accepting American military aid (d) secure Soviet use of Afghan ports on the Indian Ocean.

57. Two nations that have contested control of the Golan Heights are (a) Iraq and Iran (b) Syria and Jordan (c) Israel and Egypt (d) Israel and Syria.

58. The Iraqi nuclear facility was destroyed by an airplane attack from (a) France (b) Israel (c) Iran (d) Syria.

59. The Carter Doctrine was designed to protect (a) the Persian Gulf region from Soviet control (b) Central America from Fidel Castro (c) Taiwan from mainland China (d) Lebanon from Syrian control.

60. The Central American nation that overthrew the Somoza regime and established a leftist government is (a) El Salvador (b) Nicaragua (c) Honduras (d) Guatemala.

——————————— **CHRONOLOGY QUESTIONS** ———————————

Harry Truman	John Kennedy	Richard Nixon	Jimmy Carter
Dwight Eisenhower	Lyndon Johnson	Gerald Ford	Ronald Reagan

For each of the following events in American foreign affairs, select the President in whose administration the event took place.

1. A quarantine was placed upon ships bound for Cuba with offensive weapons.
2. An army general was dismissed by the commander in chief on grounds of insubordination.
3. Congress overrode the President's veto and enacted the War Powers Resolution.
4. Air strikes were first ordered against North Vietnamese military targets.

5. American troops were sent into the Dominican Republic.
6. American forces were not returned to Vietnam despite Hanoi's violation of the peace agreement by forcibly seizing control of South Vietnam.
7. The Caribbean Basin Initiative proposed American economic aid for friendly nations in that area.
8. Diplomatic relations were broken with Cuba.
9. The Camp David summit meeting reached two accords for Middle East peace.
10. An airlift was used to break the Berlin blockade.
11. A Presidential visit to China began a period of improved Sino-American relations.
12. The Alliance for Progress was inaugurated to improve conditions in Latin America.

———————————————— **MATCHING QUESTIONS** ————————————————

Column A	*Column B*
1. Prime Minister of India	a. Yuri Andropov
2. President of Nationalist China	b. Menachem Begin
3. President of Egypt	c. Fidel Castro
4. Chancellor of West Germany	d. Chou En-lai
5. President of South Korea	e. Indira Gandhi
6. Chairman of Communist party of China	f. Chun Doo Hwan
7. President of North Vietnam	g. Chiang Kai-shek
8. Prime Minister of Israel	h. Henry Kissinger
9. United States negotiator of Vietnam peace agreement	i. Ho Chi Minh
10. Premier of Cuba	j. Anwar al-Sadat
	k. Helmut Schmidt
	l. Rafael Trujillo
	m. Mao Tse-tung

———————————————— **ESSAY QUESTIONS** ————————————————

1. United States foreign policy is most often defined by what the policymakers say is our national interest. Throughout history our national interest has been influenced by and, at times, dictated by the actions of other nations. *(a)* For *each* of the following regions, describe *one* way in which the national interest of the United States has been involved: (1) Europe (2) Latin America (3) Middle East (4) Far East. *(b)* For *one* region, discuss to what extent a United States foreign policy decision has had a positive or negative effect on the United States national interest. You may discuss both positive and negative effects. *(c)* Discuss *two* reasons why the United States, since World War II, has increasingly used joint actions with other nations in attempting to solve international problems.

2. Discuss American foreign policy toward *either* Germany *or* Japan from 1930 to the present. Include in your answer the following topics: *(a) one* cause for ill-feeling, during the period from 1930 to 1941, between the United States and the country you have selected *(b)* a major aim of United States policy toward that country fol-

lowing World War II *(c)* *two* specific American attempts to carry out the aim given in your answer to part *(b)*.

3. "Who does not see, then, that the Pacific Ocean, its shores, its islands, and the vast regions beyond, will become the chief theater of events in the world's great hereafter?"—Senator William H. Seward (1852)

   Discuss *three* events or developments in Asia or the Pacific region since 1898 that indicate that Senator Seward was correct in his prediction that this region would become increasingly important in history.

4. To understand the problem of Vietnam, Americans should know the history of that country and of our involvement there. *(a)* Explain *two* reasons why the Communists in Vietnam were able to win popular support against French rule. *(b)* State *two* agreements reached at the Geneva Conference of 1954 regarding Vietnam. *(c)* Trace the development of United States involvement in Vietnam by describing *one* action of each of the following Presidents: (1) Kennedy (2) Johnson (3) Nixon. *(d)* Discuss *one* argument supporting and *one* argument opposing United States involvement in Vietnam.

5. The United States has faced serious problems in its relations with Latin America during recent years. *(a)* Describe *two* developments affecting the relations between Cuba and the United States since 1898. *(b)* Show how policies of the United States since 1898 toward *two* Latin American countries other than Cuba have been criticized by Latin America. *(c)* Describe *two* policies of the United States during the 20th century that have gained favor in Latin America.

6. The majority of the people in Latin America live in poverty. Some Latin Americans contend that their poverty is the result of the actions of industrialized nations. *(a)* Cite *two* factors that may lead to people living in poverty. For *each* factor mentioned, describe *one* way in which that factor may have helped to cause poverty in Latin America. *(b)* Describe *one* action taken by Latin Americans to raise their standard of living. *(c)* Tell how this action taken affected the area's relations with one or more of the industrialized nations.

7. Agree or disagree with *each* of the following statements and give *two* reasons to support your opinion: *(a)* The dispute between the Soviet Union and Communist China has both ideological and nationalistic roots. *(b)* Germany will remain a divided nation for the foreseeable future. *(c)* The Middle East will have peace only after the Arab nations accept the existence of Israel. *(d)* The problems of Latin America were not caused and cannot be solved by the United States alone. *(e)* From its experiences in Vietnam, the United States should learn many lessons. *(f)* By the mid-1970s, the United States was turning away from the role of world policeman.

8. The following paragraph is a model representing events that led to war:

   A long series of minor conflicts strained relations between *A* and *B*. Using all means available to them, molders of public opinion on each side aroused hostile feelings. The public on each side was only partially informed. As a result of limited information, each side increased its bitterness toward the other. An event took place which triggered strong emotional reactions and demands for war. Public officials were caught up in the excitement and gave in to demands for military action. War followed.

   (a) Select any *two* wars and, using specific events, discuss the extent to which the model does or does not apply to *each* war chosen. *(b)* For *one* of the wars discussed in *(a)*, discuss possible events or actions that might have prevented the war.

9. The military government of Omega has been in power since January, when it overthrew the democratically elected president in a bloodless coup. The new president, General Hector Ramir, is demanding that United States corporations which hold in-

vestments and properties in Omega pay back taxes to his government.

The corporations have so far refused to yield to General Ramir's demands, with the result that the general has given the corporations 30 days in which to meet his demands. Should the corporations refuse, Ramir has been authorized to seize and nationalize the properties and assets of the United States corporations. The corporations have appealed to the United States State Department and the President for assistance.

(a) Based on the situation and your knowledge of foreign affairs, judge the seriousness of the threat in terms of the legitimate interests of the United States government.

(b) In its response to the appeals of the corporations, the United States government would probably decide on an immediate action to take, along with a series of follow-up actions if the immediate action did not result in the desired outcome.

(1) From the list of possible actions below, select the *one* which you think the United States government should take as the immediate action and indicate the outcome the U.S. government would desire from this action.

(2) If the immediate action does not result in the desired outcome, consider the actions below and indicate which further actions might be taken. In your answer, describe the decisions that would be involved. Support your choices by citing specific historical examples of similar decision-making in the handling of foreign affairs.

A. Do nothing.	D. Invoke economic sanctions.
B. Intervene with armed forces.	E. Request assistance from the UN.
C. Conduct bilateral negotiations.	F. Break diplomatic relations.

PART 5. The United States Is Concerned With Scientific Developments

NUCLEAR ENERGY

NUCLEAR ENERGY: FOR HUMANITY TO USE

1. Military Uses for Mass Destruction. The single *atom bomb* (A-bomb) dropped on Hiroshima in 1945 contained about two pounds of uranium and had the explosive power of 20,000 pounds of TNT. It killed or injured 130,000 people and destroyed 60 percent of the city. Subsequently, scientists developed the *hydrogen bomb* (H-bomb), which can generate up to several thousand times the explosive power of the Hiroshima bomb. A single hydrogen bomb can wipe out all life within a 60–100-mile radius.

The destructiveness of nuclear weapons results from their explosive blast, tremendous heat, and radioactivity, which can contaminate whole areas. Widespread fear exists that a nuclear war could mean the end of civilization.

2. Peaceful Uses for Mass Benefit. Atomic scientists devised methods to control nuclear reactions and utilize the tremendous heat to change water into steam. In turn, steam can be used to propel boats and to generate electricity. The United States possesses a fleet of atomic-powered surface ships and submarines and a number of atomic-powered plants for the production of electricity. (For opposition to the use of nuclear power plants, check the Index.)

Atomic scientists also produced radioactive chemical substances called *isotopes.* These have significant uses (1) in *medicine,* to diagnose body ills, (2) in *agriculture,* to study plant growth and to preserve foods, and (3) in *industry,* to measure the flow of oil in pipelines and to uncover flaws in metal.

Within the United States *(a)* the *Department of Energy* is responsible for research and development of nuclear and other energy supplies, and *(b)* the *Nuclear Regulatory Commission* (NRC) oversees the use of nuclear materials.

3. Nations Possessing Nuclear Power. The United States led the way in developing nuclear energy, exploding the first atomic bomb in 1945. Other nations followed: The Soviet Union in 1949, Great Britain in 1952, France in 1960, Communist China in 1964, and India in 1974. A number of other nations, scientists believe, possess the technical know-how to become nuclear powers.

The United States and the Soviet Union—the two superpowers of today— each has more than enough nuclear weapons and delivery systems to inflict upon the other incredible death and destruction. The two superpowers have been deterred somewhat from provoking each other into a major war because they realize that they live in the shadow of a nuclear "balance of terror."

FIRST EFFORT FOR INTERNATIONAL CONTROL: A FAILURE

1. United States Proposes the Baruch Plan. To 1949 the United States held a monopoly over nuclear weapons. *Bernard Baruch,* the American representative to the *UN Atomic Energy Commission,* proposed international control according to the following generous plan: The United States would destroy its atom bombs and share its technical know-how with other nations on condition that an international authority *(a)* supervise the use of atomic energy for only peaceful purposes, and *(b)* be permitted unlimited inspection of atomic facilities without the restrictions of the Big Five veto in the UN Security Council.

2. The Soviets Reject the Baruch Plan. The Soviet Union criticized the Baruch Plan, especially the proposals to eliminate the veto power and to provide unlimited inspection. In the Security Council in 1948, the Soviet Union vetoed the Baruch Plan. Unrestricted by any international controls, the Soviet Union exploded its own atom bomb in 1949, and ended the United States monopoly. Thereafter, both nations continued to develop and test nuclear weapons.

EFFORTS TO HALT NUCLEAR BOMB TESTS: A PARTIAL SUCCESS

In the mid-1950s the people of the world became increasingly fearful of the rising level of radioactivity resulting from nuclear weapons testing. Their fears moved the Soviet Union, the United States, and Great Britain to seek agreement for halting nuclear tests.

1. Conflicting Proposals for Halting Nuclear Tests

The Soviets proposed the immediate cessation of nuclear tests without any provision for enforcement. The Western powers rejected an unpoliced ban. Instead, they proposed a test ban coupled with a system of inspection and control. Western leaders feared that the Soviets could violate an unpoliced ban without the free world's knowledge. The Soviet Union vehemently rejected the Western proposal as a plot to establish, on Soviet territory, spy rings disguised as inspection stations.

In 1961 the United States proposed a treaty to ban nuclear tests that could be detected without on-site inspection, but to exclude underground blasts, since these could be confused with earthquakes and therefore could not be detected from far away. Two years later, the Soviets agreed to this American proposal.

2. Limited Nuclear Test Ban Treaty (1963)

a. Provisions. The Big Three powers (1) agreed not to conduct nuclear tests in the atmosphere, in space, and under water (these tests can be detected, by air-sampling and monitoring devices, without on-site inspection), (2) excluded underground tests from the ban, (3) invited all other nations to sign the treaty, and (4) provided an escape clause permitting each signatory to withdraw from the test ban if it feels that the treaty jeopardizes its national interests.

b. France and China Abstain. Although about 100 nations joined the Big Three in signing this treaty, two key nations did not. (1) France. President de Gaulle insisted that France continue atmospheric testing and develop its own H-bomb. De Gaulle wanted to end France's dependence upon the nuclear strength of the United States. (2) China. Chinese leaders denounced the treaty as an attempt by a few powers to monopolize nuclear weapons.

FURTHER EFFORTS TO HALT THE NUCLEAR ARMS RACE

1. Outlawing Nuclear Weapons in Outer Space.

In 1966, the UN General Assembly approved a treaty prohibiting nations from placing weapons of mass destruction in outer space or on any heavenly body.

2. Outlawing the Spread of Nuclear Weapons.

The *UN Disarmament Committee* sought a treaty to outlaw the *proliferation* (spread) of nuclear weapons. The committee reasoned that as more nations gain nuclear weapons, the more difficult it will be to prevent their accidental or deliberate use. In 1968, the United States and the Soviets agreed upon a treaty providing that the *(a)* nations without nuclear weapons agree not to develop them and to accept an international system of inspection, *(b)* nuclear powers assist the other nations in developing peaceful uses of atomic energy, and *(c)* nuclear powers strive to halt the arms race.

The *Nuclear Nonproliferation Treaty* was approved by the UN General Assembly. However, some nations without nuclear weapons expressed strong doubts. They were being asked to forgo atomic weapons, which could be vital to national defense.

3. Nuclear Proliferation in Asia

a. Pakistan. In 1979 the United States ended its economic and military assistance to Pakistan after the Central Intelligence Agency reported that Pakistan secretly was building a plant to produce nuclear weapons. Pakistan denied the report but was unwilling to place its atomic facilities under international safeguards. After the Soviet invasion of Afghanistan in 1979 placed Soviet troops at the Pakistani border, President Reagan resumed American aid. The United States explained that this aid was designed not against India but against the "serious threat" posed to Pakistan by Soviet troops in Afghanistan. The United States further stated that it was firmly committed to halt the spread of nuclear weapons and warned Pakistan that the aid package would be terminated if Pakistan exploded a nuclear device.

b. India. Having refused to sign the Nuclear Nonproliferation Treaty, India in 1974 exploded an underground nuclear device that it claimed was for peaceful purposes. India refused to accept international safeguards on all its nuclear facilities, however, and refused to rule out production of nuclear weapons.

In 1980 President Carter, citing a 1963 agreement, decided to ship India enriched uranium fuel. Although this fuel was meant for peaceful electric power production, it could be diverted to the making of atomic bombs. The President's decision was political, observers felt, intended to keep India from moving closer to the Soviet Union, but to the detriment of America's nonproliferation policy.

c. Other Third World Nations. Other Third World nations that have contracted with industrial powers for nuclear plants, fuel, and technology—supposedly for peaceful purposes—include Argentina and Brazil with West Germany and Iraq with France. (In 1981, fearing that the Iraq facility was about to become operational and produce nuclear weapons for use against Israeli targets, Israel bombed and destroyed it. (For details, check the Index.)

4. Outlawing Nuclear Weapons on the Seabed. In 1970 the UN General Assembly overwhelmingly approved a treaty prohibiting any nation from placing nuclear weapons on the seabed outside its 12-mile limit.

5. Strategic Arms Limitation Talks (SALT). (Check the Index.)

MISSILES

TYPES OF MISSILES

Since 1945 the United States and the Soviet Union have developed rocket-propelled missiles capable of delivering either conventional or nuclear warheads. The smallest are tactical missiles that have a short range and carry warheads of low explosive power. They can be used as battlefield artillery for close support of troops. The largest missiles, for offensive purposes, are the *intermediate-range ballistic missile* (IRBM) and the *intercontinental ballistic missile* (ICBM); and for defensive purposes the *antiballistic missile* (ABM).

1. Intermediate-Range Ballistic Missile (IRBM). These missiles soar into space and then descend to earth, hitting a target up to 2500 miles away from the launching site. The United States has produced several types of IRBMs. Our main reliance is on the *Polaris* and on its newer version, the *Poseidon*. Both missiles can be launched from a surface ship or from a submarine.

Patrolling Norwegian and Mediterranean waters, American missile-carrying submarines are close enough to the Soviet Union to expose its major military targets to IRBM attack. The Soviets also have IRBM's for use *(a)* from land-based sites against our European allies, and *(b)* from missile-carrying submarines in the North Atlantic against major American targets.

2. Intercontinental Ballistic Missile (ICBM). These missiles soar into space, travel at a speed up to 20,000 miles per hour, and descend to earth, hitting a target over 6000 miles away from the launching site. The earliest ICBMs carried a single warhead. More recent models are capable of carrying multiple warheads, with each warhead aimed at a different target. These are named *multiple individually targetable reentry vehicles* (MIRVs).

The ICBM has been called the "ultimate weapon" because its speed and its nuclear explosive power make any defense against it extremely difficult. The United States relies chiefly on the solid-fueled *Minuteman*. The Soviets have ICBMs, which can be launched from sites in the Soviet Union against the United States.

3. Antiballistic Missile (ABM). These missiles are designed to destroy offensive missiles in space. When radar indicates that enemy missiles are en route, the ABMs are to be launched to explode in the path of the approaching missiles and destroy them by explosive force, heat, and radiation.

BEGINNING ABM DEFENSE SYSTEMS

1. In the Soviet Union. By 1967, the Soviets had begun installing an ABM system around Moscow. Western observers surmised that Soviet ABMs were meant for defense against American as well as Chinese missiles.

2. In the United States. In 1969 Nixon won Congressional approval for two ABM sites. Their purpose was to protect not our cities but our ICBM launching sites against any Soviet initial attack, or *first strike,* so as to preserve our retaliatory, or *second-strike,* capacity.

TWO SALT I ACCORDS—SIGNED IN 1972

After almost three years of talks, American and Soviet negotiators completed two SALT I accords. Signed at Moscow by President Nixon and Communist party leader Brezhnev, the accords provided as follows:

1. The Treaty on ABMs. The United States and the Soviet Union *(a)* agreed to protect by ABM defense systems only two sites each (later reduced to one site each), *(b)* accepted a ceiling of 100 ABM launchers for each site, and *(c)* provided that the treaty be of unlimited duration but allowed each nation, upon notice, to withdraw from the treaty.

Observations. This treaty reflected the belief that the United States and the Soviet Union each has the ability to absorb a "first strike" and to retaliate powerfully upon the other nation, thereby making a nuclear war between them improbable. This belief has been known as "*mutual and assured destruction,*" or MAD. The treaty was overwhelmingly ratified by the United States Senate.

2. The Interim Agreement on Offensive Missiles. The United States and the Soviet Union "froze" at the current level their offensive-missile systems: *(a)* for the United States—1054 land-launched ICBMs and 656 sub-marine-launched missiles, and *(b)* for the Soviet Union—1618 land-launched ICBMs and 710 submarine-launched missiles.

Observations. This agreement *(a)* did not cover the number of warheads per missile, thereby giving the United States, with its advanced MIRV technology, the advantage of 5700 warheads as compared to 2500 for the Soviet Union, *(b)* did not cover the explosive power of each warhead, thereby giving the Soviet Union with its larger warheads a 3-to-1 lead in explosive power, *(c)* did not cover the number of long-range bombers capable of delivering nuclear bombs, thereby giving the United States a lead of 460 strategic bombers to 140 for the Soviet Union, *(d)* did not limit the construction of strategic bombers and did not prevent the replacement of existing missiles and submarines by more destructive models, and *(e)* did not provide for on-site inspection to prevent violations.

Although an executive agreement, not requiring ratification, it was submitted by Nixon to Congress and received an overwhelming "concurrence."

THE SALT II TREATY—SIGNED IN 1979

After seven years, American and Soviet negotiators reached agreement on a treaty to replace the 1972 Interim Agreement on Offensive Missiles. The SALT II Treaty, signed at Vienna by President Carter and Soviet leader Brezhnev, was a highly technical 100-page document.

1. Provisions. *(a)* The United States and the Soviet Union each accepted, as of 1982, an overall ceiling of 2250 strategic nuclear-delivery vehicles. These included land-based intercontinental ballistic missiles (ICBMs), submarine-launched ballistic missiles (SLBMs), heavy bombers, and air-to-surface ballistic missiles (ASBMs) with a range of over 375 miles. The treaty also set limits on the number of MIRVs, or warheads, per missile and the weight per missile. *(b)* The United States and the Soviet Union both agreed to test and deploy no more than one new type of ICBM. *(c)* The treaty placed no limits on the Soviet *Backfire* bomber, which they insisted was an intermediate-range plane, but the Americans considered a strategic long-range bomber. The Soviets pledged not to increase

Western and Soviet Bases Facing the North Polar Region

WESTERN BASES
PROBABLE SOVIET BASES

the current rate of *Backfire* production—about 30 per year. *(d)* The treaty limited, until 1982, America's air- or sea-launched cruise missile to a maximum range of 375 miles. (The cruise missile is a low-flying, pilotless vehicle that can be guided to its target.) *(e)* The treaty did not provide for on-site inspection to verify compliance. Both nations, however, agreed not to conceal missile activities and not to impede verification by "national technical means" (NTM)—such as satellites and intelligence listening posts. *(f)* The SALT II Treaty was to expire in 1985. Both nations agreed to work for further limitations in nuclear weapons as part of a SALT III Treaty.

2. Arguments for the SALT II Treaty: *(a)* It furthered the principle of equality in the two superpowers' strategic missile arsenals. *(b)* It required the Soviets, by 1982, to dismantle over 10 percent of their strategic nuclear missile systems so as to conform to the 2250 ceiling. Also, by its various other ceilings, the treaty inhibited the growth of Soviet missile power, which without any treaty could expand greatly. *(c)* The restriction to 1982 on America's cruise missile was not vital, since the United States could not produce longer-range cruise missiles within that time period. *(d)* President Carter claimed that the treaty would "lessen the danger of nuclear destruction while safeguarding our military security."

3. Arguments Against the SALT II Treaty: *(a)* Although the treaty limited both nations equally regarding overall nuclear-delivery vehicles, the Soviets had a major advantage in that their missiles were larger and more destructive than those of the United States. *(b)* By limiting new-type ICBMs to only one, the treaty handicapped American efforts to deploy varied mobile missile systems. These are needed, since the existing, fixed, land-based *Minuteman* missiles are vulnerable to a surprise attack by increasingly accurate Soviet missiles. *(c)* The treaty placed no limits on the Soviet *Backfire* bomber, which could be used for a one-way attack upon the United States targets. By providing exceptions and permitting modernization of existing weapons, the treaty would not halt the nuclear arms race and would not permit any reduction in military spending.

4. President Carter's Moves to Obtain Senate Ratification. The SALT II Treaty required a two-thirds vote of the Senate for ratification. Many Senators feared that the treaty confirmed Soviet nuclear superiority over the United States. To quiet such fears, President Carter agreed to increase American military spending and to proceed with the *MX mobile missile system*. This system would move new, more powerful land-based missiles back and forth through 20-mile-long trenches so as to disguise their exact location from the Soviets. The MX system would be built in sparsely inhabited areas of Nevada and Utah, would cost some $30 billion, and would be fully operative by 1989.

5. Factors Causing the Senate to Indefinitely Postpone Consideration of SALT II

a. Soviet Combat Force in Cuba (1979). American intelligence reported the existence of a Soviet combat brigade, of up to 3000 men, in Cuba. Although President Carter held that this force posed no direct military threat to the United States, its presence in Cuba raised questions of Soviet motives. President Carter announced plans for increased surveillance of Cuba and increased economic aid for Caribbean nations.

The President still urged ratification of SALT II. A number of Senators, however, argued that the Soviet combat force in Cuba was an additional reason for rejecting the treaty.

b. Soviet Invasion of Afghanistan (1979–1980). With the Soviet invasion of Afghanistan, President Carter requested the Senate to delay consideration of SALT II. While the President still held SALT II to be in the national interest, he concluded that the Soviet invasion made consideration of SALT II "inappropriate."

The Carter administration—and the Reagan administration for a time—indicated that, as long as the Soviets honored the SALT II terms, the United States would do likewise.

6. United States Breaking of the SALT II Treaty. Arguing that the Soviet Union had not fully complied with the SALT II Treaty, the United States broke the unratified treaty's limits in 1986 by deploying one more cruise missile than the treaty allowed. Officials declared that the United States "couldn't afford to reduce our future deterrent force structure" by dismantling any missile-carrying submarines, as would have been required to keep within treaty limits. The Reagan administration took this action against the advice of Congress. Congressional critics argued that compliance with the treaty's limits was "in the national security interests of the United States," since the Soviets were ready to deploy new strategic weapons. Supporters of the United States move said it was a long-overdue response to Soviet treaty violations.

7. President Reagan's Weapons Policies. President Reagan altered some of the weapons policies of President Carter while carrying on others. *(a)* President Reagan sought funds for 100 long-range, multiple-warhead MX missiles, to be placed in hardened missile silos. Congress agreed to 50, the first of which were to be operational in 1986. *(b)* Congress approved funds for a smaller, mobile, long-range missile to be called *Midgetman,* which the Reagan administration had not sought. *(c)* President Reagan revived the B-1 bomber program canceled by President Carter. The first of the fleet of 100 planes, known as B-1Bs, went into operation in 1986. These planes were to replace aging B-52s. *(d)* President Reagan expanded the *Stealth* program to build a new generation of planes and missiles designed to be "invisible" to enemy radar. Much of the *Stealth* program was kept secret. Its technology was reportedly applied to fighter

planes, cruise missiles, and ballistic missiles. *(e)* President Reagan revived production of chemical weapons, suspended by President Nixon in 1969. Congress approved a new generation of nerve-gas weapons, designed to be more stable than earlier weapons and thus safer to store.

PRESIDENT REAGAN'S STRATEGIC DEFENSE INITIATIVE ("STAR WARS") PROGRAM

Declaring a goal of making nuclear weapons "impotent and obsolete," President Reagan in 1983 announced a sweeping program of research into space-based defenses aimed at shielding the United States against nuclear attack. He labeled his program the *Strategic Defense Initiative* (SDI). Because of the program's emphasis on exotic techniques such as particle beams and orbiting mirrors, observers soon called it "Star Wars."

President Reagan described SDI as a system for destroying Soviet missiles soon after launching, before they had time to get close to their targets. The program would depend heavily on technology that was still in the early stages of research. By providing "insured defense" against attack, the President said, the SDI program aimed to "save the West from mutual nuclear terror, to make ballistic missiles obsolete, and, ultimately, to eliminate them from the face of the earth." The President rejected the traditional theory (*"mutual and assured destruction,"* or MAD) that nuclear war could be deterred if each superpower had overwhelming nuclear power with which to threaten retaliation. Administration officials described the SDI program as one of *"mutual and assured survival,"* or MAS.

Critics said that SDI would (1) cost untold billions of dollars, (2) touch off a new arms race, (3) increase rather than decrease the risks of nuclear war, and (4) militarize American society by vastly enlarging the defense industry. Besides, said critics, (5) the plan would never work—it called for far more precision than was technically feasible. Defenders of the plan said it (1) was indeed feasible, (2) was needed to match Soviet antimissile efforts, (3) would have technological spinoffs that benefited everyday life, (4) would be less expensive than critics thought, and (5) would give the United States greater bargaining power in negotiations with the Soviets.

Congress approved funding for SDI, but at lower levels than requested by President Reagan. The program was budgeted at just over $3 billion a year in the mid-1980s.

UNITED STATES-SOVIET ARMS NEGOTIATIONS IN THE 1980s

The Reagan administration deemphasized arms control talks in the early 1980s. President Reagan argued that the United States had fallen behind the Soviet Union in military strength and should not negotiate from a position of weakness. The Reagan administration accelerated the military buildup begun by the Carter administration.

1. START Talks and INF Talks. United States and Soviet negotiators met in Geneva, Switzerland, to discuss two types of nuclear arms. One set of meetings, called *Strategic Arms Reduction Talks* (START), dealt with long-range missiles that could strike one of the two superpowers from the other's heartland. The second set, called the *Intermediate Nuclear Force* (INF) meetings, dealt with medium-range missiles based mainly in Europe. Neither set of meetings made significant progress. In 1983, when the United States began to install medium-range cruise and *Pershing* missiles in Europe, the Soviet Union broke off both sets of talks.

2. A Resumption of Arms Talks. In 1984, worried about American "Star Wars" research, the Soviet Union proposed talks on preventing the militarization of outer space. After some debate over the scope of the talks (the Soviets wanted a narrow focus), new talks began in Geneva on medium-range, long-range, and space-based weapons.

3. Geneva Summit in 1985: Reagan Meets Gorbachev. In November 1985, holding his first summit meeting with a Soviet leader, President Reagan met in Geneva with Mikhail Gorbachev. Although the two spoke frankly about arms control and human rights, they reached no significant agreements.

4. Reykjavik Meeting in 1986: Sweeping New Proposals. After further talks between arms negotiators for the two sides, Reagan and Gorbachev held a second meeting at Reykjavik, Iceland, in October 1986. (Reagan declined to call this a "summit" meeting, saying it was a preliminary encounter to prepare for a later summit.) The Reykjavik talks produced a serious give-and-take in which each side made major new proposals. President Reagan proposed the elimination of "all United States and Soviet offensive ballistic missiles of whatever range or armament" within ten years, with a 50 percent reduction in the first five

"What now?"

Wallmeyer, Long Beach Press-Telegram

years. Gorbachev offered concessions on medium-range missiles while insisting that the "Star Wars" program be limited to laboratory research. Gorbachev wanted to bar testing and deployment of any space-based defense system for ten years. Reagan refused to agree to the "Star Wars" restrictions. The talks ended without agreement, and lower-level negotiations resumed in Geneva.

President Reagan's proposal for eliminating all ballistic missiles had far-reaching implications. The proposal alarmed leaders of the NATO nations, which have depended on a United States nuclear "shield" for defense against the Soviet Union. Without ballistic missiles, any confrontation in Europe would be between conventional armies. The NATO leaders saw no hope of matching the Soviet Union in conventional forces, even with the assistance of the United States. In the aftermath of the Reykjavik conference, NATO proposed new negotiations on reducing conventional forces in Europe. Western European leaders also turned new attention to the prospects of building a joint European nuclear deterrent.

The Reagan administration's arms control policies evoked a mixed reaction in Congress and among the American people. Some people criticized the administration for refusing to agree to a freeze on arms construction and on nuclear testing. Critics argued that President Reagan was not serious about arms control and was missing opportunities to halt the arms race. The administration's supporters argued that the Soviet Union could not be trusted to keep an arms-control agreement, and that President Reagan's SDI program offered better protection against nuclear war. They said that Reagan would agree to any genuine Soviet proposals that protected United States interests and had verification provisions allowing experts to detect Soviet violations.

For developments in 1987, see page 713.

SATELLITES AND OTHER SPACE VEHICLES

THE SOVIET UNION LAUNCHES ITS SPUTNIKS

The *International Geophysical Year* (1957–1958) was a worldwide effort to increase humanity's knowledge of the physical environment. As part of the program, the United States and the Soviet Union each announced plans to place into orbit around the earth data-gathering satellites. The Soviet Union was first to fulfill this promise. In 1957 Russian scientists orbited the first satellites: the 184-pound *Sputnik I* and the 1120-pound *Sputnik II*.

EFFECT OF THE USSR's SATELLITES UPON THE UNITED STATES

The Soviet's initial lead in the space race greatly perturbed the American people. Why had the United States fallen behind? (1) As a dictatorship, the USSR was able to concentrate all necessary resources toward achieving its goals. As a democracy, the United States had to heed demands for other goals such as more consumer goods and lower taxes. (2) Soviet education, critics said, was ahead of that in the United States in science, mathematics, and technical subjects. (3) The Communists channeled their best students into science, mathematics, and engineering. In America many capable students selected nontechnical fields.

THE UNITED STATES SPEEDS UP ITS SPACE PROGRAM

(1) Congress approved additional funds for missile and satellite research, development, and production. (2) Congress passed the *National Defense Education Act* (1958) to improve education, especially in science and mathematics. (3) Congress established a new agency to direct the nonmilitary aspects of space exploration—the *National Aeronautics and Space Administration* (NASA).

INITIAL AMERICAN SPACE FLIGHTS

In 1958, from *Cape Canaveral,* Florida, the United States placed into orbit its first satellite, the 18-pound *Explorer I* and later the three-pound *Vanguard I* and the 18-pound *Explorer III.* Soviet Premier Khrushchev gibed at the American satellites, calling them "grapefruits" in relation to the much larger Soviet Sputniks.

Thereafter, both the Soviet Union and the United States achieved considerable progress in space.

MAJOR SOVIET EFFORTS IN SPACE

1. Unmanned Flights. *(a) Around the Earth.* The Soviets have placed many satellites of their *Cosmos* series into orbit to test equipment for military and peaceful uses, to provide military communications, and to gather weather data. *(b) To the Moon.* The Soviets sent many *Luna* space vehicles to the moon, some reaching its surface and sending back pictures. In 1970 *Luna 17* landed on the moon, carrying a self-propelled vehicle, *Lunokhod I.* It roamed the lunar surface, analyzing lunar soil, and relayed the data back to earth. In 1972 *Luna 20* returned to earth with a cargo of moon rocks. *(c) To the Planets.* The Soviets sent several spaceships to the planets Mars and Venus and in 1982 again achieved soft landings on Venus. The more recent ships sent back scientific data such as the surface temperature and atmospheric composition of these planets.

2. Manned Flights. The Soviets achieved a number of space firsts. In 1961 *Vostok 1* orbited the earth once, carrying the world's first cosmonaut, *Yuri Gagarin.* In 1963 *Vostok 6* completed a 48-orbit flight carrying the first woman cosmonaut, *Valentina Tereshkova.* In 1964 *Voskhod 1* became history's first multipassenger space capsule. In 1971 the Soviets orbited *Salyut 1,* the first unmanned space station, and later sent there a three-person scientific team. In 1979 a two-person Soviet team lived in the *Salyut 6* space station for 175 days.

MAJOR AMERICAN EFFORTS IN SPACE

1. Unmanned Flights. *(a) Around the Earth.* The United States placed many satellites into orbit—the *Explorer* series to increase our scientific knowledge of space; *Transit* satellites to assist airplane and ship pilots in navigation; *Telstar, Early Bird,* and *Intelsat,* all privately financed satellites, to build a global telecommunications system; and the *Tiros* series to gather weather data. *(b) To the Moon.* The United States sent a number of spacecrafts to the moon; some landed on the moon's surface and sent back thousands of photographs. *(c) To the Planets.* The United States sent to Mars and Venus a number of *Mariner* spaceships that sent back pictures and scientific data. In 1973 *Pioneer 10* ended a 21-month journey to Jupiter and provided photographs of that outer planet. (Pioneer 10, carrying a pictorial plaque, was expected to escape from our solar system and travel into the Milky Way—where it might be seen by other intelligent beings, if any exist.) In 1974 *Mariner 10* reached and photographed Mercury, the planet closest to our sun. In 1976 two *Viking* vehicles reached the vicinity of Mars and each placed a landing craft on that planet's surface. The Viking landers sent back photographs of the terrain, data regarding the atmosphere, and analyses of the Martian soil. In 1979, after a six-year trip, *Pioneer 11* swept past and sent back data about the rings, moons, and atmosphere of the planet Saturn. In 1980 *Voyager 1* flew by Saturn and revealed the existence of three previously unknown Saturn moons, making a total of fifteen. (Voyager 1 eventually is expected to leave our solar system and wander in interstellar space.) In 1981, after a four-year trip, *Voyager 2* sent back pictures and data as it flew by Saturn. The spacecraft sent back similar information about Uranus in 1986 and headed for a rendezvous with Neptune in 1989.

What great discoveries lie ahead?

Palmer in The Springfield (Mo.) Leader & Press

2. Manned Flights. At first behind, the United States eventually caught up with and then surpassed the Soviets in the number and complexity of manned flights. In 1962 the United States sent *Friendship 7* to circle the earth three times with America's first orbiting astronaut, *John Glenn.* Thereafter, the United States orbited numerous multipassenger space vehicles. American astronauts practiced docking, or the joining together, of spacecraft in orbit, and then guiding a lunar module or landing craft to leave and return to the command ship.

In 1969, with the eleventh flight of the *Project Apollo* series, the United States achieved an historic first. While *Michael Collins* orbited the moon in the command ship *Columbia, Neil Armstrong* and *Edwin Aldrin* descended to the moon's surface in the lunar module *Eagle.* Armstrong, the first human to set foot on the moon, spoke the historic words "That's one small step for a man, one giant leap for mankind." The two astronauts gathered rock samples, set up scientific experiments, stationed a plaque saying, "We came in peace for all mankind," and then ascended to the command ship. The three men then returned safely to earth. Five subsequent Apollo flights repeated the moon-landing triumph.

In 1973 the United States placed into orbit its first space station, *Skylab.* Successive teams of American astronauts lived in the space station, performing experiments and gathering data.

In 1981 NASA launched the first reusable winged *space shuttle,* the *Columbia.* A manned vehicle carrying two astronauts, it was placed into orbit, circled the earth 36 times, and glided to a safe landing in southern California. Because it can be reused for many trips, the space shuttle will be less costly than previous single-use orbiting vehicles. Thereafter, the *Columbia* space shuttle successfully completed four more space flights.

In 1983 a companion craft, the *Challenger* space shuttle, went into orbit. It released and then retrieved a satellite in space. This *Challenger* flight carried a crew of five, including the nation's first female astronaut, *Sally Ride.* Later that year, another space shuttle carried the nation's first black astronaut, *Stewart Bluford, Jr.,* into space.

3. Developing a Permanent Manned Space Station. In 1984 NASA was directed by President Reagan to develop and launch within a decade a permanent manned space station. Estimated to cost more than $8 billion, this space station would serve to *(a)* permit various scientific experiments, *(b)* enhance our knowledge of the solar system and the universe, and *(c)* manufacture metals and medicines that can be produced only in a gravity-free environment.

4. Coping With the *Challenger* Tragedy. In 1986 the *Challenger* space shuttle exploded soon after takeoff, killing its seven crew members—including *Christa McAuliffe,* a schoolteacher who was to have been the first "ordinary" American in space. A Presidential investigating commission blamed the explosion on a faulty booster rocket. Critics argued that NASA had stressed speed over safety in the shuttle-launching program and that the companies that built the rocket should share in the blame. Shuttle flights were suspended for two years pending the revision of preflight procedures and the redesign of the shuttle's booster rocket.

OTHER SPACE EFFORTS

(1) In 1972 President Nixon and Soviet leader Brezhnev agreed to a joint American-Soviet space venture, the *Apollo-Soyuz Test Project.* The project, to link up and exchange crews, took place in 1975 and was successful. (2) Other nations that launched satellites into orbit include Great Britain, France, Italy, Japan, and China. (3) In 1975 ten West European nations, to further space research, established the *European Space Agency* (ESA).

SPACE EXPLORATION AND OUR DAILY LIVES

Advocates of space exploration point out that—in addition to having military uses and providing enhanced knowledge of the solar system—it benefits our daily lives. Orbiting satellites are used to provide long-distance communications and television broadcasts, to improve weather forecasting, and to map the earth for water and mineral resources. Smoke detectors, now found in many homes, were first developed for use in *Skylab.* Space exploration needs spurred the growth of computer technology.

PART 6. American-Soviet Relations Follow a Fluctuating Pattern

Since World War II, relations between the United States and the Soviet Union have varied from periods of great tension to periods of comparative calm.

1947–1953: PERIOD OF TENSION

While Stalin ruled, the Soviet Union pursued a "hard line" toward the free world, and the United States responded by its policy of containment. Evidences of tension were (1) Truman Doctrine (1947), (2) Berlin Blockade (1948–1949), (3) creation of NATO (1949), and (4) Korean War (1950–1953).

1954–1959: COMPARATIVE CALM

In the years after Stalin's death, Khrushchev espoused peaceful coexistence, and relations between the Soviet Union and the United States improved.

1. Summit Conference of 1955. President Eisenhower met at Geneva with the leaders of Great Britain, France, and the Soviet Union. They discussed East-West problems in a calm and friendly atmosphere but reached no settlements.

2. Scientific and Cultural Exchanges (1958). The United States and the Soviet Union inaugurated a scientific and cultural exchange program. Since then, reciprocal visits have been made by athletes, scholars, concert artists, orchestras, ballet companies, writers, and scientists.

3. Khrushchev's Visit to the United States (1959). Khrushchev visited the United States and received a friendly reception. Khrushchev showed great interest in many facets of American life. He met with President Eisenhower, and the two men initiated plans for another summit conference.

1960–1962: ANOTHER PERIOD OF TENSION

1. U-2 Incident and the Summit Conference of 1960. Two weeks before a new summit conference was to be held in Paris, the Soviets shot down, deep inside their territory, an unarmed American U-2 reconnaissance plane. The Soviets, who maintained an extensive espionage system in the West, had known of such U-2 flights but had not previously protested against them. In Paris, Khrushchev accused America of aggression, vilified Eisenhower, and demanded an apology. Eisenhower denied the charge of aggression and refused to apologize. The summit meeting was dead.

2. Building of the Berlin Wall (1961). (Check the Index.)

3. Cuban Missile Base Crisis (1962). (Check the Index.)

1963–1968: COMPARATIVE CALM

Following the peaceful settlement of the Cuban crisis and the deepening of the Soviet-Chinese split, Soviet-American relations improved.

1. Limited Nuclear Test Ban Treaty (1963). The United States and the Soviet Union agreed to a ban on all but underground nuclear tests. This was the first agreement to emerge from 18 years of East-West disarmament negotiations.

2. Hot Line (1963). The Soviet Union and the United States established a "hot line," or emergency communications link, between Washington and Moscow to reduce the risk of war by blunder or miscalculation.

3. Wheat Sale (1963). With the Soviets suffering from a poor grain harvest, the United States sold substantial quantities of wheat to the Soviet Union.

4. Nuclear Nonproliferation Treaty (1968). The United States and the Soviet Union agreed upon a treaty to outlaw the spread of nuclear weapons.

1969 TO PRESENT: COMPARATIVE CALM AND A SEARCH FOR DÉTENTE

American and Soviet leaders all voiced support for moving relations into a new era of détente. Secretary of State Kissinger defined détente as the "process of managing relations with a potentially hostile country in order to preserve peace while maintaining our vital interests." A Soviet expert on foreign policy explained that détente "sets limits on what each side can do without risking war and gets officials concerned—Soviet and American—talking with each other."

SUCCESS OF DÉTENTE

1. Four-Power Agreement on Berlin (1971). (Check the Index.)

2. Nixon's Journey to Moscow (1972). Despite Soviet-American tensions over Vietnam, President Nixon journeyed to Moscow to a summit meeting with Communist party chief Leonid Brezhnev. Nixon received a restrained but correct welcome. Nixon and the Soviet leader signed a number of accords: *(a) on space*—to cooperate in 1975 in a joint Soviet-American docking and flight of manned spacecraft, *(b) on health*—to coordinate Soviet-American research on cancer, heart disease, and public health, *(c) on incidents at sea*—to set rules so that Soviet and American naval vessels operating near each other will avoid collisions, *(d) on environment and technology*—to cooperate in the study of pollution problems and in other scientific research, *(e) on trade*—to resolve trade problems so as to increase Soviet-American trade, and *(f) on nuclear arms*—to limit ABM sites and "freeze" current offensive-missile arsenals.

3. Strategic Arms Limitation Talks; Two SALT I Accords (1972). (Check the Index.)

4. Brezhnev's Visit to the United States (1973). Soviet leader Brezhnev visited the United States, projected a spirit of friendship, and spoke to the American people via television. He and President Nixon signed a number of accords: to make *every* effort to avoid a military confrontation, to promote trade, to continue cultural and educational exchanges, and to cooperate in oceanography, transportation, and agricultural research.

5. Helsinki Pact (1975). Leaders of the United States, Canada, and 33 European nations met at Helsinki, Finland, to conclude the *Conference on Security and Cooperation in Europe.* They signed a charter containing two major provisions:

a. Accepting the Post-World War II Boundaries in Europe. By this provision the Western powers held that they were being realistic—acknowledging a situation they could not alter peaceably. The Soviets were jubilant because this provision formally recognized Soviet territorial gains in Europe, the division of Germany into two nations, and Soviet domination of Eastern Europe.

b. Agreeing to Further Human Rights. By this provision the Soviet Union and its satellites promised to ease the movement of individuals across frontiers, assist in the reunion of separated families, reduce restrictions on journalists, and increase East-West cultural exchanges. Western observers wondered, however, whether these promises would be kept.

DISILLUSIONMENT ABOUT DÉTENTE

1. United States

a. Members of Congress protested the internal Soviet crackdown on dissident intellectuals and minority groups. Congress members pointed to the forced exile in 1974 of the Russian author and dissident *Alexander Solzhenitsyn.* In his book *The Gulag Archipelago,* published only in the West, the famed Nobel Prize winner documented the history of Soviet prison camp tyranny and asserted that tyranny was an integral part of the Soviet system. Members of Congress also pointed to Soviet harassment of persons, chiefly Jews, seeking to leave the Soviet Union. Would-be emigrants, upon making their intentions known, were fired from their jobs, expelled from their living quarters, kept waiting for months and years enmeshed in bureaucratic red tape, and—if permitted to leave—required to pay exorbitant exit fees. In 1974 Congress approved a trade bill permitting

"Détente."

Drawing by Richter; © 1974 The New Yorker Magazine, Inc.

trade benefits for the Soviets on condition that they allow emigrants to leave the Soviet Union promptly and without harrassment.

b. American experts concluded that Soviet words and actions in the 1973 Arab-Israeli war were indistinguishable from the bitterest of cold war days.

c. American military leaders pointed out that the Soviet Union had accelerated its building of offensive nuclear weapons. Although permitted by the SALT I accord, these additional offensive weapons did not indicate peaceful intentions.

d. American critics of détente pointed out that the Soviet Union had provided the massive weapons used by Hanoi to triumph in South Vietnam and by the pro-Soviet faction and the Cubans to triumph in Angola. They further quoted Brezhnev's statement in 1976 that the Soviet Union saw détente as "the way to create more favorable conditions for peaceful socialist and Communist construction" and that détente did not "abolish or alter the laws of class struggle." American critics of détente claimed that it was a "one-way street" benefiting only the Soviet Union.

e. In 1977, President Carter announced that one aspect of his administration's foreign policy would be concern for human rights. Accordingly, the United States charged Czechoslovakia with violating the Helsinki Pact provision on human rights by harassment of Czechoslovak dissidents, who had called for civil liberties and cultural freedom. The United States also stated that the Soviet Union would be in conflict with "accepted international standards of human rights" by continued efforts to silence dissidents.

Among the most prominent dissidents were *Andrei Sakharov,* an atomic scientist who won the Nobel Peace Prize in 1975; *Anatoly B. Shcharansky;* and *Yuri F. Orlov.* All three were part of a group formed by Soviet citizens to monitor Soviet compliance with the Helsinki Pact. All suffered for their outspokenness. Sa-

Reprinted with special permission of King Features Syndicate, Inc.

kharov was confined to "internal exile" from 1980 to 1986 at Gorky, a city closed to foreigners. Shcharansky spent nine years in prison and a labor camp before being freed in an East-West spy exchange in 1986. He settled in Israel. Orlov was sent to "internal exile" in northeastern Siberia.

In the mid-1980s, some Americans took hope from signs such as the release of some imprisoned dissidents that Soviet leader *Mikhail Gorbachev* was encouraging a "thaw" in Soviet life. Others said the "thaw" was illusory and that Soviet repression remained as cruel as ever.

2. Soviet Union

a. Soviet trade experts protested that the United States Congress, despite administration promises, had long delayed a sweeping trade agreement. The Soviets wanted substantial credits and loans with which to purchase American machinery and technology, pay for imports of American grain, and develop Siberian oil and gas resources. The Soviets also wanted the United States to tax its imports of Soviet products at the lowest regular tariff rate—such treatment being known as "most-favored-nation" status. The Soviets resented the 1974 legislation passed by Congress that tied trade benefits to the easing of Soviet emigration policies. In early 1975 the Soviet Union canceled the 1972 Soviet-American trade accord.

b. Soviet political leaders objected to efforts by Congress to change Soviet policies regarding dissident intellectuals and minority groups. These policies, the Russians insisted, dealt with internal Soviet matters beyond the scope of American concern and would be maintained in the interests of the Communist state. The Soviets also expressed resentment against President Carter's human rights campaign as unwarranted interference with internal Soviet policies. The Soviet Union warned the United States against raising human rights issues as dangerous to the cause of détente.

c. Communist foreign policy experts complained that the United States was seeking to erode Soviet influence in the Arab Mideast.

DEVELOPMENTS IN THE 1980s

1. An End to Détente? With the Soviet invasion of Afghanistan (1979–1980) and the American responses by the Carter administration—delaying consideration of the SALT II Treaty, restricting grain and high-technology exports to the Soviet Union, and calling for a boycott of the 1980 summer Olympic Games in Moscow—observers believed that the two superpowers were abandoning détente and returning to the tensions of the Cold War.

While expressing the desire for "fair agreements" with Moscow, the Reagan administration accused the Soviets of (1) responsibility for "international terrorism" by maintaining terrorist training camps in the Soviet Union, in its East European satellites, and in its North African ally Libya and (2) imperialist adventurism to expand Soviet control in the Persian Gulf, South Asia, Africa, and Central America. The Soviets accused the Reagan administration of (1) bringing the "world closer to a nuclear catastrophe" by installing American nuclear weapons in West Germany (where they face Soviet missiles in Eastern Europe), (2) "playing the China card" by selling China modern American weapons and by jointly operating an intelligence-gathering station in western China to monitor Soviet missile tests, and (3) speeding the arms race by sharp increases in American military spending. With charges and countercharges flying high, observers foresaw the continued unraveling of détente.

2. Soviet Downing of a Korean Commercial Airliner. In 1983 a Soviet fighter plane shot down a South Korean airliner that was crossing Soviet territory in the Far East. All 269 passengers and crew members were killed. President Reagan called the Soviet action "barbaric" and a "massacre." The Western nations took relatively minor measures in protest—mainly halting, for limited periods of time, air flights to and from the Soviet Union.

The Soviet Union said it had shot down the plane because the pilot had deliberately invaded Soviet airspace on a spying mission. Western governments denied the charge, citing evidence that the plane had strayed from its course by mistake. The evidence was open to more than one interpretation, however, and searchers could not find the plane's flight recorder to settle the dispute.

3. Toward an Easing of Tensions? President Reagan and Soviet leader Mikhail Gorbachev held face-to-face meetings to try to resolve major differences. Their first meeting was at Geneva, Switzerland, in November 1985, and their second was at Reykjavik, Iceland, in October 1986. The conferences dealt with arms control, human rights, and other issues.

The course of human events.

Shanks in The Buffalo Evening News

4. Intermediate Nuclear Force (INF) Treaty. In a December 1987 summit conference at Washington, D.C., President Reagan and Premier Gorbachev signed a treaty agreeing that within three years the United States and the Soviet Union would dismantle their intermediate-range nuclear weapons, destroy the launchers for these weapons, and establish elaborate systems to verify each other's compliance with the treaty. (These weapons included the United States Pershing 2 missiles in West Germany.) Reagan and Gorbachev also discussed the war in Afghanistan and the possible reduction of their ICBM arsenals.

——————— MULTIPLE-CHOICE QUESTIONS ———————

1. The *least* important factor in explaining the destructiveness of nuclear weapons is their great (a) heat (b) radioactivity (c) blast (d) weight.

2. The Baruch Plan for international control of atomic energy did *not* propose (a) an international authority in which no nation would have the veto power (b) unlimited inspection (c) stockpiling of atomic bombs (d) sharing American atomic know-how with other nations.

3. The Baruch Plan never went into effect because of (a) the UN's lack of interest in the problem (b) American opposition to international control (c) a Soviet veto in the UN Security Council (d) Britain's refusal to cooperate.

4. Since World War II, the United States has *not* (a) developed atomic artillery (b) exploded hydrogen bombs (c) built nuclear submarines (d) used the atom bomb in Korea.

5. The chief factor that long blocked agreement between the Soviet Union and the United States on a nuclear test ban was the dispute regarding (a) admission of Communist China to the test ban conference (b) the war in Vietnam (c) effective measures of inspection and control (d) the building of the Berlin Wall.

6. The limited nuclear test ban treaty permits testing (a) in the atmosphere (b) in space (c) below the ground (d) under water.

7. A leading European nation that refused to sign the limited nuclear test ban treaty was (a) Communist China (b) Czechoslovakia (c) France (d) Italy.

8. The "proliferation" of atomic weapons refers to their (a) spread to many nations (b) complexity (c) radiation (d) use to produce electricity.

9. In regard to the SALT I accords, which statement is *most* valid? (a) They did not provide for limiting ABM systems. (b) They called for on-site inspection to prevent violations. (c) They enabled the United States and the Soviet Union to significantly reduce their military defense spending. (d) They did not call for any reduction in existing offensive missile arsenals.

10. The SALT I accords were significant because they (a) provided an example of UN effectiveness (b) provided for joint American-Soviet space flights (c) were a first step toward limiting a nuclear missile arms race (d) ended the cold war.

11. The realization by major world powers that a "balance of terror" exists in international relations is best evidenced by the major powers' (a) reliance upon the United Nations to settle disputes (b) attempts to limit armaments (c) continuation of the cold war (d) adoption of world trade agreements.

12. Which statement is an opinion rather than a fact? (a) France originally was involved in the Vietnam conflict. (b) There are tensions between China and the Soviet Union. (c) Arms limitation agreements between the United States and the Soviet Union will lead to world peace. (d) Britain has joined the Common Market.

13. The "hot line" and the nuclear test ban treaty are indications that (a) the alliance systems headed by the Soviet Union and the United States are being strengthened (b) to some extent, cold war tensions between the United States and the Soviet Union could be eased (c) the United States is relying more heavily on its policy of containment (d) the great powers are seeking closer cooperation on the peaceful uses of space.

14. In 1957 the first satellite was placed into orbit around the earth by (a) a UN team of scientists (b) the Soviet Union (c) the United States (d) Great Britain.

15. Which is *not* the name of a Soviet space vehicle? (a) Sputnik (b) Vostok (c) Luna (d) Vladivostok.

16. Which term is *not* associated with the United States space effort? (a) NASA (b) Project Apollo (c) the Carter Doctrine (d) Cape Canaveral.

17. The *Poseidon* is (a) an atomic-powered submarine (b) the name of the project for the flight to the moon (c) an intercontinental ballistic missile (d) an intermediate-range missile capable of being fired from a submerged submarine.

18. Yuri Gagarin of the Soviet Union was the first human being to (a) design a space vehicle (b) achieve space flight (c) die on a space flight (d) take close-up photographs of the moon.

19. The chief object of Project Apollo was to (a) send space teams to the moon and back (b) gather data about Venus and Mars (c) establish a worldwide telecommunications system (d) improve the forecasting of weather.

20. "We came in peace for all mankind" was said (a) by President Carter and Soviet leader Brezhnev at their 1979 Vienna meeting (b) by American and Soviet negotiators at the SALT II meetings (c) on a plaque left on the moon by the two American astronauts who first set foot there (d) by Alexander Solzhenitsyn, the Soviet author and dissenter, who spoke for his family upon being exiled from his homeland.

21. The purpose of an antiballistic missile system is to increase the nation's (a) defensive strength (b) offensive power (c) scientific knowledge (d) ability to carry on nuclear testing below the ground.

22. The term "summit conference" refers to a meeting of the (a) heads of the world's leading nations (b) foreign ministers of the NATO powers (c) members of the UN Security Council (d) chiefs of staff of the United States Armed Forces.

23. Which event immediately preceded the 1960 summit conference and led to its collapse? (a) a Soviet nuclear test series (b) the Soviet intervention in Hungary (c) the invasion by Cuban exiles at the Bay of Pigs (d) the downing of an American U-2 spy plane inside the Soviet Union.

24. Détente is *best* explained as (a) an American policy of protection for intellectuals and minority groups (b) a Soviet policy of seeking large loans and expanding trade (c) a policy of both the United States and the Soviet Union to reduce tensions and improve relations between the two countries (d) a joint American-Soviet policy to impose peace terms upon the Middle East.

25. Which event indicated a Soviet "hard line" toward the West? (a) establishing the "hot line" communications link (b) signing the limited nuclear test ban treaty (c) placing missiles in Cuba (d) differing with China regarding peaceful coexistence.

26. In recent years United States involvement in world crises has *most* clearly shown that (a) solutions to major international problems require the cooperation of the major world powers (b) isolation is the only way to assure the safety of the United States (c) international affairs have come to be dominated by the small nations (d) meaningful settlements can only come about through the UN.

27. Based on world history, which prediction would be easiest to defend? (a) Europe will have a single economic system by 1995. (b) Unsettled areas of Africa will pro-

vide space for the expanding population of North America. (c) The human race's problems and the need to solve those problems will grow at an ever-increasing rate. (d) As more people become literate, conflict among nations will decrease.

28. Which action taken by the Soviet Union has been most consistent with Communist philosophy? (a) purchasing wheat from the United States (b) giving financial rewards to Soviet athletes (c) supplying aid to revolutionaries in other countries (d) permitting members of minority groups to emigrate freely.

29. One reason why the Soviet Union and the United States have not had a direct military conflict in the Middle East is because of the (a) sharp reduction of nationalism in both nations (b) general disarmament between the two nations (c) general lack of interest in the area (d) fear of an outbreak of nuclear war.

30. Détente, as applied to United States foreign policy, holds that (a) where peaceful coexistence fails, a display of force frequently leads to suitable compromise (b) formal alliances should be avoided, since they often cause small conflicts between two countries to broaden into international wars (c) ideological differences need not prevent peaceful economic and cultural contacts among countries (d) internal problems of foreign countries are best solved by a joint agreement of major powers not to intervene.

31. Recent United States negotiations with China and the Soviet Union are attempts to (a) decrease the necessity for the United Nations (b) implement a policy of peaceful coexistence (c) accelerate the movement toward state socialism in the United States (d) lessen the tension on the Chinese-Soviet border.

32. "We must somehow learn to live together in this world, to tolerate one another, or else we cannot survive." The author of this statement would most likely support a policy of (a) nativism (b) coexistence (c) conformity (d) isolation.

DISCUSSION ANALYSIS QUESTIONS: STATEMENTS OF ———— AMERICAN SECRETARIES OF STATE ————

Secretary A It has been a splendid little war, begun with the highest motives, carried on with magnificent intelligence and spirit, favored by the fortune which loves the brave. It is now to be concluded with that fine good nature which is the distinguishing trait of the American character.

Secretary B Our policy is not directed against any country or doctrine but against poverty, desperation, and chaos. . . . We of the United States are deeply conscious of our responsibilities toward the world.

Secretary C Support of the United Nations, development of regional organizations, economic cooperation, readiness to negotiate, and a firm adherence to the fundamental purposes and principles of our society constitute [our] national policy.

Secretary D A potential for massive attack will always be kept in a state of instant readiness. . . . A potential aggressor should know in advance that [it] will be made to suffer more for [its] aggression than [it] can possibly gain from it.

Secretary E The political trends have . . . been in the direction of improved and more normal relations. . . . Our interests will certainly continue to clash at many points. Nevertheless, the number of areas in which these interests are similar is growing.

1. Secretary A is most probably describing United States involvement in which war? (1) United States Civil War (2) Spanish-American War (3) World War I (4) Vietnam War.

2. Which secretary presents the most accurate description of the term "balance of terror"? (1) A (2) B (3) C (4) D.

3. Which two secretaries of state expressed the most similar views on the role of the United States in world affairs? (1) A and E (2) B and C (3) C and D (4) D and E.

4. Which is the most valid generalization based on all five statements? (1) A strong military is the best deterrent to war. (2) The United States has consistently followed a policy of expansionism. (3) The United States has adopted foreign policies that are most consistent with the goals of the time. (4) Isolationism has been a primary goal of most United States policy decisions.

5. Which secretary probably most favors a policy of détente? (1) B (2) C (3) D (4) E.

6. Which secretary probably would most favor economic aid for Europe after World War II? (1) A (2) B (3) D (4) E.

7. Which secretary probably most favors a buildup of American military power? (1) B (2) C (3) D (4) E.

—————————————— **ESSAY QUESTIONS** ——————————————

1. While we continue to develop the peaceful uses of atomic energy, we must find a way to deal with the problem of more and more countries possessing nuclear weapons. *(a)* Mention *one* military development in nuclear energy since 1945 *and one* development of nuclear energy for a peaceful use. *(b)* Name *two* international agreements regarding nuclear energy or missiles. Evaluate *each* agreement named as a means of reducing the possibility of nuclear warfare.

2. Science has taught us how to put the atom to work, but to make it work for good instead of evil is a problem in human relations. *(a)* Prove briefly that science has "put the atom to work." *(b)* Give *two* facts to show how the atom can "work for good instead of for evil." *(c)* Show why the major world problem today is not progress in science, but the relationship of human beings to one another.

3. Give *two* reasons for agreeing or disagreeing with *each* of the following statements: *(a)* It would have been better for humanity if nuclear energy had never been discovered. *(b)* The development of nuclear energy has increased the military security of the United States. *(c)* The SALT I accords were a major step toward world peace. *(d)* The space age will affect humanity as much as did the 16th-century age of discovery and exploration. *(e)* If détente is to succeed, the United States and the Soviet Union must place the goal of world peace ahead of other national interests.

4. United States foreign policy since 1945 has had *three* specific goals: *(a)* defense of the United States against attack *(b)* the maintenance of world peace *(c)* the promotion of economic and social welfare abroad. Discuss *two* specific means used by the United States in an effort to accomplish *each* of these goals. Explain how *one* foreign policy goal listed above has interfered or conflicted with a foreign policy goal of another nation since 1945. Use specific information in your answer.

5. Relations between the Soviet Union and the United States have been in the process of continual change since the end of World War II. *(a)* Describe and compare *one* relationship that existed between them at the end of World War II with *one* relationship that exists between them today. *(b)* Explain why the relationship that existed between them at the end of World War II was different from the relationship that exists today. *(c)* Discuss the effects of the change in the relationship mentioned in answer to *a* on another area, nation, or group of nations.

6. The following news article describes foreign policy actions of the United States government.

The United States will reduce its aid to countries *X*, *Y*, and *Z* because of human rights violations in those countries," the secretary of state said in presenting the administration's foreign aid program to the Senate Appropriations Subcommittee on Foreign Operations. "But," the secretary said, "there will be no cuts in aid to country *W* or to other strategically situated allies, no matter what human rights violations may exist in such countries, because security commitments are the overriding consideration.

(a) Discuss *two* traditional foreign policy values of the United States government which appear to be in conflict in the article.

(b) The actions below are possible responses by nations *X*, *Y*, or *Z* to the United States foreign policy described above. Select *one* of these actions. Discuss *one* reason why nation *X*, *Y*, or *Z* might choose that action.

> Nationalize United States businesses in the country
> Refuse to accept United States aid
> Break diplomatic relations with the United States
> Remove all restrictions on human rights in the country

(c) Identify *one* other situation when United States foreign policy decision-makers were faced with a conflict in values. Your answer should include a statement of the conflict and the steps taken by the government of the United States to resolve the conflict.

7. To answer this question, refer to the cartoon entitled "The course of human events" on page 712. *(a)* Briefly state the major idea or concept presented in this cartoon. *(b)* Name *two* foreign policy crises of the past and explain how *each* was solved. *(c)* Name *two* foreign policy crises of the present and indicate your ideas of what the solutions might be. *(d)* In your opinion what might be *one* foreign policy crisis in the near future? Give *one* reason to support your opinion.

8. One philosopher has said, "Ignorant heads read only the past in history, wise ones also read the future."
   (a) Explain the meaning of the quotation.
   (b) Following is a list of predictions that have been made by social scientists for the year 2000. Select *two* predictions that you believe are likely to occur and select *two* other predictions that you believe are *not* likely to occur. In *each* case, explain, by referring to specific historical evidence, why you believe the prediction will or will not occur.

1. Oil-rich nations will control oil-hungry nations.
2. Existing nuclear weapons will be destroyed and their production outlawed.
3. The United States will withdraw from its defense alliances and follow a policy of isolation.
4. The United States will spend a smaller percent of its budget on defense and more on improving the quality of life for its people.
5. Communism will become the dominant form of social, economic, and political organization in the world.
6. The United Nations will become a genuine world government; national boundaries will disappear.
7. China will become the leader of world communism.
8. The number of Asians living at or below the subsistence level will increase.
9. There will be a federation of African nations ruled by one central government.
10. Worldwide concern for human rights will tend to dominate international relations.

THE DECLARATION OF INDEPENDENCE

*Unanimously Adopted by the Thirteen United States of America
Through Their Representatives Assembled in Congress, July 4, 1776*

Introduction: An Address to Humanity*

When, in the course of human events, it becomes necessary for one people to dissolve the political bands which have connected them with another, and to assume, among the powers of the earth, the separate and equal station to which the laws of nature and of nature's God entitle them, a decent respect to the opinions of mankind requires that they should declare the causes which impel them to the separation.

Democratic Philosophy: Rights of Individuals and the Purpose of Government

We hold these truths to be self-evident: That all men are created equal; that they are endowed by their Creator with certain unalienable rights; that among these are life, liberty, and the pursuit of happiness.

That to secure these rights, governments are instituted among men, deriving their just powers from the consent of the governed.

That whenever any form of government becomes destructive of these ends, it is the right of the people to alter or to abolish it, and to institute new government, laying its foundation on such principles and organizing its powers in such form as to them shall seem most likely to effect their safety and happiness. Prudence, indeed, will dictate that governments long established should not be changed for light and transient causes; and, accordingly, all experience hath shown that mankind are more disposed to suffer, while evils are sufferable, than to right themselves by abolishing the forms to which they are accustomed. But when a long train of abuses and usurpations, pursuing invariably the same object, evinces a design to reduce them under absolute despotism, it is their right, it is their duty, to throw off such government, and to provide new guards for their future security.

Grievances Against Great Britain: Reasons for Separation

Such has been the patient sufferance of these colonies; and such is now the necessity which constrains them to alter their former systems of government. The history of the present King of Great Britain is a history of repeated injuries and usurpations, all having in direct object the establishment of an absolute tyranny over these states. To prove this, let facts be submitted to a candid world:

* The headings are not part of the Declaration of Independence but have been provided to assist the reader.

He has refused his assent to laws the most wholesome and necessary for the public good.

He has forbidden his governors to pass laws of immediate and pressing importance unless suspended in their operation till his assent should be obtained; and, when so suspended, he has utterly neglected to attend to them.

He has refused to pass other laws for the accommodation of large districts of people unless those people would relinquish the right of representation in the legislature, a right inestimable to them and formidable to tyrants only.

He has called together legislative bodies at places unusual, uncomfortable, and distant from the depository of their public records, for the sole purpose of fatiguing them into compliance with his measures.

He has dissolved representative houses repeatedly for opposing with manly firmness his invasions on the rights of the people.

He has refused for a long time, after such dissolutions, to cause others to be elected; whereby the legislative powers, incapable of annihilation, have returned to the people at large for their exercise; the state remaining, in the meantime, exposed to all the dangers of invasion from without and convulsions within.

He has endeavoured to prevent the population of these states; for that purpose obstructing the laws for naturalization of foreigners, refusing to pass others to encourage their migrations hither, and raising the conditions of new appropriations of lands.

He has obstructed the administration of justice by refusing his assent to laws for establishing judiciary powers.

He has made judges dependent on his will alone for the tenure of their offices and the amount and payment of their salaries.

He has erected a multitude of new offices, and sent hither swarms of officers to harass our people and eat out their substance.

He has kept among us, in times of peace, standing armies, without the consent of our legislatures.

He has affected to render the military independent of and superior to the civil power.

He has combined with others to subject us to a jurisdiction foreign to our constitution and unacknowledged by our laws; giving his assent to their acts of pretended legislation:

For quartering large bodies of armed troops among us;

For protecting them, by a mock trial, from punishment for any murders which they should commit on the inhabitants of these states;

For cutting off our trade with all parts of the world;

For imposing taxes on us without our consent;

For depriving us in many cases of the benefits of trial by jury;

For transporting us beyond seas to be tried for pretended offences;

For abolishing the free system of English laws in a neighbouring province, establishing therein an arbitrary government and enlarging its boundaries so as to render it at once an example and fit instrument for introducing the same absolute rule in these colonies;

For taking away our charters, abolishing our most valuable laws, and altering fundamentally the forms of our governments;

For suspending our own legislatures, and declaring themselves invested with power to legislate for us in all cases whatsoever.

He has abdicated government here by declaring us out of his protection and waging war against us.

He has plundered our seas, ravaged our coasts, burnt our towns, and destroyed the lives of our people.

He is, at this time, transporting large armies of foreign mercenaries to complete the works of death, desolation, and tyranny already begun with circumstances of cruelty and perfidy scarcely paralleled in the most barbarous ages, and totally unworthy the head of a civilized nation.

He has constrained our fellow citizens, taken captive on the high seas, to bear arms against their country, to become the executioners of their friends and brethren, or to fall themselves by their hands.

He has excited domestic insurrections among us, and has endeavoured to bring on the inhabitants of our frontiers the merciless Indian savages, whose known rule of warfare is an undistinguished destruction of all ages, sexes, and conditions.

In every stage of these oppressions we have petitioned for redress in the most humble terms. Our repeated petitions have been answered only by repeated injury. A prince whose character is thus marked by every act which may define a tyrant is unfit to be the ruler of a free people.

Nor have we been wanting in attentions to our British brethren. We have warned them from time to time of attempts by their legislature to extend an unwarrantable jurisdiction over us. We have reminded them of the circumstances of our emigration and settlement here. We have appealed to their native justice and magnanimity, and we have conjured them by the ties of our common kindred to disavow these usurpations, which would inevitably interrupt our connections and correspondence. They too have been deaf to the voice of justice and of consanguinity. We must therefore acquiesce in the necessity which denounces our separation, and hold them, as we hold the rest of mankind, enemies in war, in peace friends.

Conclusion: Dissolution of Bonds to Great Britain and Affirmation of Independence

We, therefore, the representatives of the United States of America, in General Congress assembled, appealing to the Supreme Judge of the world for the rectitude of our intentions, do, in the name and by authority of the good people of these colonies, solemnly publish and declare: that these united colonies are, and of right ought to be, free and independent states; that they are absolved from all allegiance to the British crown, and that all political connection between them and the state of Great Britain is, and ought to be, totally dissolved; and that, as free and independent states, they have full power to levy war, conclude peace, contract alliances, establish commerce, and to do all other acts and things which independent states may of right do.

And for the support of this Declaration, with a firm reliance on the protection of divine Providence, we mutually pledge to each other our lives, our fortunes, and our sacred honor.

Signed by John Hancock of Massachusetts as President of the Congress and by the Fifty-Five Other Representatives of the Thirteen United States of America

THE CONSTITUTION
OF THE UNITED STATES

Preamble: Purposes of the Constitution*

We, the people of the United States, in order to form a more perfect Union, establish justice, insure domestic tranquillity, provide for the common defense, promote the general welfare, and secure the blessings of liberty to ourselves and our posterity, do ordain and establish this Constitution for the United States of America.

Article I. The Legislative Branch†

Section 1. The Bicameral Congress

All legislative powers herein granted shall be vested in a Congress of the United States, which shall consist of a Senate and House of Representatives.

Section 2. The House of Representatives

1. Representatives: Election and Term of Office. The House of Representatives shall be composed of members chosen every second year by the people of the several states, and the electors in each state shall have the qualifications requisite for electors of the most numerous branch of the state legislature.

2. Requirements Set for Representatives. No person shall be a Representative who shall not have attained to the age of twenty-five years, and been seven years a citizen of the United States, and who shall not, when elected, be an inhabitant of that state in which he shall be chosen.

3. Apportionment of Representatives Among the States. Representatives [*and direct taxes*] shall be apportioned among the several states which may be included within this Union, according to their respective numbers, [*which shall be determined by adding to the whole number of free persons, including those bound to service for a term of years, and excluding Indians not taxed, three-fifths of all other persons.*] The actual enumeration shall be made within three years after the first meeting of the Congress of the United States, and within every subsequent term of ten years, in such manner as they shall by law direct. The number of Representatives shall not exceed one for every 30,000, but each state shall have at least one Representative; [*and until such enumeration shall be made, the state of New Hampshire shall be entitled to choose three; Massachusetts, eight; Rhode Island and Providence Plantations, one; Connecticut, five; New York, six; New Jersey, four; Pennsylvania, eight; Delaware, one; Maryland, six; Virginia, ten; North Carolina, five; South Carolina, five; and Georgia, three.*]

---

* The headings—for the Articles, Sections, and clauses—are not part of the Constitution but have been added to assist the reader.

† Those portions of the Constitution no longer in effect are printed in italics and enclosed in brackets.

4. Filling House Vacancies. When vacancies happen in the representation from any state, the executive authority thereof shall issue writs of election to fill such vacancies.

5. Special Powers: Election of House Officers and Impeachment. The House of Representatives shall choose their Speaker and other officers; and shall have the sole power of impeachment.

Section 3. The Senate

1. Senators: Number, Election, and Term of Office. The Senate of the United States shall be composed of two Senators from each state, [*chosen by the legislature thereof,*] for six years, and each Senator shall have one vote.

2. Expiration of Terms of Senators; Filling Senate Vacancies. [*Immediately after they shall be assembled in consequence of the first election, they shall be divided as equally as may be into three classes. The seats of the Senators of the first class shall be vacated at the expiration of the second year, of the second class at the expiration of the fourth year, and of the third class at the expiration of the sixth year,*] so that one-third may be chosen every second year; [*and if vacancies happen by resignation, or otherwise, during the recess of the legislature of any state, the executive thereof may make temporary appointments until the next meeting of the legislature, which shall then fill such vacancies.*]

3. Requirements Set for Senators. No person shall be a Senator who shall not have attained to the age of thirty years, and been nine years a citizen of the United States, and who shall not, when elected, be an inhabitant of that state for which he shall be chosen.

4. Vice President as President of the Senate. The Vice President of the United States shall be president of the Senate, but shall have no vote, unless they be equally divided.

5. Other Senate Officers. The Senate shall choose their other officers, and also a president *pro tempore*, in the absence of the Vice President, or when he shall exercise the office of President of the United States.

6. The Senate as Jury in Impeachment Cases. The Senate shall have the sole power to try all impeachments. When sitting for that purpose, they shall be on oath or affirmation. When the President of the United States is tried, the Chief Justice shall preside; and no person shall be convicted without the concurrence of two-thirds of the members present.

7. Punishment in Cases of Impeachment. Judgment in cases of impeachment shall not extend further than to removal from office, and disqualification to hold and enjoy any office of honor, trust, or profit under the United States; but the party convicted shall nevertheless be liable and subject to indictment, trial, judgment, and punishment, according to law.

Section 4. Congressional Elections and Sessions

1. Regulations for Congressional Elections. The times, places, and manner of holding elections for Senators and Representatives shall be prescribed in each state by the legislature thereof; but the Congress may at any time by law make or alter such regulations, except as to the places of choosing Senators.

2. Sessions of Congress. The Congress shall assemble at least once in every year, [*and such meeting shall be on the first Monday in December,*] unless they shall by law appoint a different day.

Section 5. Organization and Rules of Each House of Congress

1. Control Over Members: Election Returns and Attendance. Each house shall be the judge of the elections, returns, and qualifications of its own members, and a majority of each shall constitute a quorum to do business; but a smaller number may adjourn from day to day, and may be authorized to compel the attendance of absent members, in such manner, and under such penalties, as each house may provide.

2. Rules of Procedure; Further Control Over Members. Each house may determine the rules of its proceedings, punish its members for disorderly behavior, and with the concurrence of two-thirds, expel a member.

3. Journal or Record of Proceedings. Each house shall keep a journal of its proceedings, and from time to time publish the same, excepting such parts as may in their judgment require secrecy; and the yeas and nays of the members of either house on any question shall, at the desire of one-fifth of those present, be entered on the journal.

4. Adjournment. Neither house, during the session of Congress, shall, without the consent of the other, adjourn for more than three days, nor to any other place than that in which the two houses shall be sitting.

Section 6. Congressional Privileges and Restrictions

1. Salaries and Special Privileges. The Senators and Representatives shall receive a compensation for their services, to be ascertained by law and paid out of the Treasury of the United States. They shall in all cases, except treason, felony, and breach of the peace, be privileged from arrest during their attendance at the session of their respective houses, and in going to and returning from the same; and for any speech or debate in either house, they shall not be questioned in any other place.

2. Restrictions. No Senator or Representative shall, during the time for which he was elected, be appointed to any civil office under the authority of the United States, which shall have been created, or the emoluments whereof shall have been increased, during such time; and no person holding any office under the United States shall be a member of either house during his continuance in office.

Section 7. Procedures for Passing Bills

1. Revenue Bills. All bills for raising revenue shall originate in the House of Representatives; but the Senate may propose or concur with amendments as on other bills.

2. Bills Subject to Presidential Approval or Veto. Every bill which shall have passed the House of Representatives and the Senate, shall, before it become a law, be presented to the President of the United States; if he approve, he shall sign it, but if not, he shall return it, with his objections to that house in which it shall have originated, who shall enter the objections at large on their journal, and proceed to reconsider it. If after such reconsideration two-thirds of that house shall agree to pass the bill, it shall be sent, together with the objections, to the other house, by which it shall likewise be reconsidered, and, if approved by two-thirds of that house, it shall become a law. But in all such cases the votes of both houses shall be determined by yeas and nays, and the names of the persons voting for and against the bill shall be entered on the journal of each house respectively. If any bill shall not be returned by the President within ten days (Sundays excepted) after it shall have been presented to him, the same shall be a law, in like manner as if he had signed it, unless the Congress by their adjournment prevent its return, in which case it shall not be a law.

3. Other Congressional Actions Subject to Presidential Approval or Veto. Every order, resolution, or vote to which the concurrence of the Senate and House of Representatives may be necessary (except on a question of adjournment) shall be presented to the President of the United States; and before the same shall take effect, shall be approved by him, or being disapproved by him, shall be repassed by two-thirds of the Senate and House of Representatives, according to the rules and limitations prescribed in the case of a bill.

Section 8. Powers Granted to Congress

1–17. Delegated or Enumerated Powers. The Congress shall have power

1. To lay and collect taxes, duties, imposts, and excises, to pay the debts and provide for the common defense and general welfare of the United States; but all duties, imposts, and excises shall be uniform throughout the United States;

2. To borrow money on the credit of the United States;

3. To regulate commerce with foreign nations, and among the several states, and with the Indian tribes;

4. To establish a uniform rule of naturalization, and uniform laws on the subject of bankruptcies throughout the United States;

5. To coin money, regulate the value thereof, and of foreign coin, and fix the standard of weights and measures;

6. To provide for the punishment of counterfeiting the securities and current coin of the United States;

7. To establish post offices and post roads;

8. To promote the progress of science and useful arts by securing for limited times to authors and inventors the exclusive right to their respective writings and discoveries;

9. To constitute tribunals inferior to the Supreme Court;

10. To define and punish piracies and felonies committed on the high seas and offenses against the law of nations;

11. To declare war, [*grant letters of marque and reprisal,*] and make rules concerning captures on land and water;

12. To raise and support armies, but no appropriation of money to that use shall be for a longer term than two years;

13. To provide and maintain a navy;

14. To make rules for the government and regulation of the land and naval forces;

15. To provide for calling forth the militia to execute the laws of the Union, suppress insurrections, and repel invasions;

16. To provide for organizing, arming, and disciplining the militia, and for governing such part of them as may be employed in the service of the United States, reserving to the states, respectively, the appointment of the officers, and the authority of training the militia according to the discipline prescribed by Congress;

17. To exercise exclusive legislation in all cases whatsoever, over such

district (not exceeding ten miles square) as may, by cession of particular states, and the acceptance of Congress, become the seat of government of the United States, and to exercise like authority over all places purchased by the consent of the legislature of the state in which the same shall be, for the erection of forts, magazines, arsenals, dock-yards, and other needful buildings;—and

18. Implied Powers: The Elastic Clause. To make all laws which shall be necessary and proper for carrying into execution the foregoing powers, and all other powers vested by this Constitution in the government of the United States, or in any department or officer thereof.

Section 9. Powers Denied to the Federal Government

1. May Not Interfere With the Slave Trade Prior to 1808. [*The migration or importation of such persons as any of the states now existing shall think proper to admit shall not be prohibited by the Congress prior to the year 1808; but a tax or duty may be imposed on such importation, not exceeding ten dollars for each person.*]

2. May Not Suspend the Writ of Habeas Corpus Except in Emergency. The privilege of the writ of habeas corpus shall not be suspended, unless when in cases of rebellion or invasion the public safety may require it.

3. May Not Enact a Bill of Attainder or an Ex Post Facto Law. No bill of attainder or ex post facto law shall be passed.

4. May Not Levy a Direct Tax Except in Proportion to Population. [*No capitation or other direct tax shall be laid, unless in proportion to the census or enumeration herein before directed to be taken.*]

5. May Not Levy an Export Tax. No tax or duty shall be laid on articles exported from any state.

6. May Not Favor the Ports of One State Over Those of Another. No preference shall be given by any regulation of commerce or revenue to the ports of one state over those of another: nor shall vessels bound to, or from, one state, be obliged to enter, clear, or pay duties in another.

7. May Not Spend Federal Funds Without Congressional Approval and Public Accounting. No money shall be drawn from the Treasury, but in consequence of appropriations made by law; and a regular statement and account of the receipts and expenditures of all public money shall be published from time to time.

8. May Not Grant Titles of Nobility. No title of nobility shall be granted by the United States; and no person holding any office of profit or trust under them, shall, without the consent of the Congress, accept of any present, emolument, office, or title, of any kind whatever, from any king, prince, or foreign state.

Section 10. Powers Denied to the States

1. Unconditional Denial of Various Powers. No state shall enter into any treaty, alliance, or confederation; grant letters of marque and reprisal; coin money; emit bills of credit; make anything but gold and silver coin a tender in payment of debts; pass any bill of attainder, ex post facto law, or law impairing the obligation of contracts, or grant any title of nobility.

2. Conditional Denial: May Not Levy Import and Export Taxes Without the Consent of Congress. No state shall, without the consent of the Congress, lay any imposts or duties on imports or exports, except what may be absolutely necessary for executing its inspection laws; and the net produce of all duties and imposts, laid by any state on imports or exports, shall be for the use of the Treasury of the United States; and all such laws shall be subject to the revision and control of the Congress.

3. Conditional Denial: May Not Prepare For and Wage War (Except in Emergency) Without the Consent of Congress. No state shall, without the consent of Congress, lay any duty of tonnage, keep troops, or ships of war in time of peace, enter into any agreement or compact with another state, or with a foreign power, or engage in war, unless actually invaded, or in such imminent danger as will not admit of delay.

Article II. The Executive Branch

Section 1. The President and the Presidential Office

1. Term of Office. The executive power shall be vested in a President of the United States of America. He shall hold his office during the term of four years, and together with the Vice President, chosen for the same term, be elected as follows:

2. Number of Presidential Electors per State. Each state shall appoint, in such manner as the legislature thereof may direct, a number of electors, equal to the whole number of Senators and Representatives to which the state may be entitled in the Congress; but no Senator or Representative, or person holding an office of trust or profit under the United States, shall be appointed an elector.

3. Election Procedures of the Electoral College and Congress. [*The electors shall meet in their respective states, and vote by ballot for two persons, of whom one at least shall not be an inhabitant of the same state with themselves. And they shall make a list of all the persons voted for, and of the number of votes for each; which list they shall sign and certify, and transmit sealed to the seat of the government of the United States, directed to the president of the Senate. The president of the Senate shall, in the presence of the Senate and House of Representatives, open all the certificates, and the votes shall then be counted. The person having the greatest number of votes shall be the President, if such number be a majority of the whole number of electors appointed; and if there be more than one who have such majority, and have an equal number of votes, then the House of Representatives shall immediately choose by ballot one of them for President; and if no person have a majority, then from the five highest on the list the said House shall in like manner choose the President. But in choosing the President the votes shall be taken by states, the representation from each state having one vote. A quorum for this purpose shall consist of a member or members from two-thirds of the states, and a majority of all the states shall be necessary to a choice. In every case, after the choice of the President, the person having the greatest number of votes of the electors shall be the Vice President. But if there should remain two or more who have equal votes, the Senate shall choose from them by ballot the Vice President.*]

4. Nationwide Election Day. The Congress may determine the time of choosing the electors, and the day on which they shall give their votes; which day shall be the same throughout the United States.

5. Requirements Set for the President. No person except a natural-born citizen, [*or a citizen of the United States, at the time of the adoption of this Constitution,*] shall be eligible to the office of President; neither shall any person be eligible to that office who shall not have attained to the age of thirty-five years, and been fourteen years a resident within the United States.

6. Filling a Presidential Vacancy. In case of the removal of the President from office, or of his death, resignation, or inability to discharge the powers and duties of the said office, the same shall devolve on the Vice President, and the Congress may by law provide for the case of removal, death, resignation, or inability, both of the President and Vice President, declaring what officer shall then act as President, and such officer shall act accordingly, until the disability be removed, or a President shall be elected.

7. Salary of the President. The President shall, at stated times, receive for his services, a compensation, which shall neither be increased nor diminished during the period for which he shall have been elected, and he shall not receive within that period any other emolument from the United States, or any of them.

8. Presidential Oath of Office. Before he enter on the execution of his office, he shall take the following oath or affirmation:—"I do solemnly swear (or affirm) that I will faithfully execute the office of President of the United States, and will to the best of my ability, preserve, protect, and defend the Constitution of the United States."

Section 2. Powers of the President

1. Military, Executive, and Judicial Powers. The President shall be Commander in Chief of the Army and Navy of the United States, and of the militia of the several states, when called into the actual service of the United States; he may require the opinion, in writing, of the principal officer in each of the executive departments, upon any subject relating to the duties of their respective offices, and he shall have power to grant reprieves and pardons for offenses against the United States, except in cases of impeachment.

2. Treaty Making and Appointive Powers With the Consent of the Senate. He shall have power, by and with the advice and consent of the Senate, to make treaties, provided two-thirds of the Senators present concur; and he shall nominate, and by and with the advice and consent of the Senate, shall appoint ambassadors, other public ministers and consuls, judges of the Supreme Court, and all other officers of the United States, whose appointments are not herein otherwise provided for, and which shall be established by law; but the Congress may by law vest the appointment of such inferior officers, as they think proper, in the President alone, in the courts of law, or in the heads of departments.

3. Appointments During Recess of the Senate. The President shall have power to fill up all vacancies that may happen during the recess of the Senate, by granting commissions which shall expire at the end of their next session.

Section 3. Further Powers of the President: Legislative, Diplomatic, and Executive

He shall from time to time give to the Congress information of the state of the Union, and recommend to their consideration such measures as he shall judge necessary and expedient; he may, on extraordinary occasions, convene both houses, or either of them, and in case of disagreement between them, with respect to the time of adjournment, he may adjourn them to such time as he shall think proper; he shall receive ambassadors and other public ministers; he shall take care that the laws be faithfully executed, and shall commission all the officers of the United States.

Section 4. Impeachment of Civil Officers

The President, Vice President, and all civil officers of the United States, shall be removed from office on impeachment for, and conviction of, treason, bribery, or other high crimes and misdemeanors.

Article III. The Judicial Branch

Section 1. The Federal Courts: Supreme and Lower Courts; Tenure and Salary of Judges

The judicial power of the United States shall be vested in one Supreme Court, and in such inferior courts as the Congress may from time to time ordain and establish. The judges, both of the Supreme and inferior courts, shall hold their offices during good behavior, and shall, at stated times, receive for their services a compensation, which shall not be diminished during their continuance in office.

Section 2. Jurisdiction of the Federal Courts

1. **Cases Tried in Federal Courts.** The judicial power shall extend to all cases, in law and equity, arising under this Constitution, the laws of the United States, and treaties made or which shall be made, under their authority; to all cases affecting ambassadors, other public ministers and consuls; to all cases of admiralty and maritime jurisdiction; to controversies to which the United States shall be a party; to controversies between two or more states; [*between a state and citizens of another state;*] between citizens of different states; between citizens of the same state claiming lands under grants of different states, and between a state, or the citizens thereof, and foreign states, citizens, or subjects.

2. **Original and Appellate Jurisdiction of the Supreme Court.** In all cases affecting ambassadors, other public ministers and consuls, and those in which a state shall be a party, the Supreme Court shall have original jurisdiction. In all the other cases before mentioned, the Supreme Court shall have appellate jurisdiction, both as to law and fact, with such exceptions, and under such regulations as the Congress shall make.

3. **Rules Regarding Trials.** The trial of all crimes, except in cases of impeachment, shall be by jury; and such trial shall be held in the state where the said crimes shall have been committed; but when not committed within any state, the trial shall be at such place or places as the Congress may by law have directed.

Section 3. Treason

1. Definition of Treason; Requirements for Conviction. Treason against the United States shall consist only in levying war against them, or in adhering to their enemies, giving them aid and comfort. No person shall be convicted of treason unless on the testimony of two witnesses to the same overt act, or on confession in open court.

2. Punishment of Treason Limited to the Guilty Person. The Congress shall have power to declare the punishment of treason, but no attainder of treason shall work corruption of blood or forfeiture except during the life of the person attainted.

Article IV. Relations Among the States and With the Federal Government

Section 1. Relations Among States Regarding Official Acts

Full faith and credit shall be given in each state to the public acts, records, and judicial proceedings of every other state. And the Congress may by general laws prescribe the manner in which such acts, records, and proceedings shall be proved, and the effect thereof.

Section 2. Relations Among States Regarding Citizens and Fugitives

1. Exchange of Privileges of Citizenship. The citizens of each state shall be entitled to all privileges and immunities of citizens in the several states.

2. Extradition: Return of Fugitives From Justice. A person charged in any state with treason, felony, or other crime, who shall flee from justice, and be found in another state, shall on demand of the executive authority of the state from which he fled, be delivered up, to be removed to the state having jurisdiction of the crime.

3. Return of Fugitive Slaves and Indentured Servants. [*No person held in service or labor in one state, under the laws thereof, escaping into another, shall in consequence of any law or regulation therein, be discharged from such service or labor, but shall be delivered up on claim of the party to whom such service or labor may be due.*]

Section 3. New States and Territories

1. Admission of New States. New states may be admitted by the Congress into this Union; but no new state shall be formed or erected within the jurisdiction of any other state; nor any state be formed by the junction of two or more states, or parts of states, without the consent of the legislatures of the states concerned as well as of the Congress.

2. Regulations for Federal Territories and Properties. The Congress shall have power to dispose of and make all needful rules and regulations respecting the territory or other property belonging to the United States; and nothing in this Constitution shall be so construed as to prejudice any claims of the United States, or of any particular state.

Section 4. Federal Protection for the States

The United States shall guarantee to every state in this Union a republican form of government, and shall protect each of them against invasion; and on application of the legislature, or of the executive (when the legislature cannot be convened) against domestic violence.

Article V. Proposing and Ratifying Amendments to the Constitution

The Congress, whenever two-thirds of both houses shall deem it necessary, shall propose amendments to this Constitution, or, on the application of the legislatures of two-thirds of the several states, shall call a convention for proposing amendments, which, in either case shall be valid to all intents and purposes, as part of this Constitution, when ratified by the legislatures of three-fourths of the several states, or by conventions in three-fourths thereof, as the one or the other mode of ratification may be proposed by the Congress; provided that [*no amendments which may be made prior to the year 1808 shall in any manner affect the first and fourth clauses in the Ninth Section of the First Article; and that*] no state, without its consent, shall be deprived of its equal suffrage in the Senate.

Article VI. Miscellaneous Provisions

1. Acceptance of Previously Contracted Public Debts. All debts contracted and engagements entered into, before the adoption of this Constitution, shall be as valid against the United States under this Constitution, as under the Confederation.

2. The Constitution: Supreme Law of the Land. This Constitution, and the laws of the United States which shall be made in pursuance thereof, and all treaties made, or which shall be made, under the authority of the United States, shall be the supreme law of the land; and the judges in every state shall be bound thereby, anything in the constitution or laws of any state to the contrary notwithstanding.

3. Official Oath of Office; No Religious Test. The Senators and Representatives before mentioned, and the members of the several state legislatures, and all executive and judicial officers, both of the United States and of the several states, shall be bound by oath or affirmation, to support this Constitution; but no religious test shall ever be required as a qualification to any office or public trust under the United States.

Article VII. Ratification of the Constitution: Assent Required of Nine States

The ratification of the conventions of nine states shall be sufficient for the establishment of this Constitution between the states so ratifying the same.

Amendments to the Constitution

Amendment I (1791). Freedom of Religion, Speech, Press, Assembly, and Petition

Congress shall make no law respecting an establishment of religion, or prohibiting the free exercise thereof; or abridging the freedom of speech, or of the press; or the right of the people peaceably to assemble, and to petition the government for a redress of grievances.

Amendment II (1791). Right to a State Militia and to Bear Arms

A well-regulated militia, being necessary to the security of a free state, the right of the people to keep and bear arms shall not be infringed.

Amendment III (1791). Regulations for Quartering of Troops

No soldier shall, in time of peace, be quartered in any house, without the consent of the owner; nor in time of war, but in a manner to be prescribed by law.

Amendment IV (1791). No Unreasonable Searches and No Vague Search Warrants

The right of the people to be secure in their persons, houses, papers, and effects, against unreasonable searches and seizures, shall not be violated; and no warrants shall issue but upon probable cause, supported by oath or affirmation, and particularly describing the place to be searched, and the persons or things to be seized.

Amendment V (1791). Rights of Accused Persons; Protection of Private Property

No person shall be held to answer for a capital, or otherwise infamous, crime, unless on a presentment or indictment of a grand jury, except in cases arising in the land or naval forces, or in the militia, when in actual service in time of war or public danger; nor shall any person be subject for the same offense to be twice put in jeopardy of life or limb; nor shall be compelled, in any criminal case, to be a witness against himself; nor be deprived of life, liberty, or property, without due process of law; nor shall private property be taken for public use, without just compensation.

Amendment VI (1791). Further Rights of Accused Persons

In all criminal prosecutions, the accused shall enjoy the right to a speedy and public trial, by an impartial jury of the state and district wherein the crime shall have been committed, which district shall have been previously ascertained by law, and to be informed of the nature and cause of the accusation; to be confronted with the witnesses against him; to have compulsory process for obtaining witnesses in his favor, and to have the assistance of counsel for his defense.

Amendment VII (1791). Trial by Jury in Most Civil Cases

In suits at common law, where the value in controversy shall exceed twenty dollars, the right of trial by jury shall be preserved, and no fact tried by a jury shall be otherwise reexamined in any court of the United States than according to the rules of the common law.

Amendment VIII (1791). No Excessive Bail or Cruel Punishments

Excessive bail shall not be required, nor excessive fines imposed, nor cruel and unusual punishments inflicted.

Amendment IX (1791). Unlisted Rights Reserved to the People

The enumeration in the Constitution, of certain rights, shall not be construed to deny or disparage others retained by the people.

Amendment X (1791). Powers Reserved to the States or People

The powers not delegated to the United States by the Constitution, nor prohibited by it to the states, are reserved to the states respectively, or to the people.

Amendment XI (1798). No Suits in Federal Courts by Individuals Against a State

The judicial power of the United States shall not be construed to extend to any suit in law or equity, commenced or prosecuted against one of the United States, by citizens of another state, or by citizens or subjects of any foreign state.

Amendment XII (1804). Revised Procedures for Electing the Presiden.. and Vice President

The electors shall meet in their respective states, and vote by ballot for President and Vice President, one of whom, at least, shall not be an inhabitant of the same state with themselves; they shall name in their ballots the person voted for as President, and in distinct ballots the person voted for as Vice President, and they shall make distinct lists of all persons voted for as President, and of all persons voted for as Vice President, and of the number of votes for each, which lists they shall sign and certify, and transmit, sealed, to the seat of government of the United States, directed to the President of the Senate; the President of the Senate shall, in the presence of the Senate and House of Representatives, open all the certificates and the votes shall then be counted; the person having the greatest number of votes for President shall be the President, if such number be a majority of the whole number of electors appointed; and if no person have such majority, then from the persons having the highest numbers not exceeding three on the list of those voted for as President, the House of Representatives shall choose immediately, by ballot, the President. But in choosing the President, the votes shall be taken by states, the representation from each state having one vote; a quorum for this purpose shall consist of a member or members from two-thirds of the states, and a majority of all the states shall be necessary to a choice. And if the House of Representatives shall not choose a President whenever the right of choice shall devolve upon them, [before the fourth day of March next following,] then the Vice President shall act as President, as in the case of the death or other constitutional disability of the President. The person having the greatest number of votes as Vice President shall be the Vice President, if such number be a majority of the whole number of electors appointed, and if no person have a majority, then, from the two highest numbers on the list, the Senate shall choose the Vice President; a quorum for the purpose shall consist of two-thirds of the whole number of Senators, and a majority of the whole number shall be necessary to a choice. But no person constitutionally ineligible to the office of President shall be eligible to that of Vice President of the United States.

Amendment XIII (1865). Abolition of Slavery

Section 1. No Slavery in the United States. Neither slavery nor involuntary servitude, except as a punishment for crime whereof the party shall have been duly convicted, shall exist within the United States, or any place subject to their jurisdiction.

Section 2. Enforcement. Congress shall have power to enforce this article by appropriate legislation.

Amendment XIV (1868). Protection of Civil Liberties Against State Infringement; Measures Against Former Confederate Leaders and Bondholders

Section 1. Definition of Citizenship; Due Process of Law and Equal Protection of the Laws. All persons born or naturalized in the United States and subject to the jurisdiction thereof, are citizens of the United States and of the state wherein they reside. No state shall make or enforce any law which shall abridge the privileges or immunities of citizens of the United States; nor shall any state deprive any person of life, liberty, or property, without due process of law; nor deny to any person within its jurisdiction the equal protection of the laws.

Section 2. Reduction of Representation of States Denying Vote to Citizens. Representatives shall be apportioned among the several states according to their respective numbers, counting the whole number of persons in each state, excluding Indians not taxed. But when the right to vote at any election for the choice of electors for President and Vice President of the United States, Representatives in Congress, the executive and judicial officers of a state, or the members of the legislature thereof, is denied to any of the male inhabitants of such state, being twenty-one years of age and citizens of the United States, or in any way abridged, except for participation in rebellion, or other crime, the basis of representation therein shall be reduced in the proportion which the number of such male citizens shall bear to the whole number of male citizens twenty-one years of age in such state.

Section 3. Exclusion of Former Confederate Leaders From Public Office. No person shall be a Senator or Representative in Congress, or elector of President and Vice President, or hold any office, civil or military, under the United States, or under any state, who, having previously taken an oath, as a member of Congress, or as an officer of the United States, or as a member of any state legislature, or as an executive or judicial officer of any state, to support the Constitution of the United States, shall have engaged in insurrection or rebellion against the same, or given aid or comfort to the enemies thereof. But Congress may, by vote of two-thirds of each house, remove such disability.

Section 4. No Repayment of the Confederate Debt. The validity of the public debt of the United States, authorized by law, including debts incurred for payment of pensions and bounties for services in suppressing insurrection or rebellion, shall not be questioned. But neither the United States nor any state shall assume or pay any debt or obligation incurred in aid of insurrection or rebellion against the United States, or any claim for the loss or emancipation of any slave; but all such debts, obligations, and claims shall be held illegal and void.

Section 5. Enforcement. The Congress shall have power to enforce, by appropriate legislation, the provisions of this article.

Amendment XV (1870). Right of Citizens to Vote

Section 1. Conditions Irrelevant to Suffrage. The right of citizens of the United States to vote shall not be denied or abridged by the United States or any state on account of race, color, or previous condition of servitude.

Section 2. Enforcement. The Congress shall have power to enforce this article by appropriate legislation.

Amendment XVI (1913). Power to Levy Income Taxes

The Congress shall have power to lay and collect taxes on incomes, from whatever source derived, without apportionment among the several states, and without regard to any census or enumeration.

Amendment XVII (1913). Direct Election of Senators

Section 1. Election by the People. The Senate of the United States shall be composed of two Senators from each state, elected by the people thereof, for six years; and each Senator shall have one vote. The electors in each state shall have the qualifications requisite for electors of the most numerous branch of the state legislatures.

Section 2. Regulations Regarding Vacancies and Temporary Appointments. When vacancies happen in the representation of any state in the Senate, the executive authority of such state shall issue writs of election to fill such vacancies: *Provided* that the legislature of any state may empower the executive thereof to make temporary appointments until the people fill the vacancies by election as the legislature may direct.

Section 3. Provisions Not Retroactive. [*This amendment shall not be so construed as to affect the election or term of any Senator chosen before it becomes valid as part of the Constitution.*]

Amendment XVIII (1919). National Prohibition

Section 1. No Manufacture, Sale, or Transportation of Intoxicating Liquors. [*After one year from the ratification of this article the manufacture, sale, or transportation of intoxicating liquors within, the importation thereof into, or the exportation thereof from, the United States and all territory subject to the jurisdiction thereof for beverage purposes is hereby prohibited.*]

Section 2. Enforcement. [*The Congress and the several states shall have concurrent power to enforce this article by appropriate legislation.*]

Section 3. Ratification Required Within Seven Years. [*This article shall be inoperative unless it shall have been ratified as an amendment to the Constitution by the legislatures of the several states, as provided in the Constitution, within seven years from the date of the submission hereof to the states by the Congress.*]

Amendment XIX (1920). Right of Women Citizens to Vote

Section 1. Woman Suffrage. The right of citizens of the United States to vote shall not be denied or abridged by the United States or by any state on account of sex.

Section 2. Enforcement. Congress shall have power to enforce this article by appropriate legislation.

Amendment XX (1933). Various Governmental Details, Especially No "Lame Duck" Congressmen

Section 1. Revised Dates for Terms of President, Vice President, and Congressmen. The terms of the President and Vice President shall end at noon on the 20th day of January, and the terms of Senators and Representatives at noon on the 3rd day of January, of the years in which such terms would have ended if this article had not been ratified; and the terms of their successors shall then begin.

Section 2. Revised Date for Sessions of Congress. The Congress shall assemble at least once in every year, and such meeting shall begin at noon on the 3rd day of January, unless they shall by law appoint a different day.

Section 3. Presidential Succession in Unusual Circumstances. If at the time fixed for the beginning of the term of the President, the President-elect shall have died, the Vice President-elect shall become President. If a President shall not have been chosen before the time fixed for the beginning of his term, or if the President-elect shall have failed to qualify, then the Vice President-elect shall act as President until a President shall have qualified; and the Congress may by law provide for the case wherein neither a President-elect nor a Vice President-elect shall have qualified, declaring who shall then act as President, or the manner in which one who is to act shall be selected, and such person shall act accordingly until a President or Vice President shall have qualified.

Section 4. Congress and Presidential Election in Unusual Circumstances. The Congress may by law provide for the case of the death of any of the persons from whom the House of Representatives may choose a President whenever the right of choice shall have devolved upon them, and for the case of the death of any of the persons from whom the Senate may choose a Vice President whenever the right of choice shall have devolved upon them.

Section 5. Effective Date of This Amendment. [*Sections 1 and 2 shall take effect on the 15th day of October following the ratification of this article.*]

Section 6. Ratification Required Within Seven Years. [*This article shall be inoperative unless it shall have been ratified as an amendment to the Constitution by the legislatures of three-fourths of the several states within seven years from the date of its submission.*]

Amendment XXI (1933). Repeal of Prohibition

Section 1. Repeal of Eighteenth Amendment. The eighteenth article of amendment to the Constitution of the United States is hereby repealed.

Section 2. Control of Liquor Left to the States. The transportation or importation into any state, territory, or possession of the United States for delivery or use therein of intoxicating liquors, in violation of the laws thereof, is hereby prohibited.

Section 3. Ratification Required Within Seven Years by State Conventions. [*This article shall be inoperative unless it shall have been ratified as an amendment to the Constitution by conventions in the several states, as provided in the Constitution, within seven years from the date of the submission hereof to the states by the Congress.*]

Amendment XXII (1951). Limitation on Presidential Terms

Section 1. No More Than Two Elected Terms as President. No person shall be elected to the office of the President more than twice, and no person who has held the office of President, or acted as President, for more than two years of a term to which some other person was elected President shall be elected to the office of the President more than once. [*But this Article shall not apply to any person holding the office of President when this Article was proposed by the Congress, and shall not prevent any person who may be holding the office of*

President, or acting as President, during the term within which this Article becomes operative from holding the office of President or acting as President during the remainder of such term.]

Section 2. Ratification Required Within Seven Years. [*This article shall be inoperative unless it shall have been ratified as an amendment to the Constitution by the legislatures of three-fourths of the several states within seven years from the date of its submission to the states by the Congress.*]

Amendment XXIII (1961). Presidential Electors for the District of Columbia

Section 1. Number of Electors. The District constituting the seat of Government of the United States shall appoint in such manner as the Congress may direct:

A number of electors of President and Vice President equal to the whole number of Senators and Representatives in Congress to which the District would be entitled if it were a State, but in no event more than the least populous State; they shall be in addition to those appointed by the States, but they shall be considered, for the purposes of the election of President and Vice President, to be electors appointed by a State; and they shall meet in the District and perform such duties as provided by the twelfth article of amendment.

Section 2. Enforcement. The Congress shall have power to enforce this article by appropriate legislation.

Amendment XXIV (1964). No Poll Tax in Federal Elections

Section 1. Citizens to Vote Without Payment of a Poll Tax. The right of citizens of the United States to vote in any primary or other election for President or Vice President, for electors for President or Vice President, or for Senator or Representative in Congress, shall not be denied or abridged by the United States or any state by reason of failure to pay any poll tax or other tax.

Section 2. Enforcement. The Congress shall have the power to enforce this article by appropriate legislation.

Amendment XXV (1967). Presidential Disability and Succession

Section 1. Filling a Presidential Vacancy. In case of the removal of the President from office or of his death or resignation, the Vice President shall become President.

Section 2. Filling a Vice Presidential Vacancy. Whenever there is a vacancy in the office of the Vice President, the President shall nominate a Vice President who shall take office upon confirmation by a majority vote of both houses of Congress.

Section 3. Presidential Disability: Vice President as Acting President. Whenever the President transmits to the President pro tempore of the Senate and the Speaker of the House of Representatives his written declaration that he is unable to discharge the powers and duties of his office, and until he transmits to them a written declaration to the contrary, such powers and duties shall be discharged by the Vice President as Acting President.

Section 4. Resumption of Power by the President. Whenever the Vice President and a majority of either the principal officers of the executive departments or of such other body as Congress may by law provide transmit to the President pro tempore of the Senate and the Speaker of the House of Representatives their written declaration that the President is unable to discharge the powers and duties of his office, the Vice President shall immediately assume the powers and duties of the office as Acting President.

Thereafter, when the President transmits to the President pro tempore of the Senate and the Speaker of the House of Representatives his written declaration that no inability exists, he shall resume the powers and duties of his office unless the Vice President and a majority of either the principal officers of the executive department or of such other body as Congress may by law provide transmit within four days to the President pro tempore of the Senate and the Speaker of the House of Representatives their written declaration that the President is unable to discharge the powers and duties of his office. Thereupon Congress shall decide the issue, assembling within forty-eight hours for that purpose if not in session. If the Congress, within twenty-one days after receipt of the latter written declaration, or, if Congress is not in session, within twenty-one days after Congress is required to assemble, determines by two-thirds vote of both houses that the President is unable to discharge the powers and duties of his office, the Vice President shall continue to discharge the same as Acting President; otherwise, the President shall resume the powers and duties of his office.

Amendment XXVI (1971). Right of Younger Citizens to Vote

Section 1. Voting Age Set at Eighteen. The right of citizens of the United States, who are eighteen years of age or older, to vote shall not be denied or abridged by the United States or any state on account of age.

Section 2. Enforcement. The Congress shall have the power to enforce this article by appropriate legislation.

INDEX

739